A Deep Plough:
Unscrambling Major
Post-Marxist Texts
From Adorno to Zizek

Zhang Yibing

Translated by He Chengzhou, He Huiming, etc.

D0920780

CANut

Preface

It is a great honor to be able to write this preface for the work of Professor Zhang Yibing. I have been closely following the changes in Marxist philosophy studies in China in the last two decades, and have witnessed the astonishing achievements realized since then. Scholars in China, and those from the other parts of the world, have actively participated and promoted exchanges and dialogs, which produce valuable progress both in Marxism studies and contemporary western philosophies.

Regretfully, those achievements and progress is rarely reflected in publications or shared by the larger philosophy community in our globe. In the last three decades, Chinese scholars have been enjoying the third generation of translations of those books or texts from Marxist and Post-Marxist trend of thoughts written by thinkers in the West. Studies on them and methods of study have gradually developed and a great amount of valuable works have been produced, published in Chinese. I think, for the sake of a more vigorous development of contemporary philosophy and Marxist philosophy, the limitations of language still pose a great challenge before us.

I appreciate Canut that they have started a series of philosophy books from Chinese scholars to bridge that gap. This book is the second volume of the two-volume book written by Zhang Yibing; the first volume includes classical Western Marxism texts, and this second includes what he calls "post-Marxian" texts. Born in 1956, he belongs to the second generation of scholars studying "Western Marxism" philosophy in China. His first article was published in 1982 and in the second half of 1980s, he started his books. Zhang Yibing has chosen a brand new method for China—textual studies—which was very rarely applied. With his sharp critical reflections, and deep background investigation on how those thinkers have developed their ideas, he is one of the outstanding names in that generation. His influential books include *Back to Marx: The Philosophical Discourse in the Context of Economics*; *Back to Lenin—A Post-Textological Reading on Philosophical Notes*; *The Impossible Truth of Being: Imago of Lacanian Philosophy*; *Symptom Reading and Ideology: A Textological Reading of Althusser*; *The Subjective Dimension of Marxian Historical Dialectics*; *Atonal Dialectical Imagination: The Textual Reading of Adorno's Negative Dialectics*; and *Against Baudrillard—Deconstruction of a Post-Modern Academic Mythos*. And, I am happy to know that this publisher is preparing more works from him to be published in English, which gives me an exciting hope for the future of contemporary Marxism studies.

Through my several readings on this book, I have again and again come to remember Marx's call for philosophizing that the real human and sensuous activity, namely revolutionary, practical-critical activity should be the starting point or premise of philosophical theory. I hope this book will give more impulse to further global exchanges to develop Marxist philosophy works, including all parts of our globe and also those recent efforts realized in China.

Dennis Simon
London, December 2010

Contents

Chapter 5 Hollow Man: Perpetual Constitution of a Fantastic Scene—Textual Interpretation of Slavoj Zizek's *Sublime Object of Ideology* ···················413

Introduction

Ever since Xu Chongwen first introduced the concept of "Western Marxism" to China in 1982, the study of foreign Marxism has experienced a vicissitudinous time of 20 years. The introduction of foreign Marxism is of vital importance for the academia of Marxism study in China. Although there is still disagreement over the usage of the keyword "Western Marxism," it has in effect opened up a new range of questions in its relatively definite realm of study. In my opinion, it has transformed the traditional research of Marxism and given rise to new creative theories.

However, I have to admit that most of the achievements of Chinese scholars in this field in the past 20 years were confined to translations and general commentaries of individual texts. The translation of the classical texts of traditional "Western Marxism" (up to the 1970s) [1] had mainly focused on philosophy, culture, aesthetics, and psychology, but the subjects such as sociology, economics, politics and history were neglected (of course, some recent researchers have come to notice these aspects and made significant achievements). There is still much to be desired from our present research, especially on the theoretical positioning of this trend since the end of the 20th century. And this critical disadvantage suggests two important prospects worthy of our consideration: *a deep understanding of the classical texts and the construction of a new paradigm.*

First of all, when we look back into the classics of Western Marxism ever since the publication of *History and Class Consciousness*, it is not difficult to find that most of our achievements are still at the level of commentaries; although there are some studies on different specific topics,

---

[1] Here are some exceptions: Henri Lefebvre's *Critique of Everyday Life*, *Everyday Life in the Modern World*, and Ernst Bloch's *The Principle of Hope*. This might be caused by problems in understanding and translation.

they cannot be even counted as intensive and meticulous examinations. We can see everywhere lots of second-hand data retelling views of others and naming them as a certain "-ism", and what we really lack is a philosophical discourse leading to a deep research that understands the original context. I have once pointed out major reasons for this phenomenon: First, we have never seriously faced the classics of Marxism that have been under scrupulous studies by the Western Marxists. Then how can we come up with the "Marxist criticism"? To be specific, "Marxist criticism" presupposes the intensive reading of the classics of Marxism, what I call "Back to Marx." Without this, any simplistic comment and assertion can be branded as "illegal" or "ideological," leading to a rootless theoretical research. Second, the Western Marxism schools are ready to integrate Marx with various philosophical and cultural trends so as to construct new radical discourses opposite to or beyond the main stream of modern western capitalist ideology. In addition, a number of researchers themselves are masters of contemporary western philosophy. They tend to explain Marx through their original philosophical discourses, for example, Georg Simmel's aesthetics of modern life held by the young Lukacs before he enters Marxism, the sociology of Max Weber, the early Existentialism of Jean-Paul Sartre, the early phenomenology of Merleau-Ponty, the Fromm-Marcuse psychoanalysis, and the theory of the atonal music by Theodor W. Adorno. Without complete understanding of the perspectives of these philosophical backgrounds, it would prove futile to master the problematic matter (the "-ism" taken for granted) of what we are going to discuss, not to say the possibility for us to deconstruct the profound theories of our critical objects. Besides, we are still unfamiliar with certain historical contexts where the western researchers have been situated despite several tides of translations of the western Marxist works ever since the 1980s. This absence of background support, again, leads to the loss of the special discourses and their contexts that the Chinese researchers are supposed to have. Therefore, what is most important for the present research in China is that we should turn back, face the texts and philosophers that we deem as "present-at-hand," construct particular historical contexts, and find out the "symptoms" of their theoretical logics and main ideas. Only by the intensive reading can we start a new round of profound criticism.

In the second place, a precondition of contemporary Marxism research is about the transformation of paradigms. Since the 1968 "Red Storm" in France, there have been great changes in the New Left and the traditional Western Marxism camp. In particular, the paradigm of the traditional "Western Marxism" (two subjects, for example, *the "authenticity" of Marx* and *the political criticism of capitalism*) cannot support its original connotation and denotation any longer, with the failure to understand a postmodern world. If we do not re-define the paradigm, another wave of chaotic theories will strike us. In my opinion, we need a new definition of historical theories and logics, that is, *to identify the historical ending of the Western Marxism* and construct a new pattern where *the post-modern Marxism, the post-Marxian trend and the late Marxism* are put next to each other. This is the only way for us to review the new trends of Marxism.[1]

As noted above, Adorno's criticism of totality and identity signified the ending of Western Marxism as a necessary historical existence in the 1960s. This ending, in its practical sense, was realized through the revolutionary movements of the western students at the end of the 1960s and the failure of "Rose Revolution."[2] It was well-known that the special theoretical trend of Western Marxism was unconsciously established against the "orthodox Marxism" of the Second International by several European Marxist philosophers in the 1920s. They refused any ideological and official structuring of Marxism, especially, the unscientific interpretations to idolize Marx by those classical Marxist authors. They also attempted to re-interpret the texts of Marxism and differentiate an un-orthodox "neo-Marxism" from the Engels-Stalin system. And yet this new-born Marx is usually situated in a western cultural and philosophical school. Most of all, these Left theories persistently claim for their own *authenticity* of Marxism although

---

[1] To be accurate, this also involves post-Marxism in the sense of political practice. This term is acceptable to the western contemporary socialism and studies of revolutionary strategies.

[2] Paris "May Storm" is also called the revolution for the Invisible Thing.

they are actually ideologies against the capitalist political system within the framework of industrial civilization.

In the early theoretical construction of Western Marxism, Georg Lukacs' historical dialectics of the totality, Antonio Gramsci's hegemonism of practice and Karl Korsch's identity of subject and object contributed to opposing the split of theoretical logic from its capitalist reality. After the 1930s, a humanistic Marxism came into being, based on the young Marx's *The Economic and Philosophic Manuscripts of 1844*. In addition to the early activities of the Frankfurt School, it includes the humanistic construction by Ernst Bloch, Jean-Paul Sartre, Erich Fromm and Henri Lefebvre. This humanistic Marxism reached its peak in the mid-1960s and, experienced major strikes from scientism led by Althusser and other western Marxists, who rejected the non-historical human and subjectivity, thus reproducing a modern disintegration of rationality in the academic unconsciousness—a paradox of humanism and scientism.

After this, the *Dialectic of Enlightenment* co-authored by Theodor Adorno and Max Horkheimer started a theoretical breakthrough in the late development of the Frankfurt School. And Adorno's *Negative Dialectics* generated a new logic trend of the internal refusal of *the whole industrial civilization*. The enlightenment, as the capitalist liberal discourse, the wing of instrumental reason to enslave nature and dominate man, and any attempt to pursue the freedom and liberation based on certain *identical* essence (whether on man or laws) all take part in the hidden conspiracy of the capitalist totality. The violent relation imposed on nature by man is under critical introspection. Now, the most important foundation of the growth of productive forces and the logic of human liberation are negated. Different from the materialized production of the young Lukacs along with the alienated practice of Sartre and other ontological uncertainties, Adorno's philosophy ran over the edge of western Marxism and ended it. He set a theoretical starting-point to the post-modern trend, with his new attitude toward Marx. I posit it as the *post-Marx* trend, which radically denies the critical foundation of Marxism but essentially inherits the tradition of Marx's criticism in terms of methodology and the basic standpoints. Their writings no longer piously refer to Marx's "classical texts"; instead, they display a free and relaxed agreement or disagreement. This post-Marx trend represents the theoretical image of a great many former western Marxism researchers and Center-Left thinkers in the 1970s. It is on the basis of Adorno's thought that the Frankfurt School has a great theoretical turn to the center of the new post-humanism. For example, Fromm, the humanistic Marxist philosopher of the second generation, wrote his last work *Haben oder Sein* (1976), in which he abandoned the abstract subject-centrism and distinguished the "possessive" humanistic subject from the non-possessive, non-central subject. He was strongly against the old humanism of "self-center, self-interest and the lust to have," against "enslaving nature" and man's "hateful attitude" towards nature. Later on, both Friedrich Pollock and Jürgen Habermas established their theories on the very theoretical turn. Without attention to this point, it would be very hard to understand Habermas' non-identical communication theory, which transcends the economy of labor. Therefore, it was Adorno who started the post-(modern) Marxian trend. In addition, another important event occured almost at the same time. It was the transformation of the French philosopher Henri Lefebvre in his late academic studies, that is, the criticism of *modern* life after 1962. Lefebvre identified the conversion from the production-economy domain to the consumption-sign domain in the control and slavery structure of the capitalist society. Lefebvre is the first to overturn the foundation of the historical mode of material production; in his later studies of space, he argued for the existence of a hyper-real representational space to replace that of the social relations in Marx's historical materialism (the traditional space, which means the absolute space of nature, the political historical space and the economic abstract space). His viewpoint directly prompted Jean Baudrillard's post-Marx turn. It is worthy of notice that Adorno and Lefebvre have always been among the western Marxists, but they are also the initiators of the post-Marx trend.

In the Marxian camp after Adorno, there appeared a radical trend, which negated the industrial civilization and all of its cultural forms. Its main force derived from the post-modern Marxism which was established in and influenced by the post-modern trend, for instance, the ecological Marxism and new feministic Marxism. Although these theorists take themselves as Marxists, they fundamentally depart from the traditional western Marxism. The essential difference lies in their denial of the most important principles in Marxist philosophy. For instance, the ecological Marxism is against the idea that the level of productive forces is the base of historical development; this view that the human subject enslaves nature actually rejects the growth of the productive forces in historical materialism. As for the feministic Marxism, it refutes that the Marxist social class is only paternal because Marx only notices the labor materialized in the exchange market but ignores the position of the housework of woman in the *abstract* total labor, which neglects that the "shadow labor" also creates value. These theories, despite their claim of Marxism, have departed from the "authentic Marxism" asserted by the traditional western Marxists as well as the basic intention of modern capitalist criticism.

After the "May Storm," a group of young western Marxists in Europe bid farewell to Marxism and turned to a more radical post-Marxian thought in the post-modern trend. The vigorous thinkers, for example, Gilles Deleuze, Jean Baudrillard, and Jacques Derrida, openly expressed their disagreements with Marxism but declared that they had inherited something critical of Marx. The theoretical trend is characterized by post-modern mainstream initiated by Roland Barthes, Jacques Lacan and Jerry Fodor; at the same time, it is different from the political standpoint of the post-modern right trend, for example, Jean-François Lyotard, Richard Rorty and Ihab Hassan, along with a new comer, Slavoj Zizek, a Lacanist from Slovenia. They reject modern capitalism but cautiously keep certain distance from Marxism, including the post-colonialism and the cultural criticism of new historicism. This is what I term the *post-Marxian Trend*, which is a theoretical mutation of the Western Marxism during its abrupt turn to the right in the post-modern context. It should be noted that these Marxist philosophers are *not* or *no longer* Marxists. In this regard, they are different from Adorno and Lefebvre. And their political position quite differs from the post-modern Marxism which is self-appointed as Marxism as we mentioned above and the late Marxism which we are going to discuss later.

The post-Marxian philosophy boasts of its historical transcendence over the basic framework of Marxism, which is not different from the post-modern Marxism in terms of historical ontology: they are built on the transcendence of the modern by the post-modern. The post-Marxian philosophers believe that the foundation of social history, on which Marxism is built, will be inevitably reduced to the residue of history. An entirely new social civilization is supposed to come up with a heterogeneous reality for this radical criticism. Therefore, most of the post-Marxian thinkers criticize Marx from a certain perspective while constructing their own critical platform, for example, Baudrillard, with his *Mirror of Production* and *For a Critique of Political Economy of Sign* published in the 1970s. As a student of Lefebvre, Baudrillard is also influenced by Roland Barthes and Guy Debord. In *Society of Spectacle*, Debord rewrites the beginning of Marx's *Capital*, in which "an immense accumulation of spectacle" replaces Marx's "immense accumulation of commodities." From the *Society of Spectacle* to *The Consumer Society*, the commodity exchange of Marx is turned into the exchange of signs. The mirror of production on which Marx relies is broken while the fantasy of post-modern media becomes the real ruler in today's capitalist society. In addition, Baudrillard declares the death of modernity and industry (the mode of material production), which also accounts for his refutations of Marxism. The latest events include Mark Poster's replacement of Marx's mode of production with his *mode of information* and Zizek's adoption of the Lacanian *symptoms* in place of Marx's material relations. In general, the post-Marxian philosophy attempts to stride beyond the old Marxist domain, which is a significant heterogeneity in theory.

After the post-modern trend came to the center of the western radical thought, there appeared another kind of Marxist discourse, which was very close to the traditional western Marxism. It still retains the post-modern space-time relationship with the traditional Western Marxism and abides by its basic principles with the firm belief that the philosophical framework of Marxism is insuperable to the post-industrial thought. In face of the rapid development of capitalism, it refuses to acknowledge any essential change, which is but identified as the late capitalism (Ernest Mandel) or global capitalism. I prefer to define this trend as the *Late Marxism*. The representatives include such avant-guard members as Fredric Jameson, Terry Eagleton, Arif Dirlik, Steve Best and Douglas Kellner, among whom, the flexible production proposed by Dirlik is perhaps the most creative idea. The Late Marxism transcends the traditional western Marxism in that it comes up with an entirely new theoretical discourse to deal with the problems in the post-industrial society and globalization, in spite of the reliance on the basic framework and principles of their predecessors. It must be pointed out that both the Late Marxism and the post-Modern Marxism come to confront the same new history. However, the post-Modern Marxism asserts the post-modern renewal of Marxism with the conversion of modernity to post-modernity while the Late Marxism ignores that post-modernity and considers the new historical era as a later period of capitalist development. Both the Late Marxism and the post-Modern Marxism identify themselves as Marxism and insist to uphold Marxism, which is essentially different form the post-Marxian trend.

We cannot establish a scientific platform to study the Western Marxism without understanding the two theoretical preconditions above. Thus, it is indispensable to read the classical texts written by foreign Marxist scholars. As a focus of my study, the reading gives rise to two monographs, *Atonal Dialectical Imagination*: *The Textological Reading of Adorno's Negative Dialectics*, and *Problematic, Symptomal Reading and Ideology*: *A Textological Illustration of Althusser*. I have started a systematic reading of the Western Marxism, the post-Marxian trend, the post-Modern Marxism, and the Late Marxism. This project started after my book, *Back to Marx—Philosophical Discourse in Economic Context* (1998), and was expected to finish within 5 years. But now it has to last longer. I am determined to go on with this project.

Before the publication of the first volume of *A Deep Plough*: *Unscrambling Major Post-Marxist Texts from Adorno to Zizek*, I started to write this second volume in the year of 2003. However, I had never expected the texts that I was to deal with in this book would prove so thrilling an experience to me. In addition to the finished part about Theodor W. Adorno, which was already awful enough, other post-Marx thinkers and texts were all disturbing, frightening and distressing. These three years turned out to be a very difficult time.

For example, the meaning of the book *The Sublime Object of Ideology*, written by Slavoj Zizek, a very popular academic star in Europe and America, only became clear to me when I read it for the fourth time. It had never happened before. I remember that I could recognize every word Zizek wrote, in particular, the initial part about the discussion of the Marxist economy and philosophy, but I was simply at a loss of what he meant, annoyed. Moreover, as Zizek obtained his theoretical support from Lacan, I had to painfully concentrate my attention on Lacan and his witch-like mysterious discourse. A year passed and something interesting happened: the original plan of writing a treatise about Zizek produced a book about his theoretical father, Lacan. It added another unexpected result to my writing.

Then, I wrote about Jacques Derrida's *Specters of Marx* and Guy Debord's *Society of the Spectacle*. Although they were profound as well, I felt comparatively easy to handle them. In the fall of 2004, I began to write my interpretation about Derrida's *Specters of Marx* and finished the draft during my visit in England. The year of 2005 was mainly spent on Lacan and at the end of it I finished with Debord's *Society of the Spectacle*. But these comfortable days slipped too fast. Then, I encountered Jean Baudrillard's *Mirror of Production*, which seemed to be so difficult a task that I once hesitated whether I would go on or not. Speaking of Baudrillard, who enjoyed a great popularity in Europe and America, people are generally attracted by the hyperbolic illustration of contemporary social existence in his later years, like "implosion" "simulacrum," etc., while less concerned about his early works, especially, *The Mirror of Production*, which was used by him to bid farewell to Marx and which, in my eyes, has become so far one of the most significant books against Marxism. It is important because it steps over the dogmatic Marxism in Stalinist context and directly targets the essential contents in Marxist texts, particularly, the critical conclusions of late Marx's economic manuscripts as well as the political economy and historical materialism in *Das Kapital*. Moreover, Baudrillard structures his logic on the research of primitive tribes by the French anthropologist Marcel Mauss who influenced the whole European academia in the 1960s and 1970s. And he absorbs the relevant grassroots philosophy by Georges Bataille. As a result, I was often choked when reading *The Mirror of Production*, like being hit by someone but unable to fight back. It was a very uncomfortable feeling. Different from the text of Zizek, this book by Baudrillard is against what we are to re-interpret and sincerely follow every day. I could not retreat but fought my way out. This time, I rebuked Baudrillard as he did Marx in the 1970s. I think Baudrillard should deserve it.

The selection of the texts in this book was made using the same standard with that of the first volume. I do not want to address every appropriate aspect of the theories or choose the theorists with general social influence. My emphasis is on the texts that can be counted as the classics in the post-Marx trend. For this reason, I finally removed some texts after a careful consideration to generate a thoughtful shock in a certain logical dimension. This book is still in line with the modern textual study I have started in *Back to Marx*, instead of the textological method of *theoretical scene-construction* that I am concurrently applying in my research of Lenin's *Notes of Philosophy*.

Here, I would like to give my special thanks to Dr. Fang Xianghong, who helped me with the foreign materials, and Zhou Jiaxin and Cai Yu, who spent much time in material collection and typing. Last but not least, many thanks to my editors Li Yanhui and her colleagues for their support.

Zhang Yibing
May 20, 2003
Nanjing

Notes on Translation

This book is a critical reading, of the most well-known post-Marxian theorists in the West and their major works. A large number of Western and Chinese philosophical texts that the author has discussed or referred to do not have English translations, so we would like to highlight a few issues that we have encountered in the process of our translation.

1. There are quite a few philosophical terms or expressions invented by the author himself, which do not have English equivalents. Those terms are repeatedly used in the book and often with different emphases so that readers are advised to grasp their meanings in different contexts.

2. There are a few places in the book where the author refers to the speeches or interviews made by Western theorists when they were in China. The Chinese translations are based on the sound recordings or notes for which the original material is hard to assess. Thus our English translations are done from the Chinese records.

3. Most of the citations of Western sources (mostly German or French) in the original book are taken from the Chinese translations. In our translation, great efforts are made to access the English versions wherever possible. However, there still remain some citations for which the English versions are not available. In that case, translation was done from the Chinese.

Translation of contemporary Chinese philosophical texts into English has rarely been done. Painstaking as it is, we feel fortunate to have undertaken the translation of this exciting and inspiring monograph, which will benefit the scholarly exchange of philosophical thinking between the

East and the West, Marxism in particular.

The translation work was shared among four people, Chapter 1 by Chen Lin, Chapter 2 by Fan Shuying, Chapters 3 & 5 and Preface by He Huiming, and Chapter 4 by He Chengzhou. While He Huiming made great efforts in solving problems such as unified format, footnotes and references, He Chengzhou has proofread the whole book.

He Chengzhou
March 2009, Providence (RI)

Chapter 1

Atonal Dialectical Imagination: Reading of Adorno's *Negative Dialectics*[1]

Dialectics for Adorno is rather a critical theory than a type of knowledge of correlation and development in the textbooks of conventional Marxist philosophy. This is the way in which Western Marxism, following Lukács, defines dialectics. Accordingly, Adorno's representation of dialectics necessarily loses a logic system of totality, being a negative thinking movement of the deconstructive and anti-system, which never ceases to break its own solidification. In what the present chapter talks on— the introduction and Part Two of *Negative Dialectics*—Adorno unfolds his negative dialectic as a functional critical discourse, a modern musical poem and a dynamic impressionist painting. In other words, the object of this

---

[1] This chapter was translated by Chen Lin.

chapter is the best part in Adorno's work in question.

Introduction: A Preparative Work of Critical Methodology

In Adorno[1]'s view, the construction of theory is a tribe of thoughts—interaction of the non-hierarchical. As a result, he chooses the "constellation" and "field of forces" to represent such a new decentralized and non-slavery idea. In reality it sets a barrier which later researchers still using the conventional interpretative discourse cannot surpass. Therefore, I have to make a declaration here, that the logical deployment in this chapter has little relationship with the one in Adorno's text of *Negative Dialectics*. It merely serves as a deconstructive measure and mirror to accord facilities for the readership. Readers are expected to follow this point so that they can reach Adorno in their comprehension.

---

[1] Theodor Wiesengrund Adorno (Sep 11, 1903-Aug 6, 1969), a well-known German sociologist, a musicologist and a philosopher in Western Marxism, a member of the first generation of Frankfurt School. He was the founder of the social critical theory. Adorno was born in Frankfurt at Main in Germany, and died of a heart attack on a vacation to Visp, Switzerland. He entered University of Frankfurt and studied philosophy, musicology, psychology and sociology. By the end of 1924, under the supervision of Hans Cornelius, he graduated with a dissertation on phenomenology of Edmund Husserl. In 1931, he began his two years as a university instructor at the University of Frankfurt after his manuscript *Kierkegaard: Construction of the Aesthetic* was appreciated. When Nazis came into power in Germany, Adorno was expelled by the Nazis and had to immigrate to England, obtaining a teaching position at the University of Oxford. Soon after, following the way of several other friends from Frankfurt School, he emigrated to the U.S. During the period of 1938-1941, he was accepted as an official member by Horkheimer's Institute for Social Research in New York. From 1941 to 1948, he carried out research during his participation in Lazarsfeld/Stanton Analysis Program at Princeton, focusing on the study of totalitarianism. And then he was appointed as co-director of the Research Project on Social Discrimination at the University of California, Berkeley (1948-1949). In 1949, Adorno returned to Germany and assisted Horkheimer in his reconstruction of Institute for Social Research. Meanwhile, Adorno obtained a professorship on philosophy and sociology at the University of Frankfurt. In August of 1950, he acted as vice director of Institute for Social Research. In 1958, he took the place of Horkheimer and acted as director of the Institute. Some of his masterpieces are: *Dialectic of Enlightenment* (co-authored with Horkheimer, 1947), *Minima Moralia: Reflections from Damaged Life* (1951), *Negative Dialectics* (1966).

1. A critical principle of deconstruction and theoretical structure?

The reason I put the interrogation mark with caution at the end of the title is that there is never a fixed principle or logical framework of identity in Adorno's own discussion. In original German version of atonal *Negative Dialectics*, there are no subsections for each topic; while English version (Chinese version, Chongqing Press, 1993) paraphizes each section for the convenience of reading. The sub-titles in English version are put deliberately at the end of the whole body of text in the original German one, providing a kind of reference for reading. However, reading of Adorno is undoubtedly painful, because we have to offer a kind of logical analysis to account for the so-called "semi-postmodernist text" that he has destructuralized into the ideal field of forces. Thus, we can say that the measure is actually an illegal appropriation for the benefit of the readers.

At the very beginning of the Introduction in *Negative Dialectics*, Adorno makes a manifest announcement that dialectics will be discussed here. It marks a significant difference that to talk of dialectics after Nietzsche and Hegel. Adorno's discussion of dialectics is inevitably influenced by Hegel and Marx, on the one hand; while on the other hand, obviously does not remain at the level of **affirmative** description of external matters within the discourse of "correlation and development"; rather, it finds its right place in the critical and revolutionary context of **historical** dialectics. Accordingly, he states, in the way of Heidegger, that "as early as Plato, dialectics meant to achieve something positive by means of negation."[1] It seems to refer to Socrates' dialectics of dialog which is to produce through reduction to absurdity. To be sure, it involves young Lukács' critical identification of Engels' definition of dialectics.[2]

Revolutionary and Critical Dialectics between the Subject-Object Relationship: In *History and Class Consciousness*, Lukács

---

[1]　Adorno, Theodor. *Negative Dialectics*. New York: The Seabury Press, 1973. p. xix.

[2]　Lukács, Georg. *History and Class Consciousness*. London: Merlin Press, 1971. p. 4.

defines demonstrably "the crucial determinants" of dialectics "the interaction of Subject and Object, the unity of theory with practice."[1] He thus confirms a logical presupposition that dialectics is no more than a *historical* theory of a way how the Subject transforms the Object. The reason is that, there are not any self-conscious subjects in the materialist nature which is external to human subjects. In a later chapter, young Lukács states that "dialectics is not imported into history from outside, nor is it interpreted in the light of history (as often occurs in Hegel), but is *derived* from history, made conscious as its logical manifestation at this particular point in its development."[2] Dialectics is nothing but dialectics of subject. Accordingly, Adorno argues against Engels' position that it is an inevitable trend to extend dialectics into nature (early Marxism shares an idea in common that dialectics is qualified merely in the field of *history*). From young Lukács' view of point, Engels' misunderstanding of dialectics leads to a fact that dialectics is not revolutionary any longer. As mentioned above, young Lukács insists that dialectics is dialectics of history, and its crucial determinants are the interaction of subject and object. However, "Engels—following Hegel's mistaken lead— extended the method to apply also to nature."[3] It is undoubtedly a kind of illegal appropriation. Indeed, Engels never touches on the *"dialectical interaction of subject and object within the process of history,"* let alone put his accent on this very important topic. As a result, dialectics must have been no more revolutionary with absence of such a moment, despite its attempt to maintain (finally proved to be fruitless) the characterization of *fluidity*. Young Lukács comments that the mistake of Engels lies in his pursuing of so-called "dialectics of nature" in external nature where self-conscious subjects as such cannot be found; whereas in the field of nature external to subject

---

[1] Lukács, Georg. *History and Class Consciousness*. London: Merlin Press, 1971. p. 24, note 6.
[2] Ibid., p. 177.
[3] Ibid., p. 24, note 6.

it is impossible to produce spontaneously historical dialectics which functions revolutionarily. Thus, "if this central function of the theory is disregarded, the virtues of forming 'fluid' concepts become altogether problematic: a purely 'scientific' matter."[1] The quoted sentence obviously argues against Engels' statement that "dialectics is in general the theory of relation and development of things." Here Lukács actually intends to emphasize that, "fluidity" of dialectics (of nature) would remain a natural process external to human beings where dialectics fails to involve the interaction between subject and object. If, Marxist theory becomes a kind of positivist science, it will inevitably result in its degradation into the level at which an on-looking fetishism of capitalist ideology (positivism) does. What is known as "vulgar and non-critical Marxism" it demonstrates a further inaccuracy of reading of Marx by The Second International. For it is possible for "a theory of 'evolution' without revolution and of 'natural development' into Socialism without any conflict" [2]only when one removes the essential activity of dialectics and wait for a revolution from subject-object relationship, looking on with folded arms. As a result, such kind of 'Marxism' dooms to degrade into an anti-revolutionary dogma that is resolutely divorced from reality. This point is young Lukács' reiteration of essential negativity of materialist dialectics.

Adorno directly states that he intends to release dialectics from "the affirmative character." To do this, he singles out one of Hegelian qualifications, namely negative dialectics. It is a referential definition that transforms the functional property of dialectics (in Hegel and Marx) into the fundamental qualification.

In my views, such a negative qualification implies something like an ontological meaning. Because, Hegel had ever affirmed Spinoza's idea that "Negation is at one with affirmation"! Thus, for Adorno, negativity—

---

[1] Lukács, Georg. *History and Class Consciousness*. London: Merlin Press, 1971. pp. 3-4.
[2] Ibid., p.5.

objective contradiction inherent logic of dialectics—is an ontic pulse of dialectics. Adorno attempts to construct dialectics as negativity and critique, "without reducing its determinacy." Obviously, Adorno denounces any ontology, but his ultimate theoretical goal is to deconstruct the external affirmation of dialectics and to construct an affirmation upon negativity. It is probably the origin of his later predicament.

Another further qualification is that "*negative dialectics* is a phrase that flouts tradition."[1] Here, it is worth clarifying that, the alleged tradition is not the tradition of interpretation of dialectical theories, but the overall tradition of metaphysics from Nietzsche to Heidegger. *It is namely, according to Nietzsche-Heidegger's logic, the history of western philosophy since Descartes.* Adorno believes that, in such a metaphysical logic, things grow out of a foundation according to the dominant view of philosophy. In other words, the departure of this dominant metaphysics is *the elementary problem of primacy*, and Adorno intends to criticize such a philosophy of *foundation* or *primacy*. It is undoubtedly a great theoretical revolution. I have to make a clarification here without which it is likely to cause a kind of unnecessary negative effect in general philosophical knowledge. Indeed, Adorno's struggle against all philosophy of *ontology*, philosophy of *–ism* and philosophy of *system* is based upon a position of alleged negative dialectics and *historical philosophy* (he considers it the authentic logic of Marxist philosophy, something like a musical poem). So his enemies cover all the idealist philosophy and materialist philosophy that advocate the principle of "the foundation concept as well as the primacy of substantive thought." It obviously derives from Nietzsche and Heidegger's subversive and reflective logic of western philosophy. It consists two key points:

First, every traditional philosophy—commitment in the primacy of either substance or idea, or more recently, of either unconsciousness or transcendental structure of reason—never escapes from a great logical trap. In other words, each presupposition of any primacy is objectively *an outcome of thinking*. What does it mean? It means that, although the

---

[1] Adorno, Theodor. *Negative Dialectics*. New York: The Seabury Press, 1973. p. xix.

preceding philosophers have claimed the so-called foundation of the world is certain actual substantiality; however, the fact is, long after the philosophers has discussed things, those various kinds of alleged primacies ("substance", "mind", "nature", "human", "species", "noumenon", "logos", "reason", "practice", "unconsciousness", "will", "life", "intent" and "being", etc.) "will here be developed." Because, these primary matters are merely time-restricted concepts (the primary "Oneness") that were the historical and abstract definitions of all kinds of things and phenomena by human beings. It also means that, "a thought of whose movement the thinker becomes aware only as he performs it." When we transfigure those outcomes of our thinking into a foundation of the world, we produce certain abstract ideal essence (Seiende) within the process of thinking. It is thus the metaphysics of the *dead* concept in the sense of Sein. The secret of the philosophy of primacy lies in the fact that we are enslaved by the concepts and ideas we have produced. Such a situation in reality represents a profound *self-enslavement*, which undoubtedly was created originally by Heidegger, not Adorno.

Secondly, the metaphysics constructs, according to *the coercive logic of identity*, various *hierarchical* systems of concepts which are dominated by the primary and paramount concepts. Different from the first point, the second one does not derive directly from Heidegger, because in Adorno's view, Heidegger has been trapped into the logic of identity in the same token. Rather, it relates to later Derrida and Deleuze. So the conclusion can be drawn that the so-called post-modern theory of deconstruction can find its departure point here. Accordingly, to break all the hierarchical structures of philosophical systems, Adorno tries "putting his cards on the table" (thus puzzles the readers non-identical with Adorno, including me). He constellates all of his ideas in a non-hierarchical way, attempting "by means of logical consistency to substitute for the unity principle, and for the paramountcy of the supra-ordinated concept." In this sense, negative dialectics must be an *anti-system*.[1] It is a point to which we need to pay attention, because it figures out the key concepts and the framework of Adorno's thought in

---

[1] Adorno, Theodor. *Negative Dialectics*. New York: The Seabury Press, 1973. p. xx.

advance.

The deconstruction and reconstruction of texts: Adorno has successfully done it. In *Aesthetic Theory* which he began to write at the same time with *Negative Dialectics*, Adorno acknowledges that, "the first draft is always an organized self-deception; in the second, I maneuver myself into the position of critic of my own work."[1] The reason is that, even in his own process of writing, Adorno often confronts tempts of "primary philosophy." Usually, the writing of the first draft is still within the logic of identity, at this time, "my theorem that there is no philosophical 'first thing' is coming back to haunt me." Namely, he produces a text of primary philosophy in the first place, and then deconstructs it. It is Adorno's mode of writing. In the second draft that is self-critical, he intentionally ceases to construct a universe of reason in a conventional way, and "I have to put together a whole from a series of partial complexes which are concentrically arranged and have the same weight and relevance." It also means that, the composition of the second draft has to "be written concentrically such that the paratactical parts have the same weight and are arranged around a center of gravity which they express through their constellation"[2]. This kind of text, in which each section or each opinion "has equivalent ponderance," is an ideal constellation of theories and a montage of texts produced by Adorno. More or less, it reflects Benjamin's "indeterminate writing." For Benjamin has ever said that, a text is simply a mask of death, so one can only find truth that had not been structured by logic in "fragments" where it is on construction.[3] Actually, after the completion of the edifice of theory by the first draft, Adorno deconstructs it into the field on construction. Thus, it is reasonable to draw a conclusion that,

---

[1] Adorno, Theodor. *Aesthetic Theory* (London, Boston, Melbourne and Henley: Routledge & Kegan Paul, 1984), translated by C. Lenhardt, edited by Gretel Adorno and Rolf Tiedemann, p. 495

[2] Ibid., p. 496.

[3] Benjamin, Walter. *Works of Walter Benjamin*. Beijing: Chinese Social Science Press, 1999. p. 352.

the secret of *Negative Dialectics* just lies in such a writing mode which is in the way of deconstruction. What I intend to do, is to reconstruct what has been deconstructed by Adorno. It is probably the inchoation of the history of post-modern thinking. However, before the 1950s, Adorno still remained in the conventional way of logical construction, which Wolin called "micro-phylosophy," "a kind of self-descriptive 'logic of decomposition,' which produces 'the universal' only after the baptism of the particular."[1] Indeed, it remained dominant that the analytical logic of semi-field research as far as his work of *Against Epistemology: A Metacritique*. Besides studies on culture and music, *Negative Dialectics* is the first constellated poetic text among Adorno's discussion of philosophy. Moreover, there is another proof worth noting: in the last part of the book which collects several drafts about the very work, the readers can find the remnant of the conventional mode of writing, although Adorno has intentionally deconstructed them.

The preface, guidance for Adorno's writing, summarizes the content of *Negative Dialectics*: the introduction interprets the concept of philosophical experience. In this part, Adorno does not define some abstract concepts to construct readers' interests in theories, but introduce a new exciting philosophical experience. Adorno aims to bring the readers a new philosophical impulse by the introduction: it is due to some heterogeneous *experience* produced by a critical and dialectical thinking, not logic of *reason* which centers on some certain system of concepts. This affirmation signifies three dimensions: firstly, in the dimension of philosophical premise, Adorno advocates thinking of non-totality and *jeu*, against totality and absolute essence in conventional construction of philosophy; secondly, in the dimension of concepts, he definitely denounces logic of identity, approving of deconstruction and unattainability of nonidentity; thirdly, in the dimension of dialectics, he argues against contradictions for pseudo-unity, spark-plugging heterogeneous dialectics that tries to break away from reign of totality,

---

[1] Wolin, Richard. *The Concept of Cultural Critique*. Beijing: Commercial Press, 2000. p. 84.

namely, negative dialectics. It implicates the importance of the introduction.

The subject of Part One of *Negative Dialectics* is ontology. And it mainly criticizes Heideggerian philosophy that is important and popular in Germany. It is Adorno's another liquidation of contemporary German philosophy besides his critique of Kierkegaard and Husserl. In his view, "rather than judged from above, this ontology is understood and immanently criticized out of the need for it, which is a problem of its own."[1] It actually is Hegel's strategy of critique. Part Two, proceeds to idea of a negative dialectics. It focuses on several categories which are retained as well as qualitatively altered. Here, what I intend to remind readers of such a fact: Adorno shows his brilliance in critique of other philosophers while he loses his light in his positive construction. Part Three, elaborates models of negative dialectics. It consists in three sections: 1) philosophical ethics is done by a dialectics of freedom; 2) philosophy of history is done by "World Spirit and Natural History"; 3) to give the Copernican revolution an axial turn by critical self-reflection around metaphysical question.[2]

At the end of German version, there is an essay "excursus on *Negative Dialectics*" by Adorno (the translator of English version missed this part, so did the translator of Chinese one). From this essay, we know that: 1) *Negative Dialectics* was written during 1959-1966; in 1967, he supplements the section of "qualitative moment of rationality" into the instruction of the second version, and a footnote about the problem of contingency and inevitability; and 2) the kernel subject of the book is based on the drafts of three seminar given by Adorno at Collège de France in Paris in 1961; and 3) the former two drafts constitute Part One of *Negative Dialectics*; Part Two is based on the modification and supplement of third draft; Part Three is derived from his earlier academic movement in which the first draft of Chapter 1 "Freedom" was written in 1937, and Chapter Two "World Spirit and Natural History" from a speech at the Academy of Kant; and 4) that Adorno said himself, the most important idea of "the concept of logic disintegration" was originally

---

[1] Adorno, Theodor. *Negative Dialectics*. New York: The Seabury Press, 1973. p. xx.
[2] Ibid.

formed during his studenthood. The excursus is of great use for our historical orientation of *Negative Dialectics*.[1]

In my view, Adorno successfully achieves this goal. In the following part of this chapter, we'll try to approach Adorno's philosophical thinking which is something like a sonata.

2. Re-interpreting dialectics: the downfall and salvation of philosophy in market

Different from every other bourgeois philosopher, Adorno starts out from current state of society and then proceeds with the destiny and actuality of philosophy. He states that, since 1845 when Marx insists on changing the world, not merely interpreting it, philosophy appears to *relate theory to practice* or to approach reality. However, due to in "inadequate" understanding of Marxist impulse of changing the world, the movement of actualization of philosophy is reduced to a vulgar pragmatism. I do not think Adorno has narrated clearly his context here, for dominant Western philosophy never tries to understand Marx; on the other hand, it is not veracious to refer to traditional Marxist philosophy since Stalin in terms of "marketization." On the contrary, it would be more reasonable if Adorno states directly that, the overall contemporary western ideology is turning philosophy into *all types of theoretical stalls in the marketplace*. This phenomenon is a historical echo: in the past, the foundation of philosophy is the "primacy" that is abstracted from sensible and actual multiplicity; while nowadays it goes back to the multiple phenomena which are much more complicated than before. Here, in the modern capitalist civilization of industry, "the introverted thought architect dwells behind the moon that is taken over by extroverted technicians."[2] It means that, the conventional and mysterious abstract speculation has been broken by commodity and technique. In the old times, philosophers elaborate the essence of reason behind sensible phenomena from above, and claim a power discourse

---

[1] Adorno, Theodor. *Negative Dialektik* (Frankfurt am Main: Suhrkamp, 1982), see Excursus.

[2] Adorno, Theodor. *Negative Dialectics*. New York: The Seabury Press, 1973. p. 3.

in the right of such a mental ability of insight; but at present, everything can be taken into the marketplace and decoded by technique, "the will to this understanding bespeaks a power claim denied by that which is to be understood." The hand of industry, which made no sense of the rainbow of poets and killed those happy eidolons in the forest, has reincarnated a huge manipulator of technology that jugulates thinking. In the marketplace where no one can find poetry and mental interest, "only advertisements for the world through its duplication and the provocative lie which does not seek belief but commands silence."[1] *Today, in China who is approaching materialization, we really encounter what Adorno bears in his mind and texts. A simple question for philosophers raised by the masses is: "What can you benefit?" In this utilitarian world, philosophers are no more than a group of buskeens.*

It is accurate for Adorno to announce that "no theory today escapes the marketplace" under the reign of capitalist system. Actually, no theory can avoid the fate of merchandise so far as there is marketplace. In China, an old saying says, "A contented mind is a perpetual feast." However, so long as philosophers and their families are still in the real world, they can never cease to concern about their own earthy conditions, either consciously or unconsciously. A fact comes to Adorno: Hegel knew already in the nineteenth century that, philosophy is not something above the real word; rather, it is purely an element of reality, an activity of the division of labor. As a result, he made some restricts for the development of metaphysical philosophy. In Adorno's view, each theory of philosophy, either its immanent structure or its alleged "truth", has to build upon the actual totality of history. It is probably the inversion of Marxist famous announcement that "philosophy is the essence of the spirit of its times." Another lamentable fact is, in today's merchandized world, philosophy has "in view of the immense expansion of the society and of the strides made by positive natural science come to seem like relics of a simple barter economy amidst the late stage of industrial capitalism"[2]. In other words, in such a times where utility becomes main

---

[1] Adorno, Theodor. *Prisms* (Cambridge: MIT Press, 1967), p. 34.

[2] Adorno, Theodor. *Negative Dialectics*. New York: The Seabury Press, 1973. p. 3.

concern, the special sciences compels philosophy to turn back into a special science, *a special science who speaks nonsense for the profit*. For example, in the dominant logic of "rejecting metaphysics" by positive sciences (particularly in China), there appears philosophy of technology which pays attention to instrumental reason, following science; economical philosophy which focus on benefit and profit, following economics; political philosophy which regards mechanism of power, following politics, etc. But for Adorno, philosophy is still metaphysical.

For Adorno, it is the failure of philosophy itself. For it has become a special science. And the reason lies in logical structure of traditional philosophy itself that is the inevitable outcome of compelling system of *Identity* (in Foucault's words, the overall process of philosophy "is developed as thought of *Identity*"[1]), not in the immense pressure caused by the alternation of extrinsic social conditions. In a theoretical inertia which compulsively comprises every thing and phenomenon in a conceptual framework, philosophy inevitably with the real world goes through a "square inside a circle" (it is the shape of Chinese ancient money. It usually means money). It shows an isomorphic framework. Under the circumstance, a new erect relationship appears; "money becomes God of our times"[2]. In the reality of market economy, the monarch is no doubt the abstract and objective "One", the equivalent which relates everything: money (the capital). It is the inescapable situation of philosophy in the trap of identity derived from globalization of market.

Adorno points out that, the only way to escape logic of identity and avoid death is: dialectics. It looks like an old-fashioned identification. However, dialectics for him is rather distinct. He indeed signifies a history of

---

[1] Foucault, Michel. "*Words and Things*" in *Philosophical Discourse in Postmodernism*. Hangzhou: Zhejiang Renmin Press, 2000. p. 3.

[2] Georg Simmel, *Money, Gender and Modern Life Style* (Shanghai: Academia Press, 2000), p.12. In theological discourse, the relationship among human beings is horizontal while the relationship between God and human beings is erect. However, the new erect relation between money and human beings does not create another world, but deprives human of the status of subject and turns them into things.

interpretation of dialectics; but such a history has been misread by readers.

Adorno states that, "the name of dialectics says no more, to begin with, than that objects do not go into their concepts without leaving a reminder."[1] Here, the term "to begin with" is obviously a critique of affirmative dialectics at its beginning. These ambiguous words need to be clarified. Adorno knows, "to think is to identify." On the threshold of each civilization, there was a process of abstract identification from "many" to the concept of "one". According to history of philosophy, since Eleatic School defined the characteristic of the concept of "Being," the process from "many" to "one" is regarded as the progress of culture and the development of cognition from phenomena to essence in the history of ideas. Now, Adorno begins his speculation from the other side, namely, the dimension of Nietzsche and Hegel. However, in Introduction (even in the whole book), Adorno consciously disguises such a source of his ideas.

Adorno does not ignore the fact that the appearance of identity is inherent in thought itself, in its pure form. The reason is simple. There is no identified abstraction from multiple objects, there is no concepts (For Lenin, concepts are the same type of definitions with essences and laws), or thought which operates in terms of concepts. It is worth noticing that Adorno does not denounce it, or, in other words, he does not deny general identity. But for him, metaphysical philosophy as the thinking of thinking, had begun to construct a *hierarchical* system of concepts, since Plato, where it formed multiple secondary concepts surrounding certain primacy. It is a strictly hierarchical kingdom. Identity as a despotism of idea, is what Adorno aims at. To this regard, the history of ideas is obviously a history of self-enslavement of the concept of Identity. Then, under the rule of Identity, conceptual order is content to screen what thinking seeks to comprehend, and ultimately becomes *ideology of cognition*. In *Aesthetic Theory*, Adorno makes a famous declaration that "oneness is an illusion." Since in each process of abstraction by a concept, "the appearance of thought" intertwines with "the truth of thought" (the actuality grasped by concepts) all the time.

---

[1] Adorno, Theodor. *Negative Dialectics*. New York: The Seabury Press, 1973. p. 5.

There is a simple fact that, whatever outside the cognition is decreed away, as by an avowal of finite definitions the *totality*. It actually explains why Adorno believes for affirmative dialectics of concepts, "objects do not go into their concepts without leaving a reminder." To begin with, a concept is "substitute of presence" (in Derrida's terms); while finally, it is *believed as an actual presence*. It is problematic, because each concept historically and finitely reflects a particular object. Once it is believed as the totality, what happens is the ideology of Identity in which *falsity takes place of actuality*. It is an illusion. Even in dialectical form, it is still ideological.

Adorno compares Kant to Hegel. For Kant, the transconceptual "in itself" is void, being wholly indefinite. Hegel argues against Kant. He proposes the "conceptual totality" is mere appearance and whatever differs from it in quality comes to be designated as a contradiction. It is a definition of dialectics by negativity. However, Hegel's contradiction comes to its end as unity and conciliation. That is why Adorno calls it non-identity under the aspect of identity.

3. Dialectics is not a freezing position

Following Hegelian redefinition of negativity of dialectics, Adorno offers a positive characterization: "Dialectics is the consistent sense of non-identity. It does not begin by taking a standpoint."[1] The title of this section is "dialectics not a standpoint"! It may cause some misunderstanding. Here the term "standpoint" means a solidified position or a fixed theoretical presupposition that unfolds the logic of theories in an omniscient and theological way. In my judgment, what Adorno intends to emphasize refers to the specific negation of the "ready-made conclusion" of traditional metaphysics. Dialectics is self-consciousness of *non-identity*. However, non-identity is not sufficient to define dialectics.

In one of the variations of dialectics—the absolute ideal totality in Hegelian philosophy, although contradiction signifies non-identity to some degree, it is no more than a complicated mechanism that serves

[1] Adorno, Theodor. *Negative Dialectics*. New York: The Seabury Press, 1973. p. 5.

the Idea to proceed to the ultimate identity of logic. The reason is that, in Hegel, the contradiction of totality is nothing but the falsity in the process of identification of totality. In this sense, Hegelian contradiction is indeed welded with identity; both of them obey the same law. In Hegelian philosophy, one can find the dialectical movement of Idea here and there, whose momentum is the alleged non-identical contradiction. However, every progress or upgrade of Idea is realized by the identification which eliminates nonidentity. It is similar to the symphony of Beethoven whose position in music, in my opinion, is equivalent to that of Hegel in philosophy, in which although the movements exhibit abundant non-identity, they still represent the same theme and tuning in a way of partita, a deployment of contradictions. They never really break the identity of theme and tuning. In a like manner, the non-identical appearance and presentations always expose the essential identity of Idea. God is unique. This is the intrinsically view of theology.

Adorno interprets the Hegelian law of identity as "the law of reality, not the law of thinking." Here, like Marx, he grasps the relationship of Hegel to Adam Smith and Ricardo.[1] Actually, Hegelian absolute identity derives from identity of capitalistic market economy; his universalism of Idea implies the universalism of commodity production conquers the whole world in the way of free competition in capitalistic world. *In Part Three of Negative Dialectics, Adorno modifies his old draft on Hegelian philosophy. The issue is unfolded in detail in the new Draft.* It is this reason that leads to Marx renaming the world history of absolute identity as *the world history of capitalism.* Obviously, Adorno here follows Marx on a new level. He affirms that the law of identity in mind is consolidated in contemporary world. This consolidation is caused by the "administered world" in which we live. *We have grasped the meaning of the "administered world" with the discussion of the penetration and domination over the social life by the instrumental reason in Section Three of Introduction.* Adorno states that, in the world where instruments are reversed and become motives, "... the impoverishment of experiences by

---

[1] The very point is demonstrated in Section 2, Chapter 1 of my book, *Go Back to Marx – Philosophical Discourse in Contexts of Economics* (Nanjing: Jiangsu Renmin Press, 1999).

dialectics … proves appropriate to the abstract monotony of that world."[1] In other words, in the process of identification (it can be called modernization or civilization) of capitalist market economy, everything is dominated by the standardization of technology; everything is administered by incorporation of science; everything is identified by the homogeneity (quantification) of exchange: it must result in a *monotone* and impoverished life of experience (later we will discuss that, the heterogeneous living experiences of subject, in Adorno's eyes, imply the authentic significance of life). Then, we could discover a new expression, on the basis of rewriting Hegel: here, gold is the only thing that makes sense; varieties are no more than the different representations of an equivalent. This "oneness" is capital. It is the law of identity in the history of capitalist world (in today's world, it is the globalization of capitalism) that produces the law of identity in the subjective area. Adorno believes that, human being cannot escape the despotic world of identity in which subjects and objects are isomorphic. He has to make a choice between two: either approve of negative dialectics, or yield to omnipresent and sweet bourgeois ideology.

Secondly, Kantian philosophy is a mutation of dialectics. It attempts to challenge the world at the cost of the separation of subject and object. Kantian philosophy restricts the cognitive ability of human beings to the objective phenomena of this world. Thus, dialectics can only be *negatively* and paradoxically reached in the subjective other world. Adorno interprets this is a "feeble revival" of dialectics. In Adorno's eyes, either Hegelian dialectics or Kantian dialectics serves the end of reconcilement of theories. Generally speaking, it is required by the need of "defeating the enemy in mind" for the dominion of bourgeois. In this sense, either Hegelian dialectics or Kantian dialectics, "as idealistic dialectics, it was bracketed with the absolute subject's predominance as the negative impulse of each single move of the concept and of its course as a whole."[2] This type of negative dialectics is on the basis of a pre-existent and idealistic standpoint. Once it

---

[1] Adorno, Theodor. *Negative Dialectics*. New York: The Seabury Press, 1973. p. 6.

[2] Ibid., pp. 6-7.

is confronted the powerful capitalist kingdom of instrumental technique and exchange, it would quickly degenerate into a riddle of ideas or a component of market culture in its own operating process.

Thirdly, Adorno classifies Stalinist traditional Marxism in such type of theory that translates dialectics into a standpoint. "Yet re-opening the case of dialectics, whose non-idealistic form has since degenerated into a dogma as its idealistic one did into a cultural asset."[1] For Adorno, it is a tragic in the history of interpretation of Marxist dialectics. Such dialectics, which continue to "materialist dialectics" in the system of philosophy of identity, even gives up "the right and ability to concretely think" obtained by Hegel, turning philosophy into a "barren, futile and boring analysis of cognitive forms" that is quite "indifferent" to real world. It is Gramsci's critique of the misunderstanding of historical dialectics by the Second International.[2] Actually, for Adorno, materialist dialectics, in the interpretation framework of traditional Marxism, has been transformed into a theoretical observation (reflection) outside the objective world: only laws are *within its insight*; it is knitting an *affirmative* net of theories that can hold the whole administered world. In Hegelian philosophy, dialectics has demanded that a concept must historically penetrate into the concrete contradiction of subject and object, when it attempts to realize its own reification. Contrarily, materialist dialectics in traditional philosophical system has once again become a "methodology" that talks of several everlasting characteristics, such as "relation" and "development" outside the objective things. Indeed, the judgments derive from young Lukács' dialectics of subject and object.

Dialectics of Subject and Object: In *History and Class Consciousness*, Lukács criticizes Engels for transforming dialectics into a non-revolutionary and abstract science about relation. In young Lukács, dialectics signifies historical dialectics whose kernel is the relationship of subject and object. "Engels—following Hegel's mistaken

[1] Adorno, Theodor. *Negative Dialectics*. New York: The Seabury Press, 1973. p. 7.

[2] Antonio Gramsci, "Revolution of Anti-Capital", from *Gramsci's Works*, Volume 1 (Beijing: Renmin Press, 1992), p. 10.

lead—extended the method to apply also to nature."[1] It is an action of illegal appropriation. "But he does not even mention the most vital interaction, namely the *dialectical relation between subject and object in the historical process*, let alone give it the prominence it deserves. Yet without this factor dialectics ceases to be revolutionary, despite attempts (illusory in the last analysis) to retain 'fluid' concepts."[2] Young Lukács believes that, Engels' mistake lies in the attempt to seek the so-called "natural dialectics" in the exoteric nature where there is never self-conscious subject. And with the absence of the self-conscious subject, nature cannot spontaneously create revolutionary historical dialectics. "If this central function of the theory is disregarded, the virtues of forming 'fluid' concepts become altogether problematic: a purely 'scientific' matter."[3] This sentence is obviously a critique of Engels' statement that dialectics is a theory about universal relation and development of matter. Here young Lukács means that fluid concepts of (natural) dialectics are no more than a natural process outside human being if the interaction between subject and object is no longer the center of dialectics. And if Marxist theory becomes a pragmatic science outside human being, it must degenerate into a kind of on looking fetishism of capitalist ideology (positivism).[4]

The statement above is Adorno's negative definition of his special negative dialectics. It makes references to three mutations of pseudo-negative-dialectics. Then, what about its affirmative definition?

Adorno points out, the real *purport of philosophy* is "non-conceptuality, individuality and particularity" in what the idea-essentialism of identity (the tradition of philosophy since Plato) such as Hegel is not interested. Here, Adorno is not frank enough to mark the sources of idea: Stirner and

---

[1] Lukács, Georg. *History and Class Consciousness*. London: Merlin Press, 1971. p. 24.

[2] Ibid., p. 3.

[3] Ibid., pp. 3-4.

[4] *See* my essay "Revolutionary Dialectics and Critical historical Materialism" in *Shangdong Social Science*, issue 2, 2000.

Kierkegaard. In the following, he interprets these "things which ever since Plato used to be dismissed as transitory and insignificant, and which Hegel labeled 'lazy Existenz'."[1] In faith, Hegel's absolute idea annihilates non-identical individuality and particularity. So to oppose Hegel is to fight against *non-conceptuality* in the first place. Generally speaking, non-conceptuality means concretely heterogamous objects, namely the individual and particular presence. Indeed, it is the field exploited by new humanist Kierkegaard's "this one" or Heidegger's "Dasein." There is a point to be noted that, Adorno does not oppose to the rational nature in thought or turn to coarse external phenomena; rather, he attempts to reach the individual characteristics of things in profound thought. It is something like the concept of "intuition" mentioned by Bergson and Husserl. It means not a sensible intuition but a rational one that produces the changeability and the unattainability of the concretionary concepts.

First of all, the term of "non-conceptuality" is employed to be against the absolute and abstract essence ("oneness") in traditional philosophy. For in identified conceptualization and abstraction, "the dialectical salt was washed away in an undifferentiated tide of life; solidified reality was disposed of as subaltern, not comprehended along with its subaltern-ity" (p.8). What negative dialectics concerns is concrete individuality of the thing. Secondly, Adorno argues against the timelessness which Bergson chides in metaphysics since Plato and Aristotle. For in the abstract conceptualized essence, historically concrete existence has been annihilated; only concepts survive. Eternity is the opposite of the historical time. Heidegger borrows these two logical expressions from Marx: *individual/particular Dasein and historical time*. It is the creed of Adorno's discourse.

Adorno believes that to this regard, two modern idealists, Bergson and Husserl, confront the idea of eternal essence with philosophy of life and phenomenology. Bergson says the hater of the rigid general concept established a cult of irrational immediacy, of sovereign freedom in the midst of un-freedom. Solidified reality was withdrawn as a bad matter by him.

---

[1] Adorno, Theodor. *Negative Dialectics*. New York: The Seabury Press, 1973. p. 8.

And he pursues "absolutized duration, pure becoming" in time. Husserl would indeed sharply distinguish the mode of apprehending the essence from generalizing abstraction—what he had in mind was a specific mental experience capable of perceiving the essence in the particular. However, these two idealist attempts come to an end of failure. The reason is that, "Bergson's bearings, like those of his positivistic arch-enemies, came from the *donnees immediates de la conscience*; Husserl's came in similar fashion from phenomena of the stream of consciousness. Both men stay within range of immanent subjectivity."[1] Adorno always insists on a position: *a philosophy would be an accessory of certain ideology despite its profundity if it never intends to be confronted with reality*. This is the same judgment in his critique of western philosophers since the 1930s. In the following text, we can also see his insistence in a new "materialism" and fighting against idealist philosophy in every form, which serve the revolutionary critique of reality by philosophy.

Adorno states that he does not agree with Wittgenstein's negative silence to what cannot be expressed; he insists to "express what cannot be expressed." Who is it then? Speaking of the myth that cannot be spoken of, still is the King of Nothing—Heidegger. Speaking of what cannot be spoken of, i.e., seeking for the motionless in the motional, for the difference in the unity, for the unlimited in the limited, for concrete abstraction, etc. which is just the *irreconcilable* contradiction different from Hegel's dialectic. However, it is pity that while Adorno teases this dialectic skill of Heidegger in Part One of *Negative Dialectics*, he no longer rethinks of complicated heterogeneous relation between them. It is Adorno's ideal dialectics of philosophy, a dialectical thinking that abolishes affirmation and ceaselessly negates itself.

4. The totality and the antagonistic world that cannot be engulfed

Adorno wants to go further. According to him, traditional philosophy

---

[1] Adorno, Theodor. *Negative Dialectics*. New York: The Seabury Press, 1973. p. 9.

is trying to establish a true system of spiritual totality and with the logic of identity all the time. It seems that *no system, no philosophy*. It is a fact on work in today's Chinese academia of philosophy. But actually, this type of systematic philosophy is always *illegally* confronted with a world which is "in itself antagonistic in reality." The situation never changes. Thus, any totality or systematic philosophy has "the coercive state of reality, which idealism had projected into the region of the subject and the mind."[1] Even it is named "materialist dialectics and historical dialectics."

In reality, the totalized philosophical system does not derive from one of "absolute spirit" or God; rather, it is a system in a real life that enslaves human beings, who have it and cannot even know how much it is their own, for example, the unconscious connection between ideology of liberalism and market. It is **psychic unconsciousness**. Adorno reveals that, the secret of system does not lie in the logical structure of system, but in the reality it translates unconsciously. Therefore, to grasp its secret, one has to translate metaphysics to its original version, namely, to uncover the mundane foundation of the logic of totalized identity. Such an opinion of Adorno is very close to Marx's critique of Feuerbach's religion.

The foundation in today is surely the current society; as Adorno puts it more exactly, it is *the process of production of material in society* (Marx).

We'll see soon, Adorno bases his philosophical discussion on a political-economical foundation. It is similar to Marx's strategy in his *Economic Manuscripts from 1857 to 1858*. He uses few words to talk directly the economical subject, but his philosophical discussion constantly rests on the critique of economics, as Jameson puts it, the premise of Adorno's theoretical interpretation is law of value.[2] In my view, Adorno's understanding of Marx's economical theory began from his text "Study of Sociology and Experience" in 1957. The text demonstrates that *it is impossible to understand the essence of Marxist*

---

[1] Adorno, Theodor. *Negative Dialectics*. New York: The Seabury Press, 1973. p. 10.

[2] Jameson, Fredric. *Gratification: Culture and Politics*. Beijing: CSSPW, 1998. p. 214.

philosophy without a reading of his economical theory. However, Adorno's deducing of culture from the means of material production is controversial: he considers it "productivism."[1]

Adorno states that, the subjective precondition of the material production process in society is the unresolved part, the part un-reconciled with the subjects. In other words, people know little about the material production process in society, namely, the commodity (market) economy. The dominating economics in western society has degenerated into an operational level of handicraftsman. Even Keynes' government interventionism is not an outcome that comes from authentic understanding of the essence of market economy. Therefore, the rationality of market economy still remains irrational and unconscious to people: it is an "invisible hand." People may catch hold of one or two of its pulses, but it remains mysterious in the wholesale.

To put it on a deeper philosophical level, the real system of identity is *the subject as the subject's foe.* The sentence seems elusive because *Adorno has passed over too many backgrounds. He supposes that readers can integrate the fragments of his theory into a grand building of logic.* He means that, the totality of idea is the system of logic; and system is not merely an ideal matter, but a conscious or unconscious reflection of real mechanism. In the capitalist reality, the mechanism is the totality of identity produced by the exchange value in the marketplace. Different from extrinsic identity in feudalism, the identity in capitalism is no longer an extrinsic coercion, but an unconscious constitution made of subject and object. It is a *spontaneous and unforced* constitution. Identity at the service of market is homogeneous quantitative money, while "what defies subsumption under identity" in reality is the use value.[2] In other words, market economy is the real foundation of contemporary logic of identity, because all "incomparable subjects" in the marketplace are identified through barter trade. Here, it does not mean that Adorno fails to grasp the differences between commodity exchange and barter

---

[1] Johnson, Richard. "What Is Study of Culture?" in *Works on Study of Culture*. Beijing: CSSPW, 2000.

[2] Adorno, Theodor. *Negative Dialectics*. New York: The Seabury Press, 1973. p. 11.

trade; rather, he signifies that subject is inverted as matter in the process of exchange, so that make itself a co-generic term which is not subject ("common denominator" = exchange value). Accordingly, the subject's foe (money or capital) becomes the *identified* subject (master) in economic world, which is created by subject of human beings. As a result, the real world of identity remains intact, so that identity in the kingdom of idea cannot be cleared up. It is why Adorno says that, "a world that is objectively set for totality will not release the human consciousness."[1] It is the *worldly secret* of contemporary logic of totality and the real foundation of bourgeois ideology of liberalism as eternal and natural truth.

In Adorno's belief, the logic of identity—that intends to *keep a everlasting domination*—is illusory, because the relation of capital—in Hegelian term, the "oneness" (universality) of ether (or in Marxian term, "illuminated lights")— is actually an outcome in a certain stage of the development of material production. The identity takes place and dies out historically. Exactly, in real life, people doest not consume homogeneous money, but heterogeneous commodities ("use value"). The universality of abstraction must be reverted to particular interests of real consummation. Non-identity in economics is "use value," namely, the practical commodities. However, in Market economy, the non-identity has to be represented by identity of homogenous commodity—the price. In Scheler's expression, "the structure in the hold of value deviates from virtual wealth, and spontaneously transforms itself into the hold of 'commodity', namely, the exchange object in terms of money."[2] As a result, identity (money or capital) that veils non-identity becomes God in this world which Adorno attempts to reveal. It is actually follows Marx's criticism of capitalist society. *Modern bourgeois scholars bear a bad mode of writing from Simmel, Sombart and Webber: they seldom indicate the resource of Marx's thought.* Here, Adorno gives a considerable comment, "this is why a philosophical critique of identity transcends philosophy."[3] It is the departure of Adorno's philosophy, and also

---

[1] Adorno, Theodor. *Negative Dialectics*. New York: The Seabury Press, 1973. p. 17.

[2] Scheler, Max. *Subversion of Value*. Beijing: SDX Joint Publishing Company, 1997. p. 21.

[3] Adorno, Theodor. *Negative Dialectics*. New York: The Seabury Press, 1973. p. 11.

the real reason why many of the researchers of Adorno cannot virtually reach him.

I. Dialectics: Disintegrated Logic

As we see, the title of the second section in *Negative Dialectics* consists of two parts: one is "Negative Dialectics," which, obviously, is Adorno's own identification of his theory; the other is "concept and categories," which I believe is his "ontological" manifesto, that is, Negative Dialectics neither directly addresses the primary "eternal world," nor immediately deals with the "absolute essence" of any concept. Negative Dialectics confronts the world *through concepts and categories in a historical and theoretical sense*. That is all. Consequently, Adorno self-consciously breaks from the aberrance of the systemized logic of totality all through his discussion. Here, we are no longer supposed to find the old, basic philosophical propositions and discussions of the traditional dialectics. Of course, in a close theoretical identification, we can manage with great efforts to catch vaguely Adorno's basic philosophical tendency—a dialectics of *disintegrated logic*. This is the painful cost paid for obtaining truly valuable thoughts in the rational thinking movement. It is interesting that he fires rejections and oppositions in array even before he provides an explanation of Negative Dialects. Much like Heidegger, he keeps dancing in order to avoid solidification. When constantly saying no, he manages to identify with some of the affirmative "syndromes,"[1] through which his post-modernist and post-Marxist thoughts are comparatively better manifested.

1. Against "the first philosophy"

When starting to explain his Negative Dialectics, Adorno solemnly declares that "in criticizing ontology we do not aim at another ontology, not

---

[1] A term derived from psychoanalysis study by Althusser, referring to non-identified and non-defined functional characteristics in theoretical thoughts.

even at one of being non-ontological."[1] This draws the demarcation line between him and the unsuccessful Heidegger. To be more specific, it can also be put in this way that Adorno's philosophical thinking abandons the hope for the "originary" *first* and "total philosophy."[2] For this purpose, he has to fight a bloody way out.

In my view, Adorno's theoretical thinking is usually of grand scale. His *opposition to ontology and crush of system's totality* is far more than a slogan, for it is practiced all through his theoretical operation. Above all, Adorno fights against any idealistic abstraction that is illusory and un-rooted in nature. Without hesitation, he declares, "There is no Being [Sein] without entities [Seiendes]."[3] This is a principle to observe. Obviously derived from Heidegger, this entity or das Seiendes is different from the entity in the narrow sense of the traditional materialism, but rather referring to any objects, phenomenon and objective process (not referring to the metaphysical solid in Heidegger's illegitimate metaphor of ideal). Simply speaking, it is an object or a something in certain relations. The concept of "Something" has certainly absorbed Heidegger's concept of "Being in the world." "Being as **something** is perhaps the *basic* thing of thinking (*die* Sache des Denkens)"[4]. *Japan's new Marxist philosopher Hiromatsu, thereby put forwards the idea of "Ontology of Something."* Contrary to Hegel and Heidegger in terms of the object and the dimension of thought, Adorno insists that the premise of all abstract concepts is Something. Thus, he refers to "Something" as "a cogitatively indispensable substrate of any concept, including the concept of Being." Hegel rejects the sensible "something" due to his belief in the absolute apperception of consciousness. Heidegger, in his pursuit of an originary Being, plays with this Being in the world (or falling into the world), excluding the petrified entities. His pursuit of an absolute form that might

---

[1] Adorno, Theodor. *Negative Dialectics*. Trans. E. B. Ashtion. New York: The Continuum Publishing House, 1990. p. 136.

[2] Ibid.

[3] Ibid., p. 135.

[4] Heidegger, Martin. *Zur Sache des Denkens*, Trans. Chen Xiaowen and Sun Zhouxing. Peking: Commercial Press, 1996. p.4.

enable the thinking to shake off the subject-matter is illusionary. *Adorno is unable to forget Heidegger*. In fact, without a certain historical entity/ something as subject-matter, thought would not exist; at the counter pole, the function of thought is not to be separated from the entity—"I (Dasein)."

Adorno points out, "idealism's prôtou pseudos [Greek: proto-falsity] ever since Fichte was that the movement of the abstraction allows us to get rid of that from which we abstract."[1] People climbed up to the mount of idea through the ladder of Something, but kicked it off on the clouds of thoughts. *Being without entity, thinking without subject*—this is indeed a weird metaphysical meditation. "The contents of philosophical thinking are neither remnant after deducing space and time nor general findings about spatial-temporal matters. Philosophical thinking crystallizes in the particular, in that which is defined in space and time."[2] It should be emphasized that despite Adorno's anti-idealism stance, he abandons the issue of the primacy. Instead, *he makes casual identifications of the something*. In this sense, both Hegel and Heidegger used to stand "Beyond the Clouds" (the name of a film directed by the famous Italian director Michelangelo Antonioni in the 1990s).

Wherein does the problem lie? In Adorno's view, these two philosophical masters are dialectically self-deceit, rather than apparently shallow. Hegel refuses to begin with Something instead of with Being, because he believes that the "something" in any (individual) concept is prescribed and constructed by a general idea in self-consciousness. Thus, he emphasizes "the primacy of the subject"[3], namely, a coercive logic of identity originated from the primacy of concept. Hegelian philosophy sets up a hierarchical system crowned by the absolute concept. The absolute concept dominates all other inferior concepts and material objects. This is a kind of metaphysical white terror in the legacy of theodicy. As far as Heidegger is concerned, he incisively perceives the problem of essentialism

---

[1] Adorno, Theodor W. *Negative Dialectics*. Trans. E. B. Ashtion. New York: The Continuum Publishing House, 1990. p.135.

[2] Ibid., p. 138.

[3] Ibid., p. 135, note 1.

embedded in the traditional metaphysics of Hegel, and therefore endeavors to break from the solidification of the pure concept, liberating the current function of thinking in order to correspond to the real Being (the entity or the something). The profoundness of Heidegger's theory also lies in the fact that he situates the thinking of an individual subject in its historical correlates in the world. Inquiry is preconditioned by *de*-being-in-the world. However, this is no more than a *"return home in an unusual way."* Heidegger is still trapped in the fundamental ontology, for he believes that the originary being is the first. He does not recognize that, "wherever a doctrine of some absolute 'first' is taught there will be talk of something inferior to it, of something absolutely heterogeneous to it, as its logical correlate."[1] This will inevitably bring out such a result: the First Philosophy has an *absolute hierarchical structure*, in which the originary upper concepts enslave those being dominated. Heidegger, who abandons the substantive metaphysics in name, does not in fact escape the prison of the metaphysical logic.

To see this, Adorno makes clear his conviction: the dialectics he advocates cannot be maintained as a structure that will stay basic, no matter how it is modified. As noted above, he will not try to contradict Hegel and Heidegger by simply "positing another downright 'first'—not absolute identity, this time, not the concept, not Being, but non-identity, facticity, entity."[2] It means that dialectics is not a logical framework. It is unnecessary to create a basic philosophy of entity in order to counteract Hegel's idealistic conceptuality; it is unnecessary to positing entity as the "First" merely because Hegel advocates Being as the original, which is in fact on the other side of the same coin. It is particularly important to pay attention to this, especially when we are about to enter the contexts which involve Adorno's discussion of nonidentity and non-totality.

Adorno demonstrably states that he does not hope for a "total philosophy," because dialectics essentially rejects any kind of First principle,

---

[1] Adorno, Theodor W. *Negative Dialectics*. Trans. E. B. Ashtion. New York: The Continuum Publishing House, 1990. p.138.

[2] Ibid., p. 136.

namely, *the identity philosophy originated from basic ontology*. The "First," as a philosophical concept, is itself a form of an ideology. In the same sense, any metaphysical "category of root, of the origin" is inevitably a "category of domination" and an "ideological principle."[1] Heidegger's inquiry into the *origin* of Being, asking for a return home of the forgotten *homeless* being, fancies to construct an innate hierarchy in a new disguise, which is essentially an ideology of thinking in poetic sense. However, once we dismiss such identity in principle, the peace of the concept as an Ultimate will be engulfed in the fall of the identity. The identity thought that rejects the primacy philosophy and systematization constitutes the premise of Adorno's dialectics. It is a brand-new discourse created by Adorno in his ontological thinking: It is post-Modernism and must be post-Marxism.

Here, it should be pointed out that with Adorno, there is a problem that he is reluctant to face, that is, the relationship between the disintegrated ontic being and the general base in man's historical being (not the theoretical logic of the "First") as well as the dominated social framework. This is also the pivotal issue that the latter postmodern streams have to avoid wherever. The dissolved game of concept faces the same embarrassment with the super global capitalism which is developing with giant steps forward.

2. Nothingness and being in non-dualistic Gestalt

An ontological framework must give birth to a homogenous cognitive structure. In Adorno's view, any kind of hierarchical structure of identity logic will inevitably lead to a *dualistic* cognitive framework. The First philosophy and dualism inevitably go together with each other. In other words, the polarity of subject and object in the traditional metaphysics may well appear to be an un-dialectical structure. Obviously, Adorno's notion of dualism is neither identical with Spinozaian substantive dualism nor with the Kantian binary world, but rather referring to the segregation of subject and object in all kinds of philosophies, which can be traced back to Heidegger's

---

[1] Adorno, Theodor W. *Negative Dialectics*. Trans. E. B. Ashtion. New York: The Continuum Publishing House, 1990. p. 155.

critical discourse.

In Adorno's view, subject and object, as abstractions, are thought products. In normal process of thinking, "without dichotomy there might be no thought. Every concept, even that of being, reproduces difference of thinking and the thought."[1] The problem lies more deeply in the fact that the supposition of their anti-thesis inevitably declares thinking to be primary. Therefore, the separation, which makes the object the alien thing to be mastered and possessed, is indeed subjective, the result of *orderly preparation*. That is to say, dualism ultimately leads to the unity of thoughts. Thus, "absolute duality would be unity."[2] Adorno is right in saying so. Hegel absorbs the subject-object polarity into his logic of concept in order to bridge the gap in Kant and surpass Fichte and Schelling. By doing so, he turns the dialectics of subject and object (the reflective relations of idea itself) into an absolute subject. He directly identifies this kind of dialectics as "the structure of Being" (Heidegger also formulates the similar *ontology of relations* which is non-dualistic, non-falling and self-reflective). It seems that, the non-dual relations piece a *third* out of the opposition between the two, a rescuer. However, Adorno insists, "the third would be no less deceptive."[3]

Why? Because for Hegel, the passionate being (the individual subject) is an isolated subject, and the material object is an isolated object, and then comes the subject-object relation (reflection of idea) which is posited as a superior third element. However, Hegelian notion of this relation is still the logic of totality itself. As opposed to an independent subject and the object, the absolute essence of the quasi-subject is deified. Adorno certainly knows that Heidegger has already recognized this problem, and hence uses monism to govern this dualistic framework, trying to avoid "the unwise" mention of the First as possible as he can. It should be acknowledged that Heidegger's philosophical endeavor has more or less engendered something different. Heidegger opposes to the dualistic metaphysical categorization of any ideas

---

[1] Adorno, Theodor W. *Negative Dialectics*. Trans. E. B. Ashtion. New York: The Continuum Publishing House, 1990. p. 175.

[2] Ibid., p. 174.

[3] Ibid., p. 175.

and things and he consequently directs our attention to the functional being of things in the Now. On account of this, he always starts with the subject and the predicate verb "is." He has been trying to break the substantive (existent) subject and object, defining this being, the variant of subject, as the relation of being-in- the-world (the relation embodied in the "at-hand" nature of a entity and in "being with" others), and thinking as an inquiry into relation, which is based on this being and aiming at being, as well as being-in-itself as an ontological and functional deifying of the intentional relation. With this, the traditional substantive dualism is seemingly dissolved. However, Adorno seriously points out that Heidegger's being is, at best, a covert relational third, which is unable to release itself from an identification with the identity logic. The reason is that derived from this functional "be" (being) is still a kind of more profoundly originary primacy (ontology of being) which consequently demands an unconscious and coercive identity. Being and entity, originality and fallingness, isn't this the more covert duality? Obviously, Heidegger's fear of this metaphysical reification of the concept ends with idealism, "a thinking without the thinker." His struggle against dualistic framework turns out to be illusory and futile.

Both Hegel and Heidegger want to solve the problem embedded in Kant's dualistic framework by means of dialectics, but the dialectics applied by them (in Heidegger's case, it is an anonymous illegitimate appropriation) is still potentially subject to the traditional metaphysics of *identity logic*. It can also be put in this way that both Hegel and Heidegger have detected the contradiction embedded in subject-object relation and matter-concept relation. However, they formulate their dialectics within the old frame of *First philosophy*. Adorno says, "The summation of identical determinations would correspond to the wish fulfillment picture of traditional philosophy, to the a priori structure and to its archaistic late form, ontology."[1] He wants to make a true step forward, truly smashing identity logic. *What is his way out? We will soon get to know that the all-dimensional constellation departing*

---

[1] Adorno, Theodor W. *Negative Dialectics*. Trans. E. B. Ashtion. New York: The Continuum Publishing House, 1990. p. 145.

from any coercive framework is the means by which to reject the "oneness" and to break the duality of identity.

3. Logic of identity: "metaphysical thaumatrope"

Then what on earth is the concept of identity that Adorno attempts to negate? In his view, the concept of identity, which has dominated the Western philosophical culture for thousands of years and passed down to the modern philosophy, has four meanings: firstly, it designates the unity of personal consciousness, the illusionary self-contained-ness of the subject. The starting point of identity is the absolute "oneness" of the subject. Here, it refers to the unchangeable "I" in Descartes' fundamental notion, "I think, therefore I am," which assumes that the subject remains the same in all its experiences. *In fact, ever since Freud in the last century, particularly Lacan, the individual "I" in its mirror-image identification suffers from alienation and the essence of a social "I" is identified as paranoia.[1] After Derrida, Deleuze, and Foucault, this proposition was completely subverted in the slogans such as "the death of human being," "the death of the subject" and "the death of the author."* Secondly, it designates the logical universality generated from the identity logic. Identity of individual subject is the premise of the universality of identity, and thereby comes the unified species subject which is the basis of universality. Without identity of consciousness, without special identity, there won't exist any universality (*as I mentioned above, Stirner was the first one to oppose this universal species identity in modern Western philosophical history, and then came the New Humanism, following Kierkegaard*). Thirdly, it designates the equality with itself of every object of thought, the simple A=A. This principle presupposes oneness and stability of the object, which is no more than a metaphysically non-historical supposition—*the ready-made nature of the concept had been rejected after Husserl, and through Heidegger and Gadamar, its unarrestability was eventually confirmed in the post-modern context.* Finally, it means that subject and object coincide;

---

[1] Jiang Min'an. *Postmodern Philosophical Discourse—From Foucault to Said.* Hangzhou: Zhe Jiang People's Publishing House, 2000. pp. 173-177.

whatever their media is, the subject always swallows the object. This is the idea of immediate knowing embedded in the old binary epistemological framework, which is either manifested in the immediacy of reality or in the notion advocating the external correspondence with the truth. *These are the very ideas that Adorno intends to attack.*[1]

"Identity is the primal form of ideology (die Urform von Ideologie/ the primal form of ideology)."[2] Since Tracy, particularly after Marx and Mannheim, ideology usually designates an invisible conceptual coercion which makes use of the illusionary relations to cover the true structure of reality. Identity exists on the premise of a kind of *adequacy* which is always subject to dominant purposes, and in this sense, identitarian thought, in a deeper logic level, collaborates with ideology in its resistance to enlightenment. It is not groundless for Jameson to say that for Adorno, identity itself has been functionally reduced to domination and suppression. Adorno's analysis reveals the historical causes of this identitarian logic:

First, as the root of thinking, identity grows together with *anthropocentrism.* When the subject proclaims itself a Baconian master of all things, and finally their idealistic creator, it takes an epistemological and metaphysical part in this delusion. This is an identitarian principle of the subject and a thematic refinement of *Dialectics of Enlightenment.* It has already referred to the modern context of eco-philosophy. Adorno says, under the powerful discourse of anthropocentrism, the circle of identification— which in the end always identifies itself alone—was drawn by a thinking that tolerates nothing outside it; its imprisonment is its own handiwork. "Such totalitarian and therefore particular rationality was historically dictated by the threat of nature. That is its limitation. In fear, bondage to nature is perpetuated by a thinking that identifies, that equalizes everything unequal."[3] I personally believe that Adorno profoundly reflects on and probes into the

---

[1] Adorno, Theodor W. *Negative Dialectics.* Trans. E. B. Ashtion. New York: The Continuum Publishing House, 1990. p. 142, note 2.

[2] Ibid., p. 148.

[3] Ibid., p. 172.

identitarian logic. Obviously, he disagrees with the notion of productive forces based on Marxist historical materialism which *works on the premise of conquering the nature*. This is also Adorno's ultimate door to the late-Marxism.

In section three of the book, Adorno has applied the concept of causality, a concept taken for granted by science, to expose the enslaving nature of identity, namely, identity as an intellectual principle is only the reflection of the real control of nature. In his view, the concept of causality can directly teach us "what identity has done to noni-dentity." Subjectively or objectively, causality is "the spell of dominated nature." Why? Because reason, by which nature has been interrogated since Bacon, "finds causality in nature wherever it controls nature."[1] Man can *find* causality wherever nature is controlled and dominated. Does causality *exist* naturally or as a result of the coercive identity imposed by man on nature? This is a counter-question to Kantian notion of "man prescribes laws of nature."

Second, when Adorn says concept is of oneness, he means that at the beginning of culture, the concept was produced when "multiple" perceptual phenomena were summarized into "one." For any kind of culture, the concept's immanent claim is its order-creating invariance as against the change in what it covers. Viewing this through the colored glasses of Negative Dialectics, Adorno has made exaggerations. According to him, "the unchangeable in all changes" (being) pursued by Eleatic School, the "live fire" (logos) that Heraclitus searched for behind the objects, City of God (theocracy and patriarchy) that rejects the secular world, and the human being that resurrected in Enlightenment all result from the enforcement of identity. The construction of any philosophies such as Plato's realm of ideas, Hegel's absolute concept, and Stalin's text-book system, goes together with the building of a logical structure of identity, in which the heterogeneity is penetrated by a spiritual oneness and they would repeat themselves as in a vast analytical judgment, leaving no room for the qualitatively new. Therefore, Hegel says that there is nothing new (the heterogeneous nature)

---

[1] Adorno, Theodor W. *Negative Dialectics*. Trans. E. B. Ashtion. New York: The Continuum Publishing House, 1990. p. 269.

under the sun (the absolute idea). Here is decoded by Benjamin's statement that the progress of civilization guided by the identity logic is at the same time a savage process.

Third, subjectivity, thinking itself, is explicable not by itself but by facts, especially by social facts. Therefore, Adorno believes that *the identical barter principle in commodity economy* is today's social foundation of the principle of identification. This theoretical point has been identified in his **Introduction**.

"The barter principle, the reduction of human labor to the abstract universal concept of average working hours, is fundamentally akin to the principle of identification. Barter is the social model of the principle, and without the principle, there would be no barter; it is through barter that non-identical individuals and performances become commensurable and identical. The spread of the principle imposes on the whole world an obligation to become identical, to become total."[1] In Adorno's analysis, use value is something of the non-identical, heterogeneous and other nature in a commodity, whereas exchange value is what coerces the heterogeneous into identity. Therefore, he says, "compared with use value, exchange value is a creation of mind, which controls people's need and replaces it—illusion controls reality."[2] In this sense, the **modern** identity based on the barter principle of commodity economy is more fundamental and formidable than the externally imposed identity by the feudal agriculture. Thus, the barter principle tends to be a more philosophical topic in Adorno's works. On the other hand, Adorno identifies that the cover concepts of social roles resulting from the spread of the instrumental rationality in society and life are in accordance with the identity logic. He believes, when a man enters the social structure, the technique of the logic subsumption of his role is inevitably embedded with "manipulation" and enforcement of some cover concepts

---

[1] Adorno, Theodor W. *Negative Dialectics*. Trans. E. B. Ashtion. New York: The Continuum Publishing House, 1990. p. 146.

[2] Adorno, Theodor W. "Sociology and Empirical Research" in *The Positivist Dispute in German Sociology*. Trans. Glyn Adey and David Frisby. New York: *Hernemann Educational* Books Ltd., 1976. p. 78.

that will make the crucial differences vanish. This is the current concept of industrial society, which "ignores the social conditions of production by resorting to the technological productive forces—as if the state of these forces alone were the direct determinant of the social structure. This theoretical switch can of course be excused by the undeniable convergences of East and West in the sign of bureaucratic rule."[1] This identification is profoundly significant. It has become an open secret in the tradition of the contemporary orthodox Marxism following Weber that *the development of productive forces* is emphasized, whereas the issue of production relations is intentionally covered.

Obviously, Adorno objects to the limitless development of productive forces with the instrumental rationality as guidance or in other words, he believes the practical impulse of production for production's sake is what fundamentally maintains the lasting violence of identity. Therefore, he naturally objects to the philosophical notion that *practice is the first*. This could be a serious theoretical problem of the late Marxism's nature.

4. Against practice: the spell of "production for production's sake"

Adorno asserts that the capitalist Enlightenment reason has achieved a full-scale success in the process of industrialization, but this success at the same time abounds with sufferings and mistakes, because the unity of capital in the universal history is no more than "the unity of the control of nature, progressing to rule over men, and finally to that over men's inner nature. No universal history leads from savagery to humanitarianism, but there is one leading from the slingshot to the megaton bomb. It ends in the total menace which organized mankind poses to organized men, in the epitome of discontinuity."[2] It is one of Adorno's famous warnings. According to him, such a totality of mandatory identity would be the absolute of suffering,

---

[1] Adorno, Theodor W. *Negative Dialectics*. Trans. E. B. Ashtion. New York: The Continuum Publishing House, 1990. p. 152.

[2] Ibid., p. 320.

because "under the all-subjugating identity principle, whatever does not enter into entity, whatever eludes rational planning in the realm of means, turns into frightening retribution for the calamity which identity brought on the non-identical."[1] It is worth noting that he says such suffering and mistakes are not merely the problems of production relation, as was purposefully differentiated by Marx. Adorno has dug too deep: he wants to make a *critique of productivity* through Marx. The young Lukács's unconscious critique of the innate materialization of production (technique) against Webb is now transformed into a conscious idea. Furthermore, in the basic logic of philosophy, he *opposes the principle of "Practice First"* and thereby topples the *ontology of Practice*. This indeed is the very philosophical cornerstone of Post-Marxist thoughts.

In the following discussion of Freedom in the third part, Adorno explicitly argues *against practice*. "Marx received the thesis of the primacy of practical reason from Kant and the German idealism, and he sharpened it into a challenge to change the world instead of merely interpreting it. He thus underwrote something as arch-bourgeois as the program of an absolute control of nature."[2] He couldn't be more wrong here. According to Adorno, the primacy of practice is a special product of the industrial civilization; it is equal to Productionism and Anthropocentrism. Adorno's visionary conception is post-modern, but these multiple equations are too simplistic. To exclusively label the primacy of practice as "the program of arch-bourgeois" is Adorno's *post-Marxist tendency*. Of course, it seems to be different here. As analyzed by Adorno, Marx's stance of practice is to call for a so-called "*telos* of due practice," which was the abolition of the primacy of practice in the form that had prevailed in bourgeois society. Marx suggested, "It would be possible to have contemplation without inhumanity as soon as the productive forces are freed to the point where men will no longer be engulfed in a practice that wants exacts from them, in a practice which then becomes automatic in

---

[1]   Adorno, Theodor W. *Negative Dialectics*. Trans. E. B. Ashtion. New York: The Continuum Publishing House, 1990. p. 320.

[2]   Ibid., p. 244.

them."[1] Later on, Adorno says, historical materialism's "dialectics of practice called for the abolition of practice, of production for production's sake, of the universal cover for the wrong practice."[2] Still, Adorno is obviously not supportive of this opinion. He argues that the dependency of human freedom on practice itself is unworkable, in spite of "the possible reduction of labor to a minimum." Adorno denies the *subjugating* subjectivity as derived by Marx from *On an Outline about Feuerbach*. Anything that is built upon a dominion over the others can never be free. The happiness acquired as such is unreal, either. Theoretically, Adorno *objects to everything that is related to practice*. (It is the starting point where Arendt delineates labor, work and action, and where Habermas suggests that inter-subjective *non-utilitarian* free communication be differentiated from *objective labor practice*.)

Adorno illustrates this with a specific example: since practice is unscrupulously placed in an all-governing position, the Stalin-like socialist countries have in their realities witnessed the vicious repercussion brought about by their ignorance about theory and blindness of practice. In such a case, the impulse for the primacy of practice has made theory "the prey of power." Even the Marxism itself, on account of the so-called slogan of "combining theory with practice," has been degraded to a servant's role. Because the authentic theory has been paralyzed and disparaged by the all-governing bustle, theory is no longer a scientific conception, or a sober criticism of and reflection upon the reality, but is reduced to a royal tool for justifying policies. Thus, "the visa stamp of practice which we demand of all theory became a censor's placket."[3]

I should acknowledge that Adorno's arguments are really remarkable, but his understanding of historicity in the marrow of Marxist philosophy is not completely satisfactory. As we know, practice according to Marx refers to the creative and sensible material activities done for human existence

---

[1] Adorno, Theodor W. *Negative Dialectics*. Trans. E. B. Ashtion. New York: The Continuum Publishing House, 1990. p. 244.

[2] Ibid., p. 389.

[3] Ibid., p. 143.

under certain historical conditions (or as Heidegger put it, *Das In-der-Welt-Sein* since being *zuhanden* in dealing with the material object). In different historical periods, the contents of practical activity are completely heterogeneous, and so are the complexities. Under certain historical conditions, different practical activities within practical structure would vary greatly, in terms of their status in the process of history making realized by men. What has happened since self-production in the prehistoric period, agricultural work in the agricultural civilization, exchange based upon the industrial production, and information operation in the post-industrial time, a one-liner as romantic as "Against Practice" simply cannot dismiss. It is correct to object to the destructive exploitation of the nature, but ludicrous to oppose controlling the nature on a whole. When criticizing the simple-minded slogan of "Against Anthropocentricism," I once said, "Heidegger reflected upon the un-rootedness of our industrial civilization, in which the lust and the instrumental reason render human beings homeless, whereas the technical structure elicited by the '*zuhanden*' (readiness-to-hand) not only builds an unnatural center of human power, but empties the authentic side of nature's being and men's existence: humankind is not the end; rather, like the material, it is the means of instrumental reason's 'presence-every-time'. The decline of Rhine's utility and the 'Normalization' of humanity have envisioned the questioning of ecology and the critique of mass culture. Nonetheless, even Heidegger's poetic dwelling is by no means a proposition of 'uprooting' the existence of humankind. In fact, the absolute 'non-centralism' in postmodern thoughts is no more than a neo-Romantic fantasy. The hegemony of human beings should be removed, but the realistic and historical dominance of human race's existence in, as Engels put it, an 'Earth-centered' place could never be disavowed. Let's ask a question: is it really possible that men survive, but 'subject to the object' non-centrally, without constructing the object of nature, without feeding on the flesh of other creatures? Ecology is not anti-humanism, but to eradicate the blindness of human initiative and over-exploitation. The ecological balance is after all to serve human race."[1] If men do not carry out practical activities so as to exchange with the external nature for the human existence, can we survive? To oppose the bourgeois industrialism in practical philosophy and to deny the historical basis of practice as a whole are two different issues. In this regard, Adorno is not particularly clear-minded.

Of course, Adorno is versed in Marxism. According to his interpretation, behind the primacy of practice lies the girder of material production, or, the sustainable development of productive force. He thinks periods of harmony with the world spirit, of a happiness more substantial than the individual's, tend to be associated with the unleashing of productive forces. It is correct. Marx did suggest that the improvement of collective material conditions of social existence (a happiness of "US") replace the individual and subjective value request. However, in Adorno's opinion, "The unleashing of productive forces, an act of the spirit that controls nature, has an affinity to the violent domination of nature. Temporarily that domination may recede, but the concept of productive force is not thinkable without it, and even les is that of an unleashed productive force. This very word 'unleashed' has undertones of menace."[2] Such is theoretical description in negative sense. The *infinite* development of production is indeed the essence of all industrial civilizations, and the infinite demand of instrumental reason of the Enlightenment. The premise of such a demand is the anthropocentric control of nature. What Adorno believes is that Marx does not go beyond this kind of industrialism. In their critical meditation on the Enlightenment philosophy, Adorno and Horkheimer once asserted that the unleashing would go to its opposite; in other words, the enslavement of nature would turn into the enslavement of men. This view is hereafter referred to as "Enlightenment dialectics."

Importantly, Adorno notices that Marx has censured capitalism (Ricardo) which "ruthlessly compels mankind to produce for production's

---

[1] Zhang Yibing. "Anthropocentrism: In and Out" in *Philosophical Trends*, Vol. 6, 1996.

[2] Adorno, Theodor W. *Negative Dialectics*. Trans. E. B. Ashtion. New York: The Continuum Publishing House, 1990. pp. 306-307.

sake."[1] In other words, during the operation of capitalist economy, material production, previously used as the means to enhance the living standard of human race, has now been inverted as the end, whereas men become the means. Marx objects to the nature of capitalist production, which strikes the fetish which the barter society makes of the production process. Adorno maintains the unleashing of forces no sooner parts with the sustaining human relations than it comes to be as fetishized as the orders. In such phases, the world spirit may "pass into that which it buries." It seems quite confounding at first. Some explanations are necessary here.

Marx and Engels, of course, opposed capitalism and bourgeois philosophy of practice, but both of them would have rejected the doubts of the inevitability of totality.[2] At most, they attempted to replace the capitalist totality with a conscious identity of human liberation. However, what they didn't foresee is the domination brought about by identity may outlast the planned economy (which the two of them, of course, had not confused it with state capitalism). In other words, Marx wanted to overthrow the capitalist relations of production, notwithstanding its tenacious survival after the downfall of what had been the main object of the critique of political economy, because this is the ideology that "will prophesy dominion an infinite an infinite future, for as long as any organized society exists."[3] So did the young Lukács; the only difference is that he replaced the golden capitalist totality of universal history with the pink color of revolution. It is an issue on another level. In this regard, some of Adorno's ideas deserve further discussion.

Whether or not Marx could transcend the thinking paradigm contextualized by the industrial civilization he lived in so as to address the bondage features in man-nature relations and to pinpoint the totality of industrialism, is not necessarily an answered question. What is crucial here

---

[1] Adorno, Theodor W. *Negative Dialectics*. Trans. E. B. Ashtion. New York: The Continuum Publishing House, 1990. p. 307.

[2] Ibid., p. 321.

[3] Ibid., pp. 322-323.

is: Should Adorno oppose the development of practice and production forces in reality? How would he face the historical reality? A more straightforward question might be: How the Constellation faces the World, not of conception, but of survival. In fact, Adorno is so strong in theory that the transcendental reflection he envisions has gone as far as his time allows for. Nevertheless, he never thinks on how his negative dialectics could be transformed into social reality. It's not an impossible mission to reject in ideology "primacy," to refuse identity, or to disavow totality, but Adorno has no answer to abolishing identity, which is even inevitable to socialism, in our real social history. He is indeed a *metaphysical talker*. On this phase, his negative attitude to practice is reactionary. Negative dialectics is just a theoretical stance. He, of course has an insightful interpretation that the practical attitude of arch-bourgeois industrialism constitutes the base of modern identity's tyranny, but the theoretical stance of non-industrialism he advocates is negligible in terms of its operation and realization in reality. In this respect, his objection to Marcuse is inevitable. Marcuse's "Culture Abnegation" is doomed to fail in practice, but he at least has the guts of revolution; Habermas resorts to bourgeois social reform ("Amend the Heaven"), which is also a sort of practice. But Adorno is a musician of beauty. He should have known that the rebellions, no matter how audacious in music and conception, cannot shake even slightly the real world. In this regard, he is no better than Heidegger, who uses the spiritual homecoming of being in conscience to salvage the secular world. Therefore, when Adorno deliberately categorizes his negative dialectics as conceptual dialectics, such a strategy of thinking is inevitably overshadowed by ill omen.

Let's look back at Adorno's conceptual revolution. Now, we needn't always look up to it.

II. Non-identity: Categorical Constellation in Negative Dialectics

From the discussion above, Adorno from the approach of falsification illustrates what negative dialectics objects to. In our view, in such a negative reflection upon First Philosophy, totality and identity logic, he almost declares a capital punishment for all human cultures and history of ideas. This is an extremely subversive re-writing logic characteristic of Nietzsche and Heidegger, also the primordial form of postmodern thinking. He disagrees with the primacy of practice and industrialism, making himself, as it were, smarter than Marx. Adorno seems to be more thorough; so, he has to showcase something that carries more weight. This time, we see the exhibition of constellation on the sky of non-identity dialectics. I think, underneath the dialectic constellation, the moral law within has been replaced by the musical poem of beauty, which I am afraid would fall into the category of aesthetic Romanticism. Frankly speaking, when he is criticizing others, Adorno's vigor is absolutely undaunted; however, when presenting his own ideas, his ego would not be as lofty. When it comes to something pivotal, he is always equivocal and unintelligible.

1. Dialectics: consciousness of non-identity (the Other)

Adorno's positive description of negative dialectics originates from his critical analysis of Hegelian dialectics. In his opinion, Kant, in the Copernican revolution of "destroying the illusion of an immediate knowledge of the Absolute," attempts to use Dualism to avoid the contradiction of appearance and essence, and of finite subject and infinite knowledge; by circumscribing the phenomenal of the empirical subject and suspending the thing-in-itself of that-world, dialectics is confronted in the context of Zenonian Dialectical reason. For Kant, "Dialectics as a philosophical mode of proceeding is the attempt to untie the paradoxicality by the oldest means of enlightenment."[1] But Hegel is not content with Kant's dichotomy; rather, Hegel uses "the philosophy of the absolute and total subject" as a dialectics, which is *negative*, to dissolve contradiction and difference in its own logic. This kind of negativity concedes the contradiction between difference and

---

[1] Adorno, Theodor W. *Negative Dialectics*. Trans. E. B. Ashtion. New York: The Continuum Publishing House, 1990. p. 141.

nonidentity, but it concerns identity that coincides with positivity to include all non-identical and objective things in a subjectivity expanded and exalted into an absolute spirit. To put it in another way, Hegel's endorsement of heterogeneity is strategic, for difference and contradiction are no more than the tools which help with the fulfillment of the ultimate and identical totality (the absolute); his acknowledgement of non-identity is for the purpose of abolishing in the end anything that is non-identical or contradictory. Therefore, Adorno says that Hegel's dialectics is in its essence a "violence of equality-mongering"[1], though in the form of negativity; considering the time when the negative dialectics of totality rubbed shoulders with the Prussian tyranny in history, this observation makes even better sense. I think, Adorno's analysis is basically apt and accurate.

He rightly holds that from Hegel's identical logic of First Philosophy, "the turning to non-identity" started with the "Left Hegelists" (often referred to as the "Young Hegelians"), of which the young Marx was of course a member. This is a historically accurate identification, which *carries the vector of time*. The individualized self-consciousness is a denial of the old Hegel's idea of the Absolute of identity. In the young Marx's doctoral dissertation, it is manifest as Epicurus's atomic deviation in the natural philosophy, which cracked the vertically descending identity as claimed by Democritus. However, when Marx really faced the objective contradictions in the real society, dialectics "bids farewell to Hegel," which is right as well. The new dialectics differs from Hegel's in that "its motion does not tend to the identity in the difference between each object and its concept; instead, it is suspicious of all identity. Its logic is one of disintegration: of a disintegration of the prepared and objectified form of the concepts which the cognitive subject faces, primarily and directly."[2] *Marx coincides with Adorno in terms of "the logic of disintegration," an idea Adorno came to realize since he was young.* Speaking of its philosophical premise, it refers to *"On an Outline about*

---

[1] Adorno, Theodor W. *Negative Dialectics*. Trans. E. B. Ashtion. New York: The Continuum Publishing House, 1990. p. 143.

[2] Ibid., p. 145.

Feuerbach" (1845), in which Marx used historically evolutionary sensible practice to dissolve the concept of material entity. When the historical negativity of production was confirmed in "The German Ideology," Marx established his really revolutionary dialectics of history. Adorno knows this point very well, but what he purports is obviously more ambitious then Marx. The negative property of dialectics is not only meant to prove the historicity and temporality of capitalist system, to smash the identity of capital logic, but, more importantly, to pull down *ALL* identities. The real dialectics never builds up a new identity, even if it's a communist identity ("Plan"). The negative dialectics has to be critical, revolutionary, and fearless. It has become an alternative post-Marxist interpretation of the revolutionary nature of dialectics.

With such a theoretical tendency, Adorno claims that the negative dialectics, as the logic of disintegration, is neither *a pure method* nor a sort of reality. His interpretation is unique. Firstly, dialectics is not a pure method because the unreconciled matter—lacking precisely the identity surrogated by the thought—is contradictory and resists any attempt at unanimous interpretation. It is the matter, not the organizing drive of thought that brings us to a dialectics. This is to illustrate the realistic dynamics of negative dialectics; that dialectics is revolutionary is not because of its logical method, but primarily due to the immanent differences among the objective entities. The nonidentity of matter, phenomena, and process constitutes the foundation of negative dialectics. Only after realizing this point can the Hegel-and-the-young-Lukács-style negative dialectics of totality really be freed from the conceptual framework of logic. Secondly, dialectics is not a simple reality, either. That is to say, negative dialectics would not, for acknowledging the foundation of nonidentity derived from the objective reality, turn itself into "the reflection of outside laws." That dialectics "[proceeds] dialectically means to think in contradictions, for the sake of the contradiction once experienced in the thing, and against that contradiction. A contradiction in reality, it is a contradiction against reality."[1] "*Against reality*" is very close to

---

[1]   Adorno, Theodor W. *Negative Dialectics*. Trans. E. B. Ashtion. New York: The Continuum Publishing House, 1990. p. 145.

destroying the existing prescriptions as used in Lenin's *Notes on Philosophy*; it means that negative dialectics does not correspond with objective dialectics in a simple way. Both the human individual and the historical subject are the authentic "sources of negative entropy" that create heterogeneity.

To Practice Against Reality. In *Notes on Philosophy*, Lenin quotes a long paragraph of Hegel's statements, and then on the right top of the page's margin, marks a comment: "In other words, human consciousness not only reflects the objective world but also creates the objective world."[1] Here, "in other words" follows the top box, which concerns the meaning of Marx's "On the Outline of Feuerbach," the title of the comparative recognition we use here. We find that this proposition, in Lenin's early reading (before p.150), was exactly the target of Lenin's disparaging criticism. Of course, this proposition is not to say that human thoughts can create the world, but to verify (whether with our approval or not) that Nature is still the premise of men's survival, while men, by means of objective material practice (Note: this is the "agent" of human reality) provide themselves with some new basis of their objective existence, realizing the ("reflexive") impulse for subjective ends. "That's to say, the world won't make men satisfied; men resolve to change it with their actions."[2] There are two "real matters" here, one being the external object and another the objective practice of men; the former is an inherent premise, whereas the latter offers a new basis.

Thereby, Lenin, with lots of insights, goes further to argue, "By drawing a vista of the objective world, men change the external reality, annihilate its prescriptiveness (= modify its appearance or property here and there), and thus wipe off its characteristics in terms of its look, surface and nihility, making it a self-containing entity (= objective

---

[1] Lenin, Vladimir. *The Collected Works of Lenin*. Beijing: People's Publishing House, 2nd Ed, Vol. 55, 1990. p. 182.

[2] Ibid., p. 183.

and true)."[1] In this paragraph, Lenin for the first time stipulates that practice should paint the vista of the objective world, which eventually establishes practical dialectic's important role in the philosophical sense of ontology. Men's painting of the objective world is not a verisimilar reflection of the outside world; weaving the warp or weft thread is to change the external reality; that is, in light of men's objectives (ends), to alternate the object's appearance or quality here and there. For instance, when innovating the natural conditions, we repress or reduce in the targeted environment those factors which are disadvantageous to human beings (such as "calamities," and "disasters" imposed by the Heaven), and at the same time, keep, select and maximize those natural elements which are advantageous to our existence (such as crops, energies, and ecosystems optimized for intensive utilization). The purpose is to "abolish" in nature the externality irrelevant to men, and transform the nature into a "pro-human" being (serving for human existence) insofar as practical utilities are concerned.[2]

Under particular historical conditions, the reality usually gives rise to some identical and coercive totality in history (say, the external despotism in the Middle Ages or the spontaneous totality in market). Negative dialectics, in such a situation, highlights its antagonism against the reality. The difference, however, is that Lenin and Marx specifically suggest material practice should turn against reality, whereas Adorno, who opposes practice, does not tell us what is the weapon against reality.

Of course, Adorno understands that negative dialectics, when it comes to abolishing the logic of identity, does not simply abandon identity at all. As he mentioned before, thinking is identifying, and so is the concept. Without identity, thoughts would be inconceivable. Therefore, on the rational phase, "we can see through the identity principle, but we cannot think without

---

[1] Lenin, Vladimir. *The Collected Works of Lenin*. Beijing: People's Publishing House, 2nd Ed, Vol. 55, 1990. p. 187.

[2] Zhang Yibing. *The Collected Works of Zhang Yibing*. Guang Xi Normal University Publishing House, 1999. pp.272-273.

identifying. Any definition is identification."[1] This is an unromantic factual acknowledgement. In his view, the mistake in traditional thinking is that identity is taken for the goal, and therefore, it gives rise to the identical logic of the coercive absolute. This is indeed what he objects to, but what is similarly true is that Adorno does not oppose the identity a concept entails. He wants to abolish the identity of the *Absolute*, and excavates a *nonidentity within identity*. I think, it is the blind point in most of the previous research on identity. Adorno never attempts to negate identity in terms of common sense (as some post-modern thoughts next to nihilism do). It is in this regard that we should scrutinize carefully.

Nonidentity, as is confirmed by negative dialectics, is "the secret teleo of identification. It is the part that can be salvaged."[2] It is an in-depth dialectic relationship. For example, when we say "Phoenix tree is a sort of tree," it points to two layers of meanings: one is to define what a phoenix tree itself is, while another is to categorize phoenix tree not as itself but a species of tree. The former is non-identical cognition, but the latter is identitarian thinking. Adorno says, "This [non-identical] cognition seeks to say what something is, while identitarian thinking says what something comes under, what it exemplifies or represents, and what, accordingly, it is not itself."[3] In the traditional thinking, people simply pay much attention to inclusive identifying thinking and make it an abstract absolute, without heeding the nonidentity that identifies the object's immanent properties. The nonidentity *within* the identity is the starting point of Adorno's dialectics. *This is also the starting point of all the postmodern contexts. Barthes's "Evasiveness of Concept," Derrida's "Deconstruction of Differance," Lyotard's "Non-grand Narrative," and Foucault's "Anti-power Distribution" are all the operation and execution of nonidentity that repels the hegemony of identity.*

---

[1] ˙Adorno, Theodor W. *Negative Dialectics.* Trans. E. B. Ashtion. New York: The Continuum Publishing House, 1990. p.149.

[2] Ibid.

[3] Ibid.

2. Non-identical semantic field

Firstly, I should particularly point out that nonidentity for Adorno is not saying "No" from outside. Neither is it simple objection and destruction. It is a kind of nonidentity and difference based on identity and *internalized in identity's logic*, which means a difference *irreconcilable* in the contradictory unity. I find that it is the primary disparity between Adorno and Marcuse in terms of their understandings of nonidentity's negativity. *I notice that some researchers infer merely from the dates and then conclude that the nonidentity in Adorno's negative dialectics is an imitation of Marcus's negative thinking, but none of them has ever made an accurate distinction in theory, in terms of the essential heterogeneity between the two.*[1] Unlike Marcuse, Adorno by no means advocates a simple negation of identity and unity, because "(an) abstract denial of unity would not befit thinking either. The illusion of taking direct control of the Many would be a mimetic regression," a myth that cannot be realized.[2] Moving from a simple identity to an extreme negativity and nonidentity seems to be absolutely radical, but in fact such a move would never shake the identity in reality because of its innate impossibility. Eventually, it would end up with a sort of complicity with the reality. This is probably one of the essential reasons why Adorno later resolutely disagrees with those leftist students who practice Marcuse's "Culture Rejection" movement.

In fact, Adorno advocates nonidentity in identity, which is not only the demand of thinking but the requirement of the reality. For example, we have seen from above his critique of the correlation between the barter principle and identity, but he has no intention of destroying such a relation realistically. He once said with much insight that if we denied the barter principle abstractly, if we proclaimed, to the greater glory of the irreducibly qualitative, that parity should no longer be the ideal rule, we would be

---

[1] Li Zhongshang. *The Third Road*. Academy Press, 1994. p. 219; Yu Wujin and Chen Xueming. *Foreign Marxist Schools*. Fudan University Press, 1990. p. 162.

[2] Adorno, Theodor W. *Negative Dialectics*. Trans. E. B. Ashtion. New York: The Continuum Publishing House, 1990. p. 158.

creating excuses for recidivism into ancient injustice. It reminds me of the war communism during the early period of the October Revolution when barter was idealistically abolished, and of the crazy and stupid "People's Communes" in 1958 in China. Adorno says, "The main characteristic of the exchange of equivalents has been that unequal things would be exchanged in its name, that the surplus value of labor would be appropriated. If comparability as a category of measure were simply annulled, the rationality which is inherent in the barter principle—as ideology, of course, but also as a promise—would give way to direct appropriation, to force, and nowadays to the naked privilege of monopolies and cliques."[1] His analysis is really brilliant. To criticize the identity in barter principle and to disclose the essence of bourgeois ideology in the principle of the exchange of equivalents, are by no means at the expense of *regressing back to the direct violence of feudal autocracy*; on the contrary, only by realizing the barter principle can we "transcend barter." He adds that the self-reflection of enlightenment is not to abolish enlightenment and freedom can come to be real only through coercive civilization, not by way of "Back to nature." The explanations are similar here. As to this issue, we have experienced too much historical pain in practicing the socialist movements in reality. I believe that Adorno's analysis goes deeper than *Enlightenment Dialectics*. The reasoning is incisive, but how to carry it out? We are still fruitless.

Second, nonidentity is heterogeneity in identity, and *objective contradictoriness*. Negative dialectics is self-awareness of the deep contradictory disparity within the historical existence. In this regard, Adorno revives Hegel's concept of contradiction. "Yet objective contradictoriness does not designate only whatever entity remains outside our judgments; it also designates something in what we judge."[2] Therefore, Hegel is "the first man to envision it." Adorno is supportive of this body of opinion, that is, envisioning the innate contradictoriness of entity is the kernel of dialectics. In

---

[1] Adorno, Theodor W. *Negative Dialectics*. Trans. E. B. Ashtion. New York: The Continuum Publishing House, 1990. pp. 146-147.

[2] Ibid., p. 152.

this respect, he is in line with Marx and Lenin, who really understand secrets of Hegelian philosophy. Of course, unlike Hegel who turns contradiction into a sort of "vehicle of total identification," negative dialectics takes contradiction as an agent to dialectically resolve the identical logic. "Objectively, dialectics means to break the compulsion to achieve identity, and to break it by means of the energy stored up in that compulsion and congealed in its reifications."[1] Such nonidentity in identity is contradiction itself. As Hegel puts it, it is "its otherness." Again, what we read here is a deep dialectics. Actually, the primary form of this formula is Fichte's self-realizing "non-I"; the *I as non-I* illustrates a deep correlation. Afterwards, Hegel in ontology uses the reflective rule of *"toward otherness"* to realize subjectivity. The most brilliant explanation of metaphorical relation is what *Phenomenology of Spirit* says on master-slave relationship. The "Other" in Derrida and Said's post-colonialism is a latter appropriation of this point. Adorno says, "The inside of identity is its relation to that which it is not, and which its managed, frozen self-identity withholds from it."[2] Different from Hegel's "indifference to the other," Adorno wants to examine closely the heterogeneous other within identity.

Third, nonidentity of dialectics is a *nonstop resistance* against identity on the part of the other. Adorno maintains that, for the other, the non-identical is not to be obtained directly, as something positive on its part, nor is it obtainable by a negation of the negative. Adorno intends to create something new here. He thinks, for Hegel, what, thus wins out in the inmost core of dialectics is the anti-dialectical principle, which means *the negation of negation is positivity*. Although Hegel acknowledges contradictoriness, he always uses "identity to ease contradiction"; he advocates negation and critique as well, but the goal of such negation is still affirmation. Therefore, "the negation of negation would be another identity, a new delusion, a projection of consequential—and ultimately of the principle of subjectivity—

---

[1] Adorno, Theodor W. *Negative Dialectics*. Trans. E. B. Ashtion. New York: The Continuum Publishing House, 1990. p. 157.

[2] Ibid., p. 163.

upon the absolute."[1] Adorno says, such logic of double negation getting to positivity is a slyer "core of identification." From the standpoint of our real life, the cunning plan of the bourgeois is that it differs from the simple positivity of feudal autocracy (Saying "No" is Forbidden); rather, you are encouraged to say "No," to protest in the congress hall in an institutionalized way, to demonstrate in the street on the prescribed street route. The purpose is nothing but affirming this "democratic" system. This is a kind of worship for positive thing-in-itself. *Negation is for the purpose of confirming the status quo more deeply*, which is the reason why "the spread of its ideology prevails in the world." It calls to my mind what Foucault later said on the invisible distribution of power discourse, as well as Mintz's theory of "Sweet Power." Adorno believes that true negativity is always negative; it would never "acknowledge the *status quo*." The essence of nonidentity is *permanent negation*; only through non-stop "resistance which otherness offers to identity (can we find) the power of dialectics."[2]

Fourth, nonidentity does not turn the particular opposed to the universal conception into a metaphysical ultimate because of objection to abstract identity. What Adorno obviously critiques here is the individual-oriented new humanism after Kierkegaard. He says, if we are for objecting to rational identity turn to irrational individual existence, the self-reflective thinking mode of individual subject is bound to result in the nimbus and the authority of intellectual impenetrability and rigor. A theory shows "obedience" to the pure particular, and the result is still "preserve the status quo."[3] Such identification is very incisive. Because when a theory (like Husserl's or Heidegger's) turns into an introspective meditation done by a pure individual, or some sort of amusement enjoyed by some thinkers poetically, people can by no means extract power from it. It is very correct. But my question is— can people understand Adorno's stuff?

---

[1] Adorno, Theodor W. *Negative Dialectics*. Trans. E. B. Ashtion. New York: The Continuum Publishing House, 1990. p. 160.

[2] Ibid., pp. 160-161.

[3] Ibid., p. 161.

All in all, nonidentity proposed by Adorno is a heterogeneity that admits objective contradictoriness as unity (Derrida's difference is derived from it). This is a non-central, non-hierarchal, and non-subjugating relation of dialectics. He vividly says that it is *constellation*. Eventually we are going to live "a celestial life."

3. Constellation: the existential form of non-identity

From "Introduction," we have known that the so-called *constellation* is nonidentity caring for heterogeneity, a new type of relation between being and ideas described in Adorno's negative dialectics that acknowledges contradiction and differentiation. It not only applies to what is between subject and object but will be used between two objects, between object and species, between mind and existence, between concept and experience, between value and techniques, etc. Where there is relationship, there should be among different elements such a "peaceful" partnership, that is, "peaceful and differentiating coexistence in which no part controls the other part, but each part is subject to the influence from the other."[1] I think, Adorno's theory learns the lesson of Heidegger, that is, after abolishing an external binary opposition between subject and object, yet he reconstructs a new deity's supremacy; compared with the Real, such supremacy foregrounds a host of secondary, un-Real being and the being of the ordinary. Nevertheless, Adorno's constellation wipes off all subjugating relations and introduces a brand new companionship.

Speaking of such brand new *non-subjugating relation*, Adorno gives it original names, which are non-central, non-hierarchical "constellation" and the non-constructive status of "force field." To our best knowledge, force field and constellation are terminologies Adorno borrows from physics and Benjamin; both names refer to a compound of variables, which are juxtaposed, without being assimilated into a centre. All these variables cannot be reduced to a common denominator, a kernel, or a First Principle of essence. Constellation is used by Benjamin to illustrate the noncompulsory

---

[1] Adorno, Theodor W. *Negative Dialectics*. Trans. E. B. Ashtion. New York: The Continuum Publishing House, 1990. p. 210.

dialectic relation between concept and object, by making analogy to the loose but connected status between stars and constellation. Benjamin often says that "constellation is not the law of stars"! Adorno follows this idea to relocate the concept of constellation. He points out, "Constellation should not be deduced to an essence, for what exist within the constellation are not the essence."[1] As Eagleton puts it, Constellation refuses to nail itself on a metaphysical essence. The value of constellation lies in that it maintains a non-identical particularity, giving the target a new life in the explosion of identity. For Adorno, "the universality of reason is replaced by the gap between every particular instant, which in turn opens to the next unexpected particular instant."[2]

However, I don't think Adorno has very perfectly elucidated in theory this category; his explanation, either in terms of quantity or quality, is quite weak. I cannot judge whether this is a theoretical strategy, which increases the difficulty of our discussion. To illustrate Adorno's innovative definition, we can begin with his specific analysis of how to understand constellation.

As aforementioned, to oppose the subjugating identical thinking doesn't mean to abandon anything unified in thinking; the scientific unification of negative dialectics is constellation cognition. Here, unity is not "step-by-step progression from the concepts to a more general cover concept. Instead, the concepts enter into a constellation."[3] Unlike the compulsory "Oneness" in traditional metaphysics, constellations represent from outside what the concept has cut away within: the "more" which the concept is equally desirous and incapable of being. By gathering around the object of cognition, the concepts potentially determine the object's interior. They attain in thinking, what was necessarily excised from thinking. In the previous

---

[1] Adorno, Theodor W. *Negative Dialectics*. Trans. E. B. Ashtion. New York: The Continuum Publishing House, 1990. p.193.

[2] Eagleton, Terry. *The Aesthetics of Ideology*. Trans. Wangjie etc. Guang Xi Normal University Press, 1999. pp. 329-330. On page 356, Eagleton asserts that the concept of constellation is "the most creative endeavor" in Benjamin and Adorno's fight against totality and identity.

[3] Adorno, Theodor W. *Negative Dialectics*. Trans. E. B. Ashtion. New York: The Continuum Publishing House, 1990. p.162.

oneness-oriented essentialist cognition, the concept, forever as the result of historical cognition, assumes itself as the object itself. Therefore, unhistorical representation of concept (essence) is to excise the object crudely. Those which don't enter into the concept have been thus severely shadowed. Constellation cognition is a historical *anti-excision*. In brief, it admits a cognitive tolerance of history. For instance, "Cognition of the object in its constellation, theoretical thought circles the concept it would like to unseal, hoping that it may fly open like the lock of a well-guarded safe-deposit box: in response, not to a single key or a single number, but to a combination of numbers."[1] It is similar to an example given by Maslow when he criticizes linear causality and the theory of restoration: today, on the billiards desk of science cognition, a ball is no longer hit by another ball, but more often than not hit by ten or more balls hit at the same time! It is not simply the relation between object and subject, or substance and spirit. All conditions or elements existing in this world of object form a constellation-like connection as is in nature. It is a brand-new cognition of science, in which any linear and subjugating enforcement, any theoretical systems or "-isms" are abolished, any human-centered utilitarian intention is resolved. Here, negative dialectics presents a real picture of the world.

Hence, Adorno cites Weber as an instance. He argues, "From Weber's standpoint, constellation replaces taxonomy." This is a very meaningful commentary. Adorno says, "When Weber, in his treatise on Protestant ethics and the spirit of capitalism, raised the question of defining capitalism, he—in contrast with current scientific practice—was as well aware of the difficulty of defining historical concepts as previously only philosophers had been. He explicitly rejected the delimiting procedure of definition, the adherence to the schema *genus proximum, differentia specifica*, and asked instead that sociological concepts be 'gradually composed' from 'individual parts to be taken from historic reality. The place of definitive conceptual comprehension cannot, therefore, be the beginning of the inquiry, only the end.'"[2] This is to

---

[1] Adorno, Theodor W. *Negative Dialectics*. Trans. E. B. Ashtion. New York: The Continuum Publishing House, 1990. p. 163.

[2] Ibid., p. 165.

say, in Weber's discussion on the spirit of capitalism, he no longer focuses on definition or essentialist assertions, but attempts to make specific description of history as it happens. Such identification makes some good sense. Adorno also notices that Weber's analyses "are not mere conceptual fixations. Rather, by gathering concepts round the central one that is sought, they attempt to express what the concept aims at, not to circumscribe it to operation ends."[1] He probably means that, when Weber describes capitalism, he is not obsessive with a fixed conclusive statement, but represents a constellation-like history-function entity in details and from multiple perspectives (such as the instrumental formalistic rationalization on the level of reason, computability and standardization on the level of technique, multiple logging in economic operation, and bureaucracy in the political and legal systems). Adorno even believes that Weber's analysis is very close to Marx; furthermore, Weber's constellational analysis of capitalism is not conceptual fabrication, but based on the complexity of capitalism in reality: Its multiple variables are interwoven into an increasingly reliable function correlation. Therefore, "we need no epistemological critique to make us pursue constellations; the search for them is forced upon us by the real course of history."[2] Such a statement is by no means nonsense.

Interestingly, Adorno seems to agree with Weber's writing style. He says the "composing" is much like music composition. Constellational cognition and writing are identified with a musical thinking. However, Weber has exerted such far-reaching an influence on Western Marxism, particularly Frankfurt School that their theoretical critique of contemporary capitalist system is largely based on the inversion (since the young Lukács's *History and Class Consciousness*) of Weber's concept of instrumental reason. But that Adorno speaks so many favorable words of Weber in regard to methodology which actually surprises me.

Speaking of the music composition and thinking, the reader has already

---

[1] Adorno, Theodor W. *Negative Dialectics*. Trans. E. B. Ashtion. New York: The Continuum Publishing House, 1990. pp. 165-166.

[2] Ibid., p. 166.

known that Adorno is strong in theoretical analysis of music. Nevertheless, musical thinking is not born with the similarity to constellation. It is a matter of historical construction. In the previous introduction, we have gained preliminary acquaintance with Adorno's negative dialectics, an important origin of which is the revolution of modern new music. Compared with the tonal system of western music in accordance with the industrial system, which is characterized with "innate persistence, motivation, spread of subject matter, complete and extending structure of melody, logic development in musical routines,"[1] Wagner's half-tonal structure has made a significant breakthrough, while Schönberg further pulls down the tonal system and develops the principle of atonality adored by Adorno. Particularly, Schönberg establishes the twelve-tone technique, which finishes the constellational revolution in music composition. In *The Philosophy of New Music*, Adorno elaborates on the properties of such constellational technique in music composition. In his point of view, the main components of traditional music composition—musical elements—are situated in a divided and confrontational position for a long time. Frequently, one element takes the lead, and the others are subordinate. This is the hierarchy in music. For example, in romantic music, harmony takes the dominant role, while melody is subordinate to the structure of harmony; counterpoint is no more than the decoration of the main tone's composition. In Schönberg's new music, all the elements in musical composition for the first time are integrated into a non-hierarchal, mutually-complementary, and mutually-transcending constellation of music. Hereafter, an atonal, formless, and revolutionary new music comes into being.

4. The categorical constellation of negative dialectics

I've said that Adorno never discusses dialectics in the *ontological* sense. His negative dialectics is, as it were, a theoretical constellation, a concept and category placed subject to the change of history. Therefore, Adorno stresses,

---

[1] Yu Runyang. *An Introduction to Philosophy of Modern Western Music*. Hunan Educational Press, 2000. p. 410.

"When a category changes, as those of identity and totality do in negative dialectics, a change occurs in the constellation of all categories, and thus again in each one."[1]

It is worth noting that, to grasp a constellational category, the vital thing is to get rid of the idea of *singularity* and *primacy* in categorical relationship, that is say, the either-or logic in metaphysics, or the habit of assuming one concept or category as the decisive one, while dismissing another related concept or category as determined or subordinate. Such is the consequence of the tyranny of identity before. Constellational relationship is *equal coexistence, but with difference. Such an opinion is manifest very clearly in Deleuze's idea of "(ET and)." For him, rejecting the primacy of "the One" of identity and emphasizing inter-categorical "ET (and) means diversity and the destruction of identification."*[2] Next, let's look at some constellations of dialectical relation as discussed by Adorno.

First of all, *constellation of subject and object*. Adorno maintains that the rejection of dualistic framework does not mean "the difference between subject and object" should be simply denied. To deconstruct dualism doesn't mean a non-historical regression back to Heidegger who argues for a primitive chaotic status that makes no distinction between subject and object. The subject-object relationship standing in constellation is "neither an ultimate duality nor a screen hiding ultimate unity. They constitute one another as much as—by virtue of such constitution—they depart from each other."[3] The boundary between subject and object is a positive and bilateral construction. "Mutual-construction" is very important, because it neither simply stresses the material independence, nor favors the wrath of subject. This is an *ontologically equal* mutual construction. Obviously, Adorno requires a sort of definite negation of individual element. Such a specific negation is to face the fact that "subject is not completely subject, neither is

[1] Adorno, Theodor W. *Negative Dialectics*. Trans. E. B. Ashtion. New York: The Continuum Publishing House, 1990. p. 166.

[2] Deleuze, Gilles. *Philosophy and Critique of Power*. Commercial Press, 2000. p. 51.

[3] Adorno, Theodor W. *Negative Dialectics*. Trans. E. B. Ashtion. New York: The Continuum Publishing House, 1990. p. 174.

object completely object," and both can't be separated from each other. At the same time, they are not "connected by a transcendental third party"[1]. Relationship cannot be materialized into the third party, nor can it constitute a new ontology of relationship. It is different from both Hegel and Heidegger.

In Adorno's point of view, "(subject and object) differ in the same way, cannot be brought to pure identity with one side or the other, and mutually qualify each other because no object is determinable without the subject, the determinant that makes an object of it, and because no subject can think anything it does not confront, not even that subject itself. Thinking is tied to entities."[2] That is to say, the subject-object relationship hinges on the realization of *peace* between men and between mankind and their objects. The essence of such peace is a differentiated and equal communication between things, and between subject and object. It is constellational relationship. Elsewhere, Adorno describes it as *Three-Star-Assembly* among collective subjectivity, individual subjectivity, and the objective world. (Habermas develops a communicative theory out of it.)[3]

Second, the *constellation of essence and appearance*. Of course, essence and appearance are not a couple of ontological categories, but *epistemological* ones, because, only insofar as object *faces* subject, there is the distinction between appearance and essence. This point is a brilliant idea Hegel fails to find in Kant. In this regard, Adorno specifically rejects positivism and dislikes the simple negation of essence (essentialism). He holds that in Hegel the logic of identity makes him regard essence as "unattained self spirit." Thereby, essence is different from appearance's "pure, spiritual thing-in-itself." This is an absolute, which is the result when the idealist positively wipes off "the identification between subject and object." But Adorno argues that we should understand this pair of categories in the contradiction of nonidentity between subject and object: "It can be recognized only by the contradiction between what things are and what they

---

[1] Adorno, Theodor W. *Negative Dialectics*. Trans. E. B. Ashtion. New York: The Continuum Publishing House, 1990. p. 175.

[2] Ibid., p. 103.

[3] Adorno, Theodor W. "Letters to Walter Benjamin" in *Aesthetics and Politics*, New York: 1977. p. 113.

claim to be."[1] In other words, in Hegel's epistemology, cognition is always self-knowledge of absolute essence, for *there is nothing new in appearance!* It proves the point that in the logic of identical cognition, there is no such thing as new possibility of cognition, since "freedom is the recognition of the inevitable." On the ontological basis of epistemology, the outcome is always *prepared*. Adorno is against such a theological teleology. He acknowledges the preexistence (what it is) of cognitive object, but is more aware of that cognitive activity is in historical existence a construct; "essence" is not non-historical solid entity, but fluid and unstable. Therefore, in our cognition, there is of course something new that is homogeneous to the historical movement of things and appearances. Cognition should always point to some new possibility. Cognition is always generated historically, rather than a reflection.

At the same time, compared with the alleged fact, "this essence also is conceptual rather than immediate."[2] That is to say, in human cognition, essence is always rendered through the mediation of abstract concept. More importantly, the conceptuality of essence is not to prove that essence is an absolute existence of subjectivity, but to confirm that, in terms of men's cognition of essence, "no matter how much blame may attach to the subject's contribution, the conceived world is not its own but a world hostile to the subject."[3] It is also at this point that Adorno criticizes Husserl. He thinks, though Husserl dislikes "the thinking subject's universal rule" and objects to taking essence as "an element sprung from a source," his idealism, an ontologization of the pure mind, was hypertrophied. As a result, his idea about essentialist intuition also falls into another identical logic of the absolute. Adorno rightly points out, "phenomenology forbade the prescription of laws by a subject that was already obliged to obey them."[4] This means that Husserl attempts to suspend constructive *ponens* that cannot

---

[1] Adorno, Theodor W. *Negative Dialectics*. Trans. E. B. Ashtion. New York: The Continuum Publishing House, 1990. p. 167.

[2] Ibid.

[3] Ibid.

[4] Ibid.

be suspended as the existential form of consciousness; it also reaches the presupposition of restoration. Adorno says, in fact, Husserl feels strongly that the identical conceptual framework imposed upon object shadows a sort of nonidentity, which is "objective matter." However, since Husserl like all the idealists believes that intermediacy always belongs to subjective thinking, he can only understand this objective matter as an immediacy sui generis, and he was forced to commit an act of epistemological violence and copy the mediations from sense perception. Essentialist intuition is such thinking freak developed out of this idealist enforcement. Heidegger follows suit later on.

On the other hand, Adorno cites the lunatic Nietzsche to discuss positivism as far as the essence-appearance relationship is concerned. He holds that, "Nietzsche, the irreconcilable adversary of our theological heritage in metaphysics, had ridiculed the difference between essence and appearance. He had relegated the 'background world' to the 'backwoodsmen', concurring here with all of positivism."[1] As radical as Nietzsche may be, it never occurs to him to deny essence. Essence is what must be covered up and to deny that there is an essence means to side with appearance, because when the distinction between essence and appearance was cancelled off, the immediate "fact" would become ontologized. Yet, when we can only "treat with all appearances equally," not essentially, the result must be our collaboration with appearance, which is may be what Nietzsche didn't anticipate. Thereby, we can also reflect upon a contemporary issue, which is that the radical postmodern thoughts derived from Nietzsche also deny essence, rules, and any cognition of depth. When the actual consequence of these thoughts is to deprive men of the real critical reason, the postmodern thoughts are then reduced to an evil accomplice for those in power. This is worth our attention.

To cancel the distinction between essence and appearance, to reject the truth behind the immediate "facts" people care about, are the essence of positivism as the most important ideology of the bourgeois. Adorno comes to realize that in the contemporary capitalist society, when positivism in the

---

[1] Adorno, Theodor W. *Negative Dialectics*. Trans. E. B. Ashtion. New York: The Continuum Publishing House, 1990. p.169.

mainstream social sciences is leveling essence and appearance, men are losing their judgment to distinguish essence and appearance. The boundary between happiness and suffering or pain is gone. "No background world would annoy the latest type of backwoodsmen; he happily buys what the foreground world would sell them on, in words or in silence. Positivism becomes ideology...."[1] Positivism is the controlled premise of utmost significance.

Third, *the indirectness of the objective*. As we know, since the young Lukács, the category of meditation is always what the western Marxism focuses on. In the non-identical negative dialectics, Adorno also reinterprets the category of meditation. His discourse on it is very abstract.

In traditional philosophy, meditation is an extremely significant category of idealist dialectics. Compared with the immediate type of epistemology (which probably consists of old materialism and all metaphysics starting from immediate experience and object), the idealist dialectics excavates the prescription of indirect meditation. The idealist dialectics starts from the *indirectness* of meditation. "The triumphant finding that immediacy is wholly indirect rides roughshod over indirectness and blithely ends up with the totality of the concept, which nothing non-conceptual can stop any more. It ends up with the absolute rule of the subject."[2] In other words, in human cognition, any direct prescriptiveness in deeper context is actually indirect, for "there is nothing which is not indirect." Furthermore, in traditional idealism, since indirectness is always connected with subjectivity, *indirectness is equal to concept*. As mentioned above, the conceptuality of indirectness is essentialist: indirectness is essential, and the concept itself is indirect by its immediate nature. Therefore, due to the findings of the idealism in indirectness, the absolute rule of the conceptual (subjective) identity is thus established. The enslavement of all the indirect is then inevitable. Hegel starts from subjective referent's being mediated by self consciousness (and turned into apperception), and finally identifies idea with

---

[1] Adorno, Theodor W. *Negative Dialectics*. Trans. E. B. Ashtion. New York: The Continuum Publishing House, 1990. p.170.

[2] Ibid., p. 172.

absolute indirectness so as to establish his kingdom of the absolute idea. In modern time, of the cognitive theory in sciences, Popper and Piaget's "theory precedes observation" is derived from the same source.

Theory Precedes Observation: The modern philosophy's epistemology suddenly comes in our view when Popper puts forth in the philosophy of science. At first, he brings forward the idea that "theory precedes observation." Bacon's "science starts with observation," an important principle in modern experimental sciences, is called by him "an out-of-date mythology," because modern science never starts with experimentation, but is based on a specific framework of scientific theory. Popper from the perspective of modern science history reasserts Kant's proposition: there is no such thing as pure observation, for any observation in experiment must be conducted according to a certain theory as the axis of reference; it is "a purposeful activity led by certain questions and a range of expectation."[1] At this point, Popper and Piaget think alike. In their pint of view, human cognitive activity is engendered and developed within a specific theoretical framework; some deep structures of theory (or, scientific cognitive structure) always decide specific cognitive activities, whereas the change of such theoretical framework's cognitive axis of reference will certainly result in the Gestalt transformation of all knowledge activities. This is the theory-framework determinism in the epistemology of modern philosophy. Kant seems to come back to life in a new scientific basis, though what differs is that Kant's priori framework of reason is replaced by the dynamic theory development in history. Furthermore, agnosticism has been dumped in grave.[2]

Adorno obviously is not supportive of such idealist concept of mediation. We have seen this in his criticism of young Lukács.

---

[1] Popper, Karl. *Unended Quest*. Trans. Qiu Renzhong. Fu Jian People's Press, 1984. p. 50.

[2] Zhang Yibing. "On the Constraints of Theoretical Framework of Scientific Truth and Social Basis." *The Collected Works of Zhang Yibing*. Guang Xi Normal University Press, 1999. p. 93.

First of all, in negative dialectics, indirectness is no longer a subjective and conceptual element, but an objective mediation. "What transmits the facts is not so much the subjective mechanism of their pre-formation and comprehension as it is the objectivity heteronomous to the subject."[1] Adorno's analyses sometimes are very straightforward. He says there would be no mediation without something. The directness of the objective is not equal to the *immediacy in illusion.* Acknowledging mediation shouldn't deny the objective directness. In this regard, I think he also criticizes the young Lukács and so forth who exaggerate mediation inappropriately to a degree of idealist thinking. Secondly, the idealist dialectics uses thinking's mediation to establish an absolute rule of conceptual identity, which is however illegal. Because, for Hegel, Husserl and Heidegger, rejecting immediacy (the directness of being "ready-for-hand") would eventually end up with the ontologization of thinking's mediation, which in turn leads to a rule of idealist identity. According to Adorno, acknowledging indirectness can make people realize the difference which had been stolen away mysteriously (that is, the fake direct identification of immediacy and the thing), but which can "destroy the spell of identity."

What we talk about here is conceptual constellation, the speaking of which is more often than not tinted with aesthetic atmosphere. As to how to constellate the social and historical existence of human reality, or more specifically, as to how to transform the "administered world" critiqued by Adorno into a sky covered with constellations, Adorno is but speechless, putting his hands on the leg, silently facing the piano of non-identity.

III. The Primacy of Subject and the Priority of Object

Adorno's description of Negative Dialectics is as simple as that. It

---

[1] Adorno, Theodor W. *Negative Dialectics*. Trans. E. B. Ashtion. New York: The Continuum Publishing House, 1990. p. 170.

is after all a theoretical posture (not a stand), a vacant spirit (not a logical framework), a purely critical "City of God," and thus can never settle down on the land of reality. Nevertheless, in order to show his difference from all idealisms, Adorno has to demonstrate a basic viewpoint, that is, the *practical legitimacy* of concepts and categories of Negative Dialectics. From the above analysis, we have clearly observed in Negative Dialectics a firm and fundamental idea which used to be referred to as "materialism." Adorno insists on this materialistic tendency in order to reject the old ontology. This tendency in Adorno's theoretical framework is usually misunderstood by some scholars who haven't read Adorno correctly. They arbitrarily assert that Negative Dialectics is "a negation of the objective dialectics," taking dialectics as something "purely subjective"[1]. Is it really true? Let's find out what on earth Adorno wants to tell us. As we see, Adorno starts to draw a theoretical borderline in the field of traditional epistemology and then extends it to other theoretical fields related to the discussion.

1. The transcendental character of idealistic subject and social unconsciousness

Adorno says, "The prevailing trend in epistemological reflection was to reduce objectivity more and more to the subject."[2] It should be noted that the subject with Adorno here differs from the subject of cognition and practice with Marx in his *Theses on Feuerbach*; it is rather *the subject of concept*. In this context, it seems that Adorno is identifying himself with the trend in the study of epistemology following Hume and Kant, especially the trend in the philosophical studies of the 20th century which pays increasing attention to the cognitive framework and the observation (cognition) of the objective relations. Adorno witnesses an internal restaging of Kantian *transcendentalism* on the modern stage. Externally, both the philosophical generalization of the uncertainty law in the quantum mechanics and the

---

[1] Li Zhongshang. *Analysis of "New Marxism"*. China Renmin University Press, 1987. p. 222.

[2] Adorno, Theodor W. *Negative Dialectics*. Trans. E. B. Ashton. New York: The Continuum Publishing House, 1990. p. 196.

proposition that "theory is prior to observation" (Popper, Piaget) attribute the cognitive results to the medium (transcendental) power in the subject's cognitive framework, thereby denying the absolute objectivity of cognition. This only weakly rebuts and dissolves the traditional belief that cognition is "the mimesis of the existents." At a deeper philosophical level, the show also includes Husserl's phenomenological reconstruction of the transcendental intuition after giving up a rational framework, and Heidegger's objection to the ontological questioning of being behind the existents. After all, this is no more than a reduction to a certain hidden transcendental subject. Adorno has clearly opposed to this *idealistic* tendency in epistemology. He says, "the very tendency should be reversed" (very much like a Marxist tone). In fact, he has interpreted the genetic root of this erroneous trend in a very profound and exciting way. I even think that in quite a few issues, Adorno's critique of idealistic epistemology has surpassed Lenin's *Materialism and Empirio-Criticism.*

In modern Western epistemology, the recognition of the cognitive support system initiated by the Gestalt Psychology is an important progress in the scientific epistemology.

In the development of modern philosophy, rationalism first of all paid attention to the decisive role the rational subject played in men's cognitive experience. Kant developed from a whole set of logic from rationalism, thereby deserving to be entitled the forefather of the restriction theory in the theoretical framework of modern epistemology. In Kant's theory, a "thing-in-itself" as the essence of the world has been banished to the other bank of the real world. Kant has deepened Locke's idea that science is the process of "questioning nature" in that he believes it is a process in which man consciously makes use of a rational framework to organize and process the materials from intuitive experience; "setting laws for nature" is the essence of science. In other words, *the law of nature that we have identified in the past is actually "man-made," no more than an outcome resulting from the acting of man's cognitive subject on the perceptual object*. Kant's thought is admittedly a significant breakthrough in the history of modern epistemology, because it is indeed the first probe into the essence of science from the standpoint of idealism. In Kant's eyes, all the cognitive activities of man result from the activities of the subject: "sense is formed," rather than a simple visualization of the object by the subject. The mechanism that processes the perceptual materials is produced by apperception of the subject, an innate synthetic function. Obviously, Kant's theory of apperception has evolved from Leibniz's external unity of the organic low senses into the formulation of a new theory. Here the whole perceptual world is firstly constructed and organized by the transcendental frames such as time and space. Next, all the high cognitive movements are further prescribed by the cognitive categories and rational framework. Then, with Kant, the truth of science is produced by the constraint of a transcendental rational framework which starts as being-in-itself and develops "for me."

In the later history of Western thought, Kant's theory of constraint of a theoretical framework has been applied by Herbart and Wundt to build a psychological road beyond philosophy. Apperception is further regarded as a kind of subjective context of the psychological cognitive process. It directly emphasizes the unifying effect of the past experiences and consciousness on the present intuition, and its attention gradually shifts from the unity of psychological phenomena to the constraints of psychological contexts, which eventually leads to the famous Gestalt Psychology. The Gestalt Psychology opposes Wundt's reductionism concerning elements of consciousness and his belief of knowledge development. It also develops the theory of apperception from a theory which loosely connects consciousness and determines the psychological unity into *a theory of constraints on the deeper unity of the psychological consciousness*. They for the first time put forwards the idea of psychological receptive field, pointing out that the occurrence and development of a psychological phenomenon is constrained by an inner structure of the consciousness, and the fixing and stability of all psychological phenomena all depends on the unity constraint of a certain conscious context. This point is a great contribution that Gestalt Psychology has made to the development of modern epistemology. It is Piaget who has highly advocated Kantian epistemology. He starts with the Children's psychological genesis and development, and further investigates into the genesis and development of the whole cognitive system of all human beings, on the basis of which he formulized the theory of theoretical constraint. Piaget's genetic epistemology becomes a hugely popular philosophy.

The attention that the scientific epistemology paid to the mediating function of the cognitive structure has promoted a new round of various idealisms in modern time. It is against this background, Adorno says definitely that it is shallowly misleading to deny the objectivity of cognition because of the mediating function of the subject's cognitive structure. The key point here is that people "forgot the mediation in the mediating subject,"[1] namely how the cognitive framework of the subject, as a transcendental constitution, is *constructed*. To be specific, isn't it true that both Kant's transcendental apperception, the essential intuition of *"I"* that derived from the reduction of phenomenology and Heidegger's limited historical existence in face of death, if not in the light of the divine power of theodicy, are constructed? Adorno starts his analysis from a mock, saying that as though to punish it, the subject will be overcome by what it has forgotten. This is a dialectics which Adorno calls as "the reversal of the subjective reduction," which he used to entitle the section. I have to give a warning that this is the most unfathomable part of Adorno's text, much like a secret bottle thrown into the sea.

Adorno says, "the subject's essentiality is an existence raised to the second potency and, as Hegel did not fail to state, presupposes the first

---

[1] Adorno, Theodor W. *Negative Dialectics*. Trans. E. B. Ashton. New York: The Continuum Publishing House, 1990. p.176.

potency: factuality. Factuality is a condition of the possibility—even though negated—of essentiality."[1] Obviously, Adorno maintains a principle *similar* to materialism (later we will see this is a misunderstanding). It seems that the subject's transcendental constitution or the essential intuition of I is a more profound essentiality of understanding, but the condition that prevents people from perceiving the deeper is just the potency of factuality which rises to the constitutive potency of the subject. The stronger the subject negates this, the more constraints it gets from this basic consciousness. Is the "I"—the reduced essential intuition after the suspension of foresight, the entity that makes self-reflection and introspection through "being," really an originary perception? Adorno analyzes that the immediacy of primary reactions was broken, first, in the formation of the *I*; and broken with these reactions was the spontaneity which the pure *I*, according to transcendental custom, is to contract into. This means, the so-called *immediacy* of essential intuition is no more than a transcendental spontaneity. *This is a complex false image after the simple false image is eliminated.* The reason is that "the centristic identity of the *I* is acquired at the expense of what idealism will then attribute to it. The constitutive subject of philosophy is more of a thing than the specific psychological content which is excreted, as naturalistic and reified."[2] What lies in the immediacy of essence? What is in the "de-being"? These are the questions that the masters do not want to ask. As Adorno de-masks, the contribution of idealism to the history of thought is its emphasis on the subjective initiative, whereas this initiative relies on entity. If this initiative is ontologized, it is bound to be materialized. That is to say, as this being, the more autocratically the *I* rises above entity, the greater its imperceptible objectification and ironic retraction of its constitutive role. Once the I and this being become an imperative identity, the reasonable initiative is sacrificed. Not only the pure I is ontically transmitted by the empirical I, the transcendental principle itself, the supposed "first" of philosophy as against

---

[1] Adorno, Theodor W. *Negative Dialectics*. Trans. E. B. Ashton. New York: The Continuum Publishing House, 1990. p.176.

[2] Ibid., p. 177.

entity, is so transmitted. Neither Husserl and Heidegger have recognized this point.

Adorno points out, if the secret of the transcendental subject is to be deciphered, to expose the reality of the social and historical basis is the most important. "Beyond the magic circle of identitarian philosophy, the transcendental subject can be deciphered as a society unaware of itself."[1] This is the Marx's legacy that Adorno does not want to shake off, and is also his identification of the above statement that subjectivity is called explicable especially by social facts. Adorno identifies that ever since mental and physical labor were separated under the mind's domination, there has emerged an idea to defend the dominance, "it is primary and original." However, this idealistic idea "makes every effort to forget the source of its claim." He says, the dominance of the mind (Marx's "the dominance of the abstract or Adorno's "the dominance of the illusion") is no mental rule at all, but lies in the physical force at its disposal. "Abstraction—without which the subject would not be the constituents at large at all."[2] However, the abstraction has not been achieved by the subject in the subjective contexts; it is above all a kind of social facts, which takes place in *the general functionality* of the society. This is an in-depth revelation of Heidegger's objection to the functional being of the entity, but why?

As Adorno explains, Kant has made an important identification that the essence of the transcendental subject has been "functionality" of "the pure activity." With Kant, it is a projection of freely suspended labor on the pure subject as its origin; the *freely suspended* labor here is in fact what Marx later refers to as the abstract social labor. Kant has correctly noticed that "the social labor is a labor on something"[3], an abstraction from the concrete labor. Hegel also gives a deep perception into this historical fact which for the first time emerges from the classical economics.[4] Adorno further analyzes that

---

[1] Adorno, Theodor W. *Negative Dialectics*. Trans. E. B. Ashton. New York: The Continuum Publishing House, 1990. p.177.

[2] Ibid.

[3] Ibid., p.178

[4] Please refer to the 2nd section of Chapter one in Zhang Yibing. *Back to Marx—the Philosophical Discourse in the Context of Economics*. Jiangsu People's Publishing House, 1999.

"the generality of the transcendental subject is that of the functional context of society, of a whole that coalesces from individual spontaneities and qualities, de-limits them in turn by the leveling barter principle, and virtually deletes them as helplessly dependent on the whole. The universal domination of mankind by the exchange value—a domination which a priori keeps the subjects from being subjects and degrades subjectivity itself to a mere objects—makes an untruth of the general principle that claims to establish the subject's predominance. The surplus of the transcendental subject is the deficit of the utterly reduced empirical subject."[1] That is to say, the isolated transcendental subject is actually an internalization of generality of social functionality. Heidegger thus uses the functionalized "being in the world" and the transcendental "being" to negate the reification of the empirical subject. I think that Adorno has really understood Marx's economics correctly and has perceived the philosophical tone behind it. As mentioned above, in *1857-1858 Economics Manuscripts*, Marx has for the first time scientifically explained the social-historical source, particularly the economic base of the conceptual idealism, especially of the transcendental subject. There, Marx shows very clearly that the abstraction becomes the basis of the dominant economic relations. Adorno's view here is substantially profound.

Here Adorno once again aims at Heidegger, thinking that Heidegger's transforming the transcendental subject into a universal essence of being quested by the functional limited "this being" is "the self-preservation of the species." In face of the reality, Heidegger's "language mythology," the apotheosis of the objective spirit would be unhinged. In this mythology "reflection on the material process jutting into the spirit is banned from the outset, as inferior."[2] It points out Heidegger's illusion against the objective reality. With Adorno, "the transcendental generality is no mere narcissist self-exaltation of the *I*, not the hubris of an autonomy of the *I*. Its reality lies in the domination that prevails and perpetuates itself by means of the principle

---

[1] Please refer to the 2nd section of Chapter one in Zhang Yibing. *Back to Marx—the Philosophical Discourse in the Context of Economics*. Jiangsu People's Publishing House, 1999. p.179.

[2] Ibid., p. 177.

of equivalence. The process of abstraction—which philosophy transfigures, and which it ascribes to the knowing subject alone—is taking place in the factual barter society."[1] This transcendental generality is in fact the unity of the individual consciousness, an objective unity of people's relations in social reality. "It is the conceptual reflex of the total, seamless juncture of the productive acts in society."[2] The completeness of the objective abstraction itself results from the evolving of the objectified I; a functional transcendental generality ("being") is a true unconscious portrait of the objectification system. Thus, Heidegger's impulse of opposing objectification is dissolved in the reverse sense. It is really ironical that Heidegger, the one who strongly advocates the historicity of being, emphasizes the least on the social historicity of reality.

I have to admit that Adorno's theoretical horizon here can never be reached by the abstract philosophical rationality.

2. The illusion of the primacy of subject and self-alienation of anthropocentrism

In the philosophy of idealism, the I, as the core of the conceptual subject is usually defined as a solid, lasting and impenetrable entity which mimics the outside world as perceived by a primitive consciousness, the process of which is actually a bi-direcational projection. For in primitive consciousness the nature is also personified (the pantheism of the nature). Moreover, the projection of human's subject also initiates the exaltation of the conceptual subject, which is a hidden illusory anthropocentrism. Feuerbach's famous saying goes like this, the more impotent the human gets, the higher he sours in the sky of delusion, and Adorno, hence says that the subject's real impotence has its echo in its mental omnipotence. This originates in the primacy of subjectivity in all idealisms.

As we see, as for as his philosophical stand is concerned, Adorno make resolute opposition to idealism, to all overt and covert *primacy of subjectivity*.

---

[1] Please refer to the 2nd section of Chapter one in Zhang Yibing. *Back to Marx—the Philosophical Discourse in the Context of Economics*. Jiangsu People's Publishing House, 1999. p. 178.

[2] Ibid., p.179.

He says, "The primacy of subjectivity is a spiritualized continuation of Darwin's struggle for existence. The suppression of nature for human ends is a mere natural relationship, which is why the supremacy of nature-controlling reason and its principle is a delusion. When the subject proclaims itself a Baconian master of all things, and finally their idealistic creator, it takes an epistemological and metaphysical part in this delusion. The practice of its rule makes it a part of what it thinks it is ruling."[1] It should be noted that the above quotation from Adorno has a very profound meaning, which, I believe, deepens the pertinent theme in *Negative Dialectics*.

Firstly, the controlling of nature for human ends is a basis for a Darwinian natural existence. It is a spiritual continuation of Darwinism to take the subject, especially human's idea (category of "essence" and "discipline") as the essence of the world and the laws guiding nature. This is truly the secret of all idealisms. Here clearly identifies Adorno that human's domination of nature is a mark of its existence within *the natural relationship*. Adorno uses the "natural relationship" as a derogatory term inferior to human's real social-historical existence (we will see Adorno's discussion of this issue later). It also accounts for Marx and Engels' previous statement that human being does not truly get rid of his animal nature. However, what makes Adorno essentially different from Marx is that Adorno's arrow aims at the production power, namely human being's conquer over nature and the external world, which Marx had never questioned. This is also one of the key point of post-Marxism that I have penetrated above several times. Adorno identifies that "the nature-controlling reason"—the tool reason is a delusion of idealism, thereby declaring *the illegality of the tool rationalism justifying the nature controlling*. This is a fundamental concept in Adorno on which the later ecologies and post-modernism are based.

Next, once the subject's primitive delusion about controlling as a master is realized by means of technology and scientific knowledge, human, in another sense, actually makes itself a part of what it thinks it is ruling, the

---

[1] Please refer to the 2nd section of Chapter one in Zhang Yibing. *Back to Marx—the Philosophical Discourse in the Context of Economics*. Jiangsu People's Publishing House, 1999. pp. 179-180.

controlling relationship reverting to the subject itself. Adorno illustrates for this that Plato made a great stride toward de-mythologization by identifying the role the ideas play in the process of consciousness, but because under the name of essences it perpetuates the conditions of dominance which man took over from nature and is now practicing, which is no more than a shift from nature as master (human is enslaved by nature) to the ideas as master of the world. Under the delusion of primacy, Plato "reiterates the myth." In the same context, he points out that the very subject Kant calls free and exalted is part of that natural context, because any thing is natural provided it is based on rules of dominance. What is more horrible is that if the control of nature was a condition of demythologization and a step in it, this dominance would have to spread to that other kind, in other words, the *human-controlling by the tool reason* (the scientific management of objectification). We have seen the detailed analysis of this point in the previous article *Studies of Experiences and Sociology*. Here Adorno only gives a vivid metaphor that "this is how animal species like the dinosaur Triceratops or the rhinoceros drag their protective armor with them, an ingrown prison which them seem—anthropo-morphically, at least—to be trying vainly to shed. The imprisonment in their survival mechanism may explain the special ferocity of rhinoceroses as well as the un-acknowledged ant therefore more dreadful ferocity of homo sapiens." [1] When the subject becomes the object, we call it *objectification*; when the subjective dominance turns to self–governing, we call it *alienation*. This is *an enlightening dialectics, a rational dialectics and the subject-inverted dialectics*. Therefore, Adorno says that "it reveals the extent to which in consuming the object it [subject] is beholden to the object. What it does is the spell of that which the subject believes under its own spell. The subject's desperate self-exaltation is its reaction to the experience of its impotence, which prevents self-reflection. Absolute consciousness is unconscious."[2] We have to gasp in admiration of Adorno's perception.

---

[1] Please refer to the 2nd section of Chapter one in Zhang Yibing. *Back to Marx—the Philosophical Discourse in the Context of Economics*. Jiangsu People's Publishing House, 1999. p. 180.

[2] Ibid., p.180.

In Adorno's view, philosophy's stress on the constitutive power of the subjective moment always blocks the road to truth as well. For in fact the constitutive power that the conceptual subject imagines to impose on the object is restricted by the objective elements. Idealism is a pair of hands coving its own eyes. Adorno intends with whole-heartedness to penetrate it.

3. Vacancy of emperorship: precedence and mediation of object

Now the readers should be warned against a hasty and simple conclusion that: Adorno is affirmative for the general philosophy of materialism. One reason for his opposition to the transcendental subject is that society pre-exists the individual consciousness and all his experience, which he has provided an elaborate analysis above. However, the insight into the fact that thinking is mediated by objectivity does not negate or depreciate thinking, for "there is no way to get out of thinking." Adorno asserts that "it is not the purpose of critical thought to place the object on the orphaned royal throne once occupied by the subject. On that throne the object would be nothing but an idol. The purpose of critical thought is to abolish the hierarchy."[1] The ultimate goal of Adorno's dialectics is to abolish all the hierarchies resulted from identity and all the centers of theoretical logics. This point will certainly negate the idea that he easily accepts the materialism with its ontological root in the abstract entity, the object, the objectivity and even social reality. This idea also becomes the logical initiative of the anti-*"ism"* in post-modern thoughts.

After a definite opposition to any ontological principle of primacy, Adorno says, "The critique of identity is a groping for the preponderance of the object."[2] It should be noted that Adorno uses "preponderance," a choice made after careful consideration, because he intends to avoid using those with ontological sense. Any kind of identitarian concept (of course no exception to the object-first materialism) is subjective. Opposing to identity

---

[1] Please refer to the 2nd section of Chapter one in Zhang Yibing. *Back to Marx—the Philosophical Discourse in the Context of Economics.* Jiangsu People's Publishing House, 1999. p. 181.

[2] Ibid., p. 183.

is opposing to subjectivity, and thus it is important to admit objectivity or taking an objective perspective. Taking the subject-object relations as an example, "an object can be perceived only by a subject but always remains something other than the subject, whereas a subject by its very nature is from the outset an object as well. Not even as an idea can we conceive a subject that is not an object, but we can conceive an object that is not a subject."[1] What he identifies is a fact. He even smartly says, one can write a primeval history of the subject, but one cannot write a primeval history of the object. Here, Adorno once again challenges Heidegger. He says, "the I is an entity," a subject as an object among objects, because "without this 'my' there would be no 'I think,'" and consciousness is a function of the living subject, and no exorcism will expel this from the concept's meaning. The he "being" could for a period of time be "being in the world," could think must have a precondition of the objective existence of the "I." This fact will not change even if Heidegger has elevated the function of "-ing" to a position of dominance, because "the copula 'is' always conveys some objectivity already."[2] For Husserl, without any relation to an empirical consciousness, to the living *I*, there would be no transcendental, purely mental consciousness. Analogous reflections on the object's genesis would be meaningless.

However, when coming to this point, Adorno immediately defines that his grant to the preponderance of the object "does not mean that objectivity is something immediate, that we might forget our critique of naïve realism."[3] This clearly shows his objection to the natural materialism. The grant to precedence to the object means to make progressive qualitative distinctions between thinks which in themselves are indirect from the ideal object of natural materialism. It is import to mark this point. Also in this context, Adorno makes a critique of Kant's anti-dialectics nature when he turns the object into the thing-in-itself after seeing the meditation of the object. Particularly, Kant's construction of the transcendental subjectivity is a

---

[1] Please refer to the 2nd section of Chapter one in Zhang Yibing. *Back to Marx—the Philosophical Discourse in the Context of Economics*. Jiangsu People's Publishing House, 1999. p. 183.

[2] Ibid., p. 184.

[3] Ibid., p. 187.

magnificently paradoxically fallible effort to master the object in its opposite pole. It is a big failure to make a high exaltation of "setting laws for nature." Adorno holds that "the object takes precedence even though indirect itself."[1] The view has been executed by his student Schmitt in a slightly erroneous way.

The double mediation of nature and society: Schmidt above all defines that nature is not something to be created although it is related to the purpose of human action. However, the natural substance for Marx is something that has been created, which is certainly not accurate. The substance itself can not be created—human can only alter the form of its existence. Schmidt wants to emphasize the double mediation between nature and human practice: human's experience must be mediated by nature and natural substance must be mediated through social history. I believe that Schmidt's opening statement is not scientific. Nature is projected through the medium of human practice, and consequently entering into the social history, which is a elevation of the substance in existence, whereas the existence of society is on the premise of the existence of other substances. These two medications are not at all equivalent. When Schmidt says, the possible realization of the substance "depends on the condition of the material and scientific conditions of the productive power" and "the concept of substance is gradually modified in the development of natural science, the history of which is closely related to the history of social practice."[2] It is true if we say it is a social historical mediation of nature that human confronts. However, in a similar sense, to say that all human's purposes can only be realized through the medium of nature has a logical problem, because natural substance and movement have always relied on the social existence. Biological nature is a condition, but it is not necessary for human being to exist through the medium of biological nature. The logical error is

---

[1] Please refer to the 2nd section of Chapter one in Zhang Yibing. *Back to Marx—the Philosophical Discourse in the Context of Economics*. Jiangsu People's Publishing House, 1999. p.186.

[2] Schmidt, Alfred. *Concept of Nature in Marx*. Commercial Press, 1988, p.59.

resulted from the reflectivity of the term mediation which Lukacs had inherited from Hegel. In addition, it is not reasonable for Schmitt to take the base of natural substance as a premise of this discussion. We don't deny his correctness in opposing the idealism, which is necessary in a general logical sense, but, he is not aware that to start from the natural substance will reduce the problem to the level of the materialism philosophy.[1]

This is the subject-object dialectics, also *a dialectics of immediacy and indirectness* between the two. Marx and Engels have elucidated this kind of dialectics in *The German Ideology*.

IV. Reification, Alienation and the Resistance

Adorno sees the dialectic relationship between the immediacy and indirectness of the object, confronting and challenging the contemporary empiricism in a face-to-face manner. After achieving significant improvement in theory, he then turns to another important theoretical issue for further study, which is the critical logic of reification and alienation (which is always the theoretical logic's focus in the Western Marxism since the early-young Lukács). Adorno's analysis here is very complex and nuanced. He begins with questioning the genesis of empirical idealism in the history of epistemology, and then finds that the fountain of anti-reification struggle is none other than the ideal calling of idealism, which constitutes the important premise of thinking for social critical theories since Marx. Obviously, Adorno is against the reification of reality in capitalism, because it is the realistic foundation of identical logic rejected devoutly by the negative dialectics. However, surprisingly, he objects to the alienation logic of individualism re-approved by the traditional Western Marxism. I think, in this regard, he takes the same side with Marx. Admittedly, Adorno rejected the anthropocentricism

---

[1] Refer to my article: "Double Mediations of Nature and Society" in *Study and Exploration*. Vol.3, 2003.

Marx never frowns upon.

1. Resolving of "object" and new illusion about experiential immediacy

As we know, the critique of epistemological immediacy has become a theoretical tradition in the Western Marxist philosophy since the early Lukács' *History and Class Consciousness*. However, the existing discussions are not in-depth. I find that Adorno's analysis of the relationship between epistemological immediacy and indirectness is an important breakthrough of theory in this regard.

The study of the traditional idealist epistemology, when rejecting the naïve realism, puts immediacy on the side of the subject, while the object is no longer the target of the immediacy, but taken as "material or property of the subject." Therefore, it is not a surprise that the conclusion is "existence is being sensed," a white joke. For the empiricist, experience is a wall, as Lenin says; men cannot penetrate the sensible experience to face the object, so Berkeley and Hume reject realism according to the immediacy of reducing the objective target and matter to the material of sensation. Adorno says, "The entire empiricist critique of naïve realism, culminating in Hume's abolition of the thing, was tied to the factitious character of immediacy and skeptical of the subject *qua* creator."[1]

In a certain sense, empiricism asks us to start with the individual subject's immediacy, so as to reject mistaking the integrated apperception occurring as the material of sensual perception for the exterior thing. It is not unreasonable. Hence, empiricist "immediacy requires to stop idolatry of derivation," and thereby to smash the object's illusion in naïve realism. Developed out of it, Kant's radical action is to expand the immediacy as empirical material into a phenomenal world, while the ontology of the object is suspended as that-worldly thing-in-itself. As such, a tragedy of dividing the world is staged. Adorno points out that the problem of empiricism is that they

---

[1] Adorno, Theodor W. *Negative Dialectics*. Trans. E. B. Ashton. New York: The Continuum Publishing House, 1990. p. 187.

are unaware of that the empirical immediacy deemed as subject is "something abstracted from the object," and the immediacy of sensual experience cannot complete avoid objective contact. Otherwise, the present empirical result of immediacy, such as touch, smell, and taste, couldn't occur. In fact, sensual material "is merely the borderline value which the subject, having confiscated the concrete object, cannot fully master in its own domain."[1] Therefore, no matter how empiricism resolves the thing, the confirmation of the immediacy of experience itself cannot deny the priority of the object.

Of course, it then involves another side of the issue. Adorno says in a Heideggerian language that, "What we may call the thing itself is not positively and immediately at hand."[2] *Vorhandenheit* is used by Heidegger to make negative description of the subject positioned in an external being (an ideal and ready-made object), whereas he asserts that *Dasein* specifically constructs in this world "karma-organic world" from the starting point of "readiness-to-hand," which indeed is a thinking variant of practical activity mentioned by Marx. Yet, clarifying this point is not for our moving to another simple polarity, "abandoning any requirements for immediate understanding."[3] We cannot turn the idealistic intuitive "thing" in naïve realism directly into the component of thought so as to sustain the identity of ideal subject. In the following discussion, Adorno points out that in Husserl and Heidegger, among other people, "The total liquefaction of everything thing-like regressed to the subjectivism of the pure act. It hypostatized the indirect as direct. Pure immediacy and fetishism are equally untrue."[4] Such is a bigger illusion of idealism.

Adorno points out that, where we get rid of the idealist apriori-ism, there is a way to exorcise the pervert witchcraft. In Kant's solution to Hume's question, the intuitive object is restored to some fragmented sensual materials.

---

[1] Adorno, Theodor W. *Negative Dialectics*. Trans. E. B. Ashton. New York: The Continuum Publishing House, 1990. p. 187.

[2] Ibid., p. 189.

[3] Ibid., p. 189.

[4] Ibid., p. 374.

Then, within the framework of a priori ideal form (from time-space, quality, to all existential rules), people acquire various specific "intuitive things" from the immediate phenomenal world. In fact, Kant's rules which make the object into the specific are absolutely imposed on the object, and these rules are but applicable where people unshakably believe in the primacy of subjectivity. "Kant had already taught that consciousness performs [them] identifications, as it were, unconsciously and automatically. That the activity of the mind, and even more the activity which Kant ascribe to the problem of constitution, is something other than the automatism he equates it with—this, specifically, makes out the mental experience which the idealists discovered, albeit only in order to castrate it on the spot."[1] So, from the naïve realism's fantasy of intuitive entity to Kantian priori construct of the subject, both reflect *prima philosophia* which is obsessed with a sort of ultimate identity. Therefore, "[The] the object's residue as that which remains given after subjective appendages have been subtracted is a delusion of *prima philosophia*." [2] Yet, it never occurs to Kant that the subjective framework presumed by him as priori and changeless is in fact historical; it is priori in the sense of preceding some individual subject's certain universal ideas, which can never be the "cognitive ultimate(s)." With the development of history, "as its experience progresses, cognition can break through them."[3] Adorno is absolutely correct. In contrast with the extremely complex cognitive structure formed in present natural sciences and social life, the priori ideal structures mentioned by Kant then are very primordial prescriptions of thought. A simple example is that, "the evolution of physics since Einstein has burst the visual prison as well as that of the subjective apriority of space, time, and causality."[4]

2. Rejecting objectivity and opposing reification

Acknowledging the criticism of naïve realism is reasonable, we find

---

[1] Adorno, Theodor W. *Negative Dialectics*. Trans. E. B. Ashton. New York: The Continuum Publishing House, 1990. pp.188-189

[2] Ibid., p. 187.

[3] Ibid., p. 187.

[4] Ibid., p. 188.

that rectifying the mistake of idealist empiricism is a complicated theoretical project. Nonetheless, Adorno, with his unique depth of history, suggests further what the social origin of such an idealist wrath is. This theoretical identification is shocking: *the foundation of idealist rejection of objectivity is a deformed variant of the objection to the status of reification in reality.* I think it is an important finding.

According to Adorno, the majority of conceited philosophies, as it were, wouldn't simply acknowledge the priority of the object; hence, *the rejection of any visual object* has become a label of depth in philosophical thinking. He says, since Fichte, the dislike of it has been institutionalized. As we have seen above, Adorno disproves the empirical idealism since Hume. Yet, he continues to say, "Such philosophical subjectivism is the ideological accompaniment of the emancipation of the bourgeois I. It furnishes reasons for that emancipation."[1] What does it mean? Adorno implies that Fichte's disparaging attitude of subjective idealism toward the object originates from a *critique of the historical reification in social reality.* Of course, such a rejection is deformed. "Its tenacious vigor is drawn from a misdirected opposition to the status quo, from opposition to its thing-ness. In relativating or liquefying the thing-ness, philosophy believes to be above the supremacy of goods, and above the form of subjective reflection on that supremacy, the reified consciousness."[2] His theoretical discovery here is very incisive, which is even overlooked by Marx and Engels. I further observe that in human history of cultures and thoughts, all idealisms are a deformed rejection of subjectivity and reification in our realistic history. It then posits a way more complex question in theory.

Adorno's retrospection of such a theoretical phenomenon is in the sense of social historicity. He points out that modern idealism is a penetration for the reification in modern society. Of course, it is also a sort of logic reactionary against the fetishistic positivism. So, Adorno calls Fichte's

---

[1] Adorno, Theodor W. *Negative Dialectics.* Trans. E. B. Ashton. New York: The Continuum Publishing House, 1990. p. 189.

[2] Ibid.

egotistic and hegemonic impulse "an impulse against ideology." The remaining question then is, has Fichte been aware of it? I have observed that, Hegel expresses a sublime awareness of the modern capitalist system of reification as described in the classical economics in England; on this base, he rejects the alienated secondary nature by virtue of a god-centered, objective, and absolute essence. Accurately speaking, Adorno identifies a conscious rejection of the reified reality, which is supposed to be the neo-humanist impulse in philosophy after Kierkegaard. However, "this" I for Kierkegaard differs essentially from Fichte's big I.

Adorno analyzes, "[d]espite the preponderance of the object, the thingness of the world is also phenomenal. It tempts the subjects to ascribe their own social circumstances of production to the noumena (thing-in-itself)."[1] His argument is quite illuminating. His meaning is that, the preponderance of the object is right, but the world we face today (mostly "our world" in social and historical context) presents an objectivity which inverts the reification of social relations. Adorno explicitly tells us that the key to understanding this statement is Marx's account of the critique of fetishism in *The Capital*. Furthermore, Marx's opinion is a part of "the legacy of classical German philosophies," and even the motivation of the system of classical German philosophies is extant in this section. I find that it is one of the most brilliant discussions in this section. *I believe, the universal acknowledgement of the supremacy of the object is relative to the subject's subjective world, while the objectification of social historical existence is a deeper critique of cognition in historical **phenomenology**.*[2] *Adorno has reached such a point of depth,*

---

[1] Adorno, Theodor W. *Negative Dialectics*. Trans. E. B. Ashton. New York: The Continuum Publishing House, 1990. p. 189.

[2] I put forward this term to break through the old framework of Marxist illustration and reach a scientific and critical understanding of Marxism. In the economic life of capitalism, the phenomena and essence are contradictory: the social relations are subverted to the material relations: the economy expresses itself via an inverted representation; the social structure demonstrates itself with a logic in antithesis to the real historical development. The capitalist political-economy, including its social materialism, is premised on the pseudo-phenomena. These multiple complex inversions require a non-intuitional, non-ready-made critical phenomenology to remove the ideology for the authenticity of the economic reality. This is the basic content of the Marxist historical phenomenology.

and yet has no intention of elaborating on it.[1] What a great pity!

Adorno says, "The fetish character of goods is not laid to a subjectively errant consciousness, but objectively deduced from the social a priori, the exchange process."[2] The commodity fetishism is not derived from the mind, but a result of realistic social existence, particularly constructed out of such a special *social a priori* in the exchange relation of capital market economy in reality. The significance of pointing to social a priori cannot be exaggerated. Actually, it for the first times reveals the real foundation of the ideal a priori, which is indeed the *a priori of social relations*. Moreover, being the social a priori, "reification itself is the reflexive form of false objectivity."[3] It highlights that, under certain specific conditions of socio-historical development, particularly in the case of capitalism, the inversely reified goods, currency (money), and capitalistic relation's *pseudo-apriority* are homogeneous with ideology. Adorno says, "Marx already expresses the difference between the object's preponderance as a product of criticism and its extant caricature, its distortion by the commodity character." For him, "[b]arter as a process has real objectivity and is objectively untrue at the same time, transgressing against its own principle, the principle of equality. This is why, by necessity, it will create a false consciousness: the idols of the market."[4] Adorno's analysis here cannot be recognized from the lens of traditional philosophies; its interpretation has to be set on the rich canvas of Marxist political economics.

Adorno points out that, "[i]t is only in a sardonic sense that the barter society's natural growth is a law of nature, that the predominance of economics is no invariant."[5] Obviously, it is a step further than the early

---

[1] Zhang Yibing. *Back to Marx—The Philosophical Discourse in the Context of Economics*. Jiangsu Renmin Publishing House, 1999. Please refer to the part discussing Hegel's relations to classical economics in Chapter 1, and the part analyzing the Marx's economic manuscripts in Chapter 8.

[2] Adorno, Theodor W. *Negative Dialectics*. Trans. E. B. Ashton. New York: The Continuum Publishing House, 1990. p. 190.

[3] Ibid.

[4] Ibid.

[5] Ibid.

Lukács's critique of the natural laws in society.

Adorno's discussion is not only farther but deeper. What he meant to say is that it is right to reject the reification in reality, the thing-ness, fetish alienation, and the ideal pseudo-objectivity, but it is an unpardonable error to ideally reject objectivity. I agree with Adorno here, but the problem is whether or not these idealist masters set their thoughts before such a realistic backdrop? It is a question worth further study.

3. Alienation logic: fantasy of philosophical imperialism

Adorno finds that in face of such reified reality, apart from the ideal resistance of thinking in idealist apriorism which has been criticized earlier on, there is a more direct social critical theory worth our attention, that is, the humanist *alienation* logic which objects to realistic reification. Herein, Adorno makes some good theoretical analysis. His target is the critique of philosophical humanist ethics which makes "ought to" (essence of the real) opposed to "is" (reified or alienated reality). Nietzsche, Scheler and Heidegger's negative thinking is largely in this direction, and particularly the early (young) Lukács, Lefebvre, the late Sartre, and other Western Marxist philosophers.

In face of the reification of capitalist market economy, some thinkers directly voice the slogan of anti-reification. Yet, until now, such resistance is no more than a humanist critique starting from abstract *suspending of values* in theory. "The thinker may easily comfort himself by imagining that in the dissolution of reification, of the commodity character, he possesses the philosophers' stone." And "centering theory around reification, a form of consciousness, makes the critical theory idealistically acceptable to the reigning consciousness and to the collective unconscious."[1] It is a logic cracker. Adorno specifically notes that, it is because of what was raised in Marx's early writings—in contradistinction to *Das Kapital*—to their present popularity, notably with theologians. Of course, he refers to the early Marx's

---

[1] Adorno, Theodor W. *Negative Dialectics*. Trans. E. B. Ashton. New York: The Continuum Publishing House, 1990. p. 190.

1844 Manuscripts of Economics and Philosophy, worshipped as the Holy Bible by the humanist Western Marxists. Adorno's stance is clear.

Adorno mentions that the former Eastern U.S.S.R's ideological institutions had reasonable anger toward the reification theory in the early Lukács's *History and Class Consciousness*, because they have in another sense smelt the idealism in it. Obviously, Adorno disagrees with the early Lukács on his humanist theory of reification, and he opposes all alienation theories. He disagrees with the early Lukács because he has turned Marx's historical dialectics into a humanist ethical campaign centering on the critique of reification (alienation). Adorno's assertion that we can't restore dialectics of reification is: to confront the Western Marxism's humanist trends. If it is still an implicit humanist logic for the early Lukács, when Marx's 1844 Manuscripts of Economics and Philosophy was published in 1932, an explicit humanist Marxism was rapidly incubated among the Western Marxist trends, and the early Marx's labor alienation theory becoming the kernel to the logic construction of their *neo-individualism*, which then gave birth to various concepts of alienation (that is, the alienation theories of the early Fromm, Lefebvre and others). According to Adorno, they do critique the capitalism's economic and cultural reality, but in a deeper sense, "[t]he cause of human suffering, meanwhile, will be glossed over rather than denounced in the lament about reification."[1] Why? Adorno analyzes that the "disasters" brought about by the capitalist development of social economy are indeed caused by some objective conditions and economic relations which condemn mankind to impotence and apathy, and the conditions are yet produced by human action. Therefore, the key to the problem is not to evince these relations and to criticize these conceptual ethics. Compared with the whole of capitalist economic relation, "reification is an epi-pheneomenon," and even the alienation is no more than the subjective state of consciousness about the reified reality. Reification and alienation are not the causes, but the results, which constitutes the essential yardstick that distinguishes Marx

---

[1] Adorno, Theodor W. *Negative Dialectics*. Trans. E. B. Ashton. New York: The Continuum Publishing House, 1990. p. 190.

from humanistic individualism. At this point, Adorno's understanding is remarkably accurate.

First of all, the first evidence is the *genus man* in classical individualism. According to Adorno, the universality (as mankind's genus essence) is obtained secretly from present ruling form. It strikes the chord of Stirner, who criticizes Feuerbach by revealing that the universal (essential) genus man is indeed a *man-god* after the demise of God. But, at that time, he couldn't decipher the realistic genesis of genus man. As a genus man, its charisma is borrowed from the irresistibility of the universal. From the discussion domain above, we have inferred that the "universal" is actually the social a priori constructed by the capitalist reified reality, and different from the absolute in the traditional mythology, this time the genus essence is internalized from the exchange relation formed spontaneously in the market. Therefore, the principle of bourgeois genus man is that the unshakable unity which makes out its selfhood, defiantly repeats dominion in the subject. Adorno says, "[the person] is ancient spell of the universal, entrenched in the particular." Such an assertion resembles the tone of Foucault. But Foucault says the person is a modern product; Adorno believes that the person is the new trick of the ancient witchcraft. Anyhow, "[t]he person is the historically tied knot that should be freely loosened and not perpetuated."[1]

Next, the second evidence is Heideggerian neo-personalism. Here, the person becomes a tautology for those left with nothing but the concept-less "being there" of their existence. As to this point, we have learned a lot from the previous chapter. Heidegger's "being there" is no more than human consciousness. Men are human only where they do not act, let alone posit themselves, as persons. Adorno identifies that the Heideggerian limited individual "subject is a lie, because for the sake of its own absolute rule it will deny its own objective definitions." It is also a baleful "human ideology."[2] In such an ideological illusion, a non-existent human "substantiality" fabricates

---

[1] Adorno, Theodor W. *Negative Dialectics*. Trans. E. B. Ashton. New York: The Continuum Publishing House, 1990. p. 276.

[2] Ibid., p. 277.

a sort of values suspense, which is what men *should* become (real being), as opposed to the "being" (the existent) in reality. This is the logic of "self-alienation," which has become "the stock in trade" of apologists, "who will suggest in paternal tones that man has apostatized, that he has lapsed from a being-in-itself which he had always been. Whereas, in fact, he never was that being-in-itself, and what he can expect from recourses to his *apxai* is therefore nothing but submission to authority, the very thing that is alien to him." Adorno talks with a serious overtone of an exegete that in Marx's *Das Kapital* the concept of self-alienation plays no part in it any more. It is not only due to the economic themes of this study; it makes philosophical sense.[1] In this regard, Adorno is obviously different from the early Lukács and other Western-Marxist humanists. We have already discussed it in the preface.

The abstract alienation theory is essentially a romanticist fantasy, particularly when the basis of such a personalism surge is the logic of "*back to the past*"; the typical concepts are Schiller's fragmentation of personality and Heidegger's interpretation of Hölderlin's journey of "going home." Adorno holds, "the beautification of the past serves an additional denial of the later time, a denial experienced as a dead-end; only when it was lost could the past be appealing." Indeed, it is a critique of Nietzsche and Heidegger, who pine for a Grecian classicalism. Actually, the prehistoric society prior to the industrial civilization is not a paradise as idealized by the romanticists; at that time, "humanity was still dominated by the impersonal things," because men were, as Engels put it, "the slave of nature," and human consciousness, overall, is at the stage of reifie-tional mimesis. This is the spiritual nature of the entire period of agricultural civilization. Therefore, before the natural science was separated from other sciences, humanity "went hand in hand with reified forms of consciousness, while indifferent to things, appraising them as mere means and reducing them to the subject, helped to tear down humanity." His arguments in this paragraph is somewhat difficult

---

[1] Adorno, Theodor W. *Negative Dialectics*. Trans. E. B. Ashton. New York: The Continuum Publishing House, 1990. p. 278.

to understand. What Adorno intends to say is that in the prehistoric society human consciousness is obviously reified, but the instrumental existence of finite things in the natural economics was unconsciously, but directly, taken as subjective consciousness, subject projecting universalized to the object; the split is the weak human subject's split, as well as reification in the most immediate sense. But with the development of capitalism, particularly when the world has become the target of industry, men started constructing a brand-new surrounding world, really from the standpoint of production's "readiness-to-hand," whereas the *instrumental system created by men* began to turn against the subject, and at the same time, there comes a new realm of reification, in which "there is the an intermingling of both the object's un-identical side and the submission of men to prevailing condition of production."[1] "This is the reification in the scientific sense of Marx." Herein, "the object's un-identical side" refers to the heterogeneity between the new production force created by mean and human subject's will; men cannot control "the causal whole" they themselves create, and when men cannot see in perspective the prevailing capitalistic production relations, they are bound to kneel down in front of the historically existing "functional relations" (such as commodity, money and capital) which they inversely reify. His historical analysis is in line with Marxism here.

Adorno accurately says, Marx's treatment of reification and alienation however leads to two distinct theoretical attitudes in his early and late periods. "The mature Marx, in his quite few remarks on the character of a liberated society, had changed his position on the cause of reification, the division of labor. He now began to distinguish the state of freedom from original immediacy. In the moment of planning—the result of which, he hoped, would be production for use values for the living rather than for profit, and thus, in a sense, a restitution of immediacy—in that planning he preserved the alien thing; in his design for a realization of what philosophy

---

[1] Adorno, Theodor W. *Negative Dialectics*. Trans. E. B. Ashton. New York: The Continuum Publishing House, 1990. p. 192.

had only thought, at first, he preserved its mediation."[1] This philosophical treatise is correct in principle, but in need of specific explanations. Derived from Adorno's remarks, we observe he has identified an *immature* Marx, who is supposed to be the early Marx who wrote *1844 Manuscripts of Economics and Philosophy*; at that time, the early Marx had identified men's freedom with an un-alienated natural status (of immediacy), whereas the labor alienation incurred by the division of labor is the crucial reason for humanity's degeneration. Hence, to sublate (*aufheben*) alienation and thus to restitute human immediacy had become the targets of liberation. It is ethical critique when personalism suspends values. But "the mature Marx" (Adorno accurately identifies such a Marx in the fourth chapter of *Das Kapital*, Vol. 1) no longer deems the primordial immediate existence of humanity as freedom itself; he objectively acknowledges the progress in the social history, particularly the enormous development of production brought about by the capitalist production means—the machines; he only criticizes that in capitalism there is an essential inversion of aim (that is, profit), and thereby proposes a "planned-economy" scheme that can solve the disorder of social operations. Herein, men's life itself becomes the re-inverted objective, which is "a restitution of immediacy," but he also gives full credit to the complex social relations of mediation as a progressive reality in history. At the same time, Adorno emphasizes that "planning" is by no means a compulsory identity.

V. Negative Dialectics and Materialism

The discussion of "materialism," which usually appears in the initial parts in general philosophy, is picked up by Adorno as late as the second section of *Negative Dialectics* where it nearly comes to an end. He declares finally that he is in favor of materialism. However, we have confirmed that the materialism with Adorno is not an ontology, not an "-ism" of the First

---

[1] Adorno, Theodor W. *Negative Dialectics*. Trans. E. B. Ashton. New York: The Continuum Publishing House, 1990. p. 192.

Philosophy, so we strategically call it the materialistic theory. It is discovered that Adorno wants to draw a borderline for his correlations with and difference from Marx by elaborately defining the "materialism." It seems to be Adorno's intentional thoughtful theoretical planning.

1. Critical theory and materialism

In concluding his theoretical logic, Adorno admits that negative dialectics is materialistic. "It is by passing to the object's preponderance that dialectics is rendered materialistic."[1] This is a theoretical confession. Negative Dialectics theoretically identifies with materialism not in the sense of the originary ontology but in the sense of the object's preponderance. However, this statement involves many particular boundaries.

Firstly, Adorno makes an analysis of *the object's subjectivity*, a debate originated from Husserl's phenomenology. By Husserl, "once the object becomes an object of cognition, its physical side is spiritualized from the outset by translation into epistemology."[2] What does this mean? It means that compared with the being-in-itself advocated by the objects-deification of the naïve realism, phenomenology circumscribes a subjective cognitive zone centered on an intentional subject, and only the object that enters this zone can be identified as a subjective object. It "is called 'object' only from the viewpoint of a subjectively aimed analysis in which the subject's primacy seems beyond question."[3] It is a subjective exaggeration of Hume and Kant's empiricism to draw a conclusion with idealism based on the idea that the subject and the object are related in epistemology and consequently the objects rely on the subject. Here, the identification "presented" by Kant's nature is non-historically ontologized. Internally, the idea is still in consistent with the old, unavoidable logic of identity. But why can't people break this false, coercive identity of the subject?

---

[1] Adorno, Theodor W. *Negative Dialectics*. Trans. E. B. Ashton. New York: The Continuum Publishing House, 1990. p. 192.

[2] Ibid., pp. 192-193.

[3] Ibid., p. 193.

Also in discussion of the subject-object relations, a historical, non-identical perspective will expose the subjective cognitive zone "as inseparably fused with material things." Adorno firstly takes "sensation" as an example to explain the materialistic basis of epistemology. Generally speaking, sensation is the crucial part of the entire body of epistemology, and many idealistic philosophers, for example, Hume, believes that to the subjectively immanent reconstruction of the world of things, sensation is the basis of its hierarchy. However, the simple fact is that there is no sensation without a somatic moment. This statement plainly calls the spade: a spade. "Every sensation (Empfindung) is a physical feeling (german, köerpergefüehl) also. The feeling does not even 'accompany' it, for that would presuppose a tangibility of the sensation's *chorismos*."[1] In fact, Berkeley, Kant and Hegel have more or less related to the *composition* of the fundamental sensation ("compound," "apperception" and construction of consciousness), but without exception, all of them went towards idealism of different kinds. But, why don't we consider those material elements that also participate in the construction? Adorno thinks the somatic moment as the not purely cognitive part of cognition is irreducible. It cannot be reduced to subjectivity and thus the radical empiricism is bound to collapse. Obviously, Adorno demands a non-identical constellational mastery of the physical object (the somatic) in the subjective understanding of sensation.

It can be certain that Adorno is not without awareness of idealistic critique of the vulgar materialism and naïve realism, but he figuratively says that idealism's critique is knocking down "the straw men" in theory. Indeed, materialism is a "straw man," not worthy of a theoretical and logical refutation. Even so, while it is firmly opposed to the idealism, it in no way intends to return to the crude materialism of the same identitarian nature. Adorno advocates a reconstruction of a new, more profound philosophical thought, that is, the Marxist historical materialism. *If I am not mistaken, this is the first time in this book that Adorno has made a clear identification*

---

[1] Adorno, Theodor W. *Negative Dialectics*. Trans. E. B. Ashton. New York: The Continuum Publishing House, 1990. p. 193

of his own relations with Marx. He directly points out, "It was Marx who drew the line between historic materialism and the popular-metaphysical version."[1] This is a very important line. Adorno says, "Materialism is not the dogma indicated by clever opponents, but a dissolution of things understood as dogmatic." That historical materialism is a dogma but a guide to action has been also affirmed by both Engels and Lenin, but Adorno wants to emphasize that Marx's materialism is not intended to preserve the ready-made existents affirmatively, but rather to break the idea of transforming things into solidified objects advocated by the traditional philosophy of materialism. In his view, the critical theory of the Frankfurt school, following Horkheimer, has never taken materialism as a simple theoretical premise, such as an "amateurish explications" of the world as "the thing outside the consciousness" but rather make it a "theoretically self-consciousness," a true *negative* criticism. This is the truly dialectical and historical materialistic view which constitutes the essence of Marx's theory.

Consequently, Adorno says that historical materialism cannot be a "sociology of knowledge" as advocated by Horkheimer. That is to say, the Marxist historical materialism will not directly and affirmatively confirm all kinds of social function; otherwise, the historical materialism will turn defective, reducing to a sort of positivism. He says bitterly that this "applied philosophy," which is pragmatic in nature, is much like the "beggarly broth" obtained from other theories such as economics and politics. I think, Adorno also makes a critique of the expository framework of the traditional philosophy which distorts historical materialism into a technical description of the operation of society, particularly the sociological-historical materialism in the academic spheres of the former Soviet Union. This sociology of knowledge is still an *ideological* illusion.[2] It is the theoretical task of negative dialectics to expose the falsity of this ideology. In his view, the sociology

---

[1] Adorno, Theodor W. *Negative Dialectics*. Trans. E. B. Ashton. New York: The Continuum Publishing House, 1990. p. 195.

[2] It is interesting that Horkheimer's identification of "a sociology of knowledge" is based on his defining of "ideology" and "utopia." Refer to Horkheimer. *Ideology and Utopia*. The Commercial Press, 2000.

of knowledge denies not only the objective structure of society but the idea of the objective truth and its cognition. Therefore, "to this sociology— as to the type of positivist economics to which its founder Pareto belonged— society is nothing but the average value of individual reactive modes."[1] Submerged in today's positive science, it is worthwhile for us to contemplate on this identification.

2. The concept of spirit understood by idealism

Different from Vulgar materialism's attack against idealism, Adorno starts his philosophical attack from the historical materialism. If there is an objective factor in feeling, does it also exist in those spiritual ideas taken by various idealisms as the ontological basis of philosophy? Is it really a primary, self-contained and originary thing? We can see that Adorno's answer to this question opens a very special perspective, that is, a historical analysis of the social reality which is the basis of spiritual concepts' formation.

Adorno believes that the secret of the objectification of the mind lies in the mystification of the "I." Instead of starting with the general philosophy of logic, a common method employed by the traditional philosophical discussion, he explores the relationship between the experience and reason, between the concept and the self-consciousness, pointing to the social-historical basis on which the mind is constructed. Adorno disproves of the old materialistic view which explains the essence of the mind as a reflection of the external world. He believes, "It is looked up in the real living process, in the legalities of the survival of the species, of providing it with nutriments."[2] The I, as the spiritual subject, is actually a enhanced *social-species relationships* among us. He says that this idea was firstly identified by Hegel in his *Phenomenology of Mind*. "We know that Hegel, in his famous chapter on master and the servant, develops the genesis of self-consciousness from the labor relation, and that he does this by adjusting the I to its self-

---

[1] Adorno, Theodor W. *Negative Dialectics*. Trans. E. B. Ashton. New York: The Continuum Publishing House, 1990. p. 198.

[2] Ibid.

determined purpose as well as to heterogeneous matter."[1] In his view, this might be the most import perspective into the concept of the mind. Here it means that concept is neither a reflection of the external objects (including substance and laws) according to the traditional materialism, nor a subjective intention or self-recognition. The essence of the concept originates from the social relation: *the self-consciousness of the concept is based on the object of the labor and the objective relations*. This is very profound. Adorno believes that Hegel makes use of this to spiritualize the *species relationships* of the individual involved in social labor and to transform the purpose of the subject that evolves from the object of the labor into absorption of the entity by a totality. As a result, the mind is objectified and "hypostatized" as a "totality." In this sense, it is not entirely unreasonable for Feuerbach to criticize Hegel's idea as an elaborate theodicy, because God is generated from an alienation of species essence of man, by Hegel, God is simply replaced by idea. Adorno says, "The idealist concept of the spirit exploits the passage to social labor: it is easy to ignore the general activity that absorbs the individuals."[2] This is the real root of the modern objective idealism. I thought, Adorno's analysis is brilliantly penetrating. He gets away from the naïve method of simply turning the idealism upside-down, which is based on the idea that Hegel's idealism can be transformed into materialism, the idealistic dialectics into materialistic dialectics, as long as the "absolute idea" is replaced by "material." This is a mixture from before (past). It is overlooked that the abstract "entity" in idealism is in fact still an unconscious solidification of social labor or in Heidegger's sense, a metaphysical-ized "Being."

Of course, Adorno also disproves of the supremacy of the individual advocated by the new humanism after Kierkegaard, which was created by simply turning the species philosophy upside down, because in reality Marx's economics has revealed the social-species relationships of the materialized man, that is, "capitalism realizes the law of value over the heads of men."

---

[1] Adorno, Theodor W. *Negative Dialectics*. Trans. E. B. Ashton. New York: The Continuum Publishing House, 1990. p.198.

[2] Ibid., 199.

He obviously can not be sure of the simplification and forcing negation of species philosophy after Stirner; he advocates a dialectical constellational relationships between the species and the individual, the particular and the universal. Adorno points out, "The dialectical transmission of the universal and the particular does not permit a theory that opts for the particular to overzealously treat the universal's pernicious supremacy in the status quo or the idea of conditions which in giving individuals their due would rid the universal of its wretched particularity."[1] "A theory that opts for the particular" mentioned by Adorno here is the individual-oriented new humanism after Stirner, particularly after Kierkegaard, which also includes the humanistic concepts embedded in traditional Marxism.

Adorno says, idealism, in a deeper sense, defines the mind as an "activity"; "the mind as an activity is a sort of becoming."[2] In Fichte, Hegel, and later Bergson, Husserl and Heidegger, there is a hierarchy of existence. The object is ready-made, whereas the mind, as an activity of becoming is more creative, and thus the simple concept of mental activity makes it intra-temporal and historic, generating history and spiritual construction. Compared to the old intuitive materialism, this is deeper in thinking. However, we can only decipher the secret from the above-mentioned Adorno's historical materialism, that is, it is not the mental activity, but rather man's social activity that generates history. Adorno wins the upper-hand in this interpretation, for he grasps the problem that the idealists have to answer when they identify the mind as an activity, that is, *what* is to be active? In fact, "no activity is without a substrate," The becoming nature of the mind activity must have precondition. It is not a becoming nature of an object, but rather the becoming nature of social subject. In this context, Adorno is in consistent with Marx's notion that the mind is "non-historic."

Adorno says, the idealists neglect the fact that "it is the mind's definition as an activity which immanently compels philosophy to pass from the mind

---

[1] Adorno, Theodor W. *Negative Dialectics*. Trans. E. B. Ashton. New York: The Continuum Publishing House, 1990. pp.199-200.
[2] Ibid., p. 201.

to its otherness."[1] As mentioned in the above discussion, the "other" actually originates the real social history that the mind attempts to rid but fails in vain. Therefore, with Fichte, "only if the I on its part is also not I does it react to the not-I. Only then does it 'do' something. Only then would the doing (das tune) itself be making."[2] Without object, the subject turns into nothingness; only in face of the object and in domination of the object, the subject is constructed, its ruling activity becoming mental and ontological. This is the secret accounting for the genesis of Hegel's absolute concept and Heidegger's abstract and functional interpretation of being. Adorno hence believes that thinking breaks the supremacy of thinking over its otherness, because thinking always is otherness already, within itself. Hence the supreme abstraction of all activity, the transcendental function, does not deserve to be ranked above the factual geneses. This precisely breaks the primacy principle of idealism itself. After all, "the subject would be liberated only as an I reconciled with the not-I."[3] This is a profound dialectics. Adorno then points out that when Heidegger's doctrine of Being "turns ideological as it imperceptibly spiritualizes the materialist moment in thought by transposing it into pure functionality beyond all entity—as it removes by magic method whatever critique of a false consciousness resides in the materialist concept of Being."[4] *When through a mysterious speculation a philosophy makes the true reality evaporate and make the enslaved people to pursue truth, faith and kindness on the cross and to accept suffering poetically, it is no exaggeration to call this philosophy a new type of "spiritual opium for people."*

3. Negative dialectics and materialism

I have pointed out that Adorno's penetrating critique of idealism does not mean that he agrees with any forms of the old materialism. Adorno

---

[1] Adorno, Theodor W. *Negative Dialectics*. Trans. E. B. Ashton. New York: The Continuum Publishing House, 1990. p.200.

[2] Ibid., p. 200.

[3] Ibid., p. 283

[4] Ibid., p. 200.

specifically points out the line that consciousness depends on Being was not a metaphysics in reverse. In other words, although he is against idealism, against the idea of viewing spirit as a self-contained totality and the domination of spiritual identity, and aiming to expose its dependence on Being, he does not mean to turn the objective entity man confronts into a self-contained material entity in reverse, and to return back to construct the same abstract identity and totality logic of *materialist philosophy*. For example, in terms of the mind-body relations, some materialists in fighting against the primacy of the mind advocates the primacy of the body in reverse. This is ridiculous in the same sense. Adorno sharply points out, the controversy about the primacy of mind and body is a pre-dialectical proceeding. It carries on the question of a "first." According to him, the binary segregation of body and mind, which is an abstract formulation in imagination, results from the identitarian philosophy, but body and mind can not be separated in reality, nor is there supremacy of one over the other with the abstract boundaries.

In fact, I found Adorno in the final part of this section does not really intend to give a positive description of the basic theory of historical materialism. Instead, he excitedly dedicates this important concluding part to criticizing the materialist model in the traditional philosophical framework of the former Soviet Union. Adorno says very bluntly, when materialism becomes the official ideology, or in other words, when materialism becomes dogmatism under distortion, serving as a tool of political power, it is terribly deformed so as to become an extremely irrational *theoretical apocrypha*. At this point, materialism is the least of materialism. He thinks the apocryphal part of materialism reveals the one of high philosophy, the untruth in the sovereignty of the spirit. Here, Adorno speaks against the Stalinist ideology of the former Soviet Union and Eastern Europe, "On the threadbare pretext of a dictatorship (now half a century old) of the proletariat (long bureaucratically administered), governmental terror machines entrench themselves as permanent institutions, mocking the theory they carry on their lips. They chain their vassals to their most direct concerns and keep them stupid."[1] (In my view, this critical identification is also appropriate in criticizing Chinese people's mind during the period of China's "Cultural Revolution." When man does not have an independent spiritual personality, the theory itself—even if it claims to be materialism—because of its direct totality and identity, becomes a horrible prison of mind. The individual spirit remains for a long time in a low state of ignorance, boasting materialism on lips while at the same time practicing idealism. In 1958, when the old farmers used stones in the field to advocate materialism, people were acting ridiculously on the falsehood that "the bigger lie you can tell, the more you can produce in the farm." In the mid-1970s, when Chinese were studying Marxist classics "seriously," the period was marked by the rampant contamination of metaphysics of the "Gang of Four.") Adorno says, it is in the similar state, "Materialism comes to be the very relapse into barbarism which it was supposed to prevent."[2]

I have noticed that in the same critical domain, Adorno spends more ink to discuss epistemology, which has always been one of his important theoretical concerns. Adorno has said in the epistemological sense that "it is not the old intention recta that is restored by insight into the object's primacy"[3], or to speak more directly, "the supposedly pure object lacking any admixture of thought and vision is the literal reflection of abstract subjectivity."[4] This claim is in conformity with his above-mentioned negative attitude towards materialism. In his view, materialism in the traditional philosophical framework of the former Soviet Union had a huge theoretical defect, that is, a pursuit of totality and identity in *systematic philosophy*. Epistemologically, the defect lies in a belief in the image character of consciousness, a castrated objectivism. It is problematic to view the object as a total and identitarian thing and consciousness as a direct "image" of the

---

[1] Adorno, Theodor W. *Negative Dialectics*. Trans. E. B. Ashton. New York: The Continuum Publishing House, 1990. p. 204.

[2] Ibid., p. 205.

[3] Adorno, Theodor.W. "Subject and Object." *The Essential Frankfurt School Reader*, 1st vol. The Commercial Press, 1998. p. 212.

[4] Ibid., p.214.

thing. But, they forget that "if matter were total, undifferentiated, and flatly singular, there would be no dialectics in it."[1] This is a deadly defect of the metaphysical ontology, namely *non-historical* logical prescription. The same is true of man's cognition in that consciousness comes into being only under certain historical conditions, which means it is not a direct image of the object. Therefore, in official materialist dialectics, epistemology was skipped by fiat; epistemology's revenge has been the image doctrine. The thought is not an image of the thing (it becomes that only in an Epicurean-style materialist mythology which invents the emission by matter of little images); the thought aims at the thing- itself.

In the cognitive framework of the traditional philosophy, "the totality of images blends into a wall before reality. The image theory denies the spontaneity of the subject, a ***movement*** of the objective dialectics of productive forces and conditions. If the subject is bound to mulishly mirror the object—necessarily missing the object, which only opens itself to the subjective surplus in the thought—the result is the non-peaceful spiritual silence of integral administration."[2] The image theory misleads the people's cognition of the object under certain historical conditions to be the object itself, and thus blocks the subject's cognition of the object with a "wall." Here, self-claimed materialistic epistemology slips back into the idealism again. Adorno emphasizes the spontaneity of the subject and the subjective "surplus" which is a sort of temporal movement generated when the subject engages itself with the productive forces under the social-historical conditions. Otherwise, the image theory is bound to assist in enforcement of oneness. On this point, Adorno says, nothing but an indefatigably reified consciousness will believe, or will persuade others to believe, that it possesses photographs of objectivity. The illusions of such a consciousness turn into dogmatic immediacies. Therefore, Marx scarcely put too much weight on terms such as "reflection."

---

[1] Adorno, Theodor.W. "Subject and Object." *The Essential Frankfurt School Reader*, 1st vol. The Commercial Press, 1998. p. 205.

[2] Adorno, Theodor W. *Negative Dialectics*. Trans. E. B. Ashton. New York: The Continuum Publishing House, 1990. pp. 205-206.

Adorno believes that the critical epistemology created by Marx must be reflective in nature. In this critical reflection, the object of theory is not something immediate of which theory might carry home a replica. "Knowledge has not, like the state police, a rogues' gallery of its objects. Rather, it conceives them as it conveys them; otherwise it would be content to describe the façade. As Brecht did admit, after all, the criterion of sense perception—overstretched and problematic even in its proper place—is not applicable to radically indirect society. What immigrated into the object as the law of its motion, inevitably concealed by the ideological form of the phenomenon, eludes that criterion."[1] What Adorno identifies here is not the abstract philosophical epistemology, but rather a historical and *social epistemology*. Theory can not be a tool to demonstrate the politics, otherwise, the so-called "the unity of theory and practice" is nothing but a fraud. Adorno points out that "no theory may, for agitation simplicity's sake, play the fool about objectively attained knowledge. Theory must reflect the state of this knowledge and promote its advance. The unity of theory and practice was not meant as a concession to weakness of thought, which is a tarantism spawned by the repressive society."[2] The image theory is non-historical and non-critical. This non-reflective image theory is called by Adorno "a representational thinking." He says, representational thinking would be without reflection—an un-dialectical contradiction, for without reflection there is no theory. A consciousness interpolating images, a third element, between itself and that which it thinks would unwittingly reproduce idealism. A body of ideas would substitute for the object of cognition, and the subjective arbitrariness of such ideas is that of the authorities. Adorno firmly opposes the immediate cognition. If people are trained to naively affirm the objectivity of the existing things, what they see, hear and touch, then this is no more than a demonstration that "subjective positivism is conspiring with the powers." It sounds horrible, but it is true.

---

[1] Adorno, Theodor W. *Negative Dialectics*. Trans. E. B. Ashton. New York: The Continuum Publishing House, 1990. p. 206.

[2] Ibid., pp. 206-207.

On a deeper level of social life, materialism based on the immediate things will inevitably nourish a materialistic desire. In other words, once the pursuit of material interests becomes the sole purpose of man, materialism starts to turn vulgar. Therefore, Adorno believes that at its most materialistic, materialism comes to agree with theology. Its great desire would be the resurrection of the flesh, a desire utterly foreign to idealism, the realm of the absolute spirit. Adorno means that to oppose idealism should not turn to: living in a society with absolute pursuing of material interests, because "the perspective vanishing point of *historic materialism* would be its self-sublimation, the spirit's liberation from the primacy of material needs."[1] Adorno's statement is not wrong, but it is intertwined with a very profound logical distortion. The reason is that Adorno does not understand the distinction between the general historical materialism and special historical materialism in Marxist philosophy.

General historical materialism and special historical materialism: I have made a specific analysis of the issue in *The Subjective Dimension of Historical Dialectics* (1995) and *Back to Marx—Philosophy in Economics* (1999). In fact, this is a corresponding study of the huge defect that I had found in the entire Western Marxist philosophy. In those two books, I have carefully distinguished the heterogeneous progress along the main theoretical line of Marxist philosophy: First, "the materialistic desire" concept of Adorno here to discuss correlates with the reason for which the young Marx, who still in the idealist framework around 1840, had rejected materialism. At that time, materialism was the vulgar fetishism of "three coins" inherited from Junker Landlords of Germany. Second, in the course of Marx's reconstruction of the historical materialism in the years from 1845 to 1858, the historical materialism gradually went into two dimensions: one affirmed that material production was always the general basis

---

[1] Adorno, Theodor W. *Negative Dialectics*. Trans. E. B. Ashton. New York: The Continuum Publishing House, 1990. p. 207.

of human history and society. This is and was general historical materialism. The other had maintained that under certain historical conditions, especially in the commercial-economic kingdom created by the capitalist industry, people's blind pursuit of materialistic interests distorted economic power produced by them into a ruling power. Thus, "the primacy of material" is just the very bourgeois-fetishism by nature. In this latter regard, Marx did (narrowly) make historical materialism an ideological weapon transcending the realm of necessity. Adorno mixes these theoretical aspects and expresses a concept which was already clear in Marx, but getting more and more confusing when discussed further.

However, regardless of the defect, Adorno's warning has a significant meaning for the modern social life of today's China: in pursuit of an idealized conceptual goal, the past era has mistakenly made spiritual orientation of value the basis of social life, whereas the romantic revolution did not last long in the barren soil; once we realize that material production is the basis of historic existence, it is right to return to the laws of historical materialism, but any social life cannot gain a healthy development solely relying on materialistic interests and to prevent materialistic desire is a very important warning especially for the development of a nation aiming an advanced socialist future. It is right for Dell to say that Negative Dialectics does not simply dissolve the subject, but aims to build a dialectical tension between the ruling principles and the counter-forces against social system. It is difficult to arrive at a true dialectics.

Chapter 2

The Pseudo-Being
Presented by Images:
Reinterpreting Guy
Debord's *The Society*
of the Spectacle[1]

The *Society of the Spectacle* of Guy Debord[2] well deserves a position among the most significant ruptures of the cultural logic

---

[1] This chapter was translated by Fan Shuying.

[2] Guy Ernest Debord (1931-1994), was a renowned contemporary French thinker, experimental cinematic artist, and radical left-winged forerunner of Situationist International. He was born into a Parisian businessman's family on 28, December, 1931. He graduated from Cannes Public School in spring 1957 and pursued no further education. Debord organized Situationist International in 1957 and edited journals like *Potlatch* and *Internationale Situationniste*. His major works include: Hurlements ern faveur de Sade (Howls for Sade), a 1952 film, "Introduction to a critique of urban geography" (1954), "Theory of the Derive" (1956), "Methods of Detournment" (1957, co-authored with Wolman), "Preliminaries Toward Defining a Unitary Revolutionary

of western Marxist philosophy. In this book written in the mid-1960s, he for the first time theorizes the reified reality of industrial capitalism into a general visual representation of the contemporary capitalist ideology which parts its way from material production. And the labor relationship between human beings which according to Marx is inverted into that between objects in the market exchange is again abstracted into a pseudo desire-oriented structure represented in a commercial spectacular appearance. Such is the spectacle of the society. Debord holds that the spectacle is the dominating pattern of the relationship between human beings in contemporary society. Though indisputably people are all aware that the spectacle is a manufactured phenomenon, they still lose themselves in it so much so that they forget their real social existence. This is a new form of alienation. Therefore Marxist critique of economic fetishism in turn becomes a critique of spectacle fetishism. In general, the book has a theme of social criticism and cultural argumentation in which the projects of social reforms like "the revolution of everyday life" and the construction of artistic "situation"[1] proposed by Debord and other Situationists are not particularly highlighted. Thus, compared with the negative dialectics initiated by Adorno, Debord opens another important realistic passage to access the post-Marxian trend. Debord's ideas have a direct influence on Baudrillard, Kellner and the like. In this

---

Program" (1960), "Report on the Construction of Situations and on the International Situationist Tendency's Conditions of Organization and Action" (1957), "Theses sur la revolution culturelle" (1958), "Theses on the Paris Commune" (1962, coauthored with Vaneigem), "The Decline and Fall of the Spectacle-Commodity Economy" (1965), and *The Society of the Spectacle* (1967). In his late years he wrote his half-autobiographical work and completed *Comments on The Society of the Spectacle*, in which he further developed his critical theory on the capitalist spectacular society. In 1994 he finished his last film, Guy Debord: His Art and His Time, coauthored with Brigitte Cornand. He committed suicide in his reclusive residence the same year on 30, November at the age of 63.

[1] Debord made the film *La Société du Spectacle* in 1973 which lasts 1 hour and 28 minutes. In 1974 he made another 21-minute film Réfutation de tous les jugements, tant élogieux qu'hostiles, qui ont été jusqu'ici portés sur le film "La Société du spectacle." He wrote the playscripts and directed both of the films. At the beginning of the latter film, Debord made a resolute monologue to defend his views. He forbade the play of his own films when he was alive. Only after he died did the several films of his come to the public. In the 2001 Venice Film Festival relevant Dobord films were on show.

chapter I will give a brief interpretation of some key concepts in *The Society of the Spectacle*. As Debord made a film based on this book, I will give an introduction to some particular situations of this film as well.

I. Reversal of the Inverted World of the Spectacle

Debord wrote *The Society of the Spectacle* with a self-evident intention to announce a new historical rupture, i.e., that the reified era Marx faced had been transformed into an overturned world in which visual representation he recognized usurped the foundation of the social reality. In other words, it has been changed into a realm of the spectacles. Debord makes it clear that in today's society the relationship between the spectacle and spectator is at the core of the secure foundation of the capitalist order. Best and Kellner "interpret the emergence of Debord and the Situationist International as an attempt to update the Marxian theory in the French post-World War II conjuncture."[1] It hits the point. Best also acknowledges another important stratum of its supportive theoretical background, saying that "[a]lso influenced by Gramsci, the Situationists saw the most recent stage in social control as based on consensus rather than force, as a cultural hegemony attained through the transformation of commodity society in to the 'society of the spectacle.'"[2] In the first as well as the most important chapter, Debord describes the fundamental contents and characteristics of this significant transition, which strictly speaking define the basic ways and features of the existence of the spectacle.

1. The ontological presentational aberrance of social existence

In the introductory part of Chapter I, Debord quotes a paragraph from the Preface of the second edition of Feuerbach's *The Essence of Christianity*[3],

---

[1] Best & Kellner, *The Postmodern Turn*, New York: Guilford Press, 1997. p. 81.

[2] Kellner, (ed.) *Baudrillard: A Critical Reader*, Oxford: Wiley-Blackwell, 1994. p. 47.

[3] Debord divides his *The Society of the Spectacle* into nine chapters, consisting of altogether 221 sections of aphorisms in a Pascal-Nietzsche style. Debord also cites from other philosophers as the introduction in the beginning of each chapter.

his well-known statement to criticize the substitution of man's real life by the illusion of the City of God in the Christian context. Debord points out vividly and poignantly that Feuerbach hits it at home when he analyzes the chaotic age as one which "prefers the sign to the thing signified, the copy to the original, representation to reality, the appearance to the essence." Bearing humanity on mind, Feuerbach of course requires a revolution of the logic of pseudo reality for purposes of effacing the theistic illusion and returning to the real being of mankind. As is known to all, Marx criticizes that Feuerbach's attack on religion does not further explain that the real reason hidden behind the emergence of the theistic world of illusion resides exactly in the "self-cleavage and self-contradictions within this secular basis" of reality, though Feuerbach is right in identifying the religious world with that of the secular. In this famous assertion, Marx points out that "the secular basis lifts off from itself and establishes itself as an independent realm in the clouds."[1] By this he means to say that the reason why Christianity builds the City of God out of theistic illusion is essentially out of the needs of the ideology for the feudal authoritarianism in the authentic world. Here Debord effortlessly and cleverly borrows this Feuerbach-Marx double context to establish his new idea. Like the City of God, the secular foundation of contemporary capitalism has separated itself and has set up an equally illusionary **society of the spectacle** with clusters of images. Debord thinks that "Feuerbach's judgment on the fact that his time preferred 'the sign to the thing signified, the copy to the original, representation to reality,' has been thoroughly vindicated by the century of the spectacle."[2] In his two films with the theme of "The Society of the Spectacle," he seems to clarify through the combination and collage of scenes a fact that images and pictures have overwhelmed over, or substituted and imitated the living existence in the contemporary capitalist society. We might as well have a look at his own theoretical arguments.

---

[1] Marx, Karl and Frederick Engels. *Collected Works*, Vol. 5. London: Lawrence & Wishart, 1976. p. 4.

[2] Debord, Guy. *Comments on the Society of the Spectacle*. Trans. Malcolm Imrie, London: Verso, 1998. p. 51.

The opening section of the book goes: "The whole life of those societies in which modern conditions of production prevail presents itself as an immense accumulation of spectacles. All that once was directly lived has become mere representation."[1] This is the most famous assertion in his book. In the namesake film, the scene that goes with the voiceover is the American astronaut going out of the spaceship onto the moon. Debord illustrates the relationship between images and reality by this scene. He notices that these images look as if linked with our lives.

Spectacle[2] is the key word of Debord's new social critique. It originally means a perceptible and objective scene or sight demonstrated, and it also means a subjective and conscious show or act. By it Debord embodies the new characteristics of the contemporary capitalist society, the *dominating* essence of which is manifested as the spectacle. The trancelike state of people in the spectacle deprives them of their desire and requirement for the authentic life, and the capitalists manipulate the social life en bloc through the production and change of spectacles. In Debord's eyes, the spectacle is the most important feature of modern capitalism. It is also his most important theoretical finding. Apparently what supports Debord's concept of the spectacle derives from the logic of a humanistic binary value hypothesis, as he sees both the spectacle and the real of a society are placed within a critical tension between "be" and "should be." As a matter of fact, the deep logic of Debord's theory is entirely heterogeneous from that of Marx's horizon of historical materialism formed since 1845. For Debord, the spectacle is an illusion constructed by the images of perceptual representation. Its existence

---

[1] Debord, Guy. *The Society of the Spectacle*, Trans. Donald Nickleson-Smith, New York: Zone Books, 1994. p. 12.

[2] The word "spectacle" derives from Latin words "spectae" and "specere," meaning to look, gaze, or to be looked at. Taiwan scholars translate it as "a spectacular scene" as well. In my opinion "spectacle" is nothing like a spectacular scene. It is just appearance with no direct coercion of cluster of images, and is a prescription in the ontological sense. It means being is inverted into an ostentatious appearance. When appearance substitutes being, it becomes a spectacle. Debord used "spectacle" in a film review on Hiroshima Mon Amour published in *Situationist International* Vol. 3, 1959. According to Husserl, the word "spectacle" originates in Nietzsche's *The Birth of Tragedy*.

is underpinned by representations with various images as their form of appearance. What's more, *the presence of the spectacle obscures social reality*. Baudrillard later coined on top of this word "simulation," which however orients doubtlessly on an ontological usurpation, for it is more real than the authentic being. Besides, Debord continues to promote the logic of Marxist critique, deducing that the emergence of the spectacle essentially results from the self-alienation of the social reality of contemporary capitalism. And he says it right. We will later find that the separation Debord points out is an ontological event, the realistic foundation of the alienation of social being. It goes without saying that Debord's theory is a negative one. In his film *La Société du Spectacle*, he expresses clearly his disapproval of the so-called "writing-degree zero" attitude and the passive confrontation with reality. He affirms the revolutionary and critical nature of dialectics. This is where Debord differs from the structuralist idea of "not to take to the streets." Interestingly enough, along with this heavy discussion in the film goes the war scene in which the defense soldiers choose to retreat before their ever-charging enemies and, when stopped and reproached by an officer, they once again return to their position and defeat the students.

Debord does not theorize the definition of the spectacle in the book. Rather he attempts to refer to this phenomenon through research and discussions.

Definition of the Spectacle. Belden Fields and Steven Best once gave a clear definition of the spectacle. "Immediately, the term implies some sort of circus or show put on by a few and watched by the masses."[1] The so-called "a few" undoubtedly refers to the capitalists who, by controlling behind the curtain, make the spectacles permeate the entire contemporary life. The masses refer to the dominated audience, the ordinary people, "who stare dumbfoundedly in amusement and amazement"[2] at the performance produced and manipulated by the

[1] Fields, Belden and Steven Best, "Situatinonist International," in Robert A. Gorman (ed.), *Bio-graphical Dictionary of Neo-Marxism*, Westport: Greenwood Press, 1985. p. 384.

[2] Ibid.

minority. This enthralled gaze "implies control and passivity, separation and isolation."[1] So Baudrillard applies "the silent majority" to those bewitched people.[2] Debord likewise vividly portrays the "masses," saying, "The spectator is simply supposed to know nothing, and deserve nothing. Those who are always watching to see what happens next will never act: such must be the spectator's condition."[3] Secondly, the spectacle is not an external approach of coercion. It is neither a violent political ideology, nor a forced buy and sell in the process of trade. Instead, "the term *spectacle* subsumes all the means and methods power employs, outside of direct force, to relegate potentially political, critical, and creative human beings to the margins of thought and behavior. The spectacle then is de-politicization par excellence: 'The very principle of the spectacle [is] non-intervention.'"[4] The most profound enslavement is the covert, non-interfering one. Third, bewildered by the entertainments manufactured by the spectacle, the masses are bound to alienate from their real critical and creative aptitudes and are reduced to mere slaves of the spectacle. This idea is of course the re-summarization and reanalysis of his successors. Best defines that the truth of the spectacle is a social institution of class domination, an ideology based on the social condition of reality, which has become practical and justified materially and which is able to stimulate and hypnotize the spectators.[5]

Obviously the above quoted section from *The Society of the Spectacle* is a deliberate alteration Debord does to Marxian texts. In the beginning

---

[1] Fields, Belden and Steven Best, "Situatinonist International," in Robert A. Gorman (ed.), *Biographical Dictionary of Neo-Marxism*, Westport: Greenwood Press, 1985. p. 384.

[2] Kellner, Douglas. (ed.), *Baudrillard: A Critical Reader*, Oxford, Wiley-Blackwell, 1994. p. 141.

[3] Debord, Guy. *Comments on the Society of the Spectacle*, Trans. Malcolm Imrie, London: Verso, 1998. p. 9.

[4] Fields, Belden and Steven Best, "Situationist International," in Robert A. Gorman (ed.), *Biographical Dictionary of Neo-Marxism*, Westport: Greenwood Press, 1985. p. 385.

[5] *See* Best, Stevens. "The Commodification of Reality and Reality of Commodification: Baudrillard, Debord, and Postmodern Theory," in Douglas Kellner, *Baudrillard: A Critical Reader*, Oxford: Wiley-Blackwell, 1994.

of the first chapter of *Capital*, Marx informs us that "the wealth of those societies in which the capitalist mode of production prevails, presents itself as 'an immense accumulation of commodities.'"[1] He leads us from the recognition of commodity as the cell of capitalist market economy to the discoveries of the real relationship between money and capital hidden behind the miscellaneous forms of relationships between objects, in particular the secret of the capitalist's acquisition of surplus value. By contrast, Debord puts forth from the outset an assertion radically different from that of Marx, believing that the former reified economic world has been transformed into the sum existence of the spectacle in the society where "modern conditions of production prevails." The nature of this transformation resides in that "[a]ll that once was directly lived has become mere representation." It might be noted that here *a double inversion* occurs imperceptibly! The capitalist economic reality Marx faces is the reified economic inversion of the relationship between human beings, whereas Debord sees in his age the *re-inversion of representation* of the already inverted reification itself. *We will find that Debord in actuality does not really understand Marxian theoretical critique of reification. His ideas provide the significant logical clues for Baudrillard's political economy of the sign in substitution for Marxian political economy, one of the important sources of the logic of post-Marxian theories.* From my perspective, Debord applies the term "representation" in the ontological sense, which means that the reification of capitalist existence is reduced to an *intentional* representation, a new form of pseudo-being.

Debord gives a detailed anatomy of this point. He contends that the capitalist economic development can be divided into two stages:

> An earlier stage in the economy's domination of social life entailed an obvious downgrading of being into having that left its stamp on all human endeavor. The present stage, in which social life is completely taken over by the accumulated products of the economy, entails a generalized shift from having to appearing: all effective "having" must

---

[1] Marx, Karl. *Capital*, Vol. London: Lawrence & Wishart, 1977. p. 43.

now derive both its immediate prestige and its ultimate raison d'etre from appearances. At the same time all individual reality, being directly dependent on social power and completely shaped by that power, has assumed a social character. Indeed, it is only inasmuch as individual reality is not that it is allowed to appear.[1]

The nature of the capitalist mode of production is "the economic domination over social life," namely the special historical condition of the domination of the economic force external to man over the totality of social existence. It is basically true. To Debord, the first phase is "downgrading of being into having." This does not come from Marx directly. Instead, its supportive background more or less bears resemblance to humanistic logic, for what it is in its "being" is a value suspense. Later, Marx gives a scientific explanation in his special historical materialism or historical phenomenology: It is the direct labor relation between human beings in the pre-capitalist modes of production. Besides, the nature of capitalist mode of production according to Marx is far from the direct ownership of the object, but the primacy of the ownership of capital on it. To put it simply, the capitalist mode of production is exactly characterized by the change from direct ownership of objects (a feature of feudal relationship) to the ownership of means of production. What the capitalists have at hand is not material, but the ownership of capital that dominates and mediates material and man. Here lies the problem in Debord's theoretical analysis. This point coincides in a way with Fromm's humanistic theory.[2] Most important of all, however, Debord thinks that the present-day capitalist mode of production is undergoing a stage at the core of which is the generalized shift "from *having* to *appearing*," or the appearance of social being becoming the ruling paradigm. It goes without saying that Debord endeavors to reveal the new situation in the contemporary society, but his shaping view of individual

---

[1] Debord, Guy. *The Society of the Spectacle*, Trans. Donald Nickleson-Smith, New York: Zone Books, 1994. p. 17.

[2] *See* Fromm, Erich. *To Have or to Be?* London & New York: Continuum International Publishing Group, 2005.

reality degraded into social reality and individual confined by social forces is nothing new. Philosophers from Marx to Smith, Ricardo, and Hegel all have been aware of the fact that abstract labor as a social totality has, on the basis of adequate division of labor, replaced the concrete and perceptible individual labor ever since the emergence of industrial production and capitalist market economy. The value of individual labor is realized only via the recognition of the market. By contrast, Debord's statement is lack of precision and originality. Rather, his idea that "all effective 'having' must now derive both its immediate prestige and its ultimate raison d'etre from appearances" can be said to be his peculiar contribution. In fact, what he really has in mind is that the existing relationship in the previous economic society has now been transformed into a prestige dependent on appearance (Please note that he fails to grasp the reification of social relationship). His assertion that "it is only inasmuch as individual reality is not that it is allowed to appear" is essentially a revision of the Marxian view. If, according to Marx, the real and immediate relationship between human beings in the capitalist society cannot be realized effectively without being turned into a relationship between objects, then Debord holds that one will be nothing if one's individual reality fails to appear as an unreal spectacular fame. Or, to put it simply, no fame, no fortune. This perception of Debord's is insightful and acute. When we look around the world we live in, we will find that nothing seems to exist if not via newspapers or TV reports. In this sense, the appearance and spectacle of life is ontological.

For one to whom the real world becomes real images, mere images are transformed into real beings—tangible figments which are the efficient motor of trancelike behavior. Since the spectacle's job is to cause a world that is no longer directly perceptible to be seen via different specialized mediations, it is inevitable that it should elevate the human sense of sight to the special place once occupied by touch; the most abstract of the senses, and the most easily deceived, sight is naturally the most readily adaptable to present-day society's generalized abstraction. This is not to say, however, that the spectacle itself is perceptible to the naked eye—even if that eye is assisted by the ear. The spectacle is by definition immune from human activity, inaccessible to any projected review or correction. It is the opposite of dialogue. Wherever representation takes on an independent existence, the spectacle reestablishes its rule.[1]

The real world is reduced to images whereas images are elevated to seemingly real existence. Baudrillard asserts, "Primitive society had its masks, bourgeois society its mirrors. We have our images."[2] Debord says in his film *La Société du Spectacle* that the spectacle is the soul of the society. The nature of these changes resides in that the fabricated objects have lulled people into a trancelike state. Like the tricks played by the conjurors, various "specialized media" are under the spotlight, "it is inevitable that it should elevate the human sense of sight to the special place once occupied by touch." In fact, in Debord's era, the mass media was only at the preliminary stage, playing less a profound or extensive role over social life than today's hegemonic global internet network. It is in this sense that Kellner develops Debord's spectacle into the sweeping concept of Media Spectacle.[3] Of course the sense of sight is placed in the philosophical context. Debord means to say that if we changed the world by manipulating concrete material, the "special place" of touch, then what counts today is *to be seen*! It is according to this logic that some thinkers even point out that the present-day society has been "a society of the image," or theoretically "visual or pictorial turn,"[4] with "the sense of sight as the dominating form of social reality." Martin

---

[1] Debord, Guy. *The Society of the Spectacle*, Trans. Donald Nickleson-Smith, New York: Zone Books, 1994. p. 17.

[2] Baudrillard, in Luo Gang, Gu Zheng (eds.), *Visual Culture: A Reader*, Nanning: Guangxi Normal University Press, 2003. p. 76.

[3] According to Kellner, media spectacles refer to "those phenomena that embody contemporary society's basic values, serve to initiate individuals into its way of life, and dramatize its controversies and struggles, as well as its modes of conflict solution. They include media extravaganzas, sporting events, political happenings[.]"See Kellner, Douglas. *Media Spectacle*, London & New York: Routledge, 2003. p. 2.

[4] Erjavec, Ales. *Toward the Image*, Trans. by Hu Julan, Zhang Yunpeng, Changchun: Jilin People's Press, 2003, pp. 5-6.

Jay calls it "ocularcentrism." This seems to have become a common sense. Debord further points out that the nature of the spectacle is the refusal of *dialogue*. The spectacle is a deeper, invisible control, dissolving the defiance and the critical negation of the subject. Under the charm of the spectacle, the individual conforms in a one-dimensional way. Such is the essence of the spectacular ideology.

Debord responds to it like this: "The spectacle is heir to all the *weakness* of the project of Western philosophy, which was an attempt to understand activity by means of the categories of vision. Indeed the spectacle reposes on an incessant deployment of the very technical rationality to which that philosophical tradition gave rise."[1] This ontological vision is different in that it results in the representation of the being itself, while representation is just the new surviving form of capitalism. Baudrillard recognizes it as "an idealism which privileges the contents of representation."[2]

This "representation" in the ontological context reminds one of Kant's epistemological revolution. As is known to all, Kant starts from Hume's proposition and comes up with the conclusion that the natural world always represents itself with a fixed form before us (the subject), and representation itself is the result of the predominance of the transcendental structure of reason. Kant is insightful in that he perceives the following facts: the result is not substance (or Things-in-Themselves), but simply "appearance," an integrated *a priori* judgment. Hegel succeeds Kant in grasping the Creator of the structure of reasonable logic, and Marx takes the credit of relentlessly stripping the rhetoric overcoat of this Providence and consequently exposing the reality of the capitalist relationship and structure of industrial and modern age, hence recognizing the trick of reification of capitalist logic. Debord inherits his predecessors when he once again recognizes the inverted materialization as the representation of appearance, as an overturning of the

---

[1] Debord, Guy. *The Society of the Spectacle*, Trans. Donald Nickleson-Smith, New York: Zone Books, 1994. p. 17.

[2] Baudrillard, Jean. *The Mirror of Production*, Trans. Mark Poster. St. Louis: Telos Press, 1975. p. 116.

overturned. If in Marx's context commodity still maintains a tangible and perceptible material form, then in today's capitalist life, even the "table-turning," the mysterious shell of substance is vaporized to nothing. In the vast world our sense of touch is laid waste; what we have is only the spectacle juxtaposed with appealing images. However, this does not mean that the substance in actuality becomes absolute spectacle. What Debord means is that *the spectacle becomes the ruling force*. The spectacle generates desire, which in turn determines production. The material production is still objective, but is mediated by the illusion and trick produced by the spectacle. What an overturned world of inversion! "In a world that really has been turned on its head, truth is a moment of falsehood."[1] The spectacle juxtaposes spectacles, and man lives in the weird world, miserably grasping illusion as their last hope.

Images detached from every aspect of life merge into a common stream, and the former unity of life is lost forever. Apprehended in a partial way, reality unfolds in a new generality as a *pseudo-world apart*, solely as an object of contemplation. The tendency toward the specialization of images-of-the-world finds its highest expression in the world of the autonomous image, where deceit deceives itself. The spectacle in its generality is a concrete inversion of life, and, as such, the autonomous movement of non-life.[2]

The spectacle is the concrete inversion of life, juxtaposed by the "partial" scenes of reality. It constructs an autonomous movement of non-life, with its essence being the isolated "pseudo-world" woven by images. Thus, "reality erupts within the spectacle, and the spectacle is real. This reciprocal alienation is the essence and underpinning of society as it exists."[3]

---

[1] Debord, Guy. *The Society of the Spectacle*, Trans. Donald Nickleson-Smith, New York: Zone Books, 1994. p.14.

[2] Ibid., p. 12.

[3] Ibid., p. 14.

2. The forms of spectacle's dominance

Debord first poses the issue of the forms of spectacle's dominance. He divides the spectacle into two *concentrated* and *diffuse* forms:

"The concentrated form of the spectacle normally characterizes bureaucratic capitalism." This is his theoretical orientation. As a technique, the so-called concentrated form of the spectacle may on occasion be borrowed as a technique for buttressing state power over more backward mixed economies, and even the most advanced capitalism may call on it in moments of crisis. It is in essence the apparatus of the bureaucratic politics.

> Bureaucratic property is itself concentrated, in that the individual bureaucrat's relation to the ownership of the economy as a whole is invariably mediated by the community of bureaucrats, by his membership in that community. And commodity production, less well developed in bureaucratic systems, is also concentrated in form: the commodity the bureaucracy appropriates is the totality of social labor, and what it sells back to society—en bloc—is society's survival. The dictatorship of the bureaucratic economy cannot leave the exploited masses any significant margin of choice because it has had to make all the choices itself, and because any choice made independently of it, even the most trivial—concerning food, say, or music—amounts to a declaration of war to the death on the bureaucracy. This dictatorship must therefore be attended by permanent violence.[1]

In Debord's view, the fascist countries epitomize the concentrated spectacle, which also finds its expression in capitalist countries in moments of crisis. But Debord inaccurately includes Stalinism, which he illustrates as a phenomenon of the borrowing of concentrated spectacle when backward countries intend to enhance their power. *In his film, he links the scene of Hitler's inspection of his army with that of Leonid Ilyich Brezhnev at the Red*

---

[1] Debord, Guy. *The Society of the Spectacle*, Trans. Donald Nickleson-Smith, New York: Zone Books, 1994. p. 41.

Square at Moscow in order to exemplify this spectacle. Debord gives several examples here. For instance, the bureaucracy appropriates the commodity as the totality of social labor, and sells back to society only its "survival"; or that its spectacle imposes an image of the good which is a resume of everything that exists officially, and this is usually concentrated in a single individual, the guarantor of the system's totalitarian cohesiveness. "Everyone must identify magically with this absolute celebrity—or disappear."[1] Or, "the dominion of the spectacle in its concentrated form means the dominion, too, of the police."[2] In my opinion, Debord's so-called concentrated spectacle is nothing peculiar or deep in the real sense; what he does is only grafting the spectacle as a uniform image of violence to dictatorship. He states in his film, in brief, that capital is no longer an invisible center manipulated by the mode of production. The spectacle visualizes its violence. With this voiceover is the scene of police force in battle with the students. The most frequently recurring scene in the film is that of the conflict between the students and the police in the May Movement of 1968, with the most shocking one being the police beating the students with their batons. Besides, the so-called concentrated spectacle is neither a new phenomenon in the development of capitalism, nor a logical deduction of the previous theoretical description he makes of the spectacle: how come the spectacle, derived from dictatorship, is not interruptive? And this intervention is the external coercion which Debord denies existence. In this sense, his explanation of the concentrated spectacle is obviously a faulty expression.

The general form of the spectacle, the diffuse spectacle, is reckoned by Debord as the new form of capitalist dominance of society and its ideology. As a matter of fact, all the above discussions we hold focus on this form of the spectacle, which needs no further introduction. Above all, twenty one years after the publication of the book, Debord issued a new theoretical text concerning the spectacle, *Comments on The Society of the Spectacle*,

---

[1] Debord, Guy. *The Society of the Spectacle*, Trans. Donald Nickleson-Smith, New York: Zone Books, 1994. p. 42.

[2] Ibid.

revisiting the forms of the spectacle and introducing a new form, the *integrated spectacle*. At that time, Debord reaffirmed his theoretical findings he made over two decades ago and gave further expoundings and additional explanations to some of the past viewpoints. I think his new theoretical discoveries crystallize the discourse on the integrated spectacle, the new form of spectacular control.

Debord declares that in *The Society of the Spectacle* he has shown "what the modern spectacle was already in essence: the autocratic reign of the market economy which had acceded to an irresponsible sovereignty, and the totality of new techniques of government which accompanied this reign."[1] As an autocracy, the spectacle is apparently different from that of the previous tyranny in that it more often than not manifests itself as some *mild* ideological control. Debord thinks that the May Storm of 1968 is short-lived, failing to prevent the spreading of the spectacle, which "has thus continued to gather strength, that is, to spread to the furthest limits on all sides, while increasing its density in the center. It has even learnt new defensive techniques, as powers under attack always do."[2] *By contrast, he gave high praise to the May Movement in his 1973 and 1974 films.* This implies that after twenty years' development, the society of the spectacle is least impaired. Instead, "a third form has been established, through the rational combination of these two, and on the basis of a general victory of the form which had showed itself stronger: the diffuse. This is the integrated spectacle, which has since tended to impose itself globally."[3] Debord narrates the integrated spectacle in great detail:

> The integrated spectacle shows itself to be simultaneously concentrated and diffuse, and ever since the fruitful union of the two has learnt to employ both these qualities on a grander scale. Their former mode of application has changed considerably. As regards concentration,

---

[1] Debord, Guy. *Comments on the Society of the Spectacle*, Trans. Malcolm Imrie, London: Verso, 1998. p. 1.

[2] Ibid.

[3] Ibid., p. 4.

the controlling center has now become occult never to be occupied by a known leader, or clear ideology. And on the diffuse side, the spectacle has never before put its mark to such a degree on almost the full range of socially produced behavior and objects. For the final sense of the integrated spectacle is this—that it has integrated itself into reality to the same extent as it was describing it, and that it was reconstructing it as it was describing it. As a result, this reality no longer confronts the integrated spectacle as something alien. When the spectacle was concentrated, the greater part of surrounding society escaped it; when diffuse, a small part; today, no part. The spectacle has spread itself to the point where it now permeates all reality. It was easy to predict in theory what has been quickly and universally demonstrated by practical experience of economic reason's relentless accomplishments: that the globalization of the false was also the falsification of the globe.[1]

Undoubtedly Debord only stresses the ubiquity of the integrated spectacle. The spectacle "permeates all reality"; the globalization of capitalism is the globalization of the spectacle. Simultaneously, Debord identifies the five principle features of the integrated spectacle as: "incessant technological renewal; integration of state and economy; generalized secrecy, unanswerable lies; an eternal present."[2]

In fact, there is nothing new in the above analysis of the forms of the spectacle Debord makes. On the contrary, compared with his previous unique and profound assertion of the nature of the spectacle, his proclamation of its forms is an obvious theoretical flaw, betraying exactly his inadequacy in perceiving the social structure and the development of contemporary science and social practice. Especially after the end of the 20th century, the new advancement of global capitalism (flexible mode of capitalist production and EU as the regional ally of regional capitalists) together with the ebbing of international communist movements, and still the surging of post-modern

---

[1] Debord, Guy. *Comments on the Society of the Spectacle*, Trans. Malcolm Imrie, London: Verso, 1998. p. 4.

[2] Ibid., p. 5.

thoughts, in particular the hegemony of brand-new media of IT industries and the internet world all contribute to the unprecedentedly drastic transformation of the world at large. But Debord seems to turn a blind eye to all this change, and talks and thinks like a recluse in the remote mountains. Kellner's research on contemporary spectacle can be credited as a powerful refilling to his theory. He thinks that Debord's concept of the spectacle is a "rather generalized and abstract notion," while his own concept is more specific and microcosmic.[1]

3. Spectacular imperialism and irresistible hegemony

Admittedly, Debord does not see the emergence of the spectacle as the reduction of the world as a false picture of images: "The spectacle cannot be understood either as a deliberate distortion of the visual world," he argues, and one should fully understand that "the spectacle is not a collection of images; rather, it is a social relationship between people that is mediated by images."[2] Undoubtedly this is the extension of the critical logic of Marx's *historical phenomenology*. Whereas Marx views the relationship between the economic phenomena in the capitalist market as the materialized social relationship between people, Debord defines it as the spectacle. To some extent, Debord unveils the secret. Noticeably, the alteration Debord makes of Marxian theory contains a negative transcendence, that is, the determinant structure of the mode of material production in contemporary world has turned into *the mode of spectacular production* dominated by images. Later Best follows this logic and puts forth his substitute project of mode of information production. Debord argues,

Understood in its totality, the spectacle is both the outcome and the goal of the dominant mode of production. It is not something added to the real world—not a decorative element, so to speak. On the contrary, it is the very heart of society's real unreality. In all its

[1] Kellner, Douglas. *Media Spectacle*, London & New York: Routledge, 2003. p. 2.

[2] Debord, Guy. *The Society of the Spectacle*, Trans. Donald Nickleson-Smith, New York: Zone Books, 1994. p. 12.

specific manifestations—news or propaganda, advertising or the actual consumption of entertainment—the spectacle epitomizes the prevailing *model* of social life. It is the omnipresent celebration of a choice *already made* in the sphere of production, and the consummate result of that choice. In form as in content the spectacle serves as total justification for the conditions and aims of the existing system. It further ensures the *permanent presence* of that justification, for it governs almost all time spent outside the production process itself.[1]

Debord knows well that he must follow strictly Marx's foundation of material production before providing a structural orientation for his theory of the spectacle for referential purposes. Best, remarks that Debord intends in his theory to grasp the constituent relationship of a society, and decode its ideological operation.[2] This is entirely heterogeneous to Baudrillard who thoroughly abandons Marxism. (About Baudrillard's attack on Marx please see the following chapter.) To Debord, the spectacle has two essential features.

First, the spectacle has become the goal of today's capitalist mode of production, or the "core of unreality of real society." To simply put, the spectacle has become the "prevailing *model* of life." What a crucial theoretical assertion it is! According to my understanding, Debord means to say that, compared with the pursuit of the people in the past of food, attire, residence and everyday necessities, today the conception of the aim of life and model of life has undergone total changes: what we strive for is dazzling and spectacular *manifestation of the spectacle*. This epitomizes the unreal need of the contemporary people for news, propaganda, advertisement and entertainment which they do not really need so much. The existence of man no longer consists of its own real needs, instead, it is an accumulation of

---

[1] Debord, Guy. *The Society of the Spectacle*, Trans. Donald Nickleson-Smith, New York: Zone Books, 1994. p. 13.

[2] *See* Best, Steven. "The Commodification of Reality and Reality of Commodification: Baudrillard, Debord, and Postmodern Theory," in Douglas Kellner, *Baudrillard: A Critical Reader*, Oxford: Wiley-Blackwell, 1994.

demonstration and alienation the spectacle directs at. "[T]he spectacle is able to emerge as its apparent goal." Debord argues, "The spectacular character of modern industrial society has nothing fortuitous or superficial about it; on the contrary, this society is based on the spectacle in the most fundamental way. For the spectacle, as the perfect image of the ruling economic order, ends are nothing and development is all—although the only thing into which the spectacle plans to develop is itself."[1] Here a crucial turning point emerges imperceptibly. The foundation of modern industrial society (of the 1960s) is no longer the real relationship between commodity and consumption in the material production in traditional societies. The spectacle, on the other hand, takes it over, and the order of economics is ruled by *visual images*. Therefore, the real goals (including the advancement of social history and human needs) are dissolved while the spectacle is everything that counts: the spectacle is the goal. The later-day scholars all point out that in the 1960s when Debord developed his theory the spectacle was only in its budding stage. The contemporary spectacular society, according to Erjavec, has been in a fully developed stage.[2] Debord also found for himself that after twenty years "the spectacle has thus continued to gather strength, that is, to spread to the furthest limits on all sides, while increasing its density in the center."[3]

Second, *the ideological function of the spectacle*. Debord argues that the manifestations of the existence and authority of the spectacle just prove the legitimacy of the existing capitalism. The mass unconsciously affirm the governance of the present situation in their submission to the spectacle. So the spectacle is also the "permanent presence" of the justification of the ruling capitalism. This has shown the ideological function of the spectacle. To be more specific, it includes three aspects: its anchoring of the mass in the "already made choice" in the capitalist production and consumption through positive appearance; or in other words, each and every context of the detail

---

[1] Debord, Guy. *The Society of the Spectacle*, Trans. Donald Nickleson-Smith, New York: Zone Books, 1994. p. 16.

[2] *See* Erjavec, Alec. *Toward the Image*, Changchun: Jilin People's Press, 2003, p. 27.

[3] Debord, Guy. *Comments on the Society of the Spectacle*, Trans. Malcolm Imrie, London: Verso, 1998. p. 1.

we have today has to unconsciously confront a world of the object of desires decorated by the manifestation of advertisements. The ads reign in its vast territory while we, disabled, have nowhere to escape from it. The elegant and glamorous scenes, the slender images of beautiful ladies, modes and patterns of the fashionable life style and all sorts of persuasive and eloquent expertise or advice, trap each and every individual in its colorful and appealing spectacles, invariably from their superficially reasonable perception to their deep covert desires. *Debord once criticized the experts in service of the spectacle, saying,* "All experts serve the state and the media and only in that way do they achieve their status. Every expert follows his master, for all former possibilities for independence have been gradually reduced to nil by present society's mode of organization. The most useful expert, of course, is the one who can lie. With their different motives, those who need experts are falsifiers and fools."[1] The world is an omnipresent spectacle, from which we cannot escape, nor can we defy. We directly admit the existing system by purchasing the spectacle and unconsciously conforming to the model of the spectacular life. In *La Société du Spectacle*, Debord defines it as "conceited acceptance." He says, "The spectacle *proclaims* the predominance of appearances and asserts that all human life, which is to say all social life, is mere appearance."[2] Second, the censored spectacle is undoubtedly the accomplice of the justification of the existing system. The spectacle is of course a *covert* ideology. In other words, the various spectacles manifested before us either through advertising or through other images are in essence to unconsciously manipulate or identify our structure of desires. We ascertain the capitalist market system by means of fervent pursuit of commodities, or, allured by the spectacular culture, willingly changing into groveling slaves by mistaking the existing system for the real way of being. Thirdly, the spectacle realizes its overall control over modern man by dominating most of the time outside one's production, a discovery made by Debord of the new form of governance of contemporary capitalism. It is the control over man's

---

[1] Debord, Guy. *Comments on the Society of the Spectacle*, Trans. Malcolm Imrie, London: Verso, 1998. p.7.

[2] Debord, Guy. *The Society of the Spectacle*, Trans. Donald Nickleson-Smith, New York: Zone Books, 1994. p. 14.

non-production hours. The preys of the spectacle are just the leisure time outside labor. The unconscious psychological and cultural control and the manufacturing of man's false consumption take place silently outside the labor hours. Thus the capital considerably expands its reign on man in space and time. And when the spectacle subverts man's desire in all his leisure time, the material production is made farther away from man's real need and serves more directly the increase of the capital's surplus value.

But what is the virtue of the spectacle? What does it have to hold firm to modern man? Debord offers the following answer:

> The spectacle manifests itself as an enormous positivity, out of reach and beyond dispute. All it says is: "Everything that appears is good; whatever is good will appear." The attitude that it demands in principle is the same passive acceptance that it has already secured by means of its seeming incontrovertibility, and indeed by its monopolization of the realm of appearances.[1]

The things in the spectacular scenes are indisputable, and the spectacle is itself monologue after monologue of which we are unable to give a critical survey in its manifestation which demands submission rather than conversation.

In his 1974 film, Debord announces, "We are never to partake in the spectacle. We are merely spectators." He holds that "when television has shown a fine picture and explained it with a brazen lie, idiots believe that everything is clear."[2] Or we can describe this situation in de Certeau's words, "The television viewer cannot write anything on the screen of his set. He has been dislodged from the product; he plays no role in its apparition. He loses his author's rights and becomes, or so it seems, a pure reviewer."[3] (For

---

[1] Debord, Guy. *The Society of the Spectacle*, Trans. Donald Nickleson-Smith, New York: Zone Books, 1994. p. 15.

[2] Debord, Guy. *Comments on the Society of the Spectacle*, Trans. Malcolm Imrie, London: Verso, 1998. p. 22.

[3] Certeau, Michel de. *The Practice of Everyday Life*. Trans. Steven Rendall. Berkeley: University of California Press, 2002. p. 31.

instance, the average people can never say no to the tireless demonstration of the functions of the cars and digital cameras in the daily TV commercials. The video recorder may be promoted today, and the excellence of VCD may be displayed tomorrow, and the day after tomorrow we will be given a DVD with high definition. When all kinds of useless electric appliances fill each and every family, the capitalists behind the ever-disappearing and ever-generating spectacles laugh their heads off with money in their pockets. Such is the mute violence of the spectacle, with its logic being the invisible colonial one.)

> The flow of images carries everything before it, and it is similarly someone else who controls at will this simplified summary of the sensible world; who decides where the flow will lead as well as the rhythm of what should be shown, like some perpetual, arbitrary surprise, leaving no time for reflection, and entirely independent of what the spectator might understand or think of it.[1]

The imperialistic logic of the spectacle is undoubtedly that "Everything that appears is good; whatever is good will appear." In his *La Société du Spectacle*, appearing with this voiceover is none but Castro speaking before the TV camera. The manifestation is prescribed by force, and the tautological appearance of the spectacle is monopolized as well, which in turn is sustained by a one-dimensional affirmation that demands no reply. Such is the truth behind the spectacle. Debord points out that "[t]he erasure of the personality is the fatal accompaniment to an existence which is concretely submissive to the spectacle's rules, ever more removed from the possibility of authentic experience and thus from the discovery of individual preferences."[2] So we are left before us only one path: passive acceptance. Of course there exist different voices on this issue. For example, Kellner thinks that the spectacle is not ever invincible as thought of by Debord; instead, it may also sink into a

---

[1] Debord, Guy. *Comments on the Society of the Spectacle*, Trans. Malcolm Imrie, London: Verso, 1998. p. 11.

[2] Ibid., pp. 12-13.

dilemma of self-contradiction or reversion.

According to Debord, the success of the domination of the spectacular capitalism lies in its secret of removing the lived history from one's memory, or the demolishment of history. He analyzes this point in his *Comments on The Society of the Spectacle* in 1988:

> Spectacular domination's first priority was to eradicate historical knowledge in general; beginning with just about all rational information and commentary on the most recent past. The evidence for this is so glaring that it hardly needs further explanation. With consummate skill the spectacle organizes ignorance of what is about to happen and, immediately afterwards, the forgetting of whatever has nonetheless been understood. The more important something is, the more it is hidden.[1]

It is so because only being ignorant of historical knowledge and indifferent to the pre-existed time can one conform to the false presence presented by the spectacles. According to Debord, it isolates all it shows from its context, its past, its intentions and its consequences. It is thus completely illogical. Since no one may contradict it, it has the right to contradict itself, to correct its own past. It is the most forgetful. The products or "guidelines for health" that all the tabloids in the newspaper stands spare no efforts to promote today may well be under fierce attack tomorrow in the ads of promoting another product or medicine. What is more outrageous is that the spectacle can even directly hide the truth of the event that just takes place.

The precious advantage which the spectacle has acquired through the outlawing of history, from having driven the recent past into hiding, and from having made everyone forget the spirit of history within society, is above all the ability to cover its own tracks—to conceal the very progress of its recent world conquest. Its power already seems familiar, as if it had always been there. All usurpers have shared this

---

[1] Debord, Guy. *Comments on the Society of the Spectacle*, Trans. Malcolm Imrie, London: Verso, 1998. p. 6.

aim: to make us forget that they have only just arrived.[1]

In all, the spectacle manipulates everything and leaves nothing in our view except the scenes it wants to present. "When the spectacle stops talking about something for three days, it is as if it did not exist. For it has then gone on to talk about something else, and it is that which henceforth, in short, exists."[2] Debord's comment is insightful. For example, the present-day media makes it a routine to announce the "force-out" of some singer or public celebrity, and it is invariably successful. For if only absent form the spectacle for some time, however famous one is, one is doomed to disappear silently for ever without hope of making a further stir in the public, like a stone sinking in the depth of the sea. Because one's presence is just a spectacular one, and the force-out of one's spectacular presentation equals the direct murder of one's self. In *La Société du Spectacle*, Debord speaks of the stars' desperate attempts to squeeze a way into the spectacle. He says that we can only sense and concern about what the present spectacle wants us to inform us of, and we are left in the dark about where they come and how they happen like this. He says with the destruction of history, contemporary events themselves retreat into a remote and fabulous realm of unverifiable stories, uncheckable statistics, unlikely explanations and untenable reasoning. Such predications are no strange to us and fill us with indescribable fear.

Struggling in the fallacious light of the images, Debord declares with a touch of sorrow that the spectacle "is the sun that never sets on the empire of modern passivity. It covers the entire globe, basking in the perpetual warmth of its own glory."[3]

By means of the spectacle the ruling order discourses endlessly upon itself in an uninterrupted monologue of self-praise. The spectacle is

---

[1] Debord, Guy. *Comments on the Society of the Spectacle*, Trans. Malcolm Imrie, London: Verso, 1998. p. 6.

[2] Ibid., p. 8.

[3] Debord, Guy. *The Society of the Spectacle*, Trans. Donald Nickleson-Smith, New York: Zone Books, 1994. p. 15.

the self-portrait of power in the age of power's totalitarian rule over the conditions of existence. The fetishistic appearance of pure objectivity in spectacular relationships conceals their true character as relationships between human beings and between classes; a second Nature thus seems to impose inescapable laws upon our environment.[1]

He further acknowledges that "as the indispensable packaging for things produced as they are now produced, as a general gloss on the rationality of the system, and as the advanced economic sector directly responsible for the manufacture of an ever-growing mass of image-objects, the spectacle is the *chief product* of present-day society."[2] This confirms the unshakable ruling position of the spectacle in the present society, being its "chief product." This implies the following three layers of meaning: First, none of the commodity productions of today is able to break away from the packaging of the manifestation and promotion of the spectacle. We can even go so far as to say that no production of commodity is possible without the spectacle. Second, as a chief product of the society, the spectacle has established the advanced state of its self-production and manufacturing. It seems to be the most important and eminent economic sector of the present. Third, the spectacle plays a key role of representing and sustaining the basic principles of the prevailing capitalist structure. Kellner points out that "for Debord, the spectacle is a tool of pacification and de-politicization; [...] which stupefies social subjects and distances them from the most urgent task of real life."[3]

Another important viewpoint Debord makes is his definite objection to the neutral hiding of the ideological feature in the spectacle by means of *the media*. In response to the prevailing term of "the Age of Mass Media" in the western academia in the 1970s, Debord argues,

Rather than talk of the spectacle, people often prefer to use the

[1] Debord, Guy. *The Society of the Spectacle*, Trans. Donald Nickleson-Smith, New York: Zone Books, 1994. p. 19.

[2] Ibid., p. 16.

[3] Kellner, Douglas. *Media Spectacle*, London & New York: Routledge, 2003. pp. 2-3.

term "media." And by this they mean to describe a mere instrument, a kind of public service which with impartial "professionalism" would facilitate the new wealth of mass communication through mass media a form of communication which has at last attained a unilateral purity, whereby decisions already taken are presented for passive admiration.[1]

As a form of governance, Debord's spectacle and the so-called "media" in media theories are two completely heterogeneous expressions, with the latter referring to only an ordinary tool of communication. The key lies in that no neutral media ever exist. They are, instead, "officially independent but in fact secretly linked by various ad hoc networks."[2] Debord points his sword at the founder of media theory, accusing him of making single-handedly the so-called kingdom of media theory of the "extension of the body" of man. He criticizes poignantly,

> McLuhan himself, the spectacle's first apologist, who had seemed to be the most convinced imbecile of the century, changed his mind when he finally discovered in 1976 that "the pressure of the mass media leads to irrationality," and that it was becoming urgent to modify their usage. The sage of Toronto had formerly spent several decades marveling at the numerous freedoms created by a "global village" instantly and effortlessly accessible to all.[3]

Apparently in Debord's theoretical vision, there is such media as a tool which is talked about favorably by everyone. He thinks what is visible to our eyes is only the active and ubiquitous spectacle, the ever invincible weapon of the reign of contemporary capitalism, whereas the touching legend of the era of mass media is but one of the spectacular society with the bourgeois ideology.

---

[1] Debord, Guy. *Comments on the Society of the Spectacle*, Trans. Malcolm Imrie, London: Verso, 1998. p. 3.

[2] Ibid., p. 5.

[3] Ibid., p. 13.

4. Separation: the deep realistic background of presentational spectacle

According to Debord, *separation* is the direct cause of the spectacle of contemporary society. Interestingly enough, here he does not use the familiar term *alienation* as his keyword. He remarks that "Separation is the alpha and omega of the spectacle."[1] I have noticed that in his own theoretical argumentation he never deserts the logic of Marxian critique on religion in *Thesis on Feuerbach*; and the Marxian thoughts once again are carried forward:

> Philosophy is at once the power of alienated thought and the thought of alienated power, and as such it has never been able to emancipate itself from theology. The spectacle is the material reconstruction of the religious illusion. Not that its techniques have dispelled those religious mists in which human beings once located their own powers, the very powers that had been wrenched from them— but those cloud-enshrouded entities have now been brought down to earth. It is thus the most earthbound aspects of life that have become the most impenetrable and rarefied. The absolute denial of life, in the shape of a fallacious paradise, is no longer projected onto the heavens, but finds its place instead within material life itself. The spectacle is hence a technological version of the exiling of human powers in a "world beyond"—and the perfection of separation within human being.[2]

As is known to all, Marx accuses Feuerbach of not attaching importance to the separation of real life as the foundation of theology, and that the eradication of illusion lies in the change of the contradictions in life. Debord, however, thinks of the spectacle as the reconstruction of the religious illusion, which mystifies life itself. The denial of the bourgeois enlightenment of the religious mist is admittedly the reconstruction of the secular life. In

---

[1] Debord, Guy. *The Society of the Spectacle*, Trans. Donald Nickleson-Smith, New York: Zone Books, 1994. p. 20.

[2] Ibid., p. 18.

the industrial modernity built on cements and armored concretes, the brave city of God on the other shore has been the reformation of natural reality as its object. And the abstinency and otherworldliness of theology have been substituted by the emancipation of sensible desires and hedonism of this world. However, Debord thinks that the spectacle today has again turned the world into a "paradise of illusion." The real life in the spectacle is controlled fast by the ephemeral illusion. Here the illusion comes back, never in the form of the sacred paradise, but something nearby. What a profound and insightful metaphor! In a word, hardly have we stepped on the materialized and solid ground from the ephemeral religious illusion than we stumble again in Debord's mist of the spectacle.

Debord thinks that as far as the research on the geneology of theology is concerned, "religious contemplation in its earliest form was the outcome of the establishment of the social division of labor and the formation of classes. Power draped itself in the outward garb of a mythical order from the beginning. In former times the category of the sacred justified the cosmic and ontological ordering of things that best served the interests of the masters, expounding upon and embellishing what society *could not deliver*."[1] It is well said. The contradiction and separation is the original form of religious illusion, the hierarchy of the land has to be hallowed by the hierarchy in the heavens. In brief, the gods in heaven protect the profits of man on the earth. In this sense, religion has some touch of the spectacle, with its essence being a shared acknowledgment of loss, an imaginary compensation for a poverty of real social activity that was still widely felt to be a universal fact of life. But Debord also finds that compared with the spectacular side of religion, the spectacle today has an opposite function:

> The modern spectacle, by contrast, depicts *what society can deliver*, but within this depiction *what is permitted* is rigidly distinguished from *what is possible*. The spectacle preserves unconsciousness as practical changes in the conditions of existence proceed. The spectacle

---

[1] Debord, Guy. *The Society of the Spectacle*, Trans. Donald Nickleson-Smith, New York: Zone Books, 1994. p. 20.

is self-generated, and it makes up its own rules: it is a specious form of the sacred. And it makes no secret of *what it is*, namely, hierarchical power evolving on its own, in its separateness, thanks to an increasing productivity based on an ever more refined division of labor, an ever greater comminuting of machine-governed gestures, and an ever-widening market. In the course of this development all community and critical awareness have ceased to be; nor have those forces, which were able—by separating—to grow enormously in strength, yet found a way to *reunite*.[1]

Debord sees this as a significant heterogeneity. Different from the function of the religious illusion to compensate for what reality cannot, the present-day spectacle just manifests what reality can deliver. And, no! To be precise, it should only be called "what is permitted" instead of "what is possible." One is controlled covertly in the spectacle, having to submit to the rules of the game prescribed by the spectacle so that the separation that really emerges in reality is hidden. First, the development of the society has the increase of productivity, not the need of man himself, as its end; and that the growth of wealth is the only immanent driving force of the social movement while the existence of man becomes the tool for the mad pursuit of profit. This is the standpoint Marx makes of the inversion of means and ends in the capitalist mode of production. Then, the subjectivity of the individual has been fragmented into some posture, action, or the tailpiece of some external forces by the machine system and division of labor, so it is no longer the full development of himself. *I don't quite think it is a new idea, as Schiller, Marx and Young Lukacs all thoroughly argued about it.* Third, people have no choice but to identify it in front of the aberration of this external reality, so as to lose unconsciously all the critical negative dimensions of his own. (As for this point, Marcuse discusses more clearly and in greater details in his *One-Dimensional Man*.) Debord recognizes that all the aforesaid important social separations are hidden tightly in the spectacle. It is easy to find that his idea

---

[1] Debord, Guy. *The Society of the Spectacle*, Trans. Donald Nickleson-Smith, New York: Zone Books, 1994. p. 21.

only sums up again some basic concepts in certain existing critical theories of the society, and is therefore only old wine in a new bottle.

Next, Debord puts forth his theoretical critique of the separation in the spectacular society. Like before, this time he imitates young Marx and young Lukacs. Interestingly, however, he does not borrow the category of alienation from young Marx nor use the conception of reification by Marx and young Lukacs. Instead, he enumerates a demonstrative and informal word, separation. But in the film *La Société du Spectacle* he quotes in the black screen a paragraph from young Marx's *Economic and Philosophical Manuscript of 1844*. Debord argues that separation is the foundation of social reality where the spectacle is generated. In *La Société du Spectacle* this statement is accompanied by pictures of the workers at the automobile workshops. To be specific, alienation in this situation includes the following aspects:

First, the separation of the workers from their products. "Though separated from his product, man is more and more, and ever more powerfully, the producer of every detail of his world. The closer his life comes to being his own creation, the more drastically is he cut off from that life."[1] Those who are familiar with Marx's *Economic and Philosophical Manuscript of 1844* all know the origin of this quote, only that the alienation of product turns to "separation" of it. Debord's context does have something in common with that of young Marx in 1844, but he does not make clear what is the internal connection between the separation of the worker from his product with the spectacle. Clearly, this "separation" is not a new thing in the life of today's capitalist world. In *La Société du Spectacle*, the equivalent for this statement is the scene of the contrast between the workers in the worksite and the skyscrapers they have built up. Debord asserts, "Man separates himself from his own product."

Second, the separation from direct socialization between the producers. In Debord's view, the generalized separation of worker and product has

---

[1] Debord, Guy. *The Society of the Spectacle*, Trans. Donald Nickleson-Smith, New York: Zone Books, 1994. p. 24.

spelled the end of any comprehensive view of the job done, as well as the end of direct personal communication between producers. As the accumulation of alienated products proceeds, and as the productive process gets more concentrated, consistency and communication become the exclusive assets of the system's managers. The triumph of an economic system founded on separation leads to the *proletarianization* of the world. I still see nothing new in this section. But Debord no longer relies on *Economic and Philosophical Manuscript in 1844* here but sets out from the *Economics Manuscript of 1857-1858* or *Das Kapital*. Or, to be more precise, the self-sufficient process of labor activity is dissolved into fragmented activities due to the division of labor and market exchange, the producers are no longer face to face with each other, and the direct exchange relationship of the goods is replaced by the medium of the market of commodities. The difference is, in the liberal capitalist age which Smith and Marx confronts, the indirect communication completed by the market is not directly monopolized by the rulers, but Debord seems to think that in his age the play of the monopoly economic structure's overall control over society is on show and this direct control forms the most important foundation for the making of the spectacle by the capitalists. It is a pity, though, that Debord does not further elaborate on this issue.

Third, the separation of the non-work time. Please note that this is Debord's contribution. He thinks that the separation of production itself will surely result in the fact that "that fundamental area of experience which was associated in earlier societies with an individual's principal work is being transformed... into a realm of non-work, of inactivity,"[1] and will be "at least at the leading edge of the system's evolution."[2] In other words, the experience linked with the sensible and concrete work in the earlier capitalist society has been substituted by the inactive leisure life outside work. The point is that the non-work time is just a part of the separated reality.

---

[1] Debord, Guy. *The Society of the Spectacle*, Trans. Donald Nickleson-Smith, New York: Zone Books, 1994. p. 21.

[2] Ibid.

Such inactivity, however, is by no means emancipated from productive activity: it remains in thrall to that activity, in an uneasy and worshipful subjection to production's needs and results; indeed it is itself a product of the rationality of production. There can be no freedom apart from activity, and within the spectacle all activity is banned—a corollary of the fact that all real activity has been forcibly channeled into the global construction of the spectacle. So what is referred to as "liberation from work," that is, increased leisure time, is a liberation neither within labor itself nor from the world labor has brought into being.[1]

Therefore, in the capitalist production, workers are from the outset in a passive position before the immense power of manipulation of the automatic machinery system. Marx has noticed this too. What Marx fails to see is that in the supposedly pleasant leisure hours, man does not develop in a free or thorough way in hope of realizing a free creativity at his will; on the contrary, he is equally in thrall and inactive. Despair comes into being henceforward, while the reign of the spectacular control no longer is realized solely within the production time. Instead, what it is good at is the manipulation of and control over the leisure time outside work. Enslaved by the spectacular, the leisure time which hopefully permits the full play of creativity is also filled with an *inactivity* which appears active but is internally passive. At this stage, man is totally reduced to the Monkey King who cannot escape from the palm of Buddha. He lives in the spectacle whenever and wherever he is. In *La Société du Spectacle*, the scenes of people's spending their vacations on the beach and other scenic spots frequently appear.

Debord points out indisputably that the wretched inactivity in the existence in the leisure time outside work is not released from the production process, but is manufactured by the spectacle itself. Why does he say so? In the capitalist spectacular life, all goods *proposed by the spectacular system*, from cars to televisions, also serve as weapons for that system as

---

[1] Debord, Guy. *The Society of the Spectacle*, Trans. Donald Nickleson-Smith, New York: Zone Books, 1994. p. 22.

it strives to reinforce the isolation of "the lonely crowd". The spectacle is continually rediscovering its own basic assumptions—and each time in a more concrete manner. It is apparent that in the capitalist societies man has only to face what the spectacle forces upon him, and he is only an audience passively receiving all the images. One no longer conforms to his own constitution, nor even knows about his own real need. Neither does he extend his creativity and activity, as all the modes of the leisure time are pre-established by the spectacle. In all, the capital logic exercises a brand-new colonization on the non-work time. In sunny holidays we may go traveling, having outdoor exercises, or spend time in shops, restaurants, and other places of entertainment. But nearly all these activities are invisibly instigated and predesigned by the spectacle. Under the glamorous cover of activity and creativity, what really exists is a *pseudo-activity*, in essence an inactivity with no sense of individualization. Debord says accordingly, "The erasure of the personality is the fatal accompaniment to an existence which is concretely submissive to the spectacle's rules, ever more removed from the possibility of authentic experience and thus from the discovery of individual preferences."[1] Kellner claims that "in submissively consuming spectacle one is estranged from actively producing one's life."[2]

> The spectator's alienation from and submission to the contemplated object (which is the outcome of his unthinking activity) works like this: the more he contemplates, the less he lives; the more readily he recognizes his own needs in the images of need proposed by the dominant system, the less he understands his own existence and his own desires. The spectacle's externality with respect to the acting subject is demonstrated by the fact that the individual's own gestures are no longer his own, but rather those of someone else who represents them to him. The spectator feels at home nowhere, for the spectacle is everywhere.[3]

---

[1] Debord, Guy. *Comments on the Society of the Spectacle*, Trans. Malcolm Imrie, London: Verso, 1998. pp. 12-13.

[2] Kellner, Douglas. *Media Spectacle*, London & New York: Routledge, 2003. p. 3.

[3] Debord, Guy. *The Society of the Spectacle*, Trans. Donald Nickleson-Smith, New York: Zone Books, 1994. p. 23.

A ready example is the numerous film and TV media and print media, whose content and targets are pre-designed, with all the things we are supposed to expect and pursue manufactured by the business people hiding behind the curtain. Once we internalize the images as our own desires, we will lose track of the real needs of our own. This is what Debord means when he says "the more readily he recognizes his own needs in the images of need proposed by the dominant system, the less he understands his own existence and his own desires."[1] (In fact, it is only self-evident that in his expounding here he borrows the idea of alienation from *Economic and Philosophical Manuscript of 1844*.)

Finally, the spectacle is a new machine to produce and gild alienation. In today's society, "Workers do not produce themselves: they produce a force independent of themselves." It sounds like having nothing to do with separation, rather the emergence of **alienation**. This is a very important theoretical switchover. Yet it is a pity that he does not explain the significance of it.

> The *success* of this production, that is, the abundance it generates, is experienced by its producers only as an *abundance of dispossession*. All time, all space, becomes foreign to them as their own alienated products accumulate. The spectacle is a map of this new world—a map drawn to the scale of the territory itself. In this way the very powers that have been snatched from us *reveal* themselves to us in their full force.[2]

Here the discourse is overly metaphysical and paradoxical. How do the powers snatched from us reveal themselves to us? Why is the spectacle the map of this new world of alienation? Debord gives no further explanation but stresses that "[t]he spectacle's function in society is the concrete manufacture of alienation."[3] However, he forgets to give a detailed analysis of the connection between the crucial theory of alienation and separation.

---

[1] Debord, Guy. *The Society of the Spectacle*, Trans. Donald Nickleson-Smith, New York: Zone Books, 1994. p. 23.

[2] Ibid.

[3] Ibid.

This chapter ends with the statement that "The spectacle is *capital* accumulated to the point where it becomes image."[1] This certainly is a step further in his theoretical logic. Obviously the relationship between the capital and the spectacle is the next topic he is to discuss in detail.

II. Fetishism of Spectacle: The Totally Successful Colonization of Commodity

In *The Society of the Spectacle*, Debord reaffirms the critique Marx has in his historical phenomenology on the reification of capitalist economy. Debord points out in Chapter II and III that the emergence of the spectacle in contemporary mode of capitalist production reinforces the hegemonic logic constituted by the earlier commodity, money and capital. In other words, the spectacle not only fails to eradicate the three fetishisms as the bourgeois ideology; on the other hand, it colonizes the economic fetishism as the unconscious desire in the individual through the bombardment of images. I think this is one of the most important viewpoints in the whole theoretical framework of Debord's theory. The idea directly influences Baudrillard, Best, Kellner and the others in their post-modern media critique, which deserves our contemplation.

1. From fetishism of commodity to fetishism of spectacle

At the end of Chapter I, Debord makes the finishing point like this: "The spectacle is **capital** accumulated to the point where it becomes image."[2] According to my understanding, this provides an important logical orientation, which, to be exact, should be the conclusion of the logical analysis of Chapter I. Why do I say so? We might as well first have a look at Debord's analysis.

At the beginning of this chapter, Debord quotes from young Lukács'

---

[1] Debord, Guy. *The Society of the Spectacle*, Trans. Donald Nickleson-Smith, New York: Zone Books, 1994. p. 24.

[2] Ibid.

History and Class Consciousness, meaning that only when commodity becomes a generalized social category can the relationship of commodity, in particular the materialization of economy in the capitalist mode of production play its determining role upon society. As I have argued before, young Lukacs' narration is problematic: in the historical phenomenological critique Marx contends that only in the fully-developed capitalist market economy can fundamental dominating logic of reified inversion prevail when the capitalist relationship becomes the "illuminating light." Debord agrees with young Lukacs when he argues that the submission, as labor is increasingly rationalized and mechanized, is enhanced by the fact that the activities of human beings become less active and more imaginary. This corresponds to the problems stated by Debord in his previous chapter in which "**submission**" and "**absence of activity**" are highlighted. Of course his theoretical intention is to introduce his own new explanation from the statement Lukacs made forty years ago.

Debord elaborates,

"The self-movement of the spectacle consists in this: it arrogates to itself everything that in human activity exists in **a fluid state** so as to possess it in a congealed form—as things that, being the negative expression of living value, have become exclusively abstract value. In these signs we recognize our old enemy the **commodity**, which appears at first sight a very trivial thing, and easily understood, yet which is in reality a very queer thing, abounding in metaphysical subtleties."[1]

He implies that the principle for the existence of the spectacle is in reality an extension of the principle of the commodity, the demonstration of the very being in life *in an inverted manner*. However, with all its changes and variations it is in essence the principle of *commodity fetishism* which Marx repudiates: "The domination of society by things whose qualities are 'at

---

[1] Debord, Guy. *The Society of the Spectacle*, Trans. Donald Nickleson-Smith, New York: Zone Books, 1994. p. 26.

the same time perceptible and imperceptible by the senses.'"[1] This is also the story derived from that of the wooden table: a commodity realizes itself by the imperceptible value behind the perceptible material, so once the invisible value relationship transits itself from the reification of the value equivalent to sign in the form of money, it replaces the real wealth subversively in an empty form. The reason why the people are madly in pursuit and worship of money is that the possession of money means the possession of the world. Debord thinks that the spectacle carries out and develops the principle of commodity fetishism, as "this principle is absolutely fulfilled in the spectacle, where the perceptible world is replaced by a set of images that are superior to that world yet at the same time impose themselves as eminently perceptible."[2] Here *usurpation* again takes place. However, in Marx's opinion, the use value of the real commodity in the capitalist market economy is realized by submitting to its value, so money that can generate more money (the capital relationship) as the symbolic substitution takes over the throne with justification. But the real existence is replaced by its images in today's capitalist world, and people always unconsciously possess these images as authenticity. What a *spectacle fetishism*! It entails the most important logic of Baudrillard who apparently foregrounds Debord's spectacle as a more abstract symbolic sign, which he elaborates in his *For a Critique of the Political Economy of the Sign*. The internal generating mechanism of spectacle fetishism turns things into images by demolishing the real being of them and then vaporizing them into fantastic vision. Debord analyzes this mechanism in great detail.

In the previous relationship of commodity exchange, the commodity form is characterized exclusively by self-equivalence—it is exclusively quantitative in nature: the quantitative is what it develops, and it can only develop within the quantitative. Marx, Weber, Simmel, and the later-day Adorno and Horkheimer all probe into this issue. At that time man and goods of various qualities have to be represented only by the uniform currency,

---

[1] Debord, Guy. *The Society of the Spectacle*, Trans. Donald Nickleson-Smith, New York: Zone Books, 1994. p. 26.

[2] Ibid.

so the quality of things is eradicated. As a matter of fact, Debord does not concern about the deeper background behind this quantification as much as he does the abstract labor and general production as the precondition of the relationship of value quantity.

According to Debord's analysis, "the condition of existence of human groups"[1] in traditional society is conditioned by a "*real unconscious history.*"[2] By "unconscious" he means that in the early capitalist societies the axis of the relationship between man and nature is man as the "slave" (in Engels' words) of the external natural world, so man cannot consciously become the master of nature while the development of the production forces of industrial capitalism changes this condition from its very foundation.

Wherever it encountered the social conditions of large-scale trade and capital accumulation, however, such production successfully established total hegemony over the economy. The entire economy then became what the commodity, throughout this campaign of conquest, had shown itself to be—namely, a process of quantitative development. The unceasing deployment of economic power in the shape of commodities has transfigured human labor into labor-as-commodity, into *wage-labor*, and eventually given rise to an abundance thanks to which the basic problem of survival, though solved, is solved in such a way that it is not disposed of, but is rather forever cropping up again at a higher level. Economic growth liberates societies from the natural pressures occasioned by their struggle for survival, but they still must be liberated from their liberators. The *independence* of the commodity has spread to the entire economy over which the commodity now reigns. The economy transforms the world, but it transforms it into a world of the economy. The pseudo-nature in which labor has become alienated demands that such labor remain in its *service* indefinitely, and inasmuch

[1] Debord, Guy. *The Society of the Spectacle*, Trans. Donald Nickleson-Smith, New York: Zone Books, 1994. p. 27.

[2] Ibid.

as this estranged activity is answerable only to itself it is able in turn to enroll all socially permissible efforts and projects under its banner.[1]

Debord means briefly that, in the mature capitalist commodity-market economy, the previous pressure out of the conflict between man and nature is gradually reduced in the large-scale trade and accumulation of capital to the point of the so-called "state of abundance," so the principal problem of the survival of man is settled. But the development of society does not change the alienation of man, who, submitting to nature in the past, now submits to the *pseudo-nature* created by his own economic power. Hegel terms it as "second-nature." The young Lukacs and Adorno both borrow this Hegelian term. Thus, "the economy transforms the world, but it transforms it into a world of the economy." The economic power of capitalism, the liberator of man from nature, in actuality does not liberate man, but constructs another hegemony of reified economic power which equally ignores the will of man. This is apparently similar to Marx's judgment. Debord thinks that with the coming of the industrial revolution, the division of labor specific to that revolution's manufacturing system, and mass production for a world market, the commodity emerged in its full-fledged form as a force aspiring to the complete colonization of social life. This time Debord makes a really original discovery. Emergence is the specific concept with which Debord defines his spectacle. Different from the Marxian thought of the reified inversion of the capitalist social relationship, Debord attaches importance to the inverted reified reality itself which once again emerges deceivingly. Full-fledged emergence refers to the appearance and spectacle of the existence en bloc. Another point different from economy fetishism is that commodity, money and capital fetishism all take place spontaneously and unconsciously. But the manifestation of the spectacle, by contrast, is *intentional*. Later Zizek elaborates on this, poignantly too, which he refers to as "ideological cynicism." I will return to this part in the last chapter of this book.

Debord declares, "The spectacle corresponds to the historical moment

---

[1] Debord, Guy. *The Society of the Spectacle*, Trans. Donald Nickleson-Smith, New York: Zone Books, 1994. p. 28.

at which the commodity completes its *colonization* of social life."[1] It is a new stage of commodity colonization, as "[i]t is not just that the relationship to commodities is now plain to see—commodities are now all that there is to see; the world we see is the world of the commodity."[2] Or, the commodity economy has successfully covered the real and direct social relationship between men, and the spectacle further *fantasizes* this inverted material relationship into the images that veil the existence. The world is a spectacle and the spectacle is the God of life who overwhelmingly manipulates everything. So the brand-new spectacle fetishism enters with its sweeping majesty.

2. The pseudo-effect and pseudo-recreation in the process of being watched

According to Debord, the new type of spectacle fetishism has undergone two crucial qualitative changes: First, in spectacle fetishism, "exchange value eventually gained the upper hand. The process of exchange became indistinguishable from any conceivable utility, thereby placing use value at its mercy. Starting out as the condottiere of use value, exchange value ended up waging a war that was entirely its own."[3] In his film *La Société du Spectacle*, Debord states that use value finds its expression in exchange value. This is elaborated by his follower Baudrillard. The use value of commodity is for contemplation only. This is a very important theoretical statement, though it of course goes a little too far. Debord discovers,

> The spectacle is another facet of money, which is the abstract general equivalent of all commodities. But whereas money in its familiar form has dominated society as the representation of universal equivalence, that is, of the exchangeability of diverse goods whose uses are not otherwise compatible, the spectacle in its full development is

---

[1] Debord, Guy. *The Society of the Spectacle*, Trans. Donald Nickleson-Smith, New York: Zone Books, 1994. p. 29.

[2] Ibid.

[3] Ibid., p. 32.

money's modern aspect; in the spectacle the totality of the commodity world is visible in one piece, as the general equivalent of whatever society as a whole can be and do. The spectacle is money *for contemplation only*, for here the totality of use has already been bartered for the totality of abstract representation. The spectacle is not just the servant of *pseudo-use*—it is already, in itself, the pseudo-use of life.[1]

By comparing the functions of money and spectacle, Debord makes a conclusion that money as the general equivalent of commodities functions as the medium of exchange, but now it is turned into the end (wealth) so as to be elevated as an alienating force that dominates society. The instrumental function the value relationship in the past owned has been alienated imperceptibly as the desired nature of being. Once in a spectacular society, the spectacle becomes "the general equivalent of whatever society as a whole can be and do"[2], holding a position even higher than money, for "the spectacle is money *for contemplation only*."[3] And, under the contemplations from all people, the real use of commodities is usurped unavoidably by the "pseudo-use" created by the spectacle. Or, we can say that being is bartered by abstract representation. We are aware that it is Walter Benjamin who first noticed this change. In *Arcades Project*, Benjamin points out that the contemporary commodity world has been an "illusion" for contemplation, in which value is obscured by representation and demonstration. Adorno also touches upon this in his exploration of the pop culture. Debord once cites an example that even eroticism has lost its immediate real function in the spectacular society, in which the strip dance is a most obvious form of eroticism which degrades into mere spectacle. In his film he presents the scenes of strip-tease dance many times. This is an extraordinary example.

However, I think that his analysis somehow is problematic. The spectacle is indeed for "contemplation," yet it has not really and completely

---

[1] Debord, Guy. *The Society of the Spectacle*, Trans. Donald Nickleson-Smith, New York: Zone Books, 1994. pp. 32-33.

[2] Ibid., p. 33.

[3] Ibid.

replaced the use value in the original sense. It at best only makes one *ignore* the real use of things. Dominated by advertising and other media, one can only be aware of the things recognized by the spectacle, the coercion of which has been internalized into one's unconscious desire, driving one to purchase what he/she does not really need and consume what he/she does not ask for. This, however, is not identical with the so-called transformation of use value in the consumption into contemplation. Debord does not clarify the subtle connections between the two.

According to him, under the control of the spectacle,

> Replacing that necessity by the necessity of boundless economic development can only mean replacing the satisfaction of primary human needs, now met in the most summary manner, by a ceaseless manufacture of pseudo-needs, all of which come down in the end to just one—namely, the pseudo-need for the reign of an autonomous economy to continue. Such an economy irrevocably breaks all ties with authentic needs to the precise degree that it emerges from a social unconscious that was dependent on it without knowing it. "Whatever is conscious wears out. Whatever is unconscious remains unalterable. Once freed, however, surely this too must fall into ruins?" (Freud).[1]

The situation becomes more and more complicated, with even Freud as an eloquent witness to the crime of the spectacle. In fact, I do not think that Debord grasps Freud correctly.

Debord makes a justifiable analysis by recognizing the goal of the spectacular dominance is to manufacture the *pseudo-needs*, (instead of the use value of goods or commodities) and these unreal needs are constituted just by the unconscious in the manifestation of the spectacle. It is not an external coercion, but a covert manipulation with apparent non-interference. So when people live in the illusions manufactured by the spectacles, they have "the general acceptance of illusion in the consumption of modern

---

[1] Debord, Guy. *The Society of the Spectacle*, Trans. Donald Nickleson-Smith, New York: Zone Books, 1994. p. 34.

commodities. The real consumer thus becomes a consumer of illusion."[1] The consumption in the spectacle is in reality that of the illusion. It does not mean that one will have any illusion when using the goods one buys, but that one has the *illusion of motive* when thinking about *why* one wants to buy, to get involved, or to expend.

Further, if "the commodity is this illusion,"[2] then the spectacle is its "general form." If the inversion of reification is only out of one's reluctance to know the mysteries, then the logic of the commodity in the spectacle is a self-generated truth inspired by the unconscious, that is, the spectacular pseudo-truth you have identified with. Debord points out sharply that the mission of the spectacle is to persuade people to buy what they don't really need. Best and Kellner comment that the spectacle "converts direct experience into a peculiar and glittering universe of images and signs, where instead of constituting their own lives, individuals contemplate the glossy surfaces of the commodity world and adopt the psychology of a commodity self that defines itself through consumption and image, look and style, as derived from the spectacle."[3] And it is well said. Many scenes of model shows and commercials of diverse products (from underwear, food to automobiles) appear as examples in Debord's film.

If we turn our gaze back at the reality today, we know that we more often than not are not forced, but are fervent to cling to the glittering products *illuminated* by the spectacle. Or we even mistake wistfully the conspiracy of the spectacular promotion for our own desire. "Alienated consumption is added to alienated production as an inescapable duty of the masses."[4] The authentic reality by contrast often reduces one to an embarrassing situation. What Debord portrays is no legend; it has become a daily phenomenon in our lives. I wonder if it is a tragedy in China too.

---

[1] Debord, Guy. *The Society of the Spectacle*, Trans. Donald Nickleson-Smith, New York: Zone Books, 1994. p. 32.

[2] Ibid.

[3] Best, Steven and Douglas Kellner. *The Postmodern Turn*, New York: Guilford Press, 1997. p. 90.

[4] Debord, Guy. *The Society of the Spectacle*, Trans. Donald Nickleson-Smith, New York: Zone Books, 1994. p. 29.

The second important aspect of the spectacular fetishism is the direct manipulation and illusory falsification of the time outside the workers' labor hours. It strives for more commercial profits by manufacturing pseudo-leisure time and space. The truth undoubtedly makes one even more upset. Even Marx leaves open a door of hope for us by connecting the emancipation of man in the future with the dissolving of slavery labor in the realm of necessity. Now the last hope is completely colonized by the capitalists with their spectacle. Debord says,

> Whereas at the primitive stage of capitalist accumulation "political economy treats the proletarian as a mere worker" who must receive only the minimum necessary to guarantee his labor-power, and never considers him "in his leisure, in his humanity," these ideas of the ruling class are revised just as soon as so great an abundance of commodities begins to be produced that a surplus "collaboration" is required of the workers. All of a sudden the workers in question discover that they are no longer invariably subject to the total contempt so clearly built into every aspect of the organization and management of production; instead they find that every day, once work is over, they are treated like grown-ups, with a great show of solicitude and politeness, in their new role as consumers. *The humanity of the commodity* finally attends to the workers' "leisure and humanity" for the simple reason that political economy as such now can—and must—bring these spheres under its sway.[1]

This issue has much to do with the discussion we had above. As long as the capital continues to make pseudo-needs and pseudo-consumption, a great deal of non-work time must be spared for one's consumption; hence it is evidently another space the spectacle must conquer. Different from the situations in the traditional capitalist countries, the capitalists today must see to it that the workers are able to buy and have leisure for their consumption

---

[1] Debord, Guy. *The Society of the Spectacle*, Trans. Donald Nickleson-Smith, New York: Zone Books, 1994. p. 30.

in order to plunder the absolute surplus value. This new form of colonial plunder is the essence of Fordism. The "humanity of the commodity" is just the "*man-oriented*" in the manifestation of the capital. The most human designs and services are the most successful tricks played by the spectacle.

Debord thinks that the spectacle plays a crucial role in this aspect. Besides the consumption of commodities, the goals of the spectacular control include also the construction of leisure time and space. The only breathing space is now colonized as well. The capitalists "generously" turn the workers into consumers who afford time "away from production," are able to purchase and have entertainment so that they are trapped by the spectacle even in their free time. Kellner once comments, "The spectacular society spreads its wares mainly through the cultural mechanisms of leisure and consumption, services and entertainment, ruled by the dictates of advertising and a commercialized media culture. This structural shift to a society of the spectacle involves a commodification of previously non-colonized sectors of social life and the extension of bureaucratic control to the realms of leisure, desire, and everyday life."[1] The spectacular manipulation is not far from us: discounts for holidays, golden-week tours, and entertainments under various names surge in all forms of media commercials. The leisure time has been indisputably occupied by the spectacular images, which build up a pseudo-space in service of business profits. This serious event has happened, and is happening. Debord observes,

> The spectacle is a permanent opium war waged to make it impossible to distinguish goods from commodities, or true satisfaction from a survival that increases according to its own logic. Consumable survival *must* increase, in fact, because it continues to enshrine *deprivation*. The reason there is nothing beyond augmented survival, and no end to its growth, is that survival itself belongs to the realm of dispossession: it may gild poverty, but it cannot transcend it.[2]

---

[1] Kellner, Douglas. *Media Spectacle*, London & New York: Routledge, 2003. p. 3.

[2] Debord, Guy. *The Society of the Spectacle*, Trans. Donald Nickleson-Smith, New York: Zone Books, 1994. p. 31.

This is a famous section in the book. He restates it in his film. The spectacle is like an enduring opium war in which people indulge themselves and forget their demand for authentic life. In today's spectacular society, "the elevated living condition is a gilded poverty." What a heavy remark Debord makes!

3. The spectacle: counterfeiting life in the paradise of commodity

Debord thinks that separation is at the core of the spectacle, and its image of unity is constructed in its internal separation. The alienated consumption we see as a unity is likewise just built upon the immanent division between one's real need and pseudo-desire. Hence Debord remarks, "Like modern society itself, the spectacle is at once united and divided. In both, unity is grounded in a split. As it emerges in the spectacle, however, this contradiction is itself contradicted by virtue of a reversal of its meaning: division is presented as unity, and unity as division."[1] Ironically, in the introduction to Chapter II Debord borrows from an article on the issue of "one divides into two" and "two fuse into one" in China's magazine *Red Flag* (Peking), 21 September, 1964.

For him, the emergence of the spectacle always has much to do with the "abundance" of commodity. As is said above, the needs of the consumer no longer "comes from the satisfaction of the use value," but by virtue of the recognition of the **visible** spectacular value. Here,

> Each individual commodity fights for itself, cannot acknowledge the others and aspires to impose its presence everywhere as though it were alone. The spectacle is the epic poem of this strife—a strife that no fall of Ilium can bring to an end. Of arms and the man the spectacle does not sing, but rather of passions and the commodity. Within this blind struggle each commodity, following where passion leads, unconsciously actualizes something of a higher order than itself: the commodity's

---

[1] Debord, Guy. *The Society of the Spectacle*, Trans. Donald Nickleson-Smith, New York: Zone Books, 1994. p. 36.

becoming worldly coincides with the world's being transformed into commodities. So it is that, thanks to *the cunning of the commodity*, whereas all *particular* commodities wear themselves out in the fight, the commodity as abstract form continues on its way to absolute self-realization.[1]

The spectacle is an augmented epic poem, permeated with all the cunning of the commodity. All the commodities in the spectacular world are always acknowledged by the spectacular spotlight before they are introduced in the market their "sovereign authority" as if they were "the sole existence of the world." But this fabricated sovereignty is just the appearance of its brief survival. In other words, the spectacular commodity from the outset is to appear in a haste on the stage for its "sudden death" before long. If considered in this light, is it not the ironic version of "born to die"?

Each and every new product is supposed to offer a dramatic shortcut to the long-awaited promised land of total consumption. As such it is ceremoniously presented as the unique and ultimate product. But, as with the fashionable adoption of seemingly rare aristocratic first names which turn out in the end to be borne by a whole generation, so the would-be singularity of an object can be offered to the eager hordes only if it has been mass-produced. The sole real status attaching to a mediocre object of this kind is to have been placed, however briefly, at the very center of social life and hailed as the revelation of the goal of the production process. But even this spectacular prestige evaporates into vulgarity as soon as the object is taken home by a consumer—and hence by all other consumers too. At this point its essential poverty, the natural outcome of the poverty of its production, stands revealed— too late. For by this time another product will have been assigned to supply the system with its justification, and will in turn be demanding its moment of acclaim.[2]

---

[1] Debord, Guy. *The Society of the Spectacle*, Trans. Donald Nickleson-Smith, New York: Zone Books, 1994. p. 43.

[2] Ibid., p. 45.

Debord is indeed insightful! The singularity hidden behind the spectacular commodity is the mechanism of mass production, and the things that are elaborated and exaggerated today in the commercials are doomed to be the oblivious trash tucked away in tomorrow's storehouses. Whatever is glamorous and alluring in the advertisements enjoys the shortest life and once it is possessed by us, it immediately loses its luster and charm it is enshrined before. Lury calls this a *disillusioning experience*: "The actual consumption or use of goods becomes a disillusioning experience. The actuality of consumption fails to live up to the dream or the fantasy. This persistent cycle of pleasurable expectation and disappointment explains the never-ending, insatiable character of modern consumption, why people continue to shop until they drop."[1] Beyond all this Debord spots the dynamism of the spectacular capitalism at first glimpse: "It is things that rule, that are young."[2] The so-called "perpetual youth" exactly entails the *temporariness* that the spectacular things must have, the nature of them. In his film, he says that inside the freshness of commodity resides decadence.

He does not stop with all this. The spectacular things are the objects pursued by the pseudo-needs generated by the spectacle:

> It is doubtless impossible to contrast the pseudo-need imposed by the reign of modern consumerism with any authentic need or desire that is not itself equally determined by society and its history. But the commodity in the stage of its abundance attests to an absolute break in the organic development of social needs. The commodity's mechanical accumulation unleashes a *limitless artificiality* in face of which all living desire is disarmed. The cumulative power of this autonomous realm of artifice necessarily everywhere entails a *falsification of life*.[3]

The real need and desires of man all vanish in the spectacular society in

---

[1] Lury, Celia. *Consumer Culture*. New Brunswick: Rutgers University Press, 1996. p. 73.

[2] Debord, Guy. *The Society of the Spectacle*, Trans. Donald Nickleson-Smith, New York: Zone Books, 1994. p. 41.

[3] Ibid., p. 45.

which all is substituted by the shining goods manufactured by the spectacle; man's existence becomes the falsification of life. At first glance, there is actually nothing in the spectacular society but a swarm of frantic shoppers who are mediated by the alienated consumption. De Certeau thinks that this is an "enigma of consumer Sphinx." One is bewitched by the spectacle without knowing why and for what he is bewitched. The spectacular manifestation is "characterized by its ruses, its fragmentation (the result of the circumstances, its poaching, its clandestine nature, its endless but activity, in short by its quasi-invisibility, since it shows itself not in its own products (where would it place them?) but in the art of using those imposed on it."[1] On the contrary, the consumers lost in the spectacle are filled with "religious zeal," and in this way reified man proclaims his intimacy with the commodity. Following in the footsteps of the old religious fetishism, with its transported convulsionaries and miraculous cures, the fetishism of the commodity also achieves its moment of acute fervor. In the sermons of spectacular consumption, the capitalists proclaim with justification that consumers are gods. What they do is merely construct a shopping paradise for the consumers. But essentially those under the control of the spectacle are no better than a herd of wretched slaves of commodity, whose *coming to throne* is but a recognition by the other. In the shopping malls which are eulogized as paradise, they are tightly manipulated by the spectacle, and buy and consume things that are to disappear soon. The "majority" happily engrossed in the pseudo-heaven tirelessly act the role of the pathetic martyrs for the spectacle; while blessed are always those capitalists who make astounding profits. Debord gives a vivid example to illustrate this abnormal relationship:

> Waves of enthusiasm for particular products, fueled and boosted by the communications media, are propagated with lightning speed. A film sparks a fashion craze, or a magazine launches a chain of clubs that in turn spins off a line of products. The sheer **fad item** perfectly

---

[1] Certeau, Michel de. *The Practice of Everyday Life*. Trans. Steven Rendall. Berkeley: University of California Press, 2002. p. 31.

expresses the fact that, as the mass of commodities become more and more absurd, absurdity becomes a commodity in its own right. Keychains that are not paid for but come as free gifts with the purchase of some luxury product, or are then traded back and forth in a sphere far removed from that of their original use, bear eloquent witness to a mystical self-abandonment to the transcendent spirit of the commodity. Someone who collects keychains that have recently been manufactured for the sole purpose of being collected might be said to be accumulating the commodity's *indulgences*—the glorious tokens of the commodity's immanent presence among the faithful.[1]

True, capitalists manufacture the spectacle, which in turn arrests the mad mass. In this unprecedented absurd consumption of the spectacle, the initiators, the capitalists have the lion's share. To some extent, the life style shown in fashion magazines, soap operas and movies seem to be more real than the authentic life itself; a line from the film yesterday (the fun-poking slang from the character of Zhou Xingchi, or the black-humored line in a Feng Xiaogang film, to name a few) may well become a catch word overnight, and the creed of many people. A random suite of clothes some movie star wears today (the warm scarf that Bae Yong Jun, a popular Korean actor, wrapped up around his neck in the winter of several years ago, for instance) is likely to kindle a fashion storm on tomorrow's streets. It goes without saying that the spectacle not only creates pseudo consumption, it also takes a hand in the creation of life.

Not only that. Debord then points out that the spectacle not only manufactures the alienating consumption amongst the separation, but it makes spectacular pseudo-subjects, with the omnipresent **stars** and **mass** as self-evident examples. "Media stars are spectacular representations of living human beings, distilling the essence of the spectacle's banality into images of possible roles."[2] The glamour of the stars is actually set against the mundane

---

[1] Debord, Guy. *The Society of the Spectacle*, Trans. Donald Nickleson-Smith, New York: Zone Books, 1994. p. 44.

[2] Ibid., p. 38.

of the mass. This is itself a dialectics of identification with the other. "Behind the glitter of the spectacle's distractions, modern society lies in thrall to the global domination of a banalizing trend that also dominates it at each point where the most advanced forms of commodity consumption have seemingly broadened the panoply of roles and objects available to choose from."[1] Who is the star? None other than the one who has to weave dreams for our mediocre daily life. But banality does not refer to the stultification in one's career; rather, it refers to the inactivity arisen from the enslavement of everyday life by the spectacle.

Stardom is a diversification in the semblance of life—the object of an identification with *mere appearance* which is intended to compensate for the crumbling of directly experienced diversifications of productive activity. Celebrities figure various styles of life and various views of society which anyone is supposedly free to embrace and pursue in a global manner. Themselves incarnations of the inaccessible results of social **labor**, they mimic by-products of that labor, and project these above labor so that they appear as its goal.[2]

The life of the stars in totality is always imagined as the realization of a full life and individual values, and "[s]tars of decision, meanwhile, must possess the full range of accepted human qualities."[3] In his film *La Société du Spectacle*, he claims that the existence of the stars means to show the different perspectives of life. The scene on the screen is the western rock concerts and the rock stars. They have to maintain their positive and glittering images before the public, like Michael Jordan, Yao Ming, Jennifer Lopez and Maggie Cheung. They must appear before the public as shining stars without a moment of obscurity, the athletes and actors as the deputy of the commodity of the world-famous brands. For Kellner, they are "the

---

[1] Debord, Guy: *The Society of the Spectacle*, Trans. Donald Nickleson-Smith, New York: Zone Books, 1994. p. 38.

[2] Ibid.

[3] Ibid., p. 39.

icons of media culture, the gods and goddesses of everyday life."[1] The presence of the stars is just the illusion of the pseudo-subject made by the spectacle which intends to obscure the fragmentation and specialization of production of existence. So the stars become the deputy of the spectacle, whose presence arises exactly from the absence of the average man. On the other hand, Debord thinks that the nature of the stars lies in the contradiction between their glittering appearance on the stage and their real existence: "The individual who in the service of the spectacle is placed in stardom's spotlight is in fact the opposite of an individual, and as clearly the enemy of the individual in himself as of the individual in others. In entering the spectacle as a model to be identified with, he renounces all autonomy in order himself to identify with the general law of obedience to the course of things."[2] The glamour of the star is a manufactured one. One is the star just in the sense that he is not himself. Debord divides the stars that appear as the pseudo-subjects in the spectacular world into two types. One is the stars of decision, the familiar politicians who frequent TV screens and newspapers every day. The government power assumes the personified form of the pseudo-star. To some extent, politics is a completely hypocritical show, and they have achieved greatness by embracing a level of reality lower than that of the most insignificant individual life—and everyone knows it. The other type is the stars of consumption, who, thickly powdered and changing endlessly their commercial attires, never cease a moment to present themselves in the advertisements of all media. "[S]tars of consumption canvas for votes as pseudo-power over life lived. But, just as none of these celestial activities are truly global, neither do they offer any real choices."[3]

More sadly still, the spectacular life of the stars has become the illusory world admired and yearned by the mass in their banal daily life. The ordinary spectators of the spectacle often tend to sink into the false life and fake events

---

[1] Kellner, Douglas. *Media Spectacle*, London & New York: Routledge, 2003. p. 4.

[2] Debord, Guy. *The Society of the Spectacle*, Trans. Donald Nickleson-Smith, New York: Zone Books, 1994. p. 39.

[3] Ibid.

of the stars so as to beguile their boring daily existence. On the other hand they are more helplessly trapped in the abyss of the pseudo-consumption of fashionable spectacles. How about China today? Is it not just like this?

III. Pseudo-Being and the Spectacular Time

It is acknowledged that Marx penetrates the truth of historical materialism via historical time, and Heidegger realizes the secret in it by affirming the existence of the dead in the relationship between being and time. They both lay the foundation of their philosophical reforms on their clairvoyance and mastery of the real historical time. Debord on the other hand puts forth the issue of spectacular time different from historical real time in chapters V and VI in *The Society of the Spectacle*. In his view, different from the cyclical time in the traditional society and irreversible time in industrial age, the spectacular time existing in contemporary capitalist society is a consumability with a false appearance of pseudo-cyclical time, whose essence is the coverage of history and hence the manufacture of pseudo-historicity that can be consumed.

1. Static society and cyclical time

I have noticed that Debord always tries to appear more philosophical and sophisticated by virtue of turning to Hegel and Marx for help. In the arbitrary Hegelian thoughts, the natural existence of materiality has no history when he says there is nothing new under the sun. The historical time of the world is only possessed by the reason of the subject, but the people who share the subjective consciousness enter time and historical context by means of a "night" of natural being, or "the negative being." So the individual human may serve only as an apparatus of the absolute idea to realize itself via his life, but the totality of society's historical development is temporal. Entitling his fifth chapter as "Time and History," Debord denies the Hegelian concept, and tries to fuse it with Marxian idea of real socio-historical time with the movement of mode of production as its core.

Debord argues that the real historical movement is above all the slow and subtle development of the true nature of man. The existence of man initiates historical time. Debord orients time as social time. Here we can see the residue of Hegel. But in different historical stages of society, the patterns of time differ according to the modes of production. In the previous "static society," the developing history is represented as a cycle that denies time. This is where Hegel starts his logic of history in his *The Philosophy of History*.

> When a more complex society did finally attain a consciousness of time, its reaction was to deny rather than embrace it, for it viewed time not as something passing, but as something returning. This was a static type of society that organized time, true to its immediate experience of nature, on a cyclical model.[1]

To my understanding, Debord refers his static society and cyclical time mainly to the period of natural economy in human society which was based on nomadic and agricultural production. Seen from a broader time span, the society is bound to move forward slowly, but one is used to supposing the cyclical return of life and being in his natural experience due to the repetition of the natural economic mode of production and the narrow space of his existence. This is also the realistic foundation of an *imaginary* cyclical time. Debord does not formally admit this point, rather there seems to him a real objective cyclical time. Time is not the linear fluidity, but a return and cycle of some identical living condition. Debord says, among the nomads, cyclical time was already dominant in the experience of nomadic peoples, who confronted the same conditions at each moment of their roaming. And it holds true from a perspective of short-span time. The hunting and herding activities of the earlier peoples were determined by particular conditions (like the location of preys and grass), and people completed their production and reproduction in the same way in certain surroundings. Debord proposes

---

[1] Debord, Guy. *The Society of the Spectacle*, Trans. Donald Nickleson-Smith, New York: Zone Books, 1994. pp. 92-93.

that once the human society steps from nomadic life to relatively steady agrarian mode, this "cyclical time" is further enhanced as "The agrarian mode of production in general, governed by the rhythm of the seasons, was the basis of cyclical time in its fullest development. Eternity, as the return of the same here below, was **internal** to this time."[1] For thousands of years the sowing and reaping of crops are done according to the seasons. The peasants are confined to their land from generation to generation, with time forever flowing and the life style scarcely changing. This reinforces their belief in the cyclical nature of time.

Of course Debord's insight enables him to see further. He finds that a different, non-cyclical, and *irreversible* time exists just within this so-called "cyclical time": the existence of real historicity. But this is not owned by the slaves who toil and sweat on the earth, but by the new-born ruling class.

> The social appropriation of time and the production of man by means of human labor were developments that awaited the advent of a society divided into classes. The power that built itself up on the basis of the penury of the society of cyclical time—the power, in other words, of the class which organized social labor therein and appropriated the limited surplus value to be extracted, also appropriated the *temporal surplus value* that resulted from its organization of social time; this class thus had sole possession of the irreversible time of the living. The only wealth that could exist in concentrated form in the sphere of power, there to be expended on extravagance and festivity, was also expended in the form of the squandering of a *historical time at society's surface*. The owners of this historical surplus value were the masters of the knowledge and enjoyment of directly experienced events.[2]

We now meet several new concepts here. In the falsehood of cyclical time live the poor agrarian people whose cyclical labor gives rise to *non-cyclical* temporal surplus value. This is a new concept and new point, by

---

[1] Debord, Guy. *The Society of the Spectacle*, Trans. Donald Nickleson-Smith, New York: Zone Books, 1994. pp. 93-94.

[2] Ibid., p. 94.

which Debord means that the oppressed class produce for the ruling class irreversible time with their cyclical time. There is no history in the cycle, but on top of it, the rulers who consume material wealth on "extravagance and festivity" steal the temporal surplus value. Those who enjoy life are those who do not work. And they are the same people who possess the "historical surplus value" and therefore become the "masters of the knowledge and enjoyment of directly experienced events." This is an acute remark in itself. On the one hand we have the peasant masses in the dark of history in the cyclical time, a time known to the peasant masses "who—no matter what empires may crumble along with their chronologies—never change."[1] On the other hand we have the emperors and generals in the spotlight of history as the masters of cyclical time, who own historical surplus value, undergo the changes of historic events, and write "their own history." This is an important historical dialectics, a second significant point Debord makes here.

So irreversible time (history) in the beginning stage does not reflect the simple process of production and reproduction of the primitive economic structure, but is represented in turn through the politics of the dynasties of the kings and generals, the "masters" in the spotlight. To be more specific, Debord thinks of chronology as the expression of power's irreversible time. According to him, history does not first emerge in the process of real material production, but rather in the arena of the political conflict between the slave-owners and the feudal rulers. "Irreversible time was the prerogative of whoever ruled, and the prime yardstick of rulership lay in dynastic succession. The ruler's chief weapon was the written word."[2] It is true too. The dominant class not only writes history but *those who possessed history gave it an orientation—a direction, and also a meaning.*"[3] I think that the history Debord mentions here is history in quotation mark, in that it is an usurping *pseudo-history* dominating the historical reality created by the

---

[1] Debord, Guy. *The Society of the Spectacle*, Trans. Donald Nickleson-Smith, New York: Zone Books, 1994. p. 96.

[2] Ibid.

[3] Ibid.

laborers with their lives.

Meanwhile Debord finds that mythology becomes an accomplice of this pseudo-history. Under the protection of mythology, the rulers monopolize the free realm of imagination accessible to the thoughts of the mass, hence he believes all of these consequences flows from the simple fact that it is only to the degree that the masters make it their task to furnish cyclical time with mythic underpinnings, as in the seasonal rites of the Chinese emperors, that they themselves are relatively emancipated therefrom. Debord then points out that afterwards semi-historical religions replace myths as the new armor with which the rulers maintain their secular reign.

> Monotheistic religions were a compromise between myth and history, between the cyclical time which still dominated the sphere of production and the irreversible time which was the theater of conflicts and realignments between peoples. The religions that evolved out of Judaism were the abstract universal recognition of an irreversible time now democratized, open to all, yet still confined to the realm of illusion. Time remained entirely oriented toward a single final event: "The Kingdom of God is at hand." These religions had germinated and taken root in the soil of history; even here, however, they maintained a radical opposition to history. Semi-historical religion established qualitative starting points in time—the birth of Christ, the flight of Muhammad— yet its irreversible time, introducing an effective accumulation which would take the form of conquest in Islam and that of an increase in capital in the Christianity of the Reformation, was in fact inverted in religious thought, so as to become a sort of countdown: the wait, as time ran out, for the Last Judgment, for the moment of accession to the other, true world.[1]

Thus Debord unfolds before us a new historical perspective for the study of religions. He thinks that religious time entails irreversible historical

---

[1] Debord, Guy. *The Society of the Spectacle*, Trans. Donald Nickleson-Smith, New York: Zone Books, 1994. p. 99.

elements, namely the orthodox history of theism that the world again moves toward the City of God. But this irreversible time is represented as "a sort of countdown." This is literally the logic of the Millenarianistic teleology. Moreover, Debord thinks that the nature of this irreversibility resides still in the cyclical anti-historicity as it leads eventually to Eternity. "Eternity emerged from cyclical time; it was that time's beyond. Eternity was also what humbled time in its mere irreversible flow—suppressing history as history continued—by positioning itself beyond irreversible time, as a pure point which cyclical time would enter only to be abolished."[1] This is indeed insightful.

2. Bourgeois and irreversible time

Debord points out that the bourgeoisie makes its appearance with the new model of life: industrial production after the collapse of the Middle Ages. Industrial production shatters to pieces the previous static society on the basis of agricultural production, puts to an end the cyclical time and inaugurates irreversible time in the real sense.

> This diversification of possible historical life reflected the gradual emergence, following the collapse of the great official enterprise of this world, namely the Crusades, of the period's unseen contribution: a society carried along in its unconscious depths by irreversible time, the time directly experienced by the bourgeoisie in the production of commodities, the founding and expansion of the towns, the commercial discovery of the planet—in a word, the practical experimentation that obliterated any mythical organization of the cosmos once and for all.[2]

Debord's description of the history is overflowed with elegant poetics and ineffable solemnity. In his eyes, all this starts from the European Renaissance. In succession to the cyclical eternity of the above mentioned

---

[1] Debord, Guy. *The Society of the Spectacle*, Trans. Donald Nickleson-Smith, New York: Zone Books, 1994. pp. 99-100.

[2] Ibid., p. 101.

theistic discourse, he continues to contend, "The renaissance embodied the new form of possession of historical life. Seeking its heritage and its juridical basis in Antiquity, it was the bearer of a joyous break with eternity. The irreversible time of the Renaissance was that of an infinite accumulation of knowledge, while the historical consciousness generated by the experience of democratic communities, as of the effects of those forces that had brought on their ruin, was now, with Machiavelli, able to resume its reflection upon secular power, and say the unsayable about the State."[1] And it is well-reasoned. Knowledge stands against the cyclical fatuity, and the emergence of industry and experimental science as a key to the natural mysteries must break the solidification of theology in order to establish itself as a new form of historical life. What's more important, *historical consciousness* appears for the first time. Different from the former false chronicles of power, progress initiates from here as the essence of historical being. To be precise, it is a progress based on the modern industrial production. Irreversible time emerges in the real sense due to this progress. At the same time, history also represents a new form of existence as opposed to eternity, namely *temporality*. This is a significant landmark of modern theory. Debord cites a eulogy that epitomizes "the very spirit of the Renaissance": "Quant' è bella giovinezza/Che si fugge tuttavia."[2]

But then how does the bourgeois create this new irreversible time? According to Debord,

The time with which the bourgeoisie was inextricably bound up was labor-time, now at last emancipated from the cyclical realm. With the rise of the bourgeoisie, work became *that work which transforms historical conditions*. The bourgeoisie was the first ruling class for which labor was a value. By abolishing all social privilege, and by recognizing no value unrelated to the exploitation of labor, the bourgeoisie effectively conflated its own value qua ruling class with labor, and made

[1] Debord, Guy. *The Society of the Spectacle*, Trans. Donald Nickleson-Smith, New York: Zone Books, 1994. p. 103.

[2] Ibid.

the progress of labor the only measure of its own progress. The class that accumulated commodities and capital continually modified nature by modifying labor itself—by unleashing labor's productivity.[1]

It is obviously another one of Debord's profound theoretical quips. The nature of cyclical time is the natural material time, while labor (or to be more exact, industrial production) creates a new form of social wealth totally different from the natural wealth out of agricultural production. If we take it for granted that the essence of agriculture is to conform to the law of nature, then the objective of industrial production is to transform historical conditions. Thus the relationship between nature and man is no longer the mother-child bond which tightly links the one with the other. Nature becomes the object, and industry will change the world in terms of labor time and work value. "The world had a new foundation."[2] The advancement of labor becomes that of history itself, and work time constructs irreversible time that breaks the cyclical time.

The victory of the bourgeoisie was the victory of a *profoundly historical* time—the time corresponding to the economic form of production, which transformed society permanently, and from top to bottom. So long as agriculture was the chief type of labor, cyclical time retained its deep-down hold over society and tended to nourish those combined forces of tradition which slowed down the movement of history. But the irreversible time of the bourgeois economic revolution eliminated all such vestiges throughout the world. History, which had hitherto appeared to express nothing more than the activity of individual members of the ruling class, and had thus been conceived of as a chronology of events, was now perceived *in its general movement*—an inexorable movement that crushed individuals before it.[3]

---

[1] Debord, Guy. *The Society of the Spectacle*, Trans. Donald Nickleson-Smith, New York: Zone Books, 1994. p. 104.

[2] Ibid.

[3] Ibid., p. 105.

Marx defines the capitalist relationship of production as a never-ending revolution, which will not escape its destiny of perdition without changing its mode of existence. Therefore Debord is right when he points out that the victory of capitalist class is that of a profoundly historical (irreversible) time. Meanwhile he sees the two determining factors in its victory: One is the triumph of irreversible time was also its metamorphosis into the time of things, because the weapon that had ensured its victory was, precisely, the mass production of objects in accordance with the laws of the commodity. The "luxurious rarity" production revolving around the aristocratic class in the static society has now been transformed into mass production of daily products. Debord even claims that the "main product that economic development transformed from a luxurious rarity to a commonly consumed item was thus *history itself*."[1] It is interesting in itself, but not convincing.

The second factor is that the irreversible time tends "socially to eliminate all such lived time."[2] By this he implies, if the traditional cyclical time "supports the social existence", then the irreversible time of today's bourgeois is a historical one with the fervent accumulation of non-living wealth. Here entails an implicit value judgment that however bad the cyclical time in traditional society is, it is after all a time of human, while the progressive time of the bourgeois, be it magnificent, is a non-human reified time, the time of proliferation of commodities. So Debord proclaims that in the capitalist society, the irreversible time of production is first and foremost the measure of commodities. The time officially promoted all around the world as the *general time of society*, since it signifies nothing beyond those special interests which constitute it, is therefore not general in character, but *particular*. That makes sense too. The capitalist irreversible time is not a progressive one of the real being of human, but a reified historical time. For Marx, a capitalist is not human (subject), but the personification of capital, or at the best an economical animal.

Debord further points out that one should be cautious as not to believe

---

[1] Debord, Guy. *The Society of the Spectacle*, Trans. Donald Nickleson-Smith, New York: Zone Books, 1994. p. 105.

[2] Ibid.

that the capitalist class really will possess irreversible historical time, as in essence, the bourgeois ideology will be bound to reaffirm the reactive concept of historical time.

So the bourgeoisie unveiled irreversible historical time and imposed it on society only to deprive society of *its use*. Once there was history, but "there is no longer any history"—because the class of owners of the economy, who cannot break with economic history, must repress any other use of irreversible time as representing an immediate threat to itself. The ruling class, made up of *specialists in the ownership of things* who for that very reason are themselves owned by things, is obliged to tie its fate to the maintenance of a reified history and to the permanent preservation of a new historical immobility. Meanwhile the worker, at the base of society, is for the first time not materially estranged from history, for now the irreversible is generated from below.[1]

According to the above citation, in the level of politics, the bourgeois has to break with history again. Marx said that "once there was history" for the bourgeois when it met with the feudal society, but now there is "no longer any history." Judging from the point here, Debord's analysis lacks its former subtlety. The objectively irreversible time still exists, but the non-historical mark he mentions is embodied in the maintenance of political ideology in the process of the production of reified wealth and the ceaseless expansion of the capital. He does not realize that these are two different issues.

Debord concludes, in the final analysis,

The development of capitalism meant the unification of irreversible time *on a world scale*. Universal history became a reality because the entire globe was brought under the sway of this time's progression. But a history that is thus the same everywhere at once has as yet amounted to nothing more than an intrahistorical refusal of history. What appears the

---

[1] Debord, Guy. *The Society of the Spectacle*, Trans. Donald Nickleson-Smith, New York: Zone Books, 1994. pp. 105-106.

world over *as the same day* is merely the time of economic production—time cut up into equal abstract fragments. Unified irreversible time still belongs to the *world market*—and, by extension, to the world spectacle.[1]

Well, the spectacle as a new stage of capitalist development is present, but the stress here is still on time, though of course as time of the spectacle. The global history of capital is added a new spatial dimension, the global manifestation of the spectacle, which is just the new temporal element in the logic of capital.

3. Time of consumption and pseudo-cyclical time

Debord entitles his sixth chapter of *The Society of the Spectacle* as "Spectacular Time." In this chapter, he focuses his discussion on this new concept of time he defines. As a matter of fact, it is where his main focus lies. The descriptions of the cyclical time and irreversible time both serve to pave the way for the emergence of spectacular time.

This time Debord begins his discussion on spectacular time as time-as-commodity or time of production in capitalism. In plain words, it is the time which is recognized in China when they agree that "time is money."[2]

The time of production, time-as-commodity, is an infinite accumulation of equivalent intervals. It is irreversible time made abstract: each segment must demonstrate by the clock its purely quantitative equality with all other segments. This time manifests nothing in its effective reality aside from its *exchangeability*. It is under the rule of time-as-commodity that "time is everything, man is nothing; he is at the most time's carcass" (The Poverty of Philosophy). This is time devalued—the complete inversion of time as "the sphere of human

---

[1] Debord, Guy. *The Society of the Spectacle*, Trans. Donald Nickleson-Smith, New York: Zone Books, 1994. p. 107.

[2] The slogan "Time is Money" first appeared on the streets of Shenzhen City, a special economic zone in the beginning of opening and reform policy.

development."[1]

We should discuss this from the other way around. First of all, Debord makes an *implicit value hypothesis*, that is, time is the irreversible progress of man's life. The cyclical time in traditional society is not irreversible though it belongs to man. This is a theoretical yardstick *"that should exist"* but which he tries all means to conceal. Only by understanding this can we have a clue of his analytical logic here. If time is an irreversible yardstick of man, time in capitalist commodity production is not of man but some exchangeable quantity of labor time that has nothing to do with man's existence. Rather, it is an "infinite accumulation" of homogeneous fragments of time. Debord observes that the capitalist class take the production time based on labor as "the sphere of human development" when it denies the cyclical time of the Middle Ages, but they fail to understand that under the slogan of "time is money," the real development of man is never possible. In a time of infinite accumulation of material wealth, man is reduced to submission to material. And, as opposed to the time of the development of man's being prescribed by Debord, man is necessarily a complete inversion of time, for in the time with production as its aim, man is only "time's carcass."

Compared with this reified time of commodity, Debord for the first time defines the abrupt emergence of *consumable time* of contemporary capitalism. He discovers that the general time of man outside his production is now also based on this capitalist mode of production, which is demonstrated in the form of "*pseudo-cyclical time*" in daily life. Everyday life is the concern of the situationist movement. Influenced by Lefebvre, Debord and the others value critique and revolution of everyday life as the most important revolutionary practice. Situationism gets its name from the situation of merging life and art (Lefebvre) by reforming pseudo-daily life.

Pseudo-cyclical time is a time *transformed by industry*. The time founded on commodity production is itself a consumable commodity,

---

[1] Debord, Guy. *The Society of the Spectacle*, Trans. Donald Nickleson-Smith, New York: Zone Books, 1994. p. 110.

recombining everything which, during the period of the old unitary society's disintegration, had become distinct: private life, economic life, political life. The entirety of the consumable time of modern society ends up being treated as raw material for the production of a diversity of new products to be put on the market as socially controlled uses of time. "A product, though ready for immediate consumption, may nevertheless serve as raw material for a further product." (Capital)[1]

We have already known that Debord's "pseudo-cyclical time" is *leisure time* created artificially for purposes of product consumption in the capitalist society. In his view, the leisure time outside of work is not a real process in which one relaxes and luxuriates in life, rather it is a passage of time transformed by industry. Directly speaking, it is time reformed by the market, whose existence is for the efficient consumption of goods in order to promote production. In fact, it is just where a certain heterogeneity lies in the concept of time between contemporary capitalist society and traditional capitalism. If I understand it correctly, the new situation occurred after the enforcement of Fordism in the West, when Ford for the first time proposed the idea to enable workers to buy goods. Only till then did capitalist mode of production turn from exploiting the absolute surplus value (by prolonging working hours) to the exploitation of relative surplus value. If, in Marx's time, the improvement of productivity was a key issue in the relative surplus value production, then the capitalist logic has developed into a situation in which *new production is possible only when there is consumption*! Therefore, a part of time particularly for consumption of goods must be set aside. Debord is insightful enough in spotting this phenomenon.

But why is this leisure time called pseudo-cyclical time? Debord thinks that the capitalist consumption time can well be artificially divided into a general cycle of consumption to labor then to consumption again.

Pseudo-cyclical time typifies the consumption of modern economic

---

[1] Debord, Guy. *The Society of the Spectacle*, Trans. Donald Nickleson-Smith, New York: Zone Books, 1994. p. 111.

survival—of that augmented survival in which daily lived experience embodies no free choices and is subject, no longer to the natural order, but to a pseudo-nature constructed by means of alienated labor. It is therefore quite "*natural*" that pseudo-cyclical time should echo the old cyclical rhythms that governed survival in pre-industrial societies. It builds, in fact, on the natural vestiges of cyclical time, while also using these as models on which to base new but homologous variants: day and night, weekly work and weekly rest, the cycle of vacations and so on.[1]

Debord thinks that in contemporary capitalist society, man loses his opportunity and right to make real choices in one's daily life, "the natural order" is gone far away, and one has to subject to the "pseudo-natural order" derived from alienated labor. All the weekends and vacations which seem to draw a distinct line from working hours appear to be formed naturally by the previous cyclical time of work and rest, but the opposite is true. The emergence of cyclical time is for the consumption of goods outside work time. This manufactured pseudo consumption will become the immanent driving force of production itself, thus the chain of consumption-production-reconsumption-reproduction comes into being, within which consumption is vital to the existence of contemporary capitalism. Accordingly, the pseudo-consumption time is also essential to the capitalists.

Debord hence remarks, "Pseudo-cyclical time is in fact merely the *consumable disguise* of the time-as-commodity of the production system, and it exhibits the essential traits of that time: homogeneous and exchangeable units, and the suppression of any qualitative dimension. But as a by-product of time-as-commodity intended to promote and maintain the backwardness of everyday life it necessarily finds itself laden with false attributions of value, and it must manifest itself as a succession of artificially distinct moments."[2] When the first few sentences are understandable, it takes one a while to comprehend why the function of pseudo-cyclical time is to "promote and

---

[1] Debord, Guy. *The Society of the Spectacle*, Trans. Donald Nickleson-Smith, New York: Zone Books, 1994. pp. 110-111.

[2] Ibid.

maintain the backwardness of everyday life." In my view, Debord means by promot[ing] and maintain[ing] the backwardness of everyday life to say that today's capitalists always try their dazzling means to make one feel the "*backwardness*" of one's life, or to feel that it is always possible to *improve one's living standard*. We never fail to hear or read this sentence on TV and in newspapers. This feeling of backwardness is just manufactured by the capitalists who try to promote their own products. It stimulates one to endlessly buy and consume. The capitalists are Godfathers behind the omnipresent advertisements and other types of propaganda, who manufacture copiable, more "advanced" patterns by "falsely evaluating" and promoting "individuality" which caters for individual life, making one live in illusory spectacular desires and willingly sink into the traps of commodity sale.

4. Spectacular time: pseudo-events producing toy bricks

All right then, after beating about the bush for a while, Debord finally is ready to give rise to his important theoretical claim: "*Consumable pseudo-cyclical time is the time of the spectacle.*"

> Consumable pseudo-cyclical time is the time of the spectacle: in the narrow sense, as the time appropriate to the consumption of images, and, in the broadest sense, as the image of the consumption of time. The time appropriate to the consumption of images, the medium of all commodities, is at once the chosen field of operations of the mechanisms of the spectacle and the goal that these mechanisms hold up overall as the locus and central representation of every individual act of consumption.[1]

Debord in the previous chapters refers to advertising and media that produce desires of consumption, and here he more directly talks about the issue of images as the most vital element in the spectacular being. According to him, the essence of pseudo-cyclical time is a coercive importation into

---

[1] Debord, Guy. *The Society of the Spectacle*, Trans. Donald Nickleson-Smith, New York: Zone Books, 1994. p. 112.

the mind of the people of the consumptive goods behind the images through bombardment of images. The spectacle initiates pseudo-desires which constitute pseudo-consumption, for purposes of a new round of commodity production. Such is the whole play in the spectacular time. In his film, Debord remarks that when time is our consumption of the images, it becomes a commodity. Accompanying this is the scene of people on vacation. He asserts that the spectacular time is constituent of our lives.

Above all, Debord says that the spectacular time is like a box of blocks of time, as a new means of contemporary capitalism.

> This is the logic behind the appearance, within an expanding economy of "services" and leisure activities, of the "all-inclusive" purchase of spectacular forms of housing, of collective pseudo-travel, of participation in cultural consumption and even of sociability itself, in the form of "exciting conversations," "meetings with celebrities" and suchlike. Spectacular commodities of this type could obviously not exist were it not for the increasing impoverishment of the realities they parody. And, not surprisingly, they are also paradigmatic of modern sales techniques in that they may be bought on credit.[1]

The spectacular commodities promoted in the spectacular time are successfully introduced for consumption through images. Debord says, "As we know, modern society's obsession with saving time, whether by means of faster transport or by means of powdered soup, has the positive result that the average American spends three to six hours daily watching television."[2] True, modern society has saved for everyone a large amount of leisure time, a lot of blocks of spectacular time manipulated by the images which are stuffed by all kinds of spectacular deception and deliberate misleading. He thinks "[t]he self-approbation of the time of modern survival can only be reinforced, in the spectacle, by reduction in its use value. The reality of time

---

[1] Debord, Guy. *The Society of the Spectacle*, Trans. Donald Nickleson-Smith, New York: Zone Books, 1994. p. 112.

[2] Ibid.

has been replaced by its publicity."[1] It being "all-inclusive," we are nowhere to escape from the spectacular time. It is never difficult to see Debord's examples in today's China: TV, radio, newspapers, and internet media, all are permeated with various commodity advertisements and sales promotion. Top-quality daily wares, newly marketed buildings, attractive golden-week tours, all these desires created by advertising never cease a minute to attack our lives. In addition, all celebrity interviews and demonstration of the stars surround us with their spectacular desires. Undoubtedly we have already felt and experienced the spectacular phenomena and time defined by Debord. What he said is just what is happening around us now.

Secondly, spectacular time manufactures pseudo-festivals in life. The most typical pseudo-festivals are the so-called "Golden Weeks" in today's China. Common festivals in this spectacular time are no longer any meaningful celebrations in our existence, rather they have become a characteristic means of commodity promotion. So holidays are no longer holidays but capitalists' patented alienated time of consumption, in which we are forced by the spectacle to consume what we do not really need.

Our epoch, which presents its time to itself as essentially made up of many frequently recurring festivities, is actually an epoch without festival. Those moments when, under the reign of cyclical time, the community would participate in a luxurious expenditure of life, are strictly unavailable to a society where neither community nor luxury exists. Mass pseudo-festivals, with their travesty of dialogue and their parody of the gift, may incite people to excessive spending, but they produce only a disillusion—which is invariably in turn offset by further false promises. The self-approbation of the time of modern survival can only be reinforced, in the spectacle, by reduction in its use value. The reality of time has been replaced by its publicity.[2]

---

[1] Debord, Guy. *The Society of the Spectacle*, Trans. Donald Nickleson-Smith, New York: Zone Books, 1994. p. 113.

[2] Ibid.

This is no longer strange to us. From "New Year-Spring Festival Golden Week," "Valentine," to "May Golden Week," "Mid-Autumn Festival," to "October Golden Week" and "Christmas Shopping Season," all these holidays are cyclical time created in real life in China. Their sole being is based on the logic of spectacular pseudo-festivals, with the real purpose of urging one to spend money on consumption of the spectacular goods.

Third and the most important, Debord discovers in spectacular time *the forgery of the authentic life*. It is known to us that Debord's situationism is close to the idea of surrealism in their objection to banal everyday life. They propose to capture the authentic or surrealistic artistic moments of life through inversion of pseudo-reality. And Debord finds out that the spectacle makes people believe that it is the ultimate state of being and fall into its trap of consumption, by forging all kinds of artistic moments.

> The social image of the consumption of time is for its part exclusively dominated by leisure time and vacations—moments portrayed, like all spectacular commodities, *at a distance*, and as desirable by definition. This particular commodity is explicitly presented as a moment of authentic life whose cyclical return we are supposed to look forward to. Yet even in such special moments, ostensibly moments of life, the only thing being generated, the only thing to be seen and reproduced, is the spectacle—albeit at a higher-than-usual level of intensity. And what has been passed off as authentic life turns out to be merely a life more *authentically spectacular.*[1]

"Moments" are by nature the real living condition of man in Situationist revolution of daily life. But Debord sees that the spectacular time more often than not imitates and plays the role of this "moment." In particular, the excellent moments presented in ads always intoxicate one when they employ aesthetics as a means of their presentation. People tend to believe the pseudo-situations and pseudo-events produced by the spectacle are the

---

[1] Debord, Guy. *The Society of the Spectacle*, Trans. Donald Nickleson-Smith, New York: Zone Books, 1994. p. 112.

direct manifestations of life, and that the purchase of certain products and the participation of certain trips or cultural shows mean to step into the artistic moments of authentic life. We cannot help but forget our being heedlessly. Debord points out, "The pseudo-events that vie for attention in the spectacle's dramatizations have not been lived by those who are thus informed about them. In any case they are quickly forgotten, thanks to the precipitation with which the spectacle's pulsing machinery replaces one by the next."[1] Following the spectacle and vogue wears out and puts an end to life when we are lost in the juxtaposition of spectacular images. Eventually the "pseudo-self" lingering in these images will be mercilessly forgotten in the course of history.

5. Spectacular time synchronous with pseudo-cyclical time

Debord thinks that the spectacle not only makes pseudo-cyclical time but also proportionate spectacular space. Or, it is the "environmental planning" with which contemporary capitalist society uniformly molds its spatial environments. This is the title of the Seventh Chapter of *The Society of the Spectacle*. It is also the field to which Lefebvre, who wrote *The Production of Space*, later devotes his in-depth research.

Spectacular space is a *spatial alienation*, whose visible form is urbanization or *urbanism* familiar to all. In Debord's opinion, "Urbanism is the mode of appropriation of the natural and human environment by capitalism, which, true to its logical development toward absolute domination, can (and now must) refashion the totality of space into *its own peculiar decor*."[2] Urbanism here is in reality modernized metropolises, a peculiar spatial form of capitalism. In the spatial deployment of the city, the capital is capable of dominating nature and human society in a more centralized and convenient way. Living in this *social space* created by industrial capital, the existence of man and nature both lose their mystery and poetic luster. It is the silent world of metal and cement in Pascal's

---

[1] Debord, Guy. *The Society of the Spectacle*, Trans. Donald Nickleson-Smith, New York: Zone Books, 1994. p.114.

[2] Ibid., p. 121.

words, where all the buildings and streets are designed and made according to capital's commercial logic. In the straight and wide streets we see no trace of nature or human nature. We live in an era when air-conditioning and vegetable sheds annihilate the seasons, and the artificial lighting system devours the distinction between night and day. People thus can no longer live in the natural world, and our daily activities are done in the man-made commercial cities. Debord points out the requirement of capitalism that is met by urbanism in the form of a freezing of life. Contemporary capitalist spectacular society seems to go beyond this in its attempt to accelerate the spatial separation of social life by means of a more important technique. This is the so-called urbanization process.

First, in Debord's view, the goal of urbanization is the *reconstruction of pseudo-space* of the atomized workers in capitalist society. He says,

> Lewis Mumford, in *The City in History*, points out that with the advent of long-distance mass communications, the isolation of the population has become a much more effective means of control. But the general trend toward isolation, which is the essential reality of urbanism, must also embody a controlled reintegration of the workers based on the planned needs of production and consumption. Such an integration into the system must recapture isolated individuals as individuals **isolated together**. Factories and cultural centers, holiday camps and housing developments—all are expressly oriented to the goals of a pseudo-community of this kind. These imperatives pursue the isolated individual right into the **family cell**, where the generalized use of receivers of the spectacle's message ensures that his isolation is filled with the dominant images—images that indeed attain their full force only by virtue of this isolation.[1]

The spectacular space is a "controlled reintegration" of workers. Especially after mass media becomes the main framework of the society, the

---

[1] Debord, Guy. *The Society of the Spectacle*, Trans. Donald Nickleson-Smith, New York: Zone Books, 1994. p. 122.

lonely crowds constitute a strange existence in the real spatial isolation and the illusionary community manufactured by the spectacle: man is by nature lonely, but he gains a false togetherness from the "omnipresent" images (listening to the same radio program, watching the same TV program and reading the same newspaper). It is also in this sense that the spectacular space is no longer of the geographical spatial structure in the traditional sense, rather it "is termed 'psycho-geography.'"[1] This new space will be a socio-historical conception, a special form of control of the capital.

Secondly, we have the *mass pseudo-architecture* in spectacular space. Debord also finds that when in the past architecture was constructed for the ruling class, it is different now:

> In all previous periods, architectural innovation served the ruling class exclusively; now for the first time there is such a thing as a new architecture specifically for **the poor**. Both formal poverty and the immense extension of this new experience in housing are the result of its mass character, dictated at once by its ultimate ends and by the modern conditions of construction. At the core of these conditions we naturally find an **authoritarian decision-making process** that abstractly develops any environment into an environment of abstraction.[2]

This is a new spatial deployment. Debord argues that urbanization in fact took place in the beginning of industrialization. The spatial construction of the city invariably emerges everywhere in the same manner even in backward and industrially underdeveloped areas. Urbanization is done at the cost of destruction of natural environment. Debord has already described in his time what we can feel directly now:

> The explosion of cities into the countryside, covering it with what Mumford calls "formless masses" of urban debris, is presided

---

[1] Fields, Belden and Steven Best, "Situatinonist International," in Robert A. Gorman (ed.), *Bio-graphical Dictionary of Neo-Marxism*, Westport: Greenwood Press, 1985. p. 385.

[2] Debord, Guy. *The Society of the Spectacle*, Trans. Donald Nickleson-Smith, New York: Zone Books, 1994. p. 122.

over in unmediated fashion by the requirements of consumption. The dictatorship of the automobile, the pilot product of the first stage of commodity abundance, has left its mark on the landscape in the dominance of freeways that bypass the old urban centers and promote an ever greater dispersal. Meanwhile, instants of incomplete reorganization of the urban fabric briefly crystallize around the "distribution factories"—giant **shopping centers** created exnihilo and surrounded by acres of **parking space**.[1]

Highly-developed highways, forever increasing cars and immense suburban shopping malls are what Debord saw and we see today. What is different is that Debord sees some disparate things in the immoderate expansion of these material objects we crave for.

Third, we have the "**pseudo-countryside**" appearing in the spectacular space. Debord says that the global history of capitalism was "born in the city," and reached its maturation in the time when the city overwhelmingly defeated the countryside. "As it destroys the cities, urbanism institutes a *pseudo-countryside* devoid not only of the natural relationships of the country of former times but also of the direct (and directly contested) relationships of the historical cities. The forms of habitation and the spectacular control of today's 'planned environment' have created a *new, artificial peasantry*."[2] This new peasantry is in fact produced by the spectacle.

> The traditional peasantry was the unshakeable basis of "Oriental despotism," and its very scatteredness called forth bureaucratic centralization; the new peasantry that has emerged as the product of the growth of modern state bureaucracy differs from the old in that its **apathy** has had to be historically manufactured and maintained: natural ignorance has given way to the organized spectacle of error. The "new towns" of the technological pseudo-peasantry are the clearest

---

[1] Debord, Guy. *The Society of the Spectacle*, Trans. Donald Nickleson-Smith, New York: Zone Books, 1994. p. 123.

[2] Ibid., p. 125.

of indications, inscribed on the land, of the break with historical time on which they are founded; their motto might well be: "On this spot nothing will ever happen—and nothing ever has."[1]

Debord does not give any more in-depth analysis to this spectacular peasantry. I think it may refer to the mechanized agrarian workers who are equally manipulated by modern spectacles. They no longer rely on the patriarchal clan relationship of the earth and tradition, but live in the "new towns" in the spectacular space. They are "indifferent people" deprived of their attachment to nature.

Of course Debord is not pessimistic in front of this spectacular space. He still optimistically expects a critique of human geography. He harbors it in his mind that,

> The same history that threatens this twilight world is capable of subjecting space to a directly experienced time. The proletarian revolution is that **critique of human geography** whereby individuals and communities must construct places and events commensurate with the appropriation, no longer just of their labor, but of their total history. By virtue of the resulting mobile space of play, and by virtue of freely chosen variations in the rules of the game, the independence of places will be rediscovered without any new exclusive tie to the soil, and thus too the authentic journey will be restored to us, along with authentic life understood as a journey containing its whole meaning within itself.[2]

Debord still believes in proletariat revolution, thinking of its nature as "the critique of human geography." This is just the critique and revolution of spectacular time. The aim of revolution is to dissolve the alienation of space made by spectacular space, returning to people the possession of the totality of history. The new space for human beings will be a space "containing its whole meaning within itself."

---

[1] Debord, Guy. *The Society of the Spectacle*, Trans. Donald Nickleson-Smith, New York: Zone Books, 1994. p. 126.

[2] Ibid.

IV. Spectacular Ideology and Its Subversion

Besides the above mentioned ideas, *The Society of the Spectacle* contains another revolutionary view, that is, the spectacle as recognized unreservedly by Debord as the important form of expression of contemporary capitalist ideology. Debord declares that the spectacle is the realization of the concretion of bourgeois economic relationship fetishism. If the previous fetishism is only a mysterious concept in man's mind, it is now developed into a visible and palpable spectacular control. Different from before, people of the present age have unconsciously subordinated to the capitalist ideology in their unconditional support of all heaven-like spectacles. And, as a radical left-wing revolutionary, Debord also tries his hand at discussing the issue of subverting the spectacular ideology.

1. The spectacle as materialized ideology

The spectacle is a flagrant criminal for Debord. It is on the one hand the most important supporting frame of contemporary capital society, on the other the readiest accomplice of its predominance. The micro-mechanism of the spectacular ideological operation has been elaborated in the previous chapters, and the discussion here looks more like a theoretical conclusion. In the last chapter of this book, which Debord entitles "Ideology in Material Form," he significantly quotes from Hegel's *The Phenomenology of Mind*, which briefly means that the Self-consciousness exists for the other; that is, it is to gain the acknowledgement and recognition of this other self-consciousness. It stresses that the spectacle is a materialized intensification of ideology.

> Ideology is the *foundation* of the thought of a class society within the conflicted course of history. Ideological entities have never been mere fictions—rather, they are a distorted consciousness of reality, and, as such, real factors retroactively producing real distorting effects; which is all the more reason why that *materialization* of ideology, in

the form of the spectacle, which is precipitated by the concrete success of an autonomous economic system of production, results in the virtual identification with social reality itself of an ideology that manages to remold the whole of the real to its own specifications.[1]

Ideology is by no means an illusion, but a conceptual distortion of a real social relationship. This is the basic orientation since Mannheim and Althusser, but Debord aims to recognize a new form of ideological existence: the spectacle is the **direct materialization** of the whole bourgeois ideology. We live in a gaudy mediated age in which the spectacle has changed the invisible implicit hegemony of the previous ideology into palpable coercion of the false spectacular world with its overwhelming images. The spectacle amazingly realizes its direct control over man's deep unconscious structure by producing desires and inflicting ubiquitous allure of objects to us. And Debord thinks that this control has ripened into an automatic mechanism and played the role of the direct materialization of images of ideology. Thus he further recognizes that the spectacle is intensified ideology in whose deployment an unconscious social identity is realized to affirm the existing social control. Such is the coercive ideology.

Debord says that "[t]he spectacle is the acme of ideology, for in its full flower it exposes and manifests the essence of all ideological systems: the impoverishment, enslavement and negation of real life."[2] It is heart-felt assertion. Groveling under the predominance of the spectacle, we never realize that we have forsaken authentic life and real being. The life we live is no better than the puppets manipulated by the spectacle. Debord finds that in the spectacular control we encounter,

> once ideology, which is the **abstract** will to universality and the illusion thereof, finds itself legitimated in modern society by universal abstraction and by the effective dictatorship of illusion, then it is no

---

[1] Debord, Guy. *The Society of the Spectacle*, Trans. Donald Nickleson-Smith, New York: Zone Books, 1994. p. 150.

[2] Ibid., p. 151.

longer the voluntaristic struggle of the fragmentary, but rather its triumph. The claims of ideology now take on a sort of flat, positivistic exactness: ideology is no longer a historical choice, but simply an assertion of the obvious. **Names** of particular ideologies have vanished. The portion of properly ideological labor serving the system may no longer be conceived of other than in terms of an "epistemological base" supposedly transcending all specific ideological phenomena. Ideology in material form is itself without a name, just as it is without a formulable historical agenda, which is another way of saying that the history of **ideologies, plural**, is over.[1]

If it is acknowledged that in Marx's age the bourgeois conception as the governing will of the ruling class usually finds its expression in an invasion of idealism imposed on the working class, then the bourgeois fancy has become a rampant "monotonous positivist correctness" in today's era of spectacular ideology. While we bury ourselves in the ceaseless appreciation of the spectacle, we leave no time nor energy for a moment of suspicion of the truth of life values and scientific concepts transferred by the spectacle. It is held true that the spectacular ideology completely takes the place of the previous arguable political ideologies. Best once remarks, "the spectacle is a tool of pacification and de-politicization, it is 'a permanent opium war' (ibid.: Section 44), which stupefies social subjects and distracts them from the most urgent task of real life."[2] The end of traditional ideology is just the beginning of the spectacular ideology, which has no definite political bias (historical agenda). This seemingly well-meant anonymity is just where the excellent trick of the spectacle resides.

Next, Debord further elaborates on the several characteristics of the spectacular ideology by elevating them to the level of more abstract metaphysics. First he makes it clear that the spectacular ideology is the

---

[1] Debord, Guy. *The Society of the Spectacle*, Trans. Donald Nickleson-Smith, New York: Zone Books, 1994. p. 150.

[2] Best, Steven. "Commodification of Reality and Commodified Reality: Baudrillard, Debord, and Post-Modern Theories," in Douglas Kellner (ed.), *Baudrillard: A Critical Reader*, Oxford: Wiley-Blackwell, 1994. p. 47.

alienation of the existence of human life. He says, the principle which Hegel enunciated in *the Jenenser Real philosophie* as that of money—"the life, moving of itself, of that which is dead"—has now been extended by the spectacle to the entirety of social life. Here once again he recalls the idea of alienation. But he does not mind whether the logic of alienation is a humanity value hypothesis. Noteworthy is that he does not first cite young Marx, but rather turns directly to Hegel as the instructor of young Marx. And young Hegel in specific. Debord's proclamation more or less adds some chilly factors to the familiar notion of alienation. Under his pen, the spectacle turns the non-living things created by man himself into forever self-generating power which substitutes man's life and manipulates his being. In philosophical terms it is alienation itself. Furthermore,

> Materially, the spectacle is "the expression of estrangement, of alienation between man and man." The "new potentiality of fraud" concentrated within it has its basis in that form of production whereby "with the mass of objects grows the mass of alien powers to which man is subjected." This is the supreme stage of an expansion that has turned need against life. "The need for money is for that reason the real need created by the modern economic system, and the only need it creates." (*Economic and Philosophical Manuscripts*)[1]

It is easy to see that here Debord's expression is no more than the juxtaposition of citations. But this section is evidently the direct borrowing from Marx's *Philosophical and Economical Manuscript of 1844* in its overall logic. It is a pity that Debord fails to distinguish the heterogeneity of young Marx's historical outlook of alienation from his scientific method of historical materialism. He does not grasp that even before today's spectacle, the single-handed humanity value critique is still weak, with which alone no scientific clairvoyance is possible. Here it is only self-evident that Debord's theoretical foundation is only too fragile.

---

[1] Debord, Guy. *The Society of the Spectacle*, Trans. Donald Nickleson-Smith, New York: Zone Books, 1994. p. 151.

Secondly, at the level of basic philosophical assumptions, the ideology of the spectacle is the simple resurrection of the old materialism and idealism. Debord thinks that in *Thesis on Feuerbach* Marx has transcended practice and the dichotomy between traditional materialism and idealism, but the spectacle

> preserves the ideological features of both materialism and idealism, imposing them in the pseudo-concreteness of its universe. The contemplative aspect of the old materialism, which conceives of the world as representation, not as activity—and which in the last reckoning idealizes matter—has found fulfillment in the spectacle, where concrete things are automatically masters of social life. Correlatively, idealism's **imaginary activity** likewise finds its fulfillment in the spectacle, this through the technical mediation of signs and signals—which in the last reckoning endow an abstract ideal with material form.[1]

This is an interesting idea To my surprise, Debord is capable of making such significant interpretation and application of the first point in Marx's *Thesis on Feuerbach*. As is known to all, Marx at the same time criticizes Feuerbach and Hegel whereas Debord moves the critiques of these two dimensions in his reading into the critique of the spectacle. First, the realm of the appearance of the old materialism is again realized in the spectacular being, but never to refer to one's direct confrontation with the natural objects through his own senses, but his passive and inactive reception of the world of images manufactured by the spectacles; Second, the activity of idealism is embodied in the spectacle via "technological medium of signs and signals": the spectacle transforming into the materialization itself of the conceptual governance.

Third, on the level of social being, the spectacular ideology succeeds in hiding the social conflicts and contradictions. Debord argues that controlled by the spectacular ideology,

---

[1] Debord, Guy. *The Society of the Spectacle*, Trans. Donald Nickleson-Smith, New York: Zone Books, pp. 151-152.

A blocked practice and its corollary, an anti-dialectical false consciousness, are imposed at every moment on an everyday life in thrall to the spectacle—an everyday life that should be understood as the systematic organization of a breakdown in the faculty of encounter, and the replacement of that faculty by a **social hallucination**: a false consciousness of encounter, or an "**illusion** of encounter." In a society where no one is any longer **recognizable** by anyone else, each individual is necessarily unable to recognize his own reality. Here ideology is at home; here separation has built its world.[1]

Lost in the world made by the spectacle and the mad pursuit of spectacular fantasies, one can never discern the contradictions and conflicts in real society so that he is deprived of the ability to grasp the meaning of his existence and the reality of life. Such is the pivotal function of social surveillance of the spectacular ideology.

For Debord, the way one lives in the spectacular world is like;

[i]mprisoned in a flat universe bounded on all sides by the spectacle's screen, the consciousness of the spectator has only **figmentary interlocutors** which subject it to a one-way discourse on their commodities and the politics of those commodities. The **sole mirror** of this consciousness is the spectacle in all its breadth, where what is staged is a false way out of a generalized autism.[2]

It reads quite Lacanian: the spectacle is a sort of mirror image, which the individual mistakes for himself and loses his own being. The spectacular narrative, being "figmentary interlocutor which subject it to a one-way discourse," reduces the people in it to passive spectators who from the beginning to the end have no power of speech. The grotesque and gaudy spectacular mirror images galore are what we are to become, and the real self

[1] Debord, Guy. *The Society of the Spectacle*, Trans. Donald Nickleson-Smith, New York: Zone Books, 1994. p.152.

[2] Ibid., p. 153.

is cunningly murdered inside the spectacle:

> The spectacle erases the dividing line between self and world, in that the self, under siege by the presence/absence of the world, is eventually overwhelmed; it likewise erases the dividing line between true and false, repressing all directly lived truth beneath the real presence of the falsehood maintained by the organization of appearances. The individual, though condemned to the passive acceptance of an alien everyday reality, is thus driven into a form of madness in which, by resorting to magical devices, he entertains the illusion that he is reacting to this fate. The recognition and consumption of commodities are at the core of this pseudo-response to a communication to which no response is possible. The need to imitate that the consumer experiences is indeed a truly infantile need, one determined by every aspect of his fundamental dispossession.[1]

Lacan's cast of spell appears again in the spectacle: everyone is mad, and different from the pathological sense, we are lunatics who behave in a decent way. More miserably, we never know that our real selves are already dead under the control of the spectacle. And the body dancing to the will of the spectacle is but hollow.[2]

2. Revolution of everyday life: subversion of the spectacle

As a left-wing intellectual, Debord anchors his social critique of the spectacle on his advocate of some revolutionary practices. Different from Baudrillard and other post-modern representatives, Debord refuses to abandon his attempt to explain and change the social reality. On the other hand, his spectacular theory is heterogeneous to traditional Marxist theory on proletarian revolution, as he advocates the situationist *artistic* transformation of life.

---

[1] Debord, Guy. *The Society of the Spectacle*, Trans. Donald Nickleson-Smith, New York: Zone Books, 1994. p.153.

[2] As for the Lacanian philosophy, please see my new monograph: *The Impossible Truth of Being: Mirror of Lacan's Philosophy*, Beijing: Commercial Press, 2005.

For Debord, *the historical thoughts* appear in reality ever since the determining victory of capitalist mode of production. It is also the "irreversible time" he discusses previously. Now "[t]he development of the forces of production had shattered the old relations of production; every static order had crumbled to nothing. And everything that had formerly been absolute became historical."[1] In the rise of the bourgeoisie, as a conscious revolutionary class consciousness, they always endeavor to evolve "in tandem with the 'thought of history', with the dialectic—with a truly historical thinking that is not content simply to seek the meaning of what is but aspires to understand the dissolution of everything that is—and in the process to dissolve all separation."[2] However, once it predominates the society, the capitalist class will at once desert the historicity of social history in the sense of noumenon. History merely becomes an abstract conception, and the essence of bourgeois ideology is the attempt to clarify the non-historicity of capitalist system: eternity. Debord analyzes it correctly. This is also a key concept Marx has illuminated.

Debord thinks that the one who founded historical science is Marx himself. In his film *La Société du Spectacle*, he frequently quotes from Marx and inserts the portraits of Marx and Engels. The nature of the theory lies in the process of the revivification of conceptual history into real, object social history, as historical thoughts are preserved only through being turned into practical thoughts. But Debord accuses Marx of the "determinant" side of his thoughts, as Marx oversimplified his historical analysis into a linear model of the development of modes of production according to which, at each stage, class struggles would end "either in a revolutionary reconstitution of society at large, or in the common ruin of the contending classes."[3] Debord illustrates the static "asiatic mode of production." In fact, he does not even reach the threshold of Marx's late-day research on ancient

---

[1] Debord, Guy. *The Society of the Spectacle*, Trans. Donald Nickleson-Smith, New York: Zone Books, 1994. p. 48.

[2] Ibid.

[3] Ibid., p. 56.

history, the historical survey about the ancient Russian village community in particular. Just due to this, the economic determinism Marxism of the Second International comes into being:

> The "orthodox Marxism" of the Second International was the scientific ideology of the socialist revolution, an ideology which asserted that its whole truth resided in objective economic processes, and in the gradual recognition of their necessity by a working class educated by the organization. This ideology exhumed utopian socialism's faith in pedagogies, eking this out with a contemplative evocation of the course of history.[1]

Debord does not take the "necessity of socialism" for granted. At the same time, he openly rejects Russian socialism, which he thinks gives rise to the dictatorial ideology. Stalin's USSR epitomizes concentrated spectacle. "This same historical moment, when Bolshevism triumphed for itself in Russia and social democracy fought victoriously for the old world, also marks the definitive inauguration of an order of things that lies at the core of the modern spectacle's rule: this was the moment when *an image of the working class* arose in radical *opposition* to the working class itself."[2] Debord does not think this is the right path to the abolition of contemporary spectacular reign. In his film he often inserts scenes of the Russian leaders participating in mass gathering, including that of Stalin's speeches. He arranges these scenes more often than not in a derogative sense.

   With his denial of both the capital and the social, what then is exactly the attitude Debord puts forth against the spectacular society? For him, under the control of the sweeping spectacle, "[t]he proletariat has not been eliminated, and indeed it remains irreducibly present, under the intensified alienation of modern capitalism, in the shape of the vast mass of workers who have lost all power over the use of their own lives and who, once they *realize this*, must

---

[1] Debord, Guy. *The Society of the Spectacle*, Trans. Donald Nickleson-Smith, New York: Zone Books, 1994. p. 65.

[2] Ibid., p. 69.

necessarily redefine themselves as the proletariat—as negation at work in the bosom of today's society."[1] Evidently young Lukacs's class conscious awakens quietly! And also he finds out that in most developed capitalist countries, a "constantly growing sign of negation" still thrives, albeit it is misinterpreted or altered by the spectacle. What's more, Debord points out a brand new revolutionary element: the direct defiance of the youth to the society of the spectacle. "[A]t the same time rebellious tendencies among the young generate a protest that is still tentative and amorphous, yet already clearly embodies a rejection of the specialized sphere of the old politics, as well as of art and everyday life."[2] He obviously accepts Marcuse's idea of new revolutionary subjectivity and cultural revolution, the latter of which Marcuse expresses as "cultural negation." In Debord's opinion, the revolution initiated by the young generation seems to be calm in the surface, but it has already ignited the enthusiasm among the people. The artistic revolution of the young generation apparently is in accordance with the idea of Debord, who recognizes it as the real path to undo the shackle of spectacular manipulation, the essential content of his new revolution. In his 1973 film *The Society of the Spectacle*, one of the most frequently recurring scenes is the young students in street battles with the French military police. After the French May Storm of 1968, Debord held a stronger expectation on the young generation's revolutionary practice. The revolutionary scenes in Paris are frequently interwoven into the historical scenes of Russian Revolution, with the hope of telling a profound historical importance.

In fact, it is no wonder that Debord takes sides with these young people, as his Situationist International is itself a revolutionary experiment which *subverts the spectacle to artistic moments*. I contend that the emergence of Situationist International is by no means accidental, which finds its roots in the revival of the western world due to the soaring development of technology after the two heavy blows from the two world wars.

---

[1] Debord, Guy. *The Society of the Spectacle*, Trans. Donald Nickleson-Smith, New York: Zone Books, 1994. p. 84.

[2] Ibid., p. 86.

Up to the mid-1900s, mediated by Keynes's revolution and Fordism, the capitalist economy underwent a stage of unprecedented boost, with which the western capitalist countries took on a new look, and simultaneously brought about significant changes (compared with the early capitalism) in the political domination and economic structure on the one hand and prosperity of consumerism on the other due to the leaping accumulation of commodities. In fact, western Marxist Lefebvre called for the concern for the sphere of "everyday life" constructed by consumption outside the range of production as early as 1940s. His idea paves the way for the logic starting point for situationists like Debord and Vaneigem. Lefebvre's student Baudrillard makes a detailed and sharp anatomy of this new form of capitalist development in his *Consumer Society*.

This school of thought originated by Lefebvre can be summarized as the definite proposal that contemporary capitalist society has turned from the infrastructure of production superiority to that of **consumption priority**. This also can be considered as the original sources of **post-Marxian trends** in western Marxist social critiques. If, following this trend, the sphere of material production traditional Marxism focuses on has been swept aside as a secondary side in the essence of social life. Next, Debord and Vaneigem further deepen Lefebvre's concept and define that the commodity society has been replaced by the spectacular society and the concepts like production mode, productivity and production relationship have been substituted by the spectacle, space and everyday life and the ilk. As for the class struggle which points at capitalist economy and eco-political life, it too has been transformed into "revolution of everyday life" which turns being into artistic moments. Moreover, discarding alienation and rejection to fetishism also become the "drift" of the artists and "derailment" in the sense of psychology, with the essence of the so-called construction of active real situation of existence. Interestingly, situationist names after this situation. In this view, the basic stance of situationist parts its way from Marxism. Best and Kellner once summarize the difference like this:

Whereas classical Marxism focused on production, the Situationists highlighted the importance of social reproduction and the new modes of the consumer and media society that had developed since the death of Marx. Whereas Marxism focuses on the factory, the Situationists focused on the city and everyday life, supplementing the Marxian emphasis on class struggle with a project of cultural revolution and the transformation of subjectivity and social relations. And whereas Marxian theory focused on time and history, the Situationists emphasized the production of space and the constitution of liberated zones of desire.[1]

As is mentioned above, in the age of the spectacle, the form of control characteristic of political coercion and economic methods has abdicated, and control of cultural ideology succeeded its throne with august. The spectacle, by means of cultural apparatus and mass media, creates a pseudo-reality, a pseudo-world that dominates everyday life (which might be Baudrillard's "realm of simulation"). So the revolution is to unmask the alienating nature of the spectacle in everyday life and further demolish the spectacle and direct the people to return to the moment of real existence. They also aim to show the people to prove wrong the false desire demonstrated by the spectacle, liberate the real desire of our being, construct brand-new living situations and revolutionize everyday life. Best and Kellner claim that "[t]he fundamental goal of the Situationist praxis was to reconstruct society and everyday life to overcome the apathy, deception, passivity, and fragmentation induced by the spectacle. The recovery of active existence was possible only by destroying spectacular relations and by overcoming passivity through the active creation of 'situations' and the use of technology to enhance human life."[2] In this glorious revolution, Debord hopes, a new environment will be created in which the present will dominate the past and creativity of life will always prevail the repetition of life.

The revolutionary strategies of the situationists include "drift" (dérivé) "turnabout" or "derailment" (Détournement), and constructed situation.

---

[1] Best, Steven and Douglas Kellner. *The Postmodern Turn*, New York: Guilford Press, 1997. p. 81.
[2] Ibid., p. 92.

Dérivé is the ossified negation to the repressive urban life, in particular the demonstration of the architectural space. Détournement refers to the "deconstruction of capitalist images by disclosing the hidden manipulation or repressed logic," or, in other words, an inverse self-destruct with the images of ideology (as in the counterattack in advertising, architecture and comics). Constructed situation is to redesign, recreate and re-experience the process of the life of the subject according to the real wishes of the subject. For Debord, it is a moment of life carefully constructed by a collective organization of a unitary game of environment and events, a construction of revolutionary negative spectacle. The situation refers to the "non-spectacular ruptures" and the "breaking of the spectacular."[1] In a revolutionary situation, people are permitted "the expression of desires and emancipated possibilities that everyday life has suppressed."[2] They even think that Marx's reform of Hegelian dialectics is a well-known strategy of subversive derailment, and the aims of both are to expose the non-material poverty and alienation of mankind in the society of the spectacle in order to show the real nature of the selves.

This revolution urges us to actively construct a new living situation, an individual space and urban public space based on liberated desires. In the process of the revolution, art plays a crucial role (situationists being mostly artists) and is a main approach together with poetics.

Debord throughout his life confronted the overwhelming spectacles with an unbending gesture of rejection and devoted himself to the revolutionary practice of exposing and reforming the misty social reality. He made an attempt to awaken the people intoxicated in the spectacle, calling for the resolute actions of the situationists who, instead of awaiting passively the remote horn of revolution, should stand out for the thorough reform of contemporary daily life, change of people's viewpoints, and alteration of the social structure. By means of self-emancipation, we can change the power

---

[1] Fields, Belden and Steven Best, "Situatinonist International," in Robert A. Gorman (ed.), *Biographical Dictionary of Neo-Marxism*, Westport: Greenwood Press, 1985. p. 386.

[2] Ibid.

relationships in order to reform the society. The tri-missions all point to the same destination. Therefore, he tried to break conventions by constructing situations, and help people to break away from their same old groove of thinking and behavioral methods. All these refusal gestures are thought to be emblematic of creativity. The Situationist International took it as its task to enable the mass to be aware of their unconscious behaviors. Thus, they expected to reinvigorate the on-going revolution. They insisted that each individual should actively and consciously participate in the reconstruction of every minute of life. They call themselves situationists in the sense that they hold it true that each individual can make their potentials to full play and obtain their respective pleasure by reconstructing their living situations. As a matter of fact, the situationist theories can be seen as a budding of an overall criticism to the new form of modern capitalistic control in the post-war France and other western countries with the rise of consumerism.

Chapter 3

From Ape to Man, a Subversive Perspective: Critical Reading of Jean Baudrillard's *Mirror of Production*[1]

Introduction

Since my first reading of Baudrillard's *Mirror of Production*, I have been harboring an anger in my heart that is difficult to subdue. Baudrillard, the savvy and talented elf, is generally regarded a great postmodernist avant-garde. Unexpectedly, he proves to be the most

---

[1] This chapter was translated by He Huiming.

profound and dangerous theoretical enemy of Marxism we have ever seen. His attack on Marxism, especially, on historical materialism in *The Mirror of Production*, is without doubt the most vicious but comprehensive critique of contemporary history. It is true that Marx has many enemies across the bourgeois camp. Since the birth of Marxism, criticism and condemnation against it have never stopped. However, in comparison with these outside clamors, Baudrillard's philosophical outset extends from the *inner logic* of Marxism. As a disciple of the western Marxist master Henri Lefebvre and a participant of the French translation of *German Ideology*, Baudrillard has a deep understanding of historical materialism in many aspects. Therefore, his accusation of historical materialism and Marxism as a whole is almost lethally fundamental. Unlike most Marxist critics, who give shallow talks like a dragonfly skimming the water surface but missing the real target, Baudrillard's criticism seems to be developed to a quite destructive level, which we cannot be more serious to deal with. In this connection, he is quite similar to the Frankfurt School deserter, Jurgen Habermas[1], and to some extent, even goes far beyond him. In short, Baudrillard is much more profound and precise than his stupid predecessors, whose abuses are mere bluffings directed at the pseudo-image of Stalinist dogmatism but who are unable to shake the real Marxism itself at all. Baudrillard grasps the two basic Marxist concepts, the material production and the mode of production, from which he goes on to negate the basic standpoints, concepts and the methodology of the whole Marxist system. Thus, all the core concepts of historical materialism and the basic logic of Marxist political economy seem to be completely brought within the range of Baudrillard's critical fire. If he had succeeded, the building of Marxist historical materialism that weathered 160 years would have collapsed. To avoid this misfortune, we are obligatory to face Baudrillard and accept his challenge.

Early in 1973, Baudrillard's *Mirror of Production* was published.

---

[1] Young Habermas finished his *Legitimation Crisis* (1975) in 1973, which is another important inner-logic critique of Marxism. Unlike Baudrillard's choice of a pseudo-romantic return to primitive situation, Habermas straightly turned to Capitalism.

Regrettably, in the past 30 years, little attention has been paid to it by most international left-wing scholars, few of whom really explore the theoretical truth of the text except some abstract and empty rejections in the name of criticism.[1] Ironically, in other fields such as anthropology and sociology[2], *The Mirror of Production* is acclaimed as an important philosophical achievement. Even more disappointing is the situation in China. No counter-critique essay has been seen since its Chinese translation appeared nearly two years ago. How puzzling is it? Where are those slogan-shouting "theoretical leftists" and bombastic claimants who always chant about "perfect Marxism?" Why don't the orthodox old guards stand out to face Baudrillard and make high-keyed refutations? Over 30 years ago, Baudrillard threw down the gauntlet with his *Mirror of Production* before all the Marxists, while this side has been almost silent. As a Chinese Marxist scholar of a new generation, I am compelled to put off other things at hand and tackle this important theoretical enemy. Before concrete discussions of the book, there are two prerequisite questions to be clarified.

First, conventional western researchers of Baudrillard simply refer to his early theoretical development as within the framework of *neo-Marxism*, for example, Mark Poster, who implies that before 1973, Baudrillard's critique of the capitalist commodity economy can still be viewed as within the general framework of Marxist political economy and structuralism as he says, "*The Mirror of Production* (1973) marks Baudrillard's parting of the ways with Marxism."[3] Similar opinions are held by Steve Best and Douglas Kellner.[4] I find most Chinese researchers seem to accept the above opinion,

---

[1] No essay in a 1994 reader of Baudrillard has a serious discussion of *The Mirror of Production*. *See Baudrillard: A Critical Reader* (Jiangsu People's Publishing House, 2006).

[2] As far as I know, *The Mirror of Production* is enlisted in the sociological reference in many overseas universities.

[3] Poster, Mark. *Jean Baudrillard, Selected Writings*. Stanford University Press, 1988. p. 4.

[4] Kellner, Douglas. "Introduction: Jean Baudrillard in Fin-de-Millenium." *Baudrillard: A Critical Reader* (Jiangsu People's Publishing House, 2005. page 7). Kellner even said Baudrillard's early text was a semiological supplement to Marxism. For Best's similar idea, *see* page 58 of the title book.

too. However, after careful reading of Baudrillard's early works, *The System of Objects* and *The Consumer Society*, I cannot help holding doubt about this judgment. Was there a real Marxist Baudrillard? My answer is "No". Baudrillard *never* became a Marxist. Even at the very beginning, his first theoretical position is post-Marxism. Interestingly, a symbolic textual event at that time was his first book, *The System of Objects*, published in 1968[1], the year of demarcation in the history of European leftist academia. Early in the mid-1960s, Baudrillard's three teachers, Henri Lefebvre, Roland Barthes and Guy Debord did not belong to the traditional western Marxist camp. Although Barthes belonged to the European left in his later years, he was never a Marxist. In addition, Lefebvre and Debord also transcended Marxism at that time.[2] We should bear in mind this significant point.

Second, my judgment is that in his early works of *The System of Objects*[3] and *The Consumer Society*, Baudrillard converted his teachers' critique of the latest capitalist changes into abstract philosophical reflection. Especially, in *The Consumer Society*, he merely offered a popular and hyperbolic portrayal of the dominant phenomenon in contemporary society, of which Lefebvre and Debord had already been aware. Lefebvre called the bureaucratic society of controlled consumption and Debord regarded it as the consumer society with spectacle control as the dominant structure. It should be noted that Baudrillard did not base his theoretical standpoint on Marxism. Marx's historical phenomenology has a perfunctory and unconvincing

---

[1] May of 1968 sees the outbreak of a famous student-labor movement against the modern capitalist culture in Paris. It is commonly known as the "May 1968" storm, after which Western Marxism began to decline.

[2] In 1967, Lefebvre began his criticism of Marxist productivism in *Everyday Life in the Modern World*. In the same period, Debord's *Society of the Spectacle* replaced commodity production with spectacle production, which is basically a post-Marxian text. Therefore, I have reason to conclude that the young Baudrillard sets his logical outset beyond the framework of Western Marxism.

[3] *The System of Objects* does not discuss the natural material or objects outside human society but aims to explore the non-natural objects within the instrumental world of man's "circumspection (Heidegger)," that is, the objects of man's material system in social existence. In fact, such objects classified in groups do not appear until industrialization.

presence here, if any. Instead, he employed what Lefebvre taught him, the *symbolic being* of ancient life, unpolluted by utilitarian logic. Its context root traced back to the theory founded by the French sociologist Marcel Mauss in social anthropological studies. After a metaphoric philosophical-cultural hyperbole by Bataille, the thought finally reached the conception of *grassrootism* centered on the primitive/tribal gift-exchange relations and non-utilitarian consumption. This concept had a sporadic appearance in Baudrillard's two early books but was developed by leaps and bounds in *For a Critique of the Political Economy of the Sign*[1], where he commenced the attack on the second great discovery of Marx, the theory of surplus value. By semiological rewriting of Debord's "society of spectacle," Baudrillard promptly brought forward the logic of symbolic relations and symbolic value. After that, the methodology of Marxist economics, historical materialism, and other successive important Marxist concepts, especially, production-labor, history and mode of production naturally became his targets in *The Mirror of Production*. The most important theoretical foundation of this ferocious criticism is nothing else but Bataille's grassroots romanticism philosophy. It is true that Baudrillard was still left with a vestige of *post-Marxian* idea, but *The Mirror of Production* completed his position finally as a thorough anti-Marxist theorist. Finally, when it came to *Symbolic Exchange and Death*, Baudrillard announced for the first time his theoretical framework –the logic of symbolic exchange, by which he re-summarized the criticism of contemporary society. It is here that Baudrillard rejected the scientific socialist theory of Marxism. He proposed a political alternative schema of *symbolic subversion*. The actual revolution against the capitalist control is then translated into a change of concepts. During the symbolic "revolution in the depths of soul," everything is substituted by imagination.

Baudrillard continues to produce a large number of new concepts and analytical frameworks with close attention to the most significant changes in contemporary western society; hence, he becomes the center of attention

---

[1] This book is planned to be translated and published by Nanjing University Press.

with his radical negative perspective and post-modern critique in western academic world. Here, I have to remind the reader that Baudrillard is not a post-modernist. He is only a stubborn thinker, persistent in his own grassroots romanticism but reaches a distant realm along the dimension of human thinking, even beyond the domain of post-modernism. In fact, Baudrillard himself feels uncomfortable about the popular misinterpretation of him as a "post-modern" "authority of reference." To him, it is quite absurd for his critical analysis of contemporary society to be casually "patched up at hindsight" and labeled as "post-modern."[1] For this reason, we shall only *miss* Baudrillard once we extol him as a post-modern theorist.

Strictly speaking, Baudrillard's works that really belong to post-Marxian school are *The System of Objects*, *The Consumer Society* and *For a Critique of the Political Economy of the Sign*. Although *The Mirror of Production* is a transitional text that *bids farewell to post-Marxism*, its existence poses so serious a threat to Marxism that I have to include it in my research field. As a Chinese Marxist, I hope to face this fierce enemy and defend historical materialism in the following theoretical argument.

In this chapter, we are going to deal with the extremely popular Jean Baudrillard[2], who is a major figure among radical post-modern thinkers

---

[1] *See* the preface of Jean Baudrillard's *The System of Objects* translated by Lin Zhiming and published in 2001.

[2] Jean Baudrillard (July, 1929-March, 2007), the famous contemporary French thinker, was born into a common family in Reims, a remote area of Northeast France. His grandfather was an ordinary farmer, and his parents were normal civil servants, therefore, Baudrillard did not possess the deep-rooted elitism in his early mind. It might also psychologically explain his later acceptance of the Bataille-Mauss grassroots radicalism. After graduating from high school, he failed in the entrance examination of the Paris Higher Normal School, even unable to be admitted to a university through common procedures. In his own words, his enrollment was done "in a tortuous way." The failure of obtaining a teacher's certificate deepened his hatred to the mainstream western culture. Thus, in the early 1960s, Baudrillard only relied on his language talent to teach German in a middle school. At the same time, he began to receive Mauss's anthropological view and note Bataille's philosophy. In 1966, under the tutelage of Lefebvre, the renowned western Marxist master, Baudrillard defended his "These de Troisième Cycle." In the same year, he got the position of teaching assistant in Université de Paris 5. From then on, Baudrillard received two concurring impacts, Sartre'sExistentialism and the French structural-

of Europe but never embraced Marxism, or more precisely, his academic presence is acquired by betraying his teachers' leftist position. In retrospect of the "post-1968" period in Europe, this betrayal coincided with the emergence of post-Marxism. At the same time, the post-modern thought came in to being as a whole. It must be particularly noted that Baudrillard is *not a post-modernist*[1] in the strict sense. Indeed, he not only tenaciously opposes the entire modernity but also *radically criticizes and rejects anything that is post-modern*. It is safe to say that Baudrillard's theoretical root, *Mauss-Bataille logic*, is fundamentally anti-civilization. We might as well define it as *grassroots romanticism*. (I shall make a detailed explanation later.) In addition, this logic dramatically differs from the *affirmative* conclusion of postmodernism by other scholars like Jacques Derrida and Jean Lyotard. This chapter will focus on the logical framework of the young Baudrillard's *Mirror of Production* and answer his comprehensive questioning of historical materialism. Baudrillard spends his most effort in chapters One and Five of *Mirror of Production*. Accordingly, these two chapters shall be the center of my attention. Meanwhile, in order to clarify the real logic that supports the text, I think it is necessary to spend a preliminary section to discuss Mauss-

---

ism, especially, the structural semiology by Roland Barthes. Later, he taught in Université de Paris-X Nanterre. Judged from his academic career, he is not an orthodox academic scholar. His writing style is relatively free, paying little attention to reference and bibliographies in his later years. However, we have to admit the explosive power of creativity and extraordinary depths of thinking in his text. In addition, his thought displays extreme variety and nonlinear thickness. In his own words, he was a pataphysician at 20 and then "situationist at 30, utopian at 40, transversal at 50, viral and metaleptic at 60." (Quoted from Baudrillard's *Cool Memories* (Vol. II) by Lin Zhiming in his Chinese preface of *The System of Objects*.) His representative works include *The System of Objects* (1968), *The Consumer Society* (1970), *For a Critique of the Political Economy of the Sign* (1972), *The Mirror of Production* (1973), *Symbolic Exchange and Death* (1976), *Simulacra and Simulations* (1978), *On Seduction* (1979), *America* (1986), *Lautre par lui-meme* (1987), *Cool Memories* (2 volumes in 1986 and 1990), *The Illusion of the End* (1991), *The Transparency of Evil* (1993), *The Perfect Crime* (1996), *Impossible Exchange* (1999) among others.

[1] In fact, the post-modern cannot be generally viewed as an "-ism" because of its rejection of any theoretical structure. It can be translated as post-modern thought or post-modern view.

Bataille's grassroots romanticism and Baudrillard's two early books. After it, we can smoothly enter the context of *The Mirror of Production*.

I. Baudrillard: A Marxist Before?

The Young Baudrillard rose to fame with *The System of Objects*, *The Consumer Society* and *For a Critique of the Political Economy of the Sign*. They are usually classified by overseas researchers as neo-Marxist text because Baudrillard is somehow criticizing today's capitalism. Nevertheless, it is a hasty conclusion that cannot hold up after careful reconsideration. If we penetrate behind the lines of the text, it is not difficult to find that the real logic of the text is neither Marxist ideas nor the critical thinking of his left-wing teachers, like Lefebvre, Barthes and Debord. It is but Mauss-Bataille's thought of symbolic exchange. In this section, we are going to have a general discussion about the Mauss-Bataille thought at first, and then clarify the basic clues of Baudrillard's discourse in the early works to pave the way for the critique of *The Mirror of Production*.

1. Mauss's symbolic exchange and the grassroots romanticism

Strangely, in all the available biographies of the young Baudrillard, there does not seem to be sufficient attention to the important influence of the mid-20th century French anthropological-sociological thinking on the development of Baudrillard's thought. In my opinion, people, especially western researchers, are absorbed in the trendy "post-modern" ideas of his late period, while ignorant of the original discourse framework hidden in his various creative logical platforms. Therefore, Mauss's social anthropological concepts and the ensuing Bataille's philosophy; the most influential and important factor in the development of the young Baudrillard's thought is but eclipsed by the popular discourse and kept far away from people's attention. Now, I want to start from Marcel Mauss's anthropological discoveries about primitive societies achieved through his fieldwork and then investigate the inherent correlation among them.

The nephew of the eminent sociologist Émile Durkheim[1], Marcel Mauss[2] had a favorite condition to pursue his studies of sociology and anthropology. He inherited many of Durkheim's sociological doctrines. In his early studies, he was also under the guidance of other sociologists, such as Claude Lévi-Strauss and Antoine Meillet. This experience benefited him much in studying methodology and Sanskrit, laying a sound foundation for his anthropological field research later. Mauss began from the first hand investigation of the lives of primitive tribes. His most important contribution to anthropology is to abandon the conservative construction of primitive cultures through modern western discourse. Instead, he infiltrated himself into the real life of primitive tribes and the depths of primitive culture, acquired many completely new explanations from field investigations, created a new academic platform for French sociological and anthropological studies, and affected a whole generation of French thinkers. We should pay attention to the following aspects of Mauss's achievement.

First, *the whole symbolic culture dominates the material existence* in primitive social life. In 1896, Mauss published his first important paper, *A General Theory of Magic*.[3] By observation of the primitive tribes, Mauss initiated his unique thought from the social role of magic. After examining the indigenous peoples of Australia, the Melanesians and

---

[1]　Emile Durkheim (1858-1917), renowned contemporary sociologist of France.

[2]　Marcel Mauss (1872-1950), the famous French anthropologist and sociologist. He was born to a Jewish family in Epinal. His father was a small embroidery workshop owner while his mother is sister of the eminent socialist Émile Durkheim. After high school graduation in 1890, he was not admitted to Ecole Normale Super Paris but studied philosophy at Bordeaux, where he followed Durkheim and became his assistant. At the same time from 1891, he registered for the study of law. Tow years later, his learning was interrupted by military service abroad. In 1895, Mauss passed the national qualification exam for teachers of philosophy and then studied and worked in Ecole Pratique des Hautes Etudes. In 1898, Mauss founded Année sociologique with Durkheim, and began "L'École de L'Année Sociologique" in France. In 1930, he took up the chair of Sociology at the Collège de France. In 1938, he was elected dean of the religion and science section in EPHA. He died in 1950 at the age of 78. His works include *The Nation* (1920), *The Gift* (1925), *Sociology and Anthropology* (1950) and *Works* (*Vol. 1-3*) (1968-1969).

[3]　It was co-written with Henri Humbert.

Iroquois in the North Pacific region and the Mexican tribes, Mauss found that magic almost permeated every corner of the tribal life, be it primitive techniques, arts, or mystical religious ceremonies. The power of magic was observable everywhere. "Association with evil as an aspect of magical rites always provides humanity with a rough general notion of magic."[1] Various rites were centered on a supernatural power in order to structure all the material existence of man. Different from the religious tendency towards the abstract, magic usually draws to the concrete. Mauss drew three laws on magic: "contiguity, similarity and opposition." He stated that the essence of magic is to pursue the usage of ascertaining man, things and concepts as well as the specific, general or common power. Magic seeks a vigorous and shapeless *totality of symbolic relations* to attain the control of interpretations and constructions of life. Thus, Mauss made the important assertion that in primitive life "the whole adds up to much more than the number of its parts."[2] (Claude Lévi-Strauss highly praised this opinion.) In primitive tribes, things such as "nature", "Mana"[3] and "power" belong to a symbolic totality that offers real meanings to man, objects and various social phenomena and turns the material existence into *being*. Mauss discovered "the sacred"[4] positioned as the object of worship in primitive societies. At least to the primitive people, the sacred is not a hallucination, but a more "real social entity"[5] and generally structures the existence of the primitive life. (Mauss's conception had a deep influence on Bataille.) Mauss further valorized this symbolic relation as the most real being, only obscured by numerous material signs of today's society. (According to Lévi-Strauss, as early as 1924, Mauss

---

[1] Mauss, Marcel, and Robert Brain. *A General Theory of Magic*. London: Routledge & Kegan Paul, 1972. p. 27.

[2] Ibid., p. 107.

[3] An important concept with divine power discovered by Mauss in his fieldwork about the Melanesians.

[4] Mauss, Marcel, and Robert Brain. *A General Theory of Magic*. London: Routledge & Kegan Paul, 1972. p. 11.

[5] *See* the appendix of *A General Theory of Magic* in *Sociology and Anthropology* translated by Yu Biping Shanghai Translation Publishing House, 2003. p. 104.

said that the social life is in "a world of symbols,"[1] which also accounts for Marshall Sahlins's logic of symbolic culture governing the praxis.)

Second, the structure of *reciprocal symbolic exchange* in primitive societies. In *The Gift* (1925), Mauss discovered a "trading human nature" of the original people, which he named the *gift-exchange* relation. It is very different from the utilitarian economic relation that dominates today's society. Mauss drew this conclusion from his analysis of Indian tribes in the North Pacific region, especially, the phenomenon of "potlatch" between Tlingit and Haida tribes. The so-called "potlatch" is a modern name, which means the hosts endeavor to demonstrate their wealth through mutual invitations of eating. Mauss perceptively found that during the potlatch between these two tribes, people attached no importance to the eating itself but aimed to realize a process of gift exchange, for instance, they wantonly squandered and destroyed things during their enthusiastic gift exchanges. In their eyes, everything had a certain spiritual power, called "hau." In the process of gift exchanges, the responsibility and the received objects were not rigid. Even if one did not receive the gift, "hau" still belonged to him. Therefore, the act of receiving the gift actually corresponded to a symbolic essence and spirituality. That is why "hau" had to be returned to where it came.[2] Mauss believed the potlatch is very similar to the consumption and destruction in sacrificial ceremonies, only in different names of man and God but for the same purpose of mutual peace and coexistence. Mauss also found another kind of potlatch, the Kula, "the system of gift exchange" at a larger scale, in which the general sense of "wealth" circulation was brought to a halt and replaced by "killing" the exchanged gifts. This exchange turned out to be more of a *symbolic* rite, during which people exchanged their soul and meaning, and the gift became the sacré. Unlike the ubiquitous market exchange today, the primitive people not only avoid possessing the sacred thing but also revere

---

[1]   Claude Lévi-Strauss. "Introduction to Sociology and Anthropology." Trans. Yu Biping. *Sociology and Anthropology*. Shanghai Translation Publishing House, 2003. p. 5.

[2]   Mauss, Marcel. *The Gift: Forms and Functions of Exchange in Archaic Societies*. Trans. Ian Cunnison. Glencoe: Free Press, 1954. p. 9.

it and prepare to waste anything for it. This symbolic exchange produces a continual, reciprocal and equal communication and circulation. It forms the basic structure that supports the entire social activities.

Finally, Mauss drew from his anthropological research an important *judgment of value* that the relation of primitive symbolic exchange is the cure to modern social diseases. (It is the conclusion also of the ecstasy of Bataille and Baudrillard.) Mauss believed that the primitive system of symbolic exchange possesses a "common sociological value" for our society today. It can explain the historiography of human societies and should be restored as "the way to better administrative procedures for our societies."[1] According to Mauss, it is only a recent event in Western society for man to become an "economic animal (Marx)." (Michel Foucault echoed it later.) "Homo economicus is not behind us, but before, like the moral man, the man of duty, the scientific man and the reasonable man. For a long time man was something quite different; and it is not so long now since he became a machine—a calculating machine."[2] In his opinion, only recently did people begin to chase fame and wealth, while in the most Epicureanistic ethics of ancient times, people pursue goodness and happiness instead of material interest. Mauss then visualized a beautiful future, in which he attempted to substitute the primitive relation of symbolic exchange for today's utilitarian value exchange. "The producer-exchanger feels now as he has always felt— but this time he feels it more acutely—that he is giving something of himself, his time and his life."[3] Mauss was happy that "it can be seen at work already in certain economic groups and in the hearts of the masses who often enough know their own interest and the common interest better than their leaders do."[4]

This idea at last gives birth to what I call *grassroots romanticism*. It

---

[1] Mauss, Marcel. *The Gift: Forms and Functions of Exchange in Archaic Societies*. Trans. Ian Cunnison. Glencoe: Free Press, 1954. p. 69.

[2] Ibid., p. 74.

[3] Ibid., p. 75.

[4] Ibid., p. 76.

is well known that in traditional humanitarian logic the idealized man's authenticity is based on an abstract value assumption. The contradiction between the *must existence* ("ought") and the non-logical *bad reality* ("is") generates a tremendous critical tension, for instance, Rousseau's ideal natural status of man before degeneration and Feuerbach's inalienated natural sortal being of man hollowed by divine attributes. Therefore, Mauss's opinion does not belong to the traditional humanitarian discourse. In his mind he has formed a logical mode in which the primitive tribal life (the past) is employed to judge the social reality (the present). Obviously, this notion stems from under-developed primitive societies. Moreover, Mauss assumes the *ontological base* of the primitive existence and the *authentic ought* of the sortal being. Without doubt, it should be included in romanticism, and it differs from the classic romanticism centered on theological critique of late Middle Ages. I therefore hereby refer to it as grassroots romanticism. This *backward* logic appeared in previous history, for example, the Confucian vision of self-abnegation and etiquette-restoration, which regards a historical past as a gauge of value to measure the present reality. Mauss's ontological vision of the past is an important achievement in the fieldwork of modern anthropology and its theoretical value can never be overestimated. If extended to the theoretical level of social reform, it can be called practopianism, in contrast to fantastic utopianism. However, the real situation of the primitive tribal life is not as beautiful as in Mauss's poetical description. Those who could attend the potlatch were confined to a few chiefs and even women were taken as consumptions in the free exchange of gifts. Earlier, Marx commented that such a life was "natural, restricted."[1] At first glance, the primitive life is not poisoned by capitalist exchange-value, and from the perspective of symbolic exchange process, it generally "*seems* personal." After all, it is an early state of social life. Hence, when the eminent anthropologist Mauss jumps out of his research field and idealistically appoints the primitive tribal

---

[1] Karl Marx and Frederick Engels. *Collected Works*, vol. 28. London: Lawrence & Wishart, 1986. p. 100.

life as the authentic being of human modernity, he becomes what Lenin calls a "poor philosopher." The reason why Mauss's concept is first treated here is that it later becomes a theoretical tool to criticize Marxist historical materialism used by such people as the young Baudrillard and Sahlins, whom I am going to deal with in the following part. In addition, it is still popular in certain fields, such as anthropology and sociology.

It should be recognized that Mauss's impact on the French academia was enormous, which is reflected through many other theorists. For instance, in the field of philosophy, there is Bataille; in sociology, there are Lévi-Strauss, who, based on Mauss's theory, proposed structural anthropology that emphasizes the symbolic system, and his successor, Sahlins[1]; in sociology, Pierre Bourdieu first combined Mauss's concept with Marxist economy and put forward such concepts as "cultural capital" and "social capital." Later,

---

[1] Marshall David Sahlins (1930-) was born in Chicago, Illinois on December 27, 1930. He is a prominent American anthropologist. He received both a Bachelor's and Master's degree at the University of Michigan in 1951 and 1952. He then earned his Ph.D. of anthropology at Columbia University in 1954. He returned to teach at the University of Michigan from 1956 to 1973. After it, he moved to the University of Chicago, where he is today the Charles F. Grey Distinguished Service Professor of Anthropology Emeritus. In 1976, he was admitted to the American Academy of Arts and Sciences. His major works include: *Social Stratification in Polynesia* (1958), *Evolution and Culture* (ed., 1960), *Moala: Culture and Nature on a Fijian Island* (1962), *Culture and Practical Reason* (1976), *Historical Metaphors and Mythical Realities* (1981), *Islands of History* (1985), *Cosmologies of Capitalism* (1988), *Anahulu: The Anthropology of History in the Kingdom of Hawaii* (co-authored with Patrick Kerch) (1992), *How "Natives" Think: About Captain Cook, for Example* (1995), *The Sadness of Sweetness* (1996). As early as in the 1960s, Sahlins gradually gave up the traditional concept of historical evolution and accepted the so-called cultural schema neoevolutionism. In the mid-1970s, based on Mauss's anthropology, he turned his critique to economic anthropology, that is, to employ contemporary western culture, especially, economics in the illustration of primitive societies or non-western cultures. In 1976, he published *Culture and Practical Reason*. In his opinion, symbolic cultural logic is rather a deep supporting structure for social existence and movements. In this book, Sahlins quoted much from Marx's literature, with profound and accurate understanding. By comparison, Baudrillard's *Mirror of Production* is a simple negation of Marxist historical materialism. Because Sahlins's text is later than the *Mirror*, I will not have a comprehensive discussion here but rather selectively employ its contents to help illustrate the thought of the young Baudrillard.

Mauss was faithfully followed by Baudrillard[1] and others. As a matter of fact, Mauss's thought was well accepted wherever it spread in the French academia. His fame reached the summit in the 1980s, when a handful of French sociologists launched a famous interdisciplinary Movement of Anti-Utilitarianism in Social Science, in a word, "MAUSS."[2]

Next, we will examine Bataille's philosophical concept because Baudrillard's early theoretical logic derives more directly from him.

2. Bataille's non-useful philosophy of grassrootsism

Georges Bataille (1879-1962) is a very important contemporary French thinker.[3] (My book, *The Impossible Truth of Being*: *Mirror of Lacan's Philosophy*, has already touched upon Bataille's philosophical thought.[4]) As early as in the mid-1920s he had communicated with the surrealists, but Bataille kept off their elitism. He supported the "vulgar" heterogeneity of the famous pornographic writer Marquis de Sade. (It is reasonable to believe that Bataille's philosophy gets on with an anti-elitist *grassrootsism* from the very beginning.) At that time, Bataille already focused on the non-useful secular "excretion" in a society of possession and utilitarianism as well as the heterogeneous religious life.[5] In 1925, Mauss published *The Gift*, a desired treasure for Bataille, who soon devoted himself to the

---

[1] The young Baudrillard did not agree with Bourdieu's interpretation of Mauss.

[2] In French, it is "Mouvement anti-utilitariste dans les sciences socials." In short, "MAUSS."

[3] Georges Bataille (1897-1962) was born in Billom in France, Sept. 10, 1897. In his 17, he was baptized as a Catholic. After the outbreak of World War I, he was recruited to the army and retired due to illness in the same year. In 1918, he passed the university entrance examination and studied at the École Nationale des Chartes in the following years. After graduation in 1922, he was given the position of librarian in Bibliothèque Nationale. He then founded a series of journals, *Documents* in 1929, *Acephale* in 1936. He died in Paris in June 8, 1962. His major works include *The Solar Anus* (1931), *The Notion of Expenditure* (1933), *The Inner Experience* (1943), *The Accursed Share* (I&II, 1949-1951), and *On Nietzsche* (1945).

[4] *See The Impossible Truth of Being*: *Mirror of Lacan's Philosophy* (The Commercial Press, 2006).

[5] *See* Georges Bataille's "The Use Value of D.A.F. Sade" translated by Allan Stoekl, with Carl R. Lovitt and Donald M. Leslie, Jr. Excerpted from the book *Visions of Excess*: *Selected Writings, 1927-1939*, Minneapolis: UMP, 1985.

popular anthropological and sociological research of primitive tribal lives. In 1933, another book *Notion of Expenditure* was printed, which was his metaphysical summary of Mauss's theory. In 1937, Bataille, together with others, established "The College of Sociology." They honored Mauss as their spiritual leader and attempted to develop his anthropological and sociological achievements into a new philosophy to criticize social reality. (To their disappointment, Mauss gave his support only moderately, and even openly expressed his opposition to over-philosophize and over-politicize his own theory.) Bataille then discussed the subject in *The Limitations of Usefulness* (1945, draft), *The Accursed Share Vol. III* (1945-1954), *Hegel, Death and Sacrifice* (1955). These writings composed his most important philosophical thought. (It is also the logical pillar behind the critical theory proposed by the arrogant young Baudrillard.) Next, I am going to have a general discussion about Bataille.

First, his division between the *profane world* and the *sacred world*. The sacred thing is Mauss's deferential call for the non-actual existence indicated by the symbolic exchange relation in primitive life. Bataille expands the concept to philosophy. (He confirms the division of the binary world as "one of the conclusive findings of social anthropology."[1]) In his early research of Sade, Bataille put forward the division between the "profane" reality with utilitarian possession as the scale of existence and the religious reality with the useless excretion as measurement. He believed in the "division of social facts into religious facts (prohibitions, obligations and the realization of sacred action) on one hand and profane facts (civil, political, juridical, industrial, and commercial organization) on the other."[2] In his later studies, Bataille went further to state that the secular world is at the same time a *materialized* world of homogeneity, where material production

---

[1] Bataille, Georges. "Psychological Structure of Fascism." *Visions of Excess: Selected Writings, 1927-1939.* Trans. Allan Stoekl. Theory and History of Literature, V. 14. Minneapolis: University of Minnesota Press, 1985. p. 144.

[2] Ibid., p. 94.

and reproduction is put on a fundamental position as the only standard to arrogantly determine this world. (It is the logical starting point for Marxist historical materialism. Later, the young Baudrillard hounded this negative theoretical point.) In such a utilitarian profane world, any item is linked to another by human-defined means and purpose. This linkage goes on and on, composing a systematic material world of utility. (Here is easily seen what Heidegger defines the "ready-to-hand" material world. It is also here earth is turned into the earthly world.[1]) In such a world, man's thought and practice only caters for the requirement of material utility. The object sets its prime task to protect its "value of utility" from destruction and *sustain* it in a certain way.[2] Thus, the utilitarian world makes human character "an abstract and interchangeable entity."[3] (Bataille's idea had a direct impact on Baudrillard's *System of Objects*.) In Bataille's view, the production-possession oriented *progressive* world is a *projected* world. (Bataille believes it is a historical progressive logic of rationalism posited by Descartes.[4]) The so-called project refers to people's labor and creative activities under the guidance of rationality. And their purpose is not immediate pleasure but a *delayed* expectation. (This project/plan is the ontological base of the late Sartre's idealization of Marxism.) Unlike other animals that indulge in current pleasure, human beings temporarily give up present satisfaction and willingly postpone it because they believe their ongoing labor is for fruitful results which will be obtained in the future. People grow out of the direct animal existence and live for the delayed utilitarian value. Hence, anything that does not help achieve the objective or harvest the desired result will be

---

[1] *See* Heidegger, Martin, and David Farrell Krell. *Nietzsche*. San Francisco: Harper & Row, 1979.

[2] Yuasa, Hiroo. *Georges Bataille*: *Consumption*. Trans. Zhao Hanying: Hebei Educational Publishing House, 2001. p. 155.

[3] Bataille, Georges. "Psychological Structure of Fascism." *Visions of Excess*: *Selected Writings, 1927-1939*. Trans. Allan Stoekl. Theory and History of Literature, V. 14. Minneapolis: University of Minnesota Press, 1985. p. 138.

[4] Bataille, Georges. "Pain" Trans. Wu Qiong. *Eroticism, Expenditure and General Economy*. Ed. Wang Min'an: Jilin People's Publishing House, 2003. p. 49.

estimated as meaningless and thus ruthlessly abandoned. (Obviously, the profane world here is the actual society based on material production that the young Baudrillard loathed.) Bataille thinks that sacred things stand in contrast to this utilitarian secular world. They, unlike the palpable and useful items, stem from the resistance against this world and the secular time.[1] They essentially allude to the filth, sex and death of the profane world, where man escapes time and dedicates his life to expenditure.[2] "The *heterogeneous* world includes everything resulting from *non-productivist* expenditure (sacred things themselves form part of this whole)."[3] In comparison with Mauss's anthological thought, Bataille's discussion is ontological. He turns Mauss's hypothesis of grassroots romanticism into an anti-actual *philosophy of grassrootsism*.

Second, Bataille's confirmation of the *non-productive expenditure schema*. According to Mauss, the primitive tribes see the non-utilitarian expenditure happening in sacrifice, potlatch and other large-scale symbolic exchanges, which compose the social structure that supports the tribal life. Bataille's notion of expenditure is, first of all, an inheritance of Sade's "excretion" in contrary to industrial utilitarianism. In *The Use Value of D.A.F. Sade*, Bataille says that the weird but attractive thing in ordinary people's eyes is nothing else but his cognition of excrement and the ensuing pleasure.[4] Unlike the utilitarian possession in today's production realm, man undergoes an authentic existential pleasure of escaping homogeneity during the physical excretion of the waste. The same experience repeats in other situations such as sex abuse, sight of a dead body and nauseating as well as

---

[1] *See* Bataille's *History of Eroticism*. Trans. Liu Hui: The Commercial Press, 2003. p. 187.

[2] Ibid.

[3] Bataille, Georges. "Psychological Structure of Fascism." *Visions of Excess: Selected Writings, 1927-1939*. Trans. Allan Stoekl. Theory and History of Literature, V. 14. Minneapolis: University of Minnesota Press, 1985. p. 142.

[4] Lacan wrote Kant with Sade, but this is not included in the Chinese version of the Selected Works of Lacan. Bataille wrote *The Use Vale of D.A.F. Sade: An Open Letter to My Current Comrades*. (Bataille, Georges. Eroticism, Expenditure and General Economy. Ed. Wang Min'an: Jilin People's Publishing House, 2003. 1.)

the time of facing truth and sacredness. Bataille even assumed the "identical nature" "of God and excrement."[1] Based on Mauss's theory, Bataille extends the non-utilitarian sacred "excretion" to an *ontological* concept of expenditure. (In the second part of *The Notion of Expenditure*, Bataille details Mauss's discussion of the potlatch phenomenon.[2]) As stated by the non-useful excretion logic, the essence of expenditure is non-productivist and non-utilitarian. Through the primitive sacrificial ceremony, Bataille discerns a pure destructive "exhaustion," a material consumption that is separated from the utilitarian utility in real social life. This consumption of abandonment, destruction, loss and emptiness symbolizes a certain God-oriented spiritual function that is external to man's material existence. Therefore, in Bataille's opinion, the non-productivist expenditure breaks the project logic and makes the existence recover its original glow by negating the utilitarian utility. (The utility is man's insult at the object through production, if in adapting Heidegger's words, the "thing not thinged.") In this regard, Bataille says expenditure can refer to,

> luxury, mourning, war, cults, the construction of sumptuary monuments, games, spectacles, arts, perverse sexual activity (i.e., deflected from genital finality)—all these represent activities which, at least in primitive circumstances, have no end beyond themselves.[3]

This definition clearly exceeds Mauss's anthropological scope. Bataille believes that "in the market economy, the processes of exchange have an acquisitive sense."[4] In contrast to the productivist possession and acquisition during the value exchange, expenditure is a non-utilitarian and non-useful

---

[1] Bataille, Georges. "The Use Value of D.A.F. Sade" *Visions of Excess: Selected Writings, 1927-1939*. Trans. Allan Stoekl. Theory and History of Literature, V. 14. Minneapolis: University of Minnesota Press, 1985. p. 102.

[2] *See* Bataille's "The Notion of Expenditure." *Visions of Excess: Selected Writings, 1927-1939*. Trans. Allan Stoekl. Theory and History of Literature, V. 14. Minneapolis: University of Minnesota Press, 1985.

[3] Ibid., p. 118.

[4] Ibid., p. 123.

action. It concerns man's entire inner life instead of his material existence.[1] To illustrate this, Bataille employs the example of the pyramid: in the eyes of profit, pyramid building is a big mistake; instead, people could well have dug a hole and then filled it.[2] However, for the ancient Egyptians, the pyramid was the symbol of the shining sun. They firmly believed that the pyramids, although useless in today's secular world, could transform death into radiance, the endless existence.[3] The pursuit of divine attributes is prevalent. (If Bataille's thought would be actualized, it might stage the scene in Andrei Platonov's *Gradov City*[4] or the Chinese Cultural Revolution, where people denied material interest, completely stopped utilitarian production, indifferently saw the weeds growing in the cornfield, blindly shot the so-called bourgeoisie, or passionately performed the "Loyalty Dance." With incredible enthusiasm, people joined the symbolic revolutionary activities and happily allowed the detestable economy end in collapse. The miserable result is not difficult to imagine.)

Third, coexistence of the *general economy* with divine attributes. Bataille bases his philosophy on religious feelings, which differentiates him from Mauss. In the guiding light of the religious lamp, Bataille does not have Mauss's practopian complex of recovering the primitive life. In my understanding, the so-called general economy is the *road to the sacred world* in his mind. To Bataille, the secular capitalist society implements a *limited* special economy in pursuit of mundane utilitarianism while he admires and yearns for a general economy with the yardstick of "non-acquisition." Bataille thinks that the capitalist possessive economy based on utilitarianism is a kind

---

[1] Bataille, Georges. *History of Eroticism*. Trans. Liu Hui: The Commercial Press, 2003. p. 181.

[2] Bataille, Georges. "Economy." Trans. Wang Min'an. *Eroticism, Expenditure and General Economy*. Ed. Wang Min'an: Jilin People's Publishing House, 2003. p. 167.

[3] Bataille, Georges. *Eroticism, Expenditure and General Economy*. Jilin People's Publishing House. Ed. Wang Min'an, 2003. p. 236.

[4] *Gradov City* was written by the former Soviet Union writer Andrei Platonov during 1927-1928 but was delayed to be published until 1978. The Chinese translation was done by Gu Yang in 1997.

of special, socially alienated existing form and the most general authentic being is just incarnated in the "glory" existence of endless expenditure, like the shining sun never asking for returns.[1] Bataille appeals that it is indeed man's authentic mode of being and the meaning for God's existence because the essence of religion lies in man's transcendence of material possession. Apotheosization of God is then associated with de-apotheosization of human life.[2] Only in the bright city of God can we acquire the divine existence of non-productivist expenditure. In this connection, Bataille thinks that beauty is nothing and the artist is *nothing* of the material world.[3] "God is NOTHING."[4] In fact, the true, the good, the beautiful and the divine of the sacred world become the anticipated Nothing and *désoeuverment*. Due to the absence of the object, God is not an actual and useful presence but "death" in the profane world of utilitarianism. It should be admitted that Bataille aims for the City of God from the primitive grassroots *Existenz* (existence). This is his essential difference from Mauss.

Bataille has two other points that are worth our attention. First, although he noticed the sacred thing and non-utilitarian expenditure in Mauss's theory, he did not over-emphasize Mauss's symbolic exchange thought. In comparison, the idea of symbolic exchange was frequently echoed by Lévi-Strauss and Sahlins in their anthropological studies, as well as the young Baudrillard to found his philosophical ontology. Second, Bataille did not turn his critique against Karl Marx. In his early years, he admitted that Marx was "justified"[5] in his criticism of capitalism about the question of nation

[1] Bataille, Georges. "Economy." Trans. Wang Min'an. *Eroticism, Expenditure and General Economy*. Ed. Wang Min'an: Jilin People's Publishing House, 2003. p. 151.

[2] Bataille, Georges. "Origin and Reform of Capitalism." Trans. Wu Qiong. *Eroticism, Expenditure and General Economy*. Ed. Wang Min'an: Jilin People's Publishing House, 2003. p. 171.

[3] Bataille, Georges. *Eroticism, Expenditure and General Economy*. Ed. Wang Min'an: Jilin People's Publishing House, 2003. p. 265.

[4] Ibid., p. 217.

[5] Bataille, Georges. "Psychological Structure of Fascism." *Visions of Excess*: *Selected Writings, 1927-1939*. Trans. Allan Stoekl. Theory and History of Literature, V. 14. Minneapolis: University of Minnesota Press, 1985. p. 139.

and class. Later, in his talk about the whole secular world based on material production, he repeatedly confirmed Marx's idea of "going back to one's real being" through negating the material reality and believed it would open a new chapter for human liberation.[1] Like Sartre, Bataille also commended Marx's decisive impact on our era, although he at the same time pointed out that Marx's communist ideal is still preconditioned by material wealth. Exactly these ideas paved the way for young Baudrillard's avant-garde critique of Marxism.

3. Hidden logic support in *The System of Object* and *The Consumer Society*

Now we are ready to deal with the two important works by the young Baudrillard: *The System of Object* (1968) and *The Consumer Society* (1970). There has been sufficient exploration about their historical context and theoretical construction, for instance, theoretical premises from Lefebvre, Barthes, and Debord. There is also a clear distillation of the basic thoughts in the texts.[2] Therefore, these subjects will not be emphasized here again. I attempt to have a serious discussion about the *hidden but governing Mauss-Bataille idea* gradually constructed by the young Baudrillard in them.

Previous studies are drawn much to aspects such as semiology and may well overlook another important logical structure. In *The System of Objects*, the young Baudrillard's ontological concept is developed from Heidegger's ready-to-hand "circumspection." He believes that in the daily life of the capitalist system, the *functional utility chain* gradually becomes the basic existence of items, which is called "the scientificalized and structuralized process of objects."[3] Behold, Baudrillard here takes a negative attitude towards the functionality of objects. No doubt, such logic also derives from

---

[1] Bataille, Georges. "Origin and Reform of Capitalism." Trans. Wu Qiong. *Eroticism, Expenditure and General Economy*. Ed. Wang Min'an: Jilin People's Publishing House, 2003. p. 180.

[2] *See* Yang Haifeng's *Towards Post-Marx: From Mirror of Production to Mirror of Symbols*. Central Compilation and Translation Press, 2004.

[3] *See* Lin Zhiming's introduction to *The System of Objects*. Shanghai Century Publishing Group Co., Ltd., 2001. p. 3.

the late Heidegger's criticism of technology, the romantic conversion of "das ding dingt." As expected, Baudrillard says that in such a structuralized system, "many objects are confined within their own functionality and coexist in a functionalized situation according to man's needs."[1] Here, he is clearly dissatisfied with the anthropocentric discourse.

The opening of *System of Objects* seems to take the early patriarchal bourgeois tradition as the initial reference to criticize the functionality of family furniture and items. The essence of the traditional furniture layout lies in building an invisible "entity of moral order," that is, "to personify human relationships," in his borrowing of Marx's words.[2] The statement is not wrong by itself. However, in Baudrillard's consideration of the traditional structure of objects and space, I find another important evidence, the "symbolic relation." Through the presence of objects, Baudrillard says, the traditional furniture layout embodies and *symbolizes* a deep emotional relationship of family spirit. With the change of life, the current capitalist home furnishings break the traditional "density" structure. The object has been greatly functionalized and modern furniture strides toward a completely fresh utility-oriented system, speaking of which, the young Baudrillard passionately laments: Why?

In his eyes, the modern system of objects chooses the organization value to shroud the "symbolic values, and along with them use values."[3] (At that time, Baudrillard still regarded the use value as an *original* material attribute, an ideal much less radical than that of his *Mirror of Production* later.) He states that, in today's structure of objects,

> [t]hese objects are no longer endowed with a "soul," nor do they invade us with their symbolic presence: the relationship has become an objective one, founded on disposition and play. The value this

---

[1] *See* Lin Zhiming's introduction to *The System of Objects*. Shanghai Century Publishing Group Co., Ltd., 2001. p. 6.

[2] Baudrillard, Jean. *The System of Objects*. Trans. James Benedict. Radical Thinkers, 3. London [u.a.]: Verso, 2005. p. 14.

[3] Ibid., p. 19.

relationship takes on is no longer of an instinctive or an psychological but, rather, of a tactical kind.[1]

It is noticeable that Baudrillard still takes the original use value as the foundation of *symbolic value,* with a more important symbolic relation here. (In my opinion, the young Baudrillard was very similar to Sahlins at this time.) The conventional structure of objects is poetic, and their objectivity adopts closed and mutually responsive objects to stage an associated scene, that is, the system of symbolic family relations. This system is accompanied by a whole set of poetic and metaphoric symbols. "So, with meaning and value deriving from the hereditary transmission of substances under the jurisdiction of form, the world is experienced as given (as it always is in the unconscious and in childhood)."[2] (This non-utilitarian and non-reciprocal *gift* belongs to Mauss. However, Baudrillard believes it only exists in man's early life and unconscious state.) The object exists in an "anthropomorphous" presence. As a result of the present functionalized objects, "[t]he notion of a world [is] no longer given but instead produced—mastered, manipulated, inventoried, controlled: a world, in short, that has to be *constructed.*"[3] Hence, "rooms now have traded in the symbols of family for signs of social relationship."[4] Baudrillard sadly comments that "we have thus moved from the depth of a vertical field to the extension of a horizontal one."[5] (This point was later developed in *Symbolic Exchange and Death,* where the transition of vertical relation to horizontal relation referred to the transformation of the "law of commodity value" with reference frame to the semiotic "structural law of commodity value" without reference frame.)

In the second part of the text, "Structures of Atmosphere," Baudrillard even devotes an independent section "The End of the Symbolic Dimension" to the illustration of the loss of symbolic value in conventional arts. People

---

[1] Baudrillard, Jean. *The System of Objects.* Trans. James Benedict. Radical Thinkers, 3. London [u.a.]: Verso, 2005. p. 19.

[2] Ibid., p. 27.

[3] Ibid., p. 28.

[4] Ibid., p. 48.

[5] Ibid., p. 53.

in traditional handcrafts link each other with gestures and form a symbolic "theatre," where items play various roles while "gestures and physical effort are also the vectors of a whole phallic symbolism, as deployed, for example, in such notions as penetration, resistance, moulding or rubbing."[1] However, in the modern system of technical production, the traditional symbolic relation of gestures is completely retires. Technology creates, through imitation, an "artificial intelligence world", where only functionality and symbols dangle and the symbolic value that represents man's qualitative existence disappears.

At the same stroke the symbolic relationship likewise disappears. What emerges from the realm of signs is a nature continuously dominated, an abstract, worked-upon nature, rescued from time and anxiety, which the sign is constantly converting into culture. This nature has been systematized: it is not so much nature as naturalness (or, equally well, "culturalness"). Such naturalness is thus the corollary of all functionality and the connotation of the modern system of "atmosphere."[2]

Baudrillard repeatedly maintains that the present existence has lost symbolic relationship, and consequently, man's existence is not authentic anymore and nature is not the real nature. (This point is related to his view of nature advocated in *The Mirror of Production*.)

We need to clarify what exactly the young Baudrillard means by his symbolic value. From the discussion about the symbolic value of antiques, I realize that Baudrillard only has a vague and imaginary understanding of this idea despite Mauss-Bataille's influence on him. In Baudrillard's eyes, "the antique may be said, though it serves no obvious purpose, to serve a purpose nevertheless at a deeper level."[3] The reason why antiques are precious is their important use of *uselessness* (a parroting of Bataille.) With a *symbolic*

---

[1] Baudrillard, Jean. *The System of Objects*. Trans. James Benedict. Radical Thinkers, 3. London [u.a.]: Verso, 2005. p. 57.

[2] Ibid., p. 68.

[3] Ibid., p. 79.

divine presence in contrast to the utility of today's functionalized objects, the antique means complete fulfillment and answers the inquiry as an ultimate and perfect existence. If the functionalized object is "devoid of being,"[1] the existence of the antique as such should be used in "perfective aspect". Hence, the antique justifies its own existence, the "authentic presence."[2] Heidegger calls it "das ding dingt." Baudrillard also passionately chants that:

> like the holy relic, whose function it secularizes, the antique object reorganizes the world in a dispersive fashion which is quite antithetical to the extensive nature of functional organization—such organization being the very thing, in fact, from which it seeks to protect the profound and no doubt vital lack of realism of the inner self.[3]

He goes on to affirm that the more ancient the object is, the closer we are to an early era, "to 'divinity,' to nature, to primitive knowledge, and so forth."[4] Unsurprisingly, one can see here a clear Mauss-Bataille logic. The theory used to attack the capitalist system in *The System of Objects* is not Marxism at all but a nostalgic Mauss-Bataille grassroots romanticism. It is true that Baudrillard hates the capitalist utility-utilitarian system, but his alternative is not a progressive reform, rather, it is an impossible *return to the past*.

In fact, it is not difficult to find in the concluding remarks of *The System of Objects* that Baudrillard has already recognized the process of modern capitalist society walking towards the world of consumption, in which, "systematic manipulation of the activity of signs" becomes the most important existent structure.[5]

Later, in *The Consumer Society*, Baudrillard's analysis of the system of objects transits to the research of the structure of commodity circulation.

[1] Baudrillard, Jean. *The System of Objects*. Trans. James Benedict. Radical Thinkers, 3. London [u.a.]: Verso, 2005. p. 85.

[2] Ibid., p. 79.

[3] Ibid., p. 84.

[4] Ibid., p. 80.

[5] Ibid., p. 218.

(I note that from this book on he sets foot on economics, although with insufficient in-depth studies.) But his logical position changes slightly compared with his first arguments. He does not directly call it the symbolic value again. Instead, he refers to the resisting standpoint that deconstructs consumption logic as the "natural ecological laws," vis-à-vis "the law of exchange-value."[1] In the transitional part of Chapters One and Two, Baudrillard only gives a presentation of various problems in consumer society. At the end of the first section in Chapter two, we encounter an old friend, Sahlins with his famous *Original Affluent Society*. Baudrillard fully agrees with Sahlins's concept that in capitalist *productivity-oriented* society, the needs are turned into "the very needs of the order of production, not the 'needs' of man."[2] (It should be noted that Baudrillard borrows the "productivity-oriented" concept from Sahlins and changes it into a vicious slogan used against historical materialism.) In Baudrillard's eyes, the Australian primitive tribes live an "affluent" life. People there had never possessed objects nor do they have material worries. They do not have our political economic concept of utility in mind. They readily discard and consume anything they want. (In the following discussion, Baudrillard says that the primitive society does not have today's idea of time, like "time is money". To them, time is only the rhythm of existence, symbolic, unable to be abstracted or substantialized[3], and in this symbolic-value dominated existence, "gold and money are excrements." It has a non-utilitarian "sacrificial function of excrement."[4]) Baudrillard concludes that the most valuable treasure in primitive life is not material wealth but a *symbolic* social relation, which, unlike the chaotic and blind utilitarian possession of objects, is "transparent and reciprocal."[5]

---

[1] Baudrillard, Jean, Chris Turner, and George Ritzer. *The Consumer Society: Myths and Structures*.
      Theory, Culture & Society. London: Sage Publications Ltd, 1998. p. 26.
[2] Ibid., p. 66.
[3] Ibid., p. 152.
[4] Ibid., p. 155.
[5] Ibid., p. 11.

In the economy of the gift and symbolic exchange, a small and always finite quantity of goods is sufficient to create general wealth since those goods pass constantly from one person to the other. Wealth has its basis not in goods, but in the concrete exchange between persons. It is, therefore, unlimited since the cycle of exchange is endless, even among a limited number of individuals, with each moment of the exchange cycle adding to the value of the object exchanged.[1]

What value? The symbolic value. It is from this important reference coordinate that Baudrillard starts his critique of the "consumer society." His theoretic foundation is *not Marxism*. In his negation of the legitimacy of the consumer society, Baudrillard dos not adopt historical materialism to criticize the capitalist system of exploitation. On the contrary, he bases his theoretical framework on Mauss-Bataille's grassroots romanticism. He reveals the essence of the consumption logic as a symbolic manipulation in the following words:

The symbolic values of creation and the symbolic relation of inwardness are absent from it: it is all in externals. The object loses its objective finality and its function; it becomes a term in a much greater combinatory, in sets of objects in which it has a merely relational value. Moreover, it loses its symbolic meaning, its millennial anthropomorphic status, and tends to peter out into a discourse of connotations which are also simply relative to one another within the framework of a totalitarian cultural system (that is to say, a system which is able to integrate all significations whatever their provenance).[2]

The reactionary consumer logic deprives man and the object of real symbolic value; accordingly, existence itself is degraded to a useful exchange of value. Baudrillard takes sexual desire as an example; "once its total, symbolic exchange function has been deconstructed and lost, sexuality

---

[1] Baudrillard, Jean, Chris Turner, and George Ritzer. *The Consumer Society: Myths and Structures.* Theory, Culture & Society. London: Sage Publications Ltd, 1998. p. 67.

[2] Ibid., p. 115.

collapses into the dual use-value/exchange-value schema" and becomes a false consumption.[1] In the last chapter of the book, about the discussion of leisure, Baudrillard finally lets Bataille embark on the stage. He goes directly to the late Bataille's *Accursed Share* and fetches the "gift exchange" found by Mauss. In his eyes, real free time is the *exchange of meanings and symbols*, and the value of existence lies "in its very destruction, in being sacrificed."[2]

Now we know the real logic that supports the young Baudrillard's discourse in these two important works. Obviously, there is nothing Marxist in it. Critiques against capitalism are not necessarily Marxist. It can be refusal of the bourgeoisie from a theological perspective, like Pascal, or anti-capitalist speculation based on oriental populism, like Mikhaylovsky. It is only in appearance that the young Baudrillard follows his leftist teachers in the critique of the capitalist system of objects and consumer society, attached with a slight post-Marxian thought. What lies at the core is Mauss-Bataille's grassroots romanticism. The above analysis clearly breaks the delusion that Baudrillard was once as a Marxist.

In fact, the young Baudrillard follows Mauss (Sahlins)-Bataille concept from the very beginning of his theory building. Although he displays some superficial attention to Marxism in *The System of Objects* and *The Consumer Society*, it is only a background account paying respect for his teachers. The essence of Baudrillard's theory is grassroots romanticism which is qualitatively (essentially) different from Marxism. After *For a Critique of the Political Economy of the Sign*, a straight transcendence of Marxist political economy, the young Baudrillard quickly changes his post-Marxian position to the opposite of Marxism. When it comes to *The Mirror of Production*, he has grown to be a ferocious enemy of Marxism. Unlike the late Lefebvre, Debord, and Derrida, Baudrillard never possesses any favorable impression of Marx after 1973 and he spares no effort in using the symbolic exchange of primitive societies to bury Marxism and entire modern life. In my opinion, this self-righteous and absurd fantasy is doomed to fail.

---

[1] Baudrillard, Jean, Chris Turner, and George Ritzer. *The Consumer Society: Myths and Structures*. Theory, Culture & Society. London: Sage Publications Ltd, 1998. p. 150.

[2] Ibid., p. 157.

Now, we are ready to deal with the ferocious Baudrillard's *Mirror of Production*.

II. Marxism: Transgression of Historical Materialism

The Young Baudrillard's *Mirror of Production* had a big academic impact after its publication. The most important reason may be what we have mentioned previously in our introduction: as a defector of western Marxism, Baudrillard is different from other external Marxist enemies who simply attack the historical patterns derived from Marxism. He attempts a direct and accurate blasting of the principal pillars that sustain Marxist historical materialism—the basic theory of material production and the logic of historical phenomenology.[1] It amounts to a life-and-death matter about the methodological postulates of Marxism. Thus, we have to seriously deal with *The Mirror of Production*. In this section, we shall begin from several important questions and anti-propositions proposed by Baudrillard.

1. *The Mirror of Production*: what does the young Baudrillard object to?

"A specter haunts the revolutionary imagination: the phantom of production. Everywhere it sustains an unbridled romanticism of productivity."[2] Baudrillard opens his preface with a parody of the celebrated statement from *The Communist Manifesto*. This sentence has been dealt with

---

[1] They are two significant theoretical dimensions of Marxism in my understanding. To be more specific, one is about the general law of social existence and development of general historical materialism in the subjective dimension of historical dialectics; the other, the social critical theory based on special historical materialism in the objective dimension of historical dialectics, that is, historical phenomenology. *See* my *Subjective Dimension of Marxian Historical Dialectics* (Nanjing University Press, 2002) and *Back to Marx: The Philosophical Discourse in the Context of Economics* (Jiangsu People's Press, 1999).

[2] Baudrillard, Jean. *The Mirror of Production*. Trans. Mark Poster. St. Louis: Telos Press, 1975. p.17.

in numerous critiques and adapted to various theoretical contexts—Kelso and Adler's *Capitalist Manifesto*, neo-humanistic texts of ex-communists of Eastern Europe, and even today's post-modernist thought, for example, Derrida's *Specters of Marx*. However, it is different this time in Baudrillard's adaptation, which menacingly points toward the very heart of Marxism. "Revolutionary imagination" is used as a metaphor to present all radical discourses that criticize capitalism. Baudrillard attempts to identify that right before those seemingly radical revolutionary expectations there hides a wild dragon called "romanticism of productivity," whose initiator is nobody else but Marx the revolutionary. However, he admits that this dragon is set free *unconsciously* by Marx.

Baudrillard's real target is Marxist historical materialism which transcends all old ideologies along with the ensuing critical theory of the entire capitalist social historical mode of production. (I once mentioned that the critical logic of the mode of production is an important qualitative logic to define late capitalist thoughts.)[1] In Baudrillard's eyes, he seems to pinch the Achilles heel of Marx the giant. He says that:

> [t]he critical theory of the *mode* of production does not touch the *principle* of production. All the concepts it articulates describe only the dialectical and historical genealogy of the *contents* of production, leaving production as a *form* intact. This form reemerges, idealized, behind the critique of the capitalist mode of production. Through a strange contagion, this form of production only reinforces revolutionary discourse as a language of productivity. From the liberation of productive forces in the unlimited "textual productivity" of *Tel Quel* to Deleuze's factory-machine productivity of the unconscious (including the "labor" of the unconscious), no revolution can place itself under any other sign.[2]

---

[1] *See* "Preface" to this book.

[2] Baudrillard, Jean. *The Mirror of Production*. Trans. Mark Poster. St. Louis: Telos Press, 1975. p. 17.

Without my preparatory discussion of Mauss-Bataille's non-productive thought, a common reader would find it rather abrupt and thus hard to enter Baudrillard's textual context here. In fact, what Baudrillard wants to say is this: despite criticism of the capitalist mode of production, Marx is never able to touch the ontological foundation on which capitalism relies, namely, the *logic of production*; despite his discussion about the specific contents of production in different historical periods, Marx does not recognize just misses the qualitative structure ("form") of the production per se. It can be seen that Baudrillard here intends here to criticize *production*, which becomes the first negative key word of his criticism. As we all know, the conception of production is all too important to Marxist historical materialism, whether it is the initial explanation of general historical materialism founded in the *German Ideology* or the theoretical development of historical materialism; the production and reproduction of the means of subsistence is always the fundamental paradigm of Marxist philosophy. According to Baudrillard, the never-questioned logic of production (and the productive forces) hides deeply, and it grows rapidly under the cover of the cries of capitalist criticism to the extent that all the present critical discourses that seemingly transcend Marxism are haunted by this invisible evil dragon of production. In addition, Baudrillard attacks the so-called production text released from the modernity text by Barthes and Kristeva (*Tel Quel*)[1], along with the unconscious productive forces released from Deleuze's Machines désirantes. We seldom find so arrogant a person like Baudrillard, who tramples the late *Tel Quel* and proud Deleuze! Obviously, in the eyes of Baudrillard, post-modernism is tirelessly seeking a flowing, true creation of life to flee the totality of the modern industry framework, but unfortunately, it always finds itself contained within the logic of production. In my opinion, Baudrillard is a theoretical prophet, who, from the standpoint *opposite* to post-modernism, perceives the secrets of the trend that madly throws out fresh eccentric ideas. Therefore, he cannot be viewed as a *positive* post-modernist.

---

[1] *See* my "Barthes: Text is a Kind of Weaving" in *Tribune of Social Sciences* (2002. Vol. 10).

Once the mystery is revealed, Baudrillard identifies "a productive Eros" from what he considers to be behind the radical Marxist critiques, which is also deemed as a man's ideal being in the industrial framework. As a result, today's social wealth or language, meaning or value, sign or phantasm—everything is "produced" according to a labor. Good! Here appears Baudrillard's second negative key word: *labor*. (As I concluded earlier, Baudrillard was never a Marxist even from his very beginning of theoretical discoveries. Ironically, Baudrillard was engaged in the French translation of *German Ideology*, due to which the bright elf of thoughts familiarized himself with the first original document that gave birth to historical materialism and availed himself of this advantage in his criticism of Marxism.) It is now clear that Baudrillard argues against production and labor. For Marx, production is the prerequisite of man's entire social history and the general foundation of social existence and development. What is labor, then? According to Engels, it is the fundamental link that conveys man from animal existence to human being; it is the dominant subjective action in the process of material production. What Baudrillard attempts to nullify is nothing but the groundwork of Marxism: the social existence and man in the vision of historical materialism. Baudrillard's logical outset is actually the *entire logical death* of Marxism. It may shed light on why he became so prominent in European academic circles.

He believes that all present social existence is based on the production-labor logic, which is also "the truth of capital and of political economy." Baudrillard says that the Marxist critique of capitalism can be said to be precise but it never generates doubt about the logic of production, which narrows the revolutionary critique and makes it lose momentum. What Marx wants is only to emancipate the productive forces from the heavy shackles of capitalism. In his opinion, even more radical critiques of capitalism since then cannot escape the same pattern. *Liberation of the productive forces* becomes a revolutionary slogan but at the same time covers a vision that would have been more grandiose and more subversive. (On second thought, Baudrillard is also falsifying the fundamental way that China is proceeding.)

He says that,

> the capitalist system of production is to be subverted in the name of
> an authentic and radical productivity. The capitalist law of value is to be
> abolished in the name of a de-alienated hyper-productivity, a productive
> hyperspace. Capital develops the productive forces but also restrains
> them: they must be liberated. The exchange of signifieds has always
> hidden the "labor" of the signifier: let us liberate the signifier and the
> textual production of meaning! The unconscious is surrounded in social,
> linguistic, and Oedipal structures: let us give it back its brute energy; let
> us restore it as a productive machine! Everywhere productivist discourse
> reigns and, whether this productivity has objective ends or is deployed
> for itself, it is itself the form of value. It is the leitmotif both of the
> system and of a radical challenge.[1]

Baudrillard seems to spread an overwhelming net that captures Marx,
who cries for the liberation of productive forces from the shackles of
capitalist mode of production, seizes Barthes and Kristeva, who try to free
the textual production limited to the pursuit of originality of modernity, and
snares Freud and Deleon, who hope to release the unconscious Eros as man's
authentic being. Behold, all this belongs to the "discourse of productivism!"
Nevertheless, it does not simply mean the modern liberalism handed down
from Adam Smith and Ricardo but the very revolutionary discourse *critical
of capitalism*, viz. the "leitmotif of a radical challenge." Among these
radical discourses of revolution against capitalism, Marx committed the
biggest crime. Baudrillard has a specific explanation for this: Marx played
an essential role in the rooting of this productivist metaphor because he
radicalized and rationalized the *mode of production*, giving it a "revolutionary
title of nobility." Therefore, Baudrillard points the sword towards Marx
in order to erase this sort of productivism. Hence, the third key concept is
the *mode of production* that unifies the productive forces and relations of

---

[1] Baudrillard, Jean. *The Mirror of Production*. Trans. Mark Poster. St. Louis: Telos Press, 1975.
    p. 18.

production.

Marxism, in Baudrillard's criticism, has many problems. For example, he shattered the fiction of *homo economicus*, the myth which sums up the whole process of the naturalization of the system of exchange value, the market, and surplus value and its forms. (I suspect Baudrillard first learned the concept of "homo economicus" from Mauss's *Gift* before he found confirmation from Marx.) Baudrillard certainly knows that Marx transcends capitalist economics (the hypothesis of homo economicus) by mercilessly exposing and firmly negating the externalization and naturalization of the ideology of capitalist production. He does not deny this point. Nevertheless, Marx's critical method is, in his eyes, still achieved "in the name of labor power." To be specific, Marx discovers that the capitalist only pays the "value" of labor power based on the equivalent exchange relations of the market but secretly appropriates a large sum of surplus value. In this connection, Marx transcends Proudhon and other capitalist economists and establishes scientific political economy critical of the capitalist mode of production. Baudrillard goes on to point out that the theory of surplus value does uncover the secret of capitalist exploitation, but it is the same "mythical" and "naturalized" ideology for Marx to hold the view that value is *produced* through labor. Note that here appears the fourth Marxist concept violently attacked by Baudrillard: labor *power*. Baudrillard holds that man is defined via the labor power engaged in production in the philosophical discourse of Marxist historical materialism, while labor power comes to be man's authentic survival mode in all social-historical patterns. (This condemnation of Baudrillard's is absolutely groundless, which will be dealt with in a separate section.) Here, Baudrillard does not target Marx's criticism or exposure of capitalism but opposes the *social ontological base* on which the Marxist critique of capitalism relies. (We already know Baudrillard objects to Marxism due to the idea of *non-productive* existence based on symbolic relations.) He disagreeably grumbles, "isn't this a similar fiction, a similar naturalization—another wholly arbitrary convention, a simulation model bound to *code* all human material and every contingency of desire and exchange in terms of value, finality, and production?"[1] It turns out that Baudrillard's anger stems from his demurral against Marx's method of using the production-value frame to *universalize* the entire human existence and social history, especially, the non-productive "practopian" state that he learns from Mauss. With the above words, Baudrillard seems to interrogate Marx by a sharper question: is the entire history of human existence controlled by the logic of production?

Baudrillard already has his answer to it: No. He believes that Marx's logic of production leads to an illusion, "no longer a matter of 'being' oneself but of 'producing' oneself." According to him, the unseen humanistic logic brings about the situation that *I produce, therefore I am (je produis, donc je suis)*, or, if extended a little further, even *I produce, therefore history is*. To a certain extent, his summing-up of Marx's philosophical discourse is not completely wrong. It also explains why Baudrillard titles his book *The Mirror of Production*. He claims that "the *mirror of production* in which all Western metaphysics is reflected, must be broken."[2] Baudrillard explains that the title borrows Lacan's theory of mirror stage, which can be found, according to him, in every aspect of political economics as well. (I have to mention that Baudrillard's reference to Lacan is not legitimate here. Obviously, it shows his inadequate knowledge of Lacan's mirror theory.) Just have a look at his reasoning:

> Through this scheme of production, this *mirror* of production, the human species comes to consciousness *[la prise de conscience] in the imaginary*. Production, labor, value, everything through which an objective world emerges and through which man recognizes himself objectively—this is the imaginary. Here man is embarked on a continual deciphering of himself through his works, finalized by his shadow (his own end), reflected by this operational mirror, this sort of ideal of a

---

[1] Baudrillard, Jean. *The Mirror of Production*. Trans. Mark Poster. St. Louis: Telos Press, 1975. p. 19.

[2] Ibid., p. 47.

productivist ego. This process occurs not only in the materialized form of an economic obsession with efficiency determined by the *system* of exchange value, but more profoundly in this *overdetermination by the code*, by the mirror of political economy: in the identity that man dons with his own eyes when he can think of himself only as something to produce, to transform, or bring about as value.[1]

This short paragraph huddles a pile of Baudrillard's negative key words, *labor, value, political economy* and so on. (Later, Baudrillard adds to his blacklist other basic concepts like *need, labor power, use value, history, nature, law, dialectics*, etc.) As we know, Lacan's mirror theory is the negative identification of an ego's establishment that begins from a false image. Originated in the external image of an *individual*, the illusion is first mistaken by the unconsciousness as "self," and then constructed as a pseudo-self by the regulatory mirror reflection of the surrounding faces during the early period. According to Lacan, the reflection relationship (pseudo-self) that occupies the subjective self is autre (more accurately, autre I and autre II). Therefore, the mirror stage is an ontological fraud in the initial phase of self-formation.[2] Baudrillard applies Lacan's mirror theory to the generic field of human existence. It can be counted as a logical possibility, if not a mistake. However, as the objective activity of man, production does not come from the direct objective reflection of man's subjectivity. No thinker ever mistakes production as man's real being, less to mention the absence of *unconscious self-reference* in Lacan's logic of mirror. Ironically, Baudrillard's proud analogy is actually based on his misunderstanding of Lacan. In this way, his critical foundation will be nothingness. *Nothing is constructed from nothingness.* Baudrillard proves a good example of Lacan's satire of those crazy, self-righteous people.

According to Baudrillard, man acquires an imago from the Smith-Marx

---

[1] Baudrillard, Jean. *The Mirror of Production*. Trans. Mark Poster. St. Louis: Telos Press, 1975. p. 58.

[2] *See* Chapter Three in *The Impossible Truth of Being—Mirror of Lacan's Philosophy* (2006).

mirror, and then creates an illusionary objective world, a self-reference of the subject. The essence of the image is the *utilitarian logic of value*; hence, the production of mirror can be developed to *the mirror of political economy*. (He later uses such concepts as *the mirror of labor* and *the mirror of history*.) On a more profound level, Baudrillard attempts to question all anthropocentrism centered on *utilitarian value*. It is interesting to find that Baudrillard does not dispute the supreme economization or growthism in capitalist economy, but turns against Marx who stands opposite to the capitalist ideology. According to him, Marx does negate the overt ahistoricality of classical economics, whilst the productive and *expressive* discourse are still two "unanalyzed" things in Marx's critical logic, furthermore, the mirror of production hides deep in Marx's inner logic.

What does it mean? The so-called productive discourse indicates Marx's theories of material production and the development of the productive forces while the expressive discourse represents Marxist production relations and the mode of production. In the eyes of Baudrillard, the capitalist schema of production is only the superficial form of representation, or "the order of representation" of the production logic. Marx does not deny the production logic per se that sustains the whole capitalist existence. Accordingly, "it is no longer worthwhile to make a radical critique of the order of representation in the name of production and of its revolutionary formula."[1]

In fact, this discovery of Baudrillard's is not that fantastic. In my opinion, it is only a sort of critical tension with pseudo-romanticism extended from the sacred thing called by Bataille. Only the elated Baudrillard regards himself as the pure child who observes the falsehood of the entire social existence and decides to tear off the "emperor's new clothes," which, to him, is nothing else but production, the mirror of production. He wants to stand out and be the first to break this magic mirror. (According to Sahlins, Gajo Petroviæ and Alfred Schmidt already criticized the universality of historical

---

[1] Baudrillard, Jean. *The Mirror of Production*. Trans. Mark Poster. St. Louis: Telos Press, 1975. p. 20.

materialism earlier than Baudrillard.[1]) I wonder whether Baudrillard would know that his flighty conceit leads to a Don Quixotian battle and illusion. True, he is somewhat profound in some points, but he still makes the same mistake as those "cataract theorists" do. The devil that he endeavors to fight is a false image, which is nonexistent or simply is misunderstood. (Next, we are going to deal with Baudrillard with his own means and dissect his critique about Marxism, in particular, about historical materialism.)

Baudrillard's arrangement of his text is sometimes broken and often repetitious, so I intend to choose a logical path for discussion rather than strictly abide by the original textual order, which, in my opinion, will restore the critical logic more faithful than Baudrillard's own for, regrettably, reality is really dead with him. (The subject of the death of reality is discussed in his late important text, *The Perfect Crime*, which is also the background for *The Matrix*, a movie deeply influenced by Baudrillard.)

2. Rejection of the Gestalt of historical materialism

The avid critic Baudrillard targets the concept of labor because in his judgment it is the key of the Marxist logic of production. (Indeed, this is an academic misconception and logical confusion due to mixture of different research fields.) In the beginning, Baudrillard demonstrates his intention: The real critique of political economy should not be confined to the exposition of such anthropologic concepts as need and use value that conceal themselves behind consumption, but to "unmask everything hidden behind the concepts of production, mode of production, productive forces, relations of production, etc. All the fundamental concepts of Marxist analysis must be questioned, starting from its own requirement of a radical critique and transcendence of political economy."[2] Baudrillard deserves to be called a genius. This is a very accurate statement in which he perceives what others cannot see and

---

[1] Sahlins, Marshall D. *Culture and Practical Reason*. Joint Publishing Company Limited (Beijing), 2002. p. 3.

[2] Baudrillard, Jean. *The Mirror of Production*. Trans. Mark Poster. St. Louis: Telos Press, 1975. p. 20.

wield sword at the heart of Marxism. (I have to acknowledge that Baudrillard is sometimes terribly sober.) In his view, a profound critique of political economy should not make negations within the framework of itself but first strides beyond Marx's *transcendence* of political economy, that is, a thorough direct reflection of the methodology of historical materialism that Marx employs to transcend political economy. (Political economy should not be opposed within its own framework, which is the viewpoint which Marx used to criticize Proudhon but borrowed here by Baudrillard in his objection to Marxism.) Baudrillard realizes that Marx's secret of transcending bourgeois classical economics is the methodology of historical materialism. This understanding is certainly right. What is left for Baudrillard to do is to transcend Marx's transcendence in turn.

Therefore, he raises two axiomatic questions:

What is axiomatic about productive forces or about the dialectical genesis of modes of production from which springs all revolutionary theory? What is axiomatic about the generic richness of man who is labor power, about the motor of history, or about history itself, which is only "the production by men of their material life?"[1]

If interpreted in a simple way, the first historical "axiom" means why the contradiction between the productive forces and the relations of production is regarded as the driving force of social historical development, while the demand to reform the relations of production is the cause of revolution. This is an issue about social movement. The second historical "axiom" has a deeper suggestion, which can be explained as follows: why is history only the process of producing man's material life? Then, why is production is the initiative of historical development? Moreover, why does man only acquire the "generic" richness when he is taken as the "labor power"? (We are going to analyze in detail this question later. Baudrillard's simplified appropriation of the concept of "labor power" from the context of Marxist political

---

[1] Baudrillard, Jean. *The Mirror of Production*. Trans. Mark Poster. St. Louis: Telos Press, 1975. p. 20.

economy is illegitimate.) Please note that this is a systematic falsification of propositions. First, it belongs to the domain of philosophical questions. More specifically, it is a question directed against historical materialism. Again, I have to admit that Baudrillard precisely grasps the main issue in his critique. However, in the very beginning he chooses to ignore a theoretical blind spot, which has experienced a progressive development. Marx first assumes that man's generic nature is labor (power) before he regards the social history of human beings as the record of the self-movement of material production; afterward, he stipulates that the contradiction of productive forces and the relations of production during material production drives forward the entire human social history. Regarding this, my opinion is as follows:

First, after the establishment of historical materialism in 1845, Marx did not consider labor as man's generic nature in the sense of *philosophical ontology*. Since Baudrillard must have read Althusser, he should not neglect the important historical change of Marxism. He uses the humanistic discourse *thoroughly refuted* by Marx to fire at a disappeared logical outset, which cannot be counted as fair. Besides, Marx never universalized the historical view and anthropology with the *worker's labor power*, the special historical materialization only possible in the economic context of the capitalist mode of production. This does not belong to Marxism but results from Baudrillard's own confusion. Baudrillard really lacks a sufficient knowledge of Marxist history. In fact, when Marx entered the final stage of building historical materialism, he clearly opposed the stipulation of man as wage labor. In a draft about Friedrich List's book of economics in March, 1845, Marx wrote that under the capitalist system, one is reduced to a "productive force of wealth" because in this mode of production, as manpower, he is juxtaposed with other material forces, such as water-power, steam-power, and horse-power. Marx angrily asked, "Is it a high appreciation of man for him to figure as a 'force' alongside horses, steam and water?"[1] Judging from this point, Baudrillard was a poor student of Marxism. He did not carefully read the

---

[1] Karl Marx and Frederick Engels. *Collected Works*, vol. 4. London: Lawrence & Wishart, 1975. p. 285.

above statement; otherwise, he would probably not smear Marx with this *anthropological labor force.*

Second, it is known that the concept of production undergoes multiple semantic and historical changes in Marx's text. However, Baudrillard's judgment on this point seems very poor, or probably, the genius is so overwhelmed by his critical impulse and ambition that he makes a silly mistake of *absolute homogeneity* of the theory that experienced an academic progress for nearly 50 years. (I once criticized this approach of indiscriminate citation from the first volume to the last one of the *Collected Works of Marx and Engels* in a subject research. In fact, it is a Stalinist ahistorical illustration. Regrettably, this fascist-like grammar is also detectable in Baudrillard's subaltern critique under the fashion of a vanguard.) Ignorance begets impetuousness. Baudrillard is unaware that Marxist historical materialism is divided into general and special types, with several concepts of production *literally similar* but substantially different in contents and meanings.

Baudrillard should know that Marx's general historical materialism discusses the common situation and regulations of human social history, while the special historical materialism mainly accounts for the historical phenomena of the capitalist society. Production, first refers to the *general* productive activity as a given in the philosophical-historical view, which entails both the *production of man per se* as well as the material. Second, production is a *modern* concept used to understand the nature of contemporary social history. In the *Thesis on Feuerbach*, it exists as a relational being to eliminate the binary separation of subject and object, a presence of revolutionary practice; or in *German Ideology*, it appears in the most fundamental material creation process of modern industrial activities, being the kernel of the logic of historical materialism. The above two paradigms belong to the philosophical discourse. After 1858, Marx employed multiple particular concepts of *general* and *special* production in the context of political economy to mainly indicate machine production in the capitalist mode of production when commodity production and market exchange have developed to a certain level. The complexity of the Marxist theory of production above seems to confound the clever Baudrillard, who, despite his talent, started from a flimsy foundation to build his theory. No matter how magnificent his theoretical palace looks, it will collapse on a slight but vital push.

Then, Baudrillard makes a high-profile quotation from *German Ideology*—jointly translated by him—the famous statement of general historical materialism firstly put forward by Karl Marx:

> The first historical act is thus the production of the means to satisfy these needs, the production of material life itself. And indeed this is an historical act, a fundamental condition of all history, which today, as thousands of years ago, must daily and hourly be fulfilled merely in order to sustain human life.[1]

Is Marx wrong? Previous thinkers only saw history created by heroic wills while Marx simply identified the truth of history. The word "production" in the first sentence above is used in its *general* sense, not a special historical mode of existence. It refers to the basic material activity that creates the entire human society, without which man cannot survive. Accordingly, Marx and Engels would view production as the initiative of man's social history in the *German Ideology* that founds general historical materialism. In addition, the word "needs" here is also general. Marx is definitely aware of man's *specific* needs of each historical production. (Marx made a particular analysis of the different needs under different historical conditions in the *German Ideology*. Similarly, in the later *Economic Manuscripts of 1861-1863*, Marx wrote that "the extent of the so-called primary requirements for life and the manner of their satisfaction depend to a large degree on the level of civilization of the society, are themselves the product of history, the necessary means of subsistence in one country or epoch include things not included in another."[2])

---

[1] *See* "Feuerbach" in *MECW*.

[2] Karl Marx and Frederick Engels. *Collected Works*, vol. 30. London: Lawrence & Wishart, 1988. p. 44.

Although Baudrillard does not openly put down his interpretation of the aforesaid statement, we can infer that in his eyes Marx's production and requirement here are belongings of the capitalist system. Therefore, he can make the rash conclusion that the liberation of productive forces is confused with the liberation of man, and thus questions: Is this a revolutionary formula or that of political economy itself?

For this question, I really think Baudrillard needs to take supplementary instructions since Marx never equated the liberation of productive forces with the liberation of man. Instead, the former is the *material precondition* of the latter and the real objective foundation from which social revolutions take place. (This question will be analyzed in detail later.) Baudrillard means to say that it is this subject that we need to reflect upon, that is, production is deemed as the nature of history, even the unique *qualitative* aspect of man. It is for the same reason that he strongly dislikes Marx's writing in the *German Ideology*: "They [Men] themselves begin to distinguish themselves from animals as soon as they begin to *produce* their means of subsistence."[1] Baudrillard questions: why should man be differentiated from other animals? In his opinion, it is a humanistic "obstinacy" and bigotry of political economy. This opinion would strike any normal reader: Is there anybody who does not regard people as different from other animals? Can it be that man exists in the same way as other animals do? (To Baudrillard, it is not weird at all, because his spiritual teacher Bataille was always fascinated by the French pornographic writer Marquis de Sade, who claimed that man's authenticity of being was cognized through animal-like sexual impulsion and excretion.) As the analysis goes on, we shall understand the true color of the Mauss-Bataille logic to which Baudrillard clings.

In Baudrillard's eyes, given that Marx regards man's existence as his own end, he will set a means (production) other than the purpose to satisfy the needs that he has; that is, he has to produce. Accordingly, man is forced to think of himself as the labor power of production, during which man as

---

[1] Karl Marx and Frederick Engels. *Collected Works*, vol. 5. London: Lawrence & Wishart, 1976. p.31.

purpose will be separated from man as means. This is called "alienation."
Marx's critical transcendence of political economy aims to restore man
as his own end. (Of course, my paraphrasing above is a rearrangement of
Baudrillard's unclear, broken line of thought often interrupted by his own
questions. We would be at a complete loss if we follow his sequence.)
Baudrillard is wrong again! After 1845, Marx was no longer dependent on
Feuerbach's humanistic *view of alienation.* It is true that Marx still criticized
the phenomenon in which the material force created by man proves to
enslave himself in the capitalist social economy, as stated in the *Economic
Manuscripts of 1857-1858* and *Das Kapital* and that he also pointed out
the nature of alienation in capitalist economic relations, but he raised his
disproving critiques more from the perspective of the reversed materialized
social relations. Did ever make such an imprudent statement as that man
needs to be restored with his own end through denial of alienation?

Baudrillard claimed that his intention was to challenge Marx, to bring
down Marxism so that he could disprove the "political radicalism" pursued
and contributed by "generations of revolutionaries." I am pessimistic of his
wish.

3. Methodological root cause: transhistorized history

Baudrillard focuses on the critique of the Marxist concept of labor in his
first chapter, though his desultory thought makes a hasty leap from a hardly
prepared arena of historical philosophy into the economic context, which is
but an illegitimate argument. (We are going to discuss this in detail in the
next section.) I shall first analyze the philosophical conclusion of chapter
one because, in theory, it happens to be his methodological advance of the
criticism above.

In *The Mirror of Production*, almost every chapter has a so-called
summary of epistemology to show off Baudrillard's metaphysical
complacency (except Chapter IV, all the first four chapters have summaries
of epistemology.) The title of the first epistemology is "In the Shadow
of Marxist Concepts," which, judging from the entire text, is intended to

identify the methodological root cause of Marxist historical materialism. In Baudrillard's view, the specific, limited concepts are "universalized." (This critical logic is taken from the methodology of Marxist historical materialism.) It leads to an illegitimate theoretical transgression. We shall examine his critique.

Baudrillard admits that "Marxist theory has sought to shatter the abstract universality of the concepts of bourgeois thought (*Nature* and *Progress*, *Man* and *Reason*, formal *Logic*, *Work*, *Exchange*, etc.)."[1] Strangely, in retrospect of Marxist texts, one will fail to find him simply denying what Baudrillard judges the universality of the concepts of bourgeois thought. In my opinion, Marx does not reject nature and progress, but he is against the naturalization and externalization of the capitalist mode of production; he does not oppose man and rationality, rather he resists the capitalist abstraction of man and hypocrisy of rationality; a fortiori, he does not reject formal logic, labor and exchange, instead he denies the materialized social relations and fetishistic thought under the capitalist system. Ridiculously, Baudrillard states that Marx attempts to shatter the bourgeois universal thought by concepts such as "historical materialism, dialectics, mode of production, labor power" and so on, which, again, only tells his own fallacy.

First of all, historical materialism is the most universal concept, the Weltanschauung called by Marx as the single "science of history", while historical dialectics is a significant logic structure of this world view. Historical materialism is in essence historical dialectics. The mode of production is the central concept of historical materialism as well as the key perspective that Marx employs to study the nature of capitalist society. Regarding the last concept of "labor power," it belongs to the economic category, obviously different from the first three concepts. In all the published texts of Marx, it is never found to be used in a broader sense of philosophy (epistemology). (Baudrillard tends to confuse thoughts of different categories. We have to adapt ourselves to this characteristic casualty of his.)

---

[1] Baudrillard, Jean. *The Mirror of Production*. Trans. Mark Poster. St. Louis: Telos Press, 1975. p. 47.

More importantly, Marx is capable of transcending classical economics of the bourgeois ideology in that he stands on the high point of historical materialism. He bases his critique and destruction of the bourgeois ideology on the profound study of economics along with social and scientific history. After 1845, Marx abandoned his youthful declaration that the kingdom of bourgeois was dead in the philosophical sense (as written in the *Economic and Philosophical Manuscripts of 1844*). Unfortunately, Baudrillard is only self-righteous, but wrong.

After a far-fetched criticism, Baudrillard brings forward another discovery of the epistemological root cause of Marxism: despite his correct critique of the abstract bourgeois concepts, Marx again "universalizes" the concepts that are used to transcend the bourgeois ideology. As a result, Marxist epistemology is in essence "'critical' imperialism." (This sharp criticism necessitates serious attention.) Baudrillard says that the proposition that a concept is not merely an interpretive hypothesis but a translation of universal movement depends upon pure metaphysics. Marxist concepts do not escape this lapse. In his opinion, to transform a paradigm or concept into a universal formula is an old metaphysical practice, which Marx fails to avoid.

Instead, in Marxism history is trans-historicized: it redoubles on itself and thus is universalized. To be rigorous the dialectic must dialectically surpass and annul itself. By radicalizing the concepts of production and mode of production at a given moment, Marx made a break in the social mystery of exchange value. The concept thus takes all its strategic power from its irruption, by which it dispossesses political economy of its imaginary universality. But, from the time of Marx, it lost this advantage when taken as a principle of explication. It thus cancelled its "difference" by universalizing itself, regressing to the dominant form of the code (universality) and to the strategy of political economy. It is not tautological that the concept of history is historical, that the concept of dialectic is dialectical, and that the concept of production is itself produced (that is, it is to be judged by a kind of self-analysis). Rather, this simply indicates the explosive, mortal, present form of critical concepts. As soon as they are constituted as universal they cease to be analytical and the religion of meaning begins.[1]

This long paragraph of Baudrillard's is only too important. It vividly displays what Baudrillard thinks as an internal criticism and insightful perspective of Marxist historical materialism. Let me explain this "classical" statement.

Baudrillard acknowledges the Marxist effective refutation of the universality of the bourgeois political economy (the eternal existence of the market economy as natural order) in the respect that through critical analysis of historicality and dialectic Marx illustrates that the bourgeois mode of production is historical (impermanent), history is *progressive* and historical dialectic denies any attempt to solidificate the present. However, when Marx extends this historical concept, it is no longer historical and in turn joins the "dominant code" of bourgeois ideology. This time, Baudrillard is not unclear in expressing his idea, except the nonsense of radicalizing the concepts of production and mode of production. He tries to criticize Marx for extending a historical concept (*necessity of progress*) to universal social history, particularly, to the primitive society where there are *no* such concepts as *progress* or *mode of production*. It proves Marxist theoretical violence.

In my opinion, Baudrillard plays tricks with the concepts here. *After 1845*, in dealing with the social reality of human history, especially the capitalist society, Marx had several different historical concepts in his mind experiment. First, it is the historical paradigm as the nature of historical materialism—the methodological (and the epistemological) paradigm of *limited historicality* and *ontological subsistence timescale* in the heart of Marxism, that is, the analytic model "under particular historical condition" specially marked by Marx and extraordinarily emphasized by me. In other words, Marx exactly rejected any transhistorical conception. (It is from this

---

[1] Baudrillard, Jean. *The Mirror of Production*. Trans. Mark Poster. St. Louis: Telos Press, 1975. p. 48.

point that Heidegger's notion of sterbliches dasein arises.)[1]

The second is modern industrial production, the concept of history that forms during the capitalist development, which is more *fluid and revolutionary*. The dialectical nature in German classical philosophy did anticipate this historical modernity. Regrettably, Germany lacked the reality of industrial production. Marx jested in the *German Ideology* that the Germans "have no history." Obviously, history here is used in the special modern sense.

The third one only appears after the liberation of man, which is the true development of *human history*. In the eyes of Marx, capitalist society is still the world of "economic animals." (He abandoned the use of humanistic concepts like "inhuman.") He often calls it the "pre-historical society." The third concept is used in an ad hoc sense.

Fourth, Marx also uses it in the common historical sense and researches. This is unnecessary to explain here.

Clearly, only with the second meaning can Baudrillard's criticism of historical concepts make sense. In addition, he needs to prove Marx made the attempt to impose the capitalist *modern schema of time* on the entire human history. Otherwise, however rigorous the critique is, it only ends up in falsehood.

With the above background introduction, Baudrillard's accusation turns out to be unreasonable and empty.

> They [concepts] only evoke themselves in an indefinite metonymic process which goes as follows: man is historical; history is dialectical; the dialectic is the process of (material) production; production is the very movement of human existence; history is the history of modes of production, etc. This scientific and universalist discourse (code) immediately becomes imperialistic. All possible societies are called on to respond.[2]

---

[1] *See,* My book, Chapter Six in *Back to Marx: The Philosophical Discourse in the Context of Economics* (Jiangsu People's Press, 1999).

[2] Baudrillard, Jean. *The Mirror of Production.* Trans. Mark Poster. St. Louis: Telos Press, 1975. p. 48.

There is a significant problem in Baudrillard's reasoning. He is likely to equate Marx's thoughts to the old philosophical framework of Stalinist dogmatic explanation, especially by means of simplistic inference. Smart as he is, he makes such simple errors. Where can we find in Marxist texts and thought the aforementioned code imperialism? Although some Baudrillard's allegations are applicable to the conventional dogmatic textbooks of Marxism, the assertion that "the dialectic is the process of material production" is found nowhere. (Even in the textbooks of the former Soviet Union and East European socialist countries, the dialectic refers to the study of the general laws of nature, society and human thought.) Baudrillard just makes another fabrication here.

Baudrillard seems unsatisfied in this attack. Apart from his judgment of the epistemological fallacy in Marxism, he expands his target field: "What we have said about the Marxist concepts holds for the unconscious, repression, Oedipal complex, etc., as well." He thus sentences Freudian psychoanalysis to death, too.

What is more, Baudrillard is very glad about his last resort. He is confident that once he utters "check" Marx and Freud will be checkmated. The final placement is his favorite "primitive societies." (We are already familiar with primitive societies, perceived as the ontological starting point by Baudrillard. This primitive society is certainly an imagined ideal scene of human existence refracted through the Mauss-Bataille prism.) He cannot conceal his excitement in the following remark:

> There is *neither a mode of production nor production* in primitive societies. There is *no dialectic* and *no unconscious* in primitive societies. These concepts analyze only our own societies, which are ruled by political economy. Hence they have only a kind of boomerang value.[1]

Baudrillard emphasizes his conclusion with words in italics[2], which,

---

[1] Baudrillard, Jean. *The Mirror of Production*. Trans. Mark Poster. St. Louis: Telos Press, 1975. p. 49.

[2] Baudrillard attaches great importance to it.

in my opinion, is but a little trick to amuse himself. A more accurate account should be like this: In primitive societies, there is no *modern-sense* mode of production and production, and today's theories of the dialectic and unconscious are still out of sight. Marx never views today's modern production as the existential basis of primitive societies. In the discourse of historical materialism, "when we speak of production, we always have in mind production at a definite stage of social development."[1] The mode and nature of production vary at different social stages but production always exists as the material basis of the social existence and movement. "Human life has from the beginning rested on production, and, *d'une manière ou d'une autre*, on *social* production."[2] Even in primitive societies, unless our ancestors did not eat or drink, they needed to engage themselves in activities for survival of obtaining food and protection against dangers. As Marx says, it is "appropriation of nature by the individual within and by means of a definite form of society."[3] *The reason why there is* "the process by which he makes his living"[4] is that man has the characteristic superior mode of survival and obtaining food, not to make an empty show to be differentiated from animals. Otherwise, not only the gift exchange and consumption enthroned by Baudrillard and his teachers would have disappeared but also the primitive peoples would have simply lost their survival opportunities.[5] Indeed, the primitive activity cannot be called "production" by any modern language but this objective activity is the only basis for human survival. It

---

[1] Karl Marx and Frederick Engels. *Collected Works*, vol. 28. London: Lawrence & Wishart, 1986. p. 22.

[2] Ibid., p. 413.

[3] Ibid., p. 25.

[4] Ibid., p. 538.

[5] Marx cited an example of this. He said that "it is a received opinion that in certain periods people lived from pillaging alone. But, for pillaging to be possible, there must be something to be pillaged, hence production." And the mode of pillaging is itself in turn determined by the mode of production. *See MECW* vol. 46. If slightly adapted, the above statement can be retailed to Baudrillard: For gift exchange (symbolic exchange) to be possible, there must be gifts to be exchanged, hence production. Without "gifts," there would be no large-scale consumption as in the "potlatch", not to mention basic survival.

does not belong to the utilitarian value system but it is a must. It is labeled by Marx as *general* material production in general historical materialism. In this respect, it does not change its essence although Marx and Engels later noticed that material production is only "a peripheral matter" in H. Morgan's rough study of the primitive societies in the late 19th century. (Marx said that primitive people do not exchange in accordance with an overturned material relation. He inferred that they "had only a CARRYING TRADE and did not themselves produce. At least production was secondary among the Phoenicians, Carthaginians, etc."[1] In other words, material production did not become a decisive factor in primitive societies, but without it man would have lost his survival foundation, which demonstrates that Marx's anthropological view is fairly comparable with Mauss's discovery later.) This is because the form of activities by the primitive people (if not called the mode of production), superior to common animals in sustaining life, is an objective reality as well as a basic condition for man's survival. It needs to be clarified that Marx's theory that man's social history is generally based on the production of the material means of subsistence belongs not to the logic of political economy but to the philosophical discourse of historical materialism. Baudrillard's critique confuses the discourse of political economy with the discourse of philosophy, which leaves its validity very questionable.

Moreover, Baudrillard's criticism contains a paradox of which he himself is fully unaware. He accuses Marx of projecting contemporary concepts, such as production and history to primitive societies, at the same time *imposes the elementary social structure and mode of existence in primitive societies on the entire human life*. Is it not the right code imperialism? Baudrillard says he wants to break from Marxism, from psychoanalysis. This scares no one. The boomerang he throws is certain to strike back on himself.

---

[1] Karl Marx and Frederick Engels. *Collected Works*, vol. 28. London: Lawrence & Wishart, 1986. p. 155.

III. Ontology of Production: I produce, therefore history is.

The first chapter of *The Mirror of Production* is entitled "The Concept of Labor," but Baudrillard's major critical target is the core of historical materialism: material production. In his view, Marx seriously objects to the capitalist mode of production and exposes the exploitation nature of capital, but he is unaware that the discourse of the philosophy of history centered on the *useful* production of labor is still the coded product of the unconscious in the bourgeois system of value exchange. Baudrillard declares to refute this I-produce-therefore-history-is ontology, Marxism and even all the radical discourses of the post-Marxian trend. We have to respond to this arrogant misunderstanding of and vicious attack on Marxism. First, I am going to discuss Baudrillard's view about production.

1. Mis-criticism of use value and "exchange value"

The first issue in chapter one is the criticism of "use value and labor power," in which Baudrillard argues that Marxism is built on the specific stipulations constructed by the bourgeois system of utilitarian value and the logic of market exchange. Categories such as use value and labor power only make sense in the capitalist system and will end up in theoretical transgression if generally applied to the entire history.

Once more, it is Baudrillard's misunderstanding of Marxism. Marx is different from the bourgeois thinkers in that he attaches *historical restriction* in theoretical application to each paradigm of particular eras. Baudrillard's accusation exactly proves Marx's unique advantage. In fact, what Baudrillard criticizes is a non-existent "pseudo-Marxism", a demonized illusion only in Baudrillard's own perverse thinking. Baudrillard says that:

> [i]n the distinction between exchange value and use value, Marxism shows its strength but also its weakness. The presupposition of use value—the hypothesis of a concrete value beyond the abstraction of

exchange value, a human purpose of the commodity in the moment of its direct relation of utility for a subject—is only the effect of the system of exchange value, a concept produced and developed by it. Far from designating a realm beyond political economy, use value is only the horizon of exchange value.[1]

Despite this verbiage, he is not able to pick a hole in Marx. Firstly, the distinction of exchange value and use value should be counted as the early economic exercise of Smith and Ricardo instead of the contribution of Marx. Baudrillard is not reading carefully enough. It is true that Marx employs them in the arena of classical economics (until the first half of the *1857-1858 Manuscripts*) but later in *Das Kapital* he defines the duality of commodity by use value and *value*, and confirms that exchange value is merely the *superficial appearance* of value. Baudrillard ignores this point.[2] More importantly, Marx does not separate the commodity from the issues of value, exchange value and use value, nor does he simply apply economic concepts to the fields of philosophy and anthropology. In the first run, Baudrillard chooses a wrong target.

Secondly, Baudrillard does not accept the anthropological use value severed from the "system of exchange value", especially the commodity's "direct relation of utility for a subject." Understandably, he longs for proceeding with the Mauss-Bataille logic and radically wipes away the bourgeois utilitarian value system that does not allow the "thing thinged" (Heidegger), but where on earth does Marx make an ahistorical, abstract, eternalized concept of use value? On one hand, Baudrillard cites the specific points of Marxist economy; on the other, he arbitrarily makes ontological use of these points. What a misconception it is! Marx strictly limits the discussion of use value and value (exchange value) within the historical process of

---

[1] Baudrillard, Jean. *The Mirror of Production*. Trans. Mark Poster. St. Louis: Telos Press, 1975. p. 23.

[2] Marx once said that "exchange-value is merely a '*form* of appearance,' an independent way of presenting the *value* contained in the commodity." MECW.

commodity production and exchange. He never talks about the duality of commodities in primitive and communist societies, where commodity exchange relations are not found. Marx says that "the dissolution of all products and activities into exchange values presupposes both the dissolution of all established personal (historical) relations of dependence in production, and the all-round dependence of the producers upon one another."[1] Here, Marx uses "fixed personal relations" to identify the first one of the three major social forms, which, in my understanding, certainly includes the primitive tribal life of the Mauss-Baudrillard research. For example, the symbolic exchange during gift transference and sacrifice represents the close *kinship reliance* that is definitely personal; however, such ontological scales as value, exchange value and use value do not penetrate the entire human life and social relations until "bourgeois society" appears.[2] In addition, Marx stated that "when material production is no longer limited by exchange value, but [solely] by its relation to the overall development of the individual, all this business, with its convulsions and pains, comes to an end."[3] Marx's statement cannot be clearer here! In fact, I can figure out the real intention behind Baudrillard's logical violence. He means to say that he does not agree with viewing *utility* as the scale for everything. (His utility is proposed in line with Bataille's ontological uselessness, not the use value in antithesis to value, which will be discussed in detail later.) In the second run, Baudrillard makes a mess of an originally clear issue.

Thirdly, Baudrillard does not regard use value as the foundation of exchange value. He thinks that use value is "produced and developed from the system of exchange value." I have to admit that Baudrillard is not without grounds this time. His opinion had once obtained support from a classical economist, who was Adam Smith, but not Marx. In *The Wealth of Nations*, Smith first proposed that an item's usefulness determines its exchange value.

[1] Karl Marx and Frederick Engels. *Collected Works*, vol. 28. London: Lawrence & Wishart, 1986.
      p. 93.
[2] Ibid., p. 93.
[3] Ibid., p. 12.

Nevertheless, after man enters the era of machine production, the smart Ricardo opposed this point by saying that the direct factor that determines the item's exchange value is not its utility but rather the scarcity and amount of labor spent to acquire it.[1] Baudrillard does not understand that they are discussing the theory of labor value *in the economic context*. In this connection, Marx approaches from an economic perspective the relations of value and use value of the commodity, value generated from abstract labor, the amount of value determined by the amount of labor, necessary labor time being the real scale of value, etc. At the same time, Marx points out that under capitalist economic conditions commercial development "will increasingly subject production to exchange value, and force immediate use value more and more into the background."[2] All in all, Marx never deals with labor value *outside* the economic context.

Baudrillard seems to fruitlessly thrash about against Marxism. He intends to look through the Mauss-Bataille lens, goes beyond the economic field and declares: the *utility* (his appropriated "use value") of all objects, even the entire world is only the ahistorical *universal* projection of the specific mode of bourgeois existence (his "system of exchange value"). He thinks that Marx is the culprit for this blunder. Prima facie, it is a bizarre accusation: Is not Marx resolutely against the capitalist mode of production? And why does Baudrillard assert that it is Marx's fault? In fact, Baudrillard employs this attack to display his "insightfulness." In his view, Marx only criticizes the capitalist *mode of production*; denies the bourgeois economic and political structure, but he is unaware that the real problem lies in capitalist *production* per se. Consequently, Marx neutralizes the productive force by extending it to the foundation of general social existence and progress, while unable to realize it is this utility system of production that generates the entire *utilitarian* coordinate of values. Therefore, Baudrillard thinks that Marx's criticism of the capitalist mode of production not only

---

[1] Ricardo, David. *On the Principles of Political Economy and Taxation.* London, 1821. pp. 16-25.

[2] Karl Marx and Frederick Engels. *Collected Works*, vol. 29. London: Lawrence & Wishart, 1987. p. 233.

fails to solve the problem once for all but also obscures the deep truth of the matter to the extent that the radical revolution digresses. Baudrillard attempts to reject Marx, then his historical materialism and material production, and goes so far as criticizing any utilitarian economic view extended from the concept of production. In brief, he is critical of the I-produce-therefore-I-am and I-produce-therefore-history-is ontology of *utilitarian labor*. Here, Baudrillard takes it as the critique of "use value." (I shall turn to this point later.) For this reason, Baudrillard says that the final way to solve the problem is to radically rethink the *needs* of consumption, production, along with labor power as the key subject of production. (The "needs" here are not needs in the common sense. They refer to the utilitarian necessities created in the system of exchange value. In the Mauss-Bataille logic, these needs are false; consumption is evil while non-specific and non-utilitarian expenditure should be valued.)

2. Theoretical stick of symbolic exchange in primitive societies

The reader will certainly entertain the question: what is the foundation of Baudrillard's attack on Marxism? Fortunately, the same chapter provides an interesting textual event, through which we may find the answer. It is Baudrillard's critique of Julia Kristeva. Here, he unequivocally demonstrates the basic logic that he relies on—Mauss-Bataille grassrootism centered on symbolic exchange. (Baudrillard is very aggressive. He is unwilling to let go of any person within his criticism.)

Despite the title "Marx and the Hieroglyph of Value," Baudrillard focuses on the rejection of Kristeva's "defense" of Marxism. He first cites a paragraph of her *Semiotica*, among which, he is particularly enraged by the following sentences: "Marx clearly outlined another possibility: work could be apprehended outside value, on the side of the commodity produced and circulating in the chain of communication. Here, labor no longer represents any value, meaning, or signification. It is a question only of a body and a discharge…."[1] Kristeva is not wrong. Marx does recognize labor and production outside the system of commodity exchange. In his notes on anthropology, Marx stipulates life and labor activities beyond the value of commodity. In fact, Kristeva's statement was not originally meant to defend Marx. However, the intolerant Baudrillard still vents his grudge against Marx on the innocent Kristeva because he must feel that her defense for Marx threatens the truth that only his teachers and he can understand at a time when Marx is already obviously bewildered by the bourgeois system of exchange value.

Baudrillard cleverly turns to the text of the first volume in *Das Kapital*, which he cites before. He underscores the following sentence: "Productive activity, if we leave out of sight its special form, viz., the useful character of labor, is nothing but the expenditure of human labor-power."[2] Baudrillard questions: is there a conception of labor in Marx different from that of the production of useful ends (the canonical definition of labor as value in the framework of political economy and the anthropological definition of labor as human finality)? No! He is very upset.

> Kristeva attributes to Marx a radically different vision centered on the body, discharge, play, anti-value, non-utility, non-finality, etc. She would have him read Bataille before he wrote—but also forget him when it is convenient. If there was one thing Marx did not think about, it was discharge, waste, sacrifice, prodigality, play, and symbolism.[3]

What a far-fetched interpretation! Was Marx that eager to be Bataille's student? Why should Marx read the next century stuff of discharge, anti-value, non-utility by Bataille? It is ridiculous! Here, Baudrillard puts his teacher to the front to show his orthodox learning. Furthermore, he cites a

---

[1] Baudrillard, Jean. *The Mirror of Production*. Trans. Mark Poster. St. Louis: Telos Press, 1975. p. 42. *See* Note 30 of the book. Julia Kristeva, "La sémiotique et la production," *Semiotica* 2. [I have not been able to complete this reference. Translator's note]

[2] Karl Marx, *Capital*, vol. 1. London: Lawrence & Wishart, 1977. p. 51.

[3] Baudrillard, Jean. *The Mirror of Production*. Trans. Mark Poster. St. Louis: Telos Press, 1975. p. 42.

longer paragraph of Bataille to illustrate the so-called "sacrifice economy" and the theory of symbolic exchange, which also contains Bataille's criticism of political economy and complete rejection of the concept of labor. (We have learned Bataille's opinion in the first section.) For Bataille "the social wealth produced is *material*; it has nothing to do with *symbolic* wealth which, mocking natural necessity, comes conversely from destruction, the deconstruction of value, transgression, or discharge."[1] (Baudrillard's word is not often in agreement with his deeds. As an excellent photographer, he made use of his high-class camera, took many valuable pictures, held a number of personal exhibitions, and published several fine collections, from which we find no useless expenditure of "transgression and discharge.")[2] It seems reasonable for Baudrillard to accuse Kristeva of her imposition of what Marxism lacks on Marx; or, how can he prove this book against Marx valuable?

According to Baudrillard, the "discharge" of human power that Marx speaks of is not a discharge with a pure waste, a symbolic discharge in Bataille's sense (pulsating, libidinal); it is still an economic, productive, finalized discharge precisely because, in its mating with the other, it begets a productive force called the earth (or matter). It is a useful discharge, an investment, not a gratuitous and festive energizing of the body's powers, a game with death, or the acting out of a desire.[3] Baudrillard says that:

> What man gives of his body in labor is never *given* or *lost* or *rendered* by nature in a reciprocal way. Labor only aims to "make" nature "yield." This discharge is thus immediately an investment of

[1] Baudrillard, Jean. *The Mirror of Production*. Trans. Mark Poster. St. Louis: Telos Press, 1975. p. 43.

[2] Baudrillard's interest in photography began in the 1980s. A friend gave him a point-and-shoot. At first, he casually used it to take pictures. Gradually, he was fascinated by photography. He held several personal exhibitions and published a number of photo albums. I also like photography. I bought a second-hand photography collection of his from Amazon.com. Frankly, I like his unique conception of light and layout.

[3] Baudrillard, Jean. *The Mirror of Production*. Trans. Mark Poster. St. Louis: Telos Press, 1975. p. 44.

value, a *putting into value* opposed to all symbolic *putting into play* as in the gift or the discharge.[1]

As we know, the gift (exchange) here is Mauss's anthropological discovery. It is a non-utilitarian structure of symbolic exchange in primitive personal relations used by Bataille as the weapon to ward off the modern kingdom of value production. Bataille adopts the useless discharge as the scene of authentic being from Sade while Marx does not understand the importance of symbolic exchange and discharge. But why should he? Baudrillard's *theoretical terrorism* (his own words) attempts to force everybody to abide by a theory, one that contains little truth. This is pure violence. As I said before, it is impossible to replace modernity with the ancient or primitive mode of human existence. It is only a beautiful dream unworthy of mentioning. Mauss-Bataille grassrootism is in essence childish. In our daily life, we are familiar with the wish "to simply maintain childhood", but avoidance of the complexity and evils of the adult world does not justify the continual preservation of childlike simplicity and purity. A baby may feel that discharge is the most pleasant sensation or may randomly destroy or waste items, which is also seen in kittens and puppies. However, the baby has to grow up and his existence will certainly be differentiated from other animals. Human history cannot be reversed or stopped; it is only liberated through progress and revolution. There is no hope in historical reversion. For this, Marx made a wonderful comment: "An adult cannot become a child again, or he becomes childish. But does not the naiveté of the child give him pleasure, and must he not himself endeavor to reproduce the child's veracity on a higher stage?"[2] Marx's voice still echoes in our ears. He must never have expected a student of his student would attempt to transform man back into a child. This act is more than childish. It is absurd.

But, Kristeva has a hard time here. She is attacked without any given

---

[1] Baudrillard, Jean. *The Mirror of Production*. Trans. Mark Poster. St. Louis: Telos Press, 1975. p. 44.

[2] Karl Marx and Frederick Engels. *Collected Works*, vol. 28. London: Lawrence & Wishart, 1986. pp. 47-48.

reason. Baudrillard proudly claims that she "would gladly be rid of value, but neither of labor nor Marx." To his happiness, Baudrillard thinks he gets rid of Marx. He posits that Kristeva's problem lies in her blindness of Marx's lapse, the so-called "hieroglyph of value." In Baudrillard's eyes, it is an invisible but trapping snare; moreover, he stresses that Marx himself makes this definition. He cites the following paragraph in the first volume of *Das Kapital*:

> Value, therefore, does not stalk about with a label describing what it is. It is value, rather, that converts every product into a social hieroglyphic. Later on, we try to decipher the hieroglyphic, to get behind the secret of our own social products; for to stamp an object of utility as a value, is just as much a social product as language.[1]

They are indeed the exact words of Marx, but Baudrillard's citation only proves his own fault. First, Marx abandons the use of "exchange value" but chooses a precise word: value (exchange value is merely the external manifestation of value in the process of exchange). Second, Marx indicates that stipulation of useful things as valuable only occurs in a particular historical condition, the same way as language does. In other words, value does not exist in primitive societies. Does Baudrillard not understand this? Third, the hieroglyph here is meant by Marx to refer to the universal light converting everything into commodities in the *capitalist mode of production*. Marx never intends to allow this vicious light to shine on all history or forever. He is actually against viewing the logic of capital (use value and value of every object) as an ahistorical ideological hallucination in every social form. Marx concludes that capitalist production "based upon the basis of exchange value" is going to collapse.[2] Baudrillard makes his petty tricks and sometimes his consideration seems insightful. He admits that Marx is clear in meaning, even so:

> this entire analysis of the mystery of value remains fundamental.

---

[1] Karl Marx, *Capital*, vol. 1. London: Lawrence & Wishart, 1977. p. 79.

[2] Karl Marx and Frederick Engels. *Collected Works*, vol. 28. London: Lawrence & Wishart, 1986. p. 195.

But rather than being valid only for the product of labor in distribution and exchange, it is valid even for the product of labor (and for labor itself) taken as a "useful object." Utility (including labor's) is already a socially produced and determined hieroglyphic abstraction. The whole anthropology of "primitive" exchange compels us to break with the natural evidence of utility and to reconceive the social and historical genesis of use value as Marx did with exchange value. Only then will the hieroglyph be totally deciphered and the spell of value radically exorcized.[1]

Baudrillard may deem the above analysis profound: Marx only deals with the product in distribution and exchange; as long as people take the "utility" attitude, they fall to the hieroglyphs of value. Only through primitive exchange relations (symbolic exchange) can they radically reject the utility of nature and break the magic of the social hieroglyphs of value. In my opinion, even a nesting bird cannot agree with the grassrootism of "useless ontology" beloved by Baudrillard and his teachers; otherwise, how can it survive without the shielding *useful* nest? In view of all the history of thought, it is a common practice to admit the utility of objects because it is the basic condition for human survival. Why should Marx be picked out to blame? Could it be that Baudrillard does not know or just pretends not to understand the truth, and gives empty talks? If not, how can Baudrillard the photographer exist?

3. Down with the utilitarian ontology of production

The critique of "use value" leads to the falsification of the concept of labor power. Baudrillard is really good at association. He says that "the revolutionary originality of his theory comes from releasing the concept of labor power from its status as an unusual commodity whose insertion in the cycle of production *under the name of use value* carries the X element, a differential extra-value that generates surplus value and the whole process of

---

[1] *See* Note 33 of *The Mirror of Production*. Trans. Mark Poster. St. Louis: Telos Press, 1975.

capital. (Bourgeois economics would think instead of simple 'labor' as one factor of production among others in the economic process.)"[1] Baudrillard's text is characterized by leaping thoughts with insightful perspectives. We know that in solving the question of equal exchange between the worker and the capitalist in the market, Marx proposes the *value* of labor *power* from the old imprecise usage, "value of labor." (According to Althusser, Marx read out the symptomatic blankness of the Smith-Ricardo texts.) In this way, the capitalist only pays the worker for his right to use labor. Behind the seemingly equal exchange, the added value generated in the activity of the labor power contains a part that is to be appropriated by the capitalist, which is the secret of surplus value. Here, Baudrillard seems to allude to the "revolutionary creativity" of the Marxist theory of surplus value, but his statement is opaque.

He then quotes Marx's comment on Wagner's textbook of political economy. It is a famous illustration about the relationship between labor duality and commodity duality, in which Marx underscored that his explanation of use value is achieved via analysis of particular economic formations.[2] The ad hoc clarification specifies that economic concepts such as value and use value only hold for a certain economic social form. Marx does not attempt to apply the theory of value into the entire social historical existence. Strangely, Baudrillard smells some philosophical sense from this pure economic discussion. He thinks that Marx still "retains something of the *apparent movement of political economy*" and "he does not radicalize the schema to the point of reversing this appearance and revealing use value *as produced by the play of exchange value*."[3] Once more, he is raving. In the original discourse of Marx, under the capitalist system the use value of commodity is generated by concrete labor while value (not exchange value)

---

[1] Baudrillard, Jean. *The Mirror of Production*. Trans. Mark Poster. St. Louis: Telos Press, 1975. p. 23.

[2] Karl Marx and Frederick Engels. *Collected Works*, vol. 24. London: Lawrence & Wishart, 1989. p. 546.

[3] Baudrillard, Jean. *The Mirror of Production*. Trans. Mark Poster. St. Louis: Telos Press, 1975. pp. 24-25.

is produced by abstract labor. Baudrillard cannot observe the *duality* of labor differentiated as abstract labor and concrete labor in the *same* process of production. The use value emphasized by Marx is the foundation of value, that is to say, abstract labor is based on concrete labor. However, this logical sequence cannot be reversed in the economic context. The abstract is not the foundation of the concrete, except in Hegel's idealistic philosophy; value is not the basis of use value; exchange value (price) to express value cannot produce use value. In fact, what the pointless Baudrillard really wants to propose is that the *utilitarian utility* of any object is generated by the bourgeois system of commodities. I just wonder why he enters the economic context that is completely strange to him. If he goes outside the economic context, he seems capable of saying something correct:

> The definition of products as useful and as responding to needs is the most accomplished, most internalized expression of abstract economic exchange: it is its subjective closure. The definition of labor power as the source of "concrete" social wealth is the complete expression of the abstract manipulation of labor power: the truth of capital culminates in this "evidence" of man as producer of value.[1]

Look, the Mauss-Bataille logic is present here, only if we are willing to interpret it through a reversed order. First, from the perspective of the discourse of capital, man's existence is essentially for the production of value, viz. creation of useful items for the subject, which is the *ontology of production*. Second, the ontology of production is certain to posit man's existence as the labor power engaged in the activities of production, that is to say, labor power is *labor man*, which results from the "abstract maneuver" of man's existence by the discourse of capital. Third, only in the ontology of production can the fake needs of man (desire of the Other) emerge and the objects be turned into *useful* items.

I wrote a book to particularly deal with the close relations between

---

[1] Baudrillard, Jean. *The Mirror of Production*. Trans. Mark Poster. St. Louis: Telos Press, 1975. p. 25.

Marxist economic research and the philosophical discourse of historical materialism. The philosophical methods of Marxism develop with the constant achievements of economics, historiography and anthropology.[1] However, it does not mean that all the specific statements of Marxist economics can be *directly converted to* the philosophical logic. Baudrillard makes a common mistake like his fellow French thinkers, who always directly apply the achievements of Marxist political economy to other disciplines. For instance, Bourdieu transplants Marx's concept of capital and puts forward fanciful notions such as "cultural capital," "symbolic capital" and "social capital"; Lacan alters Marx's surplus value into "surplus enjoyment"; Debord draws the "spectacle fetishism" from Marx's economic fetishism, etc. Baudrillard follows suit and creates a "semiotic political economy" in his previous book. Here, he goes beside himself, radicalizing (in Baudrillard's own word) this simple logical transplant for a *metaphysical* denial of Marxist economic achievement. Now the problem rises: It is actually incongruous as chalk and cheese when he smugly analyzes the specific economic concepts of labor power, value and exchange from a philosophical perspective. He does not clarify the issue but makes the problem more confounding.

Baudrillard has more to say. In his eyes, as the ontology of production, Marxist historical materialism still conceals a humanistic logic, a *potential* anthropological framework labeled by him as the double "generic" face of man, due to the fact that the existence of man has two latent dimensions, *needs* and *labor power*.

It should be admitted that Baudrillard grasps Marxist historical materialism per se this time. According to him, in the classic discourse of historical materialism, for human activities to occur requires two conditions: needs and the production generated by these needs, whereas man is only the laborer engaged in production. Accordingly, the nature of Marxist humanity is the *humanism of production*. Baudrillard's comment seems correct except the inaccurate conception of labor. However, we will soon discover what on

[1] *See* my *Back to Marx: The Philosophical Discourse in the Context of Economics* (Jiangsu People's Press, 1999).

earth Baudrillard is opposing.

In Baudrillard's view, Marx's philosophical encoding of history is still a controlled result of the discourse of the bourgeois political economy, only he himself is unaware. This is because Marx's "needs" is in essence the "consumption of use value" of the object, which presents the same characteristics as the concrete aspect of labor: uniqueness, differentiation, and incommensurability, in short, quality (again, Baudrillard is illegitimately appropriating the specific concepts in Marxist political economy.):

> In concrete labor man gives a useful, objective end to nature; in need he gives a useful, subjective end to products. Needs and labor are man's double potentiality or double generic quality. This is the same anthropological realm in which the concept of production is sketched as the "fundamental movement of human existence," as defining a rationality and a sociality appropriate for man.[1]

Needs and labor are man's generic qualities, or double generic face. As man's potentiality or nature, they must be realized through production. Hence, production as "the fundamental movement of human existence" is the inevitable basis of Marxist philosophy. In the final analysis, the reason why we are human beings is owing to production: *I produce, therefore I am.*

I am going to first deal with Baudrillard's accusation of historical materialism. Despite several economic and philosophical misuses mentioned above, Baudrillard is not completely wrong in his understanding of Marx. His purpose is to oppose need, labor and production, the production of means of subsistence that is deemed by Marx as the foundation for human social existence. According to his Mauss-Bataille logic, the ideal personal relations occur in the non-utilitarian symbolic exchange framework, where there is no consideration of the object's usefulness and the gift's exchange value, even no utilitarian consumption and usage, and where non-useful consumption reaches its culmination. Therefore, the need of utility should not appear in man's real existence, neither should the material production that aims at

---

[1] Baudrillard, Jean. *The Mirror of Production*. Trans. Mark Poster. St. Louis: Telos Press, 1975. p. 32.

making useful items. As we know, it is a *backward* grassrootism, a western version of "self-abnegation and etiquette-restoration," and an unrealistic practopianism. I even lose interest to refute it.

In the *German Ideology*, Marx discusses the needs as a prerequisite for the historical activities of man. They stem from the *condition for life subsistence* (the most basic activities such as eating, drinking, finding or building habitation, etc.) whose development can be traced back to animals, even living organisms. Nonetheless, this condition is not generated from the living things themselves, who have to relate to their environment and make material transference (I carefully avoid the word "exchange"), in which the necessary metabolic material is obtained from outside and their waste is discharged. (I feel uncomfortable here in writing the above words. It is embarrassing to talk about common sense biology in a serious philosophical discussion. Baudrillard often plays to the gallery, like the abnormal Sade.) Marx does not talk about man's needs from the capitalist view of utilitarian value. Otherwise, would the tribes in Australia and north Pacific coastal areas have survived without eating or habitation? Obviously not. It is impossible to reject the basic needs of living things, unless we deny the complete existence of life. If Marx's perquisite is correct, then needs inevitably lead to man's superior activities of obtaining means of subsistence. We know that the animal kingdom abides by the law of the jungle and the survival of the fittest. Man distinguishes himself from other animals not merely by strength but, more importantly, by the adjustment of *the mode of existence*, which starts from change of the mode of activities that acquire survival conditions, or the mode to meet one's own needs. (The young Marx already realized it before he became a Marxist. He said the animals and nature are homogeneous while man differentiates himself from nature by transcending the present existence.) When homo sapiens (or anthropoids in the pre-historical period) want to satisfy their needs, they have to use tools and engage themselves in an activity to obtain the necessary means of life which is different from other animals, viz. *production*. This is the changing and making process of nature that other animals do not have. According to Marx, it is production that causes man to be different from other animals. Marx's production here is not what Baudrillard says about the production with the specific structure obtained from the bourgeois economic code, but the general activities that man is engaged in order to obtain the means of subsistence. It is true that *modern industrial production* is not the foundation for the entire human history, but man's survival cannot be separated from the objective action of acquiring means of subsistence, of which there is no exception, even for the primitive tribes in Mauss-Bataille logic. Without this material production of changing nature, man would have died out, like other disappeared living things in the vicissitudes of history.

Baudrillard may propose that in primitive societies objects are not secured mainly through production or man's utilitarian labor. Nevertheless, direct acquisition from nature is the major mode of the survival condition for animals, in Marx's words, the *appropriation* of nature (not the utilitarian *possession* that Baudrillard dislikes). In Baudrillard's favorite *1857-1858 Manuscripts*, Marx analyzes the alleged "naturally formed society" with the 19th century anthropology and historiography, which also deals with the primitive tribal existence to which Mauss and Bataille clung. (To be honest, Marx's discussion is not out of date even for today's standard.) Marx admits that man's initial existence starts from the appropriation of nature: "The original conditions of production appear as natural presuppositions, *natural conditions of the existence of the producer*, just as his living body, even though he reproduces and develops it, is not originally posited by himself, but appears as his own *presupposition*; his own (corporeal) being is a natural presupposition not posited by himself."[1] To survive as a race, man has to reproduce himself, which is a material presupposition. In addition, the reproduction of life (or the continuation of race) begins from the complete reliance on nature, just in the same way of animals. "Man takes possession of the ready-made fruits of the earth, to which, among others, belong the animals, especially those he can domesticate."[2] Here, "man does not

---

[1] Karl Marx and Frederick Engels. *Collected Works*, vol. 28. London: Lawrence & Wishart, 1986. pp. 413-414.

[2] Ibid., p. 416.

originally confront nature as a worker but as a proprietor."[1] However, things change soon.

> Originally the act of producing by the individual is confined to the reproduction of his own body through the appropriation of ready-made objects prepared by nature for consumption? But even where the task is only to *find* and *discover*, effort, labor—as in hunting, fishing, the care of herds—and production (i.e. development) of certain skills are soon required on the part of the subject. This means that condition in which man need merely reach for what is already available, without any tools (i.e. products of labor already destined for production), without alteration of form (which already takes place even in herding), etc., are very transitory, and can nowhere be regarded as normal; nor even as normal at the earlier stage. Of course, it has to be remembered that the original conditions of production include substances directly consumable without labor, such as some fruit, animals, etc.; thus the consumption fund is itself part of the *original production fund*.[2]

In my opinion, the above analysis is accurate. Marx clearly illustrates how the initial history of humankind comes into being, how labor and production become the real objective foundation of human society, how man possesses material items only through labor and production and will get more and more reliant on them. "Real appropriation does not occur through the establishment of a notional relationship to these conditions, but takes place in the active, real relation to them, when they are really posited as the conditions of man's subjective activity."[3] Now we know that Baudrillard imagines something impossible. His brainstorm only ends up in destruction of his own logical foundation.

---

[1] Karl Marx and Frederick Engels. *Collected Works*, vol. 30. London: Lawrence & Wishart, 1988. p. 98.

[2] Karl Marx and Frederick Engels. *Collected Works*, vol. 28. London: Lawrence & Wishart, 1986. p. 416.

[3] Ibid., p. 417.

Here, I have to give a common lesson of Marxist history to Baudrillard. Perhaps he is unaware that before making material production the core paradigm of historical materialism, Marx posited *practice* as the logical start point of his new world outlook in the 1845 *Thesis on Feuerbach*. The concept of praxis went through a gradual development from the *philosophical* conception of labor (generic nature) that Baudrillard disapproves (*the 1844 Manuscripts*), the whole process of which is too complicated to have a detailed discussion here. We are going to have a general introduction of the relations among them. In 1845, Marx discovered the fundamental problem of humanistic *generic discourse* from M. Stirner's critique, and then he eliminated the concept of labor, which he had learned from Ricardo's socialist economy, from his philosophical logic. He also understood that the real existent labor in history is only the "living" subjective activity of man.[1] Therefore, he restored man and his whole objectification process (wherein labor is one aspect of human activity) to the foundation of his philosophy, which was the *original, revolutionary* material practice. Therefore, after 1845, labor was no longer the core of Marxism or the generic nature of man. Marx stated in *Thesis on Feuerbach* that his philosophy still started from the subject, but not the Hegelian ideal initiative; instead, it is man's initiative of objective material activities. I also noted that the nature of this practice is modern, a specific *industrial* product. (It is because the labor production of natural economy cannot generate the totality of the revolutionary relations, the timing when "nature becomes the object" as Heidegger says.) Here, Marx observed history from the summit of historical development. When he and Engels wrote the *German Ideology*, they treated the praxis of man as a complex system of activities in the process of the social history when labor-material production action is the *more fundamental* aspect, since it is the universal foundation of human existence and development as well as the most basic principle of general historical materialism.

It is understandable for Baudrillard to take a Mauss-Bataille stand

---

[1] Karl Marx and Frederick Engels. *Collected Works*, vol. 28. London: Lawrence & Wishart, 1986. p. 202.

and hate the capitalist utilitarian system of production, but he should have known that Marx also takes a critical attitude of the capitalist *production-for-production's-sake* Ricardoism that turns man into a cap. For Marx, such economic relations decide "production not as the development of human productivity; but as the display of *material wealth*, in antithesis to the productive development of the human individual."[1] Baudrillard wrongly imposes the label of turning man into labor power on Marx, who radically denies the transformation of man into "hands"-like labor power in the capitalist production process.[2] (I also notice that Sahlins is more objective than Baudrillard regarding this point. In *Culture and Practical Reason*, Sahlins offers a fine division between Marx and traditional Marxist interpreters. He concludes, that "Marx did not advocate a crass economism of the enterprising individual."[3]) Marx aims for the liberation of the productive forces and then man through his critique of the capitalist mode of production while for Baudrillard, liberation of the productive forces is itself a mistake. His grassrootism may ask questions such as: Why should history make progress? Why should an object be useful? Why should man produce? Or, is not the primitive gift swapping system premised on authentic symbolic exchange man's best existential situation? Baudrillard thinks Marx still falls victim to the capitalist material foundation and the whole Western civilization that creates this foundation. In his view, besides the corrupted bourgeois economic relations and political structure, the real culprit is the *material mode of production per se*, while capitalism is only the highest level of this mode. Irritated, he says:

> And productivity is not primarily a generic dimension, a human and social kernel of all wealth to be extracted from the husk of capitalist

---

[1] Karl Marx and Frederick Engels. *Collected Works*, vol. 34. London: Lawrence & Wishart, 1994. p. 109.

[2] Karl Marx and Frederick Engels. *Collected Works*, vol. 30. London: Lawrence & Wishart, 1988. p. 55.

[3] Sahlins, Marshall D. *Culture and Practical Reason*. Joint Publishing Company Limited (Beijing), 2002. p. 165.

relations of production (the eternal empiricist illusion). Instead, all this must be overturned to see that the abstract and generalized development of productivity (the developed form of political economy) is what makes the *concept of production* itself appear as man's movement and generic end (or better, as the concept of man as producer).[1]

Baudrillard is genuinely opposed to historical materialism, to the logic of production, and to the development of the productive forces as man's end. Behind this opaque expression of political economy, his strategy is clear: He denies all social existence and historical movement established on material production, rejects the social development outlook of progressive history, and refuses to view man as the producer (labor power). Judging from the common knowledge of contemporary Western thought, Baudrillard wants to bring down *productivism*. Thus, Baudrillard's philosophy is not trivial to Marxist historical materialism. He is destined to be Marx's theoretical enemy.

In my opinion, Baudrillard's attack on Marx's theory of production is not completely original. Among the Western Marxist camp, the young György Lukács was the first to put forward this question. In *History and Class Consciousness*, when he overturned Weber's instrumental rationality based on production technology, he inadvertently came to the discovery that the controlling and exploitative character of modern capitalism is, unexpectedly, the material aspect of *production per se*, the materializing and unifying assembly line leading to the double de-totalization of the existence and conception of worker. The materialization and de-totalization here are not Schiller's slavery of capital resulting from the reversed economic relations or division of labor. It is a problem not only about the relations of production but also entails that production itself is permeated by the venom of capitalism. This concept was first noticed by Heidegger from an ontological perspective: Dasein (being there) appears through material readiness-to-hand, which is also the onset of existential alienation and oblivion. This idea

---

[1] Baudrillard, Jean. *The Mirror of Production*. Trans. Mark Poster. St. Louis: Telos Press, 1975. p. 31.

was inherited by the late Sartre. In the same line of thought, the first one to publicize this secret in neo-Marxist history was Karol Kiosk from the Czech Republic, who put forward the concept of pseudo-practice in his *Dialectics of the Concrete*.[1] When it came to the Benjamin-Adorno critical philosophy, this question was composed into a *general* negation, that is, criticism of the Enlightenment, instrumental rationality, and even the entire progressive human civilization. In my view, it is the actual outset of post-Marxian thought. Now, the concepts of practice, production and historical progression in Marxist framework are not neutral any more; the profound foundation of historical materialism is exposed to direct attack by Arendt's *Human Condition*, Habermas's *Toward a Rational Society*, and Leiss's *Domination of Nature*, all extending their criticism in this issue. They only fail to attain Baudrillard's depths and intensity.

4. Re-questioning the Marxist criticism of the capitalist mode of production

More importantly, Baudrillard's accusation of Marx also contains Marx's criticism of capitalism, which, in his view, only seizes the particular form of the capitalist material production but on a deeper level strengthens the control of this mode of production with a mere negation of the overt form.

> *And in this Marxism assists the cunning of capital. It convinces men that they are alienated by the sale of their labor power, thus censoring the much more radical hypothesis that they might be alienated as labor power, as the "inalienable" power of creating value by their labor.*[2]

Baudrillard italicizes nearly four lines to stress his meaning. It shows his great concern for this. In Baudrillard's opinion, despite Marx's criticism

---

[1] The first chapter has a specific discussion of the above conceptions. Please go there for details.

[2] Baudrillard, Jean. *The Mirror of Production*. Trans. Mark Poster. St. Louis: Telos Press, 1975. p. 31.

of capitalism, his liberation still aims at the "inalienable" labor, which is also within the capitalist system of exchange value. Here, Baudrillard has two misunderstandings: First, it is true that the young Marx did advocate the theory of inalienable labor in his writing of the *1844 Manuscripts*, and regarded communism as the restoration of the nature of labor through sublation of alienation and privatization, but after the establishment of historical materialism in 1845, this humanistic historical view of inalienable labor was abandoned by him. Second, Marx's criticism of capitalism is not that simple as Baudrillard imagines. It at least contains the following aspects: First, to analyze the systematic weakness of the capitalist mode of production from the perspective of the whole social-historical development and the prospects of productive forces; second, the exploitative nature of capitalists to occupy the surplus value in capitalist economic system; third, the materialized personal relations in the capitalist mode of production. Obviously, Marx's criticism is radically different from the view of inalienable labor and liberation in Baudrillard's humanistic logic. This time, what Baudrillard considers a fatal point is still a groundless imagination, or at most, a pseudo-target erected by the 20th century Western Marxist humanists.[1]

Of course, Baudrillard is not satisfied to stop with the criticism of the logic of the inalienable labor. His intention is to deny production and labor. In his eyes, Marx criticizes the capitalist mode of production but comes to agreement with the Western Enlightenment spirit on more fundamental concepts.

> Radical in its *logical* analysis of capital, Marxist theory nonetheless maintains an *anthropological* consensus with the options of Western rationalism in its definitive form acquired in eighteenth century

---

[1] After the 1930s, especially, after the publication of the young Marx's *1844 Manuscripts*, the second generation Marxist representatives, like early Erich From, Herbert Marcuse and Henri Lefebvre, tended to review Marxist philosophy with humanistic ideas, which had a great impact on the neo-Marxists of ex-communist Eastern Europe. *See* my *The Historic Logic of Western Marxist Philosophy*.

bourgeois thought. Science, technique, progress, history—in these ideas we have an entire civilization that comprehends itself as producing its own development and takes its dialectical force toward completing humanity in terms of totality and happiness.[1]

Indeed, Baudrillard's ultimate purpose is directed against the rationality of Western civilization as a whole. In his opinion, Marx only opposes the corruption of the capitalist mode of production but does not negate the progression of history, which, per contra, is seen hindered by the capitalist relations of production. Therefore, in his comment, Marx changed nothing basic, nothing regarding the *idea* of man *producing* himself in his infinite determination, and continually surpassing himself toward his own end.

Marx translated this concept into the logic of material production and the historical dialectic of modes of production. But differentiating modes of production renders unchallengeable the evidence of production as the determinant instance. It generalizes the economic mode of rationality over the entire expanse of human history, as the generic mode of human becoming. It circumscribes the entire history of man in a gigantic simulation model. It tries somehow to turn against the order of capital by using as an analytic instrument the most subtle ideological phantasm that capital has itself elaborated.[2]

According to Baudrillard, Marx universalizes the economic framework characteristic of capitalism, generalizes production and the mode of production that are typical of the system of exchange value over the entire expanse of human history. Subsequently, Marx fails to make critical changes of the capital logic: He is against the very capitalist economic relations but only creates an "ideological phantasm that capital has itself elaborated." Universalization of production, along with "the 'dialectical' generalization of this concept, is merely the *ideological* universalization of this system's

---

[1] Baudrillard, Jean. *The Mirror of Production*. Trans. Mark Poster. St. Louis: Telos Press, 1975. p. 33.

[2] Ibid.

postulates."[1]

Who on earth is the real producer of the bourgeois ideology and the vicious accomplice of capital?

First, it is inappropriate, if not completely wrong, for Baudrillard to say that Marx extended the production and the mode of production from the bourgeois rationality of political economy to generality of history. Without the classical economics based on large-scale machine production, in particular, Ricardo's logic, Marx could not abstract the general conception of modern production. As I said before, it is through profound research of political economy that Marx finally developed his own philosophical discourse, historical materialism, and reached the theoretical commanding heights. As early as the 1850s and 1860s, Marx already learned the basic condition of primitive societies. At that time, he even pointed out that material production is *subordinate* to human reproduction. Therefore, Marx would not project modern production and the mode of production to the entire human history. This is but Baudrillard's own fabrication.

Second, Marx never attempted the radical negation of modernity in human development and material wealth of industrial production via his criticism of capitalism. He knew material affluence is the prerequisite for human liberation and freedom. As to Baudrillard's grassrootism based on the Mauss-Bataille logic (the ancient simplicity of human existence as a rejection of the advanced human civilization), I think it is at most a possibility, one for amusement. The same question has to be asked: Can we really return to the original existence?

Third, Marx's historical materialism discourse builds its framework on the rationalistic recognition of social-historical progression; or else, he would not raise the issue from political liberation to complete liberation of humanity. For the primitive tribal life with "limited development of productive forces", Marx firmly believed that historical development of social production is to promote disintegration of this primary form, which in turn advances the development of the productive forces. "Labor is only undertaken on a

---

[1] Baudrillard, Jean. *The Mirror of Production*. Trans. Mark Poster. St. Louis: Telos Press, 1975. p. 33.

certain basis—first naturally evolved—then an historical presupposition. Later, however, this basis or presupposition is itself transcended, or posited as a transient one, which has become too narrow for the unfolding of the progressing human pack."[1] The complete social history of humankind precisely displays this progressive interaction between self-transcendence and self-sublation unmasked by Marxism. Probably, the prevailing historical trend is far beyond the narrow ideas of Baudrillard and others.

IV. Critique of Labor Ideology

Baudrillard's *Mirror of Production* reaches its first farcical climax with the onset against Marx's conception of labor. In his view, the kernel of material production is human labor. Interestingly, it is from the textual context of political economy that Baudrillard begins his interpretation of Marx's labor, but he wants to identify the illegitimate discourse of Marxist philosophy. It must be admitted that this train of thought is acute whereas his argument is regrettably invalid. I also find that Baudrillard's accusation is well prepared. He cites a number of Marxist economic remarks with irrelevant interpretations. To those who are not familiar with Marxist economics, Baudrillard is all too formidable. However, once his unsustainable logical support is detected, this magnificent building of falsification is easy to collapse.

1. Metaphysical evil of labor: the concrete vs. the abstract; quality vs. quantity

For Baudrillard, to negate the Marxist theory of material production requires further exposure of the evil nature of labor that dominates the productive activities. This time, he embarks on the issue of *reification of labor*. He discovers that the secret of the Marxist theory of labor lies in the "dialectics of quality and quantity" of the so-called theory of labor value. It is

---

[1] Karl Marx and Frederick Engels. *Collected Works*, vol. 28. London: Lawrence & Wishart, 1986. p. 420.

a more micro, more specific "profound" critique. Let us read his analysis.

Baudrillard first quotes Pierre Naville's *Le nouveau léviathan*, saying that the quaintly of labor does not appear in Europe until the 18th century because previous differences of handicraft production made labor incommensurable. It is correct that the division of labor during the industrial production process gives rise to total social labor, which leads to abstracted labor as such, which then makes the computability of labor possible. Baudrillard does not deny this. He then goes to a citation from Marx: "whereas labor positing exchange-value is *abstract universal and uniform* labor, labor positing use-value is concrete and distinctive labor, comprising infinitely varying kinds of labor as regards its form and the material to which it is applied."[1] Marx's idea is very clear here: For a commodity, its value is based on abstract labor, and use value on concrete labor, in other words, concrete labor and abstract labor are both at one production process of the same item, not two dual substances. Baudrillard seems to be more fascinated by use value, which, to him, is founded on the concrete, qualitative labor. (However, Baudrillard always forgets the fact that every time Marx mentions use value he refers to the use value of commodity. Marx never employs use value in its general or universal sense. It is another proof of Baudrillard's casualty in his analysis.)

Without any intermediate explanation, Baudrillard suddenly jumps to the value and use value of labor power.

> In contrast to the quantitative measure of labor power, labor use value, remains nothing more or less than a qualitative potentiality. It is specified by its own end, by the material it works on, or simply because it is the expenditure of energy by a given subject at a given time. The use value of labor power is the moment of its actualization, of man's relation to his useful expenditure of effort. Basically it is an act of (productive) *consumption*; and in the general process, this moment retains all its

---

[1] Karl Marx and Frederick Engels. *Collected Works*, vol. 29. London: Lawrence & Wishart, 1987. p. 277.

uniqueness. At this level labor power is incommensurable.[1]

Baudrillard does the same thing as a smart aleck would do. His spouting about what he knows little only brings disgrace upon himself. The "value" and "use value" in Marx's writing are actually used *metaphorically*. Marx does not make labor power into a common commodity that can be consumed by the public given that the duality of a commodity (value and use value) is generated through living labor (abstract labor and concrete labor). Does Marx say labor power is *created and produced by labor*? Of course, no! This is common sense! As a special commodity, labor power is used by Marx to unmask the apparent equality of capitalist exchange relations wherein the worker only receives the fees ("value") of the means of subsistence for his wage labor. Marx metaphorically calls the sale of this *usufruct* of labor power (or "disposition over alien labor"[2]) the "use value" of labor power. Here, both value and use value are only existent in relation to capitalism. Marx says that "as a free worker, he has *no value*; only the right to dispose over his labor, acquired by exchange with him, has value."[3] The last "him" refers to capital, the materialized labor. Here the value is a *relative* construct in antithesis to the existence of capital. Without the dominance of labor in employment relations, the value of labor power is out of the question. Baudrillard seems to lack the slightest knowledge of this. The so-called "use value" of labor power, viz. the worker's labor per se, is not a real commodity that can be directly sold, quite apart from being *produced* by a concrete labor. (It needs to be noted that in postmodern feminism, domestic work is an implicit labor that sustains and produces labor power, although unrecognized by the patriarchal system. They think that housework creates value through labor, which is another theoretical issue and has nothing to do with Baudrillard's mess here.) Therefore, the use value of labor power, viz. the use

---

[1] Baudrillard, Jean. *The Mirror of Production*. Trans. Mark Poster. St. Louis: Telos Press, 1975. p. 26.

[2] Karl Marx and Frederick Engels. *Collected Works*, vol. 28. London: Lawrence & Wishart, 1986. p. 211, p. 214.

[3] Ibid., p. 218.

value of living labor per se, makes sense in relation to the materialized labor that appropriates and exploits it. According to Marx:

> [p]roduction based on exchange value, on the surface of which that free and equal exchange of equivalents takes place, is basically the exchange of *objectified labor* as exchange value for living labor as use value, or, as it may also to be expressed, labor relating to its objective conditions—and hence to the objectivity created by itself—as to alien property: *alienation of labor*. On the other hand, the condition of exchange value is that it is measured by labor time, and thus living labor—not its value—is the measure of values. It is a DELUSION to believe that production in all its forms and hence society rested upon the *exchange of mere labor for labor*.[1]

As everybody can see, Marx's living labor here does not indicate that man's labor (power) has a certain inborn value and use value. The process when the worker sells this "specific commodity" is the *labor process itself*.[2] Poor Baudrillard! He does not understand it is within an ad hoc context that Marx discusses the "value" and "use value" of the specific commodity of labor power. He even cuts their association with the context, abstracts them, makes a positive proposition in the logic of value theory, and in this faked context builds a compulsory misreading of Marx. All these "theoretical insights" are already embedded with the "theoretical buts" from the very beginning. Labor power is not at all produced in the process of production, since there is no abstract labor to produce it; where does the "accountability of quantity" come from? (Allow me to make a joke here. Perhaps Baudrillard sees many sci-fic movies, in which the intelligent robots, bio-technically replicated creatures, or cloned people, are *produced* as labor power, or more often, as terrifying killers. With those reproduced men, as real specific products, it is possible to possess the value and use value jointly generated by

---

[1] Karl Marx and Frederick Engels. *Collected Works*, vol. 28. London: Lawrence & Wishart, 1986. p. 438.

[2] Karl Marx and Frederick Engels. *Collected Works*, vol. 30. London: Lawrence & Wishart, 1988. p. 54.

the abstract labor and the concrete labor. But it is another question of a higher context.) Baudrillard's use value of labor power is not sensible once outside the stipulated context by Marx. In fact, "concrete labor" as the foundation of production is just like a mother's childbearing and upbringing, which should have been the simple logic for Baudrillard to follow. However, Baudrillard is blind to his own blunder. Owing to his little knowledge of Marxist economics, he makes such an absurd mistake and goes on with it.

In the Don Quixote's journey against his imaginary Marx, Baudrillard claims the use value of labor power is the moment of "man's relation to his useful expenditure of effort." It is grammatically wrong in Marxist economics, as Marx never accepts the labor of worker who is the labor power under the capitalist working condition as a *general* useful consumption of human power. For Marx, not only the primitive societies are free of the issues of value about labor power and products but also in the future communist society—that he deems as the substitute for capitalism—it is impossible to have the problems of use value and value about labor power and products. Baudrillard may not have made a serious study of Marx's *Critique of the Gotha Programme*, in which Marx makes the following comment on the inaccurate expression of "undiminished proceeds of labor" in the "Programme" of the Social Democratic Party in Germany. It is worthwhile for Baudrillard to read it:

> Within the collective society based on common ownership of the means of production, the producers do not exchange their products; just as little does the labor employed on the products appear here as *the value* of these products, as a material quality possessed by them, since now, in contrast to capitalist society, individual labor no longer exists in an indirect fashion but directly as a component part of the total labor.[1]

Marx cannot be clearer here. Why does Baudrillard deliberately misunderstand Marx? If the formation of labor force does not involve

---

[1] Karl Marx and Frederick Engels. *Collected Works*, vol. 24. London: Lawrence & Wishart, 1989. p. 85.

concrete labor in the real economic sense (not counting the mother's reproduction), there is nothing sensible in Baudrillard's "qualitative" aspect of different concrete labors possessed by the labor power (except the different birth process of Baudrillard and Bataille). Thus, Baudrillard's next question, namely, how the incommensurable, qualitatively different labor forces can produce a *quantified* surplus value, becomes a pseudo-proposition: before answering it, I am really amazed by Baudrillard's poor level of political economy. Baudrillard should have come to China for a supplementary lesson of politics in a high school. To Marx, the "value" of labor power as a special commodity is the wage that the capitalist pay in the employment. This "value" is not based on what Baudrillard considers abstract labor (the general social labor of industrial societies) developed since the 18th century. The use value of labor power is neither what Baudrillard defines as the concrete labor useful for all the people; it only holds for the very *living* labor that is *useful for capitalist exploitation*, which is what the capitalist wants to cover. Therefore, the existence and movement of the labor force naturally become the foundation for the use vale and value of common commodities. As the abstract labor is founded on value composed by the necessary labor time, how can it become incomputable? Such a simple principle is known to any profit-seeking capitalist, or even, a Chinese high school student with some basic knowledge of Marxist political economy. But the great French thinker Baudrillard turns a blind eye to it. This is very strange, indeed.

Baudrillard wants to say that Marx's division of the duality of labor— the *qualitative and quantitative dialectic* of the computable abstract labor and the incomputable concrete labor—conceals a bigger philosophical fantasy: since the 19th century, the universalization of labor (to be accurate, it is the emergence of labor as such or abstract labor brought about by socialized industrial production and market exchange) has initiated the universalization of work "not only as market value but as human value. Ideology always thus proceeds by a binary, structural scission, which works here to universalize the dimension of labor. By dividing (or re-dividing into the qualitative structural effect, a *code* effect), quantitative labor spreads throughout the field of

possibility."[1] This mouthful remark means that in the division of the duality
of the quality and the quantity of labor, the universality (abstraction) of labor
becomes man's general nature; while labor, a special existence of man in the
market economy, also extends the ideology to man's general existence and
conceals this operation of codes.

I feel that Baudrillard often appears paranoid with his logic. Was there
not "labor" before the emergence of capitalist industrial production and the
real market economy? We should admit that in the capitalist ideology, under
the universal light (Marx's words) of the logic of capital, every conception
is inevitably tainted with a certain bourgeois color. As Baudrillard learned
Saussure's linguistics, he must understand it is possible to use the same
concept or terminology with other semantic meanings. Nevertheless, at this
point, Baudrillard is as ignorant as his predecessors, like Hannah Arendt or
Jürgen Habermas.[2]

In my opinion, Baudrillard's analysis is an intentional distortion of
Marx's duality of labor, which is proposed to solve the economic question
of labor value, and proved better than Smith and Ricardo's incomplete
and confusing answer. Furthermore, the relation between quality and
quantity drawn from the abstract labor and concrete labor is only the issue
of calculating the value quantity and the way through which to expose the
surplus value. Marx does not attempt to formulate a universal value or nature
from the relation of the quality and quantity of the capitalist characteristic
wage labor.

Here, we have to give Baudrillard another lesson about the history of
Marxism: the qualitative development of the conception of labor. The first
important concept of labor of the young Marx was proposed in the *1844
Manuscripts* as an idealized human nature, at time when Marx himself
was still influenced by Feuerbach's humanistic discourse. On one hand, he
criticized the economic exploitation of the capitalist society; on the other he

---

[1] Baudrillard, Jean. *The Mirror of Production*. Trans. Mark Poster. St. Louis: Telos Press, 1975.
     p. 27.

[2] *See* Hannah Arendt's *The Human Condition* and Jürgen Habermas's *Legitimation Crisis*.

took this illegitimate relation as the deviation from man's authentic being—
the free, independent creation of labor, in the words of the young Marx, the
alienation of labor. There are *two* concepts of labor: labor idealized as man's
generic nature; and alienated labor as the reversed and abnormal generic
nature of man found in the reality of the capitalist society. The former is the
"ought" in humanistic critique, as differentiated from the latter (the bad "is").
The paradigm of labor here in the humanistic discourse is what Baudrillard
refers to as abstract, universal human value. Even at that time, Marx did
not universalize the alienated labor of capitalist society into a human
value. Nevertheless, in his comments on Listz, March, 1845, Marx began
to dissipate the humanistic logic. He abandoned the alienation of labor and
used a quotation-marked concept of labor to illustrate the *enslaved* status of
labor. Later, in the *German Ideology* which was familiar to Baudrillard, Marx
used *wage* labor. Then, the concept of labor was replaced by the concepts
of practice and production in Marx's philosophical discourse. In his logic,
on one side "labor is the universal condition for the metabolic interaction
between nature and man, and as such a natural condition of human life it
is independent of, equally common to, all particular social forms of human
life"[1]; on the other side, labor is, in economic sense, the *"general possibility*
of wealth as *subject* and as activity."[2] It cannot become the only source for
wealth while the real foundation for social existence and development is the
material relationship of man and the external world, which is the objective
process of material production. Labor is not clearly defined in Marxist
general historical materialism. Later, Marx used it more often in the economic
context and seldom made metaphysical illustrations of the economic concept
of labor.[3] Another point is when Marx analyzed the capitalist machine
production, he found *"immediate labor* as such ceases to be the basis of

---

[1] Karl Marx and Frederick Engels. *Collected Works*, vol. 30. London: Lawrence & Wishart, 1988.
     p. 63.
[2] Karl Marx and Frederick Engels. *Collected Works*, vol. 28. London: Lawrence & Wishart, 1986.
     p. 222.
[3] *See* my student Dr. Yang Jianping's *On Marx's Conception of Labor*, which contains a detailed
     discussion about the development of Marx's conception of labor.

production"[1] because the worker's living labor is reduced to an insignificant
link in the machinery system, "the value-creating power of the individual
labor capacity is an infinitesimal, vanishing magnitude." Phenomenally,
"the production process has ceased to be a labor process."[2] What does this
indicate? It is quite clear that Baudrillard's complacent discovery is not new.
Marx already revealed it.

In retrospect of the above history of thoughts, it is not difficult to find
that Baudrillard cleverly avoids the concept of labor in the philosophical
discourse of the *1844 Manuscripts* and tightly grabs the scientific concept of
labor in Marxist economics. However, he is unaware that it is still illegitimate
to posit the concept of labor with special semantic meaning in Marxist
economics as the logical outset of the *ideology of labor*. I am going to further
explain this in the next part.

2. Guilt of the Productive Labor

Baudrillard's criticism of Marx then turns from the ideology of labor
to the production-labor ideology, in which he satires Marx with a notion
from Marxist historical phenomenology, namely, the *fetishism of labor and
productivity*.

Baudrillard is sometimes surprisingly stubborn. With a fallacious
premise, he closes himself in an assertive space without any flexibility,
blindly but happily thrashing about. He does not like the concreteness of
labor; nor is he disposed to the "abuse" of this concreteness and abstractness.
In his eyes, Marx is playing a "game" of signification, that is, from the
abstract to the concrete, from the quantity to quality, from the Labor's
exchange value to use value of dialectics, the double of the game must be the
result of labor productivity and fetishism. In that case, he questions, what are
the reasons? Baudrillard offers his own inferences.

This time, he quotes from the introduction of the *1857-1858*

---

[1] Karl Marx and Frederick Engels. *Collected Works*, vol. 29. London: Lawrence & Wishart, 1987.
  p. 95.
[2] Ibid., p. 83.

Manuscripts. (The reason why Baudrillard daunts some people is partly due to his frequent citation of the unknown Marxist economic text barely even touched by traditional Marxist philosophers, for which he is in striking contrast to Schmidt and Althusser.)

> The fact that the specific kind of labor is irrelevant presupposes a highly developed totality of actually existing kinds of labor, none of which is any more the dominating one. The most general abstractions arise on the whole only with the most profuse concrete development, when one [phenomenon] is seen to be common to many, common to all.[1]

It should be accepted that Baudrillard's reference to the Marxist text is very smart compared with traditional Marxists and Western scholars. He often shrewdly employs some of Marx's important statements which were ignored by scholars in the former Soviet Union and the East European socialist countries, only with the majority of them put in the wrong place. (I also notice that it is the same with those keen anthropologists in the 1970s, among whom, the first was Lévi-Strauss's quote from Marx and the most distinguished one was Sahlins, who was very familiar with Marxist economic and philosophical texts, for example the "Anthropology and Two Marxisms: Problems of Historical Materialism" in his *Culture and Practical Reason.*[2] Sahlins had quite a few wonderful remarks about his understanding of Marxism, far superior to Baudrillard but was still wrong with some of his conclusions as he posited the logic of symbolic culture over the praxis of material production.) With this comment, Marx intends to illustrate that the concept of general labor belongs to "a modern category." From the monetarist view of wealth as the object "capital," to the manufacturing or mercantile transference of the source of wealth from the

---

[1] Karl Marx and Frederick Engels. *Collected Works*, vol. 28. London: Lawrence & Wishart, 1986. p. 41.

[2] Sahlins, Marshall D. *Culture and Practical Reason.* Joint Publishing Company Limited (Beijing), 2002.

object to the subjective activity, the commercial labor and industrial labor, and the agricultural labor of the physiocrats, all these are big steps forward. Smith makes "an immense advance" for his discovery of *labor as such* that is neither manufacturing, nor commercial, nor agricultural labor, but all types of labor. Then, Marx continues, this abstraction of labor is the objective abstractness of modern economic activity per se, considering the individuals of industrial production "easily pass from one type of labor to another" when labor has become a means to "create wealth" in the reality of capitalism. On the other hand, general labor emerges because during the internal division of labor in production, the old collective work is replaced by professional and specific functional work, in other words, labor is de-totalized. (Schiller saw through it almost two hundred years ago. In *The Aesthetic Letter*, he reflected the detotalization from the ontological perspective of man's existence.) As a result, in the capitalist commodity exchange, "labor is *posited* as general only through *exchange*."[1] This is another abstraction of objective economic activities, which makes the *conceptual abstraction* possible. Baudrillard, do you understand now? Marx's labor as such is first an objective abstraction, which springs from the de-totalization of work in modern technical division of industrial production and the objective exchange of the market economy where different concrete labors form the homogeneous labor as such in the mirror of value. Labor as such in economics arises from the subjective cognition of the objective economic abstraction. (We will understand this mystery in the later discussion of Slavoj Žižek in this book.) Marx believes the abstraction of labor is "the point of departure of modern economics." Even applicable in all ages, they are "a product of historical conditions and retain their full validity only for and within these conditions."[2] The above remark is very precise, even perfect.

Nevertheless, Baudrillard draws a widely separated, sensational conclusion from it. He cuts off the special context and arbitrarily upgrades it

---

[1] Karl Marx and Frederick Engels. *Collected Works*, vol. 28. London: Lawrence & Wishart, 1986. p. 108.

[2] Ibid., p. 42.

to a generalized discourse in the philosophy of history. He accuses Marx of taking the mode of labor as the essence of controlling *all* human existence because his labor dominates the other, rest existential spheres of humankind. Labor replaces all forms except wealth and exchange; labor generates use value and shapes the mode of expression of human being. Baudrillard thinks that Marx's ideology of productive labor is a subjective violence against history, and this paradigm of labor postulates the "general schema of production and needs", with the law of value universalized. He argues that the analysis of all primitive or archaic organizations contradicts this, as does the feudal symbolic order and even that of our societies. How ridiculous this is! When does Marx project "modern" labor as such only found in the capitalist mode of production to the primitive and feudal societies? Nay, Marx adds a particular limitation: in social conditions prior to capitalism, "the purpose of this labor is not the *creation of value*"; rather, "its purpose is the maintenance of the individual proprietor and his family as well as of the community as a whole."[1] In addition, equipped with limited knowledge of contemporary anthropology and other materials, Marx perceives that even if the primitive communal existence, Baudrillard's favorite, provides a possible foundation for labor production, the presuppositions of the entire social existence "are not themselves the *product* of labor, but appear as its natural or *divine* preconditions."[2] This is because at that time, whether concerning husbandry or agriculture, "the chief objective condition of labor does not itself appear as the *product* of labor, but is already there as *nature*."[3] Does Baudrillard understand this time? Our world becomes the result of labor production only after the late industrial civilization. I almost lose patience when Baudrillard does not abide by general principles and often stumbles over mistakes.

He walks on an evidently wrong path but proudly deems that he grasps

---

[1] Karl Marx and Frederick Engels. *Collected Works*, vol. 28. London: Lawrence & Wishart, 1986. p. 399.

[2] Ibid., p. 400.

[3] Ibid., p. 409.

the weak point of Marx. He claims that "[Marx's] all perspectives opened up by the contradictions of the mode of production drive us hopelessly into political economy" because he fails "to conceive of a mode of social wealth other than that founded on labor and production, Marxism no longer furnishes in the long run a real alternative to capitalism."[1] (Baudrillard really deserves the name of a capable pioneer for he scolds the post-Marxian transcendence of radicalizing Marxism, which, unexpectedly, proves a disapproval of his own *System of Objects*, *The Consumer Society*, and even *For a Critique of the Political Economy of the Sign*.) It is clear that Baudrillard is unsuccessful in his theoretical innovation. He only makes some small tricks, in which he first puts into historical materialism Marx's conception of labor as such that is used for solving specific economic questions[2] along with the rough concept of production without any careful reflection; and then he sentences this fabricated theoretical "imagery" to death.

Baudrillard insists on the radical negation of the Marxist conception of labor, of use value, but his purpose is not to promote the theory of labor value from an economic perspective. His real attempt is to deny labor, production and the usefulness of any object in the sense of *philosophical ontology:*

> In fact the use value of labor power does not exist any more than the use value of products or the autonomy of signified and referent. The same fiction reigns in the three orders of production, consumption, and signification. Exchange value is what makes the use value of products appear as its anthropological horizon. The exchange value of labor power is what makes its use value, the concrete origin and end of the act of labor, appear as its "generic" alibi. This is the logic of signifiers which produces the "evidence" of the "reality" of the signified and the referent.[3]

---

[1] Baudrillard, Jean. *The Mirror of Production*. Trans. Mark Poster. St. Louis: Telos Press, 1975. p. 29.

[2] Marx made a particular note that labor here refers to wage labor under the capitalist system. It is "in the *strict economic sense in which we use it here, and no other.*"

[3] Baudrillard, Jean. *The Mirror of Production*. Trans. Mark Poster. St. Louis: Telos Press, 1975. p. 30.

We have had enough discussion on this allegation of Baudrillard's. He means to say that the fundamentals of our world, that is, the phenomena of taking usefulness as the present scale occurs due to the fabrication and imposition of the system of exchange value; this code control of the signifier makes production—production of useful things, consumption—a false satisfaction of needs, and signification—fabrication of imageries becomes the dominant order of survival. He imposes every evil onto Marx's theory of exchange value and use value of labor, which, almost amounts to a Pandora's box. He says it is the ideology of labor that makes a false productive, generic nature of man; "in this sense, need, use value, and the referent do not exist."[1] "They are only concepts produced and projected into a generic dimension by the development of the very system of exchange value."[2]

Baudrillard has been saying this over and again. Only a shallow person can make such poor repetitions.

3. Good labor and beautiful non-labor

Baudrillard is not satisfied with a common negation of the labor concept. He tries to go deeper and dig out the devil inside the logic of Marx. He believes that Marx's discourse on labor is first of all an existential ontology, which is established in the *1844 Manuscripts*. (In a given historical context, Baudrillard is not wrong.) To prove his opinion, Baudrillard cites Herbert Marcuse's note on the *Manuscripts*, which says that labor is the ontological concept of human existence. Baudrillard must have read Althusser, but he seems not to know the essential difference between the young Marx's humanistic view of alienated labor and historical materialism.

He makes a speedy juxtaposition of the *1844 Manuscripts* and *Das Kapital* under the same theme. First, in his quotation from the *Manuscripts*, labor is identified as the ideal generic nature of the subjective objectification,

---

[1] *See* Note 13 of *The Mirror of Production*. It says, "This does not mean *that they have never ex-isted*. Hence we have another paradox that we must return to later."

[2] Baudrillard, Jean. *The Mirror of Production*. Trans. Mark Poster. St. Louis: Telos Press, 1975. p. 30.

"coming-to-being for himself" and "self-confirmation."[1] Without warning, he then jumps over 20 years of space-time across different research fields to *Das Kapital*, catching two early explanations about labor that are radically different from the humanistic logic. (This is a common practice of the so-called Marxist anthropologists.) In the first explanation, useful labor as the key of the process of the material production is "a necessary condition, independent of all forms of society, for the existence of the human race; it is an eternal nature-imposed necessity."[2] The context of this statement is an example of the handcraft of making clothes, which lasted for hundreds of years, used by Marx to discuss the ontological base of the eternality of labor (production). The second explanation is from *Das Kapital*, which reads: "Labor is, in the first place, a process in which both man and Nature participate, and in which man of his own accord starts, regulates, and controls the material re-actions between himself and Nature."[3] Here, it is not difficult to find that, unlike the humanistic discourse of the *1844 Manuscripts*, Marx's elucidation of labor is not an abstract hypothesis of man's authentic being, but an emphasis on the status of labor during the process of material production and identification of material production as the eternal premise of social existence and development of humankind.

Baudrillard's strategy is actually clever. First, he carefully makes an ahistorical patchwork of the qualitatively different texts used by Marx for the same theme, then borrows the early Marcuse's misreading of Marxist humanism, and finally proves the legitimacy of his accusation. Ironically, if Marcuse is proved wrong, then Baudrillard is also wrong.

Baudrillard claims that Marx's ontological position of labor makes the Marxist philosophical discourse unfold in two directions: an ethic of labor and an esthetics of non-labor.

The former exalts labor as value, as end in itself, as categorical

---

[1] Karl Marx and Frederick Engels. *Collected Works*, vol. 3. London: Lawrence & Wishart, 1975. p. 333, p. 338.

[2] Karl Marx, *Capital*, vol. 1. London: Lawrence & Wishart, 1977. p. 50.

[3] Ibid., p. 173.

imperative. Labor loses it negativity and is raised to an absolute value. Baudrillard believes that such a conception is existent in both capitalist and socialist ideologies. In my view, if he means to criticize the *1844 Manuscripts* of the young Marx, he has an advantage; if it is the negation of Marx's assertion in *Das Kapital*, he is doomed to fail. The two statements above are not meant to explain the theory of labor value in the economic sense or illustrate labor as man's aim from the philosophical view, to say nothing of "categorical imperative" or "absolute value". Labor production, the fundament of social existence, is the activity to create the basic material means for human survival, which has no rationalistic tint of *generic philosophy* or has nothing to do with the positive value scale and coordinates of ethics. In fact, as early as in the *German Ideology*, Marx discards a concealed idealistic historical view, that is, the way of writing history according to an extraneous standard—the practice of seeking "an *ideal* to which reality [will] have to adjust itself" from outside history.[1] Baudrillard makes use of the humanistic discourse in the early *1844 Manuscripts* to assault historical materialism developed in the later *Das Kapital*. Without doubt, it is an unreasonable argument. If his early concepts in *The System of Objects* are employed to crack his subsequent texts, such as *The Perfect Crime*, we would not come to sensible conclusions. Judging from the critique per se, Baudrillard is very slippery. He adroitly takes advantage of the humanistic explanation in current Western Marxism. (It, of course, includes our own "humanistic" logic construct. They provide a ready target for Baudrillard and others.)

Baudrillard turns to Marcuse's critique of the economic concept of labor, which is a re-interpretation of Marx's logic of labor alienation in the neo-humanistic context. Marcuse stipulates labor as man's ontological basis and puts forward the substitute relation of game and labor. Baudrillard grasps this mistake and exposes him as a stand-in of Marx. He angrily questions why Marxist dialectics leads to "Christian ethics," to its own opposition.

---

[1] Karl Marx and Frederick Engels. *Collected Works*, vol. 5. London: Lawrence & Wishart, 1976. p. 49.

In Baudrillard's view, Marx's concept of labor is bound for the "aberrant sanctification of work," for the capitalist asceticism stipulated by Weber. In order to prove his distortion, Baudrillard adds the misconceptions of Benjamin and Lafargue, even going out of his way to invite Joseph Dietzgen's work Messiah. However, what does all this have to do with Marxism? As we all know, Marx and Engels dedicated their entire lives to the struggle against enslaved labor and the myths of opium-like ideologies. How could they accept an almost theological ethics of labor? It is merely illusory.

The second point is the so-called "aesthetics of non-labor." Baudrillard says that:

> [i]n the fine points of Marxist thought, confronting the work ethic is an esthetic of non-work or play itself based on the dialectic of quantity and quality. Beyond the capitalist mode of production and the quantitative measure of labor, this is the perspective of a definitive qualitative mutation in communist society: the end of alienated labor and the free objectification of man's own powers.[1]

Here, Baudrillard refers to the well-known paragraph about the realm of freedom in *Das Kapital* (*Vol. III*). Marx intends to express the idea that for man's ultimate liberation, "the realm of freedom actually begins only where labor which is determined by necessity and mundane considerations ceases; thus in the very nature of things it lies beyond the sphere of actual material production."[2] (It is almost outrageous. Does not Baudrillard know what Marx means by "beyond the sphere of actual material production" in this citation? Why does he overlook this in his criticism of Marx's universalizing the paradigm of production?) This time, Baudrillard is silent about the universality of production. Instead, he makes a feint and slips to another issue, the aesthetic meaning of the future society expected by Marx.

---

[1] Baudrillard, Jean. *The Mirror of Production*. Trans. Mark Poster. St. Louis: Telos Press, 1975. p. 38.

[2] Karl Marx and Frederick Engels. *Collected Works*, vol. 37. London: Lawrence & Wishart, 1998. p. 807.

However, he still relies on Marcuse's account of labor to oppose Marx. He concludes that Marx's communism is still a non-labor, dis-alienated play, qualitatively the same as capitalism. "This realm beyond political economy called play, non-work, or dis-alienated labor, is defined as the reign of a finality without end. In this sense it is and remains an *esthetic*, in the extremely Kantian sense, with all the bourgeois ideological connotations which that implies."[1] Baudrillard implies that Marx's communist social life only emerges from the negation of the capitalist conception of labor, which is but the trap of the bourgeois aesthetic ideology, since Marxist criticism of the alienated labor still "inherits the aesthetic and humanistic virus of bourgeois thought." (Baudrillard's aesthetics corresponds to Althusser's non-scientific ideology.)

Baudrillard speaks on volubly in self-justification:

Here stands the defect of all notions of play, freedom, transparence, or disalienation: it is the defect of the *revolutionary imagination* since, in the ideal types of play and the free play of human faculties, we are still in a process of repressive desublimation. In effect, the sphere of play is defined as the fulfillment of human rationality, the dialectical culmination of man's activity of incessant objectification of nature and control of his exchanges with it. It presupposes the full development of productive forces; it "follows in the footsteps" of the reality principle and the transformation of nature. Marx clearly states that it can flourish only when founded on the reign of necessity. Wishing itself beyond labor but *in its continuation*, the sphere of play is always merely the esthetic sublimation of labor's constraints. With this concept we remain rooted in the problematic of necessity and freedom, a typically bourgeois problematic whose double ideological expression has always been the institution of a reality principle (repression and sublimation, the principle of labor) and its formal overcoming in an

---

[1] Baudrillard, Jean. *The Mirror of Production.* Trans. Mark Poster. St. Louis: Telos Press, 1975. p. 39.

ideal transcendence.[1]

Baudrillard imposes on Marx such misinterpretations as "repression," "desublimation" and "reality principle" by the young Marcuse, a fascinated fan of Freud. He thoughtlessly makes labels or trumps up charges. Anyone who has common knowledge of Marxism understands that Marx never used such unscientific stipulations as play in his discussion of the future liberation of humankind. (Marx even criticized the interpretation of liberated labor as "pure fun, pure amusement, as in Fourier's childishly naïve conception.")[2] In his late years, Marx never made metaphorical examples, not to mention psychoanalytic terminology and context. Even in the statement quoted by Baudrillard, Marx only points out that the real, liberated social life of humankind is mainly "that development of human energy which is an end in itself"; simply put, it is the *overall and free development of mankind*. When does Marx posit the play of labor or non-labor as the communist social existence?

Baudrillard tries to refute Marxism with mistakes made by others. It only proves he has an ulterior motive, if not ignorance. Should Marx be responsible for the young Marcus's errant explanation of the Marxist discourse?

V. Marx and the Domination of Nature

In the second chapter of *The Mirror of Production*, Baudrillard develops his criticism further. This time, he transforms himself into an avant-garde of ecological ethics and anti-anthropocentric thought. In his opinion, the problem of Marxist historical materialism lies in the violent view of domination and enslavement of nature. Baudrillard thinks the ideal concept of nature is "a hidden essence" and mystical power existent in the imagery

---

[1] Baudrillard, Jean. *The Mirror of Production*. Trans. Mark Poster. St. Louis: Telos Press, 1975. p. 40.

[2] Karl Marx and Frederick Engels. *Collected Works*, vol. 28. London: Lawrence & Wishart, 1986. p. 530.

of the primitive peoples.[1] He criticizes Marx for not knowing that beneath the notion of conquering nature is nothing else but the bourgeois rationalistic logic of the Enlightenment.

1. Conception of enslaving nature in Enlightenment

Baudrillard says that the conception of nature through presence of the object of labor sits at the core of the bourgeois enlightenment, while the political economy, which is the foundation for the whole of Marxism, is also founded on this conception of nature. In the eyes of the westerners, as late as the 17th century nature signified only the totality of laws founding the world's intelligibility: the guarantee of an order where men and things could exchange their meanings [*significations*].[2] In the end, this is God (Spinoza's "*Deus sive natura*"). The above judgment is basically correct. When it comes to the 18th century, the original "nature" experienced changes with the development of industrial production. Baudrillard regards it as "Nature's entry into the era of its technical domination." It is the first *split* between subject and Nature-object and "their simultaneous submission to an operational finality." Here, nature is no longer the totality of laws but the *object* of the subject.

Nature appeared truly as an essence in all its glory but under the sign of the *principle of production*. This separation also involves the *principle of signification*. Under the objective stamp of Science, Technology, and Production, Nature becomes the great Signified, the great Referent. It is ideally charged with "reality"; it becomes *the* Reality, expressible by a process that is always somehow a process of labor, at once *transformation* and *transcription*. Its "reality" principle is this operational principle of an industrial structuration and a significative pattern.[3]

---

[1] Mauss, Marcel. *The Gift: Forms and Functions of Exchange in Archaic Societies*. Trans. Ian Cunnison. Glencoe: Free Press, 1954. p. 61.

[2] Baudrillard, Jean. *The Mirror of Production*. Trans. Mark Poster. St. Louis: Telos Press, 1975. p. 53.

[3] Ibid., p. 54.

In my opinion, this is a general rehearsal of the views of nature by
the Western technological criticism and ecological ethics since the 1960s.
Judging from the statement per se, we cannot say Baudrillard is wrong.
It is actually a post-industrial resonance that frequents the technology-
critical texts of the late Martin Heidegger, Max Horkheimer and Theodor
Adorno's *Dialectic of Enlightenment*, Leiss's *Domination of Nature*, and
so on. Baudrillard adds to this his code of production principle, the concept
of Signifier of semiotics, and the idea of pseudo-reality appropriated from
Lacan. In a lengthy note, Baudrillard emphasizes that, during production,
nature is turned into commodity and codes at once, which leaves every
product with both the exchange value and the "symbolic value"; the more
advanced a modern consumer society develops, the more important and
dominant the commodity's *manipulation of symbolic value* becomes. It
is a "new discovery" by Baudrillard in his *For a Critique of the Political
Economy of the Sign*.

For Baudrillard, the Enlightenment views nature as the object to be
conquered and dominated, or "the very reality of its exploitation." Posited
as the object, nature is dissected, utilized, made by science and technology
at man's will. "Science presents itself as a project progressing towards an
objective determined in advance by Nature. Science and Technology present
themselves as revealing what is inscribed in Nature: not only its secrets but
their deep purpose."[1] (Baudrillard capitalizes the initial letter of nature,
similar to the derogatory *generic concept* presented by Stirner, Nietzsche
and Lacan. It denotes the homogeneity of violence under man's rational
governance.) Before the brutal science and technology, Nature is forced to
reveal its secrets, which are again used by the greedy man in his endless
exploration of all the potentialities of nature. "*Nature is the concept of a
dominated essence and nothing else.*"[2] In addition, today's nature exists
for the subject, if put through the early Hegel's discourse, the existence

---

[1] Baudrillard, Jean. *The Mirror of Production*. Trans. Mark Poster. St. Louis: Telos Press, 1975.
     p. 55.
[2] Ibid.

for me. Therefore, nature loses its being-ness facing the advance of the singing science and technology. Heidegger moans that natural thing cannot be "thinged" with its existence degenerated to human nature. Baudrillard does not suppress his anger: "Everything that invokes Nature invokes the domination of Nature."[1]

According to Baudrillard, the split between the subject and nature under capitalist production principle can be traced to an earlier period:

> The separation is rooted in the great Judeo-Christian dissociation of the soul and Nature. God created man in his *image* and created Nature for man's *use*. The soul is the spiritual hinge by which man is God's image and is radically distinguished from the rest of Nature (and from his own body).[2]

This is the original sin. Baudrillard believes that Christianity is the most *anthropocentric* religion the world has ever known and it still constitutes the theoretical core of the *dominant* view of nature. I feel this opinion seems to be justified. Nevertheless, it is not his innovative thinking, but the common sense of ecological ethnics in the last century.

2. "Half-revolution" of Marxist view of nature

To Baudrillard, the concept of nature is the core of the whole Western Enlightenment thought, or the moral philosophy of the Enlightenment. He says that Marx wanted to break the myth of the capitalist conception of nature along with the idealistic anthropology sustained by this myth, but lost the name of action, and only partially dislocated the myth of Nature.

> Marx indeed "denaturalized" private property, the mechanisms of competition and the market, and the processes of labor and capital; but he failed to question the following naturalist propositions:
> —the useful finality of products as a function of needs;

---

[1] Baudrillard, Jean. *The Mirror of Production*. Trans. Mark Poster. St. Louis: Telos Press, 1975. p. 56.

[2] Ibid., p. 63.

—the useful finality of nature as a function of its transformation by labor.[1]

Baudrillard does not let go of Marx. In his view, the Marxist critique of the bourgeoisie is not unproductive for it sees through the bourgeois ideological ruse that attempts to universalize the capitalist mode of production, but historical materialism still emphasizes the conquest and transformation of nature, and ascribes social life as the finality of the usefulness of the object. Consequently, Marx's criticism of nature is only a "half-revolution."

Here, Baudrillard goes on with his criticism of the whole historical materialism. He thinks that Marx is unable to make a critical reflection of material production, and thus, is unaware of the fact that the usefulness of labor and nature is still the core of the bourgeois enlightenment ideology. Baudrillard says that:

> The functionality of Nature structured by labor, and the corresponding functionality of the subject structured around needs, belong to the anthropological sphere of use value described by Enlightenment rationality and defined for a whole civilization (which imposed it on others) by a certain kind of abstract, linear, irreversible finality: a certain model subsequently extended to all sectors of individual and social practice.[2]

Marx criticizes the capitalist mode of production, whose logic of enslaving nature still traps him. In a certain sense, Baudrillard is not completely wrong. In the *1857-1858 Manuscripts*, Marx says that "for the first time, nature becomes purely an object for man, nothing more than a matter of utility; It ceases to be acknowledged as a power for itself, and even the theoretical cognition of its autonomous laws appears merely as a stratagem for its subjection to human needs."[3] Marx does admit the

---

[1] Baudrillard, Jean. *The Mirror of Production*. Trans. Mark Poster. St. Louis: Telos Press, 1975. p. 56.

[2] Ibid., p. 56.

[3] Karl Marx and Frederick Engels. *Collected Works*, vol. 28. London: Lawrence & Wishart, 1986. p. 337.

important role of capitalism. Unlike the romantic critique in the *1844 Manuscripts*, he fully confirms the "great civilizing influence" of capitalism by calling it "a system of universal exploitation of the natural and human qualities, a system of universal utility, whose bearer is science itself as much as all the physical and spiritual qualities, and under these conditions nothing appears as something *higher-in-itself*, as an end in itself, outside this circle of social production and exchange."[1]

I think this understanding of Marxist view of nature is correct. Marx expects no liberation without social historical progress and the highest level of productive forces created by the industrial civilization, given that the reality of complete human liberation can only be achieved on an advanced level of material production. This was already proven by previous history: poverty cannot directly lead to socialism and communism. Even from a historical view, Baudrillard is also right with his ecological ethics and technological criticism of the over-exploitation and the destructive use of natural resources. In fact, Marx and Engels did not entirely ignore the same problem at that time.[2] However, overdone is as bad as undone. Baudrillard makes an absoluteness out of the reasonable reflection, turns the anti-anthropocentric view in ecological criticism into an ontological discourse, injects some Mauss-Bataille thought, then aggressively comes to negate *all the change and use* of nature by man, and finally comes to another theoretical proof of his grassrootism. In my opinion, it is a non sequitur.

Baudrillard says that "without ceasing to be ideological, the concept splits into a 'good' Nature that is dominated and rationalized (which acts as the ideal cultural reference) and a 'bad' Nature that is hostile, menacing, catastrophic, or polluted. All bourgeois ideology divides between these two poles."[3] For nature that can be utilized by man, it is good; if not, man will "dominate" nature (Heidegger). Man does the same to his own kind: he that

---

[1] Karl Marx and Frederick Engels. *Collected Works*, vol. 28. London: Lawrence & Wishart, 1986. p. 336.

[2] *See* my "Contemporary Ecological Horizon and the Logic of the Materialistic View" in *Philosophical Researches*. 8 (1993).

[3] Baudrillard, Jean. *The Mirror of Production*. Trans. Mark Poster. St. Louis: Telos Press, 1975. p. 57.

can be sublimated as a productive force is a naturally good man; if unable
to enter rational regulation, he is mad. For Baudrillard, Marxism allies with
this optimistic rationalization of man. He thinks even in the latest Freudian-
Marxist version, in which the unconscious itself is reinterpreted as "natural"
wealth, a hidden positivity that will burst forth in the revolutionary act.
(Baudrillard probably targets the aforementioned Deleuz this time.)

Clearly, in Baudrillard's eyes, nature should remain in the primordial
status when it is not objectified and dominated. He follows his teacher's
extreme admiration of the mystique and opaqueness of nature. In their
heart, nature is absolutely not the object to be planned or made. As a result,
in primitive societies, "neither Law nor Necessity exists at the level of
reciprocity and symbolic exchange."[1] For this reason, Baudrillard hates the
root of all evil. To him, Marx still falls a victim to the capitalist conception of
nation.

> The concept of production is never questioned; it will never
> radically overcome the influence of political economy. Even Marxism's
> transcending perspective will always be burdened by counter-
> dependence on political economy. Against Necessity it will oppose the
> mastery of Nature; against Scarcity it will oppose Abundance ("to each
> according to his needs") without ever resolving either the arbitrariness
> of these concepts or their idealist overdetermination by political
> economy.[2]

Baudrillard thinks the core of the bourgeois conception of nature is still
material production, which, as a basic logical start point, leads to the linear
progressive conception of history wherein nature is regulated, controlled,
enslaved, and endlessly produced by the always-unsatisfactory *human desire*
(Scarcity). In this continual production and reproduction, miserable nature
is at the mercy of man's willful control and regulation. To Baudrillard's
disappointment, Marx's communist ideal is also based on this unreflecting

---

[1] Baudrillard, Jean. *The Mirror of Production*. Trans. Mark Poster. St. Louis: Telos Press, 1975. p. 61.

[2] Ibid., p. 59.

bourgeois conception of nature, which gives rise to his vision of the material "distribution according to needs."

It is, in the eyes of Baudrillard, a revolutionary ideal built on the bourgeois *Prometheanism of productive forces*, because Marx is fooled by "the Promethean and Faustian vision of its perpetual transcendence."[1]

This dialectical voluntarism, for which Necessity exists and must be conquered, is not shaken. Scarcity exists and must be abolished; the Productive Forces exist and must be liberated; the End exists and only the means need be found. All revolutionary hope is thus bound up in a Promethean myth of productive forces, but this myth is only the space time of political economy. And the desire to manipulate destiny through the development of productive forces plunges one into the space time of political economy.[2]

Baudrillard is opposed to the development of productive forces, to the transformation and conquest of nature, to historical progression, and even to any forward-looking thought of liberation. Marxism is certainly rejected in the grassrootism that is bogged down in and redirected towards the past. However, I have to repeat the same questions: Can history really go backward? Can the primitive life, favored by Baudrillard and his dear teachers, really stop the rolling tide of history?

3. Big Law and the big Necessity of nature

To Baudrillard, Marx does not eradicate the "moral philosophy" of the Enlightenment. He rejects its naiveté and sentimentality, its fantastic religiosity, but cannot radically break the phantasm of *Nature-imposed necessity*.

By secularizing it in the economic concept of scarcity, Marxism keeps the idea of Necessity without transforming it. The idea of "natural

---

[1] Baudrillard, Jean. *The Mirror of Production*. Trans. Mark Poster. St. Louis: Telos Press, 1975. p. 61.
[2] Ibid., p. 60.

Necessity" is only a *moral* idea dictated by political economy, the ethical and philosophical version of that bad Nature systematically connected with the arbitrary postulate of the economic. In the mirror of the economic, Nature looks at us with the eyes of necessity.[1]

What Baudrillard wants to deny is Marx's eternal Nature-imposed necessity in which man creates his own social existence through production. However, Marx insists that even in primitive societies, man has to be engaged in material production. Baudrillard refers to a paragraph in *Das Kapital* (*Vol. 3*), in which Marx says that the primitive people have to struggle against nature for survival, and produce the necessary means of life; likewise, modern social existence and development is based on the same natural necessity. As for this material production and re-living during which man transforms nature, "he must do so in all social formations and under all possible modes of production. With his development this realm of physical necessity expands as a result of his wants; but, at the same time, the forces of production which satisfy these wants also increase."[2] Baudrillard strongly resists this idea. In his opinion, just like other capitalist thinkers, Marx is unable to realize "that in his symbolic exchanges primitive man *does not gauge himself in relation to Nature*."[3] It is true that the primitive people can neither possess in the modern sense self-awareness nor understand "the forces in production which satisfy these wants." However, Baudrillard misinterprets it. Marx does not really mean that the primitive society has the mode of production in modern sense. What he wants to stress is the fundamental status of common material production in social existence.

He [Marx] is not aware of Necessity, a Law that takes effect only with the objectification of Nature. The Law takes its definitive form

[1] Baudrillard, Jean. *The Mirror of Production*. Trans. Mark Poster. St. Louis: Telos Press, 1975. p. 58.

[2] Karl Marx and Frederick Engels. *Collected Works*, vol. 37. London: Lawrence & Wishart, 1998. p. 807.

[3] Baudrillard, Jean. *The Mirror of Production*. Trans. Mark Poster. St. Louis: Telos Press, 1975. p. 59.

in capitalist political economy; moreover, it is only the philosophical expression of Scarcity. Scarcity, which itself arises in the market economy, is not a *given* dimension of the economy. Rather, it is what *produces and reproduces* economic exchange. In that regard it is different from primitive exchange, which knows nothing of this "Law of Nature" that pretends to be the ontological dimension of man.[1] Hence it is an extremely serious problem that Marxist thought retains these key concepts which depend on the metaphysics of the market economy in general and on modern capitalist ideology in particular.[2]

I have to admit that this paragraph is rather sensible in Baudrillard's book. Unlike his grassrootism which is blindly against material production as the foundation of social existence, he points out a problem that is reasonable from a certain point of view.

First, regarding the natural laws in the sphere of science, Baudrillard's proposition is not false. From Kant, people gradually find that the essence of natural scientific laws is the historical cognitive effect by subjects in different ages, that is, man's legislating laws for nature. The presence of "natural laws" before the subject, viz, the existence of natural science, is indeed steadily developed with the *overall objectification* of nature in the capitalist industrial practice.

Second, Baudrillard is correct if his "Law" refers to the modern social economic regulations that are first generated in the capitalist economic process, partially revealed by classical economics, and then noticed in Marxist (special) historical materialism and political economy as an effective economic law (e.g. law of value) in a *given historical condition*. He is also right if his "Scarcity" implies false desire (e.g. the false consumption in his *Consumer Society* to echo Debord and the Frankfurt School), which can be said to be the fundamental aspect of what *produces and reproduces* economic

---

[1] Cf. Marshall Sahlins, "La première société d'abondance," Les Temps Modernes (October, 1968), pp. 641-680. (It is the original note.)

[2] Baudrillard, Jean. *The Mirror of Production*. Trans. Mark Poster. St. Louis: Telos Press, 1975. p. 59

exchange.

Third, Baudrillard says that primitive economic exchange is radically different from that of the modern society. This is a correct conclusion, too. The primitive people certainly have no idea of what we call the "natural law", which is but the mysterious might of god in their eyes.

However, when Baudrillard draws on them to blame Marx, it becomes strange. That such concepts as natural law and objective necessity depend on the metaphysics of the market economy in general and on modern capitalist ideology in particular only makes sense in a special context, that is, when they refer to natural scientific regularities and the category of necessity in the contemporary era, because these concepts appear in the very early time of Western history and have their own specific historical contents. Baudrillard is obviously arbitrary with this assertion. In addition, if natural law and objective necessity are viewed as being correlatively reliant on the bourgeois ideology, and are really necessary for people in their scientific comprehension of the world (since people cannot return to Baudrillard's preferred primitive society and understand the world with something like "hau"), then this means the universalization of the bourgeois ideology. What is more, Baudrillard is unaware that Marx's biggest contribution of criticizing the bourgeois ideology in the *special* historical materialism is the identification of the historicity of the *natural order* existent as social history and the *law of nature* as human nature in the capitalist market economy.

Baudrillard is also ignorant of the fact that natural law has a rich variation of contexts for Marxism, too. Perhaps his flat thought cannot adapt to multi-dimensional, complex history. As I mentioned in *Subjective Dimension of Marxian Historical Dialectics*, besides the concept of natural law in common sense, the young Marx already had the conception of nature with different meanings and as a category of relationship in his critique of Hegelian philosophy and the humanistic discourse before 1845.[1] After he established historical materialism, in a very special metaphorical context of

[1]   *See* my *The Subjective Dimension of Marxian Historical Dialectics* (Nanjing University Press, 2002). pp. 184-185.

the capitalist economic process, he names the commodity-market economic law—which Baudrillard hates—the natural law in social life, that is, the aimless movement in human social existence and development similar to that of the natural world, which I call *nature-likeness*.[1] For example, in Marx's criticism of Thomas Malthus in the *1857-1858 Manuscripts*, he points out the latter's ignorance of the "specific historical laws of population movement" in a given situation. (This "specific" must *not be capital* in Baudrillard's logic.) Marx also tells Malthus that these laws are "indeed the history of the nature of man, his *natural* laws. But they are the natural laws of man only at a certain level of historical development, corresponding to a certain level of development of the productive forces which is determined by his own historical process."[2] Again, Baudrillard comes to his blind spot. Marxist context is very complicated. First, when Marx observes the social-historical movement from the perspective of historical materialism, he always emphasizes the "lowercase" social life, the special state in a concrete historical situation. Second, Marx stipulates the "prehistorical society" (social existence before the final liberation of man), especially the social laws of the capitalist society, as a similar status in the aimless material movement of nature. Accordingly, he identifies these lowercase, specific social laws as natural laws. Marx uses them to illustrate that this situation is going to be developed or abrogated in future social development. Ironically, Baudrillard is precisely opposed to this progress.

Baudrillard puts forward the second epistemological summary, titled "Structural Limits of the Marxist Critique," at the end of that chapter. What a big slogan! However, in my opinion, except some aforesaid points, there is nothing substantial. It is a pseudo-transcendence failure of his logic. In particular, when he concludes that the projection of the class struggle [of Marxism] onto all previous history is led to reproduce the roots of the

---

[1] *See* my *The Subjective Dimension of Marxian Historical Dialectics* (Nanjing University Press, 2002). pp. 191-204.

[2] Karl Marx and Frederick Engels. *Collected Works*, vol. 28. London: Lawrence & Wishart, 1986. p. 525.

system of political economy, he is obviously lying. In the *German Ideology* of 1845 and the *Communist Manifesto* of 1848, Marx and Engels make a theoretical transgression due to lack of necessary materials. However, after they got to know the real situation of primitive social history through studies of anthropology and social history, they immediately revised their text and added special attributives before their assertion, which also proves the respectable matter-of-fact spirit of Marxism. Why does Baudrillard turn a blind eye to this well known fact?

VI. Marx and Ethnocentrism

The third chapter in *The Mirror of Production* is titled "Historical Materialism and Primitive Societies." According to Baudrillard's own words, this chapter focuses on Marx's concept of history, after his investigation of the Marxist concept of nature in the previous chapter. Its main critical target is the contemporary Marxist anthropologist Maurice Godelier and his *Anthropology, Science of Primitive Societies?* published in 1971.[1] Afterward, Baudrillard turns against the basic methodology of Marxist historical materialism. Next, we are going to analyze his criticism of historical materialism and then his discussion of the issues of primitive societies.

1. The Big History and the Big Dialectics

In his usual open style, Baudrillard makes a clear statement that Marxist concept of history, the same as the dominant category of nature, is a "*rewriting of History through the mode of production.*"[2] In other words, the concept of history in Marxist historical materialism is not a real reflection of history, but a re-coded effect by productive codes. Consequently, unlike dominated Nature, the Marxist concept of history is also a big "History."

Instead, the concepts of production and mode of production

---

[1] Godelie, Maurice. *Anthropology, Science of Primitive Societies?* Paris: Denoël, 1971.

[2] Baudrillard, Jean. *The Mirror of Production*. Trans. Mark Poster. St. Louis: Telos Press, 1975.
     p. 69.

themselves "produce" and "reproduce" the concepts of Nature and History as their space time. The model produces this double horizon of extent and time: Nature is only its extent and History only its trajectory. They do not need somehow to have their own names because they are only emanations of the code, referential simulations that acquire the force of reality and behind which the code legislates. These are the "laws of Nature" and the "laws of History."[1]

In a certain sense, Baudrillard is very shrewd. All the concepts in Marxist historical materialism acquire their particular historical meanings at a given level of social historical practice. The materialistic view is to observe history through the historical movement of the production. As long as Baudrillard rejects Marx's conception of material production as the foundation of social historical existence and movement, opposes the thought of understanding social history through the basic logic of the mode of production, he is bound to deny all the categories of historical materialism formed by this paradigm. Unsurprisingly, Baudrillard explains that Nature and History in historical materialism are but the effect of rewriting the model of material production and the mode of production: first, Nature is the extent horizon objectified by the scheme of production. Under the code of production, nature is the target of labor and the place to realize production; second, History is the continuous spreading of production, in which the time of life distorts into a trajectory of producing objects and history becomes the mere process of the changing mode of production. Therefore, Baudrillard thinks names are not necessary for nature and history that are only "referential simulations" of the code of production.

Here, we have to ask ourselves: Is Marx wrong? Is historical materialism wrong? Baudrillard's criticism of historical materialism stems from his primitive social guidelines based on the Mauss-Bataille symbolic exchange. He thinks that the simple original relations between people, between man and nature, are completely replaced by the utilitarian productive *readiness-*

---

[1] Baudrillard, Jean. *The Mirror of Production*. Trans. Mark Poster. St. Louis: Telos Press, 1975. p. 69.

to-hand. Everything regarding human social existence is shrouded in the shadow of exchange value; man's existence is deprived of the most authentic, non-useful happy status of survival. This is his theoretical foundation which he relies on to oppose historical materialism.

In my opinion, Baudrillard's understanding of historical materialism is one-sided. First, Marx emphasizes that general material production, namely, man's creative activity of transforming nature, is the common basis for the survival of the entire human social life, which is also called the eternal natural necessity. This cannot be denied by Baudrillard or anyone else. Even in the Mauss-Bataille symbolic exchange, the priceless consumption necessitates the previously *produced* objects. It cannot proceed with sheer natural objects like those used by animals. Therefore, Baudrillard's negation of production by the romantic grassrootism is not sensible. Second, Marx never legitimizes the utilitarian economic control generated in a given condition of material production, especially the bourgeois ideology proliferation; on the contrary, he dedicates himself to the criticism of the materialized control of the capitalist mode of production, and, of course, the distortion of nature and history by the logic of capital.

Besides nature and history, Baudrillard begins to deny the third concept in Marxist historical materialism, the *Dialectic*. In his eyes, the Dialectic is about the theory of Laws. The laws of Nature and the laws of History can only be "read in the Dialectic." As mentioned before, Baudrillard's initial letters indicate man's control and dominate logic, thus the laws of the Dialectic here denote the *rule of man*. Once again, Baudrillard misses the target. The Dialectic is not an invention by Marxism, but a philosophical category existent since the ancient time, shining in both Eastern and Western thoughts. When Heraclitus and Laozi, the ancient Chinese philosopher, used the dialectic as an ontological conception, the logic of production and exchange value in modern sense and Baudrillard's hatred was far from master of that world. Only if Baudrillard's Dialectic excludes the ancient dialectic and refers to the one that appears since the dominance of capitalist mode of production in the 18th century, I shall agree with what he says. In fact, Baudrillard's criticism of the *violent* logic of Dialectic mainly originates from Hegel, the modern German idealist great master, whose absolute idea system says that Nature and History are the alienation and restoration history of the absolute spirit; in Baudrillard's stylish words: Through the rewriting by the code of absolute idea, Nature is the space for objectified ideas; History becomes the process to materialize concepts; and Dialectic turns into the Logic of the conceptualized world. Perhaps some correlation is necessary here, for Hegel's logic is not his own creation either, but largely a philosophical mapping of modern industrial and economical development.[1] Marxist historical materialism and historical dialectics indeed reverse Hegel's reversed world. In my understanding, Marx's transcendence is his essential removal of the concepts-rape-reality capitalization. Specific analysis of certain historical existence is found everywhere in Marxist historical materialism. What is absent is exactly the abstract capitalization of the suspending hypothesis of subjective values. In his later years, Marx used the figurative "Man" but it is a philosophical positioning of human liberation. After 1845, Marx abandons the Hegelian/Feuerbachian *capitalized concepts*. But Baudrillard commits another false accusation here.

According to Baudrillard, Marxist historical materialism makes another serious mistake, namely, generalizing these concepts, for example, Nature, History, and the Dialectic, which only belong to the framework of productive materialism. In particular, Marx subjectively extends them to primitive societies where there are no such things as objectified nature, history of production, and dialectic, which directly reflect the reciprocal relation between subject and object. It is an illegitimate transgression. At the same time, Baudrillard appreciates the critical deconstruction theory of Nietzsche, which, he says, aims at "deconstructing the imaginary universality of the solidest conceptual edifices (the subject, rationality, knowledge, history, dialectics) and restoring them to their relativity and symptomality."[2] He

---

[1] *See* "Section Two" in the first chapter of *Back to Marx*: *The Philosophical Discourse in the Context of Economics* (Jiangsu People's Press, 1999).

[2] Baudrillard, Jean. *The Mirror of Production*. Trans. Mark Poster. St. Louis: Telos Press, 1975. p. 70.

counts on Nietzsche to oppose the "logos and the pathos of production."

Again, I almost lose patience with Baudrillard, who often frames Marx by the exact things which Marx opposes. When does Marx insist on the universal conception? Except the premise for the existence of common society, the basic material production and reproduction, is *specific*; *historical and actual* stipulation after historical materialism was established in 1845. He always analyzes the material production status in a given historical condition, a certain natural environment, certain conceptions and certain relations between people, which is the scientific "historical and transitory" methodology and historiography established in the 1846 "Letter from Marx to Pavel Vasilyevich Annenkov."[1] Marx's methodology is meant to deconstruct any attempt to self-solidificate concept. The zealous Nietzsche-admirer, Heidegger, valued this as the most important subversion of metaphysics. Did the profound Baudrillard not know this?

2. Categories of analysis and ideology

Baudrillard makes every effort to continue his tenacious criticism and denial of Marxism. In the end of this chapter, he provides the usual epistemological summary, titled "Materialism and Ethnocentrism." Another carefully prepared label put on Marxism! (Baudrillard did not take part in the Chinese Cultural Revolution, but his "label factory" does not fall behind those Chinese radicals. He is also of the so-called French Red May generation, probably inheriting this terrible and poor style of writing from that revolution.)

As said by Baudrillard, Marx "outlined the formula for" epistemology in his labor theory, or in the relation with labor. He likes quoting from the *1857-1858 Manuscripts*. I discover that he uses the same text source here. To be specific, it is Marx's statement about the "method of political economy" in the introduction, where Marx says that labor simply seems an economic

[1] *See* my *Back to Marx*: *The Philosophical Discourse in the Context of Economics*. Marx uses 7 givens and 2 certains to illustrate the specific historical analysis, which is the right opposition to the universalization of conceptions.

category but actually it is as modern a category as are the relations which create this simple abstraction. Therefore, Marx points out that:

> Even the most abstract categories, despite their being valid—precisely because they are abstractions—for all epochs, are, in the determinateness of their abstract, just as much a product of historical conditions and retain their full validity only for and within these conditions.[1]

Marx's description just rebuts the above criticism of Baudrillard, who does not even understand dialectical thought due to his lack of the spirit of dialectics. Baudrillard wonders why labor belongs all the times on one side, and applies it only to some certain eras on the other side. He calls it a "mystery." However, it is Baudrillard who invents the big modern mysteries if judged by his own logic. (He later uses such concepts as "implosion," "simulacrum," etc., which, obviously, are mystifications.) Indeed, Marx is very clear here: Labor, as the most important and dominating aspect of human production, runs through the entire history; wherever man exists, there is labor and production; labor belongs to all historical periods from this perspective. Nevertheless, the particular circumstances and preconditions of labor in a given period are not the same, e.g. simple labor in primitive societies observably differs from today's labor engaged in information-based production, which rightly proves that the conceptual abstraction of labor only fully applies for and within these conditions. Marx's explanation is rather plain for those who have common knowledge of dialectics. How can it be a mystery? Here, Baudrillard may have confused ignorance with sharpness.

Baudrillard is intentionally misleading since he soon fabricates another logical conversion in his following text. After criticism of Marx's mystification of labor, he instantly concocts a new logical link by saying that "this is the same mystery as the simultaneous subordination of infra-

---

[1] Karl Marx and Frederick Engels. *Collected Works*, vol. 28. London: Lawrence & Wishart, 1986. p. 42.

and super-structure, and the dialectical coexistence of a dominance and a determination in the last instance."[1] This is a trap. Infra- and super-structure, a dominance and a determination respectively refer to the economic foundation and political/legal superstructure of the social formation, enslaving dominance and control, and the decisive role that economic power plays in an economic social form. They are three important *special* conceptions of historical materialism. Obviously, these concepts are not universal for all historical periods. In Marx's late years, he often abstracts some philosophical concepts with common features when analyzing capitalist economic issues. These understandings and critical points only suit certain economic social forms. Marx is left with little time for some ad hoc limitations. For example, in the description of the general principles of the special historical materialism in the *Critique of Political Economy*, Marx does not notice that the modern economic structure and superstructure, including the decisive role of the economic power, lack universality. Such lapses are seriously misread by the Second International and the Stalinist textbook doctrines, which generate many unscientific explanations of historical materialism. Baudrillard grasps these misguided expressions and maliciously extends them to the whole historical materialism. It is his real purpose.

Therefore, he does observe a fault of Marxist expression and instantly makes a detour to the previous concept of labor. It is also true that Marx explicitly says that to posit man as a labor is itself the product of history. (A good proof of rebutting his falsification of Marx's universality of the concept of labor in previous part.) However, Marx does not say labor *activity* (not the concept of labor) is a historical product. (Marx points out that in the process of production labor becomes social labor *as such*, the modern-sense indistinguishable *abstraction* of labor, which is, without doubt, the effect of modern capitalist social development, with its abstraction as the *objective*

---

[1] Baudrillard, Jean. *The Mirror of Production*. Trans. Mark Poster. St. Louis: Telos Press, 1975. p. 84.

abstractness in the economic exchanges.)[1] Without specific analysis, Baudrillard continues his attack against Marx's concept of labor. He cites Sahlins, who says that "labor is not a real category of tribal economy"[2] and canonizes it in his criticism of Marx. When he accuses the abstraction of the concept of labor by Marx, he does not expect it.

> At the same time that it produces the abstract universality of labor (of labor power), our epoch produces the universal abstraction of the *concept* of labor and the retrospective illusion of the validity of this concept for all societies. Concrete, actual, limited validity is that of an *analytic* concept; its abstract and unlimited validity is that of an *ideological* concept. This distinction concerns not only labor but the whole conceptual edifice of historical materialism: production, productive forces, mode of production, infrastructure (not to mention the dialectic and history itself). All these concepts are in fact historical products. Beyond the field that produced them (especially, if they want to be "scientific"), they are only the metalanguage of a Western culture (Marxist, to be sure) that speaks from the height of its abstraction.[3]

Baudrillard offers a series of assertions, among which is the heterogeneous relation between an analytic category and ideology. A careful reader may find it is still the appropriation of the categories of Althusser's "science" and "ideology." The analytic category concerns the "concrete, actual, limited validity" of the concept while the ideological concept is featured with the "abstract and unlimited validity." In my opinion, there is

---

[1] *See* my *Back to Marx: The Philosophical Discourse in the Context of Economics*. In particular, pages from 566-572. Also, *see* the first chapter in *The Sublime Object of Ideology* by Slavoj Žižek.

[2] Quoted from Baudrillard's note about Sahlins's *Original Affluent Society*. To be more strict, is there a real category of "economy" in primitive societies? Or, the alleged "symbolic exchange"? Judging from Baudrillard's own logic, it is all illegitimate for Mauss-Bataille and Sahlins's modern discourse to describe the primitive societies.

[3] Baudrillard, Jean. *The Mirror of Production*. Trans. Mark Poster. St. Louis: Telos Press, 1975. p. 85.

nothing fresh here. Those methods of concrete, actual, limited (temporary) historical analysis are the kernel of the methodology of Marxist historical materialism. Ironically, Baudrillard borrows them to act against Marxism in turn. In addition, his definition of ideological categories is too limited. Universality is only an insignificant character in modern ideological research and it is difficult to be clarified once separated from the hegemonic discourse of the ruling class. More importantly, Marx should be the last one to be blamed. What we see here is that Baudrillard packs labor, production, mode of production, infrastructure, history and dialectic within the ideological category, as the rape of the whole social history by Western metacultural language (the hegemonic discourse of West-centralism).

We cannot accept this opinion. Amid Baudrillard's list of historical materialist categories, except infrastructure (the economic foundation) which does belong to special historical materialism, the majority are concepts of Marxist general historical materialism that have the common feature of the abstraction of the entire social history. According to Baudrillard, these concepts are the product of history. This is not wrong. Marx would not oppose this view. (During the establishment of historical materialism, what Marx emphasizes most is that any concept belongs to a given age.) However, it does not mean we can totally ignore the actual labor activities as the basis of human social survival, the whole life experience, the certain modes of production, the historical progress of human social history, and the dialectic relations ranging from the simple to the endless always existent in societies. They are not the same as the representation of these social existence or the dynamic, conceptual expressions of history. Baudrillard is easy to be proud of his argument. It proves but another non sequitur.

3. Is the anatomy of man a key to the anatomy of ape?

Baudrillard seems to expect the probable counter-argument. He explains that his criticism is not arbitrary but sustained by evidence. He cites Marx's view that *the anatomy of man is a key to the anatomy of ape*, which is an important metaphor in historical epistemology. (Baudrillard usually seizes the most important part in Marxist logic. I have to pay my respect for his sharpness.) The quotation is in the introduction of the *1857-1858 Manuscripts*, following Baudrillard's previous citation about labor. The statement is very important. Let us read the whole paragraph:

> Bourgeois society is the most developed and many-faceted historical organization of production. The categories which express its relations, an understanding of its structure, therefore, provide, at the same time, an insight into the structure and the relations of production of all previous forms of society the ruins and components of which were used in the creation of bourgeois society. Some of these remains are still dragged along within bourgeois society unassimilated, while elements which previously were barely indicated have developed and attained their full significance, etc. The anatomy of man is a key to the anatomy of the ape. On the other hand, indications of higher forms in the lower species of animals can only be understood when the higher forms themselves are already known.[1]

Marx has two implications here. First, it means that the capitalist society is by far the most advanced and miscellaneous society that we have ever seen, and, from the understanding of whose modern productive organization and social structure, we can more easily perceive the under-developed social and productive organization that disappeared in the past. It is a theoretical commending height. For the same reason, Baudrillard cites another remark from Marx: "It requires a fully developed production of commodities before, from accumulated experience alone, the scientific conviction springs up."[2] Marx believes that the modern capitalist mode of production is built on the ruins of the old social existence, thus inevitably bearing the relics of the past and signs of the future social development. It reflects the view of social history as a diachronic, correlative, and progressive course, as well as the

---

[1] Karl Marx and Frederick Engels. *Collected Works*, vol. 28. London: Lawrence & Wishart, 1986. p. 42.

[2] Karl Marx, *Capital*, vol. 1. London: Lawrence & Wishart, 1977. p. 79.

historical epistemology confirmed by Marx, that is, to research the advanced, the varied social structure of modern time is of help for us to understand the lower social structure that is abrogated or absorbed by itself. This view certainly belongs to scientific systematic epistemology and historical epistemology.

In fact, Baudrillard's quotation corresponds to two other statements in which Marx discusses the continuous historical development of social structure. Marx immediately follows the above words with the statement that "what is called historical development rests, in general, on the fact that the latest form regards earlier ones as stages leading towards itself."[1] (Baudrillard refers to the same words in his later discussion.) In the chapter on capital of the same script, Marx puts forward more specific view that the mode of production in any social existence does not develop from nothing. The historical development of society is a continual process of totalization, in which the new structure develops on the ground of the previous social condition and primary structures. In this respect, Marx offers an opinion about the organic movement of society.

> This organic system itself has its premises as a totality, and its development into a totality consists precisely in subordinating all elements of society to itself, or in creating out of it the organs it still lacks. This is historically how it becomes a totality. Its becoming this totality constitutes a moment of its process, of its development.[2]

This is a comprehensive view of the diachronic, organic development of social structure. For Marx, knowledge and perception of the advanced types of a social organism undoubtedly facilitate the understanding of the earlier primary social forms.

The second implication of the famous statement is its figurative sense, that is, the anatomy of man who exists as the highest life form, will help us

---

[1] Karl Marx and Frederick Engels. *Collected Works*, vol. 28. London: Lawrence & Wishart, 1986. p. 42.

[2] Ibid., p. 208.

to understand the physiology of the lower animals. (Of course, here Marx presupposes Darwinian biological evolution that man evolves from the "ape.") Marx intends to explain that it is the same with the understanding of human social history: The modern capitalist mode of production is like man whose anatomy is a key to observe the "ape," the earlier existent social structure. It is a very accurate metaphor. In my opinion, we cannot deny this Marxist epistemological assertion even though the Darwinian evolution theory seems not that scientific today.

But, Baudrillard does not think so. He does not accept Marx's degrading comparison of his beloved primitive social existence to the life of "ape." (Baudrillard says that Althusser also notices this metaphor, but he replaces it with the structuralist ideology after eliminating the residue of Marxist natural evolution.) For Baudrillard, it is an incorrect association: Biological anatomy is radically different from social life; the schemata of two different fields do not match; this linkage amounts to saying that "the adult can comprehend the child only in terms of the adult."[1] Can an adult really understand the world of the child? Baudrillard's answer is no. He says, in any case, in the presupposition of this continuity [Marx's metaphor] there is a (positivist) alignment of all analytic approaches with those of the so-called exact sciences, which does not fit for his symbolic existence and special meanings of man. Baudrillard believes that Marx is totally oblivious of the important "rupture" between different social forms. His remark is alarming: this rupture is "far more profound than the one Althusser detects."[2] Oh, yes, we are already familiar with Baudrillard's profoundness.

It is known that under the influence of Gaston Bachelard's "epistemological break." Althusser, introduces it to the research of Marxist history. Then, Baudrillard stealthily appropriates the result of the broken history of thought, the "ideological" and "scientific" paradigms. (Baudrillard only makes a simple conversion into "ideology" and "analysis.") In fact, what

---

[1] Baudrillard, Jean. *The Mirror of Production*. Trans. Mark Poster. St. Louis: Telos Press, 1975. p. 86.

[2] Ibid., p. 86.

Baudrillard wants to say is that in the common sense of social progress, not all different social forms and lives are classified by higher or lower, simple or complex relations, especially, the social existence of primitive symbolic exchange and gift circulation, which is not a lower social life at all but the right objective for human existence worthy of man's rethinking and effort to realize. In this regard, how can it be referred to as "ape"? Baudrillard cannot bear it. "Let us say in passing that the metaphor of the ape is worthless—certainly the ape's anatomical structure cannot be illuminated starting from the 'contradictions' of human anatomy." It explains why the rupture here is "more profound" than that of Althusser.[1]

Baudrillard then questions whether the capitalist economy retrospectively illuminates medieval, ancient, and primitive societies. Obviously, his reply is negative, because in the primitive life, "the magical, the religious, and the symbolic are relegated to the margins of the economy. And even when the symbolic formations expressly aim, as in primitive exchange, to prevent the emergence with the rise of economic structures of a transcendent social power that would escape the group's control, things are arranged nonetheless so as to see a determination by the economic in the last instance."[2] Baudrillard's explanation here seems to criticize Marx's simplified extension of the capitalist economic materialization to all the previous social existence, which is but a misunderstanding of historical materialism. What Marx insists through historical epistemology is the common principle of general historical materialism, that is, the production and reproduction of the material means of life is the foundation for the entire social existence and development; social existence defines man's conception. In no way does Marx attempt to inflict the specific social mode and special thinking within a certain period on other social historical periods and forms. Baudrillard's problem is made by himself. He first equates labor and material production of all human societies to the capitalist productive and economic mode, and then demonizes Marxist historical materialism into a

---

[1] Baudrillard, Jean. *The Mirror of Production*. Trans. Mark Poster. St. Louis: Telos Press, 1975. p. 86.
[2] Ibid., p. 87.

simple historical formula. In his writing, Marx becomes a crazy man labeling everything with capitalist ideology. But who on earth is the ridiculous one?

On the other side, Marx does not neglect the fact that ancient social life is not that utilitarian or "alienated" when compared with contemporary capitalist social life. "In this way, the old view according to which the man always appears in however narrowly national, religious or political a determination as the end of production, seems very exalted when set against the modern world, in which production is the end of man, and wealth the end of production."[1] However, the wonderful past has inevitably gone; history cannot go back; and we cannot return to the ancient "exaltation." To Marx, the beautiful social historical life of man is not a return to the distant past but actual forwardness and emancipation. He says that "[t]he absolute unfolding of man's creative abilities, without any precondition other than the preceding historical development, which makes this totality of this development— i.e. the development of all human powers as such, not measured by any *previously given yardstick—an end*-in-itself, through which he does not reproduce in any specific character, but produces his totality, and does not seek to remain something he has already become, but is in the absolute movement of becoming?"[2] In addition, shall we return to the primitive living condition?

4. Historical materialism and West-centrism

In Baudrillard's view, Marxist historical materialism is deeply trapped in the framework of the capitalist political economy. In the kingdom of capital, the productive force is a crucial element. As a result, Marx makes the hypothesis that productive forces exist in any society. This time, Baudrillard assaults another key concept of historical materialism.

"Productive force" in the philosophical discourse of Marxist general historical materialism is a concept used to gauge the level of development

---

[1] Karl Marx and Frederick Engels. *Collected Works*, vol. 28. London: Lawrence & Wishart, 1986. p. 411.

[2] Ibid., pp. 411-412.

of material production in a certain social historical period. Marx says in *The Communist Manifesto* that capitalism creates huge productive forces like invoking a daemon, the speed of which even far surpasses that of the previous centuries put altogether. However, it does not mean that productive forces only exist in capitalist society. In fact, if there is social material production, there is people's power to transform nature. Even in primitive societies where material production does not dominate, it still sustains life as the actual material basis; otherwise, the "hau" so much admired by Baudrillard and his teachers would not happen without those gifts to be exchanged or consumed. No matter how the primitive people degrade utility, they would not survive on symbolic exchanges or witchcrafts. Baudrillard's paranoid negation of the role of material production and productive forces in social existence even deviates from common knowledge.

Here, Baudrillard is mainly dissatisfied with what he believes to be the Marxist extension of bourgeois social economic categories to other societies. He cites the paragraph next to the metaphor of man and ape in the *1857-1857 Manuscripts*, in which Marx says it is understandable in a certain sense to utilize the capitalist economic category for the comprehension of other social forms. It is obviously an ad hoc stipulation. The "certain sense" means, as the most advanced social form so far, the contemporary capitalist social structure can carry out self-examination to observe the social forms sublated by itself. This self-critical analysis will begin a scientific perception of history. Marx says that:

> The Christian religion was able to contribute to an objective understanding of earlier mythologies. Similarly, it was not until the self-criticism of bourgeois society had begun that bourgeois [political] economy came to understand the feudal, ancient and oriental economies.[1]

This last sentence undoubtedly irritates Baudrillard, who could not tolerate the "Western Centrism" in this statement. To Baudrillard, it is true

---

[1] Karl Marx and Frederick Engels. *Collected Works*, vol. 28. London: Lawrence & Wishart, 1986. p. 43.

that Western culture firstly begins a self-critical approach, but the premise is based exactly on the interpretation of itself as a universal culture while all Other cultures are arrogantly put into a museum for the exhibition of relics imagined by Western culture. It should be admitted that Baudrillard's analysis represents a correct self-reflection, which also goes in line with later post-colonialism and Orientalism. Baudrillard says that:

> [i]t [Western culture] "estheticized" them [other cultures], reinterpreted them on its own model, and thus precluded the radical interrogation these "different" cultures implied for it. The limits of this culture "critique" are clear: its reflection on itself leads only to the universalization of its own principles. Its own contradictions lead it, as in the previous case, to the world-wide economic and political imperialism of all modern capitalist and socialist Western societies.[1]

The self-criticism is very perceptive. In fact, after a serious reading of the Russian commune and the ancient oriental societies in the final stage of his theoretical research, Marx is aware that his own special historical materialism only applies to the Western Europe; in addition, he admits the unique "Asian mode of production," from which we can know that Marx never had the idea of imposing the interpretative mode of Western culture on other cultures. Otherwise, Marx would not have advocated the view that for Russia it was possible to get over the Caudine Forks in the choice of its revolutionary road.

Baudrillard's background theory is completely correct in this issue, but his censure of Marxist historical materialism is still an improper parallel. To him, Marx illegitimately applies the schema of political economy to the primitive societies where there is no material production or economic structure at all. In my opinion, Baudrillard always confuses issues with radical differences. Marx never intends to treat the modern production schema as the basic structure of primitive societies. He only says that *in a*

---

[1] Baudrillard, Jean. *The Mirror of Production*. Trans. Mark Poster. St. Louis: Telos Press, 1975. p. 89.

certain sense our perception and knowledge of the capitalist social structure
helps clarify the existential conditions of ancient society, from which today's
society originates. For us, it can also be a reference for the Oriental societies
different from the West. Is all this worth the labeling of "Western Centrism"?

Baudrillard is arbitrary when he says that "[t]he impossibility for
historical materialism of going beyond political economy toward the past
as evidenced by its incapacity to decipher primitive societies, applies as
well for the future by the same logic. It appears more and more incapable
of outlining a revolutionary perspective truly beyond political economy. It
flounders 'dialectically' in the impasses of capital, just as it flounders in the
miscomprehension of the symbolic."[1] Baudrillard's worry is unwarranted.
Historical materialism will not flounder because this scientific methodology
never has the ambition to anchor any specific scientific mode, to directly
decipher the code of primitive societies, or to replace anthropology, let
alone a straight, concrete description of the future society. It is no more than
a research "guide" for us to know the world and the history of ourselves.
Baudrillard thinks that he knows Marxism, he understands historical
materialism, but in fact, he is always a layman with his messy understanding
of historical materialism.

VII. Riddle of Monkey Anatomy and Ape Analysis

Baudrillard makes an extensive criticism of the basic concepts of
Marxist historical materialism, in particular, the negation of the famous
metaphor that the anatomy of man is a key to the anatomy of the ape. In
order to verify the judgment, Baudrillard abruptly shifts to the analysis of
the "archaic and feudal mode" which came prior to the capitalist mode of
production, from which he chooses two typical issues for discussion: the
slave-master relationship and the labor of the artisan. Following Baudrillard's
opposition against the study of the past from a modern standpoint, we see a

---

[1] *See* Note 74 of *The mirror of production.*

fantastic scene: Baudrillard is interpreting the archaic and feudal life with the symbolic relation in primitive life! If in line with Marx's metaphor, the experience of monkey anatomy further mystifies the riddle of ape survival.

1. New dialectical interpretation of the master and the slave

The previous section discusses Baudrillard's teaching that we should get rid of West-centralism, the Western complex of enslaving Other cultures because another post-colonialism arises when we illuminate the past with the contemporary capitalist ideology, which, of course, is a conceptual colonization for the Westerners to reflect on their past, not for the culture of Others. This opinion seems persuasive. Baudrillard says that through its most "scientific" inclinations toward earlier societies[1], it "naturalizes" them under the sign of the mode of production. Here again their anthropological relegation to a museum, a process originated in bourgeois society, continues under the sign of its critique.[2] Then, how can we avoid such a silly mistake of cultural imperialism? Baudrillard goes out of his way to offer Marxists

---

[1] The most advanced bourgeois thought also exports its models (its viruses) under the cover of the most "objective" critical epistemology. For if the final aim of anthropology is to contribute to a better knowledge of objectified thought and its mechanisms, it is in the last resort immaterial whether in this book the thought processes of the South American Indians take place through the medium of theirs. What matters is that the human mind, regardless of the identity of those who happen to be giving it expression, should display an increasingly intelligible structure as a result of the double reflexive forward movement of two thought processes acting upon each other, either of which can in turn provide the spark or tinder whose conjunction will shed light on both. And should this light happen to reveal a treasure, there will be no need of an arbitrator to parcel it out, since, as I declared at the outset, the heritage is untransferable and cannot be split up (Lévi-Strauss, *The Raw and the Cooked*, trans. J. and D. Weightman. New York: Harper and Row, 1969, pp. 13-14). This is the extreme of liberal thought and the most beautiful way of preserving the initiative and priority of Western thought within "dialogue" and under the sign of the universality of the human mind (as always for Enlightenment anthropology). Here is the beautiful soul! Is it possible to be more impartial in the sensitive and intellectual knowledge of the other? This harmonious vision of two thought processes renders their *confrontation* perfectly inoffensive, by denying the difference of the primitives as an element of rupture with and subversion of (our) "objectified" thought and its mechanisms. Quoted from the note by Baudrillard.

[2] Baudrillard, Jean. *The Mirror of Production*. Trans. Mark Poster. St. Louis: Telos Press, 1975. p. 91.

a satisfactory model. He first analyzes Marx's archaic society and then selects the popular example of the dialect of master and slave in Hegel's *Phenomenology of Mind*.

Baudrillard believes that Marx's analysis of slavery stems from the status of wage labor in political economy, especially, the analysis of labor. For Baudrillard, Marx's worker does not sell his labor or product, but rather he remises his labor or product. (To be more precise, what the worker sells is the right to use his labor force.) In comparison, the slave sells neither labor nor product nor labor force. Therefore, the issue of slavery lies in the master's ownership of the slave's labor power. In Baudrillard's eyes, Marx is wrong because there is no separated labor and labor power for the slave. That the nature of slavery is alienation-exploitation just derives from Marx's economic assumption:

> We are faced again with a presumption of the economic through the grid labor-labor power. The symbolic relation master-slave is conceived as a kind of husk whose "real" kernel will be extracted in the thread of history (in fact, in the thread of the theoretical model that will impose this principle of reality). What is lost in this process is everything that is exchanged in the master-slave relation and everything not reducible to the alienation-exploitation of a labor power.[1]

Baudrillard seems very pleased because he teaches Marx a lesson who does not understand *the symbolic relation is the nature of all societies*. However, his rejoice comes too early.

First, Marx never employs the concept of labor which only exists in the capitalist mode of production to investigate slavery or other social forms prior to capitalism. What Marx does is to study certain social existences and movements preconditioned by given modes of production, in particular, the productive relation under specific historical conditions. Marx says that

---

[1] Baudrillard, Jean. *The Mirror of Production*. Trans. Mark Poster. St. Louis: Telos Press, 1975. p. 94.

"[i]n real history, wage labor arises from the disintegration of slavery and serfdom—or from the decay of communal property as among the Oriental and Slav peoples."[1] We can see that he does not take the free laborer who detaches from the means of production and possesses his independent labor power as the pre-capitalist schema of labor relations, in which the labor forms are always branded with their peculiar features. Furthermore, Marx clearly states that in slavery production "the slave does not come into consideration at all as *an* exchanger"[2] because everything of him, including his own existence, is kept by the master. For the slave it is impossible to freely exchange or sell his labor power. In this attachment relationship, there is no separated labor power. "The slave stands in no relation whatsoever to the objective conditions of his labor; rather, *labor* itself." His labor is juxtaposed with the live-stock tools or "as an appendage of the soil."[3] How can Baudrillard think that Marx trades off the economic presumption of labor power against the kernel of slavery? Or is Baudrillard talking too freely?

However, he still feels that his accusation is not enough. So, he puts on a long face and teaches us: there is not "a relation of reciprocity" between the master and the slave, that is, the value relationship defined in the individualistic and altruistic context does not exist; the slave and the master is "in the sense of an *obligation*." What obligation, then? Baudrillard does not offer a clear explanation but stresses that "in the original relation, the slave, or rather the relation master-slave, is *unalienable* in the sense that neither the master nor the slave are alienated from each other, nor is the slave alienated from himself as is the free worker in the private disposition of his labor power."[4] For that reason, Baudrillard again loses his temper. He thinks that Marx indiscriminately "projects" the "the illusion of Western humanist rationality" only found in capitalist society (the abstract and alienated social

[1] Karl Marx and Frederick Engels. *Collected Works*, vol. 28. London: Lawrence & Wishart, 1986. p.13.

[2] Ibid., p. 345.

[3] Ibid., p. 413.

[4] Baudrillard, Jean. *The Mirror of Production*. Trans. Mark Poster. St. Louis: Telos Press, 1975. p. 95.

relations) "on earlier forms of domination, explaining the differences as some historical underdevelopment is to miscomprehend all that the earlier formations can teach us about the symbolic operation of social relations."[1]

We are tired of this groundless allegation. (Baudrillard repeats the same mistake in the same text, which forces me do the same worthless repetition.) I already mentioned that Marx abandons the humanistic discourse after 1845. Nor does he use the value-hypothetic *logic of alienation* to measure any historical reality, even the capitalist economic relations, not to say the social relations of slavery. Besides, when Marx talks about slavery and serfdom in past Western societies, he marks with a particular note that "this does *not* apply e.g. to the general slavery of the Orient, [or does so] *only* from the European point of view."[2] Unexpectedly, Baudrillard even stipulates the brutal slavery control as some symbolic operation of the relations of responsibility. If this opinion is confirmed in the Mauss-Bataille discourse and slavery does turn out to be the symbolic exchange relation favored by Baudrillard, then he is to blame for all this. (Interestingly, I doubt whether Mauss would agree with this theoretical transgression.)

2. Difference between the artisan's work and the useful labor

Baudrillard tries to be unconventional with such a grand narration as "the Archaic and Feudal Mode", but he only discusses a far-off slave and master relation, and deals with the alleged "feudal mode" with the artisan's work. Is it Baudrillard's abstraction? Or, if we do him a favor, can it be interpreted as having two different modes of production? According to Baudrillard's own logic, any conception of production and labor in pre-capitalist times is illegitimate, but then what is the thing that the slave does but that cannot be called labor? Baudrillard does not offer a new paradigm and we are not able to find the answer. However, he strains after novelty by telling that the artisan's *work* differs from labor. Moreover, he profoundly points out that

---

[1]   Baudrillard, Jean. *The Mirror of Production*. Trans. Mark Poster. St. Louis: Telos Press, 1975. p. 96.

[2]   Karl Marx and Frederick Engels. *Collected Works*, vol. 28. London: Lawrence & Wishart, 1986. p. 419.

work has the meaning of "demiurge" according to etymology.

Baudrillard says it is not correct to regard the artisan as the owner of his labor or product because it is still coding the artisan with the logic of production. (Obviously, he indicates Marxism.) The artisan's work differs from labor because there is no such separation as labor power and product, or subject and object; he only views his own work as the symbolic relationship. To me, the symbolic relation seems to be Baudrillard's magic bullet. It is not only the secret of slavery but also the true meaning for the artisan to live.

> Something in the material that he works is a continuous response to that which he does, escaping all productive finality (which purely and simply transforms materials into use value or exchange value). There is something that eludes the law of value and bears witness to a kind of reciprocal prodigality. In his work, what he bestows is lost and given and rendered, expended and resolved and abolished, but not "invested."[1]

Baudrillard explains that it is in the same way as we use language, where there is no utilitarian purpose but an immediate reciprocity of exchange *through language*, without producers and consumers. "In the primitive exchange gift, the status of goods that circulate is close to language. The goods are neither produced nor consumed as values. Their function is the continuous articulation of the exchange."[2] The primitive exchange of gifts retains "the personal quality of the exchange."[3] (This is completely nonsense. In the potlatch and the "kula", a woman is given as the gift. She is clearly not an equal exchanger, not even a human being. Baudrillard's equality only refers to the chiefs or the clan rulers. It is the social nature beyond the knowledge of Mauss, Bataille, Baudrillard and other idealist thinkers.) Although the artisan's quid pro quo has clear purpose and value, he and his product are not separated.

---

[1] Baudrillard, Jean. *The Mirror of Production*. Trans. Mark Poster. St. Louis: Telos Press, 1975. p. 99.

[2] Ibid., p. 98.

[3] Ibid.

Baudrillard takes the work of art as an illustration of this unique artisan-work relationship. In his eyes, the work of the artisan resembles the creation of artists instead of labor.

> Artisanal work (according to etymology, "demiurge"), which draws a radical difference between work and labor. *Work is a process of destruction as well as of "production,"* and in this way work is symbolic. Death, loss and absence are inscribed in it through this dispossession of the subject, this loss of the subject and the object in the scansion of the exchange.[1]

For Baudrillard, if we examine the artisan from the perspective of historical materialism or define the work with the paradigm of production and labor, we shall see no truth. "The work of art and to a certain extent the artisanal work bear in them the inscription of the loss of the finality of the subject and the object, the radical compatibility of life and death, the play of an ambivalence that the product of labor as such does not bear since it has inscribed in it only the finality of value."[2]

It is true that Marx says that the artisan's labor is "half-artistic" but he mainly refers to the "particular skill" in the artisan's labor.[3] Baudrillard really confuses us. The artisan's work is neither labor nor production, and without the finality of purpose after binary separation. Like the functional consumption and destruction of artworks, it symbolizes the ambivalence of life and death play. Judging from any aspect, this statement is almost incomprehensible. I think Baudrillard should make a concrete description of the artisan's work, e.g. a shoemaker; in what sense is his making process, a kind of destruction? What specific destruction is it? Why do the pair of shoes not have the function of utility? Why do the shoes function as the sign of the mystical life and death? Most of all, how does a shoemaker survive if his

---

[1] Baudrillard, Jean. *The Mirror of Production*. Trans. Mark Poster. St. Louis: Telos Press, 1975. p. 99.

[2] Ibid.

[3] Karl Marx and Frederick Engels. *Collected Works*, vol. 28. London: Lawrence & Wishart, 1986. p. 507.

"work" only produces a useless, defective pair of shoes?

I just wonder why Baudrillard writes such incredibly ridiculous things in a serious academic work. Two radically different matters are bound together. It is common knowledge that the nature of artistic creation is of no utilitarian value. For the artist, the work of art materializes his will of life; for the audience, it is to experience another existential being. Personally, I like Itzhak Perlman very much. When listening to his violin, I do not notice his physical existence but feel a surging passion of life in that beautiful melody. In contrast, the artisan works not for creation but survival. Marx takes the patriarchal production of agricultural artisanship as an example, in which "the great majority of the population satisfies most of its needs directly by its labor, the sphere of circulation and exchange is very narrow."[1] Production is not primarily for exchange. "Here labor itself is still half the expression of artistic creation, half an end-in-itself, etc."[2] The example of craftsmanship does not have the separation later in the capitalist mode of production but in the artisan's work, "labor still belongs to the laborer; a certain self-sufficient development of limited specialised capacities, etc."[3] Although it is possible for the artisan to present his own creation in the product, it does not mean he can shake off the existential purpose for survival. In addition, most of artisans cannot reach up to a decent artistic level. "Clay Figure Zhang" and "Scissor Zhang Xiaoquan" (two renowned Chinese artisans) are only the very few who rise to fame with their high artisanal skills.

In my opinion, Baudrillard's pseudo-romanticism teems with grand, magnificent but empty talks, without much serious academic research. Here is another example: "Praxis, a noble activity, is always one of use, as distinct from poesis which designates fabrication. Only the former, which plays and acts, but does not produce, is noble."[4] Whereas someone like Baudrillard considers only the praxis that "does not produce" as "noble,"

[1] Karl Marx and Frederick Engels. *Collected Works*, vol. 28. London: Lawrence & Wishart, 1986. p. 345.

[2] Ibid., p. 421.

[3] Ibid.

[4] Baudrillard, Jean. *The Mirror of Production*. Trans. Mark Poster. St. Louis: Telos Press, 1975. p. 101.

they cannot ignore the fact that it is the common people who are engaged in those mediocre but useful productive activities, for instance, the production of Baudrillard's high-class camera or operational computer, that provide the opportunity for him to engage in such noble activities like photography or academic research.

3. The logical anatomies of man, monkey and ape

Baudrillard says that "[a]ll these facts converge toward one point: the inadequacy of the concepts of labor, production, productive force, and relations of production in accounting for, let us say, pre-industrial organization (the same holds also for feudal or traditional organization)."[1] Yes, even though Baudrillard does not mention Marx's name and quote from the Marxist texts as before, we are still able to understand what Baudrillard wants to object behind the lines. The concluding section of this chapter, titled "Marxism and Miscomprehension", reveals his intention to escalate the criticism of Marxism.

He first makes a critical summary of Marxism, in particular, historical materialism.

> The idea that in all societies the relations of production, and consequently, politics, law, religion, etc., presuppose that in all societies the same articulation of human activities exists, that technology, law, politics, and religion are always necessarily separated and separable; it is to extrapolate to the totality of history the structuration of our own society, which is inevitably meaningless outside of it.[2]

In my understanding, this summary has a very specific purpose. It targets the introduction of the *Critique of Political Economy*, written by Marx in 1858, which is seen as a classic representation of historical materialism. In that famous explanation of his research methodology, Marx does not add any historical limitation to the property relation and the corresponding

[1] Baudrillard, Jean. *The Mirror of Production*. Trans. Mark Poster. St. Louis: Telos Press, 1975. p. 101.
[2] Ibid., p. 106.

economic infrastructure, legal superstructure, etc., all of which cannot be found in primitive societies. For Baudrillard, there are at least two logical transgressions here: One is the diachronic imposition of what do not exist in pre-capitalist Western societies on those social lives; the other is the synchronically imposition of what the West has on those non-Western societies (Baudrillard's "ethno-centralism"). For a clear explanation, let us first read the complete paragraph:

> In the social production of their existence, men inevitably enter into definite relations, which are independent of their will, namely relations of production appropriate to a given stage in the development of their material forces of production. The totality of these relations of production constitutes the economic structure of society, the real foundation, on which arises a legal and political superstructure and to which correspond definite forms of social consciousness. The mode of production of material life conditions the general process of social, political and intellectual life. It is not the consciousness of men that determines their existence, but their social existence that determines their consciousness. At a certain stage of development, the material productive forces of society come into conflict with the existing relations of production or—this merely expresses the same thing in legal terms—with the property relations within the framework of which they have operated hitherto. From forms of development of the productive forces these relations turn into their fetters. Then begins an era of social revolution. The changes in the economic foundation lead sooner or later to the transformation of the whole immense superstructure.[1]

Marx's description here is not the general historical materialism that is applicable to all history. He is explaining the method to study the capitalist mode of expression, which mainly belongs to special historical materialism, the concrete exemplification of *economic social forms* of general historical

---

[1] Karl Marx and Frederick Engels. *Collected Works*, vol. 29. London: Lawrence & Wishart, 1987. p. 263.

materialism. For instance, social existence defines ideology; certain productive forces inevitably generate corresponding relations of production; it is a general law for all human history that the development of productive forces is the fundamental drive for social revolution; the material mode of production conditions all social and spiritual life; economic infrastructure and political-legal superstructure are closely related. None of these are found in primitive societies. They are only applicable for the later development of social history. Secondly, when Marx studied oriental societies in his late years, he made it clear that his special historical materialism only applies in the social development road of Western Europe.[1] In traditional explanations of the Marxist textbooks, Marx's above statement is wrongly interpreted as the *common* view of historical materialism without any necessary ad hoc limitations. In this sense, Baudrillard's criticism is not incorrect. However, Marx should not to be held responsible for this mistake. Differed from Baudrillard's simplicity and harshness, Sahlins observes the problem of understanding this statement in a general context, and even detects that the conventional "Marxism ignored Marx", which means the negligence of the specific research of oriental societies done by Marx himself.[2]

Baudrillard is quite tenacious in chasing Marx. He states that when dealing with primitive societies, Marxism "works *in the imaginary* like the man who, having lost his key in a dark alley, looks for it in a lighted area because, he says, that it is the only place where he could find it. Thus, historical materialism does not know how to grasp earlier societies in their symbolic articulation. It only finds in them what it could find under its own light, that is, its artificial mode of production."[3] Then, what is the key in the "dark alley"? Baudrillard's answer is the relation of exchange set up by the symbolic. Baudrillard tells us that:

---

[1] Karl Marx and Frederick Engels. *Collected Works*, vol. 24. London: Lawrence & Wishart, 1989. p. 346.

[2] Sahlins, Marshall D. *Culture and Practical Reason*. Joint Publishing Company Limited (Beijing), 2002.

[3] Baudrillard, Jean. *The Mirror of Production*. Trans. Mark Poster. St. Louis: Telos Press, 1975. p. 107.

The symbolic sets up a relation of exchange in which the respective positions cannot be autonomized:

—neither the producer and his product;

—nor the producer and the user;

—nor the producer and his "concrete" essence, his labor power;

—nor the user and his "concrete" essence, his needs;

—nor the product and its "concrete" finality, its utility.[1]

As we know, it is a negative delineation of the Mauss-Bataille logic, in striking contrast against the capitalist structure of value exchange. According to Baudrillard, Marxist historical materialism cannot make a correct explanation of them because "the repression of the symbolic nourishes all the rationalist political illusions, all the *dreams of political voluntarism*, that are born in the terrain of historical materialism,"[2] and because Marxism is ignorant of symbolic exchange. It cannot account for the primitive societies at all. Historical materialism has the critique of the capitalist economy and its relations of production as its object and primitive societies, kinship, language and the symbolic, are not its province. In other words, historical materialism only applies to the capitalist society but fails to explain the primitive society, in particular, the dominant kinship and symbolic exchange in it. When Marx extends the mode of historical materialism to the pre-capitalist social existence, he does the same thing that he is against, thus, he is an accomplice to eternalize capitalism. In this regard, historical materialism can explain neither the nature of primitive societies nor the radicality of separation in our societies, and therefore the radicality of subversion.

Baudrillard must have a happy catharsis through the criticism. In his eyes, Marxist historical materialism is simply stupid while his symbolic exchange mode—a conclusion from primitive social existence—is universal. A common reader may feel strange. First, as I have mentioned several times, Baudrillard's distortion of Marxist historical materialism leads to errant

---

[1] Baudrillard, Jean. *The Mirror of Production*. Trans. Mark Poster. St. Louis: Telos Press, 1975. p. 103.

[2] Ibid., p. 108.

conclusions. What Marx underscores is always the concrete, historical, actual analysis of any historical phenomenon. He would never make such a simple mistake as using a concrete social mode to explicate other societies. When Marx says it is helpful to perceive the social life in previous primary social forms by the anatomy of the Western capitalist society which is the most advanced social development we have seen so far, he just means what he says, nothing more. Marx does not have the ambition to promote the capitalist mode of existence to previous historical periods of Western society or other non-Western social existences. In dealing with pre-capitalist social history, he does not use the capitalist mode of production to simply schematize it. Instead, Marx insists on the historical, concrete and realistic investigation of general historical materialism, on such important common principals like that material production is the foundation for any social existence, but he never seeks the logic of capital in non-capitalist social existences. As obvious as the point is, Baudrillard chooses to turn a blind eye once again, which is hard to explain.

Baudrillard is against the metaphor of ape anatomy, but his own thought in turn reveals a deeper logical intention: in his textual context of opposing Marx's idea to use anatomy of man in the analysis of the ape, his own analytic logic is nothing else but *the secret use of the monkey anatomy to schematize the ape*. Why should the logic of primitive symbolic exchange (monkey) be the secret of archaic and feudal social existence (ape)? Isn't it an attempt to eternalize the logic of primitive social existence? Baudrillard's boomerang strikes himself this time.

VIII. Historical Materialism and Euclidean Geometry of History

Titled "Marxist and the System of Political Economy," the last chapter is a conclusive summary of Baudrillard's critique of Marxism. He questions historical materialism as a whole, criticizes Marxist theories of class and revolution, and most of all, denies the political economy on which historical materialism is built. Let us first analyze his ironical statement, "Euclidean geometry in history" which is targeted at historical materialism. After it, we shall deal with the other charges of Marxism one by one.

1. Legitimacy of articulating the archaic history with a contemporary discourse

According to Baudrillard, historical materialism is generated from capitalism. Its generation process is filled with the class struggles of the modern mode of production. Therefore, theory and praxis, the dialectic of the productive forces and the relation of production, the law of contradiction, the homogeneity of space—all the kernel concepts of historical materialism are organized with the ideal capitalist mode of production. For Marx, the capitalist mode of production is regarded as the highest point of historical development, which of course possesses the "absolute advantage" (man for anatomy) can perceive all the previous historical social forms. (Baudrillard bears particular dislike towards Marx's metaphor that "the anatomy of man is a key to the anatomy of ape.") No wonder Baudrillard says that "[i]n earlier formations, men blindly produced their social relations at the same time as their material wealth. The capitalist mode is the moment when they become conscious of this double and simultaneous production, when they aim to take it under rational control. This concept would appear only in the final stages of capitalism and in its critique, illuminating in one stroke the entire earlier process."[1] In my opinion, Baudrillard is generally correct in saying so. Most of the scientific concepts of historical materialism only fit the historical condition of modern production, which is defined by the contemporary capitalist mode of production in Europe.

Behind these Marxist concepts, Baudrillard continues, there are two theoretical presumptions:

—A process of historical development is already there in all earlier societies (a mode of production, contradictions, a dialectic) but they do

---

[1] Baudrillard, Jean. *The Mirror of Production.* Trans. Mark Poster. St. Louis: Telos Press, 1975. p. 112.

not produce a concept of it and hence do not transcend it.

—The moment of becoming conscious of the process (the production of the critical concept connected to the conditions of the capitalist formation) is also the decisive stage of its revolution.[1]

First, the contradiction movement and dialectic law of the mode of production already exist in early human societies, only people did not have these concepts then; second, the criticism of capitalism by Marxist historical materialism is also the crucial phase for the real, self-conscious emancipation of man. In this regard, Baudrillard's above statement is generally acceptable. However, something is wrong with his following words.

Baudrillard says historical materialism describes the general laws of society, which is indeed "perfectly Hegelian". Like the risk of absolute idea, human social history happens in a finalistic way, develops and reaches the summit in the realm of freedom, as in communism. But Baudrillard believes the early period humans knew not what the purpose of history is and "they lived neither historically nor within the mode of production."[2] Only we consider ourselves standing at the historical high point and looking down at previous ones, hence retrospectively, treating the present society "as the principle of explication of earlier formations."[3] Consequently, we schematize primitive life with conceptions and thoughts they do not understand, which is no doubt a theoretical violence. Baudrillard jauntily declares from his standpoint of the modern discourse, "[a]s if by chance, the *reality* of the mode of production enters the scene at the moment when someone is discovered who invents the *theory* of it."[4] He means that only through the conception of the mode of production can people construct the actual existence of the mode of production. This is not simplistic idealism; it is a conceptual imperialism in which the concepts rape reality.

Baudrillard is really considerate of the primitive peoples, but his opinion

---

[1] Baudrillard, Jean. *The Mirror of Production*. Trans. Mark Poster. St. Louis: Telos Press, 1975. p. 112.

[2] Ibid.

[3] Ibid., p. 114.

[4] Ibid., p. 113.

is a fallacy. For example, the existence of animals and plants is different from man, and they do not have consciousness of their own existence, least not to mention the conception of knowledge, and then, if we borrow Baudrillard's logic, would it be impossible for human beings to understand their existence via science and technology? Does Baudrillard mean that only through the languages or information code of the animals, bird, bugs, flowers, grass, trees themselves can people non-violently understand them? As a matter of fact, it is like an adult who can know more about the childhood significance than a kid can. Similarly, people at an advanced level of social development, equipped with the experience, knowledge, and wisdom accumulated through generations for thousands of years, are sure to better observe the nature of social history and movement better than their predecessors do. For this reason, Marx says that standing at the high point of the capitalist industrial development, with our scientific knowledge of outer nature, with the being-for-itself of the humanized material system brought by industrial praxis, with the unprecedented complexity and full expansion of the economic social structure, we can better understand the present, know our past, and envision the future. Marx does not say anything wrong.

It would be sensible if Baudrillard expressed it in this way: first, the primitive peoples are not self-conscious of the historical development since time is always visualized in the circle of sunrise and sunset, four seasons in the husbandry and agriculture of the natural economy. However, it does not mean history stops in progress. Or else, Baudrillard would still have been a primitive man who could not have had philosophical thoughts or have taken up his beloved photography. It cannot be a change of abracadabra. Second, primitive people do live with a mode of production but not with a modern mode of production like capitalism. So long as man exists, he must produce and live in a certain mode, even if material production is not dominant in his life; he cannot do without production and reproduction. The conception of the mode of production does not mean capitalism, although it is abstracted from the perception of the capitalist social structure. Meanwhile, it can be used to describe the previous social existences. Here, I have a question. Does the primitive society have what Mauss and Baudrillard call the symbolic conception? Or more precisely, Baudrillard's anthropological symbolic concept is proposed by the French structural linguist Lévi-Strauss in the middle 20th century. We can see that it is not only a product of capitalism, but also the product of an advanced capitalism. Then, what about Baudrillard's "symbolic exchange"? Is not it a rape of primitive society by such a modern concept? Where does the symbolic relation come from in the primitive life? If we still remember Baudrillard's accusation, it amounts to saying that "only when people create the *theory* of symbolic exchange can the *reality* of symbolic exchange enter their vision", is that right?

Another point to note is that, unlike Hegel's absolute-idea conception of history, Marx finds that his teleological and theodicial absolute-idea is only a reversed reflection of the history of human social praxis. When Marx denies Hegelian's idealism, he does not negate the self-purposeful movement of human social history, but instead reveals that in capitalism and its preceding social history there exists the contradiction between individual will and collective blindness, as well as a regular resultant purpose of the finality of history. Historical materialism is a methodological self-consciousness of the knowledge of historical laws. It offers a methodological explanation for what Baudrillard cannot see though.

2. Does historical materialism have the universality of science?

Baudrillard makes the firm conclusion that "[t]he materialist theory of history cannot escape from ideology." According to the classic negative ideological theory, the conclusion means that historical materialism replaces the actual things with imaginary relations as it always attempts to move through the entire process of history, very similar to "the Euclidean geometry of this history."[1] (Baudrillard is really eloquent with his vivacious analogy.) In this respect, he asks three questions in a row.

---

[1] Baudrillard, Jean. *The Mirror of Production*. Trans. Mark Poster. St. Louis: Telos Press, 1975. p. 114.

But what authorizes science in its scorn of magic or alchemy, for example, in this disjunction of a truth to come, of a destiny of objective knowledge, hidden from the infantile miscomprehension of earlier societies? And what authorizes the "science of history" to claim this disjunction of a history to come, of an objective finality that robs earlier societies of the determinations in which they live, of their magic, of their difference, of the meaning that they attribute to themselves, in order to clarify them in the infrastructural truth of the mode of production to which we alone have the key?[1]

Like Mauss-Bataille, Baudrillard regards witchcraft and magic in primitive societies as the authentic being of man which has not been poisoned by the system of utilitarian value. He is dissatisfied with the negation and transcendence of ignorance and darkness by modern science. In his eyes, primitive culture and modern science are not in the same timeline. Should science acquire absolute authority? Should historical materialism declare itself the only "science of history" after the non-scientific conception of historical rupture, and think of itself as the key to solve the mystery of history? No! No! No! Baudrillard says that:

[i]t is only in the *mirror* of production and history, under the double principle of indefinite accumulation (production) and dialectical continuity (history), only by the arbitrariness of the *code*, that our Western culture can reflect itself in the universal as the privileged moment of truth (science) or of revolution (historical materialism). Without this simulation, without this gigantic reflexivity of the concave (or convex) concept of history or production, our era loses all privileges. It would not be any closer to any term of knowledge or any social truth than any other.[2]

The reactionary logic of the mirror of production and the mirror of

---

[1] Baudrillard, Jean. *The Mirror of Production*. Trans. Mark Poster. St. Louis: Telos Press, 1975. p. 114.

[2] Ibid., p. 115.

history! Baudrillard dots the (i)'s and crosses the (t)'s here. He means that we are in this huge reflection mirror of production and history. Through endless material production which accumulates a utilitarian system of exchange value; through the historical dialectic which constructs a progressive, teleological human history—a double concave-convex mirror of logic; through the scientific truths that reflect cognition and historical process as well as historical materialism about social reforms (they are mutually supplementary to each other), Western culture turns itself into a universal authoritative discourse and basic code. According to Baudrillard, this history is simulated by the mirror of production and the mirror of history. Once we have this huge mirror broken and the source light of science and dialectic put out, the staged imaginary play of history will instantly disappear and the whole Western hegemony of culture will get lost for good. Baudrillard thus say that "[t]his is why it is important to begin with this *ethnological reduction and to strip our culture*."[1]

In essence, Baudrillard's accusation of historical materialism aims at opposing the schematization of all history with one discourse of historical philosophy since there is not a universal truth. In this connection, Baudrillard's anti-West-centralism and denial of the absolute discourse of universal philosophy is right. His view represents the important epistemological achievements of natural science and social practice in the 1930s and 1940s. On the other hand, he goes too far in his denial of science, historical materialism and Marxism, which, ironically, oppose the very universality that he is against. Indeed, Baudrillard's cherished anthropology is itself a scientific discipline. The reason why Mauss and other anthropologists can jump out of contemporary philosophical discourse and actually reflect the heterogeneous social relations in the primitive tribes is that they have a historical view and the materialist scientific spirit based on reality.

First, since Einstein, modern science has abandoned the metaphysical trace of universality, absoluteness and eternity in classic scientific view,

---

[1] Baudrillard, Jean. *The Mirror of Production*. Trans. Mark Poster. St. Louis: Telos Press, 1975. p. 115.

while *historicality, relativity and temporality* become the basic attribute of theoretical logic. We gradually come to the discovery that the objective truths treated as universal in the past, without exception, contain the subjective cognizance of the limited conditions in a certain historical period. At the same time, science more and more has a restricted meaning within a given framework of reference. This is a modern anatomy of Kant's proposition that man legislates universal laws for nature. The metaphysical science framework targeted by Baudrillard has already become a historical vestige left by the modern scientific view that has the same goal to fulfill as he does. Therefore, Baudrillard's sensational nihilistic denial of science makes no sense.

Second, Marxist historical materialism is not as stupidly ridiculous as in Baudrillard's description. Excluding the overshadowing of conventional interpretation, in particular, Stalinist doctrines since the Second International, the real Marxist historical materialism provides no universal formula or mirror reflection, but rather a methodological guide for people to research and face historical reality. (Engels gave a special discussion of it in his lifetime.) Marxist historical materialism, in its general sense, only discovers that material production (not limited to the modern capitalist production and economic mode) is the foundation of human social life, including primitive societies where material production does not dominate. As for this point, we Chinese have had too many tragedies, which is an experience not known by Baudrillard, who lives in an advanced capitalistic country. When a nation rejects fundamental material production and substitutes it with some *symbolic relations*, it is to end up in an actual crisis of survival. (For example, the huge political symbolic structure during the Chinese Cultural Revolution, when farmlands were removed of the "capitalist" sprouts; when social life was fully symbolized, codified by the "proletarian revolution", the whole society was just on the verge of collapse! It is a terrible memory that lingers on in many Chinese minds. The same tragedy happened during the rule of the Khmer Rouge of Cambodia.) The methodology of historical materialism does not only stress a temporal, linear historical progress; more importantly, it underscores the given context for observation and research, concluded by Lenin as the specific analysis for the specific problem. What it refuses is abstract universality. In this point, Baudrillard is wrong because what he denies is his own method in disguise.

I have to point out that the mirror of production and the mirror of history targeted by Baudrillard are not only turned against Marxism, but the complete modern human culture. This is determined by the Mauss-Bataille logic of grassrootism. This ridiculous view is itself a compulsive extension of primitive life, of certain social relations into the whole human history. It denies modern culture. It is a huge *symbolic mirror*. Since Baudrillard is opposed to the restoration of historical materialism, how can he prove the legitimacy of their *restoration of anthropology*? When he schematizes the entire human history with the abstraction of symbolic exchange, why does not he take into consideration the illusory privileged ideology?

3. Outdated economic root of historical materialism

Baudrillard then criticizes Althusser's interpretation of Marxism. However, due to his shallow understanding of Althusser, namely, his miscomprehension of Althusser's *quasi-structuralist* hermeneutic context, I do not think it is worthwhile to be entangled in this question. We should pay attention to a new issue raised in this discussion: Is the *economic root* of Marxist historical materialism outdated? The bourgeois attack on Marxism usually focuses on the foundation of natural science on which the philosophical discourse is generated. Rarely has one noticed the more important basis, the economics, not to mention the declaration of a dead Marxism by proving the historicality of this economic logic. It is a completely new subject, a virulent topic.

Baudrillard's criticism is often insidious. He makes the following reasoning: Marx thinks that he stands at the highest point of capitalist economic development, brought by the industrial mass production described in Ricardo's economics; he thinks he has got the key to analyze all history, but, today's economic development has far surpassed what Ricardo's economics can deal with; therefore, can contemporary social history still be studied by the Marxist key that is already *not the highest point of social economical development*? He gladly says that:

> But with the addition that, strictly speaking, in Marx's time, the commodity form had not at all attained its generalized form, and has had a long history *since Marx*. Thus Marx was not in a historical position to speak scientifically, to speak the truth. In that case, another break imposes itself, one that would risk making Marxism appear as a theory of a surpassed stage of commodity production, hence, as an ideology. At least, if one wanted to be scientific![1]

Regrettably, Baudrillard wastes his wisdom. In his eyes, since Marx political economy has spread into wider fields, e.g. consumption as the production of signs, needs, knowledge, and sexuality. Many things have erupted in the "infrastructure." Therefore, the distinction between Marxist superstructure and economic basis is outdated. "Something in the capitalist sphere has changed radically, something Marxist analysis can no longer respond to."[2] The most important reason is that political economy is based on material production in Marx's time but is unable to find its reliable foundation in today's life. In Baudrillard's eyes, the current social existence is definitely not founded on the decisive theory of material production. "Thus, when the system becomes monopolistic, labor time and production costs cease to be the decisive criteria (and become surplus value?)."[3] As a result, the present social reality determines that Marxist political economy critique cannot be extended into a universal theory. Baudrillard seems logical in his reasoning.

He further cites three phases of the mode of exchange value system, or the development of commodity economy, in Marx's *Poverty of Philosophy*:

---

[1] Baudrillard, Jean. *The Mirror of Production*. Trans. Mark Poster. St. Louis: Telos Press, 1975. p. 117.

[2] Ibid., p. 118.

[3] Ibid., p. 125.

first, in ancient and feudal societies, exchange is limited to surplus products, while the majority of objects are beyond the scope of commodities and exchange; second, since the capitalist development, the whole "industry" is within exchange; third, the universalization of commodity exchange, in which everything becomes exchangeable, including those beyond the sphere of commodity exchange in the past, for example, "virtue, love, conviction, knowledge, conscience, etc."[1] Baudrillard agrees to this division but discovers a problem in Marx's third phase, in which it is not some penetration into other spheres by the relation of commodity exchange, but a phase during which the "new social relation" takes effect. For him, Marx does not see through the nature of this new social existence:

> In Marx's projection this new phase of political economy, which in his time had not yet fully developed, is immediately neutralized, drawn into the wake of phase 2, in terms of the market and "mercantile venality." Even today the only "Marxist" critique of culture, of consumption, of information, of ideology, of sexuality, etc. is made in terms of "capitalist prostitution," that is, in terms of commodities, exploitation, profit, money and surplus value.[2]

According to Baudrillard, it is to employ the second-phase terms—the logic of the capitalist economic phase based on material production—to refer to today's life. Baudrillard thinks it is even the same with the French situationalist thought that he once supported, although their theory of spectacle society contains a radical transcendence of Marxist political economy; the material commodity pileup has turned out to be a splendid control of spectacles. In essence, it is still "the 'infrastructural' logic of the commodity."[3]

---

[1] Karl Marx and Frederick Engels. *Collected Works*, vol. 6. London: Lawrence & Wishart, 1976. p. 113.

[2] Baudrillard, Jean. *The Mirror of Production*. Trans. Mark Poster. St. Louis: Telos Press, 1975. p. 120.

[3] Ibid., p. 120. As for situationalism, *see* my "Introduction" to the Chinese version of Debord's *Spectacle of Society*.

In my opinion, Baudrillard's falsification of Marxist historical materialism is all nonsense. However, it at least opens a profound issue, that is, historical materialism must adapt itself to the continual change of the social economic structure and life. First, Baudrillard is unaware that Marxist historical materialism is not a metaphysical assertion or closed conclusion. A key to the mystery of history, it comes from social-historical practice and develops into a functional mode of thought. The nature of historical materialism is to break any traditional metaphysics through its own historicality of time, which is already identified by Heidegger.

Second, when Marx says that historical materialism is established on the highest level of production mode, brought by what Ricardo calls the practice of the industrial mass production, he has no intention to anchor this scientific method in the 19th century capitalist economic and political structure. On the contrary, it is the nature of the everlasting revolution in the capitalist mode of production that enables Marx to perceive the historical nature of all philosophical methodologies. Historical materialism is the science of history; it claims no invariable historical nature; it will continually guide us in our understanding of the new social historical life, as the development of actual historical praxis changes its own structure.

Third, whether it is Baudrillard's appropriated control of code or various subversive social phenomena in the "consumer society," the latest changes in capitalist society have not shaken the foundation of material production on which social existence and movements are built. (We are to have a particular discussion on it later.) Contemporary development and changes of the capitalist economic and political reality will not lead to an outdated historical materialism; on the contrary, it will provide a fresh amenable environment for it to grow, like China's rising social economy that will certainly promote the new development of Marxism in China.

4. Origin and new revolution of "the political economy of the sign"

Baudrillard then begins to sell his theory of "the political economy of the sign." (It is the major point in his near early *For a Critique of the Political Economy of the Sign*.) In his opinion, it is a new era now, more specifically, the capitalism of Marx's age has turned into a social existence controlled by another structure. "This mutation concerns the passage from the form-commodity to the form-sign, from the abstraction of the exchange of material products under the law of general equivalence to the operationalization of all exchanges under the law of the code. With this passage to *the political economy of the sign*, it is not a matter of a simple 'commercial prostitution' of all values."[1]

Here, all values are made into the "exchange-sign value under the hegemony of the code." According to Baudrillard, it is "a structure of control and of power much more subtle and more totalitarian than that of exploitation" observed by Marx. It should be noted that unlike those postmodernist philosophers who positively reflect this post-industrial social existence, Baudrillard holds a critical attitude of it. Nevertheless, he does not mean to negate capitalism, but bemoans the complete loss of his cherished relation of symbolic exchange. "The important question is not this one, but rather that of the symbolic destruction of all social relations not so much by the ownership of the means of production but by *the control of the code*."[2] It is a very important coordinate of logic which tells us with what criteria of value Baudrillard judges a true or false reality.

Another important question is that Baudrillard disagrees with the hypothesis that his political economy of the sign is a derivative of Marxist political economy. (He is always to escape Marxism.) In his eyes, today's capitalist social life has a revolution equally important to the early industrial one. For all that, Marxist logic has lost the flexibility of the "theoretical curvature" that makes it sensible in the new social existence, which is not monopolistic capitalism at all. He opposes the dialectical continuity between the political economy of the commodity and the political economy

---

[1] Baudrillard, Jean. *The Mirror of Production*. Trans. Mark Poster. St. Louis: Telos Press, 1975. p. 121.

[2] Ibid., p. 122.

of the sign. Here comes the rupture. This is a completely new hegemony of social structure which is not in the schema of the mode of production. "The monopolistic system transfers its strategy to a level where the dialectic no longer operates. In the monopolistic system, there is no longer any dialectic of supply and demand; this dialectic is short-circuited by a calculation of foreseeable equilibrium."[1] In contrast with the traditional structure of competition in capitalism, the monopolistic system constructs consumption into a control, a prohibition of the occasionality of needs, and a socialized process of code planning. It is a logic framework not dominated by labor time; it is only a construct of code play.

It means that one goes from a system of productive forces, exploitation, and profit, as in the competitive system dominated in its logic by social labor time, to a gigantic operational game of question and answer, to a gigantic combinatory where all values commutate and are exchanged according to their operational sign. The monopolistic stage signifies less the monopoly of the means of production (which is never total) than *the monopoly of the code*.[2]

The ontological dimension of social reality disappears in its formula of signification. In traditional political economy, all Marxist concepts and theoretical meanings can be connected with the economic or political reality; today, "the code no longer refers back to any subjective or objective 'reality,' but to its own logic."[3] As for this issue, Baudrillard later expresses in his *Symbolic Exchange and Death* that it is a change from the old vertical relation of signification with an actual reference object to the horizontal relation of signification among codes without any reference object. Even a common reader of Saussure can tell it is an appropriation of basic structuralist linguistics, in which generation of meanings by linguistic signs first escapes the old reflective mode. The casual relation between the signifier

[1] Baudrillard, Jean. *The Mirror of Production*. Trans. Mark Poster. St. Louis: Telos Press, 1975. p. 125.

[2] Ibid., p. 127.

[3] Ibid.

and the signified changes the relation of the object (actual existence) and its representative image in the reflection theory to the one between concept (existence=nature) and the sign that identifies this conception—the sound-image. In other words, language is essentially among relations; a system of linguistical relations, instead of one-to-one direct references of the objects.[1] No wonder Baudrillard says that:

> The signifier becomes its own referent and the use value of the sign disappears to the benefit of its commutation and exchange value alone. The sign no longer designates anything at all. It approaches its true structural limit which is to refer back only to other signs. All reality then becomes the place of a demiurgically manipulation, of a structural simulation. And, whereas the traditional sign (also in linguistic exchanges) is the object of a conscious investment, of a rational calculation of signifieds, here it is the code that becomes the instance of absolute reference, and, at the same time, the object of a perverse desire.[2]

Baudrillard believes that Marx encounters an embarrassment here. In this code control, "the final reference of the products, their use value, completely disappears. Needs lose all their autonomy; they are coded. Consumption no longer has a value of enjoyment per se; it is placed under the constraint of an absolute finality which is that of production."[3]

If put in a simple way, Baudrillard means to say that in today's monopolistic system, production under code control is no longer for the object's use value which is fabricated by the code; need and desire are not man's real appeal, but "the desire of the Other's desire"; it is the same with consumption, which is a controlled, made up event. Therefore,

---

[1] *See* Chapter Four in *The Impossible Truth of Being—Mirror of Lacan's Philosophy* (The Commercial Press, 2006).

[2] Baudrillard, Jean. *The Mirror of Production*. Trans. Mark Poster. St. Louis: Telos Press, 1975. p. 128.

[3] Ibid.

Baudrillard asks, when production loses its own fundamentality, is the dialectic of productive forces and relations of production still legitimate in its existence?

It should be admitted that Baudrillard is very astute in his analysis of the present capitalist economy and society. He perceives the dominant control structure of the logic of capital—the code control. However, he makes an error by regarding the *dominant* power of society as the ontological *base*. He then goes further to deny the only real foundation for social existence: material production. This mistake will unavoidably lead to a bigger one about the issue of actual revolution.

After Baudrillard denies the Marxist critique of the capitalist mode of production and negates political economy and historical materialism, he refuses scientific socialism which aims at overthrowing the bourgeois social reality. In the second half of the last chapter in *The Mirror of Production*, Baudrillard proposes his own substitute plan: the revolution of *symbolic subversion*.

For Baudrillard, the key of today's social control is not what Marx calls "profit and exploitation," which is only "the inaugural modality" of capitalism, "the infantile phase" of political economy. At present, "the truly capitalist phase of forced socialization through labor and the intensive mobilization of productive forces has been overturned."[1] Under the code control, the nature of social life becomes a desublimation of productive forces; there emerges the "immense social domestication"; the general public is more and more integrated by production tools; welfares and humanistic material life put out the revolutionary fire with demobilization. The capitalist system utilizes "the economic reference (well-being, consumption, but also working conditions, salaries, productivity, growth)"[2] and successfully eradicates the actual possibility of subversive revolution. (According to Baudrillard, through self-regulation, capitalism can offer Marx what his

---

[1] Baudrillard, Jean. *The Mirror of Production*. Trans. Mark Poster. St. Louis: Telos Press, 1975. p. 131.

[2] Ibid., p. 139.

revolution wants. For this reason, Marxism is the "ideology of labor" that
is utilized by capitalism.) During the process of integrated domestication,
Marx's proletarian revolution does not show up in time mainly because the
worker is degraded to being the most substantial confirmer of capitalism
in the ideology of productivism. Does not socialism want to "change life"?
Agreed! When the bourgeoisie satisfies the general affluence of society,
the "actual revolt" against economic exploitation "has placidly become the
victory of the proletariat."[1] The revolutionary proletariat disappears below
the horizon of welfare countries and finally returns to history. At the same
time, those revolutionary powers that were once beyond Marxist attention
have emerged, in particular, those marginalized people who do not directly
oppose exploitation and profit, for example, young students, women, colored
people and so on. In Baudrillard's opinion, they are the *resistance against
code control*.

> The Black revolt aims at race as a code, at a level much more
> radical than economic exploitation. The revolt of women aims at the
> code that makes the feminine a non-marked term. The youth revolt
> aims at the extremity of a process of racist discrimination in which it
> has no right to speak. The same holds for all those social groups that
> fall under the structural bar of repression, of relegation to a place where
> they lose their meaning. This position of revolt is no longer that of the
> economically exploited; it aims less at the extortion of surplus value
> than at the imposition of the code, which inscribes the present strategy
> of social domination.[2]

Baudrillard says that their resistance involves no class struggle though,
it reveals the weakness of current capitalism; they are the hope of a new
revolution in this fight without any apparent clear target. Why? Because this
cultural revolution is taking effect in antithesis to the function of Marxist

---

[1] Baudrillard, Jean. *The Mirror of Production*. Trans. Mark Poster. St. Louis: Telos Press, 1975.
   p. 159.
[2] Ibid., p. 135.

historical materialism; "this whole critique *is turned back against materialism in an integral way*."[1] The reality is that "the *production* of social relations determines the mode of material *reproduction*."[2] The matter is reversed. He says that "[i]t is directly at the level of the production of social relations that capitalism is vulnerable and en route to perdition. Its fatal malady is not its incapacity to reproduce itself economically and politically, but its incapacity to reproduce itself *symbolically*."[3] Baudrillard tells us that in primitive societies, the symbolic exchange relation is a continual "circle of giving and taking." Indeed, it is from the destruction of the ontological *mutual relations* that power comes up. Therefore, the only way out to beat down the current code capitalism is to rely on symbolic subversion; it is this fatality of symbolic disintegration under the sign of economic rationality that capitalism cannot escape. Baudrillard believes that subversion by the symbolic, to some degree, arises under the label "cultural revolution." Its kernel is the symbolic; it is a symbolic logic, the abolition of the imaginary of political economy; it makes the revolution of culture object to any Marxist economic-political revolt. His ideal is like the French Red May storm.

> Those of May, 1968—in every case the revolution does not speak indirectly; they are the revolution, not concepts in transit. Their speech is symbolic and it does not aim at an essence. In these instances, there is speech before history, before politics, before truth, speech before the separation and the future totality. He is truly a revolutionary who speaks of the world as non-separated.[4]

This is Baudrillard's substitute plan for Marx's scientific socialist revolution. As expected, it is a revolution of the symbolic, whose pursuit is but the conceptual disalienation and separation, the imaginative usurpation,

---

[1] Baudrillard, Jean. *The Mirror of Production*. Trans. Mark Poster. St. Louis: Telos Press, 1975. p. 150.

[2] Ibid., p. 142.

[3] Ibid., p. 143.

[4] Ibid., p. 166.

the fantastic rose in the dream. The worker's slogan is "Never Work."[1] "Something in all men profoundly rejoices in seeing a car burning."[2] Now, it is not difficult to understand why Baudrillard's symbolic revolution is easy to be objectified in sci-fic movies. For him, the future revolution is like Neo's magic in the blockbuster *Matrix*, where the subjective idea can bend and twist the iron spoon; imagination can shield the barrage; guerrillas can even *symbolically* escape Matrix's control through the phone line. Like all postmodern anti-Marxist thoughts, this seemingly radical revolution of conception is but the moon in the water, the flower in the dream. When the resistance against the actual political-economic framework disintegrates, people have no choice but to be hopelessly and endlessly enslaved by capital. No wonder Marx says in his late period, the postmodern is the best accomplice of the bourgeoisie at present.

We can finally make a conclusion about this aggressive *Mirror of Production*: Baudrillard is determined to deny Marxist historical materialism and replaces it with a nasty "mirror of symbol," which is just an idealistic cliché despite his gaudy, postmodernist ornament. In essence, he just imagines reality from voidness. This is the final and proper judgment of Baudrillard.

---

[1] In May, 1968, the workers of FIAT in Italy shouted the slogan "Never Work" in their strike action. Baudrillard says they do not want bread and butter but strike for strike's sake.

[2] Baudrillard, Jean. *The Mirror of Production*. Trans. Mark Poster. St. Louis: Telos Press, 1975. p. 141.

Chapter 4

Marx's Presence and Non-Presence: Reading of Jacques Derrida's *Specters of Marx*[1]

I n this chapter, I am going to have a selective interpretation of *Specters of Marx*, the most important book on Marx and Marxist thought by the great French deconstruction theorist, Jacque Derrida.[2] It is a typical piece of text in *post-Marx* thought.[3] (Just when I typed the first line on my computer, a pop-up window announced the obituary notice of Derrida on the screen.[4] All of a sudden, Jacque Derrida, one of the greatest

---

[1] This chapter was translated by He Chengzhou.

[2] Derrida, Jacques. *Specters of Marx: The State of the Debt, the Work of Mourning, and the New International*. Trans. Peggy Kamuf. New York: Routledge, 1994.

[3] In my view, the late Derrida is considered to be a follower of post-Marx thought largely due to this book.

[4] It was 2 p.m. on October 10, 2004. Derrida died in Paris the previous day.

thinkers today, became the Other in Lacan's sense, or, in his own words in *Specters of Marx*, the specter of thought that is not present but always with us in this world.) Among Derrida's academic writings, *Specters of Marx* may not be counted as the most satisfactory or important work, but behind the glaring attention given to his other works, it has been intrinsically linked to the Western post-Marx trend and attracted our attention. Derrida declares the return of the Marxist spirit from death as specters, and discusses the pedigree of the specters that both Marxism and the theory of deconstruction have been concerned with. Another important statement that Derrida makes in his book is that in today's world, all of us are successors of the legacy of Marxism. "Specters" and "legacy" are the key words that Derrida uses to illustrate the relationship between the theory of deconstruction and Marxism.

I. Radical Presence of the Absent Specters

In 1993, the bourgeoisie around the world were immersed in uproarious fever. The socialist camp of the Soviet Union and Eastern European countries, which had been founded after the "October Revolution", and had successfully prevented capital and imperialism from colonizing and carving up the world, had finally collapsed. The socialist cause received another crushing blow: the international communist movement hit the bottom of an all-round depression. The cliché of "the death of Marxism" surfaced again. At this confusing, painful moment for the world leftists, Jacque Derrida, the most renowned deconstruction master, firmly stood out with his *Specters of Marx*, loudly proclaiming the presence of Marx's specters, bravely struggling against the prevailing bourgeois trend, and clearly demonstrating his leftist position to maintain Marx's critical spirit. It is a really courageous and valuable critical spirit that "goes against the current."[1]

---

[1] Derrida, Jacques, and Elisabeth Roudinesco. *For What Tomorrow: A Dialogue (Cultural Memory in the Present)*. Stanford, California: Stanford University Press, 2004. p. 94

1. Why did Derrida write the *Specters of Marx*?

The first question to be clarified is why Derrida, the founder of a radical "post-modern" theory of deconstruction, would and could write this book about Marx. (We can only enter the textual interpretation after this important issue is solved. According to Fredric Jameson, Derrida does an important "remedial work" about Marxism. He thinks that Derrida has three intentions: first, to comment on Marx's texts; second, to "involve himself in a political environment where there is no choice for the radicals at present"; third, to "historically save the basis of Marxism."[1] I think it is a rather simplistic evaluation of Derrida. In his "Dedication," Derrida announces that he dedicates this book to Chris Hani, the assassinated general secretary of the South African Communist Party.[2] There is a tangible reason, namely, to commemorate a communist who is *not present due to death*. Derrida says in a philosophical tone that "[a] man's life, as unique as his death, will always be more than a paradigm and something other than a symbol. And this is precisely what a proper name should always name."[3] Derrida is more than sentimental. He despises the coward that kills Chris Hani. In his eyes, Hani's death amounts to "a banner," a saint's martyrdom. He has to say something about this Death.

However, the actual historical context for Derrida's writing is far more complex than what we see at a prima facie. It seems to me that there are several crucial factors hidden in the background of *Specters of Marx*.

First, Derrida's close friend and teacher, the renowned Marxist philosopher Louis Althusser died not long ago.[4] Derrida once said the book was actually a dialogue with Althusser despite his death. "*Specters of Marx* can indeed be read, if you like, as a sort of homage to Louis Althusser.

---

[1] Jameson, Fredric. *Neo-Marxism*. People's University Press, 2004. pp. 128-129.

[2] Chris Hani (1941-1993), one of the outstanding leaders of the black liberation movement in South Africa, was the general secretary of the Communist Party of South Africa. He was killed by white extremists on April 10, 1993.

[3] Derrida, Jacques. *Specters of Marx: The State of the Debt, the Work of Mourning, and the New International*. Trans. Peggy Kamuf. New York: Routledge, 1994. p. xv.

[4] Althusser died of a heart attack on October 22, 1990.

A salute that is indirect but above all friendly and nostalgic, slightly melancholic ... and of course it can be read as an address to him, a means of 'surviving' what I lived through with him, alongside him."[1] It is a dialogue with the *dead* Marxist philosopher which might not have taken place when he was alive. Althusser is regarded as a teacher of Derrida, who does not directly support his theory, because the modern structuralist logic used by Althusser to reinterpret Marxism already becomes the target of Derrida's deconstruction. Despite their major theoretical differences, they maintained a very close personal relationship all along. (Derrida said he kept important exchanges and communications with Althusser even when he fell mentally ill. Once the teacher died, Derrida felt obliged to clarify some critical matters, mainly about the theoretical relations between deconstruction and Marxism. It should be noted that the *Specters of Marx* does not imply Derrida's conversion from deconstruction to Marxism, as is claimed by some critics. Derrida was never a Marxist, even if he "saluted" Marx in his later years. I think an insuperable barrier always lies between the logic of deconstruction and historical materialism. Derrida himself singles out this radical heterogeneity in the book. He only reserves Marx's critical spirit and rejects the basic logic of historical materialism, which is the major reason why I categorize Derrida among the *post-Marxian trend*. And this trend cannot be deemed as being a part of something in Marxism.)[2]

Second, the book is also the result of a tangible "death", the "death of communism and Marxism" if put in the words of the clamorous Western bourgeoisie, that is, the collapse of the socialist camp of the Soviet Union and Eastern European countries. Amid the spreading laments and sighs, the West leftists again fell into a political depression. Derrida's *Specters of Marx* is a reflection of the publicly acclaimed *death*. Just when the Western bourgeoisie attempted to "bury" Marx and Marxism, Derrida went against the current of

---

[1] Derrida, Jacques, and Elisabeth Roudinesco. *For What Tomorrow: A Dialogue* (*Cultural Memory in the Present*). Stanford, California: Stanford University Press, 2004. p. 103.

[2] *See* my "Post-Marx Thought is not Marxism." in *Journal of Nanjing University*. 2003. Vol. 2.

the time by designing a special funeral.[1]

(This is the Funeral. Derrida puts down the word Funeral with a capital in the subtitle of this book.) In this lamentation for death, Derrida sees a real revival of Marxism in a divine sense. Like the death and resurrection of Jesus, the present physical disappearance is intended for the people to see eternal divinity. The tomb of the body becomes nothing while the Holy Spirit stays forever in our hearts. Accordingly, Derrida says that "[i]t consists always in attempting to ontologize remains, to make them present, in the first place by *identifying* the bodily remains and by *localizing* the dead."[2] This philosophical statement means that the Funeral is to ontologize the death per se: the dead thing in the eyes of the ordinary people will be present more really than ever! Derrida refers to Maurice Blanchot's *End of Philosophy* for explanation. Blanchot's logic is called by Derrida "the funeral discourse," in which spectral logic is also one of resurrection. To Blanchot, the death and end of philosophy rightly symbolizes its own "rebellion," a divine rebirth, instead of the continuation of the past living.

> Its very process consists of visibly heading the march at the moment of its "disappearance" and its "putting in the ground," it consists of leading its own funeral procession and of *raising* itself in the course of this march, of hoping at least to right itself again so as to stand up ("resurrection," "exaltation"). This wake, this joyous death watch of philosophy is the double moment of a "promotion" and of a "death of philosophy," a promotion in death.[3]

This very difficult philosophical account shows that Derrida perceives the "urgency and desire of revival" of Marx and his thoughts in the funeral

---

[1] "*Specters of Marx* is perhaps also, in fact, a book on melancholy *in politics*, on the politics of melancholy: politics and the work of mourning." Quoted from *For What Tomorrow: A Dialogue (Cultural Memory in the Present)*. Stanford, California: Stanford University Press, 2004. p. 78.

[2] Derrida, Jacques. *Specters of Marx: The State of the Debt, the Work of Mourning, and the New International*. Trans. Peggy Kamuf. New York: Routledge, 1994. p. 9.

[3] Ibid., p. 36.

for Marxism and communism. This is what the bourgeoisie and common European leftist thinkers cannot see. "Marx's burial, as the usual funeral, has a return under the pressure of the specter, that is, the wandering 'ghost.'"[1] Right in the place of Marx's death where people cheer or weep, Derrida discovers the very return of Marx.

Finally, there is a fundamental cause. Since the 1970s, Derrida became the center of attention of the so-called post-modern thought across Europe and America. After the 1980s, he was under severe criticism from the left academics who thought that his deconstruction theory lacked a clear political standing and was only an *accomplice* of ruling capitalism, because with the distraction of différance, dissemination and trace, people got lost about the conventional target of social critical theory, capitalism. Therefore, it was necessary for Derrida to make clear his attitude towards Marx; in a crucial ideological elucidation. In the eyes of the late Western Marxists, the radical revolt of post-modernism is without doubt the sinister conspirator of post-industrial capitalism.[2] Derrida must demonstrate his innocence. He needs to prove that, first of all, he does not belong to post-modernism and that he cannot forget the presence of Marx. (Derrida later says that "[s]o for a long time I was virtually reduced to silence, a silence that was also assumed, almost chosen."[3]) As a result, a profound logical relationship—the linkage between the theory of deconstruction and the traditional social critical spirit composes the narration of the text.

In my understanding, this is probably the main theoretical background for Derrida's writing of the *Specters of Marx*. In the same way, it is a dialogue with Death and the non-present Marx, or a logical association of Derrida and his theory of deconstruction with Marx, which leads to the most critical points here: the present and non-present *specter* and the *legacy* left by

---

[1] Derrida, Jacques. *Derrida's Speeches in China*. Central Compilation and Translation Press, 2003. p. 77.

[2] *See* my "What is the Late Marxism" in *Journal of Nanjing University*. 2004. vol. 5.

[3] Derrida, Jacques, and Elisabeth Roudinesco. *For What Tomorrow: A Dialogue (Cultural Memory in the Present)*. Stanford, California: Stanford University Press, 2004. p. 80.

the dead present. (I have noticed that some critics avoid such vital words as specter or legacy in their research of *Specters of Marx* but they are key terms posited by Derrida in the book. Their interpretation is bound to go astray.)

2. A memory politics of dancing with the specters

As for the relation of deconstruction and Marxism, especially, the issue of Marx in the context of deconstruction, Derrida offers a surprising description: the presence of the non-present specter. As we know, philosophers are usually not easy to understand. As a "post-modern" thinker, Derrida is even more puzzling. We hope to explicate the enigma of his.

At the very beginning, Derrida explains his unique perspective in a Hegelian tone. The first sentence is a simple and common aphorism: "*I would like to learn to live finally.*" (Derrida later said that the sentence occurred to him when the book was finished.) In fact, not everyone requests to learn to live their own life. In real life, it is often used by the elderly to discipline their misguided children. When one proposes it to himself "to learn to live alone from oneself and by oneself," it is no longer an authoritative coercion from outside but the *ethical* emphasis of value judgment. Here, ethics in Derrida's understanding is not the usual moral education, but a rather extreme and profound pathway towards categorical good. Derrida believes that one can learn to live neither by oneself nor from life itself because future life has not happened yet. Hence, "only from the other and by death" can one learn. It means that the living person has to learn from the dead *other*. ("The other", that is, the Other closely related to the existence of self in Lacan's sense.)[1] Derrida says alarmingly that it is a hetero-didactics between life and death. (In my understanding, there is the transformation of Heidegger's existential logic of Being towards death. Before his death, Derrida particularly explained that "[l]earning to live ought to mean learning to die— to acknowledge, to accept an absolute mortality—without positive out-come, or resurrection, or redemption for oneself or anyone else. That has been the

---

[1] *See* my "The Devil Other: Who Drives You Crazy" in *The Journal of Humanities*. 2004. vol. 5.

old philosophical injunction since Plato: to be a philosopher is to learn how to die."[1] Nevertheless, when writing *Specters of Marx*, Derrida is not simply following the last message of Plato by telling how to "learn to die." Instead, he tries to underscore the amazing and huge tension between life and death.)

It can happen only between life and death, neither in life nor in death *alone*. It is not to learn how to live from death but to learn "for what tomorrow" in life via the relationship of life and death. (*For What Tomorrow* is another book written by Derrida.) In Derrida's eyes, the relationship between life and death is about the *revenant* that haunts the living. In other words, it is the deceased soul that has not gone away. (Whether in the East or West, there are many stories about the ghosts or souls who would not leave due to an unfulfilled debt or wish, for example, the dead father in *Hamlet* or the many wronged ghosts in old Chinese tales. Thus, it can be said that Derrida's thinking originates in the non-secular.) If the soul never disappears, a special relationship of presence is hereby declared to exist. Derrida holds that such a relationship can only *maintain itself* with some ghost. The ontological "maintaining itself" is Derrida's "learning to live."

It is therefore necessary to have a better understanding of the soul. So it would be necessary to learn spirits. Even and especially if this, the spectral, *is not*. Even and especially if this, which is neither substance, nor essence, nor existence, *is never present as such*. The time of the "learning to live," a time without tutelary present, would amount to this, to which the exordium is leading us: to learn to live *with* ghosts.[2]

It is very difficult to illustrate the above statement in common sense. Judging from the context, Derrida seems to say that as the dead Other is closely related to us, it still leaves us with a soul other than the body, which is neither substance, nor essence, nor existence. In addition, to the secular world, the soul does not exit and "*is never present as such*." However, the

---

[1] Derrida, Jacques "I Am at War with Myself." *SV. Derrida* (*Special Issue*), 2004.

[2] Derrida, Jacques. *Specters of Marx*: *The State of the Debt, the Work of Mourning, and the New International*. Trans. Peggy Kamuf. New York: Routledge, 1994. p. xviii.

essence of learning to live is to live with the unsubstantial ghost, who, of course, is never actually present as a living ethical "tutelary." (To put it simply, if leaving the abstract theoretical field and entering our specific living situation, we shall find our ancestors and parents building and maintaining our initial value structure. They may leave us before we die, but they remain important in our hearts and will go on to be with us in our life. This non-present and present relationship is identified by Derrida here.) The flickering ghost is the *specter*, which is one of the key words in this book.

Furthermore, Derrida confirms that "[w]e cannot claim to do justice to a political reality without taking this virtual spectrality into account."[1] Consequently, co-existence with the non-present ghost leads to a *politics* of memory, of inheritance and of generation linked to Marx. Finally, Derrida begins to talk about left ethics and politics after a long time of avoiding direct contact with them. (In my opinion, Derrida shows his political stand here to answer the criticism by late Marxists, and ingenuity to speak in this historic moment when the dirge for the leftists is heard everywhere. Therefore, someone said to Derrida that "[y]ou have chosen a time to pay tribute to Marxism." It is the most appropriate time.)

It must be pointed out that the discussion extended from the memory, inheritance and generation of the ghost at the political and ethical stands is directed at the world's growing deficiency of *justice* since the 1990s. (Standing on the West land to discuss the non-present justice is undoubtedly a declaration of one's radical leftist position.) Notably, Derrida is very clear here; he does not hesitate to say that "[i]f I am getting ready to speak at length about ghosts, inheritance, and generations, generations of ghosts, which is to say about certain *others who* are not present, nor presently living, either to us, in us, or outside us, it is in the name of *justice*."[2] I find that the justice that bears obvious propensity of politics and value is not the old issue

---

[1]   Derrida, Jacques, and Elisabeth Roudinesco. *For What Tomorrow: A Dialogue (Cultural Memory in the Present)*. Stanford, California: Stanford University Press, 2004. p. 81.

[2]   Derrida, Jacques. *Specters of Marx: The State of the Debt, the Work of Mourning, and the New International*. Trans. Peggy Kamuf. New York: Routledge, 1994. p. xix.

under close attention by deconstruction, but the politics and ethics talked about by Derrida today. In his mind, justice is an existential responsibility, or a profound concern from the depths of our hearts when we hear people become the victims of wars, political or other kinds of violence, nationalist, racist, colonialist, sexist or other kinds of exterminations, victims of the oppressions of capitalist imperialism or any of the forms of totalitarianism. We all know this is the direct critical context of Marxism. However, Derrida does not want to speak of justice by Marx's discourse. He cleverly changes the logical relationship, the *indirect suspending hypothesis* of justice. (This logical conversion is also relevant to the "différance" of Marxism in Derrida's deconstruction, which we will approach later.) As a result, justice can only stem from the non-dasein ghost. (To this end, Derrida quotes Levinas' "the relation to others–that is to say, justice."[1] The others here refers to the dead but still influential ethical power, which is a questioning of value from the other's perspective) Derrida says that "[w]ithout this *non-contemporaneity with itself of the living present*, without that which secretly unhinges it, without this responsibility and this respect for justice concerning those who *are not there*, of those who are no longer or who are not yet *present and living* what sense would there be to ask the question 'where?' 'where tomorrow?' 'whither?'"[2] As a new leftist in the post-modern context, Derrida will not directly speak out about the future, like "where tomorrow?" It can only be inferred from something that is not present, that "secretly unhinges" "the living present." Here lies the meaning of the specter in Derrida's context. The specter in the form of the politics of memory makes us "exceed any presence as presence to itself." At the same time, when faced with the justice of capitalist slavery, it must carry beyond *present* life, life as *my life* or *our life*.

It is probably right. The specter is beyond us, *therefore beyond the living present in general* because it is already dead from the perspective

---

[1] Derrida, Jacques. *Specters of Marx: The State of the Debt, the Work of Mourning, and the New International*. Trans. Peggy Kamuf. New York: Routledge, 1994. p. 23.

[2] Ibid., p. xix. In his later years, Derrida put down his dialogue with Roudinesco into a book called *For What Tomorrow*. Derrida, Jacques, and Elisabeth Roudinesco. *For What Tomorrow: A Dialogue*. Stanford, California: Stanford University Press, 2004.

of life. Understandably, Derrida says that a spectral moment is a moment that no longer belongs to time. The appearance of the specter is neither in our space-time. (Derrida cites the famous line from *Hamlet* to describe the specter: "Enter the ghost, exist the ghost, re-enter the ghost." Slavoj Zizek says that "Jacques Derrida brought into play the term 'specter' in order to indicate this elusive pseudo-materiality that subverts the classic ontological oppositions of reality and illusion."[1]) Thus, we know Derrida's specter is not the brandishing wizard or ghost with bared fangs, but a particular academic reference, indicating the *value concern* for us by those seemingly dead or departed thoughts. In addition, Derrida's specter always assumes a just, fair and responsible look. It is, Derrida says, like Kant's supreme axiom, the "unconditional dignity that Kant placed higher, precisely [*justice*] than any economy, any compared or comparable value, any market price." (Derrida admits the great influence of Kant's theory of "ghost" on him. Kant's "should" in the form of moral imperative is indeed a relationship of debt. "'Should' is what for people must do, and the respect for 'debt.'"[2]) The justice in the high position rightly guides our life "for what will happen tomorrow" and leads the social existence to the place "where we should go tomorrow."

This justice carries life beyond present life or its actual being-there, its empirical or ontological actuality: not toward death but toward a *living-on* [sur-vie], namely, a trace of which life and death would themselves be but traces and traces of traces, a survival whose possibility in advance comes to disjoin or dis-adjust the identity to itself of the living present as well as of any effectivity.[3]

After all the meandering, Derrida turns to his pet tool, the theory of deconstruction. As to the "traces of traces", we will discuss this later. Now

---

[1] Zizek, Slavoj. *Mapping Ideology*. London; New York: Verso, 1994. p. 20.

[2] Derrida, Jacques. *Derrida's Speeches in China*. Central Compilation and Translation Press, 2003. p. 84.

[3] Derrida, Jacques. *Specters of Marx: The State of the Debt, the Work of Mourning, and the New International*. Trans. Peggy Kamuf. New York: Routledge, 1994. p. xx.

the most important point is, what on earth is this mystical ghost?

To our surprise, Derrida's ultimate answer is the spectral existence that can definitely break down the homogeneous coercion of the contemporary capitalist system as a spirit; or much more than a spirit, the dead but never-really-dead spirit of *Marx*. What an unexpected opening! In the 1990s, an impetuous time when the raucous shouts about the death of Marxism stirred the world, Derrida publicly called for the return of Marx's spirit to us with these words. His voice sounds in a profound tone: the revolutionary *legacy* left by Marx still fills every corner of this world; the specters are hovering and nobody can escape. Derrida hopes to relive the easily forgotten *memory* of politics, to re-*generate* the critical spirit of the time.

That difficult logical deduction of Derrida exhausts us but also excites us for he goes so far as to appeal to Marx in this era.

3. Marx and the interpretation of specters

Derrida says that "I analyze all the *phantoms*, and in particular the way in which Marx himself tried to chase (away) the phantom."[1] He says his discussion about the specters comes directly from Marx. (This reflex of basis differs from the post-Marx thought but resembles the traditional Marxist logic, which is a flaw from the general viewpoint of the text.)

In order to legitimize his own theory of the specter, Derrida explains from three different perspectives the existent phantoms in Marxist texts: Marx and Engels' *Communist Manifesto*, *German Ideology*, and Marx's *Das Kapital*. (I think this is among the few most important interpretations of Marxist texts left by Derrida.) The first part of the book describes Derrida being shocked in re-reading the *Communist Manifesto*, from whose famous "phantom" he starts his own interpretation. (Later, we shall approach the issue of the phantom of the *Communist Manifesto* in Derrida's eyes.) The analysis of *German Ideology* and *Das Kapital* is arranged in the latter part of

---

[1] Derrida, Jacques, and Elisabeth Roudinesco. *For What Tomorrow: A Dialogue (Cultural Memory in the Present)*. Stanford, California: Stanford University Press, 2004. p. 81.

the book. As for the part about the *Manifesto*, Derrida focuses on the critique of spiritual ghosts by Max Stirner and others; as to the *German Ideology and Das Kapital*, he converts Marx's theory of commodity fetishism to another conception of phantoms. Next, we are to examine Derrida's analysis of the "phantoms."

First of all, Derrida identifies a group of lingering phantoms in the German ideological circle from the *German Ideology*. Derrida observes that Marx's interpretation of phantom is built on *negativity*, which reveals a certain unconscious logical link between the ghost of the dead Hegel and the contemporary German circle. (Note that this is in exact opposition to the context of the specters in Derrida's book here.) Derrida says that the link of the play "often remains inaccessible, eclipsed in its turn in shadow, where it moves about and puts one off the trail."[1] Therefore, "the specter is *of the spirit*", to be specific, the spirit of the dead Hegel. In my opinion, Derrida's judgment is correct. According to him, the specter in Marx's eyes does not present itself through the realization of Hegel's absolute idea of "autonomization", but makes its "return" to a more abstract body "*in a space of invisible visibility*." For example, Stirner's "sole one," the absolute self seems to be against the Hegelian categorical concept, but it is through the appearance of this "megalomaniac" phantom that Hegel's specter descends lightly. Why? Because Stirner preaches the "sole one" (the ego), whose "real presence is promised here to a eucharistic Narcissus."[2] For Stirner, the Narcissus is a theoretical unconsciousness. It is clearly an insightful analysis.

Second, Derrida points out the specter of the capitalist commodity world in the form of the fetish from Marx's *Das Kapital*. (It should be noted that Marx does not directly mention such words as the "specter of commodity.") For Derrida, Marx's analysis of the "mystical character of the commodity, the mystification of the thing itself" already indicates a spectral identification. "The values of *value* (between use-value and exchange-value), *secret*,

---

[1] Derrida, Jacques. *Specters of Marx: The State of the Debt, the Work of Mourning, and the New International*. Trans. Peggy Kamuf. New York: Routledge, 1994. p. 125.

[2] Ibid., p. 133.

mystique, enigma, fetish, and the *ideological* form a chain" and the "*spectral* movement of this chain" carries itself through the commodities.[1] The reason why commodity is taken as the specter, Derrida admits, is that it has something beyond the ordinary *visible* materiality; in simple words, from "the body without body of this invisibility—the ghost is already taking shape." In Derrida's view, Marx starts from the common wooden table. When it is an item, it is a tangible thing. Once it becomes a commodity, the dramatic change takes place.

> This woody and headstrong denseness is metamorphosed into a supernatural thing, a *sensuous non-sensuous* thing, sensuous but non-sensuous, sensuously supersensible. The ghostly schema now appears indispensable. The commodity is a "thing" without phenomenon, a thing in flight that surpasses the senses.[2]

At this moment, the table as a commodity is no longer a material thing. It *transforms* into a specter "to present itself." Derrida holds that metamorphosis of commodities was already a process of transfiguring idealization that one may legitimately call spectropoetic. He rightly sees the transcendence of the invisible thing to the specter is not only the phantomalization of the commodity-form but the phantomalization of the social bond. (Marx interprets it as the social relationship between people reversed to the relationship between materials.) The actual social bonds (the relations of social labor) lose their nature and turn into specters, whose "proper" feature, "like vampires, is that they are deprived of a specular image."[3] The labor relation is covered and pressed back to an illusory material relation, while this commerce among things stems from the phantasmagoria. Without doubt, the real source of surplus value is magically erased because of this external illusion, which is exactly the secret of

---

[1] Derrida, Jacques. *Specters of Marx: The State of the Debt, the Work of Mourning, and the New International.* Trans. Peggy Kamuf. New York: Routledge, 1994. pp. 148-149.

[2] Ibid., p. 150.

[3] Ibid., pp. 155-156.

exploitation hidden behind the legitimacy of the capitalist production. Derrida says that "Marx had defined the residual product of labor as a phantomatic objectivity."[1] Obviously, the phantom here is completely different from the ghost in *German Ideology* mentioned by Derrida earlier.

I notice that the above descriptions of the specter in Marx's text are not logically associated with his own theory of the specter. They are just theoretical proofs of Marx's writing of specters. Derrida probably intends to say: Look, Marx is also concerned with the subject of specter in many texts at different times. However, Derrida's illustrational proofs stay rather in the peripheral. Thus, I do not think Derrida's reference of Marx's "specter theory" here can really support his own thought. As we know, even in *The Communist Manifesto*, communism in the form of the specter is an ironical illustration of the necessary presence as a gravedigger of capitalism, which is fundamentally different from what Derrida wants to identify with the nature of the specter. What is the historical origin of Derrida's own specter, then? We might as well carry on with the analysis.

4. Historical pedigree of Derrida's specter theory

Derrida's specter theory lies in the dense shadow of history. It is a recessive logical copy of multiple academic concepts. Derrida first introduces this subject with the "specter" in *The Communist Manifesto* by Marx and Engels, and then reiterates that his specter theory is connected with Shakespeare's *Hamlet*. It seems the ethical pull of the princess by the dead ghost of the king father drives his logic of revenge. (However, Derrida later says the specter theory here cannot be directly associated with *The Communist Manifesto* and *Hamlet*.[2]) In my opinion, deep in Derrida's thought there harbors several figures of the Other, mainly, his master compatriots.

First, Pascal-Goldman's *Hidden God* and the "wager theory." It is

---

[1] IDerrida, Jacques. *Specters of Marx: The State of the Debt, the Work of Mourning, and the New International*. Trans. Peggy Kamuf. New York: Routledge, 1994. p. 167.

[2] Derrida, Jacques. *Derrida's Speeches in China*. Central Compilation and Translation Press, 2003. p. 78.

well known that in the triumphant advance of industrial modernity after the Middle Ages, the theological thinker Pascal sees first through the helpless recession and silence of god on this new secular land, therefore, he appeals to those still with divinity in their hearts to wager on the hidden existence of an absent god. The important new logic of value hypothesis is developed later by the French Marxist Lucien Goldman, who states that in today's all-round victory of capitalism, the last hope of human liberation lies in their tenacious gambling on the Marxist and socialist *tomorrow*.

According to Pascal, although God silently secludes from the modern material world, he still watches people, who now do not fight for God but for the salvation of themselves, for the change of this world. Once giving up or yielding, people will lose the real possibility of saving and transforming their world. As long as people live, they must act and struggle, and the hidden God will be there with hope; to live, to have the opportunity, the last and only real possibility. Pascal thus says that we have no choice; *we must bet on the existence of God*; *we must bet on the existence of God's look*; *and we must bet on God's listening to our utterance*! Only in this way *can* we be saved; otherwise, we are forever sunk in the darkness. Here, wager on the existence of God does not mean complete reclusiveness; we have to learn to *co-exist with the devil*. In the above metaphor, the so-called devil refers to the silent material world in Pascal's writing. It is a tragedy to turn God, as well as the devil, into the silent spectators.[1] In today's bourgeois instrumental rationality and market kingdom, the previous evil has been legitimized into a cause, and materialistic desire is turned into a justified objective for people to pursue. The devil in Goethe's *Faust* matches *this evil not yet identified as evil*. For human beings, living in this material world is to sign a contract with God, who does not speak but gently watches and expects us to win the victory over the devil and reach the City of God. (Derrida himself once directly mentions this "invisible god."[2])

---

[1] Goldman, Lucien. *Hidden God*. [S.l.]: Taylor & Francis, Inc, 1981.

[2] Derrida, Jacques. *Specters of Marx: The State of the Debt, the Work of Mourning, and the New International*. Trans. Peggy Kamuf. New York: Routledge, 1994. p. 42.

In fact, it is also Goldman's basic positioning of the alleged "tragic man" in capitalism. The mid-1950s saw the international communist movement fall into a miserable "depression", and the 20th Congress of the CPSU generated a great division that caused the whole European left camp and Marxism to suffer from a theoretical schizophrenia. All of a sudden, the entire bourgeois world celebrated the "end of ideology" and the death of communism. And the gate to complete liberation of mankind opened by Marx 100 years ago seemed closed in an instant. A large number of European leftists fell into the abysm of despair, while many socialist enthusiasts abruptly turned to the right. This is the important historical context of Goldman's *Hidden God*. Against this background, Goldman attempts to solve the real problem, which, clearly, is not the theme or creation method of a certain literary work, but the predicament of human survival and liberation in the social historical condition of contemporary capitalism. Goldman simply wants to find a way of self-salvation in the contemporary capitalist reality through his research of Pascal, Racine and so on. In other words, Goldman does not really focus on the existence of God as Pascal does. What he wants is *the wager on the existence of Marxist and socialist hope*; neither giving up material interests nor abandoning the fight, especially, the struggling for a beautiful "tomorrow." This is the real foundation for his gambling on the theoretical logic, as well as the tragic reality of the international communist movement.

I think Derrida renders Goldman's hidden God into an absent specter, with which the helpless coexistence with the devil is turned to the joy of dancing with the specter. As a result, the specter becomes the value hypothesis that introduces the absence of real existence.

Second, the absence of Lacan's Real specter. Lacan's Real with a capital refers to *the relational existence of the impossible presence* shown after man's existence is killed by the symbolic signs. His Real is not the actual congruity of the cognition of external objects as in traditional epistemology, but an ontological stipulation, or a non-pseudo, non-false truth in personal ontology. This Real is somewhat similar to Kant's thing-in-itself. Another important view of Lacan is that *the Real with a capital means the "realistic" presence of the specter*, whose significance lies in its construction of presence by absence. In a certain sense, there is no reality without the specter. Man looks forward to "something" *impossible* that is always on the other side of reality. Here, "something" is Kant's epistemological thing-in-itself but logically transformed by Lacan's negative ontology. Interestingly, Lacan directly specifies "something" as the *Thing with a capital*. In his eyes, the Real Thing can only be confirmed through a traumatic demonstration of objet petit a (object a), which is *sent away in advance* and preset beyond this kingdom, but never realized here. However, as the metonymic object of desire, it is at the same time *the real cause for the formation of desire* and *the homesickness* brought by self-construction and subject/existence that are ontologically wanted and eliminated forever. The object little-a is an *impossible* thing with *disappearance as nature* in the ontology of human existence, which denies possibility for the subject/existence and for the *object of real desire*, as well as *the cause of desire*. This impossibility is nevertheless the real being of man.[1] (Perhaps coincidentally, Lacan wrote an essay analyzing *Hamlet* with the desire of the Other in his later years.)

I think this being-present of the impossible presence reflects the essence of Derrida's specter. (But there is a debate about who says this first and influences the other between Lacan and Derrida.)

Third, the face of the Other by Levinas. For Levinas, people only see themselves via the *face* of the Other. "Face" is a very important word in the philosophy of Levinas, who believes it is a phenomenological term. As a metaphor, it does not allude to the face of a specific person. Levinas says that the thing "which Plato posits as the soul contemplating the Ideas, that which Spinoza thinks as a mode of thought, is described phenomenologically as a *face*."[2] He suggests that face symbolizes a non-physical, non-substantial soul

---

[1] *See* Chapter X in my *Impossible Truth of Being: Mirror of Lacan's Philosophy*. Commercial Press, 2005.

[2] Levinas, Emmanuel. *God, Death, and Time*. Trans. Bettina Bergo. Stanford, California: Stanford University Press, 2000. p. 12. The following discussion of Levinas is mostly drawn from *God, Death and Time*, which consists of the transcripts from his lecture courses at the Sorbonne in 1975-1976.

in man's existence, which is occasionally called "expression." To someone who dies a face becomes a masque. The expression disappears. Levinas also discusses the Other through face, or, his Other is only present in the face. Face here is not used in its physical sense. It does not appear directly. However, it "imposes on me" its requirement. Face, as the Other, possesses a "non-violent" force, spreading a silent but meaningful and pervasive look, readily responsive to my answer at any time. Face denotes the *faceless* Other(s); more importantly, the epiphany of the face is the comprehensive language. Therefore, even if in silence, face is speaking.

Levinas makes another wonderful statement: "The human *esse* is not primordially *conatus* but hostage, a hostage of the other."[1] In his view, this ontological hostage relationship is even "generated earlier than self." In fact, Levinas' hostage relationship is the responsibility of autre for the other, which constructs the ethical nature of human beings. "The man who is hostage to all others is needed by men, for without him morality would have no place to start."[2] Man is constructed during the "irresistible summon of responsibility." "Someone who expresses himself in his nudity—the face—is one to the point of appealing to me, of placing himself under my responsibility: henceforth, I have to respond for him. All the gestures of the other were signs addressed to me."[3] It can be seen that the autre, which previously identifies itself via the other self-consciousness in Hegel, is now a self-reference accomplished through relations of responsibility. "The 'me' [*moi*] only surfaces in its uniqueness in responding for the other in a responsibility from which there is no flight, in a responsibility from which I could not be free."[4]

In my understanding, Levinas' other is an absent requirement of

[1] Levinas, Emmanuel. *God, Death, and Time*. Trans. Bettina Bergo. Stanford, California: Stanford University Press, 2000. p. 21.

[2] Levinas, Emmanuel. *Nine Talmudic Readings*. Trans. Annette Aronowicz. Bloomington: Indiana University Press, 1994. p. 87

[3] Levinas, Emmanuel. *God, Death, and Time*. Trans. Bettina Bergo. Stanford, California: Stanford University Press, 2000. p. 12.

[4] Ibid., p. 20.

relational ethics. The Other in the appearance of a debtor also reflects the tension of value for the existence of Derrida's specter.

From the above illustration of several philosophical thinkers, I believe it is not difficult for the reader to find out certain traces of the specter discourse in Derrida's book. Once the important context is clear, we shall come to Derrida's specter theory next.

II. Theoretical Logic of Derrida's Specter Theory

The specter theory is the focus of Derrida's *Specters of Marx*. At the same time, it is a sort of politically inclined critical ethics based on the logical platform of his deconstruction. However, this moral tension does not derive from an objective target in reality; it is a value hypothesis premised on an indirect real existence, that is, some kind of ideal impossibility generally accepted by the post-Marx thought. In this book, Derrida makes use of the logic of specter to maintain Marxism, which has lost its realistic foundation in capitalist globalization, in particular, the critical dimension of the capitalist system introduced by Marxism.

1. Deconstruction and the impossible specter

Derrida claims that he has studied the word "specter" for a long time. (According to Takahashi Tetsuya, since Derrida's publication of "Plato's Pharmacy," he uses the word "specter" several times to illustrate the impossible.[1] The research of the impossible is an issue closely followed and deeply discussed by both Bataille and Lacan.) As to specter, Derrida certainly has his unique understanding.

First, Derrida holds that the stipulation of spectrality possesses the meaning of value and deconstruction, precisely because the feature of being specter is neither life nor death, neither presence nor absence, neither true nor false. It is a very important theoretical positioning. He makes it clear that:

---

[1] Takahashi Tetsuya. *Derrida*: *Deconstruction*. Trans. Zhao Hanying: Hebei Educational Publishing House, 2001. p. 223.

First of all, this book is a reflection of the conception of spectrality, a long-term concern of mine. Such thought can be found in my early research. A specter is not just a soul or ghost who untimely turns back and summons us to inherit the legacy. It is neither life nor death, neither true nor false; it re-introduces the ghost dimension to politics and helps us understand the current public space, media, exchange and other structures. This is one of my major motives in writing this book. The conception of spectality dots the text, therefore, it is a mainline of this book.[1]

Derrida's conception of specter is indeed established on the platform of deconstruction. The presence and absence of the specter is the prerequisite in the deconstructionist context. As we know, the core of Derrida's theory means the deconstruction of the solidificated system and the actually existing false, in which the ontological "différance," "dissemination" and "trace" all indicate the illegitimate presence of the center. However, deconstruction is a functional construction with a dialectic negation instead of a nihilistic denial. Thus, différance is the coming of the absent, which perfectly matches Derrida's proposition of "being present or non-present," "neither life nor death" and "neither true nor false." (Imre Szeman thinks that Derrida's specter might be the highest image of deconstruction. The specter, in some way, exists outside ontology. It is an impossible possibility, shaking all the closure that ontology pursues. The image of the specter is absent, invisible, but always there, hovering above the noumenon, the invisible visibility.[2]) Accordingly, the key to Derrida's concept of specter is between "the present and absent," "visible and invisible," "possible and impossible," and "life and death." It also needs to be noted that Derrida's specter of deconstruction here is not simply an academic argument. His major purpose is to re-introduce with his effort the ghost dimension to politics. Derrida calls for the presence of Marx as the absent specter. He aims for a new criticism of the

---

[1] Derrida, Jacques. "Dialogue about Marxism." It is translated from Chinese.

[2] Imre Szeman "Ghostly Matters: On Derrida's Specters." *Rethinking Marxism* 12.2 (2000): 104-116.

comprehensive victory of the capital in world history.

Second, Derrida says that he is intentionally connecting the "spectrality" here with the conception of the descending messiah.[1] (Of course, it essentially differs from the word "God" in *The Internationale*.) This connection is mysterious because Derrida's descending messiah is set in this way: any existence, any experience is structuralized by the Other as an unpredictable arrival of reference. Without this tendency, the tendency towards the tension of the unpredictable arrival of the Other, there is no experience to speak of in time and space.[2] In Derrida's writing, the descending messiah is represented by the arrival of the Other in an event, in his words, "descendization." At the same time, Derrida's conception of the Other is actually a certain Other in the divine context, similar to Pascal-Goldman's "hidden god." Therefore, this Other may descend or may not come. He can save, or he cannot save. (Here, we see several figures of the previously mentioned thinkers.) This "descendization" of the specter as the Other inevitably displays a new *divinity*.

Third, visibility and invisibility of Derrida's specters. We can recognize that Derrida's specter is neither the icon and idol of the theological context nor the illusion in Plato's epistemological sense, because it is indeed the *having-been of the dead*. (Marx was once alive but he is dead now.) "Nor does one see in flesh and blood this Thing that is not a thing."[3]

> It *is* something that one does not know, precisely, and one does not know if precisely it *is*, if it exists, if it responds to a name and corresponds to an essence. One does not know: not out of ignorance, but because this non-object, this non-present present, this being-there of an absent or departed one no longer belongs to knowledge. At least no longer to that which one thinks one knows by the name of knowledge.

---

[1] Derrida, Jacques. *Derrida's Speeches in China*. Central Compilation and Translation Press. 2003. p. 78.

[2] Ibid., p. 79.

[3] After Lenin and Mao Zedong died, their remains were preserved. Derrida's specter does not mean the visible body but the immortal spirit of Marx.

One does not know if it is living or if it is dead.[1]

It is a thing that man cannot see. "This Thing meanwhile looks at us and sees us, while we do not see it even when it is there."[2] (It reminds me of the young Lukacs' God who silently watches us.) In the eyes of Derrida, "a specter is always a *revenant*." Nevertheless, not every dead ghost becomes a specter; only those who haunt the living through memorial and spiritual legacies can transform into specters. Haunting is an ethical association. The specter appears as *the invisible emotional reliance and value support*, therefore, it is always the revenant that was and is associated with our existence. Thus, we living are able to feel that some other's specter constantly watches us, like Hamlet's ghost-father does.

> This spectral *someone other looks at us*, we feel ourselves being looked at by it, outside of any synchrony, even before and beyond any look on our part, according to an absolute anteriority (which may be on the order of generation, of more than one generation) and asymmetry, according to an absolutely unmasterable disproportion.[3]

The Other forever watches us with this asymmetric look. We cannot see it, which does not block its eternal look at us beyond time and space. This is the Other *face* of the specter. Derrida adds that, as to this specter, "one cannot control its comings and goings because it *begins by coming back*."[4]

> Ghost or *revenant*, sensuous-non-sensuous, visible-invisible, the specter first of all sees *us*. From the other side of the eye, *visor effect*, it looks at us even before we see *it* or even before we see period.[5]

The absent Other silently watches us. It is not a simple "look", but *an*

---

[1] Derrida, Jacques. *Specters of Marx: The State of the Debt, the Work of Mourning, and the New International*. Trans. Peggy Kamuf. New York: Routledge, 1994. p. 6.

[2] Ibid., p. 6.

[3] Ibid., p. 7.

[4] Ibid., p. 11.

[5] Ibid., p. 101.

ontological look, from which the Other "makes the law" and "delivers the injunction."(Lacan would express it in an entirely negative statement.) In addition, the most important function of the specter is *questioning the real existence*. Derrida says that "if there is something like spectrality, there are reasons to doubt this reassuring order of presents, and especially the border between the present, the actual or present reality of the present."[1] As a result, Derrida's specter also plays the role of a radical scale for people to reflect on existent things. Our existence is nothing but the response from the spectral Other. Of course, such a response is not directly made. For Zizek, Derrida's view means that "[o]ur debt towards the Other can never be repaid; our response to the Other's call is never fully adequate."[2]

In the context of reality, Derrida stipulates the contemporary meaning of the specter:

> Today, the concept of "spectrality" seems to be interpreted as something such as technology, means of exchange and transformation, like television, network, telephone, mobile phone and so on, which is subject to physical space and geotropic space, and necessary to analyze these technologies and their development in our time. The "specter" indicates something neither real nor imaginary, neither living nor dead. He makes a technical image of spreading and imprinting.[3]

This is an associative illustration of the real situation of the specter theory: our immediate environment is being spectralized. Here, Derrida drops from the metaphysical level to the under-metaphysical material reality.

We find that it is in this complex environment that Derrida puts forward the conception of "the specter of Marx." In contrast to the overall victory of contemporary capitalism, Marx and Marxism lose the critical presence of the

---

[1] Derrida, Jacques. *Specters of Marx: The State of the Debt, the Work of Mourning, and the New International*. Trans. Peggy Kamuf. New York: Routledge, 1994. p. 39.

[2] Zizek, Slavoj. *Did Somebody Say Totalitarianism?: Five Interventions in the (Mis)Use of a Notion*. Wo Es War. London; New York: Verso, 2002. p. 155.

[3] Derrida, Jacques. *Derrida's Speeches in China*. Central Compilation and Translation Press. 2003. p. 78.

real being. But this impossibility in reality also makes it even nobler, so that it becomes a righteous tension in the field of reality. Therefore, the failure itself obtains spectral significance. Marx's specter finally resurrects and returns from death.

Now, Derrida is to speak of Marx's specters. "At a time when a new world disorder is attempting to install its neo-capitalism and neo-liberalism, no disavowal has managed to rid itself of all of Marx's ghosts."[1] On the other hand, as a student of the Western Marxist Althusser, Derrida has deconstruction theory deeply linked with the critical spirit of Marxist historical dialectics. In comparison, Derrida already converts Marx's direct presence in Althusser's philosophy into the indirect presence of a logical specter. Probably, this indebtedness is deeply buried in the argumentative words. However, when the current home of his teacher's thought and the spiritual temple of the logic of deconstruction face destruction, Derrida thinks it is time to stand out and pay the debt, the debt of the theoretical legacy of Marx the Other.

"At bottom, the specter is the future, it is always to come."[2]

2. Speaking for Marx's specters

"Maintaining now the specters of Marx" is the opening remark of Derrida's *Specters of Marx*.[3] The so-called "now" refers to April, 1993[4], when it was less than a year away from the collapse of the former Soviet Union. Derrida once explains that this book was written after the profound historic changes in the former Soviet Union, Eastern Europe, as well as China. (As we know, the "profound historic changes" here indicate the crisis

---

[1]. Derrida, Jacques. *Specters of Marx: The State of the Debt, the Work of Mourning, and the New International.* Trans. Peggy Kamuf. New York: Routledge, 1994. p. 37.

[2] Ibid., p. 39.

[3] Ibid., p. 3.

[4] In April 1993, the Center for Ideas and Society at the University of California-Riverside held a convention of "Whither Marxism? Global Crises in International Perspective." Derrida was invited to attend and make two speeches with the titles of "Specters of Marx, the state of the debt, the Work of Mourning, & the New International, on which his book, *Specters of Marx*, was based.

that the international communist movement is suffering.) Derrida admits the important conclusion of *Specters of Marx* means for him that Marx's end and death as well as the end of Marxism, Leninism and communism should re-interpret the conclusion of the historic event at that time, particularly in the West.[1]) This is correct. Derrida says that "[he] tried to draw a few consequences from this within the geopolitical situation that followed the upheaval referred to as the collapse of the Soviet model of communism."[2]

In other words, from the declaration of the specter of communism haunting Europe by Marx and Engels in 1848 to the "October Revolution" in 1917, this specter is held high "in the name of Marx" in Russia, as a metamorphosed historical presence of reality. However, it exits again 80 years later. (This time, communism turns from the inevitable, inextricable specter into an absent one in Derrida's eyes.) Derrida is aware that today the whole world is talking about the end of Marxism and Fukuyama's eschatological "end of history."[3]

> It proclaims: Marx is dead, communism is dead, very dead, and along with it its hopes, its discourse, its theories, and its practices. It says long lives capitalism, long live the market, here's to the survival of economic and political liberation.[4]

---

[1] Derrida, Jacques. *Derrida's Speeches in China*. Central Compilation and Translation Press. 2003. p. 76.

[2] Derrida, Jacques, and Elisabeth Roudinesco. *For What Tomorrow: A Dialogue (Cultural Memory in the Present)*. Stanford, California: Stanford University Press, 2004. pp. 78-79.

[3] Francis Fukuyama (1952-), consultant in the Rand Corporation and professor at the School of Advanced International Studies of the John Hopkins University. His major works include *The End of History and the Last Man* (1992), *Trust: The Social Virtues and the Creation of Prosperity* (1995), *The Great Disruption: Human Nature and the Reconstitution of Social Order* (1998). In June 2004, due to the second-term cooperation program of the John Hopkins University-Nanjing University Center for Chinese and American Studies, I led a delegation to visit the United States. One of the major experts in the US delegation was Professor Francis Fukuyama. If chance permitted, I would have had a deep discussion with him about his academic views. However, I still believed him to be a serious scholar.

[4] Derrida, Jacques. *Specters of Marx: The State of the Debt, the Work of Mourning, and the New International*. Trans. Peggy Kamuf. New York: Routledge, 1994. p. 52.

According to Derrida, this conclusion is not a fashion which occurred only recently. "A certain end of communist Marxism did not await the recent collapse of the USSR and everything that depends on it throughout the world."[1] All that begins as early as the 1950s and has been continuing for nearly 40 years. (My analysis of Goldman's wager theory above is actually an earlier theoretical response to this argument.) This time, however, it is not present as a real being. Derrida concludes that, because of this absent reality, the now becomes out of joint, "a disadjusted now", therefore, it "risks maintaining nothing together." The so-called "disadjusted now" indicates that Lenin's October Revolution associates Marxist theory with the reality of the proletariat in Russia, which broke up in 1992. As a result, socialism in reality, like Marx, has become a "nothing", while Derrida attempts to maintain these non-existent things, which are but the specters of Marx. This time, he is again evoking the re-presence of Marx as *hidden* specters.

Here, Derrida does not restrict his maintenance of Marx to the former Soviet socialism or Eastern European Marxism. Instead, he covers all the possible existing Marxist discourses. Thus, a unique plural form is used: the specters of Marx. Derrida's deconstruction context has "more than one" specters of Marx. After the exit of the real being of communism, they become "the *less than one* of pure and simple dispersion" in the bourgeoisie-dominated world. Whatever their names are, "the specter is always animated by a spirit," which is "a spirit of Marx, or more serious still, of a spirit of Marxism."[2] Derrida clearly understands that the specters of Marx cannot be contained in a homogeneous entity, and instead, they utter several heterogeneous voices from one Matrix. If interpreted in the standard discourse of deconstruction, it is called dissemination of Marx's spiritual debris in différance.

Derrida says he had not read Marx and Engels' *Communist Manifesto* for more than a decade before he picked it up again. (He made this statement

---

[1] Derrida, Jacques. *Specters of Marx: The State of the Debt, the Work of Mourning, and the New International*. Trans. Peggy Kamuf. New York: Routledge, 1994. p. 14.

[2] Ibid., pp. 3-4.

at a conference. Shortly before he finished this book, Derrida also studied Marx's *German Ideology* and *Das Kapital*.) He says in a regretful tone that the personal and thorough overlook of such a striking a thing in *The Communist Manifesto* is certainly a mistake. The thing he identifies in the text is nothing else but the specter. Nevertheless, this is not the same specter besieged by the Holy Alliance in the ironical context of Marx and Engels. In Derrida's eyes, it is the specter as a revenant that watches the contemporary world. There is an important semantic conversion. Derrida points out that it looks like "a hallucination or simulacrum", but it "is virtually more actual than what is so blithely called a living presence."[1] (It sounds like Lacan's discourse.) Derrida means that today's Marxism or communism again becomes a phantom of non-reality, but it is more real and important than the reified Marxism of the Soviet socialist mode.

In Derrida's eyes, the lesson drawn by Marx and Engels 150 years ago "seems more urgent *today*." Why?

> Because no text in the tradition seems as lucid concerning the way in which the political is becoming worldwide, concerning the irreducibility of the technical and media in the current of the most thinking thought—and this goes beyond the railroad and the newspapers of the time whose powers were analyzed in such an incomparable way in the *Manifesto*. And few texts have shed so much light on law, international law, and nationalism.[2]

Derrida sternly warns that if we do not repeatedly read and discuss Marx today, it will forever be a mistake, a more and more serious mistake, a theoretically and politically responsible mistake. In his view, we have no reason not to take Marx seriously, particularly at this moment when dogmatism and official ideology are both dead in the former Soviet Union and East European socialist countries. After re-reading *The Communist*

---

[1] Derrida, Jacques. *Specters of Marx: The State of the Debt, the Work of Mourning, and the New International*. Trans. Peggy Kamuf. New York: Routledge, 1994. p. 13.

[2] Ibid., p. 13.

Manifesto and several other great works by Marx, Derrida profoundly perceives the necessity of Marx.

> Not without Marx, no future without Marx, without the memory and the inheritance of Marx: in any case of a certain Marx, of his genius, of at least one of his spirits. For this will be our hypothesis or rather our bias: *there is more than one of them, there must be more than one of them.*[1]

It is a classic statement of Derrida. "Not without Marx" becomes a resonant slogan. (However, we will soon know that the expected Marx is no longer the dogmatic Marxism of the former Soviet Union and Eastern European countries; it is a non-substantial, non-ontological critical spirit of Marx.) Obviously, "[o]ne need not be a Marxist or a communist in order to accept this obvious fact. We all live in a world, some would say a culture that still bears, at an incalculable depth, the mark of this inheritance, whether in a directly visible fashion or not."[2] It implies that the specters of Marx, visible or invisible, are embedded in all the cultural existences of human beings. (Then, he lays the issue that we are all inheritors to Marx's legacy.)

More importantly, Derrida criticizes the tendency to "depoliticize profoundly the *Marxist reference*." He says that there appears a trend to welcome the *return* of Marx "by putting on a tolerant face to neutralize a potential force" of Marxism and by silencing the revolt in it.

> Now that Marx is dead, and especially now that Marxism seems to be in rapid decomposition, some people seem to say, we are going to be able to concern ourselves with Marx without being bothered—by the Marxists and, why not, by Marx himself, that is, by a ghost that goes on speaking. We'll treat him calmly, objectively, without bias: according to the academic rules, in the University, in the library, in colloquial. We'll do it systematically, by respecting the norms of hermeneutical,

---

[1] Derrida, Jacques. *Specters of Marx: The State of the Debt, the Work of Mourning, and the New International*. Trans. Peggy Kamuf. New York: Routledge, 1994. p. 13.

[2] Ibid., p. 14.

philological, philosophical exegesis.[1]

Derrida believes that this is the neutralized numbness of a new theoreticism, whose purpose is to bury Marxism. In contrast, Derrida really hopes to "return to Marx." His position is radically different from the above "fashionable" view.

> I do not like the idea of a return to the great classic philosopher Marx and accredit his philosophy to the monumental philosophical tradition. If the study of Marx is always necessary in the university, there is correspondingly the danger of taming, neutralizing the revolutionary commands of Marx. I think we should object to such neutralization.[2]

Derrida assumes an unequivocal priority of "political posturing" with which he wants to activate *the whole political and ethical* part in the spirit of Marx. He refuses to inherit some neutralized, academicalized and numb nondescript from Marx's thought. On the contrary, he will make sharp weapons out of the specters of Marx for the resistance of globalized capitalism.

Do not think that Derrida is to simply return to our traditional understanding of Marxism. His interpretation of Marxism must have an intermediary. He frankly admits that combination of his work with all the Marxist texts and conceptions cannot be "immediately given"[3] because "Marx's works are equally metaphysical" according to his logic of deconstruction.[4] Derrida uses his deconstruction to construe Marx, who can only be present in différance. Therefore, in my view, Derrida cannot be called a Marxist, or he does not really accept Marxism. His slogan even differs from

---

[1] Derrida, Jacques. *Specters of Marx: The State of the Debt, the Work of Mourning, and the New International*. Trans. Peggy Kamuf. New York: Routledge, 1994. p. 32.

[2] Derrida, Jacques. "Dialogue about Marxism." It is translated from Chinese.

[3] Derrida, Jacques. *Positions*. Trans. Alan Bass. London: Continuum Publishing Group, 2004.

[4] Derrida, Jacques, and George Collins. *The Politics of Friendship*. Phronesis. London [u.a.]: Verso, 2005. p. 247.

the Western Marxist Jean Sartre after the 1950s.

III. Marx in Différance: The Deconstructed Spiritual Legacy

As I mentioned before, the year 1993 is a special historic moment, when Derrida stands out to maintain the specters of Marx, demonstrating his commendable academic courage. In such a moment, he sees through the political and ethical look of the Other from Marx's absence, from which he reminds those forgetful people: we are all heirs to Marx's theoretical legacies. Derrida says that *Specters of Marx* is to illustrate the question of the inheritance to Marxism after the collapse of the Soviet Union and the reform of China.[1] However, in the logic of Derrida's deconstruction, the specters of Marx as a spiritual legacy are not just ready-made and real options, not even the so-called "dialectical abrogation." In his eyes, Marx's spiritual legacy can only be obtained in the sense of différance and trace after deconstruction. This standpoint is clearly opposite to Marxist views.

1. We are all heirs to Marx.

Derrida says that "all men and women, all over the earth, are today to a certain extent the heirs of Marx and Marxism."[2] This is a momentous statement. When the bourgeoisie around the world are burying Marxism, Derrida stands out, declaring that every person on this planet intentionally or unintentionally inherits Marx's legacy. It is really a deafening declaration, which significantly reveals the value of Marxism and undoubtedly requires people to inherit Marx's legacy, despite the fact that Marx and Marxism are kept reclusive and silent. Marx is dead. He leaves us no choice but to inherit the legacy.

---

[1] Derrida, Jacques. *Derrida's Speeches in China*. Central Compilation and Translation Press. 2003. p. 77.

[2] Derrida, Jacques. *Specters of Marx*: *The State of the Debt, the Work of Mourning, and the New International*. Trans. Peggy Kamuf. New York: Routledge, 1994. p. 91

For Derrida, this does not mean to rigidly, indiscriminately accept Marxism. According to the principle of deconstruction, the best way to be faithful to a heritage is to be unfaithful, that is, not to accept it literally, as a totality, but rather to take it as something in default, to grasp its "dogmatic moment."[1] The way to be faithful is to be unfaithful, which is a deconstructionist historical association. Thus, when facing the dead Marx, people *must accept* the Marxist *legacy*, accept its most "vital" part. (He does not state what the most "vital" part is.) Probably in this sense, Derrida believes that "a legacy is always a debt." In other words, "the spirits inscribed in historical memory under the proper names of Marx and Marxism" will become "an ineffaceable and insoluble debt" for everyone of us.[2] (According to Derrida, it is also why "the state of the debt" is put into the subtitle. Behind this debt, we see the subjective figures of the hostages and Levinas' Other as the debtor.) This is the original debt of all people living in this capitalist world, in the ontological sense.

In Derrida's view, "inheritance is never a *given*, it is always a task." This task can be explained as the divine historical drive, like the pervasive and silent "God's look."

> Just as unquestionably as we are heirs of Marxism, even before wanting or refusing to be, and, like all inheritors, we are in *mourning*. In morning in particular for what is called Marxism.[3]

Derrida firmly believes that we are *Being* Marx's successors. "Like my contemporaries, I am not a communist party member, but it is natural for me to be nurtured with Marxism, in addition, I try to choose an untimely opportunity to speak it out."[4] (In my opinion, these remarks of his are

---

[1] Derrida, Jacques, and Elisabeth Roudinesco. *For What Tomorrow: A Dialogue (Cultural Memory in the Present)*. Stanford, California: Stanford University Press, 2004. p. 2

[2] Derrida, Jacques. *Specters of Marx: The State of the Debt, the Work of Mourning, and the New International*. Trans. Peggy Kamuf. New York: Routledge, 1994. p. 92.

[3] Ibid., p. 54.

[4] Derrida, Jacques. "Dialogue about Marxism." It is translated from Chinese.

not "untimely" at all. In a special moment of disjunction, Derrida makes a wonderful speech.) It does not mean we are to capture some Marx's concepts or ready-made conclusions. Instead, we see the immortal spirit of Marx in this ontological "Being." If Marx's spirits still exist, they exist in us.

> That we *are* heirs does not mean that we *have* or that we *receive* this or that, some inheritance that enriches us one day with this or that, but that the *being* of what we are *is* first of all inheritance, whether we like it or know it or not.[1]

Derrida says he upholds Friedrich Holderlin's view that "we can only *bear witness* to it." The purported legacy is not a *material ready-made presence*, but instead a meaningful given of the specter of non-presence. Therefore, Marx's legacy is not something readily present-at-hand. It has a constantly generated heterogeneity, which amounts to a deconstructionist existence, ontologically produced by difference. For Derrida, "an inheritance is never gathered together, it is never one with itself because if the readability of a legacy were given, natural, transparent, univocal, if it did not call for and at the same time defy interpretation, we would never have anything to inherit from it."[2] (According to this standard, there is no real legacy of Marxism in the actual being of the Stalinist dogmatic framework.) Derrida's consideration of the spiritual legacy definitely differs from that of natural or biological heredity; the consistency is entirely based on assumption; for example, inheritance of Marx's legacy is a sort of heterogeneous dissemination, in which we do not need his permission. From Marx, we may "inherit this or that, this rather than that which comes to us nevertheless by him, through him if not from him."[3] Be sure to note that Derrida does not refer to Marx and Marxism themselves, but indicates that those come to us "through him." (His discussion here embarks on a different direction, drawn by the shrewd

---

[1] Derrida, Jacques. *Specters of Marx: The State of the Debt, the Work of Mourning, and the New International*. Trans. Peggy Kamuf. New York: Routledge, 1994. p. 54.

[2] Ibid., p. 16.

[3] Ibid., p. 34.

deconstruction logic.) Thus, as spiritual inheritors, "we are of *more than one* form of speech, as well as of an injunction that is itself *disjointed*," that is, they are the "very plural of what we will later call Marx's spirits."[1] (It sounds as if he is against an exclusive hermeneutics of Marxism.)

Then, what on earth is the legacy of Marx which Derrida wants us to inherit? The answer is the "critical *spirit* of Marxism." Moreover, such a critical spirit is the marrow of all of Marx's legacy. According to Derrida,

> to continue to take inspiration from a certain spirit of Marxism would be to keep faith with what has always made of Marxism in principle and first of all a *radical* critique, namely a procedure ready to undertake its self-critique. This critique *wants itself* to be in principle and explicitly open to its own transformation, re-evaluation, self-reinterpretation.[2]

Eventually, we get an insight of it. The common legacy of Marx asserted by Derrida for us all is not the theoretical science of Marxism but the "critical spirit" mediated by the logic of deconstruction.

Derrida says it is "to distinguish this *spirit* of the Marxist critique from Marxism as ontology, philosophical or metaphysical system, as 'dialectical materialism,' from Marxism as historical materialism or method, and from Marxism incorporated in the apparatuses of party, State, or the workers' International."[3] Derrida rejects the ontological "dialectical materialism" as systematic philosophy, as well as the methodologically generated "historical materialism." These forms of Marxism are called by him the mistake of the "ontological response," or the "rigid dogma of Marxism" and the "politicized discourse of Marxism in the 20th century."[4] (We shall return to this point later.) To Derrida, the root cause of this mistake is that they "rivet it to

---

[1] Derrida, Jacques. *Specters of Marx: The State of the Debt, the Work of Mourning, and the New International*. Trans. Peggy Kamuf. New York: Routledge, 1994. p. 16.

[2] Ibid., p. 88.

[3] Ibid., p. 68.

[4] Derrida, Jacques. "Interview" in *Writing and Difference* (Chinese version). Beijing Joint Publishing, 2001. p. 19.

the body of Marxist doctrine, to its supposed systemic, metaphysical, or ontological totality (notably to its 'dialectical method', or to 'dialectical materialism'), to its fundamental concepts of labor, mode of production, social class, and consequently to the whole history of its apparatuses (projected or real: the Internationals of the labor movement, the dictatorship of the proletariat, the single party, the State, and finally the totalitarian monstrosity)."[1] (Even so, Derrida does not agree with the behavior of inflexibly equating communism with Nazism done by some Western scholars.)[2] It is clear here that Derrida opposes Marxism as the official ideology, and all the conventional Marxist theories. His understanding of the spirit of Marx is very unconventional.

Then, what defines his understanding different from the above "mistakes"? It is *the deconstruction of Marx*, that is, to re-understand Marx through the theory of deconstruction, namely, the deconstruction of the metaphysics of the "proper," of logocentrism, linguisticism, and phonologism. Derrida believes that Marxism itself is metaphysical and logocentric. Therefore, to analyze Marx, Derrida wants to first deconstruct and deny the basic principles and theories in Marxism, and then succeed to Marx's critical spirit. This is the typical standpoint of *post-Marx thought*, to which we probably cannot agree.

In Derrida's view, the deconstruction of Marx is to re-radicalize Marx's spirit.

> Deconstruction has never had any sense or interest, in my view at least, except as a radicalization, which is today also *in the tradition* of a certain Marxism, in a certain *spirit of Marxism*. There has been, then,

---

[1] Derrida, Jacques. *Specters of Marx: The State of the Debt, the Work of Mourning, and the New International*. Trans. Peggy Kamuf. New York: Routledge, 1994. p. 88.

[2] Derrida says that "the communist idea, the ideal of justice that guided and inspired so many communist men and women, all strangers to everything resembling a "gulag," this idea can never be made to correspond—as a parallel, an analogy, or an equivalent, or even as a comparable opposite—to the slightest Nazi "ideal" of "justice." From *For What Tomorrow: A Dialogue* (*Cultural Memory in the Present*). Stanford, California: Stanford University Press, 2004. p. 82.

this attempted radicalization of Marxism called deconstruction.[1]

On what is this view based? To say that the radicalization of Marx's critical spirit is deconstruction is obviously a logical structuralization. Above all, Derrida's understanding of Marx's critical spirit is mediated by his theory of deconstruction. He openly admits that "I am not a Marxist," or "not an orthodox Marxist"[2] But he insists that his own deconstruction theory seems to exhibit a living critical spirit of Marxism.

> Deconstruction has never been Marxist, no more than it has ever been non-Marxist, although it has remained faithful to a certain spirit of Marxism, to at least one of its spirits for, and this can never be repeated too often, there is *more than one* of them and they are heterogeneous.[3]

The Marxist spirit is heterogeneous in that the legacy can actually be obtained only through *self-deconstruction*. Thus, to interpret Marx necessitates the unique "deconstructive thinking of the trace, of iterability, of prosthetic synthesis, of supplementarity, and so forth."[4] In short, where Marx cannot reach is only accessible through the deconstructive context of différance, through the indirect, roundabout or circularly-abbreviatory, or bending path;[5] and thus, we can reach Marx; and only in this way can we truly inherit Marx's legacy. This is the real intention of Derrida's slogan "Back to Marx."

2. Disjointed time and disjointed presence

Derrida mystifies by saying that it is necessary to reaffirm the specter's

[1] Derrida, Jacques. *Specters of Marx: The State of the Debt, the Work of Mourning, and the New International*. Trans. Peggy Kamuf. New York: Routledge, 1994. p. 92.

[2] Ibid., p. 88. He senses some theoretical homogeneity from Marx's words. *Derrida's Speeches in China*. Central Compilation and Translation Press, 2003. p. 77.

[3] Derrida, Jacques. *Specters of Marx: The State of the Debt, the Work of Mourning, and the New International*. Trans. Peggy Kamuf. New York: Routledge, 1994. p. 75.

[4] Ibid., p. 75.

[5] Derrida, Jacques. "Interview" in *Writing and Difference* (Chinese version). Beijing Joint Publishing, 2001. p. 13.

injunction *by choosing*, and "the injunction itself can only be one by dividing itself, rearing itself apart, differing/deferring itself, by speaking at the same time several times—and in several voices."[1] (It is the discourse of the deconstruction theory.) It also means that injunction in the spiritual legacy is always disjointed. In his view, in face of the disjointed injunction, *one must* filter, sift, and criticize, one must sort out several different possibilities that inhabit the same injunction. For example,

> what has been uttered "since Marx" can only promise or remind one to maintain together, in a speech that defers, deterring not what it affirms but deferring just *so as to* affirm, to affirm *justly*, so as to have the power (a power without power) to affirm the coming of the event, its future-to-come itself.[2]

In my view, "since Marx" in Derrida's deconstructive context is only a declaration, which intends not for the real death of Marxism, and also not for the real presence of communism ("the event"), but for telling that "the event" will take effect on reality through some form of delay. It is called *the present disjointedness*. Never believe that Derrida has absolute faith in Marxism. Behind his high-profile announcement is surging the soul of the post-Marx thought: *keeping off the real presence of Marxism and retaining a critical spirit*. On Derrida's theoretical platform, deconstruction is meant to smear the solidificated essence of logos and turn it into continuously disseminated traces. Therefore, making Marx into specters and Marxism into a certain affirmation in différance is Derrida's real intention. As a result, simple confirmation of Derrida's attitude toward Marxism is dangerous.

According to Derrida, the deferring quality of spiritual legacy derives from the nature of this age, in particular, the "post-modern" survival. He says with compassion that this is an era out of joint.[3] "The time is out of joint":

---

[1] Derrida, Jacques. *Specters of Marx: The State of the Debt, the Work of Mourning, and the New International*. Trans. Peggy Kamuf. New York: Routledge, 1994. p.16.

[2] Ibid., p.17.

[3] It comes from Act 1, Scene 5 in Shakespeare's *Hamlet*: "the time is out of joint."

time is *disarticulated*, dislocated, dislodged, time is run down, on the run and run down, *deranged*, both out of order and mad. Time is off its hinges, time if off course, beside itself, disadjusted.[1] His time here indicates the temporality of the age, or "the way things are at a certain time." That the time is out of joint amounts to saying that man's survival is out of joint. Disjoint, dislocation, disjunction, craziness and disorder are all put against the totality, homogeneity and solidification in the industrial-modern society. In Derrida's eyes, this era is a world which turns, which makes the existence of man and materials always fall off the modern (industrial) standardized system. Accordingly, anything is both in existence and non-existence; everything is in constant change. "There is at the same time more than one time in the time of the world ('time' here is also history, the world, society, the age, the current *times*, etc.)."[2] It is a non-linear conception of era. (In fact, this view is held by almost all post-modern thinkers.)

Thus, the principle of time is inevitably to "resist and defy after the fashion of a spectral thing." In other words, we will *not have original* things in the context of deconstruction. It is the same with Marx. In face of a text which has become history, we can only treat it as spectral. Its illustration is not restoration of the original context, even if we hold the banner of resurrection. "The animated work becomes that thing, the Thing that, like an elusive specter, *engineers* a habitation without proper inhabiting, call it a *haunting*, of both memory and translation."[3] It is still the present disjointedness. (Probably, this is the utmost meaning of Derrida's *Specters of Marx*.) Derrida says we shall encounter this haunting in the inescapable fuge.

According to Derrida, fuge is a term used by Heidegger, who puts forward this important idea in his lecture on Anaximander. It describes the

---

[1] Derrida, Jacques. *Specters of Marx: The State of the Debt, the Work of Mourning, and the New International*. Trans. Peggy Kamuf. New York: Routledge, 1994. p.18.

[2] Derrida, Jacques, and Elisabeth Roudinesco. *For What Tomorrow: A Dialogue (Cultural Memory in the Present)*. Stanford, California: Stanford University Press, 2004. p. 80

[3] Derrida, Jacques. *Specters of Marx: The State of the Debt, the Work of Mourning, and the New International*. Trans. Peggy Kamuf. New York: Routledge, 1994. p. 18.

absence of a disjunction or presence. For an object, its presence is shown through a temporary "stay." "It has its provenance in what, by essence, has not yet come-from [*provenu*], still less come about, and which therefore remains to come. The passage of this time of the present comes from the future to go toward the past, toward the going of the gone [*l'en allé*]."[1] This is truly a Heideggerian argument.

> The present is what passes, the present comes to pass [*se passe*], it lingers in this transitory passage (*Weile)*, in the coming-and-going, *between* what *goes* and what *comes*, in the middle of what leaves and what arrives, at the articulation between what absents itself and what presents itself.[2]

Derrida says that it is by the fugue of the presence of the present, or the temporal non-contemporariness that he "considers the ghost." (In the same way, Marx is turned into ghosts.)

More importantly, Derrida puts this idea of Heidegger's under the focus of a supposed completely new conception of justice. If justice or law "stems from vengeance,"[3] then this new concept of justice is no longer the experience *of vengeance*. (From this point of view, Derrida implicitly accuses the previous logic of taking the substantial presence of socialism as vengeance, like killing the capitalists/proprietariats, retaking the deprived wealth, etc.) This justice will be a gift without restitution, without calculation, without accountability, and in essence, it is removed from any horizon of culpability, of debt. (This is Bataille's logic of the sacred thing that shakes off utilitarian value, having all kinds of impact on Derrida and the late Baudrillard.) Derrida believes that it is also "the relation of deconstruction to the possibility of justice." Deconstruction observes forgiveness from the fire of revenge in others' eyes. (In his later years, Derrida was very concerned

---

[1] Derrida, Jacques. *Specters of Marx: The State of the Debt, the Work of Mourning, and the New International*. Trans. Peggy Kamuf. New York: Routledge, 1994. p. 24.

[2] Ibid., p. 25.

[3] Ibid., p. 21.

with the subject of forgiveness.)[1] For Derrida, it is a gentle pardon from the savior. The spectralized legacy of Marx is essentially a messianic slogan.

> We believe that this messianic remains an *ineffaceable* mark— a mark one neither can nor should efface—of Marx's legacy, and doubtless of *inheriting*, of the experience of inheritance in general. Otherwise, one would reduce the eventness of the event, the singularity and the alterity of the other.[2]

Now, it is very clear that in Derrida's différance, Marx's legacy is only a Messiah without content and identification, which is not a requirement for actual revolution, but the divine call from the savior *beyond*. In this regard, Szeman says that Derrida names Marx the specter in that it enables us to imagine the Utopian existence in contrast to the darkest reality; accordingly, it is similar to the languid Messianic force described by Walter Benjamin. It also resurrects the premature death of Marx, with the method of preserving the Marxist critical ability to reclaim the present meaning of Marx. "Despite the death of Marx, his specter is always alive."[3] This is a pertinent comment.

> In Derrida's own words, "now, if there is a spirit of Marxism which I will never be ready to renounce, it is not only the critical idea or the questioning stance… It is even more a certain emancipatory and *messianic* affirmation, a certain experience of the promise that one can try to liberate from any dogmatics and even from any metaphysico-religious determination, from any *messianism*."[4]

No wonder Zizek makes the statement about Derrida's return to Marx.

---

[1] In 2002, when I met Jacques Derrida in Nanjing, he told me that his thought was centered on forgiveness.

[2] Derrida, Jacques. *Specters of Marx: The State of the Debt, the Work of Mourning, and the New International*. Trans. Peggy Kamuf. New York: Routledge, 1994. p. 28.

[3] Szeman, Imre."Ghostly Matters: On Derrida's Specters." *Rethinking Marxism* 12.2 (2000): 104-116.

[4] Derrida, Jacques. *Specters of Marx: The State of the Debt, the Work of Mourning, and the New International*. Trans. Peggy Kamuf. New York: Routledge, 1994. p. 89.

It mainly says that reasserting the authentic spirit of the Marxist tradition means leaving behind its letter (Marx's particular analyses and proposed revolutionary measures, which are irreducibly tainted by the tradition of ontology) in order to save from the ashes the authentic Messianic promise of emancipatory liberation. Nevertheless, Derrida's "messianic promise remains forever a promise, can never be translated into a set of determinate economico-political measures."[1] Derrida probabaly hopes to evoke a savior in the form of Marx, for which he deliberately reverses the discourse of *The Internationale*. It should be noted that Derrida refuses a direct response to Marx and his scientific theories, which radically differentiates himself from the Marxists.

3. Error of the ontological response of the specters of Marx

Derrida insists that Marx is spectralized in a way that his presence is always "the disparate" of itself, called by deconstruction as "between being and non-being."[2] Put simply, it means a pluralistic interpretation of the text. However, that Marx's legacy is a disparate of itself does not mean this spectral spirit necessarily leads to logical confusion. In order to explain this, he refers to an idea in Maurice Blanchot's *Marx's Three Voices*, "to think the 'holding together' of the *disparate* itself."[3]

Not to maintain together the disparate, but to put ourselves there where the disparate itself *holds together*, without wounding the dis-jointure, the dispersion, or the difference, without effacing the heterogeneity of the other. We are asked (enjoined, perhaps) to turn *ourselves* over to the future, to join ourselves in this *we*, there where the disparate is turned over to this singular *joining* without concept or

---

[1] Zizek, Slavoj. *Did Somebody Say Totalitarianism?: Five Interventions in the (Mis)Use of a Notion*. Wo Es War. London; New York: Verso, 2002. pp. 153-154.

[2] Derrida, Jacques. "Interview" in *Writing and Difference* (Chinese version). Beijing Joint Publishing, 2001. p. 13.

[3] Derrida, Jacques. *Specters of Marx: The State of the Debt, the Work of Mourning, and the New International*. Trans. Peggy Kamuf. New York: Routledge, 1994. p. 29.

certainty of determination, without knowledge, without or before the synthetic junction of the conjunction and the disjunction.[1]

This is the theoretical attitude and political position of Derrida's deconstruction. He rejects homogenization of any totality. As the messianic inheritance to Marx's spirit, he hopes to build "the alliance of a *rejoining* without conjoined mare, without organization, without party, without nation, without State, without property (the 'communism' that we will later nickname the new International)."[2] This deconstructive politics is much more radical than conventional anarchism. However, as to the real possibility of this political revolution, he admits "it's a rather dim hope."[3]

In comparison to this deconstructive position, all the past understandings of Marx are under violent attacks by Derrida. He even coins a new phrase, "ontological response," which means various substantial illustrations and objectification of Marx's spirit in conventional studies. For Derrida, "the response of Marx himself for whom the ghost must be nothing, nothing period (non-being, non-effectivity, non-life) or nothing imaginary."[4] However, Marxist successors wherever they have drawn, practically, concretely, in a terribly effective, massive, and immediate fashion, its political consequences. Marx's spirit is noticeably nothing while you vainly attempt to sow it and expect it to bloom and fruit. Derrida opposes this objectification of Marxism, opposes the direct presence of Marx: the "substance, existence,

---

[1] Derrida, Jacques. *Specters of Marx: The State of the Debt, the Work of Mourning, and the New International*. Trans. Peggy Kamuf. New York: Routledge, 1994. p.29.

[2] Ibid. Later, Derrida says that it emphasizes the solidarity of the entire human race "as a way to counter these wounds" today (p. 96). "The International I speak of is therefore not the International of the Communist Party or of any Party whatever. (p. 96.) But I kept this word, with a capital, as a salute to the memory of what, existing no longer, will have been a great sign. Derrida, Jacques, and Elisabeth Roudinesco. *For What Tomorrow: A Dialogue*. Trans. Jeff Fort. Cultural Memory in the Present. Stanford, Calif.: Stanford University Press, 2004. p. 96.

[3] Derrida, Jacques, and Elisabeth Roudinesco. *For What Tomorrow: A Dialogue* (*Cultural Memory in the Present*). Stanford, California: Stanford University Press, 2004. p. 94

[4] Derrida, Jacques. *Specters of Marx: The State of the Debt, the Work of Mourning, and the New International*. Trans. Peggy Kamuf. New York: Routledge, 1994. p. 30.

essence, *permanence*." He sadly says that the objectification is at the cost of millions and millions of supplementary ghosts who will keep on protesting in us. (These metaphorical ghosts are the dissidents killed in the Stalinist system.) For Derrida, Marx in deconstruction means a possibility rooted from nothing and negativity; "it *can be, only if there is any*, it can be only possible." Once such a seed of possibility falls into the earth, it will certainly bear the flower of evil, for which, he criticizes, "the philosophical responses that consist in *totalizing*, in filling in the space of the question or in denying its possibility, in fleeing from the very thing it will have allowed one to glimpse."[1] (Totalizing here is not the stipulation in Sartre's context, but rather something in Adorno's critical context of negative dialectics, viz, the *evil totality* towards Auschwitz.) Previously, Marx was the bright moon outside the window which cast shadows behind us, while you chose to turn it into the commune where people shattered the pans of individual homes and ate together in public dining hall, into a goulash of beef and potato, like that of the Chinese Cultural Revolution. Naturally, the beautiful moon vanished, and we are left with a pale tangle. Derrida is complaining about the October Revolution and the socialist existence which followed it.

Why does such a mistake happen? According to Derrida's logic, it is deeply problematic. In the vision of deconstruction, there is no continuous history in the metaphysical sense at all, such as the linear, completed history from ancient society, to feudalism, capitalism and communism. To Derrida, this is another idealistic version of Hegel's "developing itself, producing itself, fulfilling itself." "The metaphysical character of the concept of history is not only linked to linearity, but to an entire *system* of implications (teleology, eschatology, elevating and interiorizing accumulation of meaning, a certain type of traditionality, a certain concept of continuity, of truth, etc.)."[2] The concept of history claimed by Derrida is of deconstruction,

---

[1] Derrida, Jacques. *Specters of Marx: The State of the Debt, the Work of Mourning, and the New International*. Trans. Peggy Kamuf. New York: Routledge, 1994. p. 30.

[2] Derrida, Jacques. *Positions*. Trans. Alan Bass. London: Continuum Publishing Group, 2004. p. 50.

namely, "a history that also implies a new logic of *repetition* and the *trace*." (In this regard, he seems to confirm Althusser's criticism of Hegel's view of history.)[1] The concept of history is just the Other. At the core of history is not linear continuity, but rather the *interval*. Therefore, the coming of history is the same with différance.

Also in this sense, Derrida warns us of the vital necessity to understand différance. In the context of deconstruction, "any promise" and "the future-to-come" indicates "deferral, lateness, delay, postponement." Marx, of course, is no exception. Without différance, there is no heterogeneity; without heterogeneity, no specificity; without specificity, no actual being here and now. "Heterogeneity opens things up, it lets itself be opened up by the very effraction of that which unfurls, comes, and remains to come—singularly from the other. There would be neither injunction nor promise without this disjunction."[2] The expectation of "given homogeneity, systematic coherence" in traditional thought is only an ideal method of response that inevitably plummets into dogmatism.

This is "what renders the injunction, the inheritance, and the future—in a word the other—*impossible*. There *must be* disjunction, interruption, the heterogeneous if at least *there must be*, *if there must be* a chance given to any "there must be" whatsoever, be it beyond duty.[3]

Derrida assumes a dividing line between the specter and the real presence. Communism is a present specter to spur us, and we cannot presumptuously regard it as reality. He says that "Marx thought, to be sure, on his side, from the other side, that the dividing line between the ghost and actuality ought to be crossed, like utopia itself, by a realization, that is, by a revolution; but *be too* will have continued to believe, to try to believe in the existence of this dividing line as real limit and conceptual distinction".[4]

---

[1] Derrida, Jacques. *Positions*. Trans. Alan Bass. London: Continuum Publishing Group, 2004. p. 51.

[2] Derrida, Jacques. *Specters of Marx: The State of the Debt, the Work of Mourning, and the New International*. Trans. Peggy Kamuf. New York: Routledge, 1994. p. 33.

[3] Ibid., p. 35.

[4] Ibid., pp. 38-39.

However, we never see such an explanation in Marx's text. Derrida is "frying" Marx in the logic of deconstruction.

In the same way, when it comes to concrete reality, Derrida approves of China's social development today. He says that "[i]t is critical about how China's Marxism is developed in the future."[1] It is particularly so when contemporary Chinese socialism inherits Marx in a different way than the simplistic split of history in former Soviet Union and Eastern European socialist countries. At the same time when China receives a certain Marxism, it enters the market economy, claiming peaceful coexistence with the United States and even the West, which surely contains some sort of "graft." In this respect, Derrida proclaims that between the current socialism in China and himself, there is a particular "consensus on Marxism," or an agreement on inheritance to Marx's legacy:

> Today, persistent criticism of capitalism, the new capitalist danger, must be carried out effectively while avoiding the deficiencies of the Marxist legacy and the ensuing historical catastrophes made in the name of Marx himself in China and the East, in short, to keep away the part that is to be abandoned from the legacy.[2]

Thus, the real meaning of what Derrida says to inherit Marx's legacy is to reject something in Marx's thought, but maintain his critical spirit and direct the critical target to today's capitalism. However, we find it hard to agree with Derrida on his post-Marx illustration of China's development today.

4. Contemporary capitalism and "the End of History"

As we see, Derrida's inheritance of Marx's legacy is mainly reflected in the deconstructive critical spirit. It refers to a tenacious negation of any presumptuous eternalization of solidificated structure; on the other hand, this

---

[1] Derrida, Jacques. *Derrida's Speeches in China*. Central Compilation and Translation Press. 2003. p. 81.

[2] Ibid., p. 81.

negation is present via différance. In *Specters of Marx*, the target of negation premised on Marx's critical spirit is contemporary capitalism and all the presumptuous bourgeois ideology. Derrida asserts that he makes an "untiring deconstructive critique of capitalistic logic" in the text.[1]

As mentioned above, Derrida chooses to write this book in 1993 because the practice of the international communist movement suffered unprecedented setbacks at that moment, while a capitalist superpower correspondingly emerged to be the sole world police dominating the globe. Derrida says that "the incoherent but organized coalition of international capitalist forces that, in the name of neo-liberalism or the market, are taking hold of the world in conditions such as the 'state' form."[2] "A new 'world order' seeks to stabilize a new, necessarily new disturbance by installing an unprecedented form of hegemony."[3] After the collapse of the former Soviet Union and Eastern European socialist countries, the Western intellectual circle was filled with the "doomsday" uproars of capitalist ideology, like the political assertions of "the end of history", "the end of Marxism," with the surging theoretical thoughts of "the end of philosophy," "the end of man" and so on. Among them, *The End of History and the Last Man* by the American scholar Francis Fukuyama is perhaps the most outstanding one in political assertions. In addition, Derrida believes a large number of young people have consequently become the audience of Fukuyama. Therefore, *Specters of Marx* mainly targets Fukuyama and his views.

Derrida's eyes, Fukuyama's presence is not different from the stuffy clown in a comedy, because this "apocalyptic tone in philosophy" already appears as early as 40 years ago. (It refers to the "end of ideology" represented by Daniel Bell in the 1950s.)[4] Derrida says with a pity that from

---

[1] Derrida, Jacques, and Elisabeth Roudinesco. *For What Tomorrow: A Dialogue (Cultural Memory in the Present)*. Stanford, California: Stanford University Press, 2004. p. 83

[2] Ibid., p. 92

[3] Derrida, Jacques. *Specters of Marx: The State of the Debt, the Work of Mourning, and the New International*. Trans. Peggy Kamuf. New York: Routledge, 1994. p. 50.

[4] Daniel Bell published *The End of Ideology* in 1960. *See* the 2001 edition translation of the Jiangsu People's Publishing House.

the view of methodology, this theory of "the end" is "no doubt the element in which what is called deconstruction." However, to those unaware of the actual context of deconstruction, this mistake predictably causes "a tiresome anachronism," which surprisingly "comes across in the body of today's most *phenomenal culture*: what one hears, reads, and sees, what is most *mediatized* in Western capitals."[1]

Derrida says in an ironical tone that Fukuyama's book is "a new gospel" of capitalism as the most mediatized, the most "successful" one on the subject of the death of Marxism as the end of history. In a certain sense, that book marks the mad presence of contemporary bourgeois ideology, and becomes "the finest ideological showcase of victorious capitalism in a liberal democracy which has finally arrived at the plentitude of its ideal."[2] Probably, Derrida's positioning of Fukuyama is no exaggeration.

Why does Derrida say so? And why is Fukuyama's book a gospel? For Derrida, this book claims to bring a "positive response" to a question whose formation and formulation are never interrogated in themselves. It proclaims that "a 'coherent and directional History of mankind' will eventually lead toward 'liberal democracy' (telos)."[3] According to Fukuyama, the noticeable change at the end of the 20th century proves the truth that liberal democracy remains the only coherent political aspiration which spans different regions and cultures around the globe, and the alliance of liberal democracy and of the "free market" is the "good news" of this last quarter of the century. Thus, the teleological progressive history founded by Hegel ends here; capitalism is all. Derrida says that Fukuyama is identifying the "ahistorical *telos* of history."[4]

Derrida does not agree with Fukuyama's optimism. He thinks that "neither the United States nor the European community has attained the perfection of the universal State or of liberal democracy, nor have they

---

[1] Derrida, Jacques. *Specters of Marx: The State of the Debt, the Work of Mourning, and the New International*. Trans. Peggy Kamuf. New York: Routledge, 1994. p. 15.

[2] Ibid., p. 56.

[3] Ibid., pp. 56-57.

[4] Ibid., p. 36. p. 57

even come close. And how can one overlook, moreover, the economic war that is raging today both between these two blocs and within the European community," the economic war with Japan, and all the contradictions at work within the trade between the wealthy countries and the rest of the world, the phenomena of pauperization and the ferocity of the "foreign debt"?[1] In antithesis to Fukuyama's opinion, Derrida holds that "the world is going very badly, it wears as it grows." As we already know, Derrida possesses Marx's spirit and the critical look from the specter. He observes what Fukuyama cannot see. In the contemporary historical context, Derrida points out "the economic wars, national wars, wars among minorities, the unleashing of racisms and xenophobias, ethnic conflicts, conflicts of culture and religion that are tearing apart so-called democratic Europe and the world today."[2] Therefore, "the euphoria of liberal-democrat capitalism" which Fukuyama pleasantly talks about actually resembles the blindest and most delirious of hallucinations, or even an increasingly glaring hypocrisy.

Derrida chooses the following ten aspects to illustrate the "plague" of the world today:

1) The widespread unemployment. The function of social inactivity, of non-work or of underemployment is entering into a new era. In capitalism, this kind of unemployment has become a more or less well-calculated deregulation of a new market, new technologies, new worldwide competitiveness, which is "at once mastered, calculated, 'socialized'", or put in various forms by the lofty economists and politicians. But essentially it is all suffering for the unemployed. 2) The deprived homeless citizens. This mainly includes the expulsion or deportation of so many exiles, stateless persons, and immigrants scattered around the world, for whom survival is the biggest problem, leaving little room to talk about freedom and democracy. 3) The contemporary economic war in developed capitalist countries. The ruthless economic wars between Europe and America, between Japan and

---

[1] Derrida, Jacques. *Specters of Marx: The State of the Debt, the Work of Mourning, and the New International.* Trans. Peggy Kamuf. New York: Routledge, 1994. p. 63.

[2] Ibid., pp. 77-80.

America control everything. As the smoke screen of political ideology evaporates, the battle of national interests impatiently unveils its true color. 4) The inability to master the contradictions in the concept, norms, and reality of the free market. Derrida is always concerned with who will protect the interests of the laborers in the West when the mad flow of international capital shifts to the Third World countries, when the interest of the capital is increasingly turned to snatching cheap resources and using lower labor cost to generate more surplus values in the developing countries. 5) The aggravation of foreign debt and other connected mechanisms are starving or driving to despair a large portion of humanity. The above misdeeds that directly trigger the anguish of the Third World people "appear to be dictated by the discourse of democratization or human rights." 6) The arms industry and trade inscribed in the normal regulation of the scientific research, economy, and socialization of labor in Western democracies. 7) The spread ("dissemination") of nuclear weapons, maintained by the very countries that say they want to protect themselves from it. 8) Inter-ethnic wars (has there ever been another kind?) are proliferating, driven by an *archaic* phantasm and concept, by a *primitive conceptual phantasm* of community, the nation-State, sovereignty, borders, native soil and blood. 9) Organized crimes, more and more phantom-like, penetrate into almost every corner of the world. They invade not only the socio-economic fabric, the general circulation of capital, but also statist or inter-statist institutions. 10) The international law which puts on a democratic and just face, with corresponding judicial, arbitrary and coordinating agencies that are closely linked to the European history and culture. It leads to such consequences as "the incoherence, discontinuity, inequality of States before the law, the hegemony of certain States over military power in the service of international law."[1]

These "ten wounds" reflect reality, the very historical reality that is actually happening, whereas Fukuyama has the audacity to neo-evangelize, to claim this world will never have violence, inequality, exclusion, famine

---

[1] Derrida, Jacques. *Specters of Marx: The State of the Debt, the Work of Mourning, and the New International*. Trans. Peggy Kamuf. New York: Routledge, 1994. pp. 81-84. *See* also *Derrida's Speeches in China*. Central Compilation and Translation Press. 2003. pp. 77-78.

and thus economic oppression affected. In an almost angry tone, Derrida says that:

> Instead of singing the advent of the idea of liberal democracy and of the capitalist market in the euphoria of the end of history, instead of celebrating the "end of ideologies" and the end of the great emancipatory discourses, let us never neglect this obvious macroscopic fact, made up of innumerable singular sites of suffering: no degree of progress allows one to ignore that never before, in absolute figures, never have so many men, women, and children been subjugated, starved, or exterminated on the earth.[1]

Here, Derrida cannot hide his anger: this is "a world that is more non-egalitarian than ever—on the billions of living beings—human and otherwise—who are denied not only basic 'human rights'… but are denied even the right to a live a decent life."[2] In face of such suffering, why do people choose to "harden their heart" or turn a blind eye? Derrida readily offers the answer: the successful operation of the contemporary bourgeois ideology. Derrida further lists two important concepts: "that of hegemony ('dominant discourse')" and the "*incontestable* self-evidence," both of which belong to those that "no one, I presume, would dream of contesting." Why? Because they are neither of some substantial existence, nor conceptions in people's self-consciousness. They are just implicitly referred to as "that which everywhere organizes and commands public manifestation or testimony in the public space." In Derrida's view, it is rightly a set constituted by *three* indissociable places or apparatuses of our culture: the official discourses of governing parties and politicians in power in the world, which is "the culture called more or less properly political"; the mass-media culture, which has been developed to center around TV and information in an absolutely unheard-of fashion; and a scholarly or academic culture, notably

---

[1] Derrida, Jacques. *Specters of Marx: The State of the Debt, the Work of Mourning, and the New International*. Trans. Peggy Kamuf. New York: Routledge, 1994. p. 85.

[2] Derrida, Jacques "I Am at War with Myself." *SV. Derrida* (*Special Issue*), 2004.

that of historians, sociologists and politologists, theoreticians of literature, anthropologists, philosophers (in particular political philosophers). Derrida calls the above three cultures "three places, forms, and powers of culture."[1] These three discourses communicate and cooperate at every moment in order to produce the greatest force with which they assure the hegemony or the imperialism in question.

It may account for why the specters of Marx are still present. Derrida wants to tell us that the spectral look of Marx allows us to see the injustice of the world; Marx's ethical heritage enables us not to yield to the hegemony of capital; and Marx's critical spirit which never dies lights up our hard road of resistance. In my opinion, this is a theoretically positive and academically respectable position. No matter how many problems are discovered in it, *Specters of Marx* deserves being considered as an enlightening masterpiece in the postmodern context.

---

[1] Derrida, Jacques. *Specters of Marx: The State of the Debt, the Work of Mourning, and the New International*. Trans. Peggy Kamuf. New York: Routledge, 1994. pp. 52-53.

Hollow Man: Perpetual Constitution of a Fantastic Scene—Textual Interpretation of Slavoj Zizek's *Sublime Object of Ideology*[1]

Introduction: Grafting Lacan onto Marx

As a very popular figure in the radical academia of America and Europe[2], Slavoj Zizek has made a great influence on a wide

---

[1] This chapter was translated by He Huiming.

[2] Slavoj Zizek was born in Ljubljana, Yugoslavia (a northwest city in the People's Republic of Slovenia), on the 21ˢᵗ of March, 1949. He received a Bachelor of Arts in Philosophy and Sociol-

variety of fields, such as psychoanalysis, philosophy, literature and cinema studies. Theoretically and politically, he can be counted as a Lacanian leftist intellectual in the Western context. In the 1970s, when he was still a postgraduate student in an Eastern European socialist country, he displayed enthusiasm for modern post-structuralist thought in the West and graduated with his Master of Arts thesis on Lacan, Derrida and Kristeva. In the 1980s, Zizek went to the University of Paris VIII for obtaining the doctoral degree, majoring in Lacan. In 1985, he obtained the doctorate of psychoanalysis. After that, Zizek became a radical dissident during the political unrest of his own country. He is the first to graft Lacan onto Marx[1] and form a unique philosophic branch. However, Zizek says that he considers himself "not being an orthodox Marxist,"[2] or even an orthodox Western Marxist successor. In spite of this, he always adheres to Marx's critical spirit of capitalism which is mediated through the Lacanian infiltration. Thus, I posit him in the framework of *Post-Marxism*. *The Sublime Object of Ideology* is one of

---

ogy from the University of Ljubljana in 1971, a Master of Arts in Philosophy in 1975, and a Doctor of Arts in Philosophy in 1981. He then received the PhD degree of psychoanalysis at the University of Paris VIII in 1985. From 1979 on, Zizek was a researcher at the Institute of Sociology and Philosophy of the University of Ljubljana (from 1992, Institute for Social Sciences, Faculty for Social Sciences). He was politically active in the alternative movement in Slovenia during the 1980s and a candidate for the presidency of the Republic of Slovenia in the first multi-party elections in 1990. In 1991, he was the ambassador of Science of the Republic of Slovenia. Soon, he quit and returned to the university, giving lectures in Europe and America while doing academic researches. As an influential scholar, especially, in the field of contemporary radical thought, he has published more than 40 works and large number of papers, including *The Sublime Object of Ideology* (1989), *Looking Awry: an Introduction to Jacques Lacan through Popular Culture* (1991), *The Metastases Of Enjoyment: Six Essays On Woman And Causality* (1994), *The Fragile Absolute or Why the Christian Legacy is Worth Fighting For* (2000), *Repeating Lenin* (2002).

[1] Jacques Marie Emile Lacan (1901-1983) is a renowned French post-psychoanalyst and thinker. As for my discussion of Lacan's philosophy, *see The Impossible Truth of Being: Mirror of Lacan's Philosophy*. Commercial Press, 2006.

[2] Zizek, Slavoj, and Glyn Daly. *Conversations with Zizek*. Conversations. Cambridge [u.a.]: Polity, 2004. p. 31.

his most famous books.[1] This chapter will focus on its textual analysis of Marx. Before entering his difficult discourse, we are going to make a brief introduction to Zizek's basic views about Marxism.

1. The contemporary world in the eyes of Marx

In today's complex context of post-modernism, Zizek claims to stand in Lenin's "fighting materialist" position against all the "*New Age* spiritualisms,*"*[2] which clearly demonstrates his heroic courage. To reply to those bourgeois theorists who consider Marxism a kind of quasi-theological sect of "Salvationism," Zizek says that this is only applicable for the "rigid", "dogmatic" Marxism, not for the essential core of the Marxist freedom. In my opinion, this is a reasonable delimitation. He wants to inherit the Marxist critical analysis along with the spirit of liberation.

Zizek opposes a model of judgment which asks questions such as "what is still alive among Marxism?"—he sings high praise for Theodor Adorno's criticism of Benedetto Croce's arrogant interrogation that what is still alive and already dead in Hegel—because in comparison with the inquiries of what is still alive or meaningful for us in Marxism, we are far more interested in such questions as "*what our contemporary world means in Marx's eyes?*"

> Marx's key theoretical achievement, which allowed him to articulate the constitutive imbalance of capitalist society, was his insight into how the very logic of the Universal, of formal equality, involves material inequality—not as a remainder of the past to be gradually abolished, but as a structural necessity inscribed into the very formal notion of equality. There is no "contradiction" between the bourgeois principle of equality in the eyes of the law, the equivalent

---

[1] *The Sublime Object of Ideology* was published by Verso in 1989. The Chinese version, translated by Ji Guangmao was published by Central Compilation and Translation Press in 2002. According-ing to Zizek, this book is not as "theoretically substantial" as his second book *For they know Not What They Do. See Conversions with Zizek*. Cambridge: Polity. 2004. p. 40.

[2] Zizek, Slavoj. *The Fragile Absolute*. London; New York: Verso, 2000. p. 1.

exchange between free individuals, and material exploitation and class domination: domination and exploitation are contained in the very notion of legal equality and equivalent exchange; they are a necessary ingredient of *universalized* equivalent exchange (since at this point of universalization, the laborer force itself becomes a commodity to be exchanged on the market).[1]

From the labor power that has become a commodity, Marx detects the *actual* factor that leads to *substantial* inequality: expansion of the production of surplus value. Thus, "Lacan proclaims that Marx discovers the symptom." (We are to specifically discuss the concept of "symptom" and its relation with Marx later.) Zizek thinks that today the capitalist mode of production still retains the essence exposed by Marx. He is correct regarding this point. (I approve of him here, but oppose some other points of his, for example, when he even disagrees with his own statement above.)

Zizek profoundly discovers that in contemporary social theories, there is a hidden shift of ideology. Some people are talking about the "end of history" or the coming of the "post-ideological pragmatic era." He says that in today's critical discourse and political analysis,

the term "worker" has disappeared, supplanted and/or obliterated by "immigrants [immigrant workers: Algerians in France, Turks in Germany, Mexicans in the USA]"—in this way, the *class* problematic of the "intolerance of Otherness," and so on.[2]

Marxist class analysis has been converted into the discussion of cultural tolerance, which, clearly, is the quiet spreading of a new ideology. (Coincidentally, in mainland China, the title of the bourgeoisie no longer denotes a derogatory sense; they have become the "successful people" and the object of worship. The proletarian class is not called the proletarians

---

[1] Zizek, Slavoj. *The Metastases of Enjoyment: Six Essays on Women and Causality*. Verso, 2005. p. 183.

[2] Zizek, Slavoj. *The Fragile Absolute*. London; New York: Verso, 2000. p. 10.

anymore; they have become the "disadvantaged group" and the object of sympathy. As for general descriptions of interpersonal relations, "comrade" changes into "boss" or "sir" and "one taking Lei Feng [a soldier always ready to help others in the early period of New China] as the example" is called a "volunteer." All this belongs to an obscure conversion of micro-discourse.) It seems that people beginning to silently assume the global order of capitalist freedom and democracy is somewhat the ultimate discovery of the "natural" political system. Capitalism is once again recognized as a natural way of social existence, and history seems to return to the previous condition where "there is no longer any history" in Marx's time.[1]

Is this the real situation? Zizek offers an exactly opposite view. He thinks that Marx's description of capitalism in *The Communist Manifesto* 150 years ago is still a powerful reality in today's world, namely, the brutal *globalization of capital.*

> Where do we live *today*, in our global "post..." (postmodern, post-industrial) society? The slogan that is imposing itself more and more is "globalization": the brutal imposition of the unified world market that threatens all local ethnic traditions, including the very form of the nation-state. And in view of this situation, is not the description of the social impact of the bourgeoisie in *The Manifesto* more relevant than ever?[2]

Following his reference to the comprehensive comment on the historical merits of capitalism by Marx and Engels in *The Manifesto*, Zizek goes on to explain that "this global dynamism described by Marx, which causes all

---

[1] In his criticism of the bourgeois externalization and naturalization of capitalism, Marx says that "when the economists say that present-day relations—the relations of bourgeois production—are natural, they imply that these are the relations in which wealth is created and productive forces developed in conformity with the laws of nature. These relations therefore are themselves natural laws independent of the influence of time. They are eternal laws which must always govern society. Thus, there has been history, but there is no longer any." *See* "The Metaphysics of Political Economy (The Method)" in *The Poverty of Philosophy*.

[2] Zizek, Slavoj. *The Fragile Absolute*. London; New York: Verso, 2000. pp. 11-12.

things solid to melt into air" is "more than ever our reality."[1] (This is correct, this "more than ever" can describe the contemporary all-round victory of the capital's world history.) Zizek believes in a globalization or universalization of capital, "not only in the sense of global capitalism, the establishment of a global world market, but also in the sense of the assertion of 'humanity' as the global point of reference for human rights, legitimizing the violation of State sovereignty, from trade restrictions to direct military interventions, in parts of the world where global human rights are violated..."[2] In addition, capitalism brings about the radical secularization of social life: it mercilessly tears apart any aura of authentic nobility, sacredness, honour, and so on. Marx says that the bourgeoisie has through its exploitation of the world market given a cosmopolitan character to production and consumption in every country. Nowadays, "Ericsson phones are no longer Swedish, Toyota cars are manufactured 60 per cent in the USA, Hollywood culture pervades the remotest parts of the globe."[3] This is the real social situation that China experiences today.

On the other hand, Zizek affirms the "fundamental lesson" that Marx identifies in his late economic research: *all heavenly chimeras to brutal economic reality generates a spectrality of its own.* Nevertheless, Zizek's spectrality here does not refer to the fearsome specter of communism which worries the bourgeoisie, but the *Real* in Lacan's philosophical context. (Zizek is obviously influenced by Derrida's *Specters of Marx.* He says that Jacques Derrida brought into play the term "spectre" in order to indicate the elusive pseudo-materiality that subverts the classic ontological oppositions of reality and illusion.)[4]

Lacan's Real. This refers to *the being of the impossible presence* demonstrated after man's existence is killed by the symbolic signs. The

---

[1] Zizek, Slavoj. *The Fragile Absolute.* London; New York: Verso, 2000. p. 14.

[2] Ibid. p. 201.

[3] Ibid. p. 13.

[4] Zizek, Slavoj. *Mapping Ideology.* London; New York: Verso, 1994. p. 13.

Real is not the actual congruity of the cognition of external objects in traditional epistemology, but rather an ontological stipulation, or a non-pseudo, non-false truth in personal ontology. This Real is somewhat similar to Kant's thing-in-itself. Zizek states that "Lacan replaces the Kantian noumenal Thing with the impossible/real Thing."[1] In opposition to the *Imaginary false* and the *Symbolic false*, this Real only blooms in the ruptures of the nets of mirror images and symbols. To expose the false leads to the real, whose presence signs the failure of the pseudo-reality. It should be also noted that Lacan's Real is not a simple judgment of value, neither does it necessarily mean the good nor vice versa. In this regard, Lacan's Real is not the epistemological representation but the ontological stipulation.[2]

Accordingly, Zizek believes that without specter, there is no reality. Only through the miraculous supplement of specters can reality complete its peripheral journey for reality; in the late Lacan's eyes, it is never the thing itself, and it is forever symbolized by the mechanism of language signs. The "problem resides in the fact that symbolization ultimately always fails, that it never succeeds in fully 'covering' the real, that it always involves some unsettled, unredeemed symbolic debt. *This real (the part of reality that remains non-symbolized) returns in the guise of spectral apparitions.*"[3] Here, the determination of reality by the specter does not indicate a simplistic linear relationship. It is from the "gap" among realities that the specter emerges. The presence of the specter makes reality always present itself via a partial failure of representation, from which reality assumes a fictional character. Zizek uses spectrality to metaphorize the reality of contemporary capitalism: the bourgeoisie tend to doll up capitalism with various ideological abstractions, but such symbolization always fails before the kernel of reality. (For example, the substantial inequality during the attainment of surplus

---

[1] Zizek, Slavoj. *The Fragile Absolute*. London; New York: Verso, 2000. p. 171.

[2] *See The Impossible Truth of Being: Mirror of Lacan's Philosophy*. The Commercial Press. pp. 334-335.

[3] Zizek, Slavoj. *Mapping Ideology*. London; New York: Verso, 1994. p. 21.

value and its impact on the myth of capitalist equality; or exposition of the abuse of the Iraqi prisoners of war by US soldiers and its devastating blow to the excuse of protecting human rights that the US made to wage that war.)

When Marx describes the mad self-enhancing circulation of Capital, whose solipsistic path of self-fecundation reaches its apogee in today's meta-reflexive speculations on futures, it is far too simplistic to claim that the spectre of this self-engendering monster that pursues its path regardless of any human or environmental concern is an ideological abstraction, and that one should never forget that behind this abstraction there are real people and natural objects on whose productive capacities and resources Capital's circulation is based, and on which it feeds like a gigantic parasite. The problem is that this "abstraction" does not exist only in our (financial speculator's) misperception of social reality; it is "real" in the precise sense of determining the very structure of material social processes: the fate of whole strata of populations, and sometimes of whole countries, can be decided by the "solipsistic" speculative dance of Capital, which pursues its goal of profitability with a blessed indifference to the way its movement will affect social reality. That is the fundamental systemic violence of capitalism, which is much more uncanny than direct pre-capitalist socio-ideological violence: this violence is no longer attributable to concrete individuals and their "evil" intentions; it is purely "objective", systemic anonymous.[1]

Zizek is very accurate in his explanation of "the violence of the capitalist basic system." Compared with the external coercion of the previous capitalist social ideology, today's rule of capitalism is materialized in a purely "objective," systematic, anonymous way; in other words, control is attained through *a violence that cannot be directly seen*, or an "anonymous horror." Therefore, Zizek says, today "the true horror lies not in the particular content hidden beneath the universality of global Capital but, rather, in the fact that Capital is effectively an anonymous global machine blindly running

---

[1] Zizek, Slavoj. *The Fragile Absolute*. London; New York: Verso, 2000. p. 15.

its course; that there is in fact no particular Secret Agent animating it."[1] This is because the rampant capitalism around the glove resembles a kind of spectral "self-fecundation" "self-engendering monster," which is equivalent to what Marx observes as the "universal light" of the capital relations in the *domination of abstraction.* Zizek only expresses this via the Lacanian discourse. According to Glyn Daly, "Zizek represents the philosophical equivalent of a virulent plague, or perhaps, to update the metaphor, a computer virus, whose purpose is to disrupt the comfortable appearances of what might be called the matrix of global-liberal-capitalism."[2] (This is a justified comment.)

For Zizek, life is divided into two: one is the perceptual life, or in Lacan's words, the reality; the other is the invisible, inaccessible Real. The former is contained in the social reality of the real man during the process of interaction and production. (Clearly, man's production process and mutual relations are the essential things of social life revealed by Marx, but they become the Lacanian *pseudo-reality* here. To Lacan, *all* positive social-cultural construction within the ontological relations of the subject is a fantasy, or an alienation to erase the actual being of the individual. The relational ontology discovered by Marx and Heidegger, that is, the Gestalt existence of any individual subject constructed in real life, is viewed by Lacan as a scam. *Relation is false.* As we know, the logical premise commonly acceptable to the ontology of Marx and Heidegger is precisely the Hegelian conception that where there is subject there is relation. It is from relational ontology that Lacan starts his falsifying critique of the subjective existence.) The latter "is the inexorable 'abstract' spectral logic of Capital which determines what goes on in social reality."[3] In the eyes of Zizek, "the spectral presence of Capital is the figure of the big Other which not only remains operative when all the traditional embodiments of the symbolic big

[1] Zizek, Slavoj. *The Ticklish Subject: The Absent Centre of Political Ontology.* Wo Es War. London; New York: Verso, 1999. p. 218.

[2] Zizek, Slavoj, and Glyn Daly. *Conversations with Zizek.* Conversations. Cambridge [u.a.]: Polity, 2004. p.1.

[3] Zizek, Slavoj. *The Fragile Absolute.* London; New York: Verso, 2000. p. 15.

Other disintegrate, but even directly causes this disintegration: far from being confronted with the abyss of their freedom… today's subject is perhaps more than ever caught in an inexorable compulsion that effectively runs his life."[1] He borrows the concept of the big Other from Lacan.

> **The Other**. This is a key logical component as well as the most obscure part of Lacan's philosophy. As early as the 1930s, Lacan began to use the word "other" but he did not distinguish the big Other and the small other.[2] In the beginning, Lacan adopted the word to illustrate the mirror image. It was very close to the concept of Autrui, is present as a reflective mirror mediator. In the 1950s, Lacan turned to linguistics. After that, he gradually came to the division of the big Other and the small other (Autre/Other and autre/other, in abbreviation, A and a), with the former representing the chain of signifiers in the symbolic language and the latter, the non-self mediator as the object of self-identification. The separation of the other into two is perhaps Lacan's original discovery.[3]

In my opinion, it is probably acceptable to say that the abstract logic of capital dominates the reality of life today. However, Zizek believes this is the Lacanian Real. (His logical shift is very questionable. We know that for Lacan, the reality of subjective existence derives from the illusory world that is constructed by mirror imagery and the symbolization of the big Other, whereas the Real presents itself where the symbolization fails. Accordingly, the material relation of capital is the big Other in social life, and equal exchange in the market of capitalism is an imaginary and symbolic legitimacy. Only from the place where such a materialized symbolization fails can it reveal the real masked by pseudo-reality: exploitation. In the

---

[1] Zizek, Slavoj. *The Ticklish Subject: The Absent Centre of Political Ontology*. Wo Es War. London; New York: Verso, 1999. p. 354.

[2] Only in the mid-1950s, Lacan began using Autre/Other (A/O) and autre/other (a/o) to indicate the specific meanings of the small Other and big Other, or "Big Other."

[3] *See The Impossible Truth of Being: Mirror of Lacan's Philosophy*. The Commercial Press. p. 267.

initial part of this chapter, there is a correct comment on it by Zizek.)

Anyway, Zizek seemingly consents to the conclusion which is said to be made by Marx: "Capitalism is a contingent monstrous formation whose very 'normal' state is permanent dislocation, a kind of 'freak of history', a social system caught in the vicious superego cycle of incessant expansion—yet precisely as such, it is the 'truth' of the entire preceding 'normal' history."[1]

2. The correlation between the contradiction and the drive of capitalism

Well, up till now, Zizek has been speaking for Marx and against the capitalist system, which may easily lead to an impression that he is a firm Marxist. Instead, Zizek does not believe that the classical Marxist logic offers a "full explanation" for today's capitalist globalization. In his eyes, the concrete social composition of capitalism in classical Marxism differs from Heidegger's to Adorno and Horkheimer's—which view the crazy capitalist dance as self-enhancing productivity as the expression of a more fundamental transcendental-ontological principle ("will to power," "instrumental reason"). Here, Zizek is trying to say that for Heidegger and Adorno, the key problem of capitalism is not Marx's relations of production, but rather the dominating violence derived from the instrumental rationality in the productive forces. In the same way, Heidegger says that "Americanism and Communism are metaphysically the same,"[2] implying the uncontrolled *production-growthism* shared by both of them.

Zizek proposes that we must admit the "fundamental mistake" by Marx, who sees the impetus of capitalism and the inner contradiction from this mode of production. "The ultimate limit of capitalism (of self-propelling capitalist productivity) is Capital itself, that is, the incessant development and revolutionizing of capitalism's own material conditions, the mad dance of its unconditional spiral of productivity, is ultimately nothing but a desperate

[1] Zizek, Slavoj. *The Ticklish Subject: The Absent Centre of Political Ontology.* Wo Es War. London; New York: Verso, 1999. p. 314.

[2] Zizek, Slavoj. *The Fragile Absolute.* London; New York: Verso, 2000. p. 16.

forward flight to escape its own debilitating inherent contradiction…"[1] However, Marx's further assumption of an ultimate communist society thoroughly free of the capitalist contradiction is an impossible imagination for Zizek. (Later, Zizek ironically calls it the communist *transparency of the Social*.) Why? According to Zizek, Marx is unaware that the impetus of the productive forces in capitalism stems from nowhere but its own contradiction.

> If we abolish the obstacle, the inherent contradiction of capitalism, we do not get the fully unleashed drive to productivity finally delivered of its impediment, we lose precisely this productivity that seemed to be generated and simultaneously thwarted by capitalism—if we take away this obstacle, the very potential thwarted by this obstacle dissipates….[2]

It is a paradox, by which Zizek means that the huge productive forces viewed by Marx in the capitalist mode of production rightly result from its own contradiction, which plays the role of the engine in a ship that drives it forward. As to Marx's communist society, where there is no contradiction, he says that:

> this notion of a society of pure unleashed productivity *outside* the frame of Capital, was a fantasy inherent to capitalism itself, the *capitalist* inherent transgression at its purest, a strictly *ideological* fantasy of maintaining the existing capitalism demonstrates—*the only possible framework of the actual material existence of a society of permanent self-enhancing productivity*.[3]

Obviously, Zizek disagrees with Heidegger, Adorno and Horkheimer. In his opinion, their inefficiency lies in the abandonment of the concrete social analysis of capitalism because what man needs today is not the passage from the "critique of political economy" to the transcendental-ontological "critique

---

[1] Zizek, Slavoj. *The Fragile Absolute*. London; New York: Verso, 2000. p. 17.

[2] Ibid. pp. 17-18.

[3] Ibid. p. 18.

of instrumental reason," but a return to the "critique of political economy." Zizek admits the reasonability of the general Western Marxist tradition since the young Lukacs, like their critique of economic determinism[1], but it does not mean people can ignore the economic realities of capitalism. What he has said sounds profound. Nevertheless, after his "return to the critique of political economy," he discovers that the "self-transparency" of the communist society designed by Marx is not real; therefore, he makes the following proposal:

> The task of today's thought is thus double: on the one hand, how to *repeat* the Marxist "critique of political economy" without the utopian-ideological notion of Communism as its inherent standard; on the other, how to imagine actually breaking out of the capitalist horizon *without* falling into the trap of returning to the eminently *premodern* notion of a balanced, (self-)restrained society (the "pre-Cartesian" temptation to which most of today's ecology succumbs.)[2]

In fact, it also shows his real opinion about Marxism: to retain the Marxist critical methods and the kernel of liberation while rejecting its fundamental principles. This is characteristic of the post-Marx trend. At the same time, he is against any attempt to completely solve the essential contradictions in human history because it is an impossible task, according to Lacan. Man's existence is contradiction, without which there is no man. The example cited by Zizek here amounts to an ecological goal, in other words, a neo-ecological ethic via the companionship of man and nature, ironically called by him as the "pre-modern concept."

More surprisingly, Zizek believes that the concept of Lacan's surplus-enjoyment imitates Marx's surplus value. He provides the proof that "the logic of the Lacanian *objet petit a* as the embodiment of surplus-enjoyment is already provided by the decisive formula used by Marx, in the third volume

---

[1] Zizek, Slavoj. *Absolute-or, Why is the Christian Legacy Worth Fighting For?*, London:Verso, 2000. p.18.

[2] Zizek, Slavoj. *The Fragile Absolute*. London; New York: Verso, 2000. pp. 19-20.

of *Capital*, to designate the logical-historical limit of capitalism: 'the limit of capital is capital itself, i.e. the capitalist mode of production.'" [1]

For this, Zizek offers two interpretations: the conventional understanding of Marxism and the Lacan-Zizek explanation. In the former context, we see a familiar schema of "common historicism: evolutionism," the productive force and the mode of production are in the dialectical contradiction of content and form.

> This paradigm follows roughly the metaphor of the serpent which, from time to time, sheds its skin, which has grown too tight: one posits as the last impetus of social development—as its (so to speak) "natural", "spontaneous" constant—the incessant growth of the productive forces (as a rule reduced to technical development), this "spontaneous" growth is then followed, with a greater or lesser degree of delay, by the inert, dependent moment, the relationship of production. We have thus epochs in which the relation of production are in accordance with the productive forces, then those forces develop and outgrow their "social clothes", the frame of relationships; this frame becomes an obstacle to their further development, until social revolution again co-ordinates forces and relations by replacing the old relations with new ones which correspond to the new state of forces.[2]

Although the metaphor of serpent is a little nauseating, it generally gives a correct description of the conventional Marxist interpretation of general historical materialism, in whose context, Zizek says, Marx's saying of capital as its own limit means that the capitalist society dies not because of the conventional social resistance against it, but rather because of "its ultimate inability to master and restrain its own inherent antagonism. The capitalist relations of production which at first made the fast development of productive forces possible became, at a certain point, an obstacle to their further development: these forces have outgrown their frame and demand

---

[1] Zizek, Slavoj. *The Sublime Object of Ideology*. London: Verso, 1989. pp. 50-51.
[2] Ibid, p. 51.

a new form of social relations. Marx himself is of course far from such a simplistic evolutionary idea"[1], because in *Das Kapital* Marx explains another idea: *the form drives the content*. According to Zizek, Marx discovers from the historical development of capital the "relation between formal and real subsumption of the process of production under Capital: the formal subsumption *precedes* the real one,"[2] that is, Capital first subsumes the process of production as it found it (artisans, and so on), and only subsequently does it change the productive forces step by step, shaping them in such a way as to create correspondence.

The second interpretation is posited in the Lacan-Zizek context. Marx's capital as its own limit is intended to account for the contradiction in the capitalist mode of production. The key point is: Does Marx really attempt to completely solve the contradiction? Zizek's stunning answer is: *Never*!

For him, it is the fundamental difference between capitalism and all the previous modes of production that matters.

> In capitalism, this contradiction, the discord forces/relation, *is contained in its very concept* (in the form of the contradiction between the social mode of production and the individual, private mode of appropriation). It is this internal contradiction which compels capitalism to permanent extended reproduction—to the incessant development of its own conditions of production, in contrast to previous modes of production where, at least in their "normal" state, (re)production goes on as a circular movement.[3]

Zizek believes that the *traumatic* kernel of the interior contradiction in capitalism keeps the momentum to change its own relations of production forever.

> *It is this very immanent limit, this "internal contradiction", which*

[1] Zizek, Slavoj. *The Ticklish Subject: The Absent Centre of Political Ontology*. Wo Es War. London; New York: Verso, 1999. p. 306.

[2] Zizek, Slavoj. *The Sublime Object of Ideology*. London: Verso, 1989. p. 51.

[3] Ibid, p. 52.

drives capitalism into permanent development. The "normal" state of capitalism is the permanent revolutionizing of its own conditions of existence: from the very beginning capitalism "putrefies", it is branded by a crippling contradiction, discord, by an immanent want of balance: this is exactly why it changes, develops incessantly—incessant development is the only way for it to resolve again and again, come to terms with, its own fundamental, constitutive imbalance, "contradiction". Far from constricting, its limit is thus the very impetus of its development. Herein lies the paradox proper to capitalism, its last resort: capitalism is capable of transforming its limit, its very impotence, in the source of its power—the more it "putrefies", the more its immanent contradiction is aggravated, the more it must revolutionize itself to survive.[1]

I have discussed this question before. In Zizek's view, the interior contradiction of capitalism is precisely its driving force, without which the development of this social mode is impossible. Thus, Zizek does not consent to the judgment of an "exterior limit" to the capitalist development. He thinks that "[c]apitalism has this incredible capacity of turning catastrophe into a new form of access;" and "[c]apitalism can turn every external limit to its development into a new field of market competition."[2]

In this connection, he openly opposes Marx despite the fact that he is a post-Marxist scholar. He also believes that the movement of socialism fails because "it [is] ultimately a subspecies of capitalism, an ideological attempt to 'have one's cake and eat it', to break out of capitalism while retaining its key ingredient."[3] In short, for Zizek, the complete "self-transparency" of communism without any contradiction designed by Marx is not real. This is the theoretical foundation for Zizek's post-Marxist political position. He is not a Marxist.

---

[1] Zizek, Slavoj. *The Sublime Object of Ideology*. London: Verso, 1989. p. 52.

[2] Zizek, Slavoj, and Glyn Daly. *Conversations with Zizek*. Conversations. Cambridge [u.a.]: Polity, 2004. p. 152.

[3] Zizek, Slavoj. *The Fragile Absolute*. London; New York: Verso, 2000. p. 19.

3. Marx's surplus value vs. Lacan's surplus enjoyment

When Zizek opposes the complete liberation of humanity in the future society predicted by Marx, he puts forward a more serious question about Marx's theory of surplus value. In his eyes, Marx makes use of the liberation to eliminate the developmental cause of the productive forces in capitalism. It is the same with a car whose engine is taken away to make it run faster. If put in the Lacanian discourse, Marx's mistake is "to assume that the object of desire (unconstrained expanding productivity) would remain even when it was deprived of the *cause* that propels it (surplus-value)."[1] In the eyes of Zizek, this is an impossible thing. As a result, surplus value is the mysterious objet-petit-a in the reality of capitalism.

> ***Objet-petit-a***. In French, objet-petit-a means the little *a* as the origin of the object of desire. It is a very important concept for the late Lacan. Its first usage is perhaps in the 1958 thesis *Remarks on the report of Daniel Lagache*: *"Psychoanalysis and personality structure."* Initially, it refers to a delusional presentation in the Imaginary; later it becomes the key word in the late Lacan's discussion of the Real. Although Lacan sometimes uses *a* for objet-petit-a, it should not be confused with the small other a in the mirror stage[2], the pseudo self-guidance of the first arrival of the objective ideal in the non-identification of a person's psyche. After Lacan enters the Real of human existence, he starts to pay attention to an *affirmative* content behind a pseudo-subjective construction, namely, the mirror identity, for example, the leftover that is missed by the mirror and something inaccessible to speech after the

---

[1] Zizek, Slavoj. *The Fragile Absolute*. London; New York: Verso, 2000. p. 21.

[2] The explanation by François Dosse is doubtful. By equating the objet-petit-a to the morphed other in the Imaginary of the mirror stage, he believes objet-petit-a is something against any symbolization (A). Nevertheless, how can it be consubstantial with the small other? Does it mean the mirror image is against the big Other? I think it is a misconception. *See* François Dosse's *From Construction to Deconstruction*: *Main Thoughts in 20th Century France*. Central Compilation and Translation Press, Vol. 1. p. 324.

existence killed by the symbolic language, in other words, *the leftover* or *the fallen* that cannot be completely symbolized. It is easy to be associated with the brutality of the conceptual homogeneity proposed by Adorno, in which an essential abstraction attempts to fantasize all the being beyond its containment; accordingly, the homogeneous abstraction always leaves a leftover *without*.[1] Jean Piaget regards this leftover as the mysterious "E" in the epistemological context, which reminds us of the "waste product" deserted from the scientific cognition suggested by Bataille, who even says that "the interest of philosophy" lies in considering such a waste production behind the violence of rational thought.[2] The residue does not have a material existence; it ultimately presents itself in the position erased by the subject, that is, *the lofty throne of vacancy*. Only in the failure of symbolization can we find this real event. Like a passing meteor in the night sky, Objet-petit-a is another proof of *the sublime object or the Thing* that we forever desire but will never touch.[3]

To understand this view, Zizek says, it is necessary to know the connection between Marx's surplus value as the driving force of capitalism and Lacan's libidinal dynamics of surplus enjoyment. He takes the familiar American Coke as an example, calling it the "ultimate commodity of capitalism," which, of course, is a metaphor. According to him, "Coke was first introduced as a medicine—its strange taste does not seem to provide any particular satisfaction; it is not directly pleasing and endearing; however, it is precisely as such, as transcending any immediate use-value (unlike water, beer or wine, which definitely do quench our thirst or produce the desired effect of satisfied calm), that Coke functions as the direct embodiment of

---

[1] *See* my *Atonal Dialectical Imagination: The Textological Reading of Adorno's Negative Dialectics.* Sanlian Bookstore Press, 2001. pp. 92-94.

[2] Bataille, Georges. *Eroticism, Expenditure and General Economy.* Ed. Wang Min'an: Jilin People's Publishing House, 2003. p. 8.

[3] *See The Impossible Truth of Being: Mirror of Lacan's Philosophy.* The Commercial Press. pp.349-350.

'it': of the pure surplus of enjoyment over standard satisfactions, of the mysterious and elusive X we are all after in our compulsive consumption of merchandise."[1] That is, Coke becomes something "superfluous" to drink when other drinks already satisfy our substantive necessity; thus, our need of it is often "insatiable": the more we drink, the thirstier we become.

> Coke is not an ordinary commodity whereby its use-value is transubstantiated into an expression of (or supplemented with) the auratic dimension of pure (exchange) Value, but a commodity whose very peculiar use-value is itself already a direct embodiment of the supra-sensible aura of the ineffable spiritual surplus, a commodity whose very material properties are already those of a commodity.[2]

Furthermore, Zizek cites another interesting example, namely, "caffeine-free diet Coke," available in any supermarket around us.[3] Zizek says that "we drink Coke—or any drink—for two reasons: for its thirst-quenching or nutritional value, and for its taste. In the case of caffeine-free diet Coke, nutritional value is suspended and the caffeine, as the key ingredient of its taste, is also taken away—all that remains is a pure semblance, an artificial promise of a substance which never materializes. Isn't it true that as far as the caffeine-free diet Coke is concerned, we almost literally 'drink nothing in the guise of something'?" (This is a very accurate and profound example.) Here, "We *drink the Nothingness itself*, the pure semblance of a property that is in effect merely an envelope of a void."[4] Zizek says that "what we are implicitly referring to there is, of course, Nietzsche's classic opposition between 'wanting nothing' (in the sense of 'I don't want anything') and the nihilistic stance of actively wanting Nothingness itself; following Nietzsche's

[1] Zizek, Slavoj. *The Fragile Absolute*. London; New York: Verso, 2000. p. 22.

[2] Ibid. pp. 22-23.

[3] Diet Coke originally has the meaning of "on diet" but the Coca-Cola Company puts this product into China's market with the Chinese name of "Healthy-Merry Coke." There is a slight difference here: Zizek's Coke refers to the production free of caffeine, while the corresponding Chinese product is free of sugar.

[4] Slavoj Zizek. *The Fragile Absolute*. London; New York: Verso, 2000. p. 23.

path, Lacan emphasized how in anorexia, the subject does not simply 'eat nothing'—rather, she or he actively wants to eat the Nothingness (the Void) that is itself the ultimate object-cause of desire."[1] In this regard, caffeine-free diet Coke is the famous Lacanian *objet petit a based on the nothingness*.

According to Zizek, the example of Coke displays the intrinsic linkage of three crucial elements:

> that of Marxist surplus-value, that of the Lacanian *objet petit a* as surplus-enjoyment (the concept that Lacan elaborated with direct reference to Marxian surplus-value), and the paradox of the superego, perceived long ago by Freud: the more Coke you drink, the thirstier you are; the more profit you make, the more you want; the more you obey the superego command, the guiltier you are.[2]

It looks like a weird association, especially when Zizek admits that, in comparison to Marx, the "Lacanian theory…is abstract, proto-Kantian, dealing with the ahistorical symbolic system, unaware of the concrete socio-historical conditions of its subject matter."[3] But Zizek's theoretical reflection is correct here. It seems that he intends to graft the abstract Lacan onto the social-historical Marx for a new *Marxian*-Lacanian philosophy, and use it as a weapon to criticize the speeding commercialization of the global capitalism. In my opinion, it is Lacan that sits in Zizek's logical center because *the Lacanian discourse takes over* Marx's critique of capitalism.

4. From tragedy to comedy: an overall take-over of Marx by the Lacanian discourse

In the eyes of Zizek, the change of times brings about the change of critical logics; thus, Marx's critique of conventional capitalism should be taken over by the Lacan-Zizek critical discourse. He thinks that with his

---

[1] Slavoj Zizek. *The Fragile Absolute*. London; New York: Verso, 2000. p. 23.

[2] Ibid, pp. 23-24.

[3] Ibid. p. 163.

own terminology, Lacan takes over and illustrates the Marxist theme in *The Manifesto*: how capitalism breaks all the stable relations and traditions and how anything settled dissipates under its impact.

To be specific, this substitution consists of two aspects. First, Marx's statement that "anything settled dissipates" mainly indicates the subversion of the solidificated patriarchal relations and narrow social life built on the agricultural-natural economy of the old societies, while the capitalist mode of production erodes the stable social structure with its own revolutions. For Zizek, the social relations have undergone a radical change: in the early industrial society of capitalism, people produced relatively durable goods for consumption, but today capitalist production mainly aims at the production of *immediately obsolete* garbage.

> Capitalism introduces a breathtaking dynamics of obsolescence: we are bombarded by new and newer products which are sometimes obsolete even before they come fully into use—PCs have to be replaced every year if one is to keep up with the Joneses; long playing records were followed by CDs, and now by DVDs. The aftermath of this constant innovation is, of course, the permanent production of piles of discarded waste.[1]

It is not a sensational opinion, but the case that happens to every Chinese today. For example, regarding the usage of computer, the continual upgrading of software, like that of Microsoft, will make your old computer useless.[2] To upgrade from VCD and LD (uncompressed laser disk player) to DVCD, DVD and EDVD takes only several years. Perhaps, every Chinese

---

[1] Slavoj Zizek. *The Fragile Absolute*. London; New York: Verso, 2000. p. 40.

[2] The IBM570 laptop that I am using to write this book was bought four years ago. Installed with the operation system of Windows 98, it can meet my need of ordinary textual writing, data processing and so on. However, the new systems of Windows 2000 and Windows XP create an artificial obsolescence with their new functions. Now it cannot automatically identify mobile hard disks, have high-speed internet port and play large video files and so on. It has already become garbage in the eyes of the other people.

family has such a pile of expensive junk.[1] For explanation, Zizek refers to his teacher, Jacques-Alain Miller (Lacan's son-in-law).

> The main production of the modern and postmodern capitalist industry is precisely waste. We are postmodern beings because we realize that all our aesthetically appealing consumption artifacts will eventually end as leftover, to the point that it will transform the earth into a vast waste land. You lose the sense of tragedy, you perceive progress as derisive.[2]

It is noticeable that Miller and Zizek want to correlate Lacan with the post-modern thought. They do not directly accept post-modernism, but believe that Lacan shrewdly exposes the false nature of today's life.

On the other side, according to Zizek, Marx himself explains that "anything settled" not only refers to material products but also indicates the stability that provides the symbolic order to confirm the identification for the subject. This is not wrong. To Marx, the bourgeois world replaces the feudal patriarchal relations with the cold and utilitarian monetary relationship. In comparison with the kinship locked to the land, the monetary relationship is fluid: anyone who can benefit me is my master. Zizek believes that this fluidity identified by Marx is even more magnified today, breeding more striking phenomena. In Miller's conclusion, the contemporary relations between people shift from the big Master, the signifier, to *objet-petit-a*. For this, Zizek explains as follows:

> In the discourse of the Master, the subject's identity is guaranteed by S1, by the Master-Signifier (his symbolic title—mandate), fidelity

---

[1] These devices cost several thousand yuans when they were first put into the market. A decade ago, an imported video recorder was 3,000 to 4,000 yuan, an LD, more than 6,000. Six or seven years ago, a DVD player was also expensive, more than 3,000 or 4000 yuan, but today, it only costs about 1,000 yuan. Now the video recorder and LD have been completely abandoned and become man-made disposable garbage. (When I revised the last draft of this book in the end of 2006, a common DVD fell to a few hundred yuan.)

[2] Zizek, Slavoj. *The Fragile Absolute*. London; New York: Verso, 2000. pp. 40-41.

to which defines the subject's ethical dignity. Identification with the Master-Signifier leads to the tragic mode of existence: the subject endeavors to sustain this fidelity to the Master-Signifier—say, to the mission which gives meaning and consistency to his life—to the end, and his attempt ultimately fails because of the remainder that resists the Master-Signifier. In contrast, there is the slippery-shifting subject who lacks any stable support in the Master-Signifier, and whose consistency is sustained by relationship to the pure remainder/trash/excess, to some 'undignified', inherently comic, little bit of the Real; such an identification with the leftover, of course, introduces the mocking-comic mode of existence, the parodic process of the constant subversion of all firm symbolic identifications.[1]

In my opinion, Zizek's explanation above further complicates the problem. The context here involves the elaboration of the signifier theory in the late Lacan's philosophy. In Lacan's early discussion about the Symbolic, the pseudo-subject is constructed by the floating chain of signifiers, and it is under the symbolic coercion of language signs that man further loses himself. In the seminar titled "Encore" in 1972-1973, Lacan had a careful discussion, in which he designated the initial symbolization of the subject entering the Symbolic; for instance, naming, as S1, the original signifier, also called the *First Signifier* or the *Master-Signifier*, which means that at the moment of the subjective loss a prerogative signifier is generated in which the subject existed to fill its vacancy and represent the nothingness of the lost subject.[2] It is this Master-Signifier that endows the subject with a relatively stable homogeneity of symbolic identity. For Zizek and Miller, in today's capitalist reality, that Master-Signifier with stable homogeneity of symbolic identity has become a new, "changed subject." Now, people do not simply maintain the homogeneity that represents identity; instead, they begin to dissipate

---

[1] Zizek, Slavoj. *The Fragile Absolute*. London; New York: Verso, 2000. pp. 42-43.

[2] Fukuhara Taihei. *Lacan: Mirror Stage*. Heibei Educational Publishing House, 2002. p. 119.

this homogeneity and keep displaying the so-called "indecent" "real" (objet-petit-a) to confirm the continuity of the subject, like, Clinton's sex scandal, Bush's slip of tongue, etc. In the past, this non-evident "real" would render some political image impossible. Nowadays, presentation of objet-petit-a will make a certain political image appear vivid and lovely. It is the post-modern "changed subject," also called by Zizek *the subject of cynicism.*

Zizek takes a more acute example for this by referring to the high-paid cultural profession in the Western academic circle. (He probably means those post-cultural white scholars, such as Fredric Jameson.) These people, he says, deem that their surging self-criticism of the Euro-centrism in Western academics can somewhat exempt themselves from being involved. Thus, they are very likely to "lie by pretending to speak out the truth."

> The full and candid admission of one's guilt is the ultimate deception, *the way* to preserve one's subjective position intact, free from guilt. In short, there is a way to *avoid* responsibility and/or guilt by, precisely, *emphasizing* one's responsibility or too readily *assuming* one's guilt in an exaggerated way, as in the case of the white male PC academic who emphasizes die guilt of racist phallogo-centrism, and uses this admission of guilt as a stratagem *not* to face the way he, as a "radical" intellectual, perfectly embodies the existing power relations towards which he pretends to be thoroughly critical.[1]

Zizek is very perceptive regarding this point. He say that today we would like to "seek the real self," which would be "two split real selves" in the Lacanian discourse.

> On the one hand, there is the Master-Signifier that delineates the contours of the subject's Ego-Ideal, his dignity, his mandate; on the other, there is the excremental leftover/trash of the symbolic process, some ridiculous feature that sustains the subject's surplus-enjoyment— and the ultimate goal of psychoanalysis is to enable the subject-analyze

---

[1] Zizek, Slavoj. *The Fragile Absolute.* London; New York: Verso, 2000. p. 46.

and to accomplish the passage from S1 to *objet petit a*—to identify, in a kind of *"Thou Art That"* experience, (with) the excremental remainder that secretly sustains the dignity of his symbolic identification.[1]

What happens now is the transformation from the Master-Signifier, which maintains the homogeneous identity of the subject, to the objet-petit-a as the leftover of the failed symbolic homogeneity, or to put it more simply, a conversion of identification from the symbolic to the leftover. For Zizek, the former is a tragedy while the latter is a comedy, because symbolic identification always ends in failure, it is thus tragic; but the identification of the leftover tends to be present in a cynical style of "anything goes", causing a comic or farcical ending. Correspondingly, conversion from S1 to objet-petit-a is also a "shift from *tragedy* to *comedy*".

This shift, theoretically, is a complete take-over of Marx's social critical theory by the Lacanian thought. Jameson makes the comment that "Zizek wants to tell us that Lacanism is also such a converting mode, a mode even superior to and inclusive of Marxism and the dialectics."[2] More importantly, Zizek once said that "we must stick to the Marxist insight that the only thing which can destroy capitalism is capital itself. It must explode from within."[3] However, regarding the specific analysis of problems, the Lacanian answer is "impossible."

Here, we have an outline of Marx and Lacan in Zizek's eyes. It paves the way for the following analysis of *The Sublime Object of Ideology* and related texts. Next, we are to discuss the first chapter of this book.

I. Impossibility: The Political Position of the Post-Marxian Trends

According to Ernesto Laclau, in contrast to those successors who

---

[1] Zizek, Slavoj. *The Fragile Absolute*. London; New York: Verso, 2000. pp. 48-49.

[2] Jameson, Fredric. *Neo-Marxism*. People's University Press, 2004. p. 143.

[3] Zizek, Slavoj, and Glyn Daly. *Conversations with Zizek: Conversations*. Cambridge [u.a.]: Polity, 2004. p. 152.

induct Lacan to the clinical field, the Lacanian School represented by Zizek features the application of Lacan to philosophy and politics. In these two fields, Zizek directly faces Marx. It is true that Zizek seemingly agrees to the "post-Marxian" logic of Laclau and Mouffe, but his theoretical logic does not belong to Marxism. Strictly speaking, Zizek's post-Marxist thought actually rejects Marx. He only takes Marx's critical spirit as an inheritable and changeable legacy, as some absent specter. (He is no different from Derrida at this point.) In his Introduction to the treatise, we already see that altered view of communism as a Lacanian impossible Real. (Glyn Daly observes that "the notion of impossibility lies at the root of Zizek's political perspective.")[1] Marx's liberation of humanity becomes an original deep trauma guiding society forward; revolution no longer aims at complete emancipation; and the actual struggle forever demonstrates a compromising hue.

1. Habermas and Foucault: two traditional ideas of subject in the shadowgraphs of contemporary theories

Zizek's discussion begins from Habermas, who is still in the center of European academic discourse. In a pretentious tone, he says that Habermas mentions Lacan five times on post-structuralism in his *Philosophical Discourse of Modernity* but Lacan's name is among a string of other names, like Bataille, Derrida, etc., in particular, Foucault, who is also a focus of discussion. It is perhaps an undiscovered conspiracy, with the implication that despite Lacan's importance, Habermas does not offer him his due status. Zizek wants us to perceive the secret reason behind it.

For Zizek, the answer to this mystery is buried in another black hole of logic, also a curious accident concerning Althusser "in a Sherlock Holmesian sense" (Zizek means it is a question worth our in-depth consideration and decision), in which "Althusser's name is not even mentioned in Habermas' book." "The Habermas-Foucault debate is masking another opposition, another debate which is theoretically more far-reaching: the Althusser-Lacan

---

[1] Zizek, Slavoj, and Glyn Daly. *Conversations with Zizek*. Conversations. Cambridge [u.a.]: Polity, 2004. p. 13.

debate."[1] (It is necessary to remind the reader that Zizek, like his teacher Lacan, usually utilizes a metaphorical and indirect discourse. We will come to understand and adapt to it.) It is Habermas as the defender of Enlightenment and modernity who reprimands such "post-modernist" advocates as Foucault with the famous saying that "post-modernism is the biggest conservatism." However, why does Zizek say that Habermas and Foucault are only conducting a theoretical shadowgraph, only masking the real meaning of Lacan and Althusser with "a metaphorical substitution." If Zizek is sober, it should be a genuine subversion of academic judgment: he regards Habermas and Foucault as nonsense.

Zizek believes that there are four ethics and concepts of subject, among which two are true and two are false. First, we are going to discuss the two false ones which appear dynamic and avant-garde but are essentially traditional. (To expose the falsity of common knowledge is a regular practice in the Lacanian philosophy.)

First, Habermas' concept of *communication subject*. "With Habermas, we have the ethics of the unbroken communication, the Ideal of the universal, transparent intersubjective community, the notion of the subject behind this is, of course, the philosophy-of-language version the old subject of transcendental reflection."[2] For Zizek, although Habermas criticizes the existing intersubjective deformation or ideological barrier in his theory of the communication subject he still holds the *transparent*, universalistic inter-subjectivity in his hypothesis of ideal value for Habermas' conception of subject is the pure communication subject rescued from dirty relations in secular ideology. Nevertheless, this ideal communication subject that acts as Habermas' salvation goal is but "the old subject of transcendental reflection" in Zizek's opinion. (Zizek even identifies it with a common sense "big Other" in another place.)[3] I think this is a correct reasoning because any form of

---

[1]   Zizek, Slavoj. *The Sublime Object of Ideology*. London: Verso, 1989. p. 1.

[2]   Ibid., p. 2.

[3]   Zizek, Slavoj. *Grimaces of the Real*. Central Compilation and Translation Press, 2004. p. 255

transparency and authenticity of the subjective existence is the fantasy of the Other in the Lacanian logic.

Second, Foucault's *concept of the pure individual*. According to Zizek, we see a rejection of "universalist ethics" with Foucault. (Universalism here should be interpreted as the rationalistic generic-Subject. I mentioned before that the most important critique of the generic-Subject begins with Max Stirner.) Accordingly, Foucault stands opposite Habermas: the old subject of transcendental reflection is accused of a violent spreading of rational (intellectual) discourse; the essentially mad presence of the individual is unconsciously enslaved by the self-servitude and self-restrain of a non-external mandatory discourse. Foucault regards it as the self-punishment law of the entire bourgeois kingdom. Zizek says that this exceptional rebellion of Foucault undoubtedly leads to an ethical "aestheticization."

> Each subject must, without any support from universal rules, build his own mode of self-mastery; he must harmonize the antagonism of the powers within himself—invent himself, so to speak, produce himself as subject, find his own particular art of living. This is why Foucault was so fascinated by marginal lifestyles constructing their particular mode of subjectivity (the sadomasochistic homosexual universe, for example: see Foucault, 1984).[1]

In fact, it is still the real individual Dasein from Stirner, Kierkegaard and Nietzsche, only ridding itself of the Heideggerian free *mad-me* in common people. Foucault thinks that the big Subject and Author is dead. Following Nietzsche's claim that God is dead, he kills the Man. As a result, the pure non-self-restrained me is born from the soft violence against all conventions and culture. (Indeed, this kind of post-modern drama repeats itself several times through Derrida's différance in the deconstruction of logo-centrism, Lyotard's "humble" small self in the anti-grand narrative, and Feyerabend's "anything-goes" method.) Zizek directly penetrates the pompous mask

---

[1] Zizek, Slavoj. *The Sublime Object of Ideology*. London: Verso, 1989. p. 2.

of post-modernism: the thought of Foucault and others belongs to the old humanism-elitism as it most reflects the ideal of the all-round development of personality of the Renaissance, which requires one to control one's passion and turn one's life into a piece of art. Foucault's subject is rather classical: the subject stimulates self-meditation makes various contradicting forces in a peaceful co-existence, and adjust the "use of pleasure" through restoring the image of self. Here, Zizek makes a big mystery. As described by Lukacs, bourgeois subjectivity is split. The early "all-round development of personality" in the Renaissance is buried in the generic-Subject of later abstract rationalism. Foucault's rebellion against the Subject inherits the *neo-humanistic* practice of Stirner, Kierkegaard, and in particular, Nietzsche and Heidegger. He demands the direct presence of the survival "passion" (in the Hegelian dictionary, it is the individual) of the real subject itself. Existence is art and art is enjoyment and indulgence. (The background here includes Heidegger's poetic survival all along to Henri Lefebvre and the situationalist slogan "to make daily life into art!")

More importantly, Zizek wisely identifies Foucault and Habermas as just the two sides of the same bourgeois coin: the front is the generic-Subject; the back, individual subject. They are like two *connected* rings in a *signifier chain* of humanistic logic.

2. Althusser and Lacan: the heterogeneity in the nothingness of the subject

Third, Althusser's *pseudo-subject*, which Zizek regards as "the real break." This is a qualitative judgment: in comparison with the false subject proposed by Habermas and Foucault, Althusser's subject is true. He radically denies any traditional conception of subject, claiming the historical "non-subjectivity." For him, the existential status of humanity in reality is falsified into a non-present explosion. From *For Marx* (1965) to *Ideology and Ideological State Apparatuses* (1969), the nothingness of the early generic-Subject (the non-alienated authentic Man) is turned into the non-substantiality of the individual subject (the small self as Dasein), during which "a certain cleft, a certain fissure, misrecognition, characterizes the human condition as such: by the thesis that the idea of the possible end of ideology is an ideological idea *par excellence* (Althusser, 1965)."[1] For Althusser, various human subjects are all ideological pseudo-images; the alienation logic of the generic-Subject is a non-scientific ideology; and the non-alienated authentic subject is only an ideal imagination of value, e.g. the transparent (authentic) intersubject free of the contamination of pathological communication. At the same time, any individual subject is the result of ideological inquiry. Accordingly, even the Foucaultian mad, perverse, free, homosexual individual "is constituted through a certain misrecognition: the process of ideological interpellation through which the subject 'recognizes' itself as the addressee in the calling up of the ideological cause implies necessarily a certain short circuit, an illusion of the type 'I was already there.'"[2] I want to escape the rational framework, eliminate the hegemony of intellectual discourse, therefore, I taking drugs, I identify with homosexuals, and I whoop my uniqueness. But all this still results from the interpellation of ideology. How miserable! For Althusser, a mere answer to a "hello" in the street will make you constituted by the invisible inquiry of the contemporary ideology. That the ideology of "grand narrative" is ending is but a more subtle ideology described as "post-modern." The queer representation of individual existence is dominated by a weird ideology. Zizek believes that Althusser's subject inquiry exposes the structural mechanism: something that produces the effect of subject as the misconception of ideology. (Zizek says that Althusser's student Michel Pêcheux provides "the most delicate version" of this inquiry theory. He also mentions the behavioral similarity of Althusser's view with the Foucaultian discipline.[3] Therefore, in Zizek's opinion, although Althusser does not dabble in ethics, he displays a "radical ethical attitude," which can be called "the heroism of alienation" or "subjective

---

[1] Zizek, Slavoj. *The Sublime Object of Ideology*. London: Verso, 1989. p. 2.

[2] Ibid.

[3] Zizek, Slavoj. *The Ticklish Subject: The Absent Centre of Political Ontology*. Wo Es War. London; New York: Verso, 1999. p. 306.

destitution." Althusser really wants to deny any subject or subjectivity. He is not interested in restoring the fallen subjectivity or sick individual subject. He sticks to the Non-subject and Non-humanity in social historical existence. (As I mentioned before, Althusser misunderstands the Marxist view that the essence of man is in its reality the ensemble of the social relations. Thus, man becomes a function in the vacancy of the mode of production.)[1]

However, to Zizek, the most important meaning of Althusser's conception of subject does not lie in bringing down the subject, but rather the announcement of the *impossible* dissipation of this ideological misconception and its ensuing eternity.

> The point is not just that we must unmask the structural mechanism which is producing the effect of subject as ideological misrecognition, but that we must at the same time fully acknowledge this misrecognition as unavoidable—that is, we must accept a certain delusion as a condition of our historical activity, of assuming a role as agent of the historical process.[2]

This is correct. Althusser once mentions that ideology is not a simple scam and it is even a necessary condition for man's survival. (A view more advanced than Gramsci's "cement" analogy.) With him, even in communism, there is still ideology. Thus, the declaration of the end of ideology is itself an unconscious product of ideology. (It should be noted that Althusser, despite being a Western Marxist, never gives up the social revolutionary view of historical materialism, the class struggle. He always imagines the future demise of capitalism, which is, of course, not a question of alienation and restoration of the true or false subject. The conversion of the mode of production in the non-subjective social structure certainly has a complete solution. That I single out this point is to prepare for unmaking the mystery that Zizek uses to attack the Marxist view of social revolution in the

---

[1] Zhang Yibing. *Problematic, Symptomal Reading and Ideology: A Textological Illustration of Althusser*. Central Compilation and Translation Press, 2003. pp. 285-286.

[2] Zizek, Slavoj. *The Sublime Object of Ideology*. London: Verso, 1989. p. 2.

next part.)

Fourth, the Lacanian *mutilated subject*, ceremoniously launched by Zizek. In fact, Althusser's questioning of the individual subject in 1969 appropriates Lacan's pseudo-subject. It is perhaps a misunderstanding of Lacan. Zizek says Althusser's concept of subject is opposite to that of Lacan's. Why? Because Althusser bases his theory on the quasi-structuralist logic, which leads to his radical denial of any real existence of human subject framed within the structures of society (mode of production) and language: various human objects identified in ideology are merely relational pseudo-images. Althusser has something true when fighting against the old subjectivity of Habermas and Foucault, but his truth comes with misrecognition, and the real concern is still the Lacanian concept of subject. This also forms the foundation for Zizek.

According to Zizek, Lacan's concept of subject can be called "the ethics of *separation*." It is difficult to comprehend this theoretical positioning. (For a Chinese reader who encounters this theoretical assertion, it is not possible to grasp the key point without previous introduction and discussion about Lacan's thought.)[1] In Zizek's view, Lacan opposes the old concept of subject, but does not agree to the Althusserian nihilistic "non-subject." At the very beginning, the individual subject misrecognizes the small other in the mirror stage (including the small other I as an image in the reflection of mirror and the small other II as the faces of others), thus rendering the real subject a vacancy in the Imaginary. When entering the Symbolic, the big Other with the backbone of the signifier chain further makes the subjective existence into an alienation floating on the conversion of signifiers. Nevertheless, in the late Lacan's thought, the Real eventually outstands; and objet-petit-a, as the leftover of symbolic engulfment, supports the mutilated subject. The S as subject is forever slashed; man has to be "Zu-sein." He withstands numerous tricks of the Other, but is still alive, still struggling as a remaining sewing (symptom Σ). It is impossible to restore himself and this

---

[1] *See The Impossible Truth of Being: Mirror of Lacan's Philosophy*. The Commercial Press, 2006.

impossibility becomes the root of his survival. He is not really dead; with the original desire of survival in reality, he *has to live*.

> The famous Lacanian motto not to give way on one's desire [*ne pas céder sur son desir*]—is aimed at the fact that we must not obliterate the distance separating the Real from its symbolization: it is this surplus of the Real over every symbolization that functions as the object-cause of desire. To come to terms with this surplus (or, more precisely, leftover) means to acknowledge a fundamental deadlock ("antagonism"), a kernel resisting symbolic integration-dissolution.[1]

I have mentioned more than once that Zizek's logic is based on the late Lacanian thought. (Obviously, Zizek's analysis above is a result of numerous metaphor-metonymy-metaphor transformations of signifiers. To most readers unfamiliar with the Lacanian philosophy, it is not easy to understand this discussion.) Here, Lacan already admits the mutilated subject of the real kernel. Do not yield to desire; it is the antagonism against the Other with no promise of ultimate liberation. Man is this antagonism itself, this forever-tied deadlock. (With Albert Camus, man's existence is ridiculous, like Sisyphus who keeps rolling up the boulder after it rolls down. The endless antagonism is the key to man's existence.) If it represents an ethical spirit, Zizek says, it is the Sisyphusian subjectivity separated from the false absolute subject or a transparent existence of alienation (the One World or communism and the free kingdom of complete human emancipation) that is attempedly reached and sublated through struggle. The false images of the subjects stick to each other every day while we try to separate them. Subject is thus hopeless *separation*. It is not the non-being but the *mutilated being*.

I find that Zizek is also "frying" Lacan. His account of the four concepts of subject here is not meant for a mere discussion of philosophy, but rather to introduce a post-Marxist guideline of revolution, a new trick whose radical nature is against the traditional Marxist revolution. I call it a trick because

---

[1] Zizek, Slavoj. *The Sublime Object of Ideology*. London: Verso, 1989. p. 3.

this is no longer a revolution but a strategy of compromise. We are soon to see its intention.

3. Deleting nostalgia: spectacle of the "post-Marxist" social revolution

For Zizek, Lacan's separation of ethics contains a resistance, which, perceived from the social historical aspect, is radically differentiated from conventional Marxism. Zizek believes that the Marxist social contradiction, as the "social antagonism", has two major features.

> 1) There exists a certain fundamental antagonism possessing an ontological priority to "mediate" all other antagonisms, determining their place and their specific weight (class antagonism, economic exploitation); 2) historical development brings about, if not a necessity, at least an "objective possibility" of solving this fundamental antagonism.[1]

If my understanding is correct, Zizek's first point refers to the basic movement of the internal contradictions within the mode of production (the productive forces and the relations of production) unmasked by Marx, which accounts for the class struggle and other social contradictions. Marx believes that the social historical development always provides the material condition to solve these contradictions, that is, the "objective possibility." In general, Zizek does not make any big mistake by the above argument. However, he aims to deny that perception of historical materialism.

According to Zizek, the Marxist revolutionary view is built on a fundamental solution of social confrontation, or complete liberation. It always warns those people in the specific contradictions (such as workers in the economic battle, the feminists in the struggle to oppose patriarchy, the ecologists fighting against the plundering of natural, etc.):

> The only real solution to their problem is to be found in the global

---

[1] Zizek, Slavoj. *The Sublime Object of Ideology*. London: Verso, 1989. p. 3.

revolution: as long as social relations are dominated by Capital, there
will always be sexism in relations between the sexes, there will always
be a threat of global war, there will always a danger that political and
social freedoms will be suspended, nature itself will always remain an
object of ruthless exploitation… The global revolution will then abolish
the basic social antagonism, enabling the formation of a transparent,
rationally governed society.[1]

Obviously, Zizek opposes the traditional Marxist goal of liberation. His
"transparent, rationally governed society" is an ironical call of the communist
kingdom of complete liberation foreseen by Marx and Engels. For a Lacanian
Zizek, this *ultimate solution* is impossible to achieve because, if Lacan's
concept of subject is right, human society per se as a self-sufficient subject
in Marx's view is a huge fantasy in the essentialist logic. The individual
subject is never himself but the deceptive existence of nothingness after
being usurped by the small other and the big Other. In addition, even if we
are disillusioned with the mortal world or tear apart the face of the other,
we can never return to the authentic dasein. There has been no authentic
existence of man. He is forever the slashed subject of impossible existence,
the symptomatic presence of impossible being. (In this sense, Zizek says that
Lacan is truly anti-essentialist.) Mutilation becomes the authentic existence
of the subject. In this context, the class struggle and economic conflict at the
level of society can never change the ontological impossibility of the subject's
"coming home." In the Lacan-Zizek logic, history itself has no authenticity; it
is only a mirage constructed by the big Other in the retrospective imagination.
Therefore, in comparison with the hegemonic coercion of the bourgeoisie
ideology, any attempt to subvert the existing framework for the restoration of
human liberation will be an ideology, only that utopian socialism is a simple
revolutionary imagination of ideology while the revolution of historical
materialism is a more complex sublime desire of ideology. For Zizek, *any
essentialist homesickness is to be resolutely deleted.*

---

[1]   Zizek, Slavoj. *The Sublime Object of Ideology*. London: Verso, 1989. p. 4.

Deletion of nostalgia. For Heidegger, being-towards-death is the tendency of original self, the possibility to "be *authentically itself*,"[1] and a fact obtained through the call of conscience[2], from which, dasein can really get out of the "not-at-home" status.[3] In Heidegger's hopeful fancy, man can go home, say "no" to alienation and finally come back singing Hölderlin's poem. This ontology is fundamentally built on a nostalgia for authentic existence. However, Lacan's objet-petit-a smashes Heidegger's last existence, and erases the final Hölderlin-Heideggerian nostalgia because "*homelessness is man's true existence.*" As a result, Zizek says, "The essence of homelessness is the homelessness of the essence itself; it resides in the fact that, in our world thrown out of joint by the frenetic search for empty pleasures, there is no home, no proper dwelling, for the truly essential dimension of man."[4]

Lacan says that "indeed, whether Socrates, Descartes, Marx or Freud, they cannot be transcended for they are engaged in research with a passion, the end of which is to discover an object: truth."[5] This truth is impossibility. The Real is the ontological failure of the never-ending logical transcendence. Therefore, "the real is always new."[6] Man forever pursues the real that is always new, always in the far distance.[7]

Thus, we can understand Zizek, whose social historical view is but the post-Marxist thought, the new socialist strategy of the "post-Marxism" of Ernesto Laclau and Chantal Mouffe. (For Zizek, it can be read as a kind of "postmodernist" or "deconstructionist" displacement of the Althusserian

---

[1] Heidegger, Martin. *Being and Time.* Blackwell, 1978. p. 308.

[2] Ibid., p. 314.

[3] Ibid., p. 321.

[4] Zizek, Slavoj. *Mapping Ideology.* London; New York: Verso, 1994. p. 16.

[5] *See* Lacan, Jacques. *ÉCRITS: A Selection.* Trans. Alan Sheridan. New York: Norton, 1977.

[6] Ibid.

[7] *See The Impossible Truth of Being: Mirror of Lacan's Philosophy.* The Commercial Press, 2006. pp. 344-345.

edifice: the distinction between science and ideology collapses since the notion of ideology is universalized as the struggle for hegemony that rends the very heart of every social formation, accounting for its fragile identity and, simultaneously, forever preventing its closure; the notion of the subject is re-conceptualized as the very operator of hegemony. It is a very interesting interpretation.)[1] In Zizek's opinion, the basic "post-Marxist" character proclaimed by Laclau and Mouffe disintegrates the logic of the essentialist ultimate liberation of Marxism for it is against any form of essentialism in social historical theories. "Affirming the irreducible plurality of particular struggles—in other words, demonstrating how their articulation into a series of equivalences depends always on the radical contingency of the social-historical process: it enables us to grasp this plurality itself as a multitude of responses to the same impossible-real kernel."[2] Simply speaking, even if man's complete liberation is *impossible*, the fight against capitalism is a perpetual *reform that recognizes its traumatic cleft.*

It is the merit of Ernest Laclau and Chantal Mouffe that they have, in *Hegemony and Socialist Strategy* (Laclau-Mouffe 1985), developed a theory of the social field founded on such a notion of antagonism—on an acknowledgement of an original "trauma", an impossible kernel which resists symbolization, totalization, symbolic integration. Every attempt at symbolization-totalization comes afterwards: it is an attempt to suture an original cleft—an attempt which is, in the last resort, by definition doomed to failure. They emphasize that we must not be "radical" in the sense of aiming at a radical solution: we always live in an interspace and in borrowed time; every solution is provisional and temporary, a kind of postponing of a fundamental impossibility. Their term "radical democracy" is thus to be taken somehow paradoxically: it is precisely *not* "radical" in the sense of pure, true democracy; its radical

---

[1] Zizek, Slavoj. *The Ticklish Subject: The Absent Centre of Political Ontology*. Wo Es War. London; New York: Verso, 1999. p. 128.

[2] Zizek, Slavoj. *The Sublime Object of Ideology*. London: Verso, 1989. p. 4.

character implies, on the contrary, that we can save democracy only by *raking into account its own radical impossibility*.[1]

In this way, the so-called "post-Marxism" displays a distinct anti-Marxist feature: in traditional Marxism, the global solution-revolution is the condition of the effective solution of all particular problems, while here every provisional, temporarily successful solutions of a particular problem entails an acknowledgement of the global radical deadlock, the impossibility, the acknowledgement of a fundamental antagonism.

4. Irremediable trauma: the post-Marxian political ideas of Zizek

Zizek thinks that Lacan goes further than "post-Marxism" does; in other words, only Lacan presents a real break with essentialist logic. As I said before, it is an ontological logic of antagonism which leads to no result. Lacan tells us that any culture of human existence is a kind of "creation-formation" of the original nature, man's original being. It is always an indigenous "imbalance" and "radical antagonism," "through which man cuts his umbilical cord with nature, with animal homeostasis."[2] Since man *is that trauma*, he can neither return to the natural originality, nor suture the wound that he cuts in the natural mother. (This is an adapted Hegelian view that "man is dark" from the perspective of natural existence. It is an irreversible logic.) Lacan makes us aware of the impossibility of eliminating this ontological "antagonism", because elimination itself is the denial of man's existence as such. In addition, there is another realistic factor, namely, "the aspiration to abolish it is precisely the source of totalitarian temptation: the greatest mass murders and holocausts have always been perpetrated in the name of man as a harmonious being, of a New Man without antagonistic tension."[3]

Therefore, according to the Lacan-Zizek logic, when we face the social trauma (the capitalist oppression and slavery described by Marx), we shall

---

[1] Zizek, Slavoj. *The Sublime Object of Ideology*. London: Verso, 1989. pp. 5-6.

[2] Ibid., p. 5.

[3] Ibid., p. 5.

undoubtedly fight against it, but it will last forever.

> There is no solution, no escape from it; the thing to do is not to "overcome", to "abolish" it, but to come to terms with it, to learn to recognize it in its terrifying dimension and then, on the basis of this fundamental recognition, to try to articulate a *modus vivendi* with it.[1]

Here, Zizek's social historical view displays an out-and-out capitulationism in the eyes of the traditional Marxism. He does not believe in a final solution to the social contradictions and all the problems between man and nature, and between man and man. What we can do is to "compromise" in that struggle.

Zizek takes an account of three parallel, Lacanized, "compromising" logics.

First, "the same logic" with ecology, with a transformed ecological struggle against "the control of nature." According to the recently amended ecological ethics, the birth and existence of man is "the wound of nature", or man is that irremediable wound. Thus, he is not able to return to the original balance of nature. To achieve harmony with the environment, what he can do is to "accept fully this cleft, this fissure, this structural rooting-out, and to try as far as possible to patch things up afterwards; all other solutions—the illusion of a possible return to nature, the idea of a total socialization of nature—are a direct path to totalitarianism."[2] (It is a caricatured repetition of Adorno's homogeneity and the assertion of Auschwitz.)

Second, "the same logic" with feminism, whose battle against patriarchy is considered as a farce because "there is no sex" (Lacan); that is, the relation between sexes is by definition "impossible", antagonistic; there is no final solution, and the only possibility for a somewhat bearable relation between the sexes is an acknowledgement of this fundamental antagonism, this basic impossibility.

Third, "the same logic with democracy." As we know, the existing

---

[1] Zizek, Slavoj. *The Sublime Object of Ideology*. London: Verso, 1989. p. 5.

[2] Ibid.

democratic system is perhaps the worst of all possible systems, and the only problem is that "there is no other which would be better" (Winston Churchill). That is to say, democracy always entails the possibility of corruption, of the rule of dull mediocrity; the problem is that every attempt to elude this inherent risk and to restore "real" democracy necessarily brings about its opposite—the abolition of democracy itself.

Zizek comes to an anti-traditional conclusion: Hegel is the first "post-Marxist" (Zizek is capable of making such strange assumptions all the time) because of the "recognition" of his Lacanian "antagonism", and because "the most consistent model of such an acknowledgement of antagonism is offered by Hegelian dialectics."

> For Hegel a systematic notation of the failure of all such attempts— "absolute knowledge" denotes a subjective position which finally accepts "contradiction" as an internal condition of every identity. In other words, Hegelian "reconciliation" is not a "panlogicist" sublation of all reality in the Concept but a final consent to the fact that the Concept itself is "not-all" (to use this Lacanian term). In this sense we can repeat the thesis of Hegel as the first post-Marxist: he opened up the field of a certain fissure subsequently "sutured" by Marxism.[1]

In my opinion, the background for this is the reinterpretation of Hegel by Zizek. In comparison with the traditional Hegelian absolute idea to put an end to everything, Zizek regards the essence of the Hegelian philosophy as "non-comprehensive," non-absolute. He believes the conclusion of "absolute knowledge" as a monster of conceptual totality which must be drawn with undue haste. He even offers a joke to illustrate it. During Wojciech Jaruzelski's reign in Poland, military patrols had the right to shoot without warning at people walking on the streets after curfew (10 o'clock); one of the two soldiers on patrol saw somebody in a hurry at ten minutes to ten and shot him immediately. When his colleague asked him why he shot when it

---

[1] Zizek, Slavoj. *The Sublime Object of Ideology*. London: Verso, 1989. p. 6.

was only ten to ten, he answered: "I knew the fellow—he lives far from here and in any case would not be able to reach his home in ten minutes, so to simplify matters, I shoot him now…" Zizek says that the old announcement of Hegel's "panlogism," just like that soldier, "shoots too fast." (It connotes a pornographic sense here.) This thought does not belong to Hegel at all.

Then, Zizek explains three theoretical objectives of *The Sublime Object of Ideology*: to introduce Lacan, to "return to Hegel," and to propose a new ideological critique based on Lacan and Marx.

The first objective is a general introduction of Lacanian psychoanalysis (the second half of the book is almost completely a discussion of the late Lacan). Zizek also explicitly opposes the act of deforming Lacan as a post-structuralist, and naturally, denies similar opinions of Chinese scholars. He believes in Lacan's radical break from the post-structuralist camp and disagrees to the consideration of the complex Lacanian theory as obscurantism. In his eyes, Lacan should be posited in the lineage of rationalism, and his "theory is perhaps the most radical contemporary version of the Enlightenment."

The second objective is to complete an academic "return to Hegel," to reactualize Hegelian dialectics by giving it a new reading on the basis of Lacanian psychoanalysis. He means to reconstruct Hegel with Lacanian logic. For Zizek, the current image of Hegel as an "idealist-monist" is totally misleading: "what we find in Hegel is the strongest affirmation yet of difference and contingency—'absolute knowledge' itself is nothing but a name for the acknowledgement of a certain radical loss."[1]

The last object is "to contribute to the theory of ideology" through a new reading of "some well-known classical motifs (commodity fetishism, and so on) and of some crucial Lacanian concepts which, on a first approach, have nothing to offer to the theory of ideology: the 'quilting point,' sublime object, surplus-enjoyment, and so on."[2] (In fact, it is probably what we should specially notice.) It is through them that Zizek realizes the logical grafting of

---

[1] Zizek, Slavoj. *The Sublime Object of Ideology*. London: Verso, 1989. p. 7.
[2] Ibid.

Lacan onto Marx, leading to a new theoretical scene, Zizek's philosophical context.

It is my belief that these three aims are deeply connected: the only way to "save Hegel" is through Lacan, and this Lacanian reading of Hegel and the Hegelian heritage opens up a new approach to ideology, allowing us to grasp contemporary ideological phenomena (cynicism, "totalitarianism", the fragile stratus of democracy) without falling prey to any kind of "post-modernist" traps (such as the illusion that we live in a "post-ideological" condition).[1]

The post-Marx context of Zizek is essentially a part of anti-post-modernism. He has a very wonderful saying: "after the fall of socialism, the knave is a neo-conservative advocate of the free market who cruelly rejects all forms of social solidarity as counterproductive sentimentalism, while the fool is a deconstructionist cultural critic who, by means of his ludic procedures destined to 'subvert' the existing order, actually serves as its supplement."[2] Liberalism is a knave; post-modernism (deconstruction) is a fool. Zizek wants to take a new road to face Marx. Let's wait and see.

II. Marx Invents the Lacanian Concept of Symptom

At the first look of the above subtitle, most readers will be puzzled: how can Marx be juxtaposed with Lacan and how is an ensuring concept called "symptom" invented? In fact, it is a common practice of Zizek to discuss possibility from the impossible. We know that "symptom" is an important concept of the late Lacan, for whom man without original nature is only the symptom of corruption demonstrated through a series of mis-recognitions of the Other. Behind the sutured symptom, there is no return to the authentic

---

[1] Zizek, Slavoj. *The Sublime Object of Ideology*. London: Verso, 1989. p. 7.
[2] Zizek, Slavoj. *The Plague of Fantasies*. Wo Es War. London; New York: Verso, 1997. pp.45-46.

dasein. Man is just symptom. Zizek's juxtaposition of Marx with Lacan is meant to illustrate the fact that that Marx's criticism of the capitalist mode of production is non-essentialism or anti-phenomenology, because in the rear of the materialized phenomenology of capitalist relations there is no possible return to authenticity, and it is through anatomizing the mysterious ideology of the commodity, money and capital that Marx obtains the unprecedented theoretical liberation. Here I must say that Zizek's proposition can only be understood after many theoretical turns. Besides, his reference to Marx is not true Marxism.

1. Non-essential mysterious form: Freud and Marx

Zizek is unambiguous, "according to Lacan, it was none other than Karl Marx who invented the notion of symptom."[1] (In the *Collected Works of Lacan*, the context of Lacan's discussion is not that straightforward. He only says that psychoanalysis introduces a symptomatic dimension, which is highly discernible although not clearly specified in Marx's critique. Even in the later *The Real, the Symbolic and the Imaginary*, Lacan only takes Marx as a certain origin in the discussion of symptom.) Zizek then puts forward a question: is this Lacanian thesis a hypothesis or a vague analogy, or does it possess a pertinent theoretical foundation? Obviously, he already knows the answer.

There is a fundamental homology between the interpretative procedure of Marx and Freud—more precisely, between their analysis of commodity and of dreams. In both cases the point is to avoid the properly fetishistic fascination of the "content" supposedly hidden behind the form: the "secret" to be unveiled through analysis is not the content hidden by the form (the form of commodities, the form of dreams) but, on the contrary, *the "secret" of this form itself.*[2]

It is well known that the Lacanian symptom means the existential form

---

[1] Zizek, Slavoj. *The Sublime Object of Ideology*. London: Verso, 1989. p. 11.

[2] Ibid., p. 11.

of the subject when it is usurped and there is no authentic, unseduced man's essence behind this mysterious symptom.

Symptom. It is one of the most significant philosophical concepts of the late Lacan. Originally, it was used by Freud to bridge psychoanalysis and conventional medical diagnosis. In the eyes of Freud, it is a revelation of the unconscious; therefore, it emerges in the dreams, slips of tongue, or wisecracks. Freud thought that symptom is "over-determined" by many complex factors.[1] Symptom later received the attention of Althusser, who turned it into "symptomatic reading."[2] For Lacan, it was initially an evident metaphor of the unconscious; later, the word becomes increasingly important. In a seminar of 1973, Lacan upgraded symptom to a key word following the Imaginary, the Symbolic and the Real. Symptom becomes a key knot to suture the disconnected Imaginary, the Symbolic and the Real. According to Fukuhara Taihei, Lacan's symptom has at least three meanings, or has experienced three different periods: from the early metaphorical symptom analyzed as the production of the unconscious, as possible interpretations gradually developed to the filling symptom that cannot speak of and imposes a basis on itself.[3] In a special seminar, which took place in 1975, on the "symptom", Lacan made it the fourth key concept besides the Imaginary, the Symbolic and the Real. It is changed into a significant *existential knot* that links the Imaginary, the Symbolic, and the Real. Lacan adopts the mathematical sign "Σ" to represent the concept of symptom, which means a functional suture in the ontological sense.[4]

In line with the re-interpretation of Freudian dreams, Zizek asks,

---

[1] Lacan, Jacques. *ÉCRITS: A Selection*. Trans. Alan Sheridan. New York: Norton, 1977. p. 271.

[2] Zhang Yibing. *Problematic, Symptomal Reading and Ideology: A Textological Illustration of Althusser*. Central Compilation and Translation Press, 2003. p. 285.

[3] Fukuhara Taihei. *Lacan: Mirror Stage*. Heibei Educational Publishing House, 2002. p. 248.

[4] *See The Impossible Truth of Being: Mirror of Lacan's Philosophy*. The Commercial Press. pp. 357-359.

since the theoretical intelligence of the form of dreams does not consist in penetrating from the manifest content to its "hidden kernel", why has the dream assumed such a form? The point is not the secrets behind the dream, but why are they transposed into the form of a dream? It is the same with Marx's analysis of commodities, which does not ask how much labor is consumed to evaluate the commodity, but rather "to explain why work assumed the form of the value of a commodity, why it can affirm its social character only in the commodity-form of its product."[1] To Zizek, both Freud and Marx are only speaking about two forms of the same Lacanian symptom, *behind which there is nothing.*

In fact, judging from Zizek's discussion of Freud above, we know he already understands Freud through the Lacanian discourse. Zizek denounces the basic relation between the realization of the unconscious desire, the hidden thought of the dream and its revealed meaning. "If we seek the 'secret of the dream' in the latent content hidden by the manifest text, we are doomed to disappointment."[2] The context of discussion is complicated. With Freud, the mechanism of the dreams acts as the metamorphic channel to realize the repressed unconscious (instinctive desire) which can acquire a masturbation-like catharsis in a dream, but is unobtainable in reality. However, when Lacan subversively designates the unconscious as the discourse of the Other, and the desire as the mere desire of the Other, Freud's interpretation of the dream generates a problem. In light of Lacan's theory, if the unconscious in the dream is the residue of the dominating big Other and small other, while the desire is an unconscious projection of the desire of the Master-Signifier in the Symbolic, what shall we realize in the dream? Lacan's logic is right to the point. More importantly, even if our survival is a fantasy created by the Other, there is no substantial essence that we can return to, and our life is a symptom that sutures various imaginary and symbolic fragments floating on the surface of forms. The Sisyphusian struggle and failure is the only real

---

[1] Zizek, Slavoj. *The Sublime Object of Ideology*. London: Verso, 1989. p. 11.
[2] Ibid., p. 12.

existence of the individual subject. In this way, can we still dig out the golden libido from Freudian interpretation of dreams? Clearly not.

It is in the same sense that Zizek warns us not to foolishly follow Freud and reduce a general explanation of the dream or symptom to a "retranslation," that is, to retranslate the abnormal "latent dream-thought" in the darkness into the "normal," everyday common language of intersubjective communication (Habermas' formula). (He often carelessly tramples others in this way.) According to Zizek, the essential constitution of a dream is thus not its "latent thought", but this work (the mechanisms of displacement and condensation, the figuration of the contents of words or syllables) which confers on it the *form of a dream.*

We must accomplish the crucial step of conceiving the hidden "meaning" behind the commodity-form, the signification "expressed" by this form; we must penetrate the "secret" of the value of commodities.[1]

The reason is as follows.

This desire attaches itself to the dream, it intercalates itself in the inter-space between the latent thought and the manifest text; it is therefore not "more concealed, deeper" in relation to the latent thought, it is decidedly more "on the surface", consisting entirely of the signifier's mechanisms, of the treatment to which the latent thought is submitted. In other words, its only place is in the *form* of the "dream": the real subject matter the dream (the unconscious desire) articulates itself in the dream-work, in the elaboration of its "latent content".[2]

The authentic unconscious regarded by Freud as the essential being beneath the activities of a conscious subject is broken up. The desire (the scheme of the big Other) floats on the surface and subordinates to the form of the dream (displacement and condensation), which is but another myth of a metaphorical and metonymical Master-Signifier. The form of the dream

---

[1] Zizek, Slavoj. *The Sublime Object of Ideology.* London: Verso, 1989. p. 15.

[2] Ibid., p. 13.

matters and its manifested symptom is all.

After an easy defeat of Freud, Zizek translates his logical framework to re-illustrate Marx's economical and philosophical critique of the commodity economy. He says that there is a fundamental homology between the interpretative procedure of Marx and Freud—more precisely, between their analysis of commodity and of dreams. (I have already mentioned Zizek's castration of the Freudian theory; now he is turn to Marx.)

Zizek says that Marx takes two steps to study the secret of the commodity-form.

First, Marx requires us to break the appearance according to which the value of a commodity depends on pure hazard—on an accidental interplay between supply and demand. Despite the fact that the price of a commodity fluctuates with the change of supply and demand, it always gravitates towards a central point, the value. This is a crucial development of classical political economy, which started to investigate what is behind the commodity-form and what it means. Zizek cites a statement of Marx, which says that the measurement of value being decided by the duration of labor is the "secret" of the apparent movement of the commodity value. However, the discovery of this secret does not solve the more important question why value should take a material form.

> Classical bourgeois political economy has already discovered the "secret" of the commodity-form; its limit is that it is not able to disengage itself from this fascination in the secret hidden behind the commodity-form—that its attention is captivated by labor as the true source of wealth. In other words, classical political economy is interested only in contents concealed behind the commodity-form, which is why it cannot explain the true secret, not the secret *behind* the form but *the secret of this form itself*.[1]

According to Zizek, it is the same with the above analysis of the dream, in which the dream remains a mystery despite Freud's explanation of its

---

[1] Zizek, Slavoj. *The Sublime Object of Ideology*. London: Verso, 1989. p. 15.

"latent thought." The classical economists found the economic secret, but they were only too absorbed in its essence, unaware that it is not sufficient to reduce the form to the essence, to the hidden kernel. For Zizek, one has to examine the process—homologous to the dream-work, by means of which the concealed content assumes such a form. Here comes Marx's example of the table. Common as it is, a table becomes a strange monster in the form of commodity, with almost upside-down weirdness. The problem is not with the table, but with the commodity-form that it assumes. Nevertheless, man is *unconscious* about that commodity-form. (Again, I have to remind the reader that this unconscious comes from the Lacanian context.)

2. "Scandal": the unconscious of the commodity form

Zizek says that Marx's analysis of the commodity form is not just about economics. It is correct. However, why did Marx's analysis generate such a great influence on the whole field of social sciences, enthralling generations of thinkers? Zizek offers his answer.

> Because it offers a kind of matrix enabling us to generate all other forms of the "fetishistic inversion": it is as if the dialectics of the commodity-form presents us with a pure—distilled, so to speak—version of a mechanism offering us a key to the theoretical understanding of phenomena which, at first sight, have nothing whatsoever to do with the field of political economy (law, religion, and so on). In the commodity-form there is definitely more at stake than the commodity-form itself, and it was precisely this "more" which exerted such a fascinating power of attraction.[1]

Correct! For Marx, the secret of the commodity form is the commodity fetishism. (Precisely, it is threefold: commodity fetishism, material fetishism, and capital fetishism, of which Zizek generally focuses on the first.) But Zizek, obsessed with that unpredictable Lacan, does not to follow the Marxist logic. In order to explore that secret, he turns to the so-called "fellow-traveler"

---

[1] Zizek, Slavoj. *The Sublime Object of Ideology*. London: Verso, 1989. p. 16.

of the Frankfurt School, Alfred Sohn-Rethel, instead of Karl Marx.[1] (They appear so distant that Zizek is almost doing a trick question.)

According to Zizek, in Sohn-Rethel's study of Marxist commodity fetishism, he made remarkable discovery: the crack of the secret of the commodity-form is not only a revolution of political economy but also directly relevant to the ontology of the Kantian epistemological revolution, that is, *the reality of foundation on which man's transcendental rationality constructs history*. What does it mean? Why does Marx's understanding of the secret of the commodity form involve Kant? (It is an insightful association about the history of thought.) Zizek summarizes Sohn-Rethel's thesis as follows.

> In the structure of the commodity-form it is possible to find the transcendental subject: the commodity-form articulates in advance the anatomy, the skeleton of the Kantian transcendental subject—that is, the network of transcendental categories which constitute the a priori frame of "objective" scientific knowledge. Herein lies the paradox of the commodity-form: it—this inner-worldly, "pathological" (in the Kantian meaning of the word) phenomenon—offers us a key to solving the fundamental question of the theory of knowledge: objective knowledge with universal validity—how is this possible?[2]

Zizek considerably enlarges the proposition. The answer to the Kantian question cannot be found in the *Critique of Pure Reason*, but in Marx's *Das Kapital*. What an earthshaking announcement! We should first make sure how these two out of left fields are correlated.

Zizek says, first of all, that Sohn-Rethel knows the frame of modern natural science: "the network of notions by which it seizes nature" or the "apparatus of categories" is not the a priori paradigm that is *self-sufficient* or self-generated. It is premised on the "effectiveness" of man's social activities. The actual foundation of the human mode of thinking is *the act of commodity*

---

[1] Alfred Sohn-Rethel (1899-1990) was a modern Western Marxist thinker in Germany.

[2] Zizek, Slavoj. *The Sublime Object of Ideology*. London: Verso, 1989. p. 16.

exchange. The philosopher does not know that before thought could arrive at pure *abstraction*, the abstraction was already at work in the social effectivity of the market. In a certain sense, it is a brilliant exposition. (In fact, from 1845 on, Marx also attempted to clarify this important question of historical epistemology, especially, in the *1857-1858 Manuscripts*.)[1] Zizek holds that Marx's commodity exchange contains two abstractions: the abstraction from "the changeable character" of the commodity, and the abstraction from the concrete material character of the commodity. During commodity exchange, whether it is the concreteness or the effectiveness of the commodity, they are all abstracted into an exchangeable value. What happens here is not a subjective abstraction of thought but an *objective abstraction* in economic activities, through which the value relationship transforms a general equivalent into money. (According to Zizek, Sohn-Rethel is thus quite justified in his criticism of Althusser, who distinguishes between the "real object" and the "object of knowledge" and "conceives abstraction as a process taking place in the domain of knowledge and refuses for that reason the category of 'real abstraction' as the expression of an 'epistemological confusion'."[2] Thus, Zizek says that:

> Before thought could arrive at the idea of a purely *quantitative* determination, a *sine qua non* of the modern science of nature, pure quantity was already at work in money, that commodity which renders possible the commensurability of the value of all other commodities notwithstanding their particular qualitative determination. Before physics could articulate the notion of a purely abstract *movement* going

---

[1] *See* Section 2 and Section 3 in Chapter VIII of *Back to Marx*: *The Philosophical Discourse in the Context of Economics*. Jiangsu People's Publishing House, 1999. And See Section 3 in Chapter IV of *To Understand Marx*: *Contemporary Illustration of Original Marxist Philosophy* by Zhang Yibing and Meng Mugui (People's University Press, 2004).

[2] Zizek, Slavoj. *The Sublime Object of Ideology*. London: Verso, 1989. p. 19. *See* Chapter III in *Problematic, Symptomal Reading and Ideology*: *A Textological Illustration of Althusser*. Central Compilation and Translation Press, 2003.

on in a geometric space, independently of all qualitative determinations of the moving objects, the social act of exchange had already realized such a "pure", abstract movement which leaves totally intact the concrete sensual properties of the object caught in movement: the transference of property. And Sohn-Rethel demonstrated the same about the relationship of substance and its accidents, about the notion of causality operative in Newtonian science—in short, about the whole network of categories of pure reason.[1]

It raises an important philosophical proposition: the premise of modern natural science is the abstraction of commodity value in social life; the premise of the operational structure of scientific theories are the commodity exchanges supported by the monetary flow; even all the pure theoretical categories confirmed by Kant are founded on the actual "social exchange activities." (Fairly speaking, this economic-philosophical logic originates from Marx. It is an extremely shrewd philosophical conclusion. However, there is a problem, namely, the ahistoricality of the proposition. The commodity economy is historically existent and not every rational operation starts from the commodity exchange. (I have discussed this question, the pattern of practice as the real foundation of the framework of scientific theories.)[2]

Thus, it relates to a well-known argument of Marx: *the domination of abstraction*. "Today's (late capitalist global market) social reality itself is dominated by what Marx referred to as the power of 'real abstraction.'"[3] Zizek continues, "in certain specific social conditions (of commodity exchange and a global market economy), 'abstraction' becomes a direct feature of actual social life, the way concrete individuals behave and relate to their fate and to their social surroundings. Here Marx shares Hegel's

---

[1] Zizek, Slavoj. *The Sublime Object of Ideology*. London: Verso, 1989. p. 17.

[2] *See Self-Selected Works by Zhang Yibing*. Guangxi Normal University Press, 1999. pp. 89-102

[3] Zizek, Slavoj. *Did Somebody Say Totalitarianism?*: *Five Interventions in the (Mis)Use of a Notion*. Wo Es War. London; New York: Verso, 2002. p. 2.

insight into how universality becomes 'for itself.'"[1] To a certain extent, "the abstraction of market relations that run our lives is brought to an extreme."[2] (As to the universality of abstraction and current ideological hegemony, Zizek cooperated with Judith Butler and Ernesto Laclau, writing an important academic book of dialogues.[3]) In addition, the domination of abstract capital has reached its highest level: "do not phenomena usually described as those of Virtual capitalism (the futures trade and similar abstract financial speculations) indicate the reign of 'real abstraction' at its purest, much more radical than it was in Marx's time?"[4] This is also a profound analysis.

"The transcendental subject," Zizek says, "the support of the net of a priori categories, is confronted with the disquieting fact that it depends, in its very formal genesis, on some inner-worldly, 'pathological' process— a scandal, a nonsensical impossibility from the transcendental point of view."[5] At last, *Lacan* comes. Of course, Zizek does not target the individual (I-think) subject in Lacan's destruction and nothingness, but rather the generic-Subject as the entire scientific thought, because in the academic operation of the scientific circle, the rational subject is a priori; however, according to Sohn-Rethel, this transcendental subject is not ready-made; it is reliant on the process of the corrupted commodity exchange from the origin of form. This view is acceptable. However, in Zizek's negative reflection, the origin is the "scandal" and "the nonsensical impossibility." (Here the "scandal" means the unconscious noumenon discovered by Freud, who believes the conscious subject that is held by man as his nature is indeed the exteriorization of the unconscious instinct. With Lacan, the individual subject

---

[1] Butler, Judith, Ernesto Laclau, and Slavoj Zizek. *Contingency, Hegemony, Universality: Contemporary Dialogues on the Left*. Verso, 2000. p. 105.

[2] Zizek, Slavoj. *The Ticklish Subject: The Absent Centre of Political Ontology*. Wo Es War. London; New York: Verso, 1999. p. 349.

[3] Butler, Judith, Ernesto Laclau, and Slavoj Zizek. *Contingency, Hegemony, Universality: Contemporary Dialogues on the Left*. Verso, 2000. p. 105.

[4] Zizek, Slavoj. *The Fragile Absolute*. London; New York: Verso, 2000. p. 16.

[5] Zizek, Slavoj. *The Sublime Object of Ideology*. London: Verso, 1989. p. 17.

does not know it is only a sign constructed with nothing by the big Other and small other. It is like a hereditarily enthroned king who suddenly discovers he is not descended from the previous sovereign or a democratically elected president who is uncovered with the "scandal" of gaining votes by bribery) Here, the scandalous context is Marx's designation of the corrupted commodity economy of capitalism, in which "pathology" indicates the materialization and subversion of the normal labor relations. Zizek is a little pretentious in saying that the scientific subject stems from the dirty tricks of money, and accordingly it rightly matches the Lacanian "nonsensical impossibility" of the ontological existence of the subject.

If we look closely at the ontological status of what Sohn-Rethel calls the "real abstraction" [das reale Abstraktion] (that is, the act of abstraction at work in the very *effective* process of the exchange of commodities), the homology between its status and that of the unconscious, this signifying chain which persists on "another Scene", is striking: *the "real abstraction" is the unconscious of the transcendental subject*, the support of objective-universal scientific knowledge.[1]

Zizek's textual context is probably difficult to understand for ordinary readers mainly because the unconscious as the ontological foundation for the existence of the subject is not interpreted in the Freudian sense but through the Lacanian logic. Consequently, the unconscious is no longer a transformation of the repressed instinct, instead, it is a result of the miserable subject that mistakes the big Other hidden in "another scene" as its ontological existence (Lacan says that "the unconscious is the discourse of the Other.") after the hegemony of the big Other (the symbolic signifier chain) successfully dominates the individual; in turn, the unconscious of the individual subject is also "another scene" in antithesis to the big Other. Obviously, it is the "scandal" of the ontological existence of the subject in the Freudian sense, which is at first meant to unmask the "scandal" of the

---

[1] Zizek, Slavoj. *The Sublime Object of Ideology*. London: Verso, 1989. pp. 17-18.

unconscious noumenon existent behind the subject, but Lacan reveals another "scandal" behind this "scandal"; the unconscious is the metaphor of the big Other, instead of coming from man's original desire. If the unconscious is the ontological existence of the subject, this ontological existence is always "in another place." The above is my understanding of Zizek's theoretical background of that important statement.

Lacan's unconscious. For Lacan, the unconscious does not indicate the repressed original desire of the Freudian Id; nor is it some unspeakable, unstopped, and inappeasable desire. "The unconscious is neither primordial nor instinctual; what it knows about the elementary is no more than the elements of the signifier."[1] Jameson offers a vivid description: the unconscious is not "a permanent, instinctive, boiling cauldron."[2] The unconscious means a signifier, that is to say, it is directly opposed to what Freud designates.[3] In Zizek's opinion, Lacan's unconscious is "the disembodied rational machine that follows its path irrespective of the demands of the subject's life-world."[4] Lacan insists that "the unconscious is that part of the concrete discourse, in so far as it is transindividual, that is not at the disposal of the subject in re-establishing the continuity of his conscious discourse,"[5] in other words, the individual subject is not in charge of the speech; there is an intangible force that dominates the subject which "*is spoken rather than speaking*."[6] It is a very famous post-structuralist saying. Most of all, the

[1] Lacan, Jacques. *ÉCRITS: A Selection*. Trans. Alan Sheridan. New York: Norton, 1977. p. 170.

[2] Jameson, Fredric. *The Cultural Logic of Late Capitalism*. Beijing: Sanlian Bookstore, 1997. p. 224.

[3] Green says that "[i]n my opinion, Lacan provides an anti-Freudian view of the unconscious." He is correct. *See* François Dosse's *From Construction to Deconstruction: Main Thoughts in 20th Century France* (Vol. 1). China Central Compilation and Translation Press, 2004. p. 330.

[4] Salecl, Renata, and Slavoj Zizek. *Gaze and Voice as Love Objects*. Durham: Duke University Press, 1996. p. 102.

[5] Lacan, Jacques. *ÉCRITS: A Selection*. Trans. Alan Sheridan. New York: Norton, 1977. p. 49.

[6] Ibid., p. 69.

unconscious is of the Other instead of the disorderly, chaotic demands and desires of the individual subject; or, "following Freud I teach that the Other is the locus of that memory that he discovered and called the unconscious."[1]

In this regard, Zizek explains that the unconscious is a form of thought, "whose ontological status is not that of thought, that is to say, the form of thought external to the thought itself—in short, some Other Scene external to the thought whereby the form of the thought is already articulated in advance."[2]

Finally, we come to understand Zizek's real concern: the ontological foundation of the transcendental subject, supported by the objective, universal, scientific knowledge, is the unconscious process of abstraction in the exchange of commodities, that is, dissolution of an item into the "real abstraction" of value. *Money is the biggest abstraction*. The item turns into money, which then becomes the abstraction of wealth. Money itself is material (stones, bones, metals or paper), but it has grown out of that material and become the *indissoluble Thing*.

3. The body of money: the indissoluble sublime material

For Zizek, the "real abstraction" (equivalent to value) has an implied meaning, in which the "real" does not refer to the substantial attribute of the commodity as a material object; rather than being based upon the use value of the commodity, it is attributed to an abstract Other: money.

"As Sohn-Rethel pointed out, its nature is that of a *postulate* implied by the effective act of exchange—in other words, that of a certain 'as if' [german.als ob]: during the act of exchange, individuals proceed *as if* the commodity is not submitted to physical, material exchanges; *as if* it is excluded from the natural cycle of generation and corruption; although on the level of their 'consciousness' they 'know very well' that this is

---

[1] Lacan, Jacques. *ÉCRITS: A Selection*. Trans. Alan Sheridan. New York: Norton, 1977. p. 215.

[2] Zizek, Slavoj. *The Sublime Object of Ideology*. London: Verso, 1989. p. 19.

not the case."[1] Judging from the above discussion, it is clear that Zizek knows that classical political economy has already discovered the secret of the measurement of value, namely, the duration of labor; naturally, abstraction here means abstract labor. Zizek wants us to take notice of the other side, that "postulate" and "as if." It seems that Zizek's "as if" points to something beyond the material commodity exchange, to be specific, the special materiality of money. As we know, money, (today's electronic money excluded) is like any other item: in circulation, it undergoes loss and deformation of its material form. However, we do not care for this material existence; we unconsciously assume "an immutable substance" of money, over which "time has no power, and which stands in antithetic contrast to any matter found in nature. (Sohn-Rethel)"[2]

According to Zizek, this is the formula of the fetishistic disavowal: "I know very well, but still ..." I know very well that the Buddha statue is made of clay painted with gold, but still I worship it. I know very well that he (the movie star) won't notice me, but still I love him. I know that money is a material object like others, but still ... [it is as if it were made of a special substance over which time has no power]. In the fetishistic logic, the "fans" are not pursuing a concrete object, but demanding something that is non-substantial and eternal, in Zizek's words, *the sublime object in the ideological fantasy*. It should be noted that this is social rewriting of the object of desire with the Lacanian big Other.

Thus, we encounter an important issue, allegedly missed even by Marx.

"Here we have touched a problem unsolved by Marx, that of the *material* character of money: not of the empirical, material stuff money is made of, but of the *sublime* material, of that other 'indestructible and immutable' body which persists beyond the corruption of the body physical—this other body of money is like the corpse of the Sadeian victim which endures all torments and survives with its beauty

---

[1] Lacan, Jacques. *ÉCRITS: A Selection*. Trans. Alan Sheridan. New York: Norton, 1977. p. 18.
[2] Ibid.

immaculate." This immaterial corporality of the "body within the body"
gives us a precise definition of the sublime object.[1]

Now, we see the key words in this book, "the sublime object."
Zizek means that in the effective social operation of the market economy,
people are in crazy pursuit of money; however, after second thoughts, it is
discovered that they are not after the material *object* of money, but instead,
they are unconsciously directed at the non-substantial sublime object of the
indissoluble Thing, which is converted into a universal material form: money.
This object is nothing; only the ideological illusion makes it look substantial.
Zizek says that in the fundamental procedure of ideology, "the 'sublime
object of ideology' is the spectral object which has no positive ontological
consistency, but merely fills the gap of a certain constitutive impossibility."[2]
We should pay attention to the other key word: sublime, not the one posited
beside beauty in Kantian aesthetics, but rather a Lacanian abstract symbolic
domination over everything. Thus, Zizek unsurprisingly says in a typical
Lacanian tone that "this postulated existence of the sublime body depends
on the symbolic order the indestructible 'body-within-the-body' exempted
from the effects of wear and tear is always sustained b the guarantee of
some symbolic authority."[3] Lacan's Symbolic scene shows up; the abstract
sublime object is indeed a social morph of the object of the Other's desire.

According to Zizek, prima facie, this "real abstraction" in commodity
exchange has no direct linkage with material substantiality. Nevertheless, it
is not the subjective abstraction of thought in one's mind; it is an *objective*
abstraction; as Sohn-Rethel says, the exchanged abstraction *is not* thought,
but it takes the *form* of thought in the market. Set in the *unconscious*, the
exchanged abstraction is not the subjective operation of thought, but it has
the *form of thought* as an objective abstraction. What is the form of thought,
then? In Lacan's magic dictionary of philosophy, it means that the mechanism

[1] Lacan, Jacques. *ÉCRITS: A Selection*. Trans. Alan Sheridan. New York: Norton, 1977. p. 18.

[2] Zizek, Slavoj. *The Plague of Fantasies*. London; New York: Verso.1997. p. 76.

[3] Zizek, Slavoj. *The Sublime Object of Ideology*. London: Verso, 1989. p. 19.

of subjective operation always *happens in another place*. In general, we think we are engaged in independent thinking and active cognition, but all these activities are only the transformed discourse by the dominant big Other which hides in the dark. That "language is speaking me" is the *unconscious*. Therefore, Zizek believes that the form of thought also accounts for the essence of the Lacanian unconscious. (I have to remind the reader that these familiar concepts should be interpreted in a non-Freudian sense since the Master-Signifier here refers to the patricide-Lacan, the Lacan who kills Freud!)

Well, we come to a general definition of the unconscious.

> Here we have one of the possible definitions of the unconscious: *the form of thought whose ontological status is not that of thought*, that is to say, the form of thought external to the thought itself—in short, some Other Scene external to the thought whereby the form of the thought is already articulated in advance. The symbolic order is precisely such a formal order which supplements and/or disrupts the dual relationship of "external" factual reality and "internal" subjective experience.[1]

The unconscious is not the Freudian instinct (desire) repressed by the conscious, but the operational mode of thought; it is beyond thought, but constructs thought with an *alternative* non-thought Other. According to Lacan, it is the order of the *big Other* in the Symbolic; man's thought is only the residue of the Other's discourse.

4. Blind: the essence of ideology

Zizek confirms the "scandalous" character of a philosophical reflection. Indeed, it is in homogeneity with the "scandal" of the scientific transcendental subject mentioned above. Whether the "I-think" subject proposed by Descartes or the non-category Dasein advocated by Heidegger,

---

[1] Zizek, Slavoj. *The Sublime Object of Ideology*. London: Verso, 1989. p. 19.

they are certainly constructed in the *external place* of philosophy.

Philosophical reflection is thus subjected to an uncanny experience similar to the one summarized by the old oriental formula 'thou art that': there, in the external effectivity of the exchange process, is your proper place; there is the theatre in which your truth was performed before you took cognizance of it. The confrontation with this place is unbearable because philosophy as such *is defined by* its blindness to this place: it cannot take it into consideration without dissolving itself, without losing its consistency.[1]

A reader may easily get lost here. In the Lacanian context, subjective philosophy has been a self-deceptive identity premised on false identification, the key of which is a *mistakable blindness*. According to Zizek, subjective thought actually takes place in the social effectivity of commodity exchange during the operation of thought. For Lacan, it is like one's name which is a given and the play of naming is finished before birth. In the early mirror stage, being fascinated with the false mirror image, the construction of subject is a process of misrecognition of the Other; as a result, the maintaining work of the subject is always built on the blindness to its own nothingness.

During the exchange of commodities, the real social existence relies on it, too. Any subject engaged in exchange is sure to misconceive the social and comprehensive function of exchange: the real abstraction in the actual social form of private property mediated through the market. As "pragmatic solipsism", this kind of misconception provides a prerequisite for exchange. If the participant notices the dimension of "real abstraction," the "effectiveness" of exchange activities will vanish. Zizek cites the following paragraph from Sohn-Rethel.

Thus, in speaking of the abstractness of exchange we must be careful not to apply the term to the consciousness of the exchange agents. They are supposed to be occupied with the use of the

---

[1]   Zizek, Slavoj. *The Sublime Object of Ideology*. London: Verso, 1989. pp. 19-20.

commodities they see, but occupied in their imagination only. It is the action of exchange, and the action alone, that is abstract... the abstractness of that action cannot be noted when it happens because the consciousness of its agents is taken up with their business and with the empirical appearance of things which pertain to their use. One could say that the abstractness of their action is beyond realization by the actors because their very consciousness stands in the way. Were the abstractness to catch their minds their action would cease to be exchange and the abstraction would not arise. (Sohn-Rethel, 1978, pp. 26-27)[1]

It is a split between the theory and practice of the subjective conscious, and a split constructed by this blind misconception. In exchange, man is materialized as a "pragmatic, solipsistic encounter" in the market. He sees no universal social dimension of his own act, in particular, the "real abstraction" existent in exchange; on the other hand, the abstraction originated from social dimension is transformed into *the universal reason* separated from social activities by an ignoring, repressive mode, while the whole network of categories of pure reason that emerges in face of nature is the conceptual framework of natural science. This is the split of the conscious, which is completely preconditioned by the ignorance of the subject. (Lacan says that the existence of the subject is premised on ignorance.) Therefore, whether it is the effectiveness of the process of social exchange or that of the scientific subject, they are all founded on that ignorance. Zizek refers to Sohn-Rethel: "this non-knowledge of the reality is part of its very essence"; "the social effectivity of the exchange process is a kind of reality which is possible only on condition that the individuals partaking in it are *not aware* of its proper logic; that is, a kind of reality *whose very ontological consistency implies a certain non-knowledge of its participants*—if we come to 'know too much', to pierce the true functioning of social reality, this reality would dissolve itself."[2]

[1] Zizek, Slavoj. *The Sublime Object of Ideology*. London: Verso, 1989. p. 20.

[2] Ibid., pp. 20-21.

In fact, far more than the effectiveness of commodity exchange which is built on such ignorance and misconception, probably numerous social realities are built on this nothingness in human social history. To Zizek, it is the basic dimension of ideology. Now, we meet another key word of this book: *ideology*, whose context, of course, is in line with Althusser.

Ideology is not simply a "false consciousness", an illusory representation of reality, it is rather this reality itself which is already to be conceived as "ideological"—*"ideology" is a social reality whose very existence implies the non-knowledge of its participants as to its essence*—that is, the social effectivity, the very reproduction of which implies that the individuals "do not know what they are doing". *"Ideology" is not the "false consciousness" of a (social) being but this being itself in so far as it is supported by "false consciousness"*[1].

As we know, in his studies of ideology, Althusser denies the assumption of ideology as false existence (a succession to Mannheim's view) and points out the necessity of ideology in the construction of social existence.[2] However, for Zizek, the essence of ideology is constituted by fantasy, "which sustains an ideological edifice" and makes the reality of the social existence get fuzzy and fade away. "Instead of a full rendering of the antagonisms which traverse our society, we indulge in the notion of society as an organic Whole, kept together by forces of solidarity and co-operation."[3] In fact, his is the fantasy generated by ideology. "Thus we have finally reached the dimension of the symptom, because one of its possible definitions would also be 'a formation whose very consistency implies a certain non-knowledge on the part of the subject': the subject can 'enjoy his symptom' only in so far as its logic escapes him—the measure of the success of its interpretation is

---

[1] Zizek, Slavoj. *The Sublime Object of Ideology*. London: Verso, 1989. p. 21.

[2] *See* Chapter V of *Problematic, Symptomal Reading and Ideology: A Textological Illustration of Althusser*. Central Compilation and Translation Press, 2003.

[3] Zizek, Slavoj. *The Plague of Fantasies*. Wo Es War. London; New York: Verso, 1997. p. 6.

precisely its dissolution."[1]

For Zizek, ideology is indeed a masked social symptom. As a result, today's ideological critique must aim "to unearth, beneath any semblance of a 'reified' ontological order, its disavowed 'political' foundation: how it hinges on some excessive 'subjective' act."[2]

Finally, we understand that the Lacanian correlation of ideology with symptom explains Zizek belief that "Marx invented the symptom."

III. Social Symptom and Incomplete Fetishism

At the beginning of *The Sublime Object of Ideology*, Zizek quotes Lacan's words that Marx invented the symptom. Nevertheless, in the following discussion of that question, he beats about the bush: first, he compares the Marxist economic critique with the Freudian psychoanalysis; then, he illustrates that the historical existence of transcendental subject lies in the objective abstraction of commodity exchange and explains the ontological status of social unconscious; finally, he justifies the inner logical connection between the unconscious ideology and symptom. Despite the meandering and tiresome account, it is a relatively lucent part in his logic; after all, he must make a comfortable preparation for his own discourse. Once Zizek begins to touch upon the so-called social symptom and incomplete fetishism, his discussion is really formidable.

1. Social symptom: the breakdown point of universal ideology

Zizek firmly sticks to the opinion of Lacan that Marx also pays attention to the question of symptom. However, Marx's symptom is clearly not the Lacanian trauma when the individual subject is absent; it is the social symptom present through suturing the *fissure* of fantasies in life by social ideology. (Perhaps, it can be counted as a social sublimation of Lacanian

---

[1] Zizek, Slavoj. *The Sublime Object of Ideology*. London: Verso, 1989. p. 21.

[2] Zizek, Slavoj. *The Ticklish Subject: The Absent Centre of Political Ontology*. Wo Es War. London; New York: Verso, 1999. p. 169.

psychoanalysis.) Zizek says that "Marx 'invented the symptom' (Lacan) by means of detecting a certain fissure, an asymmetry, a certain 'pathological' imbalance which belies the universalism of the bourgeois 'rights and duties.'"[1] (It is a farfetched juxtaposition of Marx with Lacan.) But, what does this mean? Let us follow Zizek's line of logic.

To him, Marx's critique of the capitalist mode of production is essentially aimed at the exposition of the bourgeoisie maintenance of an alleged natural and universal capitalist logic. Seeing through the formally equal exchange shown in the circulation, Marx unmasks the secret that the surplus value is produced in the production process and appropriated by the capitalist, thus breaking the myth of that ideological universality. In general, Zizek's understanding is correct. He goes on to say that the imbalance discovered by Marx is not meant to declare "the imperfect realization" of these abstract rules (freedom and equality), that is, this insufficiency can be eliminated through further development; on the contrary, Marx views that imbalance and "gap" as the *social symptom* inherent in the capitalist mode of production. In other words, these traumatic characters of the capitalist mode of production present themselves as "the constitutional elements of these principles." *Inherent corruption is the component of self existence*, which is the essence of the symptom. (For Lacan, the symptom is a way to present the corruptive existence of the subject. "You look like man, but you are not." You are but the *sinthome* sutured by symptom and fantasy.)[2] Understandably, "the 'symptom' is, strictly speaking, a particular element which subverts its own universal foundation, a species subverting its own genus."[3] The existence of symptoms, the starting point of subverting the subject itself, *shows the non-existence of self*, namely, the ontological *illegitimacy*. This looks like an ontological paradox. In fact, the symptom itself is a *paradox*. In Zizek's logic, *the social symptom is the paradox of ontological social existence*. The

---

[1] Zizek, Slavoj. *The Sublime Object of Ideology*. London: Verso, 1989. p. 21.

[2] Sinthome is created by late Lacan. It means the synthetic-artificial man constituted by symptom and fantasy.

[3] Zizek, Slavoj. *The Sublime Object of Ideology*. London: Verso, 1989. p. 21

emergence of a social symptom is always with the illegitimacy inherent in the social system.

In this sense, we can say that the elementary Marxian procedure of "criticism of ideology" is already "symptomatic": it consists in detecting a point of breakdown *heterogeneous* to a given ideological field and at the same time *necessary* for that field to achieve its closure, its accomplished form.[1]

Here, we get lost, again. Why does he say that Marx's critique of the capitalist ideology is basically symptomatic? In my opinion, the Lacan-Zizek logic interprets social ideology as a magnified *historical unconsciousness* that supports the structural symptom masked by ideology. The fundamental flaw (equivalent to a social symptom) will pillar the deconstruction of the entire social reality. Later, Zizek says that "one of the most elementary definitions of ideology, therefore, is: a symbolic field which contains such a filler holding the place of some structural impossibility, while simultaneously disavowing this impossibility."[2] For example, in Marx's analysis of the capitalist mode of production, the ideology of formal freedom and equality is but a blank propped up by the façade of a radical symptom, that is, *the substantial inequality behind the fantasy of formally equal exchange.* According to Marx, once the support is removed, the capitalist edifice collapses. It is the "breakdown point." (It should be noted that Zizek does not believe in the actual breakdown of capitalism, which is different from Marxist revolutionary thought. We shall come to know the reason for this in the following analysis.)

In this regard, Zizek gives some examples. The first is the famous bourgeois claim of freedom and equality. As we know, the Enlightenment declares freedom and equality as the innate rights of man in the fight against the feudal system, which is regarded as a universal ideology. (The noble

---

[1] Zizek, Slavoj. *The Sublime Object of Ideology.* London: Verso, 1989. p. 21.

[2] Zizek, Slavoj. *The Plague of Fantasies.* London; New York: Verso.1997. p. 76.

Son of Heaven in the zoological sense is now declared a common man by the notion that everyone is equal.) As a universal concept (generic-concept) must contain a series of sub-concepts (family-concepts), like Freedom includes such reified freedoms; regarding speech, publication, business and politics. Thus, Marx subverts all capitalist illusionary freedoms through a symptomatic analysis of the family-concepts of freedom, that is, "man is free to sell his labor-power in the market."

> That is to say, this freedom is the very opposite of effective freedom: by selling his labor "freely", the worker *loses* his freedom— the real content of this free act of sale is the worker's enslavement to capital. The crucial point is, of course, that it is precisely this paradoxical freedom, the form of its opposite, which closes the circle of "bourgeois freedoms."[1]

The second example is the capitalist market economy of fair exchange based on equivalent values. In the early period of the commodity economy, when natural economy still dominates, the owner of the means of production is simultaneously the producer that sells his products in the market; accordingly, Zizek says that "the exchange on the market is equivalent, every commodity is paid its full value." (This explanation is not accurate from the perspective of Marxist economy.) Most importantly, the capitalist market economy gives birth to a new commodity, wage labor. Zizek thinks that the commodity of labor power is itself a symptomatic paradox for its equivalent exchange is *the denial of itself.*

> The crucial point not to be missed here is that this negation is strictly *internal* to equivalent exchange, not its simple violation: the labor force is not "exploited" in the sense that its full value is not remunerated; in principle at least, the exchange between labor and capital is wholly equivalent and equitable. The catch is that the labor force is a peculiar commodity, the use of which—labor itself—produces

---

[1] Zizek, Slavoj. *The Sublime Object of Ideology.* London: Verso, 1989. p. 22.

a certain surplus-value, and it is this surplus over the value of the labor force itself which is appropriated by the capitalist.[1]

It indicates that due to Marx's confirmation of labor power as commodity, there appears the stipulation of social symptom, in Zizek's words, "*leading to the appearance of symptom.*" (We finally understand what Zizek means when he says "Marx invented the symptom." What an agony!)

At the same time, we observe Zizek's first ironical negation of Marx in this book. Marx's construction of scientific socialism via the denial of utopian socialism is still regarded by him as utopian. "And in the Marxian perspective, *utopian* socialism consists in the very belief that a society is possible in which the relations of a exchange are universalized and production for the market predominates, but workers themselves none the less remain proprietors of their means of production and are therefore not exploited— in short, 'utopian' conveys a belief in the possibility of *a universality without its symptom*, without the point of exception functioning as its internal negation."[2] (At his "post-Marxist" political standpoint, Zizek disbelieves the social prospect without social symptom.) Zizek says that Marx's proletarian revolution develops towards a society of transparency. Despite his intention, it proves his logic that capitalism contains the symptom, because in one's assumption of the current capitalist society as a rational totality there must be an irrational paradox that subverts itself; it means that the proletariat is secretly enslaved, viz., "the irrationality of rationality." The existence of the proletariat is the social symptom of the capitalist mode of production. It continually subverts the bourgeois universal rationality. However, to Zizek, this symptom will not completely disappear; otherwise, the social system as such would dissipate.

2. Fetishism: the misunderstanding of the inverted presentation

Zizek is very impressed by Lacan's view that Marx invents the concept

---

[1] Zizek, Slavoj. *The Sublime Object of Ideology*. London: Verso, 1989. p. 22.

[2] Ibid., p. 23.

of symptom. He refers to a paragraph in Lacan's *The Real, The Symbolic and the Imaginary*. "One has to look for the origins of the notion of symptom not in Hippocrates[1] but in Marx, in the connection he was first to establish between capitalism and what?—the good old times, what we call the 'feudal times'."[2] Lacan means that the concern of the symptom comes from the transition of the two modes of production: feudalism and capitalism that are under the comparative study of Marx; but for Zizek, Marx's discovery of the other important matter in the capitalist society is also what the social existence still in the phase of "person-to-person dependence" (the "old-happy-time" existence of the subject) lacks: *fetishism of commodity*. It indicates Lacan's interpretation of Marx's social symptom is a *historical* ad hoc but shrewd explanation. Zizek does not have a specific discussion of fetishism here. Later, in *The Plague of Fantasies*, he thinks the condition for fetishism to appear is "a clear common-sense distinction between what the object is 'in itself', in its external material reality, and the externally imposed fetishist aura", for instance, "a tree which is 'in itself' merely a tree acquires an additional spectral dimension as the seat of the Spirit of the Forest." Accordingly, he says that "[t]he fetish is thus at one and the same time the false appearance of In-itself, and the imposition on this In-itself of some spiritual dimension foreign to it."[3] I agree with this argument. He also mentions that "[t]he first to systematize this term and locate it clearly was Charles de Brosses who, back in 1760, defined fetishism as the first, primitive, stage of religion involving the veneration of natural objects (stones, animals)."[4]

Zizek says that Marx's commodity fetishism is a definite social relation between men, which assumes, in their eyes, the fantastic form of a relation between things. He is not wrong. As we know, Marx means that the relations of labor exchange in the market are gradually reversed to the relations

---

[1] Hippocrates, about 460 - 370 BC, an ancient Greek doctor. He is generally regarded as the father of medicine.

[2] Zizek, Slavoj. *The Sublime Object of Ideology*. London: Verso, 1989. p. 23.

[3] Zizek, Slavoj. *The Plague of Fantasies*. London; New York: Verso.1997. p. 97.

[4] Ibid, p. 98.

between things, like the relations of commodities, money and capital. Zizek does not really want to abide by Marx's political economy. He says that "the value of a certain commodity, which is effectively an insignia of a network of social relations between producers of diverse commodities, assumes the form of a quasi-'natural' property of another thing-commodity, money: we say that the value of a certain commodity is such-and-such amount of money."[1] (Despite its inaccuracy, the above description is generally acceptable.) And Zizek means more.

> The essential feature of commodity fetishism does not consist of the famous replacement of men with things ("a relation between men assumes the form of a relation between things"); rather, it consists of a certain mis-recognition which concerns the relation between a structured network and one of its elements: what is really a structural effect, an effect of the network of relations between elements, appears as an immediate property of one of the elements, as if this property also belongs to it outside its relation with other elements.[2]

Zizek wants to say that the essence of fetishism is not such a simple critique of ethics replacing the relations between men with those between things; it is a more complicated *structural misperception.* "The effect of a 'structure', of a network, is (mis)perceived as the direct property of an individual entity."[3] Initially, money is only a *symbolic* sign of the general equivalent in the value relationship of market exchanges. As it generates a structural effect on the whole network of value relations, it is mistaken as the direct wealth, as if it were *another* object beyond all the commodity relations. Zizek later calls it the "*displacement*" in his *Plague of Fantasies* and makes analogy between the uses of fetishism by Marx and Freud. "In both cases, fetishism stands for a displacement (relations between men are displaced on to relations between things; the subject's sexual interest is displaced from

---

[1] Zizek, Slavoj. *The Sublime Object of Ideology*. London: Verso, 1989. p. 23.

[2] Ibid., pp. 23-24.

[3] Zizek, Slavoj. *The Plague of Fantasies*. London; New York: Verso.1997. p. 100.

the 'normal' sexual object to its substitute); this displacement is in both cases a 'regressive' shift of focus towards a 'lower' and partial element."[1] Commodity fetishism is a misperception. In the symbolic structure of abstract value, the object loses its own existence and becomes an abstract wealth. Fetishism makes the symbolic abstraction *even* more important than real wealth, and thus abstraction determines and dominates reality. (We have discussed this earlier.) Correct as this judgment is, Zizek is still talking about a Lacanized Marxist view. (In another book, Zizek says that the "commodity fetishism does not designate a [bourgeois] theory of political economy but a series of presuppositions that determine the structure of the very 'real' economic practice of market exchange.")[2]

According to Zizek, the misconception of the commodity fetishism can happen to either the materialized relations in the market economy or the relations between men. First, he quotes Marx's description of simple commodity value, for example, a piece of leather expresses its value by 20 kilos of rice in the simple exchange of commodities, and then the natural form of rice becomes the value form of leather, or, the latter is the *mirror* that reflects the value of the former. (The Lacan-obsessed Zizek is easy to get excited, whenever he sees the word "mirror.") Again, he cites another statement by Marx, which is important for him in order to spread the Lacanian context.

It is with man as with commodities. Since he comes into the world neither with a looking glass in his hand, nor as a Fichtean philosopher, to whom "I am I" is sufficient, man first sees and recognizes himself in other men. Peter only establishes his own identity as a man by first comparing himself with Paul as being of like kind. And thereby Paul, just as he stands in his Pauline personality, becomes to Peter the type of the genus *homo*.[3]

---

[1] Zizek, Slavoj. *The Plague of Fantasies*. London; New York: Verso.1997. p. 124.

[2] Salecl, Renata, and Slavoj Zizek. *Gaze and Voice as Love Objects*. Durham: Duke University Press, 1996. p. 115.

[3] *See* Chapter One of *Capital, Volume I*.

Zizek, snatches this opportunity, saying that "this short note anticipates in a way the Lacanian theory of the mirror stage: only by being reflected in another man—that is, in so far as this other man offers it an image of its unity—can the ego arrive at its self-identity, identity and alienation are thus strictly correlative."[1]

> **Lacan's Mirror Theory**. The individual subject first recognizes itself through misrecognition of the image in the mirror—the small other I, and then identifies the physical and mental self *through alienation* in the small other II, the objective image of a group of others. Indeed, Lacan's mirror stage refers to the initial period of self-construction, in Lacan's words, "infans", when the individual subject identifies self as "me" for the first time. In his eyes, this self-formation is indifferent than all the old affirmative theses of subject construction, including the Freudian ego theory. Its essence is the change of the subject after it identifies the image, thus forming the so-called imagery relationship. The function of the mirror-stage is as a particular case of the function of the *imago*, which is to establish a relation between the organism and its reality—or, as they say, between the *Innenwelt* and the *Umwelt*.[2] However, the imagery relationship emerges in the reversed form of *self-denial*: the alienated identification of the infantile "me" in the mirror is also the initial concretization of "me." This imagery construction is achieved by the sacrifice of the Innenwelt "me," the noumenon in Hegelian sense alienated as pseudo-reality (the Umwelt).[3]

Zizek is particularly concerned with the isostructural occurrence of alienation and homogenization. He says that Marx pursues this *homology*. (If he were correct, Marx would have been the teacher of Lacan. Perhaps he goes too far with this judgment.) Rice as the material equivalent and Paul

---

[1] Zizek, Slavoj. *The Sublime Object of Ideology*. London: Verso, 1989. p. 24.

[2] Lacan, Jacques. *ÉCRITS: A Selection*. Trans. Alan Sheridan. New York: Norton, 1977. p. 4

[3] *See The Impossible Truth of Being: Mirror of Lacan's Philosophy*. Commercial Press, 2006. p. 131.

as man's image are both representation of equivalent quality. However, they assume the appearance of reflexive contradictories, thus generating a reversed effect of fetishism, which is called by Hegel the reflex-categories opposing each other, but also complementing each other. To illustrate this, Zizek quickly turns to another example of Marx: a man is a king only because other people stand in the relation of subjects to him. They, on the contrary, imagine that they are subjects because he is the king.[1] Later, Zizek says in *The Plague of Fantasies*, "in the case of commodity fetishism, the fact that a certain commodity functions as a 'general equivalent' is (mis)perceived as its direct pseudo-natural property, as with interpersonal relations in which (the example is Marx's own) subjects who hail a certain person as a King are not aware that this person is a King only in so far as they treat him as one, not vice versa."[2] With his profound learning and brilliant mind, Zizek efficiently slides to another important theory of Lacan.

"Being-a-king" is an effect of the network of social relations between a "king" and his "subjects"; but—and here is the fetishistic misrecognition—to the participants of this social bond, the relationship appears necessarily in an inverse form: they think that they are subjects giving the king royal treatment because the king is already in himself, outside the relationship to his subjects, a king; as if the determination of "being-a-king" were a "natural" property of the person of a king. How can one not remind oneself here of the famous Lacanian affirmation that a madman who believes himself to be a king is no more mad than a king who believes himself to be a king—who, that is, identifies immediately with the mandate "king"[3]

Now, Marx and Lacan dissolve into one. However, Zizek's uses this example for the sake of introducing another view, namely, the theoretical

---

[1] Marx, Karl. *Capital*. Trans. Samuel Moore and Edward Aveling. Ed. Frederick Engels. Vol. 1. Moscow: Foreign Languages Publishing House, 1959. p. 57.

[2] Zizek, Slavoj. *The Plague of Fantasies*. London; New York: Verso.1997. p. 100.

[3] Zizek, Slavoj. *The Sublime Object of Ideology*. London: Verso, 1989. p. 25.

demarcation between fetishism and incomplete fetishism.

3. The incomplete fetishism in the material dependency being exactly the "appearing point" of the social symptom

Zizek further explains that there are two modes of fetishism: a thorough one existing in "man's dependency" (Marx) under feudalism; the other *incomplete* one in "material dependency" (Marx) under capitalism. (Obviously, they are not what Marx means.) With the above distinction, Zizek further draws a definition about the social symptom.

First, in pre-capitalist society, precisely, in the feudal system, social life is still the "relations between men," (Marx uses the term "man's dependency" to represent this pre-capitalist social character) when commodity fetishism is not yet developed, because it is "natural" production. Therefore, the relations between men are represented as a simple direct fetishism, without material mediation. (In fact, Zizek's stipulation of fetishism already misrecognizes Marx since the Marxist concept is not a mere legacy of the old totemic fetishism, but rather places more emphasis on man's keeling down before his own creation. Acceptable as Zizek's fetishism is, it is at most the worship of natural relations such as kinship or patriarchiat.) It is what Zizek calls the first fetishism. "This fetishism in relations between men has to be called by its proper name: what we have here are, as Marx points out, 'relations of domination and servitude' —that is to say, precisely the relation of Lordship and Bondage in a Hegelian sense."[1] This is a clear relation of violence and, according to Zizek, the relation of *inter-subjective complete fetishism* of the king and subject mentioned by Marx and Lacan.

Second, as feudalism transforms into capitalism, the relations of direct dependency between men give way to the "material dependency" proper to capitalism, when the fetishistic relations between men change to the *mediated* fetishism of "relations between things," namely, the commodity fetishism. This is a "compensation" of the second fetishism for the first one.

---

[1] Zizek, Slavoj. *The Sublime Object of Ideology*. London: Verso, 1989. p. 26.

The place of fetishism has just shifted from inter-subjective relations to relations "between things": the crucial social relations, those of production, are no longer immediately transparent in the form of the interpersonal relations of domination and servitude (of the Lord and his serfs, and so on); they disguise—to use Marx's accurate formula—"under the shape of social relations between things, between the products of labor".[1]

Zizek believes that it is in this sense that the second fetishism, in comparison with the direct fetishism between men, is "defetishized, or, *incomplete*." This is another invention by Zizek. In capitalism, we have relations between "free" people, each following his or her proper egoistic interest. The predominant and determining form of their interrelations is not domination and servitude, but rather a contract between free people who are equal in the eyes of the law. Here, the two subjects engaged in market exchanges have shaken off all the lumber of veneration of the Master, of the Master's patronage and care for his subject.

> They meet as two persons whose activity is thoroughly determined by their egoistic interest; every one of them proceeds as a good utilitarian; the other person is for him wholly delivered of all mystical aura; all he sees in his partner is another subject who follows his interest and interests him only in so far as he possesses something—a commodity—that could satisfy some of his needs.[2]

The feudal nobility of the prince, with the external violence and coercion, disappears, people no longer fetishize directly out of the natural kinship. In this bourgeois kingdom, any social relation in the sun is of freedom, equality and universal fraternity. Zizek wants to ask the question: "does slavery and fetishism really disappear?" No. In the capitalist survival, man obtains superficial autonomy and becomes a man for the first time. Perhaps it

---

[1] Zizek, Slavoj. *The Sublime Object of Ideology*. London: Verso, 1989. p. 26.
[2] Ibid., p. 25.

is what Marx means when he says "to return man to man" after elimination of the last animality in man's political liberation. However, control and slavery are not really erased, but repressed deeper in man's existence. The apparent equality and freedom only mask a more intense, but hidden force, namely, "sweet violence." In Zizek's earlier analysis, behind all bourgeois freedom and equality hides the deeper captivity (the worker has to sell his labor power but its ownership and potential to create value belongs to the capitalist) and inequality (the fair market exchange masks the surplus-value appropriated by the capitalist). According to Zizek, all this is materialized through a paradox: the commodity fetishism. This apparent defetishized fetishism is the social symptom.

> With the establishment of bourgeois society, the relations of domination and servitude are *repressed*; formally, we are apparently concerned with free subjects whose interpersonal relations are discharged of all fetishism; the repressed truth—that of the persistence of domination and servitude—emerges in a symptom which subverts the ideological appearance of equality, freedom, and so on. This symptom, the point of emergence of the truth about social relations, is precisely the "social relations between things".[1]

The social symptom of the bourgeois kingdom indicates the emptiness and trauma of man's legitimate existence in modern society, termed by Zizek as the "hysteria of conversion" proper to capitalism. In this way, Zizek successfully grafts Lacan onto Marx. It is also Zizek's logical secret.

More interestingly, several years later when Zizek returns to the same question of fetishism, he makes two special statements. First, in contemporary capitalist reality, the conventional fetishism of man (master's charisma) and the reversed relations between men in Marx's concern are gradually disappearing.

In our postmodern age, what we witness as the gradual dissipation

---

[1] Zizek, Slavoj. *The Sublime Object of Ideology*. London: Verso, 1989. p. 26.

of the very materiality of the fetish. With the prospect of electronic money, money loses its material presence and turns into a purely virtual entity (accessible by means of a bank card or even an immaterial computer code); this dematerialization, however, only strengthens its hold: money (the intricate network of financial transactions) thus turns into an invisible, and for that very reason all-powerful, spectral frame which dominates our lives.[1]

Today, fetishism is spectralized and becomes more oppressive and pervasive.

Second, Zizek believes that the inversion of relations between things in fetishism again assumes the appearance of humanity. To Zizek, the logic of capital has subverted the Marxist fetishistic formula: "in contemporary capitalism, *the objective market 'relations between things' tend to assume the phantasmagorical form of pseudo-personalized 'relations between people.'*"[2] Zizek takes the example of the soft hegemony of Bill Gates' Microsoft Company. In his eyes, Gates has every reason to make his product under the "people oriented" banner only because he has controlled the global market of computer operation system. In fact, it is probably a typical slogan of all monopoly capital in the world. I think that Zizek's observation is very acute.

Nevertheless, in his *Plague of Fantasies*, Zizek begins to criticize the question of teleology in Marx's fetishism. In his opinion, Marx's critique of fetishism contains "a hidden teleology," thus leading to a "future Communist transparency of the Social,"[3] which, for Zizek, is absolutely impossible. In this point, he agrees with Derrida's critique of Marx.[4]

---

[1]　Zizek, Slavoj. *The Plague of Fantasies*. London; New York: Verso.1997. pp. 102-103.

[2]　Zizek, Slavoj. *The Ticklish Subject: The Absent Centre of Political Ontology*. Wo Es War. London; New York: Verso, 1999. pp. 349-350.

[3]　Zizek, Slavoj. *The Plague of Fantasies*. London; New York: Verso.1997. p. 99.

[4]　Ibid, p. 124.

IV. The Positive Cynicism and the Illusion of Ideology

As the most important part of his philosophy, Zizek's theory of ideology may also account for his quick rise to popularity among the left-wing academics of Europe and America. Although his new ideological critique follows the convention, his key mutation is a comprehensive invasion with Lacanian philosophy. In short, what Zizek does is to socialize the slavery of Lacan's big Other into an ideological domination in the historical scene. Differentiated against that of Marx and Althusser, here comes a renamed ideology: the ironical ideology of cynicism, which is built on the transparency of fantasy despite that "they know very well what they are doing, but still, they are doing it." Today, instead of being unaware or unconscious, ideology is deliberate and conspicuous; rather than being restrained by the "invisible hand," it viciously "points to its mask as it moves forward." (Barthes)

1. Marx: two kinds of ideological critiques

Zizek says elsewhere that the subject of ideology has outgrown being an obscure concept in academic circles. We can see ideological discussions and debates being made by almost every thinker despite their different political positions.

> Ideology' can designate anything from a contemplative attitude that misrecognizes its dependence on social reality to an action-orientated set of beliefs, from the indispensable medium in which individuals live out their relations to a social structure to false ideas which legitimate a dominant political power. It seems to pop up precisely when we attempt to avoid it, while it fails to appear where one would clearly expect it to dwell.[1]

For that inescapable ideology, Zizek has a vivid description: the

---

[1] Zizek, Slavoj. *Mapping Ideology*. London; New York: Verso, 1994. pp. 3-4.

generative matrix. (Zizek likes the movie *Matrix*.) The most elementary definition of ideology, in Zizek's opinion, should be a famous statement in Marx's *Das Kapital*: "*Sie wissen das nicht, aber sie tun es*: *they do not know it but they are doing it*."[1] It should be specially noted that Marx's classical definition of ideology in the *German Ideology* is to express the dominant view of the ruling class, of which Zizek is certainly aware, but still he has his own opinion. According to him, Marx's view of ideology contains two aspects or phases. One is the familiar statement in the *German Ideology*, when Marx regards it as a "paranoia", the warped reflection of the social reality in the mind of the philosophers. (It is a logic entrance of the old ideology research.) The second aspect of ideology is discovered by Marx in his mid to late studies of political economy, which has long been neglected.

> Things get complicated, however, the moment Marx engages in the "critique of political economy": what he encounters here in the guise of "commodity fetishism" is no longer an "illusion" that "reflects" reality but an uncanny chimera at work in the very heart of the actual process of social production.[2]

During this period, Marx did not use the ideological category to identify this important fact[3], but he made the sharpest exposition of the essence of the bourgeois ideology with his critique of fetishism, which is why Zizek expands the definition of ideology in the *German Ideology* to *Das Kapital*. I think that this is a reasonable analysis. But Zizek has another important view to deny the first aspect of Marx's ideology. He openly criticizes that "illusionary" ideology which reflects reality through distortion, calling it the "representationalist": "the concept of ideology must be disengaged from the 'representationalist' problematic: *ideology has nothing to do with 'illusion'*, with a mistaken, distorted representation of its social content."[4] Obviously,

---

[1] Zizek, Slavoj. *The Sublime Object of Ideology*. London: Verso, 1989. p. 22.

[2] Zizek, Slavoj. *Mapping Ideology*. London; New York: Verso, 1994. p. 30.

[3] Zizek reminds us that, in *The Philosophy of Marx* (1993), Étienne Balibar discovers that the word "ideology" completely disappears in Marx's texts after 1850.

[4] Zizek, Slavoj. *Mapping Ideology*. London; New York: Verso, 1994. p. 7.

he thinks that the Marxist ideology centered on the commodity fetishism is more important.

For the same reason, Zizek criticizes Marx's peer thinkers for their rash abandonment of the "dialectics of commodity fetishism" and their unawareness of the huge subversion and revolution that it brings about. Here, Zizek seems to treat himself as the inheritor of Marx's critique of fetishism. (This is a common logic of post-Marxian thinkers. Zizek is in this regard anticipated by Derrida.) Marx does say that the "invisible hand" unconsciously dominates all people involved in exchanges of the capitalist commodity-market economy. Everyone in the market activities has their own intentions, but unconsciously creates a complex commodity-market world beyond their personal understanding. (In *The Wealth of Nations*, Adam Smith first discovers that "invisible hand". He tells us not to thank the altruism of the baker or tailor for the bread we eat or the clothes we wear because it is their selfish desire that involuntarily creates our items.) In the market, people understand their own intention but "know nothing" of the mechanism of the "other" objectively formed in their activities. They are controlled by the *invisible* law of value that *plays a decisive role in other place* and they do not know the apparently autonomous self is actually a puppet manipulated by the Other. Therefore, Zizek proposes a view about the classical ideology, a *naïveté* ideology based on *misrecognition*. He explains that:

> The misrecognition of its own presuppositions, of its own effective conditions, a distance, a divergence between so-called social reality and our distorted representation, our false consciousness of it. That is why such a "naïve consciousness" can be submitted to a critical-ideological procedure. The aim of this procedure is to lead the naïve ideological consciousness to a point at which it can recognize its own effective conditions, the social reality that it is distorting, and through this very act dissolve itself.[1]

The naïve ideology is misrecognition, that is, to erase the difference

---

[1] Zizek, Slavoj. *The Sublime Object of Ideology*. London: Verso, 1989. p. 28.

between the reality of life and the representational of ideas. Hence, the conventional critique of ideology is to disintegrate the ideological fantasy by unmasking the truth of that difference. For example, Marx says that ideology represents the will of the ruling class and conceals the oppression and slavery in the reality of social life; therefore, to expose the class persecution and break up the ideological control becomes the major tasks of scientific socialism.

However, Zizek tells us, in the more complicated critical process of the Frankfurt School, ideology "is not just a question of seeing things (that is, social reality) as they 'really are', of throwing away the distorting spectacles of ideology" because today's ideology is no longer the simple illusion of society and life but a part of reality, even the *internal* nature of social existence. [It is rather similar to Althusser's view of ideology. Daly also notices that "Zizek developed his famous inversion of the classical 'false consciousness' thesis. Thus ideology does not conceal or distort an underlying reality (human nature, social interests, etc.) but rather reality itself cannot be reproduced without ideological mystification."[1]] If ideology is still a mask, that mask does not merely cover up the true situation, and that distortion of ideology is inscribed into its essence. That is to say, without the ideological "mystification", the social reality cannot copy itself. This is a logical blind spot that is difficult to understand. Zizek says that:

> We find, then, the paradox of a being which can reproduce itself only in so far as it is misrecognized and overlooked: the moment we see it "as it really is", this being dissolves itself into nothingness or, more precisely, it changes into another kind of reality. That is why we must avoid the simple metaphors of de-masking, of throwing away the veils which are supposed to hide the naked reality.[2]

We are no stranger to the paradox of existence, of the existence proper

[1] Zizek, Slavoj, and Glyn Daly. *Conversations with Zizek*. Conversations. Cambridge [u.a.]: Polity, 2004. p. 10.

[2] Zizek, Slavoj. *The Sublime Object of Ideology*. London: Verso, 1989. pp. 28-29.

to the capitalist society, namely, the social system. There is another important warning: not to damask this social symptom because reality breaks up with the disintegration of the paradox. Zizek then draws his Lacanian positioning of ideology. With the ironical metaphor of "The Emperor's New Clothes," he says that to know "the emperor is naked" does not help; we all know the new clothes imply nothing and the emperor runs with his bare bottoms, but speaking out the "truth" does not change reality. Even if "the media trumpet forth this fact, yet nobody seems really to mind—that is, people continue to act as if the emperor is not naked."[1]

2. Ideology: the Frankfurt School and Althusser

In my opinion, Zizek's discussion of ideology here implicates an almost incomprehensible context in contemporary critique of ideology: the scientific ideology of the Frankfurt School and the ideological state apparatuses of Althusser.

With the former, the scientific ideology takes the place of the political and legal bourgeois domination; moreover, the jurisprudential social structure with the core of instrumental rationality props up the self-production and self-copy of the social existence every day. Zizek's previous account seems to associate the view of the Frankfurt school with the second ideological critique. In fact, this is not true. According to Zizek's analysis, the context here rather represents a transformation of Western Marxism from political economy to instrumental reason:

> from Lukács's *History and Class Consciousness* and the early Frankfurt School, where ideological distortion is derived from the "commodity form", to the notion of Instrumental Reason which is no longer grounded in a concrete social reality but is, rather, conceived as a kind of anthropological, even quasi-transcendental, primordial constant that enables us to explain the social reality of domination and exploitation.[2]

---

[1] Zizek, Slavoj. *Mapping Ideology.* London; New York: Verso, 1994. p. 18.

[2] Ibid., p. 9.

Zizek thinks that this "Instrumental Reason" designates an attitude which does not simply function in the sense of social domination, but rather, it serves as the very foundation of the relationship of domination.[1] The ideology represented by knowledge and scientific technology is not the subjective misrecognition anymore; it is probably even correct. For Zizek, if the content of ideology is right and present with the appearance of truth, the role of ideology does better.

With regard to some relation of social domination ("power," "exploitation") in an inherently non-transparent way: *the very logic of legitimizing the relation of domination must remain concealed if it is to be effective.* In other words, the starting point of the critique of ideology has to be full acknowledgement of the fact that it is easily possible to lie in the guise of truth.[2]

Science and rationality in the garb of truth form the biggest ideology today. In a unique and mysterious way, they guide people to identify with today's social reality, and they disguise occupation and oppression with beautiful appearance. In Debord's "spectacle society" and Baudrillard's "consumer society," the ideological fantasy is the most important reality, which is more real than the real. (I think that today's ideological control has infiltrated into the daily life; for example, the culture of McDonald and fashion becomes the essential construction of life. The image of a Chinese girl twittering beside her lover with her face half-covered by the falling hair may be an unconscious copy of Japanese or Korean TV series.) Zizek cites another example: "some Western power intervenes in a Third World country on account of violations of human rights, it may well be 'true' that in this country the most elementary human rights were not respected, and that the Western intervention will effectively improve the human rights record, yet such a legitimization none the less remains 'ideological' in so far as it fails to

---

[1] Zizek, Slavoj. *Mapping Ideology*. London; New York: Verso, 1994. p. 8.

[2] Ibid.

mention the true motives of the intervention (economic interests, etc.)."[1]

On the other hand, Zizek relates to Althusser's view of ideology. At the same time, he puts forward his theory of the *three forms of ideology*.[2] Althusser's theory of ideology undergoes an important change after *Ideology and Ideological State Apparatuses*; I agree with Zizek regarding this point. However, Zizek calls Althusser's early ideological research the ideology *in-itself* and designates it as the first form of ideology, which is essentially "a complex of ideas (theories, convictions, beliefs, argumentative procedures)." It is "the immanent notion of ideology as a doctrine, a composite of ideas, beliefs, concepts, and so on, destined to convince us of its 'truth', yet actually serving some unavowed particular power interest. The mode of the critique of ideology that corresponds to this notion is that of *symptomal reading*: the aim of the critique is to discern the unavowed bias of the official text via its ruptures, blanks and slips."[3] Probably, it begins with Marx (the period of the *German Ideology*) and lasts until Althusser's early theory of ideology. Zizek says that Habermas is perhaps "the last great representative of this tradition" because ideology becomes "a systematically distorted communication" to Habermas, who attempts to reach the ideal subjective communication which is unpolluted via correcting this ideological distortion. Nevertheless, in Zizek's eyes, it is "what Habermas perceives as the step out of ideology", which is "probably the most prestigious tendency in the critique of ideology." (Here, other names in Zizek's critical list are Roland Barthes, Oswald Ducrot, and Michel Pêcheux.)[4]

In *Ideology and Ideological State Apparatuses*, Althusser considerably changes his aim and the critical method. The ideology in-itself is turned into the ideology for-itself. (Earlier, I mentioned that Althusser was then

---

[1] Zizek, Slavoj. *Mapping Ideology*. London; New York: Verso, 1994. p. 8.

[2] Zizek makes an ad hoc statement that all kinds of myths in pre-class society "are not ideology in the strict sense" but errors and illusions which are directly observed. In his eyes, only when the mistaken ideas lose their directness can ideology in the real sense emerge. *See* Zizek's *Mapping Ideology*.

[3] Zizek, Slavoj. *Mapping Ideology*. London; New York: Verso, 1994. p. 9.

[4] Ibid., p. 10.

under the direct influence of Lacan's symbolic pseudo-subject. Despite some misunderstandings, Althusser was very serious of it.) The second ideology is named by Zizek as the "objective ideology", equivalent to Althusser's ideological state apparatuses. Zizek summarizes it as the "otherness—externalization: the moment epitomized by the Althusserian notion of Ideological State Apparatuses (ISA) that designate the material existence of ideology in ideological practices, rituals and institutions."[1] For Althusser, the individual subject as in-itself is the mere result of ideological interpellation. Only in such an ideological construction of subject can the individual subject reproduce itself and survive.[2] According to Zizek, the Foucaultian counterpart to Althusser's view is the disciplinary procedures that operate at the level of micro-power. Althusser is clearly more preferable than Foucault because the former utilizes the Lacanian theory to develop the transferential relationship of the individual towards state power, or—in Althusser's terms—towards the ideological big Other in which the interpellation originates.

For Zizek, there is the third phase of ideological development, that is, the ideology "In-and-For-Itself", in which the original ideological unconscious disappears. It "is no longer the classic Marxian '**they** do not **know** it, but **they** are doing it'; it is '**they know** very well what **they** are doing, yet **they** are doing it'."[3] It is true that we have an ideology for itself that takes effect in the trans-ideological substantiality in itself.

3. Cynicism and modifications in contemporary ideology

Earlier, Althusser said that ideology is the mis-recognition and "false conscious" of social reality. This classic concept per se has become a part of reality. Zizek asks: Does this concept of ideology as a naïve consciousness still apply to today's world? Is it still operating today? His answer is negative.

Here, Zizek picks up an argument point in Peter Sloterdijk's *Critique*

---

[1] Zizek, Slavoj. *Mapping Ideology*. London; New York: Verso, 1994. p. 8.

[2] *See* Chapter VI of *Problematic, Symptomal Reading and Ideology*: *A Textological Illustration of Althusser*. Central Compilation and Translation Press, 2003.

[3] Zizek, Slavoj. *Mapping Ideology*. London; New York: Verso, 1994. p. 8.

of Cynical Reason (1983) to illustrate the emerging new ideology today, the *cynical post-ideology*.

> The cynical subject is quite aware of the distance between the ideological mask and the social reality, but he none the less still insists upon the mask. The formula, as proposed by Sloterdijk, would then be: "they know very well what they are doing, but still, they are doing it". Cynical reason is no longer naïve, but is a paradox of an enlightened false consciousness: one knows the falsehood very well, one is well aware of a particular interest hidden behind an ideological universality, but still one does not renounce it.[1]

For Zizek, today's ideology is neither simple nor naïve. They know very well about the ideological fantasy, but still point to the mask as they move forward. Zizek believes that the most "outstanding mode" of ideology is cynicism. It is a new ideological mode.

> With a disarming frankness one "admits everything", yet this full acknowledgement of our power interests does not in any way prevent us from pursuing these interests—the formula of cynicism is no longer the classic Marxian "they do not know it, but they are doing it"; it is "they know very well what they are doing, yet they are doing it".[2]

In the eyes of Zizek, this cynicism is very different from the classical cynicism of irony (a really difficult context), which "represents the popular, plebeian rejection of the official culture by means of irony and sarcasm, thus exposing behind the sublime *noblesse* of the ideological phrases the egotistical interest, the violence, the brutal claims to power."[3] For example, when a politician indignantly talks in the parliament about patriotism and devotion, the usual practice of conventional cynicism is to unveil selfish desire and cause a burst of laughs. Now it is different. Today, cynicism is

---

[1] Zizek, Slavoj. *The Sublime Object of Ideology*. London: Verso, 1989. p. 29.

[2] Zizek, Slavoj. *Mapping Ideology*. London; New York: Verso, 1994. p. 8.

[3] Zizek, Slavoj. *The Sublime Object of Ideology*. London: Verso, 1989. p. 29.

reversed. It does not deny the ruling class but speaks for the ideology of the ruling class in response to Kynicism: "the cynical subject is quite aware of the distance between the ideological mask and the social reality, but he none the less still insists upon the mask."[1] I think that it is the shamelessness in the logical structure. (Or, the *knavishness* of the bourgeois neo-conservatism we encountered before.) It does not follow ethics, and is "more like morality itself put in the service of immorality—the model of cynical wisdom is to conceive probity, integrity, as a supreme form of dishonesty, and morals as a supreme form of profligacy, the truth as the most effective form of a lie."[2] It sees through the essence of official ideology and adopts the "Negation of the Negation," that is, re-recognition.

This distance between the public, written law and its obscene super-ego counterpart also enables us to demonstrate clearly where cynicism, or cynical distance, as the predominant form of ideological attitude of the late capitalist subject, falls short: a cynic mocks the public law from the position of its obscene underside which, consequently, he leaves intact… the typical subject today is the one who, while displaying cynical distrust of any public ideology, indulges without restraint in paranoiac fantasies about conspiracies, threats, and excessive forms of enjoyment of the Other.[3]

According to Zizek, the old ideological critique is no longer able to deal with such cynical reasoning because we cannot subject the ideological text to "symptomatic reading", which is to compare it with the blank spots, with what must be suppressed to compose the self and maintain the continuity of the self, for the elimination of ideology because cynical reasoning "takes this distance into account in advance." (Again, Zizek beats about the bush with a critical adoption of Althusser's "symptomatic reading", which originally

---

[1] Zizek, Slavoj. *The Sublime Object of Ideology*. London: Verso, 1989. p. 29.

[2] Ibid., p. 30.

[3] Salecl, Renata, and Slavoj Zizek. *Gaze and Voice as Love Objects*. Durham: Duke University Press, 1996. pp.100-101.

refers to an affirmative illustration in the modern textological context, whereas Zizek takes it as the symptomatic decoding of the ideological text, that is, to expose the problematic broken blank of ideology.[1]) The old effective firepower of ideology has been blocked by the cushion of cynical reason, leaving a futile ideological critique. Thus, we are truly dropped into a new post-ideological world.

What is to be done, then? Zizek thinks that it is time to introduce the difference between *symptom and fantasy*. (Lacan becomes the new savior once again) Accordingly, the social symptom and the ideological fantasy become the new objects of discourse.

4. Ideological fantasy and the post-ideological era

As we know, words such as fantasy and illusion are the key points among the Western Marxist critiques of ideology. Althusser and Adorno both use them in the context of the illusory relations of ideology, where reality and truth are masked.

To understand fantasy, Zizek says, one must first return to the basic definition of ideology introduced by Marx, that is, "they *do not know* it, but they *are doing* it."[2] (I find that the first person to notice this important argument of Marx was the young Lukacs in the 1920s, when he defined the essential class consciousness: "Regarded abstractly and formally, class consciousness implies a class-conditioned *unconsciousness* of one's own socio-historical and economic condition."[3]) Zizek believes that there is an ideological fantasy or *daydream*. The question is where actually is that mysterious fantasy? Is it in the subjective "knowing" or that behavioral

---

[1] *See* Chapter II of *Problematic, Symptomal Reading and Ideology: A Textological Illustration of Althusser*. Central Compilation and Translation Press, 2003.

[2] *See Capital* (*Vol. 1*) of *MECW*.

[3] The young Lukacs discusses this question in the part about the class consciousness in his *History and Class Consciousness*. He uses the word "unconscious", which is not found in Marx's text. In addition to the above opinion, the young Lukacs makes a comment on Franklin elsewhere, in which he says that "he is unaware, but he speaks out." *See History and Class Consciousness*. The Commercial Press. p. 106. For Marx's statement, *see Capital* (*Vol. 1*) of MECW.

"doing"? Prima facie, the answer is not difficult. Because ideology reflects the relations of conceptual illusions, it naturally takes place in subjective cognition. But this is a mistake: what people think they are doing is differentiated from what they are actually doing. In ideology, man forms a false identification with the social reality in which he is posited. This misconception is generated from reality. Zizek tells us that the answer to this question has to be found in the famous commodity fetishism of Marx.

Money is in reality just an embodiment, a condensation, a materialization of a network of social relations—the fact that it functions as a universal equivalent of all commodities is conditioned by its position in the texture of social relations. But to the individuals themselves, this function of money—to be the embodiment of wealth— appears an immediate, natural property of a thing called "money", as if money is already in itself, in its immediate material reality, the embodiment of wealth. Here, we have touched upon the classic Marxist motive of "reification": behind the things, the relation between things, we must detect the social relations, the relations between human subjects.[1]

Here, Zizek's description of the Marxist money fetishism (not commodity fetishism) is essentially correct, but he does not distinguish between Marx's materialization and fetishism. Materialization means that the capitalist economic relations make the labor relations between men and men subvert to the relations between things during the market exchange. In comparison, fetishism is a *subjective* misconception of this materialization. (It separately assumes the forms of commodity fetishism, money fetishism and capital fetishism.) Marx's *historical phenomenology* is meant to lay bare that falsity and reach the truth of social history again.

However, for Zizek, such a reading of Marxian formula leaves out an illusion, an error, a distortion which is already at work in social reality itself.

---

[1] Zizek, Slavoj. *The Sublime Object of Ideology*. London: Verso, 1989. p. 31.

Fetishism is not only a subjective misconception, but also a *reality* (this is beyond Marx's definition here) because it acts "at the level of what the individuals are *doing*, and not only what they *think* or *know* they are doing." What does this mean? Zizek wants to say that when people use money, they know very well that there is nothing mysterious with that note of 10 yuan or the 50 cent coin. "Money, in its materiality, is simply an expression of social relations. The everyday spontaneous ideology reduces money to a simple sign giving the individual possessing it a right to a certain part of the social product. So, on an everyday level, the individuals know very well that there are relations between people behind the relations between things."[1] (Zizek is exaggerating a little here; most people cannot reach such a high theoretical level.) Importantly, the social activities of the individual, like the materiality of money, become the direct representation of wealth. *They are not theoretical fetishists but practitioners of fetishism*. Then, what on earth does Zizek mean? In line with the previous train of thought, he probably wants to say that that which people "do not know" under the domination of ideology, their misconception, represents such a fact: "their social reality itself, their activity, is guided by an illusion, by a fetishistic inversion."[2] This is not wrong. In a rather roundabout way, Zizek illustrates that the charisma of fetishism has gone through material subversion in reality. But it is not correct for him to say that people do not know the material inversion of social relations that had historically happened. Zizek tends to make complications; but this time his complication confuses himself.

Moreover, to illustrate this point, Zizek requires us to re-interpret Marx's *inversion* of the general and special relations. Here, I am deeply impressed by Zizek's theoretical insights, because he discovers another significant philosophical question which is hidden in the Marxist political economy. To be precise, in Marx's historical phenomenology, it refers to the issue that *abstraction becomes the ruler* in capitalist economic relations. According to Zizek, universality is merely an abstracted attribute of the particular things

---

[1] Zizek, Slavoj. *The Sublime Object of Ideology*. London: Verso, 1989. p. 31.
[2] Ibid., p. 32.

in real existence. When we enter the capitalist mode of production and man becomes the victim of the commodity fetishism,

> the concrete content of a commodity (its use-value) is an expression of its abstract universality (its exchange-value)—the abstract Universal, the Value, appears as a real Substance which successively incarnates itself in a series of concrete objects. That is the basic Marxian thesis: it is already the effective world of commodities which behaves like a Hegelian subject-substance, like a Universal going through a series of particular embodiments. Marx speaks about "commodity metaphysics", about the religion or everyday life. The roots of philosophical speculative idealism are in the social reality of the world of commodities; it is this world which behaves "idealistically"....[1]

Zizek's understanding of the philosophical thought in Marxist political economy does not differ from my relevant discussion in *Back to Marx*. Abstraction becomes the ruler.

> This *inversion* (*Verkehrung*) by which the sensibly-concrete counts only as the form of appearance of the abstractly general and not, on the contrary, the abstractly general as property of the concrete, characterizes the expression of value. At the same time, it makes understanding it difficult.[2]

Zizek says that now we can answer the question which has been haunting us: where is the illusion? It is clear that a capitalist living in the reality of capitalism cannot be a Hegelian philosopher who looks at this commodity-market world in an inverse way, as if the real concrete economic kingdom was the autonomous material realization of the abstract absolute idea; on the contrary, the capitalist must be a good Anglo-Saxon nominalist, thinking that the Universal is a property of the Particular—that is, of really existing things. Value in itself does not exist; there are just individual things which,

---

[1] Zizek, Slavoj. *The Sublime Object of Ideology*. London: Verso, 1989. pp. 31-32.

[2] *See* "Appendix" to the 1st German edition of *Capital, Volume 1* (1867).

among other properties, have value. The problem is that in his practice, in his real activity, he acts as if the particular things (the commodities) were just so many embodiments of universal Value. It is another inversion.

According to Zizek, Marxist economic philosophy (historical phenomenology) provides two measurements, namely, the material inversion and the double-inversion of abstraction becoming the ruler, on which we depend in order to understand illusion. In Marx's saying that "they do not know it, still they are doing it", fantasy does not take place with the subjective "knowing" but occurs with the reality itself, with what people are doing.

> What they do not know is that their social reality itself, their activity, is guided by an illusion, by a fetishistic inversion. What they overlook, what they misrecognize, is not the reality but the illusion which is structuring their reality, their real social activity. They know very well how things really are, but still they are doing it as if they did not know. The illusion is therefore double: it consists in overlooking the illusion which is structuring our real, effective relationship to reality. And this overlooked, unconscious illusion is what may be called the *ideological fantasy*.[1]

Zizek's ideological fantasy already indicates a new social existence, that is, the actual social relations composed by illusions. Ideology no longer refers to the mere system of conceptual reproduction that covers the truth with false relations; instead, fantasy constructs reality and becomes reality. In another book, Zizek says that today reality is formed by fantasy because "a fantasy constitutes our desire" which constitutes life itself.[2] Thus, the whole world dissipates into an ensemble of ideological fantasies.

Zizek, names the view which positions ideology in the subjective conception as the "classical ideology"; but it is no longer suitable now. In line with the old ideological scale, we live today in a so-called "post-ideological"

[1] Zizek, Slavoj. *The Sublime Object of Ideology*. London: Verso, 1989. pp. 32-33.

[2] Zizek, Slavoj. *The Plague of Fantasies*. London; New York: Verso.1997. p. 7.

society.

People no longer believe in the ideology-propagandized truth; nor do they take seriously the various tenets of ideology, no matter what it is; freedom, democracy or the communist ideal. What dominates their life is the *cynical ideology*. God is dead; man is dead; Marx is dead; there is no divinity, no real man's existence, and no revolution. Historical progress, driven by science and technology, becomes an irony, and history is coming to an end; democracy spreads around the globe together with precision bombardments, and justice is coming to an end; the market criticized in *Das Kapital* becomes the universal plan of configuration, and the old socialism is coming to an end. Everything is declared illegal and any modernity since the beginning of industrialization is coming to end. The alleged post-modern "anything-goes" develops into the rule of life, while the old ideology loses its hideout. "The fundamental level of ideology, however, is not of an illusion masking the real state of things but that of an (unconscious) fantasy structuring our social reality itself. At this level, we are of course far from being post-ideological society. Cynical distance is just one way—one of many ways—to blind ourselves to the structuring power of ideological fantasy: even if we do not take things seriously, even if we keep an ironical distance, *we are still doing them*."[1]

> If the illusion were on the side of knowledge, then the cynical position would really be a post-ideological position, simply a position without illusion: "they know what they are doing, and they are doing it". But if the place of the illusion is in the reality of doing itself, then this formula can be read in quite another way: "they know that, in their activity, they are following an illusion, but still, they are doing it". For example, they know that their idea of Freedom is masking a particular form of exploitation, but they still continue to follow this idea of Freedom.[2]

---

[1] Zizek, Slavoj. *The Sublime Object of Ideology*. London: Verso, 1989. p. 33.

[2] Ibid., p. 33.

This is very different. The former is the fate of post-modern intellectuals; the latter, the intelligence of the globalized tycoons. Zizek offers us the entrance, the only entrance: *the stepping out of* (*what we experience as*) *ideology is the very form of our enslavement to it*.[1] This is still Lacan's logic.

V. Materialized Faith and Fantasy Reality

We already know that Zizek's logic of ideology is centered on the late Lacanian philosophy. At the same time, the mirrored self and symbolic pseudo-subject, dissipated in Lacan's radical psychoanalysis, turn out to be the deconstruction of social existence and life itself; the traumatic symptom of the individual subject is now the breakdown point of the bourgeois political and economic reality. Zizek also finds that a materialized faith still exists in the faithless social life which supports and sutures our fantasy, while fantasy regulates social reality. For Zizek, the sublime ideologies we had fervently pursued in the past do not offer a way of liberation; they just spread the reality itself before us. Ideology is only a sublime dream.

1. Marx plus Lacan: the materialized faith

According to Zizek, 150 years ago, Marx successfully unmasked the inversed material relations between men in the capitalist mode of production with his commodity fetishism. Even now, it is valuable to reinterpret Marx. "In a society in which the products of human labor acquire the form of commodities, the crucial relations between people take on the form of relations between things, between commodities—instead of immediate relations between people, we have social relations between things."[2] (It is also a real order which is spreading in contemporary China.) Zizek thinks that in the 1960s and 1970s this Marxist critique was questioned by Althusser's anti-humanism. (I notice that Zizek often turns to Althusser,

---

[1] Zizek, Slavoj. *Mapping Ideology*. London; New York: Verso, 1994. p. 6.

[2] Zizek, Slavoj. *The Sublime Object of Ideology*. London: Verso, 1989. p. 33.

whether speaking for or against him. He likes taking over Althusser's points, and develops them.) In the eyes of Althusser, Marx's commodity fetishism is based on "a naïve, ideological, epistemologically unfounded opposition between person (human subjects) and things." (This has a profound meaning. As we know, Althusser is against the young Marx's humanist logic of alienation, but he does not openly reject historical materialism and the critique of fetishism. Zizek's theoretical positioning here has an implicit meaning. As a self-proclaimed Marxist philosopher, Althusser never directly criticizes Marx's science and philosophy after 1845, but he intentionally distorts Marx. When he attempts to remove concepts such as man, historical subject out of historical materialism, and calls the social history a "subjectless process", he is actually opposing Marx, and denying the Hegelian residue in Marx's logic, namely, the opposition between man and thing as well as the subjective restoration of man in materialization (the return from material realm of necessity to the realm of freedom). The relations between men opposed by Marx in fetishism are subverted to the relations between things, which, for Althusser, become the positive relations between the *unmanned* function and the functional materiality in the mode of production. In this regard, Zizek is very perceptive.) Obviously, Zizek will refute Althusser. This time, his weapon is Lacan.

Zizek says that Althusser's attitude towards Marx's commodity fetishism is completely different from that of Lacan, who is in full agreement with Marx. For Zizek, a Lacanian reading can give this formulation a new and unexpected twist: the subversive power of Marx's approach lies precisely in the way he uses the opposition of persons and things. From the previous discussion we know that this way refers to the exposition of the social symptom.

In feudal society, Zizek goes on, a whole set of ideological beliefs and superstitious mediations mystify the relations between persons. This is a *master-servant* relation, in which the master performs the natural *charismatic* power. (It is something from Hegel plus Weber.) By contrast, when people are liberated and enlightened in the bourgeois world, they consciously shake off that old religious belief of the Middle Ages. As a result, the City of God gradually drifts away; god withdraws into silence. In the new market of commodity exchanges, people contact each other not for beliefs (reasonable values), but as rational utilitarians, who are only subject to their private interest. Where the bourgeoisie sees the equal or freewill relations of individual subjects, Marx has his negative perception.

> *The things (commodities) themselves believe in their place*, instead of the subjects: it is as if all their beliefs, superstitions and metaphysical mystifications, supposedly surmounted by the rational, utilitarian personality, are embodied in the "social relations between things". They no longer believe, *but things themselves believe for them*.[1]

Zizek means to say that, true, the liberated subject in the bourgeois world does not believe in the naive mystery, but commodity takes place of man's faith with its own mystification. In other words, Marx's commodity fetishism is not equivalent to the totemic worship of objects; this *non-faithful faith* is realized and unconsciously existent during the materialization of market exchanges. If this explanation is still hard to understand, let us read Zizek's own analysis.

On second thoughts, he says, "This also seems to be a basic Lacanian proposition." (Not surprisingly, it is Lacan, again. Probably, this is Zizek's real context used to illustrate Marx.) According to Zizek, people often think that belief is something internal, while knowledge is something external. It seems to reflect the heterogeneity of different modes of spiritual existence in two eras. In Weber's words, belief is the internal purpose-rationality of the subject (or value-rationality), while knowledge is the external form-rationality. Thus, knowledge "can be verified through an external procedure." According to Lacan and Zizek, something located in extreme externality and embodied through effective activities is nothing but belief since instrumental reason is also belief, a deeper *unconscious material belief*. Weber would

---

[1] Zizek, Slavoj. *The Sublime Object of Ideology*. London: Verso, 1989. p.34.

have ironically said that *the form-reason is precisely a more subtle purpose-reason*. For this, Zizek makes a brilliant analogy.

> It is similar to Tibetan prayer wheels: you write a prayer on a paper, put the rolled paper into a wheel, and turn it automatically, without thinking (or, if you want to proceed according to the Hegelian "cunning of reason", you attach it to a windmill, so that it is moved around by the wind). In this way, the wheel itself is praying for me, instead of me—or, more precisely, I myself am praying through the medium of the wheel. The beauty of it all is that in my psychological interiority I can think about whatever I want, I can yield to the most dirty and obscene fantasies, and it does not matter because—to use a good old Stalinist expression—whatever I am thinking, *objectively* I am praying.[1]

We are often impressed by Zizek's wisdom and acuity. (In Tibetan Buddhism, there is something more than the manual prayer wheel used in material praying: the prayer flag, which, of course, does not stem from Zizek's Hegelian assumption about the "rational trick." In August 2003, I went to the Aba prefecture in Sichuan province and saw every Tibetan home surrounded by the prayer flags with religious text. As the flag waved in the wind, it was praying for man. A Tibetan told me that some people even used running water to drive the prayer wheel. It really shows the religious wisdom of our people. Zizek does not have any derogative meaning in that interesting comparison.) He wants to say that, in modern social existence, the original beliefs, values and feelings of man are replaced by an objective materialized process. People have no religion, and money becomes their god. More importantly, they do not worship god themselves, but make use of the material objects to do it for them, which leads to a Schizophrenia. Weber's Protestant ethic may well account for it: *getting rich is the mission which God gives us*. Thus, Zizek says, we can understand the reason why Lacan does not think that psychoanalysis is psychology: "the most intimate beliefs, even the

---

[1] Zizek, Slavoj. *The Sublime Object of Ideology*. London: Verso, 1989. p. 34.

most intimate emotions such as compassion, crying, sorrow, laughter, can be transferred, delegated to others without losing their sincerity."[1] Lacan offers an example of the chorus in classical tragedy, in which any internal anxiety or external problem of the audience can be solved by the open singing *outside* them. They feel the sorrow and the compassion instead of us—or, more precisely, we feel the required emotions through the medium of the Chorus.

Zizek has an example which is closer to life. He refers to the existence of the "weepers" since the ancient society. The job of these women is to weep for others who *must* be grieved. They are hired to cry instead of us: so, through the medium of the other, we accomplish our duty of mourning, while we can spend our time on more profitable exploits—disputing the division of the inheritance of the deceased, for example. However, this exteriorization, this transference of our most intimate feeling also appears in our daily life today, in the common "canned laugher" played during the TV series: after some supposedly funny or witty remark, you can hear the laughter and applause included in the soundtrack of the show itself. (In fact, we are used to such recorded laughter and applause in the TV series and radio programs broadcast in China.)

Zizek deepens his analysis of this: a possible explanation to this phenomenon is that laughter or applause means to remind us when to laugh and applaud. If this were true, it would mean that laughter is a matter of duty and not of some spontaneous feeling; but this answer is not sufficient because we do *not* usually laugh. The only right answer would be that:

> The Other—embodied in the television set—is relieving us even of our duty to laugh—is laughing instead of us, so even if, tired from a hard day's stupid work, all evening we did nothing but gaze drowsily into the television screen, we can say afterwards that objectively, through the medium of the other, we had a really good time.[2]

Lacan's big Other is present, but it still lacks immediate elucidation.

---

[1] Zizek, Slavoj. *The Sublime Object of Ideology*. London: Verso, 1989. p. 34.

[2] Ibid., p. 35.

2. Fantasy-modulated social reality

Zizek makes a very important division between Lacanian psychoanalysis and all previous ideological critiques. In his eyes, they tend to deduce the ideological form of a certain society from its effective social relations; on the contrary, Lacan's psychoanalysis first aims at "the fantasy which is at work in the midst of social reality itself." This *fantasy* acquires support from the materialized belief mentioned above.

In Zizek's opinion, "belief, far from being an 'intimate', purely mental state, is always *materialized* in our effective social activity: belief supports the fantasy which regulates social reality."[1] I have an ad hoc explanation for this: Zizek's "social reality" here does not mean the material substantial existence in society, but, it refers to the non-substantial interactive structure among subjects, viz., the functional, constructive social system. (Again, it is the Lacanian "hyper-real" logic: the real life of the individual subject is not that material living process in the common sense; instead, it is the process of the false desire of the pseudo-subject built by the pseudo-self reflection of the small other in the mirror relation and the fantasy of the big Other in symbolic relation. Here, Zizek transplants Lacan's theory onto the analysis of social life.) Thus, he means that the social system is modulated by the ideological illusion, behind which lies the materialized belief.

> What we call "social reality" is in the last resort an ethical construction; it is supported by a certain *as if* (we act *as if* we believe in the almightiness of bureaucracy, *as if* the President incarnates the Will of the People, *as if* the Party expresses the objective interest of the working class…). As soon as the belief (which, let us remind ourselves again, is definitely not to be conceived at a "psychological" level: it is embodied, materialized, in the effective functioning of the social field) is lost, the very texture of the social field disintegrates.[2]

Social reality is not as hard as we imagine. It is only a moral edifice

---

[1] Zizek, Slavoj. *The Sublime Object of Ideology*. London: Verso, 1989. p. 36.

[2] Ibid.

of the ideological fantasy structured by our materialized belief. If the subject rejects this fantasy, the social edifice will collapse. (The "Cultural Revolution" in China is a good example of this. The ideological fantasy of "the permanent revolution under the proletarian dictatorship" is really built on the materialized red revolution and social life. At first, people *believe in* the glory of the red sun and the objective of the revolution, and then, China is ethically made into a huge ship on the course towards communism. As if the great helmsman waved his hand, the ship would go straight through the billows. However, once this ideological fantasy is declared "a chaos", this fantasy-pillared ethical structure immediately falls apart.)

First, Zizek refers to Kafka, whose is known to hyperbolically describe the miserable and alienated personal life in the modern bureaucratic system, like the metamorphosis of man into an insect. This dramatic, fantastic narrative is not real, but it is Kafka's aberrant exaggeration, which "articulates the fantasy regulating the libidinal functioning of the 'effective', 'real' bureaucracy itself." (The Freudian libido is metaphorized into the driving mechanism within a system.) Although thoroughly alienated in the bureaucratic system, people get used to such an insect-like life. Kafka artistically exposes the nature of instrumental slavery in modern society. Therefore, Zizek says, Kafka's world is not a fantasy of social reality; on the contrary, it unmasks the fantasy that is at work in social reality itself. (Zizek's favorite movie *Matrix* tells a similar story. The real controller is the pervasive matrix. The individual human being is but a body silently lying in the incubator fed with fantasies generated by the tremendous system. The plot is centered on the question of whether to break or maintain the fantasies.)

Then, Zizek turns to Pascal. He says that Pascal and Althusser also notice the view that the ethical construction of social reality is supported by the ideological fantasy. (Althusser will be dealt with later.) Pascal attempts to illustrate that the internal nature of man's rationality is determined by the external, nonsensical, automatic "machine," viz., the automatism of the signifier, of the symbolic network in which the subjects are caught. (For Lacan, the subject is only a mutual referent of the signifier.) We all know the famous definition of Pascal: man is a thinking reed. However, man's rational thoughts and interior beliefs are often determined by the external daily life which self-copies itself and the conventions that run under inertia. In Lacan's words, the symbolic floating signifiers are structuring the conscious subject all the time.

Zizek cites Pascal's words to explain this.

> For we must not misunderstand ourselves; we are as much automatic as intellectual; and hence it comes that the instrument by which conviction is attained is not demonstration alone… Proofs only convince the mind. Custom is the source of our strongest and most believed proofs. It bends the automaton, which persuades the mind without its thinking about the matter.[1]

This suggests that the subject results from the constant self-copying of the unconscious, whereas this external mechanism of inertia is supported by the convention which does not need to be proven. (This is sometimes called by Lacan as the repetitious mechanism of the unconscious.) Therefore, "the external custom is always a material support for the subject's unconscious."[2] However, Zizek makes the farfetched conclusion that Pascal's definition of the *unconscious* is the same as that of Lacan. (As we know, Lacan's interpretation of the unconscious is a complete subversion of Freud's view. It is no longer the suppressed instinctive desire of the individual subject, but instead the spontaneity generated from the hidden control of the big Other.)

According to Zizek, Pascal believes that law, as the most important pillar of the social system, is a fundamental construction of the unconscious, because in reality we abide by it not for its justice, goodness and usefulness, but for the simple reason that it *is* the law—"this tautology articulates the vicious circle of its authority, the fact that the last foundation of the Law's authority lies in its process of enunciation."[3] Thus, Pascal concludes that

---

[1] Pascal, Blaise. *Thoughts.* Cosimo, Inc., 2007. p. 93.

[2] Zizek, Slavoj. *The Sublime Object of Ideology.* London: Verso, 1989. p. 40.

[3] Ibid., p. 37.

custom is the whole of equity for the sole reason that it is a accepted. This is the mystic basis of its authority. Anyone who tries to bring it back to its first principle destroys it. Law is law because it is law and we have to obey it. (Here, Zizek adds the argument of Kierkegaard, who says that to believe in Christ because we consider him wise and good is a dreadful blasphemy— it is, on the contrary, only the act of belief itself which can give us an insight into his goodness and wisdom. These words well accord with the superstitious Chinese saying: "the magic only works with your belief.") We obey the law not because we are yielding to an external force, but because we are continuing with the tradition.

> The only real obedience, then, is an "external" one: obedience out of conviction is not real obedience because it is already "mediated" through our subjectivity—that is, we are not really obeying the authority but simply following our judgment, which tells us that the authority deserves to be obeyed in so far as it is good, wise, beneficent... Even more than for our relation to "external" social authority, this inversion applies to our obedience to the internal authority of belief.[1]

For Zizek, that "Law is Law" brings about obedience, which explains at least two important psychoanalytic concepts. First, it illustrates the basic characteristic of the *superego*: an injunction which is experienced as traumatic and "senseless"—that is, it cannot be integrated into the symbolic universe of the subject. For Freud, the superego results from obedience to external social pressure; it is a prohibitive self-repression, a deep self-restrain. Second, it also describes the definition of "transference" in psychoanalysis.

> The Law is not to be accepted as true, only as necessary—the fact that *its authority is without truth*. The necessary structural illusion which drives people to believe that truth can be found in laws describes precisely the mechanism of *transference*: transference is this supposition of a Truth, of a Meaning behind the stupid, traumatic, inconsistent fact

---

[1] Zizek, Slavoj. *The Sublime Object of Ideology*. London: Verso, 1989. p. 37.

of the Law. In other words, "transference" names the vicious circle of belief: the reasons why we should believe are persuasive only to those who already believe.[1]

Frankly, I think that Zizek is sometimes mechanically transferring Lacan's philosophy. Nevertheless, what he wants to clarify seems to come out with a result. Social reality is indeed supported by some ideological fantasy.

Zizek still turns to Pascal again. This time, he discusses his "wager" theory.

The wager theory of Pascal. As we know, in the eyes of Pascal, god retires from the silent space structured by the bourgeois instrumental reason and materialized object. For the man of tragedy, despite the recluse of God, he is still present and non-present at the same time. However, god's "presence" does not mean the substantial manifestation; it is only a real attempt and hope. In Pascal's words, the indomitable man of tragedy forever *wagers on the existence of God*. Goldman says that in the heart of the man of tragedy, "God is a *practical postulate*, or a *bet*, rather than a theoretical certainty."[2] The man of tragedy is actually being in the bourgeois material world. For him, God's existence is no longer absolutely true and unquestionable; God's recluse and silence is real. But the man of tragedy never gives way to despair; instead, he increasingly strengthens his belief in the dark of that material world. He believes that it is always possible that people are saved or sent to hell, and we must act *as if* God promises to save us.[3] This "as if" is very important. God is reclusive and silent, but he is still watching us. We act and struggle not for God, but to save ourselves and change this world. If we give up, we shall lose the actual possibility of salvation. As long as we live, act and fight in this world, the hidden god will expectantly

---

[1] Zizek, Slavoj. *The Sublime Object of Ideology*. London: Verso, 1989. p. 38.

[2] Goldman, Lucien. *Hidden God*. Baihua Literature and Art Publishing House, 1998. p. 103.

[3] Ibid., p. 432.

exist and live, the prospect of salvation will be with us! This is the last and only opportunity. Therefore, we have no choice; *we must wager on the existence of God*; *we must wager on the existence of God's watch*; *and we must wager on God's listening to our speech*. Only in this way can we be *possibly* saved; otherwise, we shall fall into eternal darkness. Pascal adds, "if you win, you win all; if you lose, you lose nothing. Wager, then, that he is, without hesitation."[1] This is a very interesting conclusion. If you lose, you lose nothing; if you win, you obtain a bright life and change of this world. Why not wager then?

The reason why Zizek quotes Pascal's wager is to persuade those with rationality and sensibility in their heart to have faith, to believe in God's existence. According to Zizek, "Pascal's final answer, then, is: leave rational argumentation and submit yourself simply to ideological ritual, stupefy yourself by repeating the meaningless gestures, act *as if* you already believe, and the belief will come by itself."[2]

Then, Zizek says, this ideological conversion procedure is not limited to religion. It has a more general significance. For example, Pascal's wager theory was once very popular among the French communists. (It clearly refers to those French Marxists led by Jean-Jacques Goldman.)[3]

This is, of course, the very Lacanian definition of deception in its specifically human dimension, where we deceive the Other by means of the truth itself: in a universe in which all are looking for the true face beneath the mask, the best way to lead them astray is to wear the mask of truth itself. But it is impossible to maintain the coincidence of mask and truth: far from gaining us a kind of "immediate contract with our fellow-men", this coincidence renders the situation unbearable; all communication is impossible because we are totally isolated through

---

[1] Pascal, Blaise. *Thoughts*. Cup Archive. p. 111.

[2] Zizek, Slavoj. *The Sublime Object of Ideology*. London: Verso, 1989. p. 39.

[3] *See* Section 3 of Chapter VII in *A Deep Plough of Texts* (*Vol. 1*). People's University Press, 2008.

the very disclosure—the *sine qua non* of successful communication is a minimum of distance between appearance and it hidden rear.[1]

VI. Ideological Fantasy and Surplus Enjoyment

Zizek's Lacanian ideology forms a conspicuous scene in the western radical discourse. He constructs a heterogeneous critique with the Lacanian complex context. To Zizek, the symbolic sign machine makes the big Other generate its internal object of desire by questioning the subject. Hence, the ideological fantasy on the social level builds the illusion which masks the ultimate impossibility in the ontological sense in order to support the totality of social reality.

1. Questioning Althusser's ideological state apparatuses

Zizek says that through Pascal's discussion of the materialized belief, we understand a truth: when people succumb to the practice mechanism of external material in religious rituals, like praying and worshipping, they *unknowingly* have faith, and their faith is mechanically and automatically materialized and embodied in the routine symbolic practice. (If I am correct, this is also Althusser's thesis in his *Ideological State Apparatuses*.) Therefore, "[t]he externality of the symbolic machine ('automaton') is therefore not simply external; it is at the same time the place where the fate of our internal, most 'sincere' and 'intimate' beliefs is in advance staged and decided."[2] (Lacan uses the term "symbolic mechanism", which refers to the chain of signifiers in the symbolic language which "constitutes" the main existence of the subject, called the big Other A.) Clearly, as long as we are in this materialized ritual, the divine symbolic machine already makes us *consciously* have some belief. Accordingly, Zizek attempts to prove that the unconscious, like "a dead letter", is not the Freudian repressed inner desire

---

[1] Zizek, Slavoj. *The Sublime Object of Ideology*. London: Verso, 1989. p. 42.

[2] Ibid., p. 43.

but the magic discourse of the big Other—the symbolic network machine. (Lacan says that the unconscious is the discourse of the big Other.) We believe in God and what really happens is the obedience to our unconscious, to "the dead, uncomprehended letter." This is a paradox, between *not knowing and conversion*, between inner belief and external "mechanism." For Zizek, it forms the most subversive kernel in Pascal's theology.

Well, we now find Zizek's foreshadowing to link Pascal with Althusser. "Of course, in his theory of *Ideological State Apparatuses*, Althusser gave an elaborated, contemporary version of this Pascalian 'machine.'"[1] This means that there is an intrinsic connection between Althusser and Pascal.

Althusser's discussion of the copying process during which the Christian ideology interpellates the mirror image of the subject. In *Ideology and Ideological State Apparatuses* (1969), Althusser puts forward the question of materialization. He thinks that ideology possesses a *material* existence, that is, "an ideology always exists in an apparatus, and its practice, or practices. This existence is material."[2] The novel idea does not indicate that ideology is an object, but means its existence is always supported by the individual or the social objective practices which highly repeat themselves. For example, one who goes to the church, singing the Mass, worshiping, praying, confessing, uses the incessant sensuous activities to support his imaginary relations with the divine world. Althusser especially notes that the Christian discourse not only speaks through the bible and the priest, but also utilizes religious practice, like service and sacrament, to interpellate the subject. The "I-am-that-I-am" God (Big Subject) speaks via the bible and the mouth of priest, "Hello, Your name is Nikon. You are born. It is your origin. You are created by God. You are born in 2001 and it is your position in the world. You shall live and die. If you believe in me, you will be saved and become a part of Christ's body." Here, every individual in

---

[1] Zizek, Slavoj. *The Sublime Object of Ideology*. London: Verso, 1989. p. 43.

[2] Althusser, Louis. *Lenin and Philosophy, and Other Essays*. New York: Monthly Review Press, 1972. p. 166.

the structure of the Christian ideology is interpellated as the subject of "oneness of body and name." In every prayer, every act of worship, and every confession, it is told and proven that "I (the Christ) drop the blood for you." However, Althusser exposes, what really happens is that "God is thus the Subject, and Moses and the innumerable subjects of God's people, the Subject's interlocutors-interpellates: his mirrors, his reflections."[1] This is an amazing process of ideological structuring, in which the *Big Subject reproduces many subjects and becomes a subject.*[2]

However, Zizek is hesitant to show his agreement. Instead, he lists Althusser's weak points as follows.

He, or his school never succeeded in thinking out the link between Ideological State Apparatuses and ideological interpellation: how does the Ideological State Apparatus (the Pascalian "machine", the signifying automatism) "internalize" itself; how does it produce the effect of ideological belief in a Cause and the interconnecting effect of subjectivation, of recognition of one's ideological position?[3]

In my opinion, these are sharp and profound questions while Althusser's answer, in Zizek's view, is rash and simplistic. Althusser has the misconception that the ideological machine of representation is internalized as the self-identification of the subject through interpellation. But Zizek believes that the reality is much more complex.

This "internalization", by structural necessity, never fully succeeds, that there is always a residue, a leftover, a stain of traumatic irrationality and senselessness sticking to it, and that *this leftover, far from hindering the full submission of the subject to the ideological command, is the very*

---

[1]   Althusser, Louis. *Lenin and Philosophy, and Other Essays.* New York: Monthly Review Press, 1972. p. 179.

[2]   *See Problematic, Symptomal Reading and Ideology: A Textological Illustration of Althusser.* Central Compilation and Translation Press, 2003. pp. 184-185.

[3]   Zizek, Slavoj. *The Sublime Object of Ideology.* London: Verso, 1989. p. 43.

condition of it: it is precisely this non-integrated surplus of senseless traumatism which confers on the Law its unconditional authority; in other words, which—in so far as it escapes ideological sense—sustains what might call the ideological *jouis-sense*, enjoyment-in-sense (enjoy-meant), proper to ideology.[1]

Zizek's thesis appears very formidable regarding those concepts rather foreign to the traditional critique, like "traumatic," "non-integrated surplus," "*jouis-sense*, enjoyment-in-sense (enjoyment)." He is *re-writing* ideology with the Lacanian philosophy. As we know, Althusser's theory of ideological state apparatuses is under Lacan's influence. However, Zizek accuses Althusser of his misunderstanding of Lacan. It seems he wants to prove himself as an orthodox Lacanian successor.

We have already discussed that the Big Subject in Althusser's ideological state apparatuses refers to God and various Big Generic Natures (absolute idea, being, man, totality, -isms, etc.), whereas the individual in reality is only a duplicated mirror image of that Master. It is the functional secret of ideology, as well as a *hidden* self-operation. On every level of life, the duplication of the mirror image happens, consciously or unconsciously. In fact, Zizek sees through Althusser's difference from Lacan: the replacement of the Big Other by the Big Subject. With Lacan, God is the theological Big Other, while Althusser's Big Subject does what the Big Other did before. Lacan's mirror function in the early period of subject construction becomes the internal mechanism of ideological operation. For Lacan, the self is the imaginary project of the small other (a' = the image of a), and the subject is the residue of the killed big Other which is formed by the resolved self in further representation (S = slashed A). For Althusser, the big Other (the Symbolic of the signifier chain turns into ideology) directly reproduces the individual subject. Obviously, his interpretation of Lacan is simplistic, with inevitable miscomprehension, especially regarding the late Lacanian philosophy that is favored by Zizek. Here, the concept of the *impossible*

---

[1] Zizek, Slavoj. *The Sublime Object of Ideology*. London: Verso, 1989. pp. 43-44.

surplus in Lacan's *Real* becomes the key point.

Zizek's criticism of Althusser with the late Lacanian theory is meant to deny the complete assimilation of the subject by the ideological inquiry, because Lacan abandons the absolute nothingness of the castrated subject and accepts the Real surplus (objet-petit-a) which escapes the rape of the Symbolic totality. But Althusser cannot see the real existence of that surplus. In the above discussion, Zizek calls this ineradicable surplus the *ideological pleasure*. Why? The answer is discussed in the following part.

2. Kafka in Lacanian horizon

An important reason for Zizek's criticism of Althusser's pseudo-Lacanian ideological state apparatuses is that the latter had great influence on the leftist radical discourse during the second half of the 20th century, even in the fields of literature, art and cinema. Zizek thinks that Althusser mistakenly relays Lacan's message. (This exemplifies well Lacan's definition of truth: I always reach you through mistakes.)

Zizek's next critical weapon is Franz Kafka. In his eyes, Kafka's novels provide a possible critique of Althusser's inquiry into ideological *totality*. The characters of Kafka reveal a new rupture, a "gap" between the enormous ideological state apparatuses and their internalization within the individual body. Zizek says that "Kafka's 'irrational' bureaucracy, this blind, gigantic, nonsensical apparatus, precisely the Ideological State Apparatus with which a subject is confronted *before* any identification, any recognition—any *subjectivation*—takes place?"[1] Furthermore, Zizek asks: is the subject really assimilated by the machine?

According to Zizek, Kafka's novels can be traced to Althusser's interpellation.

The Kafkaesque subject is interpellated by a mysterious bureaucratic (Law, Castle). But this interpellation has a somewhat strange look: it is, so to say, an *interpellation without identification/*

---

[1] Zizek, Slavoj. *The Sublime Object of Ideology*. London: Verso, 1989. p. 44.

subjectivation; it does not offer us a Cause with which to identify—the Kafkaesque subject is the subject desperately seeking a trait with which to identify, he does not understand the meaning of the call of the Other.[1]

This is because the characters in Kafka's novels are usually outside the system, like the metamorphosed insect-man, which is an artistic representation. In the place where normal people enter identification and subjectification, the deformed insect-man is denied; in the place where a normal subject receives interpellation, the insect-man is simply confused. In *Contingency, Hegemony, Universality*, Zizek says that there are some people who reject the symbolic interpellation, "who do not say 'Yes!', but 'No!'—so called psychotics who, precisely, refuse to engage in the symbolic process"[2], which is just ignored by Althusser's theory of interpellation.

Before being caught in the identification, in the symbolic recognition/misrecognition, the subject ($) is trapped by the Other through a paradoxical object-cause of desire in the midst of it (*a*), through this secret supposed to be hidden in the Other: the Lacanian formula of fantasy. What does it mean, more precisely, to say that ideological fantasy structures reality itself? Let us explain by starting from the fundamental Lacanian thesis that in the opposition between dream and reality, fantasy is on the side of reality; it is, as Lacan once said, the support that gives consistency to what we call "reality".[3]

We have discussed about the reality supported by the ideological fantasy above. But we are still perplexed by the following questions: why is the subject expressed by $? What actually is *a* as the cause of the object of desire? And what is the Lacanian formula of fantasy?

In fact, Lacan believes that the fate of the individual subject is often very miserable because at the early stage, through misconception of the

---

[1] Zizek, Slavoj. *The Sublime Object of Ideology*. London: Verso, 1989. p. 44.

[2] Butler, Judith, Ernesto Laclau, and Slavoj Zizek. *Contingency, Hegemony, Universality: Contemporary Dialogues on the Left*. Verso, 2000. p. 119.

[3] Zizek, Slavoj. *The Sublime Object of Ideology*. London: Verso, 1989. p. 44.

image in the mirror and the forced face of the other (small other I and small other II), the subject conducts its identification in the Imaginary by alienation. While he enters the Symbolic whose mainstay is a chain of floating signifiers, the subject further resolves himself into a collage of concepts (the abstract nature) as the corpse of being. Now, Lacan's subject is empty and becomes a pseudo-subject which is dead but unaware of its death, in short, a $. In the eyes of the early Lacan, (*a*) refers to the mirror image that appears as the totality of the body, while for late Lacan, it is the abbreviation of objet-petit-a, the real leftover of the mistakenly identified false object of desire. In this regard, Zizek says that the ideological fantasy supports what we call reality. Reversely read, it means that the nature of reality is fantasy, because only ideology causes the continuous construction of social reality. In our previous example of the "Great Leap Forward" or the "Cultural Revolution," it is only real with the fantastic support of the "revolution under the proletarian dictatorship". Once that fantasy is broken, the red reality disintegrates. Social reality is like a dream: when one wakes up, the scenes in the dream shatter into pieces and disappear. However, in Lacan and Zizek's perception, the ideological fantasy always supports reality whether it is an individual dream or the social reality.

For this, Zizek cites the famous example of the "burning child" from Lacan's *Four Fundamental Concepts of Psychoanalysis*. A father is watching beside his sick child after the child dies, he goes into the next room to lie down, but leaves the door open so that he can see from his bedroom into the room in which his child's body is laid out with tall candles standing round it. An old man is engaged to keep watch over it. After a few hours' sleep, the father has a dream in which *his child is standing beside his bed, catching him by the arm and whispering to him reproachfully: "Father, don't you see I'm burning?"* He wakes up, notices a bright glare of light from the next room, hurries into it and finds the old watchman has dropped off to sleep and that the wrappings and one of the arms of his beloved child's dead body has been burned by a lighted candle that has fallen on them. Different from the conventional interpretation of dreams, Lacan's analysis is very complicated. He thinks that the father creates the dream to avoid awakening into reality; whereas the child's reproach: "Can't you see that I am burning?" is more terrifying than the so-called external reality itself, and that is why he awakens: to escape the Real of his desire, which announces itself in the terrifying dream.[1] Zizek says that it can be used to rewrite the "old 'hippy' motto of the 1960s": "Reality is for those who cannot support the dream" because "Reality" is a fantasy-construction to mask the Real of our desire (Lacan).

According to Zizek, Lacan's analysis is well applicable to our research of ideology.

> Ideology is not a dreamlike illusion that we build to escape insupportable reality; in its basic dimension it is a fantasy-construction which serves as a support for our "reality" itself: an "illusion" which structures our effective, real social relations and thereby masks some insupportable, real, impossible kernel (conceptualized by Ernesto Laclau and Chantal Mouffe as "antagonism": a traumatic social division which cannot be symbolized). The function of ideology is not to offer us a point of escape from our reality but to offer us the social reality itself as an escape from some traumatic, real kernel.[2]

Another intricate paragraph! In contrast to the old interpretation which regards ideology as a system of conceptual reproduction that substitutes real relations with false ones, Zizek thinks that ideology is not the illusions of the dream which we use to escape reality, but the tool for us to construct social relations in reality, since it is reality itself that insidiously hides the "traumatic, impossible kernel." It is a reversed Lacanian logic. In order to illustrate this thought, I take the example of the Chinese "Cultural Revolution" again, in which the "traumatic impossible kernel" indicates the impossibility of the thorough equality between people on this land despite the fact that it is a "sublime" object of desire, while the ideological fantasy of permanent

---

[1] Zizek, Slavoj. *The Sublime Object of Ideology*. London: Verso, 1989. p. 45.
[2] Ibid., p. 45.

revolution under the proletarian dictatorship constructs a "stormy" red "reality," which precisely conceals its own unfeasibility. This forever existent impossibility in the revolutionary development is also demonstrated by the post-Marxists Laclau and Mouffe.

3. Zhuang Zi's butterfly dream and the ideological dream

Zizek goes on to cite a second example from Lacan's *Four Fundamental Concepts of Psychoanalysis*. This time, it is the famous Chinese story of Zhuang Zi's butterfly dream, adopted by Lacan to illustrate the legitimacy of the butterfly-self relation.

First, Zizek says that Zhuang Zi is not a fool.

A fool is somebody who is not capable of a dialectically mediated distance towards himself, like a king who thinks he is a king, who takes his being-a-king as his immediate property and not as a symbolic mandate imposed on him by a network of inter-subjective relations of which he is a part.[1]

We know that Lacan has another saying: "if a man regards himself as a king, he is a madman; if a king regards himself as the king, he is also a madman."[2] The two statements above mean the same thing. Their background context directly implicates Lacan's theory of the pseudo-subject: the individual subject is not the equivalent of the self, whether in the early mirror stage or in the later period of language education. By identifying with the small other in the mirror stage (mirror and the other's look), the subject is only an alienated being in the Imaginary; while entering the symbolic network of signifiers in social communication, the subject is further transformed into a masked "me" interpellated by language. Thus, when one does not know the truth and thinks that the "me" is the real "self",

---

[1] Zizek, Slavoj. *The Sublime Object of Ideology*. London: Verso, 1989. p. 46.

[2] Lacan appends an aphorism of Lichtenberg: "a madman who imagines himself a prince differs from the prince who is in fact a prince only because the former is a negative prince, while the latter is a negative madman. Considered without their sign, they are alike." *See Ecrits: A Selection.*

he is a fool; and we are led to infer that any social character, whether it is a king, magnate or expert, is the result of a symbolic mandate imposed on him by a network of inter-subjective relations of which he is a part. You really think you are *something*? Actually, you are a fool, too. Lacan means there is always a "dialectical space" between man and himself, filled with something not of himself. In this regard, Zhuang Zi is wise: he finds that he *may not be himself.*

But Zizek does not believe that the problem is that simple. If I am not the king as a result of an external network of inter-signification of the symbolic language, am I still myself after being unmasked? Am I left with nothing? Zizek finds that the late Lacanian philosophy undergoes some changes, with the recognition of the leftover unable to be swallowed by the symbolic totality in man's existence.

If it were, the subject could be reduced to a void, to an empty place in which his or her whole content is procured by others, by the symbolic network of inter-subjective relations: I am "in myself" a nothingness, the positive content of myself is what I am for others. In other words, if this were all, Lacan's last word would be a radical alienation of the subject. His content, "what he is", would be determined by an exterior signifying network offering him the points of symbolic identification, conferring on him certain symbolic mandates. But Lacan's basic thesis, at least in his last works, is that there is a possibility for the subject to obtain some contents, some kind of positive consistency, also outside the big Other, the alienating symbolic network. This other possibility is that offered by fantasy: equating the subject to an object of fantasy.[1]

However, this obtainment does not happen in reality, but in the Lacanian Real. That is to say, it is possible to achieve the object of desire from fantasy. Zizek says that when Zhuang Zi dreams to be a butterfly, he is right in a certain sense. "The butterfly was the object which constituted the frame, the

---

[1] Zizek, Slavoj. *The Sublime Object of Ideology.* London: Verso, 1989. p. 46.

backbone, of his fantasy-identity (the relationship *Zhuang Zi-butterfly* can be written $-a). In the symbolic reality he was Zhuang Zi, but in the real of his desire he was a butterfly. Being a butterfly was the whole consistency of his positive being outside the symbolic network."[1] I need to do some explanation here. The so-called "symbolic reality" means the cultural in-itself structured by language (the chain of signifiers) in real life, while the "Real," in the late Lacan's definition, becomes the impossible existence after the individual subject flees the symbolic network. In reality, Zhuang Zi is himself; but in his own desire, he is being a flying butterfly, the "whole consistency of his being outside the symbolic network." It is a completely new illustration of Zhuang Zi's butterfly dream.

Zizek says that Zhuang Zi's example proves a Lacanian principle, and it is only in the dream that we come close to the real awakening—that is, to the Real of our desire. However, we cannot simply reverse it: because fantasy supports reality, real life is only a dream. Instead, Lacan is against this understanding. In his late years, he realizes that during the process of representation, "there is always a hard kernel, a leftover which persists and cannot be reduced to a universal play of illusory mirroring."[2] Lacan changes his early theory and accepts a reality in the subject that is not to be thoroughly assimilated by symbolization; man's only access to this "kernel" is through dreaming. (According to Zizek, it is the real difference between Lacan's philosophy and the old "naïve realism.")

> When we awaken into reality after a dream, we usually say to ourselves "it was just a dream", thereby blinding ourselves to the fact that in our everyday, wakening reality we are *nothing but a consciousness of this dream*. It was only in the dream that we approached the fantasy-framework which determines our activity, our mode of acting in reality itself.[3]

---

[1] Zizek, Slavoj. *The Sublime Object of Ideology*. London: Verso, 1989. p. 46.

[2] Ibid., p. 47.

[3] Ibid., p. 47.

The above thesis says that we tend to underestimate the significance of dreams. According to the late Lacan, the dream usually presents the most real object of desire. This *a* is the pillar of all fantasies of real life. The key is whether we can face this real in our dream.

Zizek then goes on in the direction of Lacan's logic: ideology is also a denigrated dream of the social unconsciousness. In the old critique of ideology, ideology is only regarded as a dream scene inconsistent with reality. However, what we do not know is that ideology itself reveals the real desire of history.

> It is the same with the ideological dream, with the determination of ideology as a dreamlike construction hindering us from seeing the real state of things, reality as such. In vain, do we try to break out of the ideological dream by "opening our eyes and trying to see reality as it is", by throwing away the ideological spectacles: as the subjects of such a post-ideological, objective, sober look, free of so-called ideological prejudices, as the subjects of a look which views the facts as they are, we remain throughout "the consciousness of our ideological dream." The only way to break the power of our ideological dream is to confront the Real of our desire which announces itself in this dream.[1]

Zizek thinks that here the heterogeneity between Lacan and the traditional Marxism emerges: "in the predominant Marxist perspective the ideological gaze is a *partial* gaze overlooking the *totality* of social relations, whereas in the Lacanian perspective ideology rather designates *a totality set on effacing the traces of its own impossibility*."[2] For Zizek, in the conventional Marxist critique of ideology, although the view of the ruling class represents the interest of some people who, by synecdoche, expand it to a general will of the whole society. In comparison, Lacan's ideological view explains that there is an impossible antagonistic coercion of totality in the existence of the individual subject. This is also the essence of social fantasy.

---

[1] Zizek, Slavoj. *The Sublime Object of Ideology*. London: Verso, 1989. pp. 47-48.
[2] Ibid., p. 49.

Closely related to this are the different conceptions about fetishism by Marx and Freud: the former believes that the fetish of commodity or money masks the real network of social relations, while the later thinks that the fetish uncovers some lack ("castration"), on whose nothingness the symbolic network is built.

According to Zizek, Lacan's Real is something in our conception which "always returns to the same place." Furthermore, we can even see the discrepancy of the ideological critiques between Marx, and Lacan and Zizek:

First, to Marx, "the ideological procedure *par excellence* is that of *'false' externalization and/or universalization*: a state which depends on a concrete historical conjunction appears as an eternal, universal feature of the human condition; the interest of a particular class disguises itself as universal human interest."[1] The aim of the "criticism of ideology" is to denounce this false universality, to detect behind man in general the bourgeois individual; behind the universal rights of man the form which renders possible capitalist exploitation; behind the "nuclear family" as a trans-historical constant the historically specified and limited form of kinship relations, and so on. It is the same with the logic of *taking the part as the overall*, *taking the non-history as the history*, while the Marxist key to solve the ideological paradox is the *re-historicized* truth.

Second, in the Lacan-Zizek horizon, the ideological critique refers not to an eternalized, universalized abstraction, but rather to the opposite, the "*over-rapid historicization*." Marxism employs historicization in the exposition of the non-historical abstraction of ideology in order to oppose over-rapid universalization. However, Zizek says that "if over-rapid universalization produces a quasi-universal Image whose function is to make us blind to its historical, socio-symbolic determination, over-rapid historicization makes us blind to the real kernel which returns as the same through diverse historiciations/symbolizations."[2] He even cites an embarrassing example, "the 'perverse' obverse of twentieth-century civilization: concentration

---

[1] Zizek, Slavoj. *The Sublime Object of Ideology*. London: Verso, 1989. p. 49.

[2] Ibid., p. 50.

camps." "All the different attempts to attach this phenomenon to a concrete image ('Holocaust', 'Gulag'...), to reduce it to a product of a concrete social order (Fascism, Stalinism...)—what are they if not so many attempts to elude the fact that we are dealing where with the 'real' of our civilization which returns as the same traumatic kernel in all social systems?"[1] We should not forget that the concentration camps were an invention of "liberal" England, dating from the Boer War; that they were also used in the USA to isolate the Japanese population, and so on. (In the recent Iraq war, they were used to detain and abuse the POWs, which proves an embodied "breakdown point" of human rights which the American government likes to mention every day.)

---

[1] Zizek, Slavoj. *The Sublime Object of Ideology*. London: Verso, 1989. p. 50.

Main References

Adorno, Theodor. "Letters to Walter Benjamin" in *Aesthetics and Politics*, New York: 1977.

"Sociology and Empirical Research" in *The Positivist Dispute in German Sociology*. Trans. Glyn Adey and David Frisby. New York: Educational Books Ltd., 1976.

Negative Dialectics. Trans. E. B. Ashtion. New York: The Continuum Publishing House, 1990.

Prisms. Cambridge: MIT Press, 1967.

Althusser, Louis. *Lenin and Philosophy, and Other Essays*. New York: Monthly Review Press, 1972.

Bataille, Georges. *Eroticism, Expenditure and General Economy*. Ed. Wang Min'an. Changchun: Jilin People's Publishing House, 2003.

History of Eroticism. Trans. Liu Hui: The Commercial Press, 2003.

Baudrillard, Jean. *The Consumer Society: Myths and Structures*. Theory, Culture & Society. London: Sage Publications Ltd, 1998.

The Mirror of Production. Trans. Mark Poster. St. Louis: Telos Press, 1975.

The System of Objects. Trans. James Benedict. Radical Thinkers. London [u.a.]: Verso, 2005.

Benjamin, Walter. *Works of Walter Benjamin*. Beijing: Chinese Social Science Press, 1999.

Best, Steven and Douglas Kellner. *The Postmodern Turn*. New York: Guilford Press, 1997.

"Commodification of Reality and Commodified Reality: Baudrillard, Debord, and Post-Modern Theories," in Douglas Kellner (ed.), *Baudrillard: A Critical Reader*, Oxford: Wiley-Blackwell, 1994.

Butler, Judith, Ernesto Laclau, and Slavoj Zizek. *Contingency, Hegemony, Universality: Contemporary Dialogues on the Left*. Verso, 2000.

Certeau, Michel. *The Practice of Everyday Life*. Trans. Steven Rendall. Berkeley: University of California Press, 2002.

Debord, Guy. *Comments on the Society of the Spectacle*, Trans. Malcolm Imrie, London: Verso, 1998.

The Society of the Spectacle, Trans. Donald Nickleson-Smith, New York: Zone Books, 1994.

Deleuze, Gilles. *Philosophy and Critique of Power*. Commercial Press, 2000.

Derrida, Jacques. *Specters of Marx: The State of the Debt, the Work of Mourning, and the New International*. Trans. Peggy Kamuf. New York: Routledge, 1994.

Derrida and Elisabeth Roudinesco. *For What Tomorrow: A Dialogue (Cultural Memory in the Present)*. Stanford, California: Stanford University Press, 2004.

Derrida and George Collins. *The Politics of Friendship*. Phronesis. London [u.a.]: Verso, 2005.

"Dialogue about Marxism." (Chinese)

"I Am at War with Myself." *SV. Derrida (Special Issue)*, 2004.

"Interview" in *Writing and Difference* (Chinese version). Beijing Joint Publishing, 2001.

Derrida's Speeches in China. Central Compilation and Translation Press. 2003.

Positions. Trans. Alan Bass. London: Continuum Publishing Group, 2004.

Eagleton, Terry. *The Aesthetics of Ideology*. Trans. Wang Jie, etc. Guang Xi Normal University Press, 1999.

Erjavec, Ales. *Toward the Image*, Trans. Hu Julan, Zhang Yunpeng, Changchun: Jilin People's Press, 2003.

Fields, Belden and Steven Best, "Situatinonist International," in Robert A. Gorman (ed.), *Biographical Dictionary of Neo-Marxism*, Westport:

Greenwood Press, 1985.

Foucault, Michel. *"Words and Things,"* in *Philosophical Discourse in Postmodernism*. Hangzhou: Zhejiang Renmin Press, 2000.

Fromm, Erich. *To Have or to Be?* London & New York: Continuum International Publishing Group, 2005.

Fukuhara Taihei. *Lacan: Mirror Stage*. Hebei Educational Publishing House, 2002.

Simmel, Georg. *Money, Gender and Modern Life Style* (Shanghai: Academia Press, 2000).

Godelie, Maurice. *Anthropology, Science of Primitive Societies?* Paris: Denoël, 1971.

Goldman, Lucien. *Hidden God*. Beijing: Baihua Literature and Art Publishing House, 1998.

Gramsci, Antonio. "Revolution of Anti-Capital", from *Gramsci's Works*, Vol. 1. Beijing: Renmin Press, 1992.

Heidegger, Martin, and David Farrell Krell. *Nietzsche*. San Francisco: Harper & Row, 1979.

Being and Time. Blackwell, 1978.

Jameson, Fredric. *Gratification: Culture and Politics*. Beijing: CSSPW, 1998.

Neo-Marxism. China Renmin University Press, 2004.

The Cultural Logic of Late Capitalism. Beijing: Sanlian Bookstore, 1997.

Jiang Min'an. *Postmodern Philosophical Discourse—From Foucault to Said*. Hangzhou: Zhejiang People's Publishing House, 2000.

Johnson, Richard. "What Is Study of Culture?" in *Works on Study of Culture*. Beijing: CSSPW, 2000.

Kellner, (ed.) *Baudrillard: A Critical Reader*, Oxford: Wiley-Blackwell, 1994.

Media Spectacle, London & New York: Routledge, 2003.

Lacan, Jacques. *ÉCRITS: A Selection*. Trans. Alan Sheridan. New York: Norton, 1977.

Lenin, Vladimir. *The Collected Works of Lenin*. Beijing: People's Publishing House, 2nd Ed, Vol. 55, 1990.

Levinas, Emmanuel. *God, Death, and Time*. Trans. Bettina Bergo. Stanford, California: Stanford University Press, 2000.

Nine Talmudic Readings. Trans. Annette Aronowicz. Bloomington: Indiana University Press, 1994.

Lévi-Strauss, Claude. "Introduction to Sociology and Anthropology." Trans. Yu Biping. *Sociology and Anthropology*. Shanghai Translation Publishing House, 2003.

Li Zhongshang. *Analysis of "New Marxism."* China Renmin University Press, 1987.

The Third Road. Academy Press, 1994.

Lukács, Georg. *History and Class Consciousness*. London: Merlin Press, 1971.

Lury, Celia. *Consumer Culture*. New Brunswick: Rutgers University Press, 1996.

Marx, Karl and Frederick Engels. *Collected Works*. London: Lawrence & Wishart, 1976.

Capital, vol. 1. London: Lawrence & Wishart, 1977.

Mauss, Marcel, and Robert Brain. *A General Theory of Magic*. London: Routledge & Kegan Paul, 1972.

The Gift: *Forms and Functions of Exchange in Archaic Societies*. Trans. Ian Cunnison. Glencoe: Free Press, 1954.

Pascal, Blaise. *Thoughts*. Cup Archive.

Popper, Karl. *Unended Quest*. Trans. Qiu Renzhong. Fuzhou: Fujian People's Press, 1984.

Poster, Mark. *Jean Baudrillard, Selected Writings*. Stanford, California: Stanford University Press, 1988.

Ricardo, David. *On the Principles of Political Economy and Taxation*. London, 1821.

Sahlins, Marshall. *Culture and Practical Reason*. Beijing: Joint Publishing Company Limited, 2002.

Salecl, Renata, and Slavoj Zizek. *Gaze and Voice as Love Objects*. Durham: Duke University Press, 1996.

Scheler, Max. *Subversion of Value*. Beijing: SDX Joint Publishing Company, 1997.

Schmidt, Alfred. *Concept of Nature in Marx*. Commercial Press, 1988.

Szeman, Imre. "Ghostly Matters: On Derrida's Specters." *Rethinking Marxism* 12.2 (2000).

Wolin, Richard. *The Concept of Cultural Critique*. Beijing: Commercial Press, 2000.

Yang Haifeng. *Towards Post-Marx*: *From Mirror of Production to Mirror of Symbols*. Central Compilation and Translation Press, 2004.

Yu Biping *A General Theory of Magic* in *Sociology and Anthropology*. Shanghai Translation Publishing House, 2003.

Yu Runyang. *An Introduction to Philosophy of Modern Western Music*. Hunan Educational Press, 2000.

Yu Wujin and Chen Xueming. *Foreign Marxist Schools*. Shanghai: Fudan University Press, 1990.

Yuasa, Hiroo. *Georges Bataille*: *Consumption*. Trans. Zhao Hanying: Hebei Educational Publishing House, 2001.

Zhang Yibing. "Anthropocentrism: In and Out" in *Philosophical Trends*, Vol. 6, 1996.

"Barthes: Text is a Kind of Weaving" in *Tribune of Social Sciences*. Vol. 10, 2002.

"Contemporary Ecological Horizon and the Logic of the Materialistic View" in *Philosophical Researches*. 8 (1993).

"Double Mediations of Nature and Society" in *Study and Exploration*. Vol.3, 2003.

"Post-Marx Thought is not Marxism." in *Journal of Nanjing University*. Vol. 2.

"Revolutionary Dialectics and Critical historical Materialism", *Shangdong Social Science*, issue 2, 2000.

"The Devil Other: Who Drives You Crazy" in *The Journal of*

Humanities. 2004. vol. 5.

"What is the Late Marxism" in *Journal of Nanjing University*. 2004. vol. 5.

A Deep Plough of Texts (Vol. 1). China Renmin University Press, 2008.

A Problematic, Symptomal Reading and Ideology: A Textological Illustration of Althusser. Central Compilation and Translation Press, 2003.

Atonal Dialectical Imagination: The Textological Reading of Adorno's Negative Dialectics. Sanlian Bookstore Press, 2001.

Back to Marx—the Philosophical Discourse in the Context of Economics. Nanjing: Jiangsu Renmin Publishing House, 1999.

Problematic, Symptomal Reading and Ideology: A Textological Illustration of Althusser. Central Compilation and Translation Press, 2003.

The Collected Works of Zhang Yibing. Guang Xi Normal University Publishing House, 1999.

The Impossible Truth of Being: Mirror of Lacan's Philosophy. The Commercial Press, 2006.

The Subjective Dimension of Marxian Historical Dialectics. Nanjing University Press, 2002.

Zhang Yibing and Meng Mugui. *To Understand Marx: Contemporary Illustration of Original Marxist Philosophy*. China Renmin University Press, 2004.

Zizek, Slavoj. *Did Somebody Say Totalitarianism?: Five Interventions in the (Mis)Use of a Notion*. Wo Es War. London; New York: Verso, 2002.

Zizek and Glyn Daly. *Conversations with Zizek*. Conversations. Cambridge [u.a.]: Polity, 2004.

Grimaces of the Real. Central Compilation and Translation Press, 2004.

Mapping Ideology. London; New York: Verso, 1994.

The Fragile Absolute. London; New York: Verso, 2000.

The Metastases of Enjoyment: Six Essays on Women and Causality. Verso, 2005.

The Plague of Fantasies. London; New York: Verso. 1997.

The Sublime Object of Ideology. London: Verso, 1989.

The Ticklish Subject: *The Absent Centre of Political Ontology*. Wo Es War. London; New York: Verso, 1999.

Printed in P.R.C. by order of Canut-Berlin.

Originally published as A Deep Plough: Unscrambling Major Post-Marxist Texts From Adorno to Zizek in 2007 by China Renmin University Press.

Original Chinese Edition Copyright © 2007 by Zhang Yibing
ISBN: 978-7-300-08812-9

A Deep Plough: Unscrambling Major Post-Marxist Texts From Adorno to Zizek
ISBN: 978-3-942575-02-7

Published by
Canut International Publishers
Yorck Street. 66
10965 Kreuzberg
Berlin-Germany

Canut International Publishers
12a Guernsey Road E11
London 4BJ-England-U.K.

URL: http//www.canut.us
E-Mail: canut@aol.com